6977

Endsheets: (top) Michael Ondaatje, Marie Laberge, David McFadden, Margaret Hollingsworth; (bottom) Jane Rule, André Major, Michel Tremblay, Sharon Pollock

Canadian Writers Since 1960
Second Series

Dictionary of Literary Biography

Documentary Series

Yearbooks

Concise Series

Dictionary of Literary Biography • Volume Sixty

Canadian Writers Since 1960
Second Series

6977

Edited by
W. H. New
University of British Columbia

A Bruccoli Clark Layman Book
Gale Research Company • Book Tower • Detroit, Michigan 48226

Manufactured by Edwards Brothers, Inc.
Ann Arbor, Michigan
Printed in the United States of America

Library of Congress Cataloging-in-Publication Data

Canadian writers since 1960.

    (Dictionary of literary biography; v. 60)
    "A Bruccoli Clark Layman book."
    Includes index.
    1. Authors, Canadian—20th century—Biography—
Dictionaries. 2. Canadian literature—20th century—History and criticism. 3. Canadian literature, 20th century—
Bio-bibliography. 4. French-Canadian literature—20th century—History and criticism. 5. French-Canadian literature—20th century—Bio-bibliography. 6. Authors, French-Canadian—20th century—Biography—Dictionaries. I.
New, William H. II. Series.
PR9186.2.C363   1987   810'.9'0054   87-14351
ISBN 0-8103-1738-9

Contents

Plan of the Series

The advisory board, the editors, and the publisher of the *Dictionary of Literary Biography* are joined in endorsing Mark Twain's declaration. The literature of a nation provides an inexhaustible resource of permanent worth. We intend to make literature and its creators better understood and more accessible to students and the reading public, while satisfying the standards of teachers and scholars.

To meet these requirements, *literary biography* has been construed in terms of the author's achievement. The most important thing about a writer is his writing. Accordingly, the entries in *DLB* are career biographies, tracing the development of the author's canon and the evolution of his reputation.

The purpose of *DLB* is not only to provide reliable information in a convenient format but also to place the figures in the larger perspective of literary history and to offer appraisals of their accomplishments by qualified scholars.

The publication plan for *DLB* resulted from two years of preparation. The project was proposed to Bruccoli Clark by Frederick G. Ruffner, president of the Gale Research Company in November 1975. After specimen entries were prepared and typeset, an advisory board was formed to refine the entry format and develop the series rationale. In meetings held during 1976, the publisher, series editors, and advisory board approved the scheme for a comprehensive biographical dictionary of persons who contributed to North American literature. Editorial work on the first volume began in January 1977, and it was published in 1978.

In order to make *DLB* more than a reference tool and to compile volumes that individually have claim to status as literary history, it was decided to organize volumes by topic, period, or genre. Each of these freestanding volumes provides a biographical-bibliographical guide and overview for a particular area of literature. We are convinced that this organization—as opposed to a single alphabet method—constitutes a valuable innovation in the presentation of reference material. The volume plan necessarily requires many decisions for the placement and treatment of authors who might properly be included in two or three volumes. In some instances a major figure will be included in separate volumes, but with different entries emphasizing the aspect of his career appropriate to each volume. Ernest Hemingway, for example, is represented in *American Writers in Paris, 1920-1939* by an entry focusing on his expatriate apprenticeship; he is also in *American Novelists, 1910-1945* with an entry surveying his entire career. Each volume includes a cumulative index of subject authors and articles. Comprehensive indexes to the entire series are planned.

With volume ten in 1982 it was decided to enlarge the scope of *DLB*. By the end of 1986 twenty-one volumes treating British literature had been published, and volumes for Commonwealth and Modern European literature were in progress. The series has been further augmented by the *DLB Yearbooks* (since 1981) which update published entries and add new entries to keep the *DLB* current with contemporary activity. There have also been *DLB Documentary Series* volumes which provide biographical and critical source materials for figures whose work is judged to have particular interest for students. One of these companion volumes is entirely devoted to Tennessee Williams.

We define literature as the *intellectual commerce of a nation:* not merely as belles lettres but as that ample and complex process by which ideas are generated, shaped, and transmitted. *DLB* entries are not limited to "creative writers" but extend to other figures who in their time and in their way influenced the mind of a people. Thus the series encompasses historians, journalists, publishers, and screenwriters. By this means readers of *DLB* may be aided to perceive literature not as cult scripture in the keeping of intellectual high priests but firmly positioned at the center of a nation's life.

DLB includes the major writers appropriate to each volume and those standing in the ranks immediately behind them. Scholarly and critical counsel has been sought in deciding which minor figures to include and how full their entries should be. Wherever possible, useful references are made to figures who do not warrant separate entries.

Each *DLB* volume has a volume editor responsible for planning the volume, selecting the figures for inclusion, and assigning the entries. Volume editors are also responsible for preparing, where appropriate, appendices surveying the major periodicals and literary and intellectual movements for their volumes, as well as lists of further readings. Work on the series as a whole is coordinated at the Bruccoli Clark Layman editorial center in Columbia, South Carolina, where the editorial staff is responsible for accuracy of the published volumes.

One feature that distinguishes *DLB* is the illustration policy–its concern with the iconography of literature. Just as an author is influenced by his surroundings, so is the reader's understanding of the author enhanced by a knowledge of his environment. Therefore *DLB* volumes include not only drawings, paintings, and photographs of authors, often depicting them at various stages in their careers, but also illustrations of their families and places where they lived. Title pages are regularly reproduced in facsimile along with dust jackets for modern authors. The dust jackets are a special feature of *DLB* because they often document better than anything else the way in which an author's work was perceived in its own time. Specimens of the writers' manuscripts are included when feasible.

Samuel Johnson rightly decreed that "The chief glory of every people arises from its authors." The purpose of the *Dictionary of Literary Biography* is to compile literary history in the surest way available to us–by accurate and comprehensive treatment of the lives and work of those who contributed to it.

The *DLB* Advisory Board

Foreword

DLB 60: Canadian Writers Since 1960, Second Series is the second of four *DLB* volumes devoted to Canadian writers whose main language of artistic expression is English or French. It is the companion to *DLB 53: Canadian Writers Since 1960, First Series* and hence the second *DLB* to cover authors whose careers were effectively established between 1960 and the early 1980s.

The cultural context is the same: a society in flux, concerned with empirical objects and stresses as much as with desperation and abstract dreams. The two official languages intermittently connect, cautious and barbed, expansive and self-defensive in approximately equal measure. The writers of this time are not without laughter nor without joy, but they are recurrently earnest about social causes and about the character and function of literature. They are often critics as well as creative writers; they are theorists of speech and genre, who are crafting political artifacts as well as narrative, lyric, or dramatic entertainments; they are artists shaping metaliterary designs while they seek to shake off the conventions of the status quo.

In the decades following 1959 one sees a generation of writers contending with particular manifestations of their culture. The twenty-year span of the 1960s and 1970s is unparalleled in Canadian literary history for the sheer amount of work published and the extraordinary liveliness of literary activity. The decade of the 1960s was one of militant cultural nationalism; that of the 1970s enjoyed what seemed to be the fruition of those national commitments. (It is for future historians to analyze whether, as some social critics claim, the wave of economic recession that has marked the 1980s has altered the course of literature somewhat, as it has marked daily life and political policy.) Behind these generalizations lies a specific set of events set in motion in the 1950s. The Massey Commission on Canadian Cultural Policy resulted in the establishment of the Canada Council in 1958, an organization devoted to the active encouragement and the real financial support of artistic endeavors. Almost immediately Canadian culture came out of its doldrums.

Canadian writers were published in larger numbers than before (a fact made possible in part because the large generation of postwar babies reached maturity in the 1960s); Canadian booksellers stocked Canadian books and readers read them; new critical and creative journals came into existence (*Canadian Literature, Liberté, Prism,* for example, all in 1959); Canadian theaters opened for Canadian plays; courses in Canadian literature came during the 1960s to be standard features of university and high school offerings; and Canadian-owned publishing houses (Anansi, Porcépic, Oberon, Talonbooks, Coach House, and others) came into being, all concerned primarily with publishing young Canadian writers and combating what they saw as the stranglehold which the subsidiaries of international companies held over the national culture. In 1959 three novels appeared which marked a watershed: Hugh MacLennan's *The Watch That Ends the Night,* the last of the positive political visions by a romantic realist; Sheila Watson's *The Double Hook,* a work of high modernism that many readers found experimental; and Mordecai Richler's *The Apprenticeship of Duddy Kravitz,* a bawdy, comic, irreverent, iconoclastic account of Jewish Montreal. Not his first book, *The Apprenticeship of Duddy Kravitz* was Richler's first to win a wide readership; it marked not only the effective beginning of his successful career but also a change in the direction of Canadian writing: from one that adopted the value system of the dominant British culture to one which acknowledged the vital presence of the ethnic minorities, and which challenged the received techniques of literary expression and the received conventions of literary taste.

These developments had a direct impact both on the character of Canadian writing and on the processes by which it reached readers. Theater emerged as a viable genre; poetry turned from its lyric format to longer, more sequential, more meditative forms; the short story thrived. The literature was deeply anti-American during the time of the Vietnam War, using the rhetoric of the American freedom marches to oppose what writers saw as imperialism in other guises.

Michèle Lalonde turned the language of black America against English Canada; images of the draft dodger appeared in Dave Godfrey's writing, images of victimization and creeping American technology in Margaret Atwood's, images of sellout and loss in Dennis Lee's (though in his children's verse Lee wrote more often of ways to prevail).

The technology of the early 1960s and the developments that followed computerization in the later 1970s made revolutions in publishing and printing possible; not only could small publishers locate anywhere in the country (no longer being dependent on the availability of large presses), they could also begin to design by computer, treating the page as a field of composition rather than simply as the background for print. Coach House Press became a leading exponent of the art of open-field composition, which in turn was to affect the way writers came to view the language they had available to them. Margaret Avison, Bill Bissett, Frank Davey: all to some degree saw the visual field as an element in design, but the visual field was also a means to revivify the voice as well. Poetry came back off the page in tantric chant, pun, play, song (with Leonard Cohen, for example), and idiomatic speech came to dominate the language of fiction, serving a political purpose in the process. In the hands of writers investigating ethnic minorities, it became a means of announcing a world of difference. Rudy Wiebe was one of several to reclaim the Indian past from its noble and savage stereotypes, and in his novel *The Blue Mountains of China* he also adapted forms of English and High and Low German to explore the codes of values that activated and shaped Mennonite experience. For Austin C. Clarke the world of difference was that of the black immigrant in Toronto; for Naim Kattan it was that of the Iraqi Jew; for Clark Blaise it was the sense of being alien to both the United States and Canada; for Bharati Mukherjee it was the contrast between North America and Bengal. Yet these explorations of minority experience also underscored the way in which many writers felt alienated as artists, alienated from their audience and more particularly from the very language they used. This sensibility showed up even more strongly in the work of a number of feminist writers—Nicole Brossard in particular but also Margaret Atwood, Jane Rule, Marie-Claire Blais, Jay Macpherson, Sharon Pollock, and Audrey Thomas—in whose writings one finds language being used as a process of discovery. The works (whether as "realistic" as Rule's accounts of love and the world or as "broken" as Brossard's meditative reflections on inheritance and independence) accept the conventions of received (or "male") language, then turn the language back on itself, shaking syntax or structure or vocabulary to release some glimmer of an understanding with which the characters (not always successfully) might be able to live.

Louky Bersianik, in such works as *L'Eugélionne* and *Le Pique-nique sur l'Acropole*, took received forms of language and parodically demolished them. The former book is a science-fiction fantasy which exposes the political limits that conventionally "real" society imposes on women; the latter reconstructs an independent female history, one parallel to, yet separate from, the cultural history accepted by men. The women's "picnic on the Acropolis" takes place both physically and verbally outside the perspective of Plato and his male *Symposium*, but at the same time; both the simultaneity and the differences are instructive. Other feminist writers include Madeleine Gagnon, Jovette Marchessault, Margaret Hollingsworth, and Louise Maheux-Forcier, all of them concerned with deconstructing words as a means of resisting sociological barriers. Still other forms of analytic fragmentation appeared in the plays of George Walker and the poems of Christopher Dewdney. Walker turned popular culture into a medium of comic judgment; Dewdney transformed scientific indeterminacy into a mode of lyrical meditation. In a more familiar manner, indeterminacy also affected children's literature, as in the dour adolescent realism of Kevin Major's books. Parody, technical innovation, fantasy, empirical realism: all these forms have been used to criticize and to reshape the normative politics of cultural attitude.

There was a political dimension to personal memory, as in the prose of John Metcalf, Michael Ondaatje, and Claire Martin or the poetry of Ondaatje and Phyllis Webb. Margaret Laurence turned her experience of Africa into a guide to the value of a folk culture, and her memory of Manitoba into a new history of Canada, through the eyes and the folk wisdom of the women of a single region. Region itself became a political statement. David Adams Richards made the Miramichi a region deprived of power because deprived of language. Robert Kroetsch and Jack Hodgins, in Alberta and Vancouver Island respectively, combined the conventions of magic realism and the exaggerations of local tale-telling customs into fantastic histories of the contemporary imagination. The theater became an articulate voice of regional politics. David French's Newfoundland, Michel Tremblay's Montreal, Sharon Pollock's West: these are emblems of the lost and the dispossessed as much as dramatic settings. And like other genres the plays of the period frequently called for a reinterpretation of the conventions of history. This was not history being rewritten to order; it was "real" history being reclaimed from the rhetoric of others. George Bowering's poetry and prose declared the personality of history, declared history to be an act of personal assembly; Mavis Gallant's stories probed the motivations that allow history to happen at all. Antonine Maillet reinvoked the culture of the Acadians, winning the Prix Goncourt for *Pélagie-la-Charrette*; Hugh Hood began a series of novels he calls *The New Age*, which through the life of a single man recounts the modern history of Canada. Milton Acorn's poetry espoused the worker and a left-wing political reinterpretation of power; Matt Cohen balanced the world of Loyalist inheritance against the world of Jewish culture; Timothy Findley took the wars of the twentieth century and the narratives of the Old Testament and turned them into an inquiry into the origins of violence in modern man. In Quebec, Roch Carrier and Jacques Ferron adapted folktales to the modern condition; Jacques Godbout wrote of a man with two heads, one with a French name and one with an English. Sometimes literature was playful. Sometimes the world seemed comic. Laurence J. Peter

stood back from it to produce a taxonomy of incompetence, thus explaining why things go wrong; Jean-Paul Desbiens, as Frère Untel (Brother Anonymous), satirized it. But for Hubert Aquin and Juan Butler, the world was bleak and there was no cure for the misery; both writers ended their lives with suicide. Aquin then became a political symbol.

Repeatedly, language was filtered through politics: from the politics of national independence came a rhetoric of antitechnology, anti-Americanism; from the politics of ethnicity a rhetoric of alienation; from the politics of feminism a rhetoric of power; from the politics of Quebec separatism (set in motion during the 1960s, coming to various climaxes in the 1970s–the October Crisis in 1970, the election of the Parti Québécois in 1976) a rhetoric of independence. In the case of Quebec separatism, the rhetoric (as in the works of Félix Leclerc, Claude Jasmin, and Michel Tremblay) involved the use of *joual*, the street language of Montreal, as a rebellion against received conventions of art and received notions of power, both being considered sellouts to foreign control. Using language for play and politics was a pattern reiterated across the country in a dozen different ways during the 1960s and 1970s. These decades saw a deliberate reach for nationhood and the strong grasp of a sense of cultural community. Writers claimed language for their own purposes, fed it with imagination, and made it their own, at least for a time.

                                                                                                                         —W. H. New

Acknowledgments

This book was produced by Bruccoli Clark Layman, Inc. Karen L. Rood is senior editor for the *Dictionary of Literary Biography* series. Margaret A. Van Antwerp was the in-house editor.

Copyediting supervisor is Patricia Coate. Production coordinator is Kimberly Casey. Typesetting supervisor is Laura Ingram. Lucia Tarbox and Michael Senecal are editorial associates. The production staff includes Kimberly Amerson, Rowena Betts, Mary S. Dye, Charles Egleston, Gabrielle Elliott, Sarah A. Estes, Kathleen M. Flanagan, Joyce Fowler, Cynthia Hallman, Judith K. Ingle, Judith E. McCray, Warren McInnis, Sheri Neal, Joycelyn R. Smith, Debra Straw, and Elizabeth York. Jean W. Ross is permissions editor. Joseph Caldwell, photography editor, and Joseph Matthew Bruccoli did photographic copy work for the volume.

Walter W. Ross and Rhonda Marshall did the library research with the assistance of the staff at the Thomas Cooper Library of the University of South Carolina: Lynn Barron, Daniel Boice, Donna Breese, Kathy Eckman, Gary Geer, Cathie Gottlieb, David L. Haggard, Jens Holley, Dennis Isbell, Marcia Martin, Jean Rhyne, Beverley Steele, Ellen Tillett, and Virginia Weathers.

The editor expresses special thanks to Robin Bellamy. Thanks are also due to Pamela Banting for providing information to the author of the entry on Fred Wah. Nicky Drumbolis of Letters, L. A. Wallrich of About Books, Richard Shuh and Linda Wooley of Alphabet Books, Beth Appeldoorn of Longhouse Book Shop, and Kenneth Landry of the *Dictionnaire des oeuvres littéraires du Québec* have provided valuable assistance in securing illustrative materials.

Canadian Writers Since 1960
Second Series

Dictionary of Literary Biography

Yves Beauchemin
(26 June 1941-)

Alberto Manguel

BOOKS: *L'Enfirouapé* (Montreal: La Presse, 1974);
Le Matou (Montreal: Québec/Amérique, 1981);
translated by Sheila Fischman as *The Alley
Cat* (Toronto: McClelland & Stewart, 1986;
New York: Holt, 1986);
Cybèle (Montreal: Art Global, 1982);
Du sommet d'un arbre (Montreal: Québec/Amérique,
1986).

OTHER: "Sueurs," in *Fuites et poursuites* (Montreal: Quinze, 1982).

PERIODICAL PUBLICATIONS: "En attendant
le feu d'artifice," *Liberté*, 19 (May-June
1977): 18-22;
"L'information littéraire une faillite," *L'Actualité*
(February 1978): 6;
"Etre écrivain: un métier comme les autres?," *Le
Devoir*, 18 November 1978;
"Le Pays-bonbon," *Québec/Amérique* (Summer
1982).

In the first chapter of *Du sommet d'un arbre*
(1986), a collection of autobiographical pieces written for CBC radio, Yves Beauchemin describes
his childhood as a time of total freedom. He was
born in the town of Noranda, Quebec, on 26
June 1941, but his first memories are those of
the forests of northern Quebec where, at the age
of five, he was taken to live by his parents.
Beauchemin, his younger brother François, and
his sister Danielle had the run of the small village of Clova, Abitibi, where his father, Jean-
Marie Beauchemin, had accepted a job with a
branch of the International Paper Company of
New York.

From 1947 to 1953 Beauchemin attended
the elementary school at Clova. As Beauchemin recalls, it was his mother, the former Thérèse Maurice, who "infected" him with "the reading virus."
He devoured Jules Verne and other popular fiction, as well as American comics—with such heroes as Archie, Bugs Bunny, Batman, and
Superman—whose influence can be traced in his
later work. According to Beauchemin, he was neither gifted for music nor talented at sports: instead, he was good at games that required
"inventing things," making use of his imagination.

With his entrance to the Joliette secondary
school in 1953, his life as a "city man" began.
The world of trees and open spaces was replaced
by movie theaters and bookstores, and
Beauchemin started to develop a passion for
what he calls the "Balzac effect": the sense of
fullness and concentration that only a city can provide.

In 1962 Beauchemin entered the University
of Montreal where, three years later, he obtained
a *license ès lettres* in French and history of art. Montreal, he says, made him discover that he is Quebecois in a political sense, confronted by unilingual
English posters and French-speaking people. For
a year he taught literature both at the Collège
Garneau in Quebec and at Université Laval but

Yves Beauchemin

photograph by Kèro

then accepted a position as editor at Holt, Rinehart, and Winston in Montreal, where he was placed in charge of their drama and history series. He also began to contribute stories and articles to magazines and newspapers such as *Sept-Jours* and *Dimensions.* He married Viviane St-Onge, with whom he has two children: Alexis, born in 1977, and Renaud, born in 1981.

A job as researcher at Radio-Quebec which he accepted in 1969 allowed him to dedicate more time to his writing, and in 1974 he produced his first novel, *L'Enfirouapé,* loosely based on the October Crisis of 1970. Even though *L'Enfirouapé* won the Prix France-Québec in 1975, it is a slight work. A story of revenge and kidnapping in which a naive young man becomes a pawn in Quebec politics, Beauchemin's novel

brings to mind the fantasies of Kurt Vonnegut, Jr., but lacks the seamless complexity of the American writer's works.

Le Matou, published seven years later in 1981, is a superior work. It draws on a few of the themes of *L'Enfirouapé*–the young, abused hero; the bureaucratic and unfair society; the corrupt elders–but it explores them in the context of a vaster, many-layered reality. *Le Matou* has a Faustian theme: a young man, Florent Boisonneault, is tempted by a Mephistophelean figure, Egon Ratablavasky, into entering the restaurant business. Florent accepts and soon finds out that Ratablavasky and an anglophone accomplice are using him to develop their own wicked schemes. Trying to fight back, Florent realizes that the whole of society, from the gas and phone companies to the police, is somehow in Ratablavasky's pay and that Montreal itself has become a corrupt place in which even the weather plots against the innocent. In the tradition of Balzac and Dickens, the novel chronicles the life of an entire city and is crisscrossed by subplots that lend richness and depth to its telling.

Le Matou was phenomenally successful both in Quebec and in France (where it was published in 1982), selling over half a million copies after it was picked up by the largest book club in France, France-Loisirs. Bernard Pivot, a leading French critic, called it "a revelation," and the novel won three major literary prizes: the Prix des Jeunes Romanciers du Journal de Montréal, the Prix de la Communauté Urbaine de Montréal, and the Prix du Roman de l'Eté in France. The publication of *Le Matou* in Paris led to a tour of France and Belgium, which Beauchemin described in an amusing article, "Le Pays-bonbon," published in the magazine *Québec / Amérique* in 1982. *The Alley Cat* (1986), the English translation of *Le Matou* by Sheila Fischman, was less successful, perhaps because of the difficulty in rendering in another language the many nuances of Quebec French.

International Cinema Corporation bought the film rights to *Le Matou,* and in 1985 it was made into a full-length feature and a television miniseries, both directed by Jean Beaudin. Neither the film nor the television series was a clear critical success, even though the film enjoyed a fairly lengthy run on the commercial screens and received the Prix de Public at the Montreal Film Festival of 1986.

Beauchemin has been working on a new novel, as yet untitled, scheduled to appear in the fall of 1987. Since *Le Matou,* in addition to radio scripts and magazine articles he has had two short stories published: *Cybèle,* which appeared in a limited edition in 1982, and "Sueurs," a detective story included in the anthology *Fuites et poursuites* the same year.

Beauchemin's importance currently lies in the fact that in *Le Matou,* without entirely abandoning the difficult literary experiments begun by Quebec writers in the 1960s, or the political pamphleteering of the 1970s, he has succeeded in composing a story that surpasses both these constrictions and can be read effectively outside the context of Quebec. The themes of *Le Matou* are universal, and Florent continues a tradition of literary heroes such as Balzac's Eugène de Rastignac, who succumb to, and then triumph over, the laws of society.

Interview:

"Vivre de sa plume an Québec: entrevue avec Yves Beauchemin," *Lettres Québécoises,* 44 (Winter 1986-1987): 13-14.

References:

Maurice Cagnon, *"Le Matou," L'Esprit Créateur,* 23 (Fall 1983): 95-104;

Gilles Cossette, "Signes et Pistes II-'Fuites Poursuites,'" *Lettres Québécoises,* 28 (Winter 1982): 32-33;

André Major, *"Le Matou," Liberté,* 24 (July-August 1982): 80-83;

Jean Royer, "Les Plaisirs du la terre-fiction," in his *Ecrivains contemporains; Entietiens 3: 1980-83* (Montreal: Editions de l'Hexagone, 1985), pp. 146-154;

Voix et Images, Special Beauchemin issue, 36 (Spring 1987).

Jacques Benoit

(28 November 1941-   )

Jacqueline Viswanathan
Simon Fraser University

BOOKS: *Jos Carbone* (Montreal: Editions du Jour, 1967); translated by Sheila Fischman (Montreal: Harvest House, 1974);
Les Voleurs (Montreal: Editions du Jour, 1969);
Patience et Firlipon (Montreal: Editions du Jour, 1970);
Les Princes (Montreal: Editions du Jour, 1973); translated by David Lobdell as *The Princes* (Montreal: Oberon, 1977);
L'Extrême Gauche (Montreal: La Presse, 1978);
Gisèle et le serpent (Montreal: Libre Expression, 1981);
Les Plaisirs du vin (Montreal: Libre Expression, 1985).

MOTION PICTURES: *La Maudite Galette*, screenplay by Benoit, CINAK Cie Cinématographique, 1972;
Réjeanne Padovani, screenplay by Benoit and Denys Arcand, CINAK Cie Cinématographique, 1973;
L'Affaire Coffin, screenplay by Benoit, Films Cine Scene/Productions Videofilms, 1979.

With Réjean Ducharme, Roch Carrier, Marie-Claire Blais, Jean Basile, André Major, Jacques Benoit belongs to the generation of Quebec novelists whose first book, published in the 1960s, impressed readers with its originality and formal perfection. *Jos Carbone* (1967; English translation, 1974) received the Prix de la Province de Québec. Benoit's other four novels have confirmed his talent as an accomplished writer.

Benoit, the son of Jean-Marie Benoit, an immigration official, and Yvette Denault Benoit, was born in the small French-Canadian village of Saint-Jean. His childhood and his secondary education in Catholic schools seem to have left him with few happy memories. He studied literature at the University of Montreal and at McGill and taught briefly before becoming a journalist. He has worked for several Quebec newspapers–*Le Petit Journal, La Patrie*, and *La Presse*–as well as for Radio-Canada. His award-winning series of articles on the radical Left for *La Presse* has been published in book form under the title *L'Extrême Gauche* (1978). Benoit has also written scripts for three successful films, two, *La Maudite Galette* (1972) and *Réjeanne Padovani* (1973), directed by Denys Arcand, and one, *L'Affaire Coffin* (1979), directed by Jean-Claude Labrecque. The 1973 screenplay, a collaboration with Arcand, won the Prix Génie. Benoit is currently a reporter and columnist for *La Presse*. He lives in Montreal with his wife, Michelle Gélinas. They have two children.

Like the other novels by Benoit, *Jos Carbone* creates a striking, fantastic world which captivates the reader. Jos and his girl, Myrtie, live in a cottage in the middle of an impenetrable forest. Their instinctive, unquestioning love and their sensitivity to the surrounding wilderness give them an Edenic innocence which contrasts with the middle-class urban values of most readers. The couple's peaceful happiness is disturbed by the intrusion of a mysterious stranger who threatens to take over both Jos's girl and his territory. Then follows a breathtaking manhunt through the forest. With the help of his friend Pique, Jos tries unsuccessfully to bait the stranger with his girl. Finally, the stranger is killed in a fit of jealousy by Pique's girlfriend Germaine. After this outburst of violence Jos and Myrtie return to the idyllic peace of their Edenic retreat.

The scenery and the dwellings associated with the characters are particularly fascinating in this novel: Jos and Myrtie's primitive cabin, Pique and Germaine's sinister underground den, and the outsider's shack built on a raft drifting down the river typify and differentiate the characters as strikingly as psychological features would in a more conventional novel. *Jos Carbone* contains many components of the fairy tale but these are interestingly combined with modern elements and unusually accurate descriptions of the physical world. The novel also develops some of the latent aspects of fantastic folk literature: characters seem to be moved by blind elemental forces and in-

photograph by Kèro

stincts which sometimes explode into extreme, irrepressible violence.

Although it has a more realistic setting, a poor neighborhood of Montreal, Benoit's second novel, *Les Voleurs* (1969), presents a series of adventures which are just as fantastic as the manhunt in *Jos Carbone*. In this thriller a church is robbed. The guilty threesome are soon arrested and put into prison where they are cruelly mistreated by the police. Unexpectedly—there is no lack of surprising developments in this novel—they are released at the request of their victim, the bishop. He brings them to his house and involves them in a complicated plot to rig an election. One of the three succeeds in outwitting the bishop, blackmails him, and finally punishes him with physical violence. The robbers emerge as heroes and the bishop as the villain, ridiculous, hypocritical, corrupt, and cowardly. Of particular interest are the novel's picturesque secondary characters, less stereotyped than the main figures. The dialogue, in popular Montreal French, is lifelike and witty, emphasizing the characters' linguistic inventiveness and their sharp dry humor. As folk characters of the Montreal underworld, they equal some of French writer Raymond Queneau's most successful creations.

The novel, however, has a weakness: the first half is narrated by a young boy who arrives in Montreal from a small village. The underworld is thus viewed from his naive perspective, and the major theme emerges as that of an innocent country boy's initiation to urban living. In the middle of the novel the boy disappears and a third-person narrator takes over. The story then becomes essentially a political satire of corrupt election practices focusing on the collusion between corrupt churchmen and corrupt politicians. Because it is developed in only one half of a short novel, the satire remains rather superficial.

Benoit's *Patience et Firlipon* (1970), "roman d'amour," is an entertaining love story about an in-

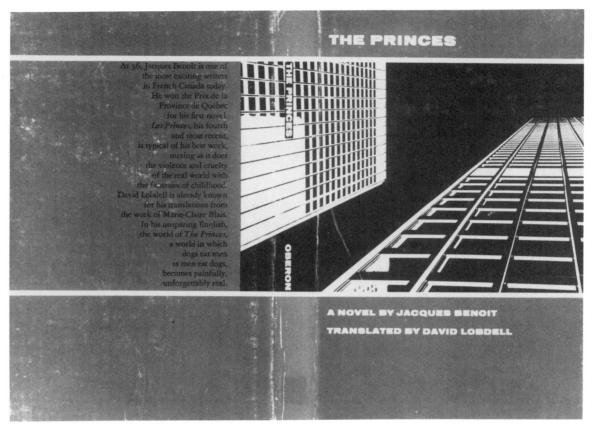

Dust jacket for the English translation of Benoit's 1973 fantasy about a mysterious city inhabited by Blue Men, Monsters, and Dogs

nocent girl and a macho man nicknamed the Gorilla. When the novel begins, Roger Firlipon is a peaceful provincial archivist, but his love for Patience transforms him until he is seized by a fit of passion which drives him to a series of crazy, violent acts. The novel depicts a manhunt during which a crowd of clumsy policemen attempt in vain to arrest the enamoured Firlipon. The two lovers go through a whirlwind courtship, and the book ends with their wedding ceremony, a bacchic orgy during which both bride and groom have to resist forceful seduction by their guests.

Patience et Firlipon may be seen as a parody of movies and television shows that exploit this same peculiar blend of sentimentality and violence. Curiously, Benoit's third novel is set in 1978. Since it was published in 1970, it was for a very brief period a "roman d'anticipation." One wonders about the author's reasons for choosing this time frame. If Benoit was interested in social commentary, the usual motivation for such a device, then he exploits this theme only superficially: the repressive police force, the highly

sophisticated television technology, the dependence on tranquilizers, and the illiteracy of the population are clichés of science-fiction literature. If, however, he wanted to make the fantastic aspects of the novel more acceptable to the reader, the time change seems unnecessary. The present public has enough familiarity with the literature of Superman and other such fanciful characters to accept a fantastic fictive world on its own terms.

The subtle balance between belief and aesthetic distance required in the reading of fantastic literature is superbly handled in Benoit's 1973 novel, *Les Princes* (translated as *The Princes* in 1977). The characters and their world are both frighteningly credible and hauntingly nightmarish. The novel is set in a highly organized, socially stratified city; place and time are unspecified. The ruling class, a small minority, lives on a mountain in the middle of the city (Westmount?); another part of the city, Nilaudante, is a clean, quiet middle-class neighborhood. The story takes place mostly in the miserable working-class areas

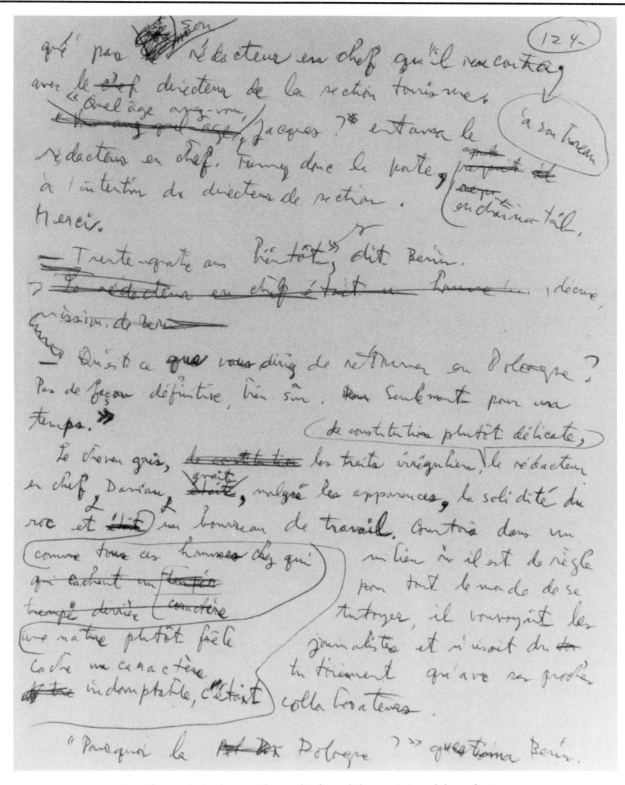

Page from a draft of a recently completed novel (by permission of the author)

where the Blue Men live in animallike conditions. Roaming around are the Monsters, half man, half animal, and the Dogs who have a highly elaborate social organization and are able to use their own complex language to communicate among themselves. One Blue Man, driven by starvation, kills and eats a Dog, an act legally forbidden. A horrible fight ensues between Blue Men and Dogs which leads to the slaughter and extermination of both groups. This fight is encouraged by the ruling class, probably to justify an even more repressive government.

The world Benoit depicts in this novel is a horrifying one in which men and animals are hardly distinguishable and where the oppressed, driven by blind instincts, succeed only in exterminating one another. Fantastic features such as talking dogs or monsters are accepted by the reader because of the hair-raising detachment and objectivity of the narration. In *Les Princes* Benoit has created a coherent fiction which unfolds in a chillingly logical and convincing fashion once the premises have been established.

If there is a symbolic meaning to this story it is not clear cut. Several interpretations are possible: by fighting among themselves the oppressed increase the power of the ruling class; laws, although their origins tend to be forgotten, should be observed or society will collapse in bloody chaos; man is basically motivated by animal instincts and the drive for power; a stable society has to be based on a lucid recognition of human nature. The more cynical of these interpretations are suggested by the Machiavellian allusion of the title.

Benoit's most recent novel, *Gisèle et le serpent* (1981), is the story of a femme fatale, Gisèle, who subjugates, with the help of her pet snake, all men who approach her. She also has the ability to change herself and her lovers into snakes. With one of her lovers, Grégoire Rabouin, Gisèle travels about Montreal and to Moscow. It is Rabouin who narrates the novel, which also includes excerpts from a black notebook supposedly written by Gisèle. On one level *Gisèle et le serpent* is a social satire aimed at extremism and fanaticism. There is, for instance, an episode describing the dissolution of a Maoist cell at Radio-Canada, and there are attacks on all forms of establishment, whether they be tyrannical civil servants in Moscow or powerful surgeons in a Montreal hospital. In Benoit's hands the supernatural and the diabolical are powerful devices with

which to ridicule social ills. A possible model for *Gisèle et le serpent* is Mikhail Bulgakov's *The Master and Margarita* (1966) which is quoted at the end of Benoit's novel.

On another level *Gisèle et le serpent* may be read as a detective novel but one in which the mystery is to be solved by the reader. There are many clues pointing to the probability that the whole story (including the black notebooks) is a figment of Rabouin's imagination. If one accepts such an interpretation, then the novel becomes the expression of the narrator's sexual fantasies and Gisèle the embodiment of his fears of women. No interpretation, however, should overlook the humor and exaggeration that pervade the novel. There is much parody of Freudian symbols and sexual clichés in this allegory of snakes and witches.

Although each novel by Benoit creates a different world of fantasy, there are common features among these books which are the stamp of the artist's personal vision and talent. Benoit's settings are always of major importance. His characters are not remarkable for their psychological subtlety; sometimes the heroes are close to stereotypes, but, driven by their elemental instincts, they have a convincing density. The deep-seated violence that explodes in Benoit's conclusions is one of the most characteristic features of his novels, which seem to expose the violence latent or camouflaged in popular fantasy literature.

It is not easy to situate Jacques Benoit in the context of contemporary Quebec literature. His books are different from the *Parti Pris* novels which are clearly committed to specific social criticism. He does not belong either to the group of Quebec writers who have switched from an attempt to change society to a subversion of literary forms and language. The comparison of Benoit with Roch Carrier, developed by Estelle Dansereau in a 1981 article in *Canadian Literature*, may be quite appropriate, not only because of the fantastic character of Benoit's work but also because of his independent position, apart from organized groups, literary or otherwise.

References:

Estelle Dansereau, "Le Fantastique chez Roch Carrier et Jacques Benoit," *Canadian Literature*, 88 (Spring 1981): 39-45;

François Ricard, "Deux romanciers de trente ans," *Liberté*, 16 (March-April 1974): 88-89.

Louky Bersianik
(Lucile Durand)
(14 November 1930-   )

Patricia Smart
Carleton University

BOOKS: *Koumic le petit esquimau,* as Lucile Durand (Montreal: Centre de Psychologie et de Pédagogie, 1964);

Le Cordonnier Pamphille, mille-pattes, as Durand (Montreal: Centre de Psychologie et de Pédagogie, 1965);

La Montagne et l'escargot, as Durand (Montreal: Centre de Psychologie et de Pédagogie, 1965);

Togo apprenti-remorqueur, as Durand (Montreal: Centre de Psychologie et de Pédagogie, 1966);

L'Euguélionne (Montreal: La Presse, 1976); translated by G. Denis, A. Hewitt, D. Murray, and M. O'Brien as *The Euguelionne* (Victoria: Press Porcépic, 1981);

La Page de garde (St-Jacques-le-Mineur, Quebec: Editions de la Maison, 1978);

Le Pique-nique sur l'Acropole (Montreal: VLB, 1979);

Maternative (Montreal: VLB, 1980);

Les Agénésies du vieux monde (Outremont, Quebec: L'Intégrale, 1982); translated by Miranda Hay and Lise Weil as "Agenesias of the Old World," *Trivia,* 7 (Summer 1985): 33-47;

Au beau milieu de moi (Montreal: Nouvelle Optique, 1983);

Axes et eau (Montreal: VLB, 1984).

OTHER: "Arbre de pertinence et utopie," in *L'émergence d'une Culture au Féminin,* edited by Marisa Zavalloni (Montreal: Saint-Martin, 1987), pp. 117-132.

PERIODICAL PUBLICATIONS: "La Maternité mâle," *Etudes Littéraires,* 12 (December 1979): 407-410;

"Tradition féminine en littérature," *Revue de l'Université d'Ottawa,* 50 (January 1980): 24-27;

"Pourquoi j'écris," *Québec Français,* 47 (October 1982): 30;

"Les réseaux de l'ecriture," *Arcade,* 4-5 (September 1983): 113-130;

"L'herbe était rouge et comme rôtie . . . (La fiction introuvable)," *La Nouvelle Barre du Jour,* 141 (September 1984): 47-48;"Y 2-Q 2-B 2-CL" and "New Cl(ear) era, Song for Ancyl of the long lashes," translated by R. McGee, *Parallelogramme,* 10 (Fall 1984);

"Women's Work," translated by Erika Grundmann, in *In the Feminine: Women and Words/ Les Femmes et les Mots* (Edmonton: Longspoon, 1985), pp. 155-165;

"Comment naître femme sans le devenir," *La Nouvelle Barre du Jour,* 172 (March 1986): 57-65;

"O nuit, qu'en est-il de la transparence?," *Estuaire,* 40-41 (September 1986): 23-28;

"Noli me tangere," translated by Barbara Godard and Erin Mouré, *Northern Literature Quarterly* (Fall 1986);

"Aristotle's Lantern," translated by A. J. Holden Verburg, in *Canadian Women Writers/Les Ecrivaines Canadiennes* (Edmonton: NeWest, 1987).

Louky Bersianik arrived on the Quebec literary scene in 1976 with her best-selling novel *L'Euguélionne,* which perhaps more than any other individual work heralded the arrival of feminism in Quebec literature. She has also produced several stories for children, a substantial body of poetry and of theoretical work, and a second novel, *Le Pique-nique sur l'Acropole* (1979). While sharing in the feminist movement which transformed the themes of Quebec literature beginning in the late 1970s, her work distinguishes itself by its broad-ranging cultural references, its use of humor and parody, and its blend of theory and fiction that is both polemical and irresistibly funny. A product of the classical college system of pre-1960s Quebec, Bersianik uses her detailed knowledge of Greek, Roman, and Chris-

photograph by Jean Letarte

ence (1952), and applied linguistics (1967).

In 1957 Durand married Jean Letarte, who worked with her on numerous productions of children's programs for radio and television. Letarte has illustrated most of her published works. She signed children's stories published during this period Lucile Durand, but for the publication of her radical feminist novel in 1976 she chose a new name neither inherited from her father nor conferred on her by marriage. Louky is a nickname invented by her husband by which she was already known to most of her friends and family; the name Bersianik was inspired by the Bersiamis River in northern Quebec, originally called Betsiamites by the Indians. A lover of word games and a fervent believer in the autonomy of language, she points out that the surname, in addition to its sonority and the association with the Indian peoples that attracted her to it, also contains the word *bercer* (to rock or cradle) as well as affectionate names for her husband (Iani) and her son (Nik). Despite the continuing affection between them, she and her husband have been divorced since 1981.

L'Euguélionne was the product of a long period of growing feminist consciousness, crystallized in particular by Bersianik's experience of reading Simone de Beauvoir and Kate Millett, both of whom are quoted on the opening page. A "triptych novel" with multiple levels of meaning, it is entirely written in chapter and verse form, like the Bible which it parodies and like the civil code which is the basis of Quebec's legal system. It is also a science-fiction novel, using the device of a visitor from another planet as the amazed observer of the subjection of women and their often unquestioning acceptance of this subjection. The power of Bersianik's novel lies in its brilliant and irreverent reversal of perspective. By placing women at the center of its worldview, it reveals the scandal of a culture which in the name of "humanity" has denied freedom and self-respect to more than half of its members, not only in its social institutions and everyday life but also in its "sacred" texts, from the Bible to the works of Freud and his influential interpreter, the French psychoanalyst Jacques Lacan, who began his rereading of Freud in the 1950s. Like Lacan, whom she satirizes in the third section of the novel, Bersianik takes seriously the link between psychoanalysis and language, but unlike him she is aware that the male bias of language (particularly the French language with its gendered nouns) must be undone in order for

tian mythology in a devastating attack on the original texts of Western patriarchal society.

Bersianik was born Lucile Durand, 14 November 1930, in Montreal. Her parents taught her the letters of the Greek alphabet on flashcards when she was three years old (a fact worth noting because the names of the characters in *L'Euguélionne* are inspired by these letters). Her father, Donat Durand, was a French professor and director of an itinerant theater troupe in which she acted for six years, and her mother, Laurence Bissonnet, had been a teacher and musician. After receiving an M.A. in literature and pursuing Ph.D. course work at the University of Montreal, she studied for five years in France, at the Sorbonne and later at the Centre d'Etudes de Radio et de Télévision. Her academic credentials also include diplomas in music (1948), library sci-

Cover for the English translation of Bersianik's "triptych novel," an "anti-Bible" in chapter and verse form whose three "books" correspond to the Old Testament, the New Testament, and the Book of Revelation

women's reality to change.

On its most basic level, *L'Euguélionne* is an "anti-Bible." As the genealogy of her name suggests, the alien Euguélionne (from the Greek *euaggeion*, meaning "good news" or "gospel") is a female Christ or anti-Christ figure. The novel's plot covers the time from her arrival on Earth in search of her "positive planet" and a "male of her species" up to her destruction at the hands of those who have been threatened by the message she brings to the Earth, and her immediate "resurrection" (the reforming of her many fragments into a new whole).

The three "books" of the novel correspond roughly to the Old Testament, the New Testament, and to the Book of Revelation, or the Apocalypse. In the first book the origins of the Euguélionne are recounted in humorous female-centered texts that parody the Bible and the Christian dogma so important in Quebec's cultural past. The doctrine of the Trinity is ridiculed in the description of the complicated "trygyny" of the three divine persons (Mother, Daughter, and Supreme Brain) who are in reality "only one Goddess" and who produced the Euguélionne. Like the patriarchal lineage of Christ, the genealogy of the Euguélionne descends in a series of "begats" from Eve through Sarah, Rachel, Mary Magdalen and the Virgin Mary to Sappho, Antigone, the Erinyes, the Brontës, Betty Friedan, and others; and the description of "Adam's pregnancy" mocks the male self-sufficiency of the Genesis account of creation. The Euguélionne's stories of her own planet of origin provide further satire of a recognizable male-centered world where language and "the Law" are used to perpetuate a master-slave relationship between the two species (the Legislators who control society and the Pedalists who are used to reproduce offspring for them). The novel is full of irreverent attacks on the concept of penis envy: the parable of the Mascles who rule over the Fems because of the magic batons they possess, the account of Eve's horror when she gazes on Adam and sees that he not only lacks breasts but has a ridiculous-looking appendage between his legs. In the third section of the novel, entirely devoted to an exposure of the male bias of psychoanalysis and language, a character named Saint Siegfried who is clearly a composite of Freud and Lacan preaches his "Sermon on the Mount" from a hill outside the Bibliothèque Nationale in Paris: "Hors du Phallus, point de Salut . . . Car . . . l'individu qui naît sans Phallus est perdant au depart. C'est un estropié. Un handicapé physique et mental qui pourrait de venir dangereux s'il lui prenait la fantaisie de se revollér contré son sort inéluctable" (Apart from the Phallus, no salvation. . . . ! For . . . the individual born without a Phallus is lost from the beginning. He is a cripple. Physically and mentally handicapped, he could become dangerous if he took it into his head to revolt against his ineluctable fate). The Euguélionne's own gospel of freedom, love, and equality for all humans is less dogmatic than either the Christian or the psychoanalytic faith: before leaving Earth, she calls on her followers to transgress her words, for "transgresser c'est progresser" (to transgress is to progress).

Bersianik's feminism is evident not only in the content of her writing but also in its form. Both *L'Euguélionne* and her second novel, *Le Pique-nique sur l'Acropole*, break radically with traditional novel form and blend fiction with linguistic and psychoanalytic theory and sociological data. What clearly designates the works as fiction and ac-

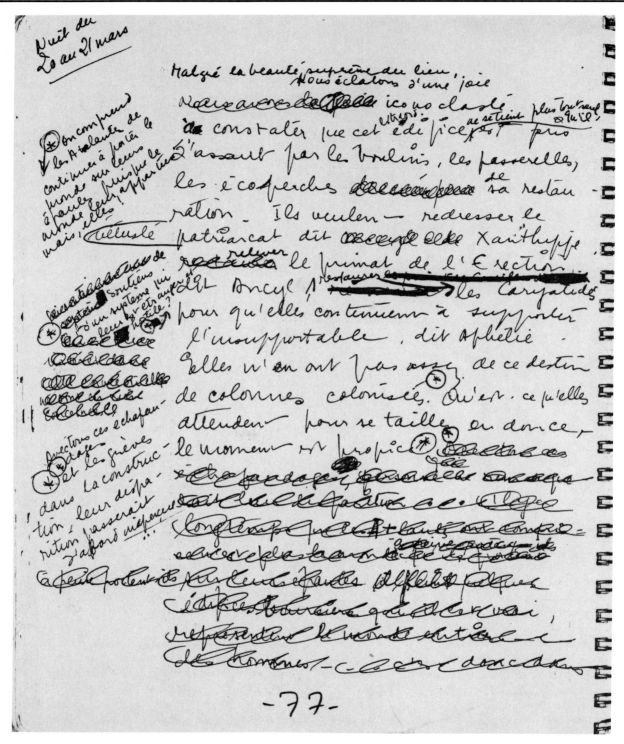

Page from the manuscript for Bersianik's second novel, Le Pique-nique sur l'Acropole, *written in Greece in 1979 (by permission of the author)*

counts for their powerful emotional impact is the presence of a group of female characters drawn from a personal mythology invented by the author, many of whom recur not only in the two novels but also in Bersianik's poetry. While on one level these women are recognizable and "realistic," they also have the immensity and resonance of mythical beings who have emerged from a long history of suffering and endurance, and who, as they grow toward consciousness, have within them the power to change human history.

This growing power of women as they discover one another as mothers and sisters and learn to trust their bodies, minds, and instincts provides the theme and the structural framework for Bersianik's second novel, *Le Pique-nique sur l'Acropole*. Whereas *L'Euguélionne* parodies the Bible, *Le Pique-nique sur l'Acropole* goes back to an even earlier text of patriarchy: Plato's *Symposium*. A parody of and response to Plato's dialogue (of males) concerning the nature of love and sexuality, Bersianik's novel centers not on a banquet but on a picnic, not on the points of view of men but on those of women. Having neither the time nor the money for a banquet, the characters make some sandwiches and picnic by night at the Acropolis (they are excluded during the day), discussing their own attitudes to life, husbands, lovers, and society's treatment of women. Among them is Xantippe, the infamous wife of Socrates who has been remembered throughout history as a shrew, but who turns out to be a strong and humorous woman somewhat skeptical of her husband's philosophizing, given his lack of participation in the responsibilities of home and family. One of Bersianik's constant concerns is to give life to the female figures of Greek mythology. As she writes in her 1982 essay, *Les Agénésies du vieux monde* (translated and published in a 1985 issue of the magazine *Trivia* as "Agenesias of the Old World"), they are part of the memory that has been stolen from women by history. Even if they were created by men, they are women and have much to tell humankind. Thus the menu of Plato's banquet as imagined in *Le Pique-nique sur l'Acropole* includes the various birds, plants, and animals into which women chose to be transformed rather than submit to rape by the gods: Procne's nightingales, baked swallows with Phiomela sauce, foods seasoned with Daphne's bay leaves, and so on.

An important theme of the novel is the relationship between writing and the body; and the form created by the arrangement of text and illustrations vividly suggests the materiality of the text and the politics of liberation associated with writing "l'ecriture du corps" (from the body). Drawings of various kinds of windows, each containing a thought-provoking quotation relating to women's situation, allow the text to "breathe" for the reader and to open onto the historical and social reality that is the inevitable outcome of women's oppression in language and myth. For the characters and their dialogue Bersianik draws liberally on such works as Shere Hite's study of female sexual preferences, the *Hite Report* (1981), and Phyllis Chesler's study *Women and Madness* (1973). The most striking example of the novel's powerful fusion of fiction and feminist theory is the character Adizetu, based on a real African child who was a victim of clitoridectomy and whose photograph is included in the text. The discussion of clitoridectomy thus becomes not only an illustration of the way patriarchal myth and symbol lead to violence and mutilation against real women; it is also an experience whose violence the reader can experience empathetically through her identification with the fictional character.

In the final scene of *Le Pique-nique sur l'Acropole*, Avertine, a madwoman based on Phyllis Chesler's account of the psychological damage done to women by their lack of female-centered mothers, escapes from her psychiatric hospital to join her sisters. Hungry for the touch and caress of a mother, she turns to one of the caryatids (the statues that support the Erechtheum of the Acropolis) and begs her for an embrace, and in response to her need the statue reaches out to her. Thus the image of women turning toward one another, mothers and daughters discovering each other at last as women, becomes the signal for the collapse of the patriarchal age and the beginning of change.

Bersianik's two volumes of poetry, *Maternative* (1980) and *Axes et eau* (1984), explore further the inner lives of various characters from the novels and their symbolic implications in terms of women's history. In this sense, the poetry is perhaps of most interest as apprentice work for the as yet unpublished novel "Pour une archéologie du futur," which Bersianik intends as the third volume of the trilogy begun by *L'Euguélionne* and *Le Pique-nique sur l'Acropole*. Similarly, the essay *Les Agénésies du vieux monde* is an exercise in feminist theory of value in itself, but at least as valuable as a background piece to Bersianik's novels. Together, the novels and the shorter works make it clear that Louky Bersianik is a writer with a transforming vision, whose compassion, intelligence, and erudition are producing a growing body of work aimed at inaugurating a new age in history. Unlike Socrates, the "sage-femme des esprits" (midwife of the mind) whom she mocks as one of the many males who have attempted to appropriate symbolically for themselves the power of giving birth, she is truly a midwife, aiding in the birth of a new and necessary system of values for women and for all humankind.

Reference:

Jennifer Waelti-Waters, "The Food of Love: Plato's Banquet and Bersianik's Picnic," *Atlantis*, 6, no. 1 (1981): 97-103.

Carol Bolt
(25 August 1941-   )

Cynthia Diane Zimmerman
York University

BOOKS: *Buffalo Jump* (Toronto: Playwrights Co-op, 1972);

My Best Friend Is Twelve Feet High (Toronto: Playwrights Co-op, 1972);

Cyclone Jack (Toronto: Playwrights Co-op, 1972);

Gabe (Toronto: Playwrights Co-op, 1973);

Red Emma (Toronto: Playwrights Co-op, 1974);

Tangleflags (Toronto: Playwrights Co-op, 1974);

Maurice (Toronto: Playwrights Co-op, 1975);

Shelter (Toronto: Playwrights Co-op, 1975);

One Night Stand (Toronto: Playwrights Co-op, 1977);

Escape Entertainment (Toronto: Playwrights Canada, 1981);

Drama in the Classroom (Toronto: Playwrights Canada, 1986).

PLAY PRODUCTIONS: *Daganawida*, Toronto, Toronto Workshop Productions, 13 January 1970;

Next Year Country, Regina, Globe Theatre, March 1971; revised as *Buffalo Jump*, Toronto, Theatre Passe Muraille, 18 May 1972;

My Best Friend Is Twelve Feet High, Toronto, Young People's Theatre, 27 July 1972;

Cyclone Jack, Toronto, Young People's Theatre, November 1972;

Gabe, Toronto, Toronto Free Theatre, 6 February 1973;

Pauline, Toronto, Theatre Passe Muraille, 22 March 1973;

Tangleflags, Toronto, Young People's Theatre, September 1973;

Red Emma, Toronto, Toronto Free Theatre, 14 February 1974;

The Bluebird, narration by Bolt, Toronto, Black Box Theatre at St. Lawrence Centre, 16 February 1974;

Maurice, Toronto, Young People's Theatre, April 1974;

Blue, Toronto, Young People's Theatre, 1974;

Shelter, Toronto, Young People's Theatre and University Alumnae Dramatic Club, Firehall Theatre, 21 November 1974;

Finding Bumble, Toronto, Young People's Theatre at the Ontario Science Centre, 3 February 1975;

Norman Bethune: On Board the S.S. Empress of Asia, Gravenhurst, Ontario, Muskoka Summer Theatre, Summer 1976;

Okey Doke, Queen's University Drama Department, Kingston Ontario, Summer 1976;

T.V. Lounge, Toronto, Redlight Theatre, 24 February 1977;

One Night Stand, Toronto, Tarragon Theatre, 9 April 1977;

Desperadoes, Toronto, Toronto Free Theatre, 5 October 1977;

Carol Bolt

Escape Entertainment (workshopped as *Deadline*, Toronto, Factory Theatre Lab, 1979), Toronto, Tarragon Theatre, 3 January 1981;
Love of Life, Toronto, Solar Stage, 9 July 1981;
Love or Money, Blyth, Ontario, Blyth Summer Festival, Summer 1981.

MOTION PICTURE: *Fidelity*, script by Bolt, Allan King Associates, 1975.

TELEVISION: "Valerie," *To See Ourselves*, CBC, 1971;
"A Nice Girl Like You," *The Collaborators*, CBC, 1974;
Distance, True North, (Ontario), 1974;
Red Emma, Performance, CBC / Allan King Associates, 4 January 1976;
Cyclone Jack, CBC, 1977;
One Night Stand, Front Row Centre, CBC / Allan King Associates, 8 March 1978;
"The Move," story by Bolt, *King of Kensington*, CBC, 1978;
"In a Far Country," *Klondike Series*, CBC, 1981;
Mayor Charlotte, The Winners, CBC, 1982;
"I Don't Care," *Fraggle Rock*, CBC, 1983;
"The Delinquent," "The School Show," "The Seance," "Invasion from Outer Space," and "Tnneers," *Edison Twins*, CBC, 1983;
"Dungeons and Raccoons," and "All the News that Fits," by Bolt and B. P. Nichol, *Evergreen Raccoons*, CBC, 1984;

"The Common Factor," *Edison Twins*, CBC, 1985.

RADIO: *Guy and Jack, Saskatchewan Writers*, CBC, 1970;
Fast Forward, CBC Stage, CBC, 1976;
Silent Pictures, Stereo Theatre, CBC, 11 June 1983;
Tinsel on my Stetson, Morningside, CBC, 5-9 March 1984;
Unconscious, Sunday Matinee, CBC, 19 January 1986;
Dancing with Each Other, Morningside, CBC, 13-17 April 1987.

Carol Bolt has repeatedly been described as one of Canada's most prolific and successful playwrights. Born on 25 August 1941 in Winnipeg, Manitoba, the only child of William Johnson, a logger and miner, and his wife, Marjorie Small Johnson, she grew up in mining towns across Canada. Settling in Vancouver for a time, Bolt received her bachelor of arts degree from the University of British Columbia in 1961. Shortly after graduating, she moved to England. Returning to Canada a few years later, she settled in Montreal where she worked as a market researcher. Partly out of boredom, she and a few friends started a small theater there in 1963. The theater closed because the building could not meet fire regulations, and she was transferred to Toronto in 1964. She decided to abandon the research job and do prop making and stage managing instead.

While stage manager for an amateur production of British playwright Christopher Fry's *The Lady's Not For Burning*, she met actor David Bolt, whom she married on 19 June 1969. Although she had written plays as an undergraduate, her professional playwriting career began when a friend showed George Luscombe her script "Daganawida," and he developed it for his theater, Toronto Workshop Productions, in 1970. After the Theatre Passe Muraille's mounting of *Buffalo Jump* in 1972, Bolt decided to write full-time, and, over the years, she saw her work move from small, impoverished alternate stages to main stages across Canada. She spent four years as resident playwright for Toronto Free Theatre when it was newly formed and struggling; three years as dramaturge for Young People's Theatre Summer Theatre School. Bolt was writer-in-residence at the University of Toronto in 1977-1978 and at the University of Connecticut in 1979. A pioneer of Canadian theater, a founding member of the Playwright's Union of Canada, and consistently active on behalf of the theater community, Bolt was recognized for her commitment in 1978 when she received the Silver Jubilee Award. Currently she lives in Toronto with her husband and her son, Alexander.

Bolt was part of the alternate theater movement of the early 1970s. Motivated by the alternate aesthetic–theater as experience, as event, as antiestablishment in its methods–as well as by the desire to put their own work on stage, the theater community committed itself to the creation of original Canadian plays. Bolt's first experience with the collaborative method of creation popular with the emerging alternate theater companies was workshopping *Daganawida* with Luscombe. The play, a revue about the hostilities between the Indians and the French settlers in seventeenth-century Quebec, was not well received, mainly because it lacked a cohesive structure–a fault common to the revue format. An early version of her next play, *Buffalo Jump*, was produced by Regina's Globe Theatre in 1971 under the title *Next Year Country*. Based on historical documents, the play is about the 1935 march to Ottawa by unemployed laborers and the ensuing riots in Estevan and Regina. The play was almost completely rewritten when Bolt returned to Toronto the following year. The script for *Buffalo Jump* used by Passe Muraille, like that for *Pauline* and a number of her plays for children, was created during rehearsals with the director and cast.

The early plays–*Daganawida, Buffalo Jump, Pauline,* and *Gabe* (the last two produced in 1973)– have significant elements in common. Plays about social issues, they are all based on actual historical figures and events (*Gabe* concerns the métis leaders Louis Riel and Gabriel Dumont and their connection to their modern descendants), but they are not documentaries. In fact, Bolt is more interested in romance, in theatricality, and in entertainment values than in historical accuracy. As she puts it, "Myth is more appealing than fact. It postulates that heroism is possible, that people can be noble and effective and change things." That optimism, that belief in heroic possibility, is central to the spirit of her characterizations. And an irreverent, freewheeling presentation of reinterpreted historical material, a kind of energetic and flamboyant theatrical style (complete with whimsical ironies and cartoonlike exaggerations), has come to be seen as Bolt's particular forte.

Her approach–bearing the imprint of the collective creation process but more strongly focused on a single character–culminated in the

Cover for the 1976 Playwrights Co-op publication of two plays Bolt wrote during her association with the Toronto-based Young People's Theatre

production of *Red Emma* in 1974. This staging of the play at the Toronto Free Theatre marked a breakthrough in her career. *Red Emma* opened to wide critical acclaim. Based on the life of anarchist-feminist Emma Goldman, it is set in New York in the 1890s and celebrates the fiery idealism of this inspirational young woman. Although it deals with a sensitive subject, the freedom fighter, the play's intention is unabashedly romantic. The work does not engage the ethics of radical political action; rather, its preoccupation is with the charismatic adventuress, with the urgency of her passion for politics and emotional entanglements. The script skillfully incorporates familiar Bolt techniques: rapid, episodic scene changes; the interweaving of songs, processions, speeches, and direct audience address; the juxtaposition of caricatures and realistic portrayals; the use of minimal props; and a large cast of characters.

In the same time period, from 1970 to 1975, Bolt was affiliated with Young People's Theatre and writing plays for children. These plays– *My Best Friend Is Twelve Feet High* (1972), *Cyclone Jack* (1972), *Tangleflags* (1974), and *Maurice*

(1975), among others—written in close association with directors Tim Bond or Ray Whelan, also explore Canadian themes and use sophisticated theatrical techniques which combine music, mime, and parade in a lively, educating, and entertaining fashion.

With the play *Shelter*, produced in Toronto in 1974, Bolt entered a new terrain. Although it presents a social issue and offers a mix of politics and heroics, *Shelter* is both fictional and contemporary. The plot focuses on a Saskatchewan widow's foray into politics after the death of her M.P. husband. A comedy about life and politics on the prairies, it is observant and witty on the role of women in public life and on the kind of sheltered lives they frequently live.

With the production of *One Night Stand* at Toronto's Tarragon Theatre in April 1977, Bolt had a hit. A riveting comedy-thriller about a young woman and the drifter she picks up in a bar, *One Night Stand* is, in Bolt's estimation, "endearing nonsense," pure entertainment without social significance. However, it remains her most popular adult piece to date. It was a runner-up for the 1977 Chalmers Canadian Play Award, and the CBC television adaptation won three Canadian film awards in 1978. It is slick, spare, amusing, and suspenseful. Although not meant as a comment on the perils of the singles scene, the play still has something serious to say about casual encounters having frightening consequences.

Shortly after *One Night Stand* came *Desperadoes*, an angry play about a writer who thinks his movie will stop the Vietnam war. Bolt claims this play, which premiered at the Toronto Free Theatre in October 1977, is a didactic comedy about money, about the artist as voyeur. In contrast to *One Night Stand*, *Desperadoes* met with strongly worded unfavorable reviews. *Escape Entertainment*, a work similar in theme, was mounted by the Tarragon Theatre in 1981. Although it has more distance on the issue, it is also a play about the Americanization of the Canadian film industry, also about idealistic individuals who want to change things. Originally workshopped at the Fac-

tory Theatre Lab as *Deadline*, the final product played to full houses in spite of bad reviews. Reviewers particularly disliked the character Laurel, a vicious critic from New York who, as a result of falling in love, is transformed into an eager participant in the making of authentic homegrown movies.

After *Love or Money*, about the strange disappearance of Canadian movie magnate Ambrose Small, staged in 1981 at the Blyth Summer Festival in Ontario, Bolt turned her energy to writing for radio and television. She now has many productions to her credit. A recent fifty-minute radio play entitled *Unconscious* was aired on CBC in January 1986. Exploring the explosive relationship between a father and his thirteen-year-old son and a murderous rage which is inadvertantly acted on, this intensely psychological work indicates that Bolt's interests and abilities are not restricted to the kind of entertainment for which she is best known. Her versatility as a writer is clearly one of her virtues. Having written the script for the 1985 *Dora Mavor Awards* and a teacher's manual on theater techniques, *Drama in the Classroom* (1986), she is currently working on an adult stage play entitled "Survival" (about an antinuclear activist and her brother), considering another series of television scripts, maintaining her hectic schedule of theater workshops in the schools, and preparing a script (about a teenage girl who wants to play hockey) for Theatre on the Move, a Toronto-based theater company which tours the Ontario schools.

References:

Diane Bessai, "Three Plays by Carol Bolt," *Canadian Drama*, 4 (Spring 1978): 64-67;

Sandra Souchotte, Introduction to *Playwrights in Profile: Carol Bolt* (Toronto: Playwrights Co-op, 1976), pp. 7-13;

Cynthia Zimmerman, "Carol Bolt," in *The Work: Conversations with English-Canadian Playwrights*, by Zimmerman and Robert Wallace (Toronto: Coach House Press, 1982), pp. 264-276.

Elizabeth Brewster

(26 August 1922-   )

Fred Cogswell
University of New Brunswick

BOOKS: *East Coast* (Toronto: Ryerson, 1951);
Lillooet (Toronto: Ryerson, 1954);
Roads, and Other Poems (Toronto: Ryerson, 1957);
Passage of Summer: Selected Poems (Toronto: Ryerson, 1969);
Sunrise North: Poems (Toronto: Clarke, Irwin, 1972);
In Search of Eros (Toronto: Clarke, Irwin, 1974);
The Sisters: A Novel (Ottawa: Oberon, 1974);
It's Easy to Fall on the Ice: Ten Stories (Ottawa: Oberon, 1977)
Sometimes I Think of Moving (Ottawa: Oberon, 1977);
The Way Home (Ottawa: Oberon, 1982);
Digging In (Ottawa: Oberon, 1982);
Junction (Windsor, Ontario: Black Moss, 1983);
A House Full of Women (Ottawa: Oberon, 1983);
Selected Poems of Elizabeth Brewster 1944-1977 (Ottawa: Oberon, 1985);
Selected Poems of Elizabeth Brewster 1977-1984 (Ottawa: Oberon, 1985);
Visitations (Ottawa: Oberon, 1987).

Elizabeth Brewster

As a young poet in the 1940s, Elizabeth Brewster wrote in an almost desperate attempt to order the chaos of her own psyche. Even then, she possessed the artistry to distance and objectify her own internal struggle by transferring it to the people and landscape of semirural New Brunswick where her childhood and adolescence were spent. Today, some forty years later, she has come to terms with herself, but the process of ordering still continues. Her current poetry is largely concerned with the spirit of place in western Canada. Having determined who she is, Brewster is now attempting to establish her proper home.

This twofold quest—first to establish identity, and second to place that identity within the context of a kaleidoscopic society—indicates that Brewster is answering creatively two of the greatest challenges that the twentieth century poses. Her prose is identical in its aims to her poetry, and her work from the very beginning has been essentially modern. It is unfortunate that because she has written realistically and effectively out of the experience of her own milieu, her reputation as a regional—and therefore minor—writer has obscured the fact that her work expresses—in its struggles, fantasies, judgments, and triumphs—what is most common and important to all.

The fact, and indeed the depth, of the struggle expressed in Brewster's poetry has also, paradoxically, been obscured by the author's technical skill. Peter Stevens writes in the 1973 *Supplement to the Oxford Companion to Canadian History and Literature*: "Her poetry is prevented from becom-

From the first draft for "Assignment," one of the selections in Oberon Press's 1985 volume covering Brewster's poetry from 1977 to 1984 (by permission of the author)

ing too obsessively gloomy, however, by the honest attitudes she takes to the individuals she remembers, and it is enlivened at times by humorous understatement and self-mockery. Furthermore, its simplicity of structure and diction express a disarming delight in ordinary objects and events." This statement is true but gives no hint of what underlies the "simplicity" and the "disarming delight in ordinary objects and events." For these things, it is necessary to look more closely at the events of Brewster's life.

Elizabeth Brewster was born in 1922 in the small lumber town of Chipman, New Brunswick. Her father, Frederick John Brewster, was an unlucky store clerk and manager who held many positions during the course of his life, but none of them for long. Her mother, Ethel Day Brewster, was an evangelical Christian, and her siblings adapted readily enough—too readily in Elizabeth Brewster's opinion—to filling humble niches in the social order to which they were born. Brewster—then a small, thin, nearsighted girl, painfully shy, and fearful of human relations—escaped into a world of order, opulence, and ideas in books and poems, determined to make learning her passport to a similar world in real life. She succeeded so well that, solely on scholarships and assistantships, she was able to attend the University of New Brunswick (B.A., 1946); Radcliffe College (A.M., 1947); the University of London; the University of Toronto (B.L.S., 1953); and the University of Indiana (Ph.D., 1962).

In the early 1940s at the University of New Brunswick, Brewster was strongly influenced by the study of English and American literature under the direction of Edward McCourt and Desmond Pacey. Also influential were the poet A. G. Bailey and the members of the Bliss Carman Poetry Society, which Bailey had founded in 1940. Brewster also received a thorough grounding in Latin and Greek language and literature. By her graduation, her characteristic styles in both poetry and prose had been formed.

While Brewster did her graduate work to obtain the requisite credits for an academic career, she worked part-time as a junior lecturer or librarian. During this time, Brewster had to cope with the old age and deaths of her parents, the loneliness inherent in changing locations, the frustration of trying to get good but unfashionable work published, and the realization that a lack of personal relationships was leading both to growing internal tensions and to employment difficulties. She turned to psychiatry and converted to

Cover for Brewster's 1983 romance about a middle-aged woman who travels backward in time and has the chance to relive a part of her life

Roman Catholicism, finally discovering that the keys to functioning successfully as an individual within society are self-acceptance and a will to survive. Brewster is currently a member of the English Department at the University of Saskatchewan, a popular, if unobtrusive, figure in literary circles, and—when time and circumstances permit—an enthusiastic traveler.

Part of Brewster's difficulty in having her early work published lay in the fact that her poetry was based on rural and small-town rather than urban experience and that it was mainly traditional in form. The problem was augmented by her elitism with respect to the places to which she submitted work for publication. She was correspondingly hard on herself in submitting very few selections, with the result that although her first three volumes—*East Coast* (1951), *Lillooet* (1954), and *Roads, and Other Poems* (1957)—were of high quality, they were too slim to have much impact upon the reading public. This defect was remedied with the publication of the full-length volume *Passage of Summer: Selected Poems* (1969), a book which established her reputation among Canada's most mature and gifted poets. That reputation has been since consolidated by her more recent volumes of verse, *Sunrise North* (1972); *In Search of Eros* (1974), *Sometimes I Think of Moving* (1977), and *The Way Home* (1982). Poems by Brewster have, during the past few years, been included in increasing numbers in anthologies designed for schools, universities, and the general public. In 1985 Ottawa's Oberon Press published two volumes entitled *Selected Poems of Elizabeth Brewster*, covering forty years of her work. The fact remains, however, that for all her seeming simplicity, she is still "a poet's poet" and apt to remain so.

In recent years Brewster has turned increasingly to prose fiction. Her novels, *The Sisters* (1974) and *Junction* (1983), are low-key accounts of New Brunswick life, written with great sensitivity and concern for form. She has also produced three well-crafted story collections, *It's Easy to Fall on the Ice* (1977), *A House Full of Women* (1983), and *Visitations* (1987). Among the awards and honors she has received are the President's Medal from the University of Western Ontario (1979) and a Litt. D. from the University of New Brunswick.

References:

Robert Gibbs, "Next Time From a Different Country," *Canadian Literature*, no. 62 (Autumn 1974): 17-32;

Desmond Pacey, "The Poetry of Elizabeth Brewster," *Ariel*, 4 (July 1973): 58-69.

Paul Chamberland
(16 May 1939-   )

David F. Rogers
University of British Columbia

BOOKS: *Genèses* (Montreal: A. G. E. U. M., 1962);
Le Pays, by Chamberland, Ghislain Côté, Nicole Drassel, Michel Garneau, and André Major (Montreal: Déom, 1963);
Terre Québec (Montreal: Déom, 1964);
L'Afficheur hurle (Montreal: Parti Pris, 1964);
L'Inavouable (Montreal: Parti Pris, 1967);
Eclats de la pierre noire d'oùrejaillit ma vie (Montreal: Editions Danielle Laliberté, 1972);
Demain les dieux naîtront (Montreal: Editions de l'Hexagone, 1974);
Le Prince de Sexamour (Montreal: Editions de l'Hexagone, 1976);
Extrême survivance, extrême poésie (Montreal: Parti Pris, 1978);
Terre souveraine (Montreal: Editions de l'Hexagone, 1980);
L'Enfant doré (Montreal: Editions de l'Hexagone, 1980);
Emergence de l'adultenfant (Montreal: Basile, 1981);
Un Parti pris anthropologique (Montreal: Parti Pris, 1983);
Aléatoire instantané & Midsummer 82 (Trois-Rivières, Quebec: Les Ecrits des Forges, 1983);
Le Recommencement du monde (Longueuil, Quebec: Préambule, 1983);
Compagnons chercheurs (Longueuil, Quebec: Préambule, 1984);
L'Inceste et la génocide (Longueuil, Quebec: Préambule, 1985).

OTHER: "De la forge à la bouche," in *Littérature du Québec*, edited by Robert Guy (Montreal: Déom, 1970), pp. 287-302.

PERIODICAL PUBLICATIONS: "Aliénation culturelle et révolution nationale," *Parti Pris*, 1 (October 1963): 10-22;
"Dans un automne à nous (nouvelle)," *Etudes du Canada Français*, 18 (1964): 129-145;
"Les Contradictions de la révolution tranquille," *Parti Pris*, 1 (February 1964): 6-29;
"De la damnation à la liberté," *Parti Pris*, 1 (Summer 1964): 53-89;
"L'Individu révolutionnaire," *Parti Pris*, 3 (December 1965): 6-31;
"Fondation du territoire–Avant-propos méthodologique," *Parti Pris*, 4 (May-August 1967): 11-42;
"Au-dessus de tout (téléthéâtre)," *Voix et Images du Pays*, 6 (1973): 181-211.

The Quebec poet Paul Chamberland was born in Longueuil, a suburb of Montreal. The son of Lucien Chamberland, an industrial designer, and German Lepage Chamberland, he was educated at the Séminaire Sainte-Croix and the Collège de Saint-Laurent. Upon completion of his studies in philosophy at the Université de Montréal *(bachelier ès arts*, in 1961; *baccalauréat*, 1963; *license*, 1964), he attended the Ecole Practique des Hautes Etudes at the Sorbonne in Paris. At the Sorbonne Chamberland worked on a thesis dealing with poetic and prosaic language, but as an act of rebellion during the 1968 Paris student revolt, he apparently burned it, terminating his formal studies. Subsequently, he taught French and philosophy at the Université de Montréal (1968-1970) and at several Quebec colleges and worked as an editor and translator for the power company Hydro-Quebec. In 1963 Chamberland was a cofounder of the periodical *Parti Pris*. From 1970 to 1973 he was involved in the design of sociocultural multimedia presentations for In-Média, a company founded by Fernand Dansereau. He is also a member of the political movement Libération Populaire and is in the forefront of a generation of socialist poets whose aim is to bring about Quebec's independence.

Since 1963 Chamberland has been engaged in a difficult experiment with other authors. Stylistic expression and the expression of the preoccupations of everyday life are his main concerns. He is particularly interested in questions of love in the general as well as in the specific sense of

Paul Chamberland (photograph by Kèro)

the term. These concerns are reflected in the periodical *Hobo-Québec*, of which he was the principal organizer in the 1970s, as well as in his works which try to bring together events, happenings, and feelings of everyday life in a way that communicates the depth of life itself, the anguished voice of an entire people, and his own personal anguish. Chamberland's poetry is difficult to penetrate, even hermetic. He has been accused of being as pretentious as Molière's Trissotin, and some critics have compared him to Victor Hugo, calling him a collector of words. Jacques Saint-Yves, for one, described Chamberland's *Terre Québec* as a seemingly random compilation of words blessed by chance with critical success: "De *Terre Québec*, on peut dire . . . : 'Des mots, des mots, des mots!' Mais des mots vides, délavés, mésalliés, perdus de sens. On croirait que le poète lauréat a renversé le dictionnaire, qu'il a ramassé pêle-mêle les mots épars, qu'il les a jetés dans un volume, et qu'un hasard merveilleux a créé un chef-d'oeuvre" (Of *Terre Québec* one might say . . . : "Words, words, words!" But empty words, washed out, mismatched, deprived of meaning. One might think that the prize-winning poet had turned the dictionary upside down, gathered words together pell-mell, thrown them into a volume, and that a wondrous stroke of chance had created a chef d'oeuvre). Chamberland did break with the logical structure of the sentence and with the traditional rules of versification; imagery and symbols convey his meaning making a paradigmatic as well as a syntagmatic reading of his poetry a necessity. Chamberland's message in his poetry resembles more closely that of Saint-John Perse, Eluard, or Aimé Césaire than that of Mallarmé because of the profusion of images and the permanence of certain themes. Three of Chamberland's important collections of poems reveal the essential concerns of the poet and his approach to what is vital to him.

The title of his first collection of poems, *Genèses* (1962), gives some insight into its content. It endeavors to be spiritual (Chamberland was at one time profoundly influenced by the Bible) and at the same time deeply pervaded by the humane (poetry of mankind rather than of the individual). Spirit and water are the two fundamental images underlying the entire work. Closely allied are secondary images such as those of the mirror, the eye, the glance, the stone, wind, and fire, which are developed in succession. *Genèses* is concerned with metamorphosis: "La pierre boit l'oeil et l'assèche"(the stone drinks the eye and dries it); the spirit becomes liquid, water becomes petrified, and one witnesses the coming of a world in which the spirit is present but not transcendental, in which man alone is responsible for overseeing and assuring the rigorous duties of justice and morality.

The first movement of *Genèses* shows the poet divided between two solutions to the problem of how man might best live in the world. The first would be to deny the flesh, "périr luminaire," that is make of death a witness to light, man having attained the ultimate point, having become solely a bearer of light. The other solution, still rather nebulous, would attempt to take the flesh into account and avoid making life a total sacrifice of the carnal. The second movement of the collection opens and ends on the evocation of the flesh; the first attempt has thus failed, and the poet suddenly discovers that he cannot regain his original unity. Wind and fire burst forth like blind forces which mock the spirit and its curiosity: "Le Feu soulèvera toutes vos questions dans un éclat de rire" (The Fire will carry off all your questions in a burst of laughter), and, in the poem "Rues digatures ciseaux," the poet speaks of a religion in which man is fundamental. The poet openly takes sides with flesh, blood, earth, and bone, the four elements: "les quatre soliveaux de la Messe précaire." However, the rejection of God is felt like a fault, a "déraison" or folly (the title of another poem). To embrace humankind (or flesh) does not require the abandonment of spirit, however. The poet chooses humankind in Christian terms. The last poem of this part of the collection indicates that the poet has gone beyond the Manichean body/mind opposition. The poem returns to light, allowing fire to manifest the truth of both sex and thought: "ton être tropical enracinera le jour à même le noeud du sexe et de la pensée" (your tropical being will implant the day at the very knot of sex and thought).

The third movement of *Genèses*, "Le Sang des blés," seems to be made of flashes which have the weightlessness of certain of Eluard's poems. The anguish as well as the intellectual endeavor which sought the resolution to conflict are abandoned. For the first time, in the last poem of this part of the collection, there is an expression of human love in precise terms, and it is the poet's country ("pays") which is to receive it: "J'abolirai tout miroir en un pays qui me regarde et m'aime" (I will abolish every mirror in a country that looks at me and loves me). However, with the fourth and last group of poems in *Genèses* the problem of man and the world resurfaces and one is confronted with despair.

The second of Chamberland's collections of poetry, *Terre Québec* (1964), won the first Prix de la Province de Québec, recognizing the poet's talent but at the same time unleashing much harsh criticism. This second collection, in which the tone becomes increasingly violent as the poems unfold, is as difficult to penetrate as the first. The title of the collection allows one to anticipate that the poems are built around nationalist themes; the poet does, however, wish to express deeper concerns. According to Maximilien Laroche in a 1964 piece for *Livres et Auteurs Canadiens*, "il se servira du thème nationaliste comme d'un levier de transformation de l'homme même." *Terre Québec* makes use of a theme already present in the first collection, that of the return to the earth, but this time it is a question of the return to the woman-earth, a return which is a love conquest:

> retourné
> . . . .
> à ton visage ô terre
> . . . .
> à la vérité du labour
> . . . .
> et de la bête brune qui bêle
> renversé d'amour sous le
> dieu immédiat
>
> (returned / . . . / to your face,
> O Earth, / . . . / and the truth
> of work / . . . / and the truth
> of the bleating brown beast/
> spelled for love under the instant
> god).

Terre Québec includes committed, patriotic, and nationalist poetry, poems with evocative titles such as "Poème de la sentinelle," "Naissance du rebelle," "Ite missa est," "Deuil 4 juin 1963," "Le Temps de la haine," "Le Poème de l'Antérévolution," titles which are perhaps less war cries than preparation or mobilization for battle. For the first time Chamberland designates clearly in his poetry the oppressor. Specifically, he rejects the multifaceted alienation of the people of Quebec. What they need is a poetry of love but it is difficult to find because it can only really exist once the "pays"–the nation of Quebec–is free. Chamberland shows that love is closely associated with patriotism and that it symbolizes the birth of the "pays" before going on to address the problems which confront people in the existing world. In this collection, as in the first, there seems to be a return to the past: illumination takes place slowly, accompanied by violence and sorrow. However, there is at least the suggestion of a possible solution to the problems by means of an indispensable return to a traditional rite of purification.

In *Terre Québec* the major themes–of freedom and its opposites, alienation and anguish–are embodied in the symbol of light. Related to the image of light is the idea of verbal communication itself, which increases or decreases, which becomes clearer or more blurred. Another motif–that of severance–allows, paradoxically, for the passage from alienation to freedom. This motif is usually associated with the image of blood. Severance, or separation, is thus potentially violent, but politically and linguistically enlivening.

From the point of view of language, which is particularly interesting in this collection of poems, one notes an abundance of nouns which reveal a yearning for the poet to name and thus to re-create, to reinvent his native "pays": "J'invente du silence un nom plus refermé que l'atome" (I invent from the silence a name more closed up than the atom).

By contrast, the poet's verbs seem, on one hand, to consolidate and affirm this re-creation and to prevent poetry from being a mere outpouring of feeling; on the other hand, the verbs are synonymous with expression: "dire," "articuler," "parler," "hurler," "sacrer," "répondre," "transverbérer," "speakwhite(r)." The verb *to speak white* recalls Michèle Lalonde's 1970 poem of that title which adopted the racist rhetoric of 1960s America to denounce anglophone Canada's treatment of francophones (a theme reiterated in Pierre Vallières's 1968 work *Nègres blancs d'Amérique*). The verb *hurler*–as in the title of Chamberland's 1964 poetry collection *L'Afficheur hurle* (The Shouting Signpainter)–anticipates energy of Quebecois political activism in the 1970s. One notices as well how many privative terms Chamberland uses with a dispossessing meaning: "déchiré," "décapité," "dépossède," "désaffecté," "déblasonné," "détraqué," "déraciné," "déministrer," "déchaussé," "démesure," "illégitime." The

Quebecois identity is not yet secure. Moreover, Chamberland's language hesitates between affectation and familiarity; it is at once lofty, distant, cheeky. Chamberland wants to be listened to but creates a dense combination of the Montreal working-class slang *joual*, English, French, and archaic terms; he also audaciously creates neologisms ("je ne ton-front-est-ceint-flon-flons-glorieuse pas"). Chamberland's mix attempts to convey a reality of everyday images: of cold, and of nude roughness–images of concrete, steel, neon, automobiles, and sign posts. Certain verses are patterned after the absurdity of telegraphic or computerized language. But "reality" is not comforting. Chamberland is a poet who knows how to alarm and how to communicate at once his fears and his aspirations.

A further example shows how Chamberland finally envisions coherence. *L'Inavouable* (1967) is a long poem of eighty-nine stanzas, a love song of life and liberty in which the themes of national alienation, childhood, violence, and flesh are interwoven, eventually coming together in harmony. *L'Inavouable* goes further than *Genèses* or *Terre Québec*; sorrow culminates in this poem in a sacred and insane sacrificial rite: "Il faut renverser l'évangéliaire prendre l'autel par les cornes saccager les tables de la loi, Moise des natives" (One must overturn the evangelistary, take the alter by the horns, plunder the Tables of the Law, Moses of the natives). At the beginning of *L'Inavouable*–the undisclosable–is a heartrending confession. The poet cleanses in blood the innumerable blemishes which stain his "compatriotes qu'on écorne comme de grands bestiaux paisibles bernés" (compatriots who are gored like great peaceful cattle deceived); "seul le sang versé est aveu extrémiste" (blood spilled is the only extremist avowal).

Because of the continuity of *L'Inavouable*, one is (more than in *Genèses* or *Terre Québec*) taken by the rhythm which is at first like that of a panting beast in flight and gradually becomes slower and more lyrical. It is the song of a poet who earlier in *Terre Québec* had the "pleasure" of flying in the face of traditional poetic forms–"le goût d'être vulgaire ét de [n]ous faire le pied de nez en alexandrins"–and who was "fier de mal écrire" (a very provocative statement, given the poetic commonplace of "writing well"); now he nearly shouts, because "il en a trop sur le coeur pour le celer en des formules polies et correctes" (there is too much weighing on his heart to conceal it in polite and correct formulas).

Chamberland's poetry is essentially poetry committed to the political situation. In *Terre Québec*, for example, an allusion to a terrorist attack names specific politicians. But one of the dangers of poetry that draws on actual events is that it limits its own significance by embedding itself in the present. "To write is to be incoherent" is a phrase that characterizes the early political *Parti Pris* period of Chamberland's career. His flowing book-length poems of the 1970s, such as *Demain les dieux naîtront* (1974) and *Le Prince de Sexamour* (1976), although they remain as hermetic as the early books, are more directly committed to eroticism as they reflect on the possibility of Marxist independence for Quebec. Typically, however, they close with a vision of disruption.

However, *L'Inavouable*, like *Terre Québec* and *Genèses*, is compelling poetry thanks to the vigor and the violence of its language, and to the fact that Chamberland is able to go from the particular to the universal, from the individual to the collective. Chamberland's poetry has a forceful and seductive lyricism that is capable of sweeping away objections to its argument. The personal confession in *L'Inavouable*, moreover, is quite simply touching. In it one witnesses the debate of the politically committed man, the collective man, and the particular man in whom there takes place a "grand ébranlement soudain qu'il [lui] faut bien appeler l'enfrance" (a great sudden tremor that he must call childhood).

References:

Carolyn Bayard and Jack David, "Paul Chamberland: la poésie, le vécu: recherche et experimentation," *Voix et Images* (December 1976): 155-172;

Jacques Bouchard, "Paul Chamberland: inexplicable restait la poésie," *Etudes Littéraires*, 5 (December 1972): 429-446;

André Brochu, "*Genèses*," *Livres et Auteurs Canadiens* (1962): 51-53;

Maximilien Laroche, "*Terre Québec*," *Livres et Auteurs Canadiens* (1964): 73-79;

Pierre Maheu, "Présentation: Le poète et le permanent," *Parti Pris*, 2 (January 1965): 2-5;

Axel Maugey, "Paul Chamberland," in his *Poésie et Societé au Québec (1937-1970)* (Quebec: Presses de l'Université Laval, 1972), pp. 200-208;

Yves Préfontaine, "Poésie pas morte," *Maintenant* (January 1965): 211-213;

Jacques Saint-Yves, "Proses poétiques ou poésie prosaique," *L'Action Nationale*, 54 (December 1964): 377-384.

Cécile Cloutier
(13 June 1930-   )

L. H. Forsyth
University of Western Ontario

BOOKS: *Mains de sable* (Quebec: Editions de l'Arc, 1960);

Cuivre et soies, suivi de Mains de sable (Montreal: Editions du Jour, 1964);

Cannelles et craies (Paris: Grassin, 1969);

Paupières (Montreal: Déom, 1970); revised as *Câblogrammes* (Paris: Chambelland, 1972);

Chaleuils (Montreal: Editions de l'Hexagone, 1978); translated by Alexandre Amprimoz as *Springtime of Spoken Words* (Toronto: Hounslow, 1979);

L'Echangeur (Trois-Rivières, Quebec: Les Ecrits des Forges, 1985);

L'Ecouté: Poèmes 1960-1983 (Montreal: Editions de l'Hexagone, 1986).

OTHER: "La Poésie canadienne-française," in *Archives des lettres canadiennes*, volume 4 (Montreal: Fides, 1969), pp. 552-556;

"La Nouvelle Poésie," in *Acta universitas uppsalientis*, series Figura, new series, volume 10 (Upsala: University of Upsala, 1972);

"Le Beau et l'avant-garde en littérature," in *Actes du VIII Congrès International d' Esthétique* (Bucharest, 1972);

"Témoinage sur Etienne Sourian," in *L'Art instaurateur* (Paris: Union Générale d'Editions, 1981);

Opuscula Aesthetica Nostra: A Volume of Essays on Aesthetics and the Arts in Canada/Un Volume d'essais sur l'esthétique et les arts au Canada, edited by Cloutier and Calvin Seerveld, includes contributions by Cloutier (Edmonton: Academic Printing, 1984).

PERIODICAL PUBLICATIONS: "Propos sur la poésie," *La Revue Dominicaine*, 65 (April 1959): 163-166;

"La Jeune Poésie au Canada français," *Incidences*, 7 (January 1965): 4-11;

"Le Nouveau Roman canadien," *Incidences*, 8 (May 1965): 21-27;

"La Machine à poèmes," *Liberté*, 8 (January-February 1966): 42-48;

"La Nouvelle Poésie," *Liberté*, 9 (July-August 1967): 118-127;

"La Poésie contemporaine du Québec," *Revue d'Esthétique* (Paris), 22, no. 3 (1969);

"Panorama de la littérature québécoise d'aujourd'hui," *Canadian Modern Language Review*, 31, no. 1 (1974): 8-32;

"L'Influence de quelques poètes français sur quelques poètes québécois," *Présence Francophone*, 9 (Autumn 1974): 48-51;

Utinam!, *La Barre du Jour*, 56-57 (May-August 1977): 93-115; translated by Josée M. LeBlond in *Rome of One's Own* (1978);

"L'Avenir de la poésie québécoise," *Possibiles*, 3, no. 2 (1979);

"Piekno w. poezji konkretnej," *Kryzys Estetyki* (Jagiellonian University, Kraków) (1983).

Cécile Cloutier is a significant Quebec poet whose work, condensed and elliptical, represents a search for intimate communion and for spiritual vision as she endeavors to establish, through language, a vital contact with the hidden forces of the natural world. Her many theoretical writings show that for her the conscious, creative act of writing, which liberates the energy of language, is a means whereby the poet can ensure that the world and human presence in the world have meaning and structure.

Cloutier is a member of the generation of poets which emerged during the Quiet Revolution in Quebec. She was one of the first of this generation to have her work published. These poets took possession of the word and used it to name both themselves and the land to which they belonged. While Cloutier does not frequently refer explicitly to the situation of the French in Quebec, her poetry has its origin in her awareness of belonging to the world's only people which are Latin and Nordic at the same time. Her roots are deep in a land of fertile ambiguities and antitheses.

Cloutier, the daughter of Adrien Cloutier, a civil servant, and Marie Lantagne Cloutier, a

Cécile Cloutier (photograph by Kèro)

nurse, was born in Quebec City on 13 June 1930. From her early formation and education in the Catholic traditions of Quebec have come great pride in her origins and a need for spiritual fulfillment, both of which are constant throughout her work. A scholar whose research covers many disciplines—aesthetics, literature, psychotherapy, philosophy—she has studied Greek, Latin, Spanish, German, Polish, Sanskrit, Inooktituk, and Chinese. She obtained a *licence ès lettres* (1953) and a *diplôme d'études supérieures* (1954) at l'Université Laval before obtaining a *doctorat de l'université* at the Sorbonne in 1961. Her thesis, directed by Etienne Souriau, was a study of aesthetics in Quebec daily life.

In 1960, when *Mains de sable*, her first volume of poetry, appeared, Cloutier was teaching Greek and Latin in Quebec City. She was also actively involved with other Quebec poets who were redefining the relationship of poetry and language, organizing meetings, creating periodicals, and founding publishing houses which would suit their newly articulated needs. Throughout the decade of the 1960s Cloutier wrote theoretical arti-

cles about poetry, her own and that of other young poets in Quebec. In these articles can be found her basic ideas on the poetic experience and on poetic language, ideas reflected in all the volumes of poetry Cloutier has written to date.

For Cloutier the poem is a window, a momentary vision, of what is finally hidden in the universe. Poetic language celebrates human creative power and the potential richness of human experience. Hers is a search for the essential word, purified of all extraneous stylistic decoration, a return to the origin of things as they are named for the first time. She perceives the world as animated by great energy and presenting signs to those who are able to listen to its pregnant silence. The poem is like a mathematical formula which acts, like Einstein's famous formula, to unlock the secrets of the universe and make them meaningful in human terms. In such a concentrated form of expression, opposites frequently come together, and, by virtue of their unexpected juxtaposition, the poet and the reader are able to perceive a field of limitless possibilities. Cloutier's surprising associations produce striking images, a process of synthesis that evokes an experience of such intensity that all the senses are aroused.

In her solitude, the poet sees beyond deceiving appearances in order to be receptive to the essential qualities of the people and things in the world. Her short elliptical poems are like snapshots of eternity, stopping the flow of time. She uses the simple past tense to evoke the stark moment of revelation as an act of birth and creation. Modifiers and subordinate clauses are used very sparingly in a poetic language whose primary function is to reveal the essential order of nouns and verbs. In place of conventional syntactic structures, she may make an entire poem of infinitives or nouns standing alone. Rather than expressing a continuous flowing thought, the poem captures and fixes a moment of rich vision, revealing fresh meanings through assonances, sounds, and rhythms which are made particularly striking by the careful placing of each word on the page.

Some have criticized Cloutier for the difficulty of her poetry; others have charged that it is insufficiently *engagée* in the social reality of Quebec. By way of response to such criticisms, she stated in a 1965 article entitled "La Jeune Poésie au Canada français" that writing such as hers, which is deeply rooted in sociocultural reality and which views that reality from a radically new

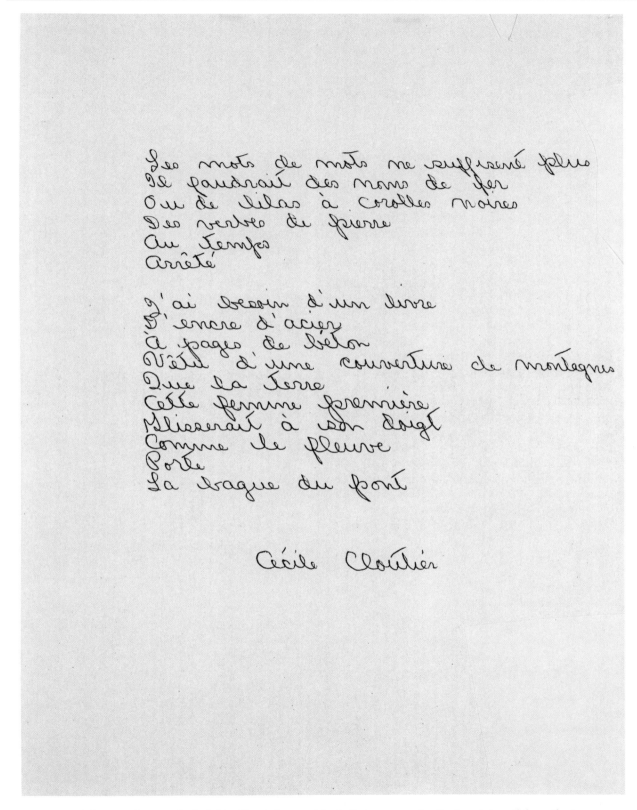

Fair copy of a poem included in Cloutier's second book, Cuivres et soies *(by permission of the author)*

perspective, is more revolutionary than poems that are explicit propaganda: "Les poésies enracinées qui partent du réel pour créer de nouvelles analogies sont des poésies en progrès. En ce sens elles sont engagées. . . . L'activité vitale transforme le monde et la conscience du poète canadien" (Deep-rooted poems that depart from the real to create new analogies are poems-in-progress. In this sense they are *engagées*. . . . Vital activity transforms the world and the conscience of the Canadian poet).

As her latest collection of poetry, *L'Echangeur* (1985), makes clear, the nature of Cloutier's poetry has not changed in the sense that it is, above all, work on the language of poetry in order to reveal essential meaning. Nevertheless, the source of her images has shifted. In *Mains de sable* the dominant image of hands reaching out to make meaningful contact with the world and to fix it in permanent form achieves fulfillment in the final poem in which the harmony between self and the universe has transformed the poet's entire body into a hand, with all voyages having become possible.

Cloutier's second book, *Cuivre et soies* (1964), represents a renewal of her experimentation in forging a poetic language sufficiently rich and precise to name the essence of things. In addition to employing the techniques already explored in *Mains de sable*, she makes even more striking use of logically contradictory associations using a favorite pattern–noun plus noun–in such evocative and seemingly paradoxical expressions as "dur feu d'eau." The work emphasizes in particular the consciousness of the poet for whom writing is of absolute importance, similar to a cosmic marriage:

> J'ai besoin d'un livre
> D'encre d'acier
> A pages de béton
> Vêtu d'une couverture de montagnes
> Que la terre
> Cette femme première
> Glisserait à son doigt
> Comme le fleuve
> Porte
> La bague du pont
>
> (I need a book
> Ink of steel
> On pages of concrete
> Dressed in a cloak of mountains
> That the earth,
> that first woman,
> would slip on her finger

> Like the river
> Wears
> The ring of the bridge).

After teaching French and Quebecois literature and aesthetics at the University of Ottawa, in 1966 Cloutier accepted a position as professor of French at the University of Toronto, where she still teaches. The same year she married Jerzy Wojciechowski, a professor of philosophy at Toronto. They have two daughters, Marie-Bérénice and Eve-Moira.

For her third volume, *Cannelles et craies* (1969), Cloutier was awarded a prize by La Commission du Centenaire de la Confédération Canadienne. The images of these poems evoke a new range of sensation and establish an important bond among revelation, poetic creation, and sensual experience: "Tu as mis en moi / La longue flûte de ta parole d'homme / Mon corps a appris la vie" (You have put in me / The long flute of your manly word / My body has learned life).

Paupières (1970) and its slightly revised version, *Câblogrammes* (1972), reflect the same desire to hear the silent voice of things and to impose on them an immunity from the ravages of time through revelation of essential being. The pure language which allows the poet to achieve this goal comes through the presence and words of the beloved man. At the end of *Paupières*, Cloutier has inserted a prose text, "Cum," dedicated to fellow Quebec poet Gatien Lapointe. This was her first theoretical formulation on poetry, given originally as an address in 1958 to the Rencontre des Poètes and published as "Propos sur la poésie" in a 1959 issue of *La Revue Dominicaine*.

Cloutier's 1978 book, *Chaleuils*, is dedicated to her father "pour tout ce qu'il n'aura jamais dit." Like the dedication, the title image evokes her Quebec roots, since the *chaleuil* is a small oil lamp used exclusively in the Quebec region. In the poems of this volume Cloutier explores even further the possibilities of language to produce meaning and sound, while developing a new range of images and sensory associations. *Chaleuils* was translated by Alexandre Amprimoz in 1979 under the title *Springtime of Spoken Words*.

In 1978 Cloutier earned a master's degree in psychology from McMaster University; in 1981 she completed a master's in theology at the University of Toronto; and in 1983 she received a Ph.D. in psychology from the University of Tours in

France. Cloutier has had articles published in a number of journals. She has also received several prizes for her poetry, most recently a Governor General's award for her retrospective collection *L'Ecouté: Poèmes 1960-1983* (1986). Her poetic expression is of impeccable precision and formal beauty, although its highly condensed nature has meant that her influence on other poets has not been widespread. She has also written a play in four "fenêtres," *Utinam!*, which has been produced in Montreal and Quebec City. As well, she is coeditor (with Calvin Seerveld) of *Opuscula Aesthetica Nostra* (1984), a book of essays on aesthetics in Canada to which she contributed two pieces.

References:

André Bourassa, "Rapprochement," *Lettres Québécoises*, 18 (Summer 1980): 30-32;

Jean Marcel, "Cécile Cloutier, alchimiste de l'image," *L'Action Nationale*, 54 (February 1965): 612-615.

Fred Cogswell

(8 November 1917-   )

Gwendolyn Davies
Mount Allison University

BOOKS: *The Stunted Strong* (Fredericton: Fiddlehead, 1954);

The Haloed Tree (Toronto: Ryerson, 1956);

Descent from Eden (Toronto: Ryerson, 1959);

Lost Dimension (Dulwich Village, U.K.: Outposts, 1960);

Star-People (Fredericton: Fiddlehead, 1968);

Immortal Plowman (Fredericton: Fiddlehead, 1969);

In Praise of Chastity (Fredericton: Fiddlehead, 1970);

The Chains of Liliput (Fredericton: Fiddlehead, 1971);

The House Without a Door (Fredericton: Fiddlehead, 1973);

Light Bird of Life: Selected Poems (Fredericton: Fiddlehead, 1974);

Against Perspective (Fredericton: Fiddlehead, 1977);

A Long Apprenticeship: The Collected Poems of Fred Cogswell (Fredericton: Fiddlehead, 1980);

Pearls (Charlottetown: Ragweed Press, 1983);

Fred Cogswell: Selected Poems, edited by Antonio D'Alfonso (Montreal: Guernica, 1983);

Charles G. D. Roberts and His Works (Downsview, Ontario: ECW, 1983);

The Bicentennial Lectures on New Brunswick Literature, by Cogswell, Malcolm Ross, and Marguerite Maillet (Sackville, New Brunswick: Mount Allison University, 1985);

Meditations: 50 Sestinas (Charlottetown: Ragweed Press, 1986).

OTHER: Robert Henryson, *The Testament of Cresseid*, translated by Cogswell (Toronto: Ryerson, 1957);

A Canadian Anthology (Poems from The Fiddlehead: *1945-1959)*, special issue of *Fiddlehead*, edited by Cogswell, 50 (Fall 1961);

Five New Brunswick Poets, edited with contributions by Cogswell (Fredericton: Fiddlehead, 1962);

"Haliburton," and "Literary Activity in the Maritime Provinces (1815-1880)," in *Literary History of Canada*, edited by Carl Klinck (Toronto: University of Toronto Press, 1965);

The Arts in New Brunswick, edited by Cogswell, R. A. Tweedie, and W. Stewart MacNutt, includes poems and articles by Cogswell (Fredericton: Brunswick Press, 1967);

Henry Green and Guy Sylvestre, eds., *A Century of Canadian Literature*, includes poems by Cogswell (Toronto: Ryerson, 1967);

Douglas Lochhead and Raymond Souster, eds., *Made in Canada: New Poems of the Seventies*, includes poems by Cogswell (Ottawa: Oberon, 1970);

One Hundred Poems of Modern Quebec, edited and translated by Cogswell (Fredericton: Fiddlehead, 1970);

A Second Hundred Poems of Modern Quebec, edited and translated by Cogswell (Fredericton: Fiddlehead, 1971);

"May Agnes Early (Fleming)," in *Dictionary of Canadian Biography*, volume 10 (Toronto: University of Toronto Press, 1972), pp. 268-269;

Robert Weaver and William Toye, *The Oxford Anthology of Canadian Literature*, includes translations by Cogswell (Toronto: Oxford University Press, 1973);

Robert H. Cockburn and Robert Gibbs, eds., *Ninety Seasons*, includes poems by Cogswell (Toronto: McClelland & Stewart, 1974);

The Poetry of Modern Quebec, edited and translated by Cogswell (Montreal: Harvest House, 1976);

"Thomas Chandler Haliburton," in *Dictionary of*

Canadian Biography, volume 9 (Toronto: University of Toronto Press, 1976), pp. 348-357;

G. Thomas, R. Perkyns, K. MacKinnon, and W. Katz, eds., *Introduction to Literature: British, American, Canadian*, includes poems by Cogswell (Toronto: Holt, Rinehart & Winston, 1981);

The Complete Poems of Emile Nelligan, edited and translated, with an introduction, by Cogswell (Montreal: Harvest House, 1983);

"Charles G. D. Roberts: The Critical Years," in *Proceedings of the Sir Charles G. D. Roberts Symposium*, edited by Carrie MacMillan (Halifax: Nimbus, 1984);

"The Classical Poetry of Sir Charles G. D. Roberts," and "The Achievement of Charles G. D. Roberts: An Assessment Panel," in *The Sir Charles G. D. Roberts Symposium*, edited by Glenn Clever (Ottawa: University of Ottawa Press, 1984);

The Atlantic Anthology, 2 volumes, edited by Cogswell (Charlottetown: Ragweed Press, 1984, 1985);

Graham Adams, eds., *The Collected Poems of Sir Charles G. D. Roberts*, introduction by Cogswell (Wolfville, Nova Scotia: Wombat Press, 1985);

"English Poetry in New Brunswick Before 1880," and "English Prose Writing in New Brunswick: World War I to the Present," in *A Literary & Linguistic History of New Brunswick*, edited by Reavley Gair (Fredericton: Goose Lane Editions, 1985).

PERIODICAL PUBLICATIONS: "Nineteenth Century Poetry in the Maritimes and Problems of Research," *Newsletter of the Bibliographical Society of Canada*, 5 (September 1961): 5-19;

"E. J. Pratt's Literary Reputation," *Canadian Literature*, 23 (Winter 1964): 6-12;

"Literary Traditions in New Brunswick," *Transactions of the Royal Society of Canada*, 15 (1977): 287-299;

"Until Time Erodes Bad Art, Maritime Writers Must Persevere," *Globe and Mail*, 14 January 1978, p. 6.

Since World War II a major force in contributing to the vitality of Canadian literature has been the poet, publisher, translator, and critic Fred Cogswell. As the guiding power behind Fiddlehead Press of Fredericton, New Brunswick, until 1981, he was responsible for the publication of more than three hundred titles and gave unstinting support to promising young writers. He has written extensively on Canadian literature, exploring the contributions of such major figures as T. C. Haliburton, Charles G. D. Roberts, F. R. Scott, and E. J. Pratt, and he has been effective in developing an overview of Atlantic Canada's literary-cultural life in the nineteenth century. His own work as a poet has earned him a place in contemporary poetry circles, while his translations of French-Canadian verse have helped to bridge the gap between the two main language groups in the country.

The son of Walter Scott and Florence White Cogswell, Cogswell was born in East Centreville, New Brunswick, on 8 November 1917. His father was a farmer and Cogswell grew up in the rural community that was to be the subject of his first volume of poetry, an environment that gave him an understanding of the social forces which have shaped his province's character. After obtaining a teacher's certificate in 1936, he served with the Canadian Army from 1940 to 1945. In 1944 he married Margaret Hynes, and they eventually had two daughters, Carmen Patricia and Kathleen Mary. Cogswell studied English at the University of New Brunswick in Fredericton (B.A., 1949; M.A., 1950) and at Edinburgh University (Ph.D., 1952). In 1952 he returned to his native province to teach at his alma mater, taking up residence in Fredericton, a city with a proud literary heritage. The names Jonathan Odell, William Cobbett, Julia Beckwith Hart, Juliana Horatia Ewing, Charles G. D. Roberts, and Bliss Carman are only a few of those associated with Fredericton's literary life from 1783 to 1880 and pride in this literary past was still strong in the city in 1952 when Cogswell returned. Combined with the activities of the Bliss Carman Poetry Society and its publication the *Fiddlehead*, Fredericton's literary tradition provided a sympathetic environment in which Cogswell could develop his creative talents and pursue his scholarly research on early New Brunswick writers.

Cogswell's first collection of poetry, *The Stunted Strong* (1954), is composed of a series of sonnets describing the Saint John River folk the poet had known in his youth. The poems are built around a set of characters including George Ernst, Miss Maybee, and Deacon Johnson, each sonnet gradually revealing the irony or tragedy which has shaped the subject's life. A certain wryness of tone permeates the entire sequence, for the speaker in the poems is both inside and outside the community. His detachment enables him to see the valley folk as parochial and unimaginative, the victims of the "narrow . . . house where we are born." Yet his status as one of them means that his irony is tinged with humanity. He knows their frustration when the Saint John River "mocks the patterned fields that we enclose," and he appreciates their need for dreams and escape as they lean upon their hoes "To watch a sea-gull glide with lazy beat / to wider regions where the river goes."

The insider-outsider tension brings an edge of disciplining irony to *The Stunted Strong*, for the potential sentimentality of the book is tempered by the speaker's dry and uncompromising observations. This control is reinforced by the tension between form and subject matter in the sixteen poems, for Cogswell has imposed the discipline of traditional sonnet conventions on lives and events which are inherently violent, ridiculous, or pathetic. His use of idiomatic phrasing creates an illusion of colloquial speech which further tests the flexibility of the sonnet form, but Cogswell succeeds in making these stylistic pulls and strains so check one another that balanced portraits of his characters emerge. However, the individual irony becomes a collective one at the end of the sonnet sequence when the poet turns to the task of characterizing the province to which all these people have contributed. Countering his interpretation of New Brunswick's weaknesses with an analysis of its strengths, Cogswell creates a qualified but dignified picture of his native region. Sparsely endowed on many levels (as are the valley folk) the area nonetheless displays the virtues of survival—the "beauty" of "stubborn strength" which its "stunted strong" have given it:

> Not soft the soil where we took root together;
> It grew not giants but the stunted strong,
> Toughened by suns and bleak wintry weather
> To grow up slow and to endure for long;
> We have not gained to any breadth or length,
> And all our beauty is our stubborn strength.

While *The Stunted Strong* reveals some of the technical insecurities of a first volume, critics found it an honest and sincere work. Northrop Frye, in an article published in the July 1960 *University of Toronto Quarterly*, commended Cogswell's "excellent eye" in creating the "vignettes of New Brunswick life" that one finds in *The Stunted Strong*. This eye for detail and human drama is also characteristic of Cogswell's subsequent books *The Haloed Tree* (1956), *Descent from Eden* (1959), *The Chains of Liliput* (1971), and *Light Bird of Life*

LIGHT BIRD OF LIFE:

SELECTED POEMS

by

FRED COGSWELL

Cover for Cogswell's tenth volume of verse, published in 1974 as a Fiddlehead Poetry Book

(1974). These titles represent only four of the fifteen poetry volumes published from 1954 to 1986, but over the years, Cogswell's ironic turns, satiric thrusts, modest humor, and epigrammatic lines have attracted a widening and increasingly eclectic readership. Not ordinarily the kind of writer to comment on his own poetry, Cogswell has nonetheless offered a useful insight into his creative process in a biographical sketch prepared for *The Arts in New Brunswick*, a volume he edited with R. A. Tweedie and W. S. MacNutt in 1967. Noting that "I write from my memory of past personal experience, from observation and from ideas suggested by a wide range of study and reading," he goes on to explain what it is that he tries to achieve as he composes: "I aim at freshness and simplicity in language and compactness in expression. I try to tone down or subordinate the details of any poem to its effect

considered as a whole. I use striking images only sparingly and at climactic points in a poem."

Cogswell's reliance on "personal experience," "observation," and "study" as catalysts for his writing is borne out by a reading of his volume of collected poems, *A Long Apprenticeship* (1980). Seen in the context of over twenty-five years of writing, the individual chapbooks and collections represented in the book reveal the consistency with which he has treated the paradoxes and contradictions of the human condition with compassion and bemusement. Style and technique may vary, but throughout Cogswell's work there is an informing and reliable presence–the wry yet vulnerable speaker who in the poem "November 11, 1979" characteristically sees life with a discerning eye:

Men do not choose.

Since then, my comrades one by one,
Without their leave, are singled out.
I read their names and numbers
In *The Legionaire*.

Not for me the cenotaph,
The march, the bagpipe, brass.
Be mine that raven-voice, crying
Against a ceremonial lie,
There is no armistice in nature.

The bald observation that "Men do not choose" sums up the situation informing much of Cogswell's work and, in its ironic implications, explains as well the modesty and qualification of the title of his volume of collected poems. Practicing the craft of poetry as well as the craft of life has been a slow and arduous learning process for the poet, an "apprenticeship" paved with ironies he might appreciate but could not always control. "I have never been a star," he notes wryly in his poem, "A Defence of Amateurism," but the honesty and ruefulness of the line illustrate the very qualities of humility and irony which Canadian readers have found so attractive in Cogswell's poetry and its persona.

The apprenticeship took an unexpected and more intensely personal turn in 1983 when Cogswell recorded in *Pearls* the death by cancer of his elder daughter just two years before. Proclaiming "I find my short-lived voice / Inadequate beneath the cosmic sky–," the poet nonetheless achieves a moving exploration of memory and death in some of the most intimate and finely controlled poems of his career. Loss of his daughter, of youth, and of the opportunity to love all find voice here and come full circle to the stoicism and sense of continuity in *The Stunted Strong*. Cogswell's "How It Was" in *Pearls* is a case in point:

> The road we travelled was the usual one.
> Uphill and down it wound its way between
> Pale fields of grain and woods of darker green,
> Skirting the river where cool waters run,
> Glassy and blue beneath a summer sun.
> Along the way, scarce noticing, we passed
> Houses, barns, pastures thick with cows. At last
> We stopped before a graveyard, journey done.
>
> At her grandparents' tomb I took a spade,
> Turned up the sod, and put her urn beneath
> To be with them in place and time and death.
> Then as I covered up the hole I made
> My ears were opened and I heard the strong
> And living sweetness of a robin's song.

Consistent with Cogswell's interest in writing poetry has been his concern that Canada's authors be published and read. His translations of French-Canadian poetry into English have illustrated this concern and have given English-Canadians access to francophone writing at a time when they urgently needed to understand the intellectual and literary forces at work in modern Quebec. His introduction to *The Poetry of Modern Quebec* (1976) indicates that in preparing an anthology that ranges from Alain Grandbois to André Major, he is presenting for the first time "in translation the work of several major Quebec poets of the last four decades in considerable depth." Cogswell's volume explores "a literary revolution" in Quebec that "has gone full circle," revealing in its contemporary poetry "a broadening and deepening of the poet's sensibility and the devising of a more elastic technique with which to deal with experience." In the words of J. M. L'Heureux in the *Canadian Forum* (July-August 1970), the translations reflect Cogswell's "technical virtuosity" and "driving energy," and like his other translations, they clearly emanate from Cogswell's expressed conviction that "the presence of another culture comparable with one's own yet possessing different values is an inestimable advantage to any writer." *The Complete Poems of Emile Nelligan*, edited and translated by Cogswell and published in 1983, gives further evidence of these sentiments, focusing on a man considered by Cogswell to be "the finest poet writing in Canada in the nineteenth century and, in terms of sensibility and use of images as a correla-

tive for his private feelings, the first modern Canadian poet."

Cogswell's interest in Canadian poetry has extended beyond writing and translation. From 1952 to 1981 he was actively engaged in publishing poetry in the *Fiddlehead*. The fiddlehead is an edible fern once regarded by the Indians as a fertility symbol and now recognized as one of New Brunswick's provincial symbols. It was thus an appropriate name for the mimeographed poetry magazine started by the Bliss Carman Poetry Society in Fredericton in 1945 and supported by the society until 1952. However, in that year it was decided that the range and format of the journal should be changed, and the editing, printing, and financial responsibilities of the *Fiddlehead* were transferred to Cogswell. Under Cogswell's guidance the *Fiddlehead* became a printed quarterly publishing contemporary poetry and reviewing the latest books. The West Coast journal *Contemporary Verse* ceased publication in 1952, and in many respects the new *Fiddlehead* was able to step into the vacuum left by its demise and provide Canadian poets with a forum in which to present their work.

By 1957 the *Fiddlehead* had expanded its size and its subscription list and had begun to receive government grants. After 1959 it also included fiction and by the 1960s it was an indisputable feature of contemporary Canadian literary life. Throughout this period Cogswell put his energies into the editing, financing, proofreading, printing, and distributing of the magazine. His dedication to the *Fiddlehead* enabled it to evolve successfully in the 1950s and 1960s and gave it the foundation on which it continues to build today. Now, as then, it provides an outlet for young and unknown writers as well as for those who are established in the field of Canadian literature. According to Roger Ploude and Michael Taylor who edited *Fiddlehead Greens* (1979), a collection of stories from the journal, the *Fiddlehead* "has always considered the encouragement of new and promising talent one of its main functions, if not its *raison d'être*." Faithful to this principle in their anthology, Ploude and Taylor have not only included stories by such well-known "Fiddlehead" writers as Margaret Atwood, Hugh Hood, Alden Nowlan, George Bowering, and John Metcalf but have also published selections by less established authors. "If their names become familiar to readers across the country in the years ahead," add the editors, they "will not be the first to achieve prominence since appearing in the *Fiddlehead*."

By 1966 Fred Cogswell was reading as many as 6,000 poems a year submitted to the *Fiddlehead* and was trying to answer each poet personally. He was actively involved in another publishing project which had emerged under the Fiddlehead name. A series entitled Fiddlehead Poetry Books, this venture, which had begun in 1954 under the auspices of the University of New Brunswick, had been the agent whereby Cogswell's own *The Stunted Strong* had been published. In 1957, however, the university withdrew its funding from the poetry series, and in an effort to keep it alive Cogswell had assumed all publishing and editing responsibilities for Fiddlehead Poetry Books. The result was that by the mid 1960s Cogswell was not only running the *Fiddlehead* magazine but was also producing several titles a year in the book series. The demands on his time and on his own creative life were extraordinarily heavy, and in an effort to afford himself more time for his own writing, Cogswell took advantage of a sabbatical in 1967-1968 to disengage himself from the journal and to transfer his publishing responsibilities to colleagues in Fredericton.

In spite of the demands the Fiddlehead poetry series made on Cogswell he remained heavily involved in directing Fiddlehead's book venture from 1957 until June 1981 when he transferred control to Peter Thomas of the University of New Brunswick. Throughout his twenty-four years as editor and publisher of the poetry series, Cogswell encouraged promising young poets by producing many books considered potentially unprofitable by major publishing houses. In the words of poet Dorothy Livesay, Fiddlehead encouraged new poets because "to Fred, they deserve to have a chance, a fair start." Though in the opinion of some, it was becoming too easy for writers to get into print in Canada, it can be pointed out that few other Canadian publishers have produced the number of poetry books or attracted the same caliber of writer as Fiddlehead. Al Purdy, Dorothy Livesay, Don Gutteridge, Anne Marriott, Dorothy Roberts, George Woodcock, and Alden Nowlan are only a few of the poets once published by Fiddlehead who vindicate Cogswell's policy of full support for talented and promising writers.

While Cogswell's reputation has rested on his creative writing and on his publishing endeavors, he has enjoyed the recognition of students and critics of Canadian literature. As a professor

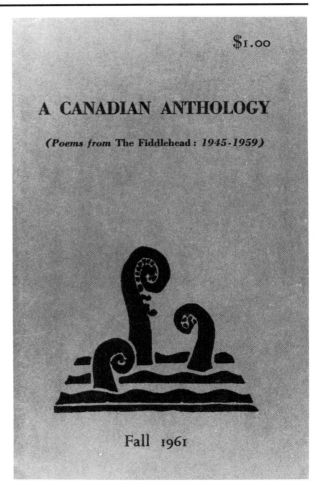

Cover for the fiftieth issue of the magazine begun by the University of New Brunswick's Bliss Carman Poetry Society in 1945. Cogswell, who compiled the anthology to secure "a larger subscription list, increased advertising, and more good poems" for the Fiddlehead, *assumed responsibility for editing and financing the magazine in 1952.*

and thesis supervisor at the University of New Brunswick he has influenced several generations of scholars and teachers who have gone on to study Canadian literature, and his own fresh appraisals of the nation's authors have stimulated new insights into Canada's literary development. Cogswell's "E. J. Pratt's Literary Reputation," published in a special issue of *Canadian Literature* devoted to Pratt (Winter 1964), is typical of his independent thinking in the way it has challenged the conventional view of the 1940s and 1950s that Pratt was, in Cogswell's words, "Canada's leading poet, the most original and the greatest in theme and execution that this country has ever had." Acknowledging that Pratt is to be admired for his "sophisticated and masterly poetic technique," "wealth of erudition," and "time-

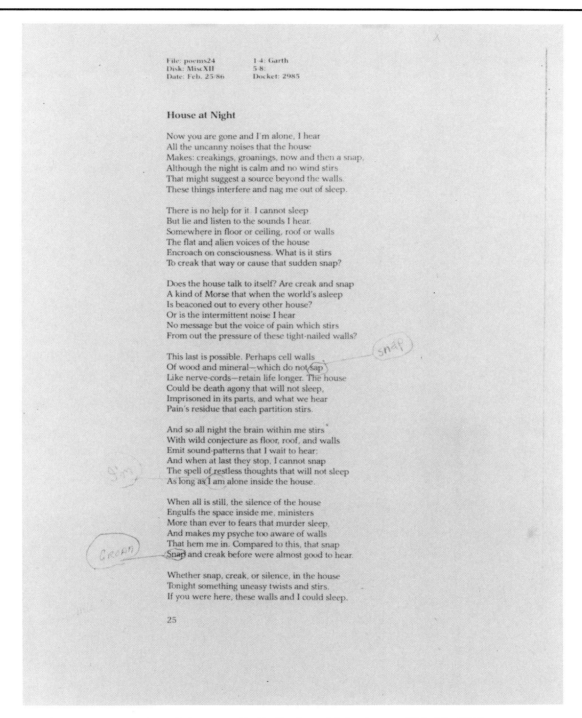

Corrected proofs for Cogswell's Meditations: 50 Sestinas, *published in 1986*

lessness in choice of themes," Cogswell nonetheless questions whether the "values of the primitive epic" which characterize Pratt's work will have popular appeal as Canada moves further and further from its frontier history. Pratt will be appreciated for his virtuosity and energetic depiction of human drama and suspense in Cogswell's view, but in the long range, he may come to be viewed as an anachronism in twentieth-century poetry, "a mid-Victorian with an eighteenth-century practicality as a writer" whose reputation will be as qualified as that of a post-Confederation poet like Bliss Carman.

In addition to the commentaries on individual writers which Cogswell has undertaken for such journals, newspapers, and books, he has contributed analyses of Maritime Canada's nineteenth-century literary development to Carl Klinck's *Literary History of Canada* (1965); to the volume he edited with Tweedie and MacNutt, *The Arts in New Brunswick* (1967); to the *Dictionary of Canadian Biography* (volumes 10 and 9, 1972, 1976); to Reavley Gair's *A Literary & Linguistic History of New Brunswick* (1985); and to other key reference works. Many of these studies have been of seminal importance, for they have approached writers in a cultural context and as representative of their time. Cogswell has been one of the few contemporary critics to discuss the importance of such secondary figures as Jonathan Odell, Peter Fisher, Douglas Huyghue, and Oliver Goldsmith, Jr., in the development of a national literature, and he has tried to present their contributions from both a literary and a social perspective. Although he considers writing in the Maritimes from 1815 to 1880 "more significant when considered as history or sociology than it is when considered as literature," he nonetheless has praise for the talent of such individuals as Thomas McCulloch and Thomas Chandler Haliburton whose satire provided a base for realistic social fiction in Canada. Furthermore, his chapter on Haliburton in *Literary History of Canada* places the creator of Sam Slick in the context of such literary reformers as Thomas McCullough and Charles Dickens, making it clear at the same time that the social ideals which Haliburton tried to preserve were not like Dickens's but were anachronisms in his own time. Cogswell has always responded to the paradoxes of life and he has recognized in Haliburton's work despair underlying the humor: "There runs through Haliburton's career a supreme irony"; "men read him for his humour and disregard what to him was the *raison d'être* of everything he wrote."

Cogswell's overview of Maritime literary development has not been limited to eighteenth- and nineteenth-century writers like Haliburton, however. One of the topics he has explored in such articles as "Literary Traditions in New Brunswick" (*Transactions of the Royal Society of Canada*, 1977) is the continuity between the writing of the nineteenth century and that of the twentieth. Charles G. D. Roberts, Bliss Carman, and Francis Sherman believed in a mystical bond between man and nature in their poetry in the post-Confederation period, and they expressed late-Victorian society's optimistic faith in progress and in the inherent goodness of man. Cogswell has commented on the influence of those values on his own development as a writer ("When I grew up as a boy on a New Brunswick farm during the 1920s and 1930s, I breathed it in so unconsciously that the revelation of reading Roberts and Carman was like the finding of words for something that was then, and still is, very much a part of me"), and he has repeated the importance of these values in his introduction to *The Collected Poems of Sir Charles G. D. Roberts*, published in 1985: "The current relative lack of esteem in which his [Roberts's] poetry is held is a testimony to how far we have departed from the beliefs, interests, and values of our ancestors." However, Cogswell has also recognized the liberating influence of the modernist movement on both his writing and that of the Fiddlehead poets of the 1940s. The Bliss Carman Poetry Society, as conceived by Alfred Bailey and his circle in 1940, was to work within the best of two literary traditions, for it was to perpetuate the poetic spirit of Roberts and Carman while "developing it to the point of contemporaneity." Thus, the influence of William Carlos Williams, W. H. Auden, T. S. Eliot, and Ezra Pound pervaded the readings at the society as much as did the tradition of Roberts and Carman, and the result was an eclectic and cosmopolitan body of poetry which defied rigid categorization. Cogswell's own first volume, *The Stunted Strong*, was created in this environment and reflects the poet's adaptation of a personal modernist sensibility to traditional poetic form and subject matter.

The sense of continuity which underlies the writing Cogswell discusses in "Literary Traditions in New Brunswick" is a feature fast disappearing from contemporary Canadian life and literature. That Cogswell regrets the loss of this continuity in an increasingly urbanized and commercial society is made clear in a 1978 article he wrote for the Toronto *Globe and Mail*. Entitled "Until Time Erodes Bad Art, Maritime Writers Must Persevere," the essay reveals that Cogswell is deeply offended by writers who allow their work to be influenced by the demands of popular taste. While never parochial in his support of Maritime writers and writing, Cogswell nonetheless champions the cause of such authors as David Adams Richards, Alistair MacLeod, and Alden Nowlan by arguing that "background, heritage, and temperament" have made the best of Atlantic Canada's contemporary writers out of fashion with critics and publishers. Literature and literary values ultimately rest on good craftsmanship, in Cogswell's opinion, rather than on trendy themes and styles, but in fashion-conscious times like the present, he notes, "many Atlantic provinces writers can only grit their teeth and persevere for the sake of the workmanship they create rather than the fame."

The views Cogswell expresses in the *Globe and Mail* piece are consistent with those which have informed his own writing and publishing. His poetry continues to treat themes of human inconsistency and abstraction with irony and quiet dignity, and his Fiddlehead publications always supported writers not considered part of the publishing mainstream. Although he has divested himself of his publishing responsibilities in recent years he continues to be important in the field of Canadian literature through his teaching, writing, editing, and translating. Few figures have been so dedicated and so influential in encouraging Canadian literary activity over the past four decades, and in recognition of Cogswell's achievement, in 1980 the Writers' Federation of Nova Scotia and the Atlantic Publishers' Association commissioned the writing and publication of "Scroll," a special collection of poetry honoring Cogswell. Presented at a private ceremony at Dalhousie University, this handprinted body of poems pays tribute to Cogswell as "a legend of Canadian letters" and

acknowledges the high regard in which colleagues and artists throughout Canada hold the poet, academic, and publisher who " . . . listened / heard them all / and knew their need to sing." In recent years, public honors have reinforced this personal tribute. Cogswell has received the Order of Canada (1982) as well as honorary degrees from Saint Francis Xavier University, Antigonish (1983), and the University of King's College, Halifax (1985). He was also awarded a Canada-Scotland Writers-in-Residence Fellowship at the University of Edinburgh in 1983-1984. Cogswell, now Professor Emeritus at the University of New Brunswick, resides in Fredericton with his second wife, poet Gail Fox, whom he married in 1985.

References:

David Galloway, "SCL Interviews: Fred Cosgwell," in *Studies in Canadian Literature,* 10, nos. 1-2 (1985): 208-225;

Robert Gibbs, "Three Decades and a Bit Under the Elms: A Fragmentary Memoir," in *Essays on Canadian Writing: Literature of Atlantic Canada,* edited by Terry Whalen, 31 (Summer 1985): 231-239;

Philip Milner, "The Apprentice's Sorcerer," *Books in Canada,* 10 (August-September 1981): 3-6.

Christopher Dewdney

(9 May 1951-   )

Stan Dragland
University of Western Ontario

BOOKS: *Golders Green* (Toronto: Privately printed, 1971);
A Paleozoic Geology of London, Ontario: Poems and Collages (Toronto: Coach House Press, 1973);
Fovea Centralis (Toronto: Coach House Press, 1975);
Spring Trances in the Control Emerald Night (Berkeley: The Figures, 1978);
Alter Sublime (Toronto: Coach House Press, 1980);
Spring Trances in the Control Emerald Night & The Cenozoic Asylum (Berkeley: The Figures, 1982);
Predators of the Adoration: Selected Poems 1972-82 (Toronto: McClelland & Stewart, 1983).

Christopher Dewdney's achievement in poetry has deep roots in London, Ontario, where he was born and raised and where he was educated in more ways than one. He attended local public and high schools and the Beal Art Annex, but he seems to have absorbed more from two other sources: his family, especially his father, and from the physical environment of his youth, particularly The Coves—an oxbow lake in a deep ravine that borders Erie Avenue where the Dewdneys lived.

Dewdney's father, Selwyn Dewdney, was a novelist and ethno-archaeologist well known for his work on Indian pictographs and the birchbark scroll legends of the Ojibway. His mother, Irene Donner Dewdney, is an art therapist. Alexander, one of two older brothers, teaches computer science at the University of Western Ontario, writes a column on computers for *Scientific American*, and is author of *The Planiverse* (1984), a novel about two-dimensional beings. Besides his home life, where interest in scholarship and the arts was a given, Dewdney's friendships with other writer-artists, particularly Robert Fones, encouraged him on his own creative path. Fones and Dewdney each have their own subjects and styles but there are certain similarities in their work—a deep interest in the natural landscape, for example, and a dadaist / surrealist, or "nonsense," strain in their writing. In fact, the two have often collaborated. Both still maintain an interest in science and poetry.

London, Ontario, is known as the Forest City and "the first block-parent community." It is noted for its plethora of insurance companies and also for its artistic community. Such internationally important artists as Jack Chambers and Greg Curnoe were active in London while Dewdney was growing up. In fact Dewdney now helps to edit the visual arts periodical *Provincial Essays* with, among others, Greg Curnoe. So London was never the middle- and upper-class haven to Dewdney that it still is to many of its citizens. Instead, London was the forested Coves and the paleozoic limestone underlying the city and the region. To one of his father's remarks about limestone Dewdney traces his obsession with the geological underpinnings of southwestern Ontario. Limestone, his father said, "was almost entirely composed of the shells and skeletons of underwater creatures, millions of years old, compacted and turned to rock." One might, in fact, say that Dewdney's entire work, with its mixture of poetry and science, rests on those limestone beds.

Dewdney is known as a poet, but since his first full-length collection, *A Paleozoic Geology of London, Ontario* (1973), he has worked in the genres of poetry, fiction, and essay and has illustrated his books with his own sophisticated collages and drawings. Each of his books, then, is a mixed-genre event. Each of them is also a theater of language pushed to and beyond the limits of what is normally considered sayable. The key manifesto piece is the essay in Dewdney's *Alter Sublime* (1980) entitled "Parasite Maintenance." The essay with its blend of neurochemistry, linguistics, and poetics, is in the "pataphysical" vein that Steve McCaffery, in "Strata and Strategy" (*Open Letter*, Winter 1976), first explored in Dewdney's work. Pataphysics, as invented by presurrealist French playwright Alfred Jarry (1873-1907), is basically pseudoscience and is often used for humorous or even satirical effects. But "Parasite Maintenance" is a mainly serious account of the workings of the

photograph by Paul Orenstein

poet's brain. It offers a highly technical and ultimately metaphorical vision of the poet as a mechanism for subverting and transcending logocentric language. It helps to provide a basis for comprehending Dewdney's work, which is often most attractive when most surreal. One always feels in Dewdney's work as well his love for the creatures, especially the nonhuman ones, who share his world. He acknowledges this feeling as his inspiration in the "Author's Preface" to his 1983 volume, *Predators of the Adoration: Selected Poems 1972-82*: "In a sense . . . this book is the voice of the land and the creatures themselves, speaking from the inviolate fortress of a primeval history uncorrupted by humans. It is a codex of the plants and animals whose technology is truly miraculous and for whom I am merely a scribe."

The formal basis for Dewdney's writing is in a sense laid down in *A Paleozoic Geology of London, Ontario*, which plays verbal and visual variations on the structure of a horizontal axis–layers of sedimented limestone–pierced on a vertical axis by wells or faults or eroding rivers. Various "strata" of reference connect, as it were, horizontally throughout the volume (and for that matter throughout Dewdney's work as a whole) while the vertical unfolding of a particular piece (down the page) seems often to work on the principle of *non sequitur*. The patient reader gradually sees Dewdney's strange universe revealed as he passes from unit to unit, volume to volume. Thematically, *A Paleozoic Geology of London, Ontario* begins to play with the concept of a prehistoric era revived and released into a somewhat disoriented and disorienting present and future. This collapse of time and space becomes one of Dewdney's trademarks. It is there already in one of his metaphors offered in the pataphysical author's preface to *A Paleozoic Geology of London, Ontario*. A man's memory is limited and of difficult access, says Dewdney, but "there do exist . . . certain three-dimensional, universally perceptible

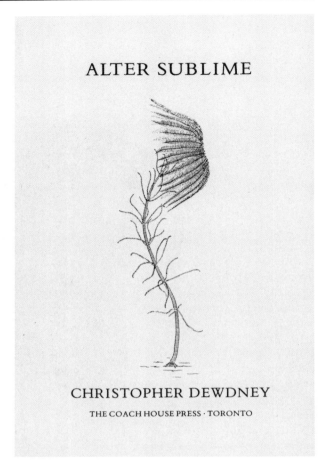

Cover and title page designed by Dewdney for the collection that includes "Parasite Maintenance," his manifesto about the workings of the poet's brain

memories posited from the workings of the evolutionary mind of form. THE FOSSIL IS PURE MEMORY." This is a formulation, in Dewdney's characteristic authoritative / oracular tone, of that germ of insight into the nature of limestone that his father gave him.

Fovea Centralis (1975), Dewdney's second full-length book, continues some of the forms and themes of *A Paleozoic Geology of London, Ontario*—the "log entries," for example, which appear again in *Alter Sublime*. These are fictional fragmentary entries in a journal kept by scientific explorers of a world or worlds whose laws are not those of our world, laws which in fact appear to shift from entry to entry. Each entry is obliquely annotated by a poem or some other sort of commentary printed vertically below it. *Fovea Centralis* also introduces one of Dewdney's most fascinating deconstructions of prose style. Entitled "The Parenthetical," this sequence begins with a conventional enough base text, about the piercing of the

"dike of your mind." Subsequent installments vary the initial text, whose words slide apart to admit parenthetical alternatives, opposites, echoes, arbitrary associations. "This (then) is the (reasoning) dike of (gold) your mind"–so goes the first metamorphosis of the phrase quoted above. The end result is prose that is both hypnotic and humorous, a linkage of responses that is unusual outside of Dewdney's work. *Fovea Centralis* is also the first volume to offer an account of the basic principles of Remote Control, a central Dewdney concept. Remote Control is the name for an operation of paranoia-mongers mysteriously charged with unsettling by degrees the mental stability of the contemporary human world. This is pataphysics again, or maybe patahistory, but it makes an uncannily compelling commentary, here and elsewhere in Dewdney's work, on the intersections of fantasy and reality, realms that other writers (Jorge Luis Borges, for instance) feel are contaminated each with the other.

While he was working on these early volumes, from 1972 to 1975, Dewdney lived with Suzanne Dennison. Their daughter, Calla Xanthoria Kirk, was born in 1974. Since 1977 Dewdney has lived with artist and fellow-Londoner Lise Downe. They moved to Toronto in 1980, where their son, Tristan Alexander, was born in 1985.

Although *Alter Sublime* was published two years after *Spring Trances in the Control Emerald Night* (1978), it is actually more like *A Paleozoic Geology of London, Ontario* and *Fovea Contralis* in terms of the variety it offers. *Alter Sublime* not only contains the key essay "Parasite Maintenance"; it also highlights in various other pieces, prose and poetry, the theoretical interest in language–its built-in limitations and the possibilities of subverting them–that is present but less insistent in all Dewdney's other works. The first section of the book, "Alter Sublime," typically mixes poems and prose poems, many of them dreamlike, some of them rendering a hallucinatory joyful experience with nature: "You are trembling at once with the chill of early morning and the incredible revelation that is unfolding itself in the small colonies of thyme and moss growing on the wall. Each cell of every tiny leaf & flower has been crystallized with living jewels of infinite detail. Every grain a vision unearthly." *Alter Sublime* passes quickly without transitional signals from such visionary celebration to a variety of other modes, such as the epigrammatic and often humorous one-liners. One sign of the containing power of Dewdney's cosmos is that it manages to hold together the parts of such a miscellaneous book.

Dewdney's most uniform texts, speaking both technically and thematically, are the two "Natural histories of Southwestern Ontario," *Spring Trances in the Control Emerald Night & The Cenozoic Asylum* (1982). These are installments in a continuing project of prose/poetry whose style mimics the radical collapse of time and space already introduced in *A Paleozoic Geology of London, Ontario.* One way to look at the two books is to see in them Dewdney's introduction of all his favorite things into a dreamlike simultaneity in one of the most effective wish-fulfillment fantasies ever created. Dewdney's language is at its most lithe and synaesthetic in these two crystallizations of the sensual and scientific thrust of his work as a whole. The books are plotless, and the narrative point of view metamorphic, so they are impossible to summarize, but one might point to the "Bibliography of Creatures" (including Mammals, Insects, Birds, Reptiles, Amphibians, Trees,

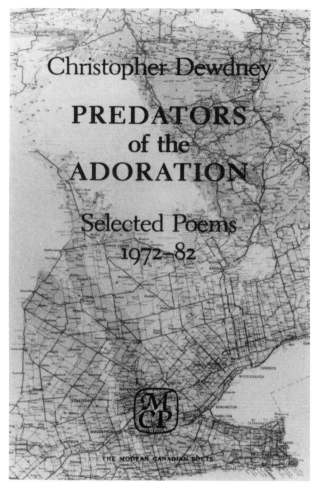

Cover for the 1983 collection drawn from five of Dewdney's previously published volumes. In the preface recalling his childhood in Southwestern Ontario, he writes: "In a sense, then, this book is the voice of the land and the creatures themselves. . . . It is a codex of plants and animals whose technology is truly miraculous, and for whom I am merely a scribe."

Plants, Weather, and Places) that ends *Spring Trances* as a skeletal summary of the contents of both books. The bibliography is annotated by the long-line incantatory poem "Grid Erectile" that opens *The Cenozoic Asylum.* These are benchmark pieces. They introduce the "characters" who are to interact across time and space in the prose poems of the natural histories proper.

Dewdney's work, being experimental or avant-garde, had been published by small alternative presses until 1983 when McClelland and Stewart brought out a volume of his selected poems, *Predators of the Adoration.* This volume contains the texts of the "log entries" and the natural histories intact and, according to Dewdney's "Note on the Text," otherwise presents a selection "ordered along slightly different lines of coherence" than any of the other volumes. Before *Predators of the Adoration* appeared, Dewdney had attracted a small but intense following, including such other poets as Steve McCaffery, David McFadden, and Michael Ondaatje, each of whom has written of his appreciation for Dewdney's work. Dewdney's delivery of "Grid Erectile" was a highlight of *Poetry in Motion*, Ron Mann's 1982 film about performance poetry, and consolidated his reputation as a dynamic reader of his own work. But it was *Predators of the Adoration* that dramatically increased interest in Dewdney's writing. The book was positively reviewed, and it made the short list for the Governor General's Awards in 1983. *Predators of the Adoration* is proof, in its selection and ordering of material from all Dewdney's works except his first, the privately printed *Golders Green* (1971), that an original and coherent vision has been unfolding from the beginning. According to David McFadden, Dewdney, like Robert Fones, is creating "a whole new set of clichés for the twenty-first century, giving the poets of the future something to rebel against." In any event it seems likely that Dewdney will be among those recognized in the twenty-first century for having made first explorations in a new sort of consciousness and for formulating a language to express it as he went along.

References:

Stan Dragland, "Afterword," in Dewdney's *Predators of the Adoration* (Toronto: McClelland & Stewart, 1983);

Steve McCaffery, "Strata and Strategy: Pataphysics in the Poetry of Christopher Dewdney," *Open Letter*, third series 4 (Winter 1976): 45-56;

David McFadden, "The Twilight of Self-Consciousness," in *The Human Elements: Critical Essays*, first series, edited by David Helwig (Ottawa: Oberon, 1978), pp. 78-96;

Michael Ondaatje, "Pure Memory/Chris Dewdney," in his *There's a Trick with a Knife I'm Learning to Do* (Toronto: McClelland & Stewart, 1979), pp. 100-103.

Pier Giorgio Di Cicco

(5 July 1949-   )

Paul Matthew St. Pierre
University of British Columbia

BOOKS: *We Are the Light Turning* (Scarborough, Ontario: Missing Link, 1975; revised, Birmingham, Alabama: Thunder City, 1976);
The Sad Facts (Vancouver: Fiddlehead, 1977);
The Circular Dark: Poems (Ottawa: Borealis, 1977);
Dancing in the House of Cards (Toronto: Three Trees, 1977);
A Burning Patience (Ottawa: Borealis, 1978);
Dolce-Amaro (Tuscaloosa, Alabama: Papavero, 1979);
The Tough Romance (Toronto: McClelland & Stewart, 1979);
A Straw Hat for Everything (Birmingham, Alabama: Angelstone, 1981);
Flying Deeper into the Century (Toronto: McClelland & Stewart, 1982);
Dark to Light: Reasons for Humanness (Vancouver: Intermedia, 1983);
Women We Never See Again (Ottawa: Borealis, 1984);
Post-Sixties Nocturne (Fredericton: Fiddlehead Goose Lane, 1985);
Twenty Poems (Guadalajara: University of Guadalajara Press, 1985);
Virgin Science: Hunting Holistic Paradigms (Toronto: McClelland & Stewart, 1986).

OTHER: "Oliver Beach," "Impersonation," "Memento d'Italia," in *Storm Warning 2,* edited by Al Purdy (Toronto: McClelland & Stewart, 1976), pp. 75-77;
"America," in *This Is My Best: Poems Selected by Ninety-One Poets,* edited by Kenneth Peregrine Gist (Toronto: Coach House Press, 1976), pp. 38-39;
"Whale-Killing," in *Whale Sound,* edited by Greg Gatenby (North Vancouver: J. J. Douglas, 1977), p. 40;
"Canzone," in *The Poets of Canada,* edited by John Robert Colombo (Edmonton: Hurtig, 1978), pp. 279-280;
"Casa Loma Birthday" and "The Educated Smile," in *Tributaries: An Anthology: Writer to Writer,* edited by Barry Dempster (Oakville, Ontario: Mosaic, 1978), pp. 53, 89;

Roman Candles: An Anthology of Poems by Seventeen Italo-Canadian Poets, edited by Di Cicco, includes his "The Man Called Beppino," "Nostalgia," "Quebec to Lévis," "Italy, 1974," "Memento d'Italia," "Paesani," "Quercianella: The Poem," "Remembering Baltimore, Arezzo," and "The Poem Becomes Canadian" (Toronto: Hounslow, 1978), pp. 31-38;
"The Bartender Speaks," in *Going for Coffee: Poetry on the Job,* edited by Tom Wayman (Madeira Park, British Columbia: Harbour, 1981), pp. 117-118;
"The Head Is a Paltry Matter," "Errore," "Male Rage Poem," and "Flying Deeper into the Century," in *The New Oxford Book of Canadian Verse in English,* edited by Margaret Atwood (Toronto & New York: Oxford University Press, 1982), pp. 458-462;
"America," "Flying Deeper into the Century," "Relationships," "The Poem Becomes Canadian," "The Explosion of Thimbles," and "Beyond Labelling," in *Canadian Poetry Now: 20 Poets of the '80's,* edited by Ken Norris (Toronto: Anansi, 1984), pp. 81-89;
"Canzone," "The Head Is a Paltry Matter," "The Man Called Beppino," "Remembering Baltimore, Arezzo," "Willing," "The Jump on Death," "Flying Deeper into the Country," "Male Rage Poem," "Relationships," "Brain Litany," and "Letter to Ding an Sich," in *The New Canadian Poets, 1970-1985,* edited by Dennis Lee (Toronto: McClelland & Stewart, 1985), pp. 80-94.

PERIODICAL PUBLICATIONS: "We Sit at the Kitchen Table" and "The Air Thick with These Things," *Descant,* 7 (Fall 1973): 11-12;
"She Comes In," *Waves,* 2 (Winter 1974): 56;
"Quebec to Levis," "Last Aunt," and "Italy, 1974," *Queen's Quarterly,* 82 (Winter 1975): 512, 513, 514;
"Poetry Bus," *Dalhousie Review,* 55 (Winter 1975-1976): 742;
"Elder" and "Fascists," *University of Windsor Re-*

photograph by B. Carey

view, 11 (Spring-Summer 1976): 86-87, 88;

"Nest" and "We Are Going Nowhere," *Fiddlehead,* 111 (Fall 1976): 5-6;

"Travelling High," *Dalhousie Review,* 56 (Autumn 1976): 552;

"Sometimes Old Age," *Waves,* 4 (Winter 1976): 55;

"Shelbourne Morning," *Canadian Author and Bookman,* 52 (Winter 1976): 34;

"Poem Against City Hospital," *Fiddlehead,* 108 (Winter 1976): 60;

"Quercianella," *Canadian Forum,* 56 (December 1976-January 1977): 34;

"Dialect," *Canadian Literature,* 73 (Summer 1977): 24;

"Paesani," "America," "Fotografia," "Branch by Branch," "Man Called Beppino," and "I Remember," *Tamarack Review,* 70 (Winter 1977): 81-87;

"Reappearances," *Waves,* 6 (Spring 1978): 68;

"Donna Italiana," *Dalhousie Review,* 58 (Autumn 1978): 553;

"Canzone," *Canadian Forum,* 58 (October-November 1978): 26;

"Empty Sleeve," *Canadian Literature,* 79 (Winter 1978): 22;

"The Beaches" and "The Sundays of St. Clair," *Descant,* no. 3/10, no. 1 (1978-1979): 39-41;

"Sixth Sensation," *Canadian Author and Bookman,* 54 (August 1979): 25;

"Morning," "How Soon Can We Refuse It," "Growing Up Big and Lonely," and "That's How Much of a Thimbleful," *Tamarack Review,* 79 (Autumn 1979): 8-12;

"The Friendship Game," *Waves,* 8 (Fall 1979): 60;

"Such Days," *Dalhousie Review,* 59 (Winter 1979-1980): 660;

"Growing Up Big and Lonely," *Descant,* 11, nos. 1-2 (1980): 34-35;

"Hatching," *Canadian Author and Bookman,* 55-56 (Summer-Fall 1980): 37;

"Mezza-Notte," *Canadian Forum,* 61 (May 1981): 35;

"Revenge for the Insides," *Dalhousie Review,* 61 (Summer 1981): 262;

"September Lirica," *Waves,* 10 (Summer-Fall 1981): 70;

"Where Were You the Day John Lennon Died?,"
"Poem Written after Reading the Thou-
sandth Bad Article on What Happened to
the Children of the Sixties," "Sixties Music,"
"Sixties Hangover," and "Old Mistakes," *Canadian Forum*, 61 (November 1981): 21-23;
"Relationships," *Saturday Night*, 96 (December
1981): 64;
"You Can't Plan What You Are About," "God
Never Remembers the Spelling of Things,"
and "Prodigal," *Quarry*, 30 (Winter 1981):
32-34;
"The Singles Galaxy," *Waves*, 9 (Winter 1981): 42;
"Quotidian" and "Lying Low," *Canadian Litera-
ture*, 91 (Winter 1981): 9, 80;
"American Love," *Descant*, 12, no. 4 / 13, nos. 1-2
(1981-1982): 108-109;
"Singles" and "Muddling Through," *Fiddlehead*,
133 (July 1982): 68, 69;
"Male Rage Poem," *Waves*, 10 (Winter 1982): 68;
"Baby Poem," *Canadian Author and Bookman*, 57
(Winter 1982): 17;
"Send Me a Postcard," *Canadian Literature*, 100
(Spring 1984): 92;
"Three Coins in the Fountain. Each One Bring-
ing Happiness," *Poetry Toronto*, 112 (April
1985): 18-19;
"Omnibiographies," "Brain Litany," "Schizo-
phrenic as the Failed Magician," *Canadian
Forum*, 65 (May 1985): 22-23;
"Multicultural Blues," "Paesani," "Going Back,"
Canadian Literature, 106 (Fall 1985): 18, 44,
and 75;
"Lazarus, the Inert," *Poetry Canada Review*, 8 (Au-
tumn 1986): 8.

In producing fourteen books of poetry in
twelve years and in placing individual poems in a
dozen Canadian anthologies and in hundreds of
periodicals around the world, Pier Giorgio Di
Cicco has proved himself a productive and perdur-
able poet. He has demonstrated a peculiarly Canadian ability to survive through small presses and
to live in little magazines. He is one of a modest
group of Canadian poets who are literary household names, whose appearances in books and journals seem matters of course. Di Cicco has
assumed a leading role in sustaining this type of literary existence, by publicizing the poetic act in
his many public readings and lectures and by promoting poetry through his editorial positions
with various literary journals and as the editor of
a poetry anthology of his own.

Because Di Cicco has worked as a poetry editor from the very beginning of his career, his editorial accomplishment sometimes seems even more
important than his poetic achievement: it has introduced him to the complete literary process
and community, provided him with a writing
framework and won him professional status, and
taught him to execute the delicate task of editing
not just the poetry of others but his own verse as
well. Although Di Cicco's intellectual, innovative
poetry has yet to receive scholarly attention (ironically, not even in the academic journals in which
it regularly appears), it consistently receives encouraging reviews. In his publications with
McClelland and Stewart in particular, Di Cicco
has found a respectability that for many Canadian poets is elusive.

The son of Giuseppe and Primetta Di Cicco,
Di Cicco was born 5 July 1949 at Arezzo, Italy.
In 1952 the Di Cicco family immigrated to Canada, living at first in Montreal and then in Toronto, and in 1958 moving to Baltimore,
Maryland, where Di Cicco received most of his
schooling. Upon the family's return to Toronto
in 1968, Di Cicco completed high school and enrolled in the University of Toronto, where he studied English literature, creative writing, physics,
and education, receiving a B.A. in 1972 and a
B. Ed. in 1973. Although in the course of his career Di Cicco has held a number of jobs (teacher,
bartender, chemist, detective), he began to pursue his literary vocation almost immediately upon
university graduation. An informing irony was
that the poet to whom spontaneity would always
take precedence over revision began his career
by editing the very journals in which he placed
his first poems.

Following the appearance of his earliest published poems (among them "We Sit at the
Kitchen Table" and "The Air Thick with These
Things" in the Fall 1973 issue of *Descant*), Di
Cicco took on three important editorial positions,
all in 1976. He founded and served as poetry editor of *Poetry Toronto Newsletter* (later *Poetry Toronto*), beginning with its first issue in January
1976 and ending his tenure in September 1977
as a consulting editor. His publication of "She
Comes In" in the Winter 1974 issue of *Waves* led
to his becoming the poetry journal's coeditor
(along with Barbara Godard and John Oughton)
in the fall of 1976. After briefly sharing the editorship with Oughton, Bernice Lever, Hédi
Bouraoui, and Robert Clayton Casto for the Autumn 1977 issue, Di Cicco withdrew from his posi-

tion to serve on the advisory board of *Waves* (in the company of Louis Dudek, Dave Godfrey, Ralph Gustafson, Al Purdy, and Adele Wiseman), becoming poetry editor again in autumn 1980, a position he held until spring 1982, when he ended his editorial affiliation with the magazine. In the fall of 1976 (just as he was beginning his tenure with *Waves*), Di Cicco became an assistant to Douglas Marshall during Marshall's editorship of *Books in Canada,* over the course of the next three years serving the magazine as editorial assistant (September-November 1976), assistant editor (December 1976-April 1977), associate editor (May 1977-October 1978), and small-press editor (November 1978-July 1979).

During his associations with *Poetry Toronto Newsletter, Waves,* and *Books in Canada,* Di Cicco also succeeded in placing poetry in some of Canada's most prestigious journals, including *Queen's Quarterly, Fiddlehead, Dalhousie Review, Tamarack Review,* and *Canadian Literature.* But it was his very earliest submissions to little magazines which caught the attention of Al Purdy in 1974 and inspired him to include three of Di Cicco's poems in his anthology *Storm Warning 2* (1976). Although Di Cicco already had a volume of poetry (*We Are the Light Turning*) published the previous year, Purdy's anthology gave him an invaluable literary endorsement and plucked him out of chapbook obscurity. With his work appearing in a series of anthologies throughout the 1970s and 1980s, Di Cicco has continued to enjoy the reputation of a young and innovative poet, in particular as he is represented in Margaret Atwood's *The New Oxford Book of Canadian Verse in English* (1982), Ken Norris's *Canadian Poetry Now* (1984), and Dennis Lee's *The New Canadian Poets* (1985).

Di Cicco's individual volumes of poetry reflect his growing preoccupation with the mystic dimensions of human geography. Although his verse is often lauded (and sometimes dismissed) as "surreal," its true focus is less on what-is-more-real-than-real than on what-underlies-reality in ordinary human experience. Di Cicco's earliest publications graphically (if somewhat simplistically) illustrate this poetic. His three collections from 1977—*The Sad Facts, The Circular Dark,* and *Dancing in the House of Cards*—all maintain an indelicate balance between observation and reflection, the poet doing little more than perceiving the ordinary within the extraordinary, as in the bathetic conclusion of "World's End":

Finally it came to an end with

stillness
Darkness sprawled
The last glimmers of light went off like candles
before our eyes

And we heard talk, voices sounding
finally as if the whole world meant it.

This kind of laconic verse is symptomatic of the poet's struggle through most of the 1970s to develop a personal technique and to find his own voice.

Toward the end of the decade, Di Cicco started to take a dialectical approach to verse, developing edifying hypotheses and memorable conceits, his style becoming increasingly dense and cerebral without losing its inherent clarity. In *A Burning Patience* (1978), for example, phrases such as "The man with no arms / is picking up the world," "The bodies of dead relatives /are piled outside the door," and "When death finds me, my grin will have widened into something / resembling a horizon" typify the poet's concern with startling images almost at the expense of thematic development. In *The Tough Romance* (1979), his first poetic volume to appear under the imprint of a large commercial press (in contrast to *Dolce-Amaro,* published the same year), Di Cicco combines imagery-in-rigor-mortis with a lively conversational style, as in "Passagio":

It is time I announced my desire to be a field,
a stone with one arm, a blue wind rising.
All the boxes of the heads of my friends
exploding, but gathering at dusk, after the
    fanfare
of sun and shadow. I am a little tired of the
    fireworks
over the lake, the confetti of cars, the ribbons
of a lover's tongue. It is time I announced that
the grave I walk in is not mine. I change it,
as of now. If you follow, you will have to dance.

Here Di Cicco not only delineates the roles of speaker and audience but also invites the audience to engage in poetry's dramatic process. He has endeavored to keep this invitation open in all of his published verse.

Standing out among Di Cicco's publications in the late 1970s is his most enduring contribution to Canadian literary scholarship, *Roman Candles: An Anthology of Poems by Seventeen Italo-Canadian Poets* (featuring Mary di Michele, Alexandre L. Amprimoz, and Mary Melfi, as well as Di Cicco himself). The poet's editorial accomplishment here echoes those of J. Michael Yates

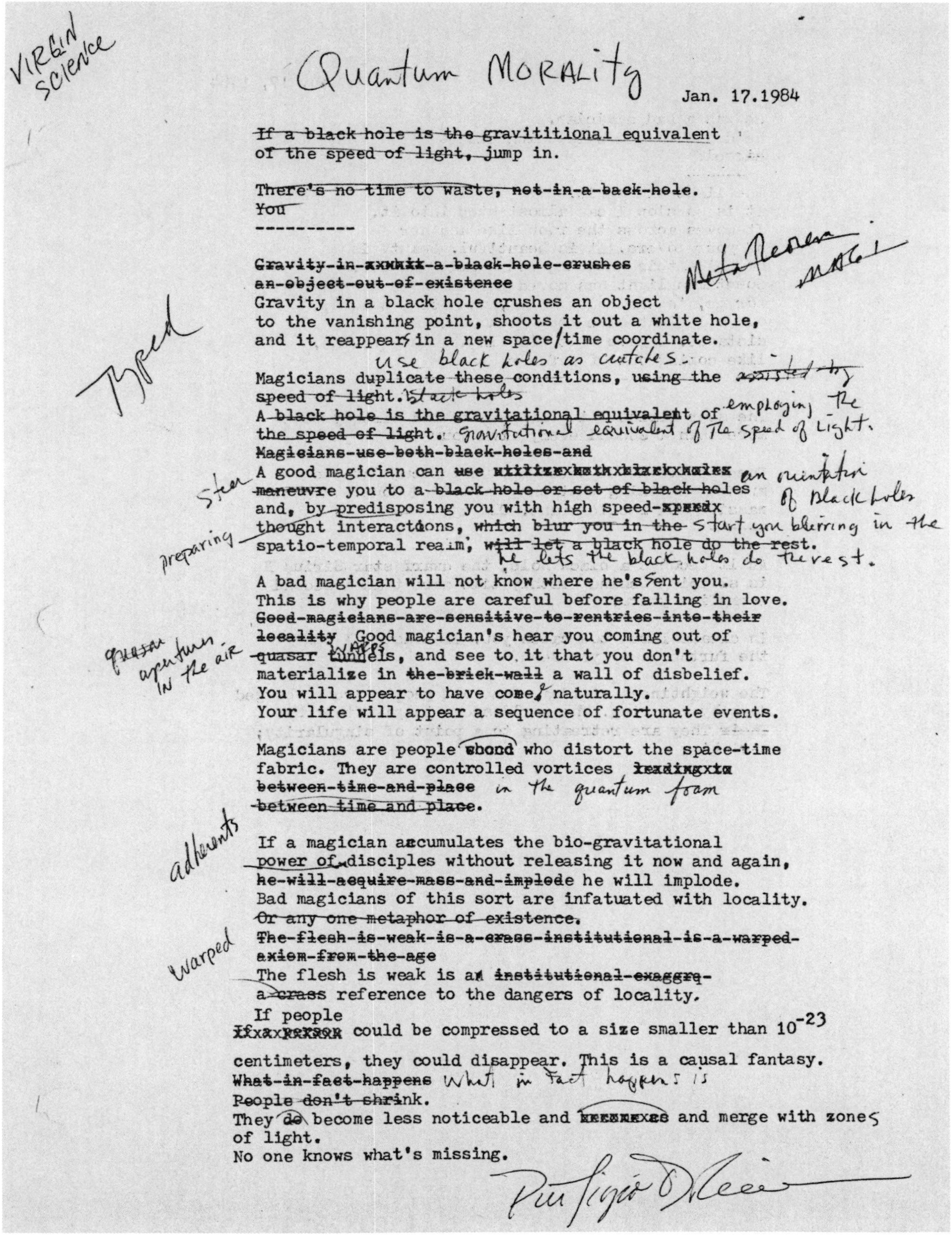

Virgin Science (handwritten margin note)

Quantum MORALity

Jan. 17.1984

~~If a black hole is the gravititional equivalent
of the speed of~~ light, jump in.

~~There's no time to waste, not in a back hole.
You~~

~~Gravity in a black hole crushes
an object out of existence~~ *Metaphora* *note:*
Gravity in a black hole crushes an object
to the vanishing point, shoots it out a white hole,
and it reappears in a new space/time coordinate.

                    use black holes as crutches
Magicians duplicate these conditions, ~~using the~~ *assisted by*
~~speed of light.~~ *black holes*
~~A black hole is the gravitational equivalent of~~ *employing the*
~~the speed of light.~~ *gravitational equivalent of The speed of Light.*
~~Magicians use both black holes and~~
A good magician can ~~use xxxxxxxxxxxxxxxx~~ *an orientation*
star ~~maneuvre you to a black hole or set of black holes~~ *of Black holes*
preparing and, by predisposing you with high speed-~~speed~~
thought interactions, ~~which blur you in the~~ *start you blurring in the*
spatio-temporal realm, ~~will let a black hole do the rest.~~
                    he lets the black holes do The rest.

A bad magician will not know where he's sent you.
This is why people are careful before falling in love.
~~Good magicians are sensitive to reentries into their
locality~~ Good magician's hear you coming out of
quasar ~~quasar tunnels~~, and see to it that you don't
apertures materialize in ~~the brick wall~~ a wall of disbelief.
in the air You will appear to have come naturally.
Your life will appear a sequence of fortunate events.

Magicians are people ~~whond~~ who distort the space-time
fabric. They are controlled vortices ~~leadingxto~~
~~between time and place~~ *in the quantum foam*
~~between time and place.~~

adherents If a magician accumulates the bio-gravitational
power of disciples without releasing it now and again,
~~he will acquire mass and implode~~ he will implode.
Bad magicians of this sort are infatuated with locality.
~~Or any one metaphor of existence.~~
warped ~~The flesh is weak is a crass institutional is a warped
axiom from the age~~
The flesh is weak is an ~~institutional exaggra-~~
~~a crass~~ reference to the dangers of locality.
If people
~~Ifxaxpxxxxx~~ could be compressed to a size smaller than 10^{-23}

centimeters, they could disappear. This is a causal fantasy.
~~What in fact happens~~ *What in fact happens is*
~~People don't shrink.~~
They ~~do~~ become less noticeable and ~~xxxxxxxx~~ and merge with zones
of light.
No one knows what's missing.

Revised typescript for one of the poems collected in Di Cicco's Virgin Science *(by permission of the author)*

and Charles Lillard in *Volvox: Poetry from the Unofficial Languages of Canada* (1971) and Stephen M. Green in *Green Snow: An Anthology of Canadian Poets of Asian Origin* (1976), and it anticipated such works as Gerry Shikatani and David Aylward's *Paper Doors: An Anthology of Japanese Canadian Poetry* (1981), the "Italian-Canadian Connections" issue of *Canadian Literature*, 106 (Fall 1985), and even the CBC *Anthology* program "Writing About the Italian Immigrant Experience" (March 1985), showcasing Di Cicco, di Michele, and others. *Roman Candles* moved Di Cicco to see himself within a widening poetic collective.

His social sensitivity is attributable to his everyday involvement in the Toronto artistic community. In 1982, for example, Di Cicco conducted a poetry workshop at Humber College in January and February, gave a reading at the Axel-Tree Coffee House in May, and served as a poet-in-residence (along with Margaret Atwood, George Faludy, B. P. Nichol, Al Purdy, and others) at the Great Canadian Poetry Weekend in June. Through these kinds of activities, year after year, Di Cicco has meticulously executed the role of practicing poet.

During the early 1980s, in *Dark to Light: Reasons for Humanness* (1983) and *Women We Never See Again* (1984), Di Cicco shifted his poetic focus from striking imagery to characters who seem inseparable from their settings and who effectively speak for place. Notable for this kind of placement of people are "The Beat Poets, 1976" ("Black jackets / at the table. They believe in stones, in wives.") and "The Blue-Eyed Man" ("The incredibly hard-earned existence of the / blue-eyed man is coming close to you."). An earlier collection, however, *Flying Deeper into the Century* (1982), featured even more accomplished verse, longer poems with more ambitious lines and carefully catalogued figures and images, Di Cicco demonstrating his poetic versatility for the first time. In "Poem Written after Reading the Thousandth Bad Article on What Happened to the Children of the Sixties" and "On Religious Talk Shows" he reveals an engagingly droll humor, in "Relationships" and "Male Rage Poem" an admirable cynicism toward hollow community, in "Skylab" and "Where Were You the Day John Lennon Died?" a subtle awareness of political inequity, and in "Flying Deeper into the Century" and "Mid-century" a timely fascination with the metaphysics of philosophy and science.

In his next collections, *Post-Sixties Nocturne* and *Twenty Poems*, both published in 1985, Di

Cover for Di Cicco's most recent poetry collection, in which he draws on principles of quantum physics and Thomist philosophy

Cicco exploits a more ponderous style, cramming his poetic line and ramming one line into the next. As in "Neighbourhoods," the verse demands an actor's sensitivity to bring it to life from the page: "A touch would do it, faint as a fossil, the hard / meanderings of flesh asking forgiveness; there is a touch / in things, like a fly caught in amber, like a kiss locked / in an eye." His most recent collection of verse, *Virgin Science: Hunting Holistic Paradigms* (1986), is even more deliberate and stylized, as Di Cicco attempts a metapoetic based on principles of quantum physics and Thomist philosophy. This volume accurately (if idiosyncratically) reflects current movements in our technocentric culture. The three sections of the book—"Dying to Myself," "Virgin Science" (which includes "The Problem of Time," "The Escape from Matter," "The Gallery of Holistic Science," "The Epistemography of Hell," and "The Future with a Human Face"), and "Hearing the Bridegroom's Voice"–transform a Dantesque cosmos into a scientific blueprint, positing a Cartesian universe that is at once the place Di Cicco inhabits and the poetry he writes.

Although mainly a Toronto poet, Di Cicco does occupy an important place in Canadian literature, partly because of his success in popularizing poetry in his community and promoting the works of other poets in magazines, but mainly because of his success in having his own verse published in journals ranging from *Malahat Review* (Victoria) to *Fiddlehead* (Fredericton), from *Argomenti Canadesi* (Rome) to *Italia-America* (San Francisco), from the *Critical Quarterly* (Hull, England) to *Poetry Australia* (Sydney). Though he has recently become an Augustinian brother, Pier Giorgio Di Cicco is the paradigm of a living Canadian poet, living beyond the means of his Canada Council and Ontario Arts Council grants, living around the world in a universal language.

Interview:

Robert Billings, "*Virgin Science:* The Hunt for Holistic Paradigms: An Interview with Pier Giorgio Di Cicco," *Poetry Canada Review,* 8 (Autumn 1986): 3-4, 8-9.

References:

Douglas Barbour, "Canadian Poetry Chronicle: VI," *Dalhousie Review,* 58 (Autumn 1978): 555-578;

Barbour, "Canadian Poetry Chronicle: VII," *Dalhousie Review,* 59 (Winter 1979-1980): 154-175;

Antonio D'Alfonso, "Per Pier Giorgio Di Cicco," *Canadian Literature,* 106 (Fall 1985): 41;

Greg Gatenby, "Poetry Chronicle," *Tamarack Review,* 77-78 (Summer 1979): 77-94;

Bruce Whiteman, "Big Seeing and Necessary as Breath," *Essays on Canadian Writing,* 10 (1978): 57-60.

Réjean Ducharme
(12 August 1941-)

Myrianne Pavlovic

BOOKS: *L'Avalée des avalés* (Paris: Gallimard, 1966; Montreal: Editions du Bélier, 1967); translated by Barbara Bray as *The Swallower Swallowed* (London: Hamilton, 1968);
Le Nez qui voque (Paris: Gallimard, 1967);
L'Océantume (Paris: Gallimard, 1968);
La Fille de Christophe Colomb (Paris: Gallimard, 1969);
L'Hiver de force (Paris: Gallimard, 1973); translated by Robert Guy Scully as *Wild to Mild* (Saint-Lambert, Quebec: Héritage, 1980);
Les Enfantômes (Paris: Gallimard, 1976);
Inès Pérée et Inat Tendu (Montreal: Leméac, 1976);
HA ha! ... (Ville Saint-Laurent, Quebec: Lacombe/Paris: Gallimard, 1982).

PLAY PRODUCTIONS: *Le Cid Maghané*, Sainte-Agathe des Monts, Quebec, Théâtre de la Sablière, 27 June 1968;
Inès Pérée et Inat Tendu, Sainte-Agathe des Monts, Quebec, Théâtre de la Sablière, 31 July 1968;
Le Marquis qui perdit, Montreal, Théâtre du Nouveau Monde au Théâtre Port-Royal, 16 January 1970;
L'Hiver de force, adapted by Ducharme from his novel, Montreal, Université du Québec à Montréal, December 1974; revised as *La Fonne c'est platte ou La Chair est triste et j'ai vu tous les films de Jerry Lewis*, Montreal, Université de Montreal, 23 March 1977;
Prenez-nous et aimez nous, Montreal, Organisation O at Théâtre de la Maine, 5 May 1976;
Ah! ah, Montreal, Théâtre du Nouveau Monde, 10 March 1978;
Les Sept Péchés capitaux, opera-ballet adapted by Ducharme from a play by Berthold Brecht, Montreal, Grands Ballets Canadiens at Place des Arts, 10 November 1978.

MOTION PICTURES: *Les Bons Débarras*, script by Ducharme, Les Productions Prisma, 1979;
Les Beaux Souvenirs, script by Ducharme, National Film Board of Canada/Lamy, Spenser, 1981.

PERIODICAL PUBLICATIONS: "Lettre de Réjean Ducharme à Pierre Tisseyre," *Le Devoir*, 5 November 1966, p. 44;
"Lettre de Réjean Ducharme à Jean Basile," *Le Devoir*, 14 January 1967, p. 13;
"Témoinages d'écrivains-Nez Lit Gant," *Etudes Françaises*, 3 (August 1967): 306-307;
"Inès Perée et Inat Tendu sur la terre," *Châtelaine*, 9 (March 1968): 22-23, 56-63;
"Mot de l'auteur," *Le Devoir*, 25 May 1968, p. 17;
"Fragment inédit de L'Océantume," *Etudes Françaises*, 11 (October 1975): 227-246.

In 1966 there appeared in Paris a novel by a twenty-four-year-old Quebec writer who was totally unknown and who wanted to remain so. The author was Réjean Ducharme–and his book *L'Avalée des avalés*–revealed such an extraordinary literary maturity that many questioned the authenticity of the publisher's assertion that the work was indeed by this unknown young man. The publication of Ducharme's first novel turned into a literary event, which for a long time was considered "news" both in France and in Quebec. Translated immediately into four languages–and hailed by some as the "discovery of the century"– the book was one of six finalists for the Prix Goncourt, sponsored by several eminent French writers and literary critics. The author, however, continued to evade the public. None knew anything about him except what he himself had chosen to reveal in a blurb on the cover of *L'Avalée des avalés*. He shunned interviews and literally fled journalists, changing domiciles every two or three days, repeating his wish to remain anonymous.

When the press and public learned through various reports that, besides *L'Avalée des avalés* Ducharme had submitted three other manuscripts to Gallimard–ironically using as a pseudonym the name of the seventeenth-century classic French writer Jean Racine–and, moreover, that Gallimard was about to publish them, they de-

Réjean Ducharme at the time of L'Avalée des avalés
(courtesy of Kenneth Landry)

manded proof of Ducharme's identity. The affair took on unusual proportions. People found it difficult to believe that a young man from the Quebec village of Saint-Félix-de-Valois could be the sole author of a work so important and began to insist that he show himself, that he demonstrate that the surname Ducharme did not hide a hoax. Enquiries about Ducharme began to assume the character of a police enquiry whose object was to uncover concrete details which might illuminate Ducharme's background and establish some connection between the personality of the man and that of the author as it was revealed in the book. Ducharme's audience wanted especially to know why Ducharme so determinedly fled the press and why he avoided public contact, too.

It took two years for a journalist—in disguise—to catch up with Ducharme and to get some photographs of him. They were not good photographs, but they quickly became the best evidence available in favor of Ducharme's existence: there was a clear resemblance between them and the pictures that had been put into circulation at the time *L'Avalée des avalés* was published. Since the late 1960s Ducharme has neither been seen in public nor interviewed. He preserves his anonymity fiercely, and even those people with whom he has occasionally collaborated have been able to maintain contact with him only by mail.

Recent research suggests that Ducharme was born in Saint-Félix-de-Valois, in Berthier County, on 12 August 1941, the son of Omer Ducharme, a taxi driver, and the former Nina Lavallée, and that he was educated at the Juvénat des Clercs de Saint-Viateur at Berthierville, and at the Ecole Polytechnique in Montreal, which he left after a single year. Briefly registered in the Canadian Air Force, he became by turns an encyclopedia salesman (1963-1965), a Yukon mineworker, and a proofreader for Québec-Presse (1972-1973). But none of these details is confirmed; readers should treat them with caution.

The sustained search for Ducharme occurred in part because his readers were scarcely prepared for the difficulty of his work. Ducharme's entry into the world of letters in a sense altered that world. In fact francophone criticism generally agrees that there is a "pre-Ducharme" and a "post-Ducharme" period in Quebec writing, because Ducharme's first book marks a threshold both in subject and in form.

L'Avalée des avalés (translated as *The Swallower Swallowed* in 1968) presumes to be the interior monologue of an antisocial girl named Bérénice Einberg, whom we follow from age nine to age fifteen. With a bitter clarity, and consumed by a need for absolutes—for perfection and uncompromised passion—Bérénice voices her deep rejection of the adult world and of the power which rests in adults' hands. The novel reads as a sustained shout: Bérénice expresses her hatred first against her family—repeatedly attacking her caricatured, authoritarian father, Mauritius. She has to work harder to detest her mother as much, for her mother's beauty and sweetness fascinate and possess her. To her brother Christian she longs to confess her lack of self-esteem, but she resists that impulse and any connection with him. Bérénice's only friend, Constance Chlore—her opposite, a representative of purity—escapes her ferocious hatred. Death, however, soon removes Constance from the scene. The young narrator is then animated by a furious will to destroy, her revolt fastening on a single purpose: to create herself anew and thereby to establish another world which will counter the one in which she lives. This frantic reinvention of the world happens through the taking of the realm of the Word: the heroine invents a language for herself she calls "bérénicien," in which words take on new meaning, overcome old realities and create new ones.

In *L'Avalée des avalés* (which was written after Ducharme's later-published works, *Le Nez qui voque* and *L'Océantume*), one finds the characteristics that confer upon Ducharme's world its specificity: the principal character is a child, as are most of Ducharme's main characters. She is a precocious and demanding child, torn between the desire to clear away the reality which stifles her and a diametrically opposed need for tenderness which could annihilate her; between possessing and being possessed (Bérénice chooses the first). Another constant that emerges is the presence of a vaguely incestuous and androgynous couple, in which one person is presented as the opposite of the other: Bérénice/Christian, Bérénice/Constance, Constance/Christian. Finally, the characters are subjected to an all-powerful maternal figure who is worshipped and despised at the same time.

Ducharme's works are introspective, and they also burst grammatical structures, which gives them some of their difficulty. Critics have praised Ducharme's linguistic virtuosity. A dictionary reader, Ducharme exploits all the resources of the codified language but manages at the same time to subvert order with what amounts to a game with words.

In *Le Nez qui voque* (1967), Mille Milles, the narrator and protagonist, questions in his private journal the semantic values that words usually possess. Mille Milles is a sixteen-year-old boy who wishes he were eight, cultivating equivocation and deriding everything he sees so that he might experience the full tragedy of his impending passage to adulthood. Adulthood repels him but at the same time attracts him, entices him—which further repels him—and he comes to despise himself. Therefore, with Chateaugué, his girlfriend, or "sister," as he would have it, he shuts himself into a little room in Old Montreal, where the two of them decide to commit suicide so as not to leave childhood and therefore never to drown in the degradations of the adult world. While Chateaugué is the living symbol of a mythic "natural" purity (associated in the book with the poet Emile Nelligan), Mille Milles must put up a spir-

ited battle to resist the progressive slide that will lead him to succumb to the sensuality of Questa, the mature woman, who horrifies but inescapably attracts him. Anguish and a heightened feeling of guilt grip Mille Milles, who is so ashamed of himself that he brings all his forces to bear to put his plan into motion. But he alone respects the suicide pact; Chateaugué does not. Is this a form of treason, a farewell to childhood, or a way of immortalizing childhood on the other side of death? The book gives no answer, but tells, with an intensity born of its ambiguity, particularly moving in this case, of the adolescent world that always traps Ducharmean heroes.

L'Océantume (1968) closes a cycle that some critics have treated as a trilogy. Though this, Ducharme's third published novel, is a repetitive and uneven dreamlike epic, it has won praise as a lyrical "odyssey." *L'Océantume* in effect explores and reinvokes the obsessive characteristics of the first two novels. The narrator, Iode Ssouvie, a girl of ten, joins the gallery of giant children (or dwarf adults?) in Ducharme's world. Iode lives with her family on a broken-down steamer half-buried on the banks of the Ouareau River. Like Bérénice, who involves Constance Chlore in her strange adventures, and like Mille Milles, who persuades Chateaugué to participate in his project, Iode finds a faithful and passionate friend in Asie Azothe, a young Finnish girl who has recently settled with her eight brothers in the manor house across the way. Like Bérénice, Iode has a brother, Inachos, who plays the submissive role that Christian did in *L'Avalée des avalés*. There are other recurrent patterns: a father, Van der Laine, is unaware of what happens around him; a superlative mother, Ina Ssouvie, figures prominently in the story; there is a quest (to sail along the coast and get to the sea) that carries the hope of rebirth; and the desire to push beyond limits is expressed through delirious language which prevents one from distinguishing between dream and reality.

Three years after the publication of *L'Avalée des avalés*, critics who had been watching the progress of Ducharme's career began to take stock of his accomplishment. The studies that appeared were laudatory, but clearly the critics were impatient for another work. *La Fille de Christophe Colomb* (1969) soon appeared, but after the amount of commentary which had accompanied the preceding works, the critical silence which greeted this publication resounded loudly. It was scarcely reviewed; it has hardly been recognized

First Canadian edition (courtesy of Kenneth Landry) and first English translation of Ducharme's revolutionary novel. After
L'Avalée des avalés *was published in 1966, francophone critics divided Quebec writing*
into two eras: "pre-" and "post-Ducharme."

even in recent anthologies; and though Ducharme's novels have been the subject of dozens of theses and dissertations, not one has been devoted to *La Fille de Christophe Colomb*.

Of all the creations born of the author's truculent imagination, this one is undoubtedly the most extravagant. A lyrical epic written in rhymed verse quatrains, this "novel" tells of the travels around the world of a woman named Colombe, daughter of the renowned explorer Columbus and a leghorn chicken. After the death of the chicken, with which the work begins, Colombe lives peacefully with her father on the Isle of Man; the two lead a life of perfect happiness until Columbus dies, poisoned by a fish which Colombe had served him. Alone, her only inheritance being her mother's golden heart which she decides to throw into the sea, Colombe leaves the Isle of Man for a vagabond life marked by hunger and various disastrous encoun-

ters. Tired of the wickedness of humans and no longer hoping to win friendship, Colombe adopts first one, then two, then a hundred, then all the animals of the earth in the course of her wanderings through the different continents. Elected queen of this adoring collection of animals—naming, nourishing, and caring for each in turn—she is soon confronted with the evils of civilization when she comes to preside over the thousandth anniversary of her father. The humans attack the animals, which respond with murderous bloodshed and a declaration of war. Colombe, powerless, can only cry over the fate of her brothers before everything is overcome in an apocalyptic deluge of blood. The narrator intones:

Cette belle histoire, croyez-le ou non, fut vécue.
Elle m'a été imposée comme un passé par
    quelque chose
Que j'ai dans la tête mais que je n'entends plus,

Par une sorte de soleil obligatoire noir et rose.

(This beautiful story, believe it or not, was lived.
It has been imposed on me like a past by something
In my head that I no longer understand,
By an obligatory sun that is black and red.)

Like a dreamed enchantment ruled by free associations–in which Colombe's body is wounded, mutilated, broken up, then put back together, part human, part animal, and part divine–this initiation story conveys an experience which has bothered many readers.

Ducharme's first four novels appeared at one-year intervals; four years, however, separated *La Fille de Christophe Colomb* from *L'Hiver de force*. Again critics were baffled by the veritable "voodoo" of the work, and in reviews they simply quoted large extracts from the novel. Realistic in structure, it presents the journal of André and Nicole, who decide to note down assiduously a detailed list of their daily activities. Proofreaders working under deadlines, eking out their lives as best they can, tempted by high-paying jobs but never bringing themselves to apply for them, they quit and give themselves over to the ambitious project of doing nothing. Living as recluses, Nicole and André sever all links with the consumer society they detest, gradually getting rid of everything they possess: the television set they have watched for hours, the record player, the telephone, the refrigerator, the stove, and so on. Then a woman named Catherine appears, countering the process of giving everything away. Unstable and inconstant, excessive but warm, Catherine represents to the couple everything they want–tenderness, love, time–which she can give them. They want her to occupy their home, but Catherine, the mirror of their wishes, ends up rebounding against them.

Aged twenty-eight and twenty-nine, Nicole and André (one never knows if they are truly brother and sister or just "temporarily" so, like Mille Milles and Chateaugué) repeat, but in other ways, fundamental patterns from the other novels. Faithful replicas of each other, like Bérénice, Mille Milles, and Iode Ssouvie, they find themselves as though by error in the bodies of adults. Their aversions are the same, as are their nostalgic memories and their amorous fixations. However, the apparent nonchalance of the novel gives Ducharme's treatment of these recurrent patterns a new tone. The deluge of puns and wordplay in the preceding works–apparent in the titles, the characters' names, and the book-

ishness which pervaded Ducharme's masterly style–has gone; here the writing owes a debt to the spoken language and is distinguished by its simplicity. This simplicity gives a deep and poignant intensity to the anguish of the characters, who are in essence Oedipal children facing the emptiness of a pointless existence.

Ducharme's next novel, *Les Enfantômes* (1976), poses, in a more extreme way, questions raised in the preceding works. When they are very young, the central characters, twins named Vincent and Fériée, find their mother brutally murdered. From that point on they quite literally stop growing. Beside Alberta Turnstiff, the English-speaker whom he marries, Vincent looks like an arrested child. *Les Enfantômes* purports to be his memoirs, memoirs haunted by his dead mother and more explicitly by Fériée, who also dies and with whom Vincent is madly in love. "Le temps commençait où je m'apercevais que j'avais fait une erreur, qu'il fallait aimer une femme c'est tout, qu'il n'y en a plus qu'une au fond, que toutes les autres recouvrent pour effacer son nom et son visage" (I began to realize that I had made a mistake, that to love a woman was all that was necessary, that when you come right down to it there's only one, and that all others repeat her in order to erase her name and her face).

"SHE"–"Woman"–whose phantom presence takes form in characters such as Constance Chlore, Chateaugué, Asie Azothe, and Colombe Colomb, appears here crudely unmasked. This story of voluntary regression asks in the most radical and perhaps the most troubling way the questions which Ducharme's previous works bring up about the nature of femaleness. The writer takes the *rétro style* aesthetics used here to the limits, shaping a past, arrested universe. The style consists mainly of a distorted, dissonant, phonetic transcription of a deprived fringe vernacular. "Story" somehow exists prior to "speech," and is embodied in the notion of femaleness, which both contains and erases all that might happen. "SHE," therefore, is both the book and what the book stands for: both the writing and its message.

Ducharme has published little since *Les Enfantômes*, except for the reworked text of a play which was written in 1968 for a theater festival, *Inès Pérée et Inat Tendu*, whose central characters are a couple of children, and *HA ha! . . .* (1982), which won a Governor General's Award. *HA ha!* is the printed version of the 1978 play *Ah! ah*. It's title punningly mirrors Ducharme's original title, a phrase of recognition that recurs throughout the play. *HA ha!* . . . begins when four characters, to offset the cost of rent, share one apartment. Sophie is a passionate woman, Roger, a poet, Mimi, a perennial victim, and her husband, Bernard, an alcoholic. A series of anecdotal revelations follows. The text, not without Ducharme's characteristic punning–"l'éden de dead end," for example–is both more lyrical and more direct than previous works; and at the heart of the play is a concern for the revolutionary power of game playing. The interchanges among the characters are all games–plays, "shows," through which the four act out their own lives. As J. P. Ronfard, the director of the Théâtre du Nouveau Monde performance, asserts in his preface to the published edition, the result is not so much comedy as a kind of "fête infernale," a hellish carnival of illusions in which the characters admit their own weaknesses only to have the others exploit them– in the name of love. Only when Mimi, the victim, frees herself does the world of masks (illusions, mirrors, negations, "play") finally end.

Since 1970 Ducharme has also been the anonymous lyricist for several of Robert Charlebois's songs, and he has turned recently to film. But he is still known primarily for his novels and for his dense style. Disconcerting, profoundly original, virtually impossible to assimilate because it plays off so many contradictions, Ducharme's work often taxes the reader's tolerance. Reading these texts, rich in nuances of fascination, enchantment, disenchantment, and discomfort, is demanding activity. But Ducharme's work holds us, brings us back to itself; it reveals us to ourselves.

Interviews:

Gérald Godin, "Gallimard publie un Québecois de 24 ans, inconnu," *Le Magazine Maclean*, 6 (September 1966): 57;

Hermine Beauregard, "J'ai rencontré Réjean Ducharme," *Châtelaine*, 9 (March 1968): 23, 54-55;

Normand Lassonde, "J'ai vu Réjean Ducharme en face," *Le Figaro Littéraire* (Paris), no. 1184 (13-19 January 1969): 22.

References:

Avez-vous relu Ducharme, special issue of *Etudes Françaises*, 11 (October 1975);

Georges Bélanger and James de Finney, "*Le Nez qui voque*," *Revue de l'Université Laurentienne* (February 1968): 34-40;

D. J. Bond, "The Search for Identity in the Novels of Réjean Ducharme," *Mosaic*, 9 (Winter 1976): 31-44;

Raoul Duguay, "L'avalée des avalés ou l'avaleuse des avaleurs," *Parti Pris*, 4 (November-December 1966): 114-120;

Bernard Dupriez, "Ducharme et des ficelles," *Voix et Images du Pays*, 5 (1972): 165-185;

Claude Filteau, "Réjean Ducharme et le poétique du desir," *Voix et Images*, 1 (April 1976): 365-373;

Monique Genuist, "Mille Milles et la Femme dans *Le Nez qui voque*," *Atlantis*, 2 (Spring 1977): 56-63;

André Gervais, "L'Hiver de force, comme rien," *Etudes Françaises*, 10 (May 1974): 183-193;

Patrick Imbert, "Révolution culturelle et clichés chez Réjean Ducharme," *Journal of Canadian Fiction*, 25-26 (1979): 227-236;

Gabrielle Poulin, *Romans du pays, 1968-1979* (Montreal: Bellarmin, 1980);

Georges-André Vachon, "Le Colonisé parle," *Etudes Françaises*, 10 (February 1974): 61-78;

André Vanasse, "Analyse de textes–Réjean Ducharme et Victor-Lévy Beaulieu: les mots et les choses," *Voix et Images*, 3 (December 1977): 230-243;

Michel van Schendel, "Ducharme l'inquiétant," in *Littérature canadienne-française–Conférences J. A. de Sève* (Montreal: Presses de l'Université de Montreal, 1969), pp. 217-234.

David Fennario

(26 April 1947-   )

Aviva Ravel
Concordia University

BOOKS: *Without A Parachute* (Montreal: Dawson College, 1972; Toronto: McClelland & Stewart, 1974);

On The Job (Vancouver: Talonbooks, 1976);

Nothing To Lose (Vancouver: Talonbooks, 1977);

Balconville (Vancouver & Los Angeles: Talonbooks, 1980);

Blue Mondays, by Fennario and Daniel Adams (Verdun, Quebec: Black Rock Creations, 1984).

PLAY PRODUCTIONS: *On The Job*, Montreal, Centaur Theatre, 29 January 1975;

Nothing To Lose, Montreal, Centaur Theatre, 11 November 1976;

Toronto, Montreal, Centaur Theatre, 2 February 1978;

Balconville, Montreal, Centaur Theatre, 4 January 1979;

Without a Parachute, adapted by Fennario from his book, Toronto, Theatre Passe Muraille, 6 February 1979;

Moving, Montreal, Centaur Theatre, 2 February 1983;

Joe Beef: A History of Montreal, Verdun, Quebec, Black Rock Theatre, 31 March 1984;

Neil Cream: Mysteries of McGill, Montreal, McGill University, 17 October 1985.

David Fennario, acclaimed as English Canada's first working-class playwright, was born in Verdun, Quebec. His father, James Wiper, English in origin, is a house painter; his mother, Margaret Kerr Wiper, part Irish, emigrated from Scotland at the age of five. The second of six children, David Fennario dropped his original surname, Wiper, and adopted his new one from Bob Dylan's song "Pretty Peggy-O." Although he found high school tedious and his peers scoffed at education, he became a voracious reader. "I can remember my mother saying, 'all that reading is gonna hurt your eyes.'" He left high school after one year, worked at unskilled jobs, and hitchhiked through the United States. He re-

turned to school but left before completing grade nine, and he subsequently worked as a shipper and mail clerk. In 1966 he drifted around Toronto with other "flower children" and spent a month in jail for vagrancy. In 1969 he worked as a packer and releaser in a Montreal dress factory which became the setting for his first play, *On The Job*, produced in 1975.

Realizing that factory jobs did not offer him the opportunities for self-development and advancement that he wanted, he registered at Dawson College where his creative writing teacher, Sally Nelson, initiated the publication of his journal, *Without A Parachute* (1972), by the college. The vigorous dramatic situations, dialogue, and strong characterizations in the work attracted the attention of Maurice Podbrey, artistic director of the Centaur Theatre, who invited Fennario to spend a year as playwright-in-residence. Fennario had never seen live theater before, but after a few months of watching rehearsals he wrote *On The Job*.

All of Fennario's work is closely related to his life, his community, and culture: "As a writer and as an artist, I'm writing about what I come from, that reality." According to David Payette in a 12 February 1977 article in the Montreal *Gazette*, Fennario's "dramas of working-class life are written with a bitter intensity that reflect his struggle to survive on the pavement and in the back alleys overshadowed by the smokestacks that dominate his neighborhood." Fennario proclaims himself a Marxian Socialist (he discovered Marx when he read Erich Fromm's *The Art of Loving*) and is a member of the Socialist Labor Party. In recent years he has left mainstream theater in favor of developing a community theater in Verdun, and his work focuses less on current workers' issues and more on Canadian proletarian history. The author regards himself as a cultural worker: "I think today the great majority of artists are working class. I define 'working class' as people who must sell their labor to people who control the means of production and distribu-

Talonbooks publicity poster

tion." Fennario resides in Verdun, Quebec, with his wife, Elizabeth, an art student, and one son.

Fennario launched his career with *On The Job,* which is set in the shipping room of a Montreal dress factory on Christmas Eve, 1970. The play, which, in the words of Dianne Allison of the Montreal *Gazette,* "captures the despair and frustration of its working class with ironic humour," features Billy, a timid, elderly man who accepts his lot and looks forward to his pension; Jacky, a ribald young man, and his sidekick, Mike; and Gary, a disillusioned hippie. When an emergency order arrives, the workers' traditional afternoon off before the holiday is cancelled. While the men pack dresses, an office party is in progress upstairs. The factory owner arrives in his impeccable suit and fresh tan and distributes Christmas bonuses; unexpectedly he sympathizes with the workers' protest and releases the men for the afternoon. However, the manager, who is directly responsible for operating the factory, rescinds the boss's order. René, the kindly French Canadian foreman, afraid of being fired, is torn

between workers and management. The slick union leader has no compassion for the workers' grievances; as long as "the contract" has not been violated, they must stay on the job. Anarchy and violence ensue when the workers, defying the union and the manager, stage a wildcat strike, creating chaos in the shipping room. René cries out, "It's bad the way we have to live when you don't want to live this way. . . . It's bullshit what I got to do just to work. To yell and scream and tell you to sit up and sit down. It's bad." Billy replies, "It's not your fault." The play progresses at a brisk pace, the dialogue is lively and trenchant, and the characters are recognizable and sympathetic. *On The Job* played to full houses across Canada. It has been shown on CBC television and toured Quebec in a French-language version.

Fennario's second play, *Nothing To Lose,* premiered at the Centaur Theatre in 1976. In the words of Jamie Portman of the Montreal *Gazette,* it is "more than just a profanely funny attack against middle-class complacencies and a call to arms against the capitalist system. It is also a crude, accurate, and endearing evocation of . . . the Montreal of dingy streets and dingier lives. . . ." The action occurs in a tavern in Montreal's Pointe-Saint-Charles district where a group of truckers considers a strike to protest the conduct of a severe foreman. Murray, the union man, urges the men to refrain from taking action until he has contacted his superior. Thirty-year-old Jackie is drinking heavily to avoid facing the realities of his unfulfilled, dull life. Jerry, his former friend, a character who obviously represents the playwright, has returned to the Pointe after having written a successful book and play. The main conflict is between Jerry and Murray, with Jackie caught between the two but eventually deciding to lead the workers in a takeover of the warehouse.

The most memorable character is a bum and alcoholic, Chabougamou, who crouches in a corner of the tavern and waits for the news that the lotto ticket he bought two years ago has won. In the course of the play he mooches drinks, wets himself, and is beset by the shakes. While he is thrown out of the tavern for being a nuisance, the other men watch him with pity, wondering if they too will sink to such depths of despair. In Fennario's words, "The system has to be overthrown because 90 percent of . . . the workers have no control over their lives, over where they work. Companies can hire or fire them" at will. In *Nothing To Lose* the workers attempt to assume

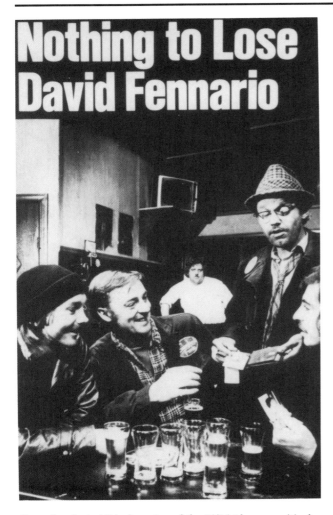

Cover for the published version of the 1976 play one critic described as "a call to arms against the capitalist system." In Fennario's words, "The system has to be overthrown because 90 percent of . . . the workers have no control over their lives. . . ."

control over their lives, but, significantly, the play does not reveal the outcome of their precipitate action.

Toronto, produced in 1978, is set in a hotel room where an artistic director, a stage director, and a playwright are occupied with casting the writer's second play. None of the three actors who audition for the roles is hired. A journalist, who arrives to interview the reluctant playwright, delivers a lecture on his political views. Despite the occasional comic antics, the play, arising out of the playwright's experiences in the theater, succeeds neither as satire nor comedy and strains to maintain the momentum of his previous work.

Balconville, produced at the Centaur Theatre in 1979, is a bilingual drama with one-third

of the dialogue in French. The play is set during the summer in Balconville, a slum in Montreal's Pointe-Saint-Charles. The characters—three families, two English and one French—spend the summer on their dilapidated verandas, drinking beer, bickering, and venting their grievances. Cecile, the francophone matron, wanders about in her housecoat feeding the birds, her "air force"; her husband, Claude, the only male in the vicinity with a steady job, is about to join the ranks of the unemployed because the company is moving to Taiwan; his daughter, in stiletto heels, dreams of escaping from the slums. In the English households Muriel, whose sailor husband deserted her, continually scolds her wastrel son. Johnny, a young rebel, hangs around making witty remarks about the "system" that forces him to wait ten weeks for his unemployment insurance. His wife, who has been supporting him by working as a waitress, has been introduced to feminism and threatens to leave. The simpleton delivery boy (like Chabougamou in *Nothing To Lose*) provides moments of bittersweet humor. Though the French and English families do not live amicably with one another (in one scene Johnny displays a maple-leaf flag, while Claude hangs up Quebec's fleur-de-lis), a moment of reconciliation occurs when they both realize they share similar problems—untrustworthy politicians, slum landlords, and capitalists exploit workers regardless of nationality. The play culminates with a fire set by the landlord to collect insurance. As Balconville goes up in flames, the characters unite to rescue their possessions.

The finest drama by Fennario to date, *Balconville* won the 1979 Chalmers Award for "the best original Canadian play seen in and around the Toronto area." According to Fred Blazer, in the *Toronto Globe and Mail* (10 February 1979), Fennario's play is a "work that has genius. It is angry, bitter, cruel and funny . . . a real vision of the country." Mark Czarnecki, in *Canadian Forum* (April 1983), states that "Fennario's bald Marxism comes wrapped in humor and humanity with guarantees for universal appeal." *Balconville,* which toured Canada, was also performed at the Old Vic Theatre in London.

Moving, produced in 1983 at Montreal's Centaur Theatre, is a fictionalized rendition of Fennario's intricate relationships with his family. Set in an apartment in Verdun, the Wilson family, having accepted the precepts of Marxism, are inspired to fight for social change. In Czarnecki's words, this play is a black comedy in which

Cover for the published version of Fennario's play set in a Montreal slum neighborhood. Balconville, *Fennario's fourth play and Canada's first bilingual drama, won the 1979 Chalmers Award.*

"gross suffering casually co-exists with hysterical buffoonery."

Blue Mondays (1984), a partly fictionalized journal interspersed with poems by Daniel Adams and illustrations by Sheila Salmela, was published by the Black Rock Community Centre formed in Verdun in 1981. Black Rock derives its name from the memorial stone the workmen, who built the Victoria Bridge in the 1850s, pulled out of the St. Lawrence River and placed near the bridge to mark the grave of immigrants who had died a decade earlier of ship fever. The journal chronicles David Wiper's life from the late 1960s to the early 1970s. Essentially a political manifesto, the journal highlights the situation of the unskilled anglophone Montreal worker in French Quebec of the 1970s. Many of the episodes, skillfully rendered, present those personal experiences which have had a strong impact on Fennario's life. The journal is a good introduction to the plays which also draw on the author's experiences at work, at home, and in the Verdun working-class community.

Joe Beef: A History of Montreal was produced in 1984 by the Black Rock community theater of which Fennario is a founding member. The play features Joe Beef, a tavern keeper on the Montreal waterfront, who, according to legend, fed a thousand strikers and their families during the Lachine Canal strike in 1877. In his tavern, where the play is set, Beef serves drinks and delivers the message of revolt to the working class. French explorers, Indians, priests, farmers, workers, and landowners of English, French, Irish, and Scottish origins, all in class and social conflict, appear in a series of vignettes. The loosely connected skits, songs, and dances often parody current political issues. In this strident agitprop revue the author urges the exploited to rise up against their oppressors. "Do not be afraid to throw the first punch," says Joe Beef.

In his first book, *Without A Parachute,* Fennario writes: "Where do these people get the strength to keep on living in the face of such despair and hopelessness? The whole area stinks of broken dreams and insanity. Little taverns hugging the corners of the street. Factory chimneys, match-box houses, solitary street lamps. Second-hand, everything is second-hand, including their lives." This is Fennario at his best, depicting the plight of the people who inspire him, calling out in his writing for radical social change.

References:

Dianne Allison, "On The Job An Impeccable Performance," *Gazette* (Montreal), 8 October 1976;

Michael Benazon, "From Griffintown to Verdun: A Study of Place in the Work of David Fennario," *Matrix*, 19 (Fall 1984): 25-34;

Mark Czarnecki, "Suffering and Buffoonery," *Canadian Forum*, 63 (April 1983): 38-39;

W. Grigs, "Bard From Balconville," *Canadian* (20 January 1979): 16-18;

D. Hamel, "Class Acts: David Fennario Moves His Show From the Mainstream To the Waterfront," *Books in Canada,* 13 (May 1984): 4;

Deirdre King, "The Drama of David Fennario," *Canadian Forum*, 60 (February 1981): 14-17;

M. Knelman, "Bilingualism Among The Hopeless," *Saturday Night,* 94 (November 1979): 101, 103-104;

Knelman, "The Playwright As Star of the Play," *Saturday Night,* 93 (April 1978): 59-60, 62;

Paul Milliken, "Portrait of the Artist As a Working Class Hero: an Interview With David Fennario," *Performing Arts,* 17 (Summer 1980): 22-25;

Jamie Portman, "Le Gout du Québec Flavours Toronto Theatre Fare," *Gazette* (Montreal), 28 January 1978;

David Payette, "Fennario Still Sees Red," *Gazette* (Montreal), 12 February 1977;

Don Rubin and Alison Cranmer-Byng, eds., *Canada's Playwrights: A Biographical Guide* (Downsview, Ontario: Canadian Theatre Review Publications, 1980), pp. 50-51;

Cynthia Zimmerman, "David Fennario," in *The Work: Conversations with English-Canadian Playwrights,* edited by Zimmerman and Robert Wallace (Toronto: Coach House Press, 1982), pp. 292-303.

Jacques Ferron

(20 January 1921-22 April 1985)

Paul Matthew St. Pierre
University of British Columbia

BOOKS: *L'Ogre* (Montreal: Cahiers de la File Indienne, 1949);

La Barbe de François Hertel; Le Licou (Montreal: Editions d'Orphée, 1951);

Le Dodu; ou le prix du bonheur (Montreal: Editions d'Orphée, 1956);

Tante Elise; ou le prix de l'amour (Montreal: Editions d'Orphée, 1956);

Le Cheval de Don Juan (Ottawa: Editions d'Orphée, 1957); revised as *Le Don Juan chrétien,* in *Théâtre,* volume one (Montreal: Déom, 1968);

Les Grands Soleils (Montreal: Editions d'Orphée, 1958); translated by Julie Stockton as "The Flowering Suns," Ph.D. dissertation, York University, 1973;

Corolles (Paris: Grassin, 1961);

Contes du pays incertain (Montreal: Editions d'Orphée, 1962);

Cotnoir (Montreal: Editions d'Orphée, 1962); translated by Pierre Cloutier as *Dr. Cotnoir* (Montreal: Harvest House, 1973);

La Tête du roi (Montreal: A.G.E.U.M., 1963);

Cazou; ou le prix de la virginité (Montreal: Editions d'Orphée, 1963);

Contes anglais et autres (Montreal: Editions d'Orphée, 1964);

La Nuit (Montreal: Parti Pris, 1965); revised as *Les Confitures de coings* in *Les Confitures de coings et autres textes* (Montreal: Parti Pris, 1972); translated by Ray Ellenwood in *Quince Jam* (Toronto: Coach House Press, 1977);

Papa Boss (Montreal: Parti Pris, 1966); revised in *Les Confitures de coings et autres textes* (Montreal: Parti Pris, 1972); in *Quince Jam* (Toronto: Coach House Press, 1977);

La Charrette (Montreal: HMH, 1968); translated by Ellenwood as *The Cart* (Toronto: Exile, 1981);

Contes—Edition intégrale: Contes anglais, Contes du pays incertain, Contes inédits (Montreal: HMH, 1968);

Théâtre, volume one: *Les Grands Soleils, Tante Elise, Le Don Juan chrétien* (Montreal: Déom, 1968);

Historiettes (Montreal: Editions du Jour, 1969);

Le Ciel de Québec (Montreal: Editions du Jour, 1969); translated by Ellenwood as *The Penniless Redeemer* (Toronto: Exile, 1984);

L'Amélanchier (Montreal: Editions du Jour, 1970); translated by Raymond Y. Chamberlain as *The Juneberry Tree* (Toronto: Harvest House, 1975);

Le Salut de l'Irlande (Montreal: Editions du Jour, 1970);

Les Roses sauvages; petit roman suivi d'une lettre d'amour soigneusement présentée (Montreal: Editions du Jour, 1971); translated by Betty

Bednarski as *Wild Roses: A Story Followed by a Love Letter* (Toronto: McClelland & Stewart, 1976);

Le Saint-Elias (Montreal: Editions du Jour, 1972); translated by Cloutier as *The Saint-Elias* (Montreal: Harvest House, 1975);

La Chaise du maréchal ferrant (Montreal: Editions du Jour, 1972);

Les Confitures de coings et autres textes (Montreal: Parti Pris, 1972); translated by Ellenwood as *Quince Jam* (Toronto: Coach House Press, 1977); revised and enlarged as *Les Confitures de coings et autres texts, suivi de Le Journal des confitures de coings* (Montreal: Parti Pris, 1977);

Tales from the Uncertain Country, translated by Bednarski (Toronto: Anansi, 1972);

Du fond de mon arrière-cuisine (Montreal: Editions du Jour, 1973);

Théâtre, volume two: *Le Dodu, ou le prix du bonheur; La Mort de Monsieur Borduas; Le Permis de dramaturge; La Tête du Roi; L'Impromptu des deux chiens* (Montreal: Déom, 1975);

Escarmouches: La Longue Passe, 2 volumes (Montreal: Leméac, 1975);

Gaspé-Mattempa (Trois-Rivières, Quebec: Editions du Bien Public, 1980);

Rosaire précédé de L'Exécution de Maski (Montreal North: VLB, 1981);

Selected Tales of Jacques Ferron, translated by Bednarski (Toronto: Anansi, 1984);

Le Choix de Jacques Ferron dans l'oeuvre de Jacques Ferron (Charlesbourg, Quebec: Laurentiennes, 1985).

OTHER: Antonine Maillet, *Les Crasseux*, preface by Ferron (Montreal: Holt, Rinehart & Winston, 1968);

Louis Hémon, *Colin-Maillard*, preface by Ferron (Montreal: Editions du Jour, 1972);

Faucher de Saint-Maurice, *De tribord à babord*, "présentation" by Ferron (Montreal: L'Aurore, 1975).

PERIODICAL PUBLICATIONS: "La Jeune Nonne," *Liaison*, 9 (September 1950): 333-334;

"Nella Mariem," *Amérique Française*, 12 (September 1954): 182-189;

"Les Rats," *Amérique Française*, 12 (November-December 1954): 326-335;

"L'Américaine; ou le triomphe de l'amitié," *Situations*, 1 (September 1959): 15-28;

"La Grande Jupe," *Liberté*, 2 (March-April 1960): 100-101;

"Un Miroir de nos misères; notre théâtre," *Revue Socialiste*, no. 5 (1961): 27-30;

"Le Tricorne de Mister Thompson," *Situations*, 4 (July 1962): 15-17;

"J'aime la langue anglaise," *Situations*, 4 (July 1962): 31-40;

"La Soumission des clercs," *Liberté*, 5 (May-June 1963): 194-207;

"La Sortie," *Ecrits du Canada Français*, no. 19 (1965): 109-147;

"Une Question, des réponses," by Ferron and others, *Liberté*, 9 (November-December 1967): 74-82;

"La Mort de Monsieur Borduas," *Les Herbes Rouges*, no. 1 (1968): 3-8;

"Le Coeur d'une mère," *Ecrits du Canada Français*, no. 25 (1969): 57-94;

"Parti Pris a eu lieu, c'est déjà beaucoup," *La Barre du Jour*, 31-32 (Winter 1972): 88-92;

"Premier Episode," *Le Québec Littéraire*, no. 2 (1976): 9-11;

"Vers une récollection des jeux," *Modern Language Studies*, 6 (1976): 7-12;

Brick, special issue on Ferron, includes essays and stories by Ferron, 16 (Fall 1982).

During the final twenty-five years of his life, Jacques Ferron emerged among the Quebecois working class and intelligentsia as one of the most charismatic figures not just of his period but of the whole literary history of Quebec. The extent of his medical, political, and literary gifts and accomplishments has become known to the rest of Canada through a steady trickle of good translations of his novels and stories and through the publicity attending his sudden death. Although he had already turned forty when he first met with the kind of literary success that all writers seek (in his case winning a Governor General's Award for fiction for his 1962 short-story collection *Contes du pays incertain*), Ferron in fact had served a long and very practical literary apprenticeship.

During the 1950s he wrote a series of culturally durable plays, and, even more significant, in the years before the publication of his first play, *L'Ogre* (1949), he worked indefatigably as a physician (not unlike fellow Canadian Norman Bethune), serving the people of his beloved Gaspé Peninsula and somewhat unwittingly observing the human nature that would later serve him so faithfully in his writing. Such was his dedication to the people and the country of Quebec, in fact, that upon his death the whimsi-satirical

Jacques Ferron three months before his death in April 1985 (photograph by Kèro)

Rhinoceros Party, which he had founded in 1972, decided to disband in honor of his memory.

Two years before founding the Rhinoceros Party, Ferron played a far more grave political role when, during the October Crisis, the FLQ (Front de Libération du Québec) selected him as a mediator in its negotiations following the kidnapping of Pierre Laporte. By assuming these positions at the nadir and zenith of Canadian politics, Ferron established for himself a unique literary and historical perspective on the Quebecois condition, assuming one of the most memorable voices to emerge from the Quiet Revolution and the separatist movement. Although Ferron's voice has been silenced by death, his voluminous writings continue to speak on behalf of a country silenced both by the referendum of 1980 and by the constitutional accord of 1987.

Born 20 January 1921 in Louiseville, Quebec, Jacques Ferron was the oldest child of Joseph-Alphonse Ferron and Adrienne Caron Ferron. His father, a lawyer active in the Liberal Party, was an imposing figure in his early life, a type against whom (especially after Ferron père's death in 1947) the younger Ferron would speak

quite vociferously in politics and literature. The death of Ferron's mother in 1931 (from tuberculosis, a disease he himself would contract in 1949) precipitated his lifelong fascination with death. As a child Ferron and his siblings did enjoy a stimulating artistic climate in the home; his sister Madeleine went on to become an innovative writer, and another sister, Marcelle, became an influential Automatiste painter.

After receiving his early education in Trois-Rivières, Ferron was educated by the Jesuits at the Collège Jean-de-Brébeuf in Montreal, where, a contemporary of the young Pierre Elliott Trudeau and other affluent children, he had his first exposure not just to the cultural heritage of Quebec but also to a kind of intracultural prejudice that would steer him toward socialism and eventually to a variety of other ideologies and causes. Such was his youthful disdain for Quebecois caste distinction that in 1943, in the middle of his medical studies at Université Laval in Quebec City, he entered a brief marriage with a communist woman named Madeleine Therrien, with whom he had a daughter in 1947. (With his second wife, Madeleine Lavallée, whom he married in 1952, Ferron had three children.)

Upon graduating from medical school in 1945, Ferron joined the Canadian Army, serving as a doctor at camps in Quebec and New Brunswick before leaving military service and going into private practice in 1946. For the next two years, in the community of Rivière Madeleine in the Gaspé Peninsula, Ferron served a literary and political apprenticeship as a country doctor and in the process chanced upon the kind of fantastic down-to-earth characters that supported his activism and inspired his writing for nearly forty years. An even more important professional move was his decision in 1948 to establish a medical practice in Montreal, specifically, across the St. Lawrence River in the working-class suburb of Ville Jacques-Cartier, later called Longueuil. In *Nègres blancs d'Amérique: Autobiographie précoce d'un "terroriste" québécois* (1968), Pierre Vallières, who grew up in Jacques-Cartier, acknowledges the enormous contribution of Ferron to the people of this region of Quebec, citing his great "fraternity" and his "revolutionary action."

Such selfless medical service gave Ferron an intimate and dynamic introduction to the common women and men (and also to the mentally and psychologically disabled people) he would idealistically dedicate himself to championing in his literature and in his political activities of the 1950s and 1960s. For example, beginning in 1951 and for the next thirty years, Ferron made regular scholarly contributions on medical, philosophical, political, social, cultural, and literary subjects to the periodical *L'Information Médicale et Paramédicale*. During the same period, he was also a compulsive observer of the print medium, addressing to the editors of Montreal newspapers and journals an incessant series of clever letters on a plethora of timely subjects. These letters were collected and published shortly after his death in *Jacques Ferron: Les Lettres aux journaux* (1985), a book edited by Pierre Cantin, Paul Lewis, and Ferron's daughter Marie.

Ferron began his literary career in 1949 with the publication of his play *L'Ogre,* the first of a series of dramatic works that, while heartily invoking traditional French theatrical values and devices, are nevertheless unremarkable both in content and in execution and have been almost completely eclipsed by the author's original treatments of Quebecois stories and storytelling techniques in his later works of prose fiction. Like *L'Ogre,* a romance in which an ogre, a virgin, a chevalier, a prisoner, and an amazon assume mildly

Cover for Ferron's second story collection, published the year after he won the Governor General's Award for French-language fiction (courtesy of Kenneth Landry)

existentialist roles, *Le Dodu; ou le prix du bonheur* (1956) presents a title character who is at once a figure in a *petit rien* and the historical figure for whom Ferron wrote the play, the poet André Pouliot. The other one-act plays in his "prix" series—*Tante Elise; ou le prix de l'amour* (1956) and *Cazou; ou le prix de la virginité* (1963)—continue *Le Dodu's* deflation of lofty absolutes, not just success, love, and virginity, but also, and more particularly, the courting rituals and marriage rites which they support so absolutely. Similar in tone, *Le Licou* (1951) and *Le Cheval de Don Juan* (1957) satirize romantic conventions of lovemaking amid equine accoutrements.

Departing from these comic social satires, two relatively memorable and lasting plays, the first fruits of Ferron's burgeoning ideological consciousness, offer comparative historical treatments of Canadian political themes. *Les Grands Soleils* (1958) measures the synchronicity of 1950s Duplessis Quebec and of Patriotes Quebec in the years leading up to the rebellions of 1837 and 1838 (which Ferron believed marked the cultural naissance of all Quebecois); and *La Tête du roi* (1963) focuses on parallels between the FLQ's 1963 mutilation of a statue of James Wolfe on the Plains of Abraham and Louis Riel's 1870 and 1885 métis rebellions on the plains of Manitoba and Saskatchewan. Although they have had political and cultural influence, these plays have received scarcely any theatrical productions. (A production in 1968 by the Théâtre du Nouveau Monde of *Les Grands Soleils*, for example, was only a modest success.)

The virtual culmination of Ferron's dramatic writing with the publication in 1968 of the first volume of his collected plays, *Théâtre* more accurately marks the beginning of the truly gifted storytelling on which his literary reputation rests. A second volume of *Théâtre* appeared in 1975, introducing some new material but extending his dramatic accomplishment only marginally.

The Governor General's Award that Ferron won in 1963 acknowledged his first major work of fiction, the short-story collection *Contes du pays incertain* (1962), and effectively inaugurated his career. Although his satirical novel *La Barbe de François Hertel* had been published in 1951, it was with *Contes du pays incertain* that he found his métier and his Quebecois audience. In 1964 he produced a second volume of stories, *Contes anglais et autres*, followed in 1968 by a collection, *Contes*, incorporating stories from the first two volumes and several new stories (*Contes inédits*). Ferron had such an affinity for the *conte*, in all its manifestations—short story, fable, tall tale, legend, folktale, anecdote—that it became both the building block and the capstone for all his works of prose fiction, for novels and *nouvelles* no less than for short-story collections. The metaphor of the first collection, "le pays incertain," became as much a figure for the internally exiled country of Quebec as Hugh MacLennan's "two solitudes" became a figure for the externally partitioned country of Canada.

Actually, the literary process was for Ferron a persistent quest for "*le pays certain.*" His stories are characterized by subtle mixtures of fantasy and realism, sentimentality and satire, simplicity and obfuscation, humor and hostility, spontaneity and contrivance, allegory and absurdity. But perhaps the greatest mixture is that of fiction and fact. In "The Dead Cow in the Canyon," for example, a woman is raped and killed by a bull. Her husband, upon discovering the scene and slaying the beast, notices "a baby girl, lying there, kicking, in the blood of her mother and the

monster." The mysterious child is baptized Chaouac, the name of Ferron's eldest daughter. Similarly, the eponymous narrator of the stories "Martine" and "Martine Continued"–this character bearing the name of Ferron's youngest daughter–recounts her quasi-mythic family relationships with choral variety and precision. These and numerous other examples in the *Contes* series suggest Ferron's propensity for blurring the lines separating the imaginary and the real.

Like many francophone Governor General's Award-winners, Ferron took English Canadians largely by surprise, and their literary and cultural acceptance of him is still not complete, despite the appearance of two excellent translations of *contes* by Betty Bednarski: *Tales from the Uncertain Country* (1972) and *Selected Tales of Jacques Ferron* (1984). Even in Quebec Ferron's acceptance as a *conteur* by nonacademic Quebecois was gradual, his public notoriety arising at first more from his accomplishments as a doctor and politician than from his production as a writer. In fact, throughout Quebec Ferron was for a considerable time largely a political media *célébrité*.

His formal entry into politics coincided with his introduction to writing in the 1950s. His initial activities were with the postwar peace movement: he demonstrated against the North Atlantic Treaty in 1949, for example, and in 1954 was elected leader of the Canadian Peace Congress. Ferron joined the CCF (Cooperative Commonwealth Federation, forerunner of the New Democratic Party) in 1956, running for parliament in the federal election of 1958, but resigning from the CCF in 1960 over what he saw as the party's weak policy on Quebec. Three years later he founded the Rhinoceros Party, the original purpose of which was to lampoon the election process itself, but which developed into a genuine (if very ironic) political movement, fielding candidates (including, on several occasions, Ferron himself) in every federal election since its foundation.

Ferron subsequently ran as a candidate for the RIN (Rassemblement pour l'Indépendance Nationale) in the 1966 Quebec provincial election, and thus consolidated his moderate position in the separatist movement and on separation itself, an issue to which he remained passionately close for the rest of his life. In 1969 he became a member of the PQ (Parti Québécois). During the October Crisis of 1970, when the FLQ named him as their choice for a government mediator, Ferron exercised an important role in bringing

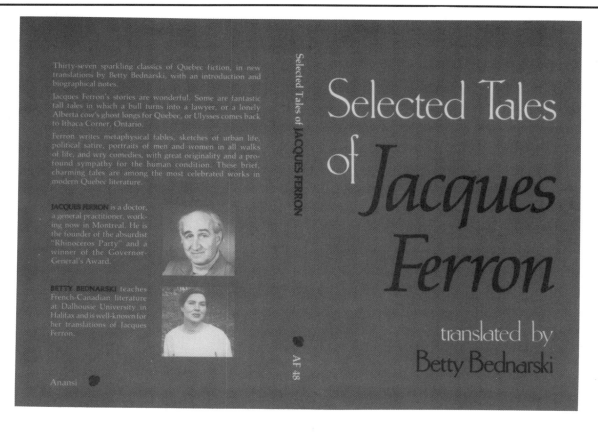

Dust jacket and cover for Betty Bednarski's translations of selections from Contes du pays incertain, Contes anglais et autres, *and* Contes inédits

about the surrender of Paul and Jacques Rose and Francis Simard. His political activism reached a climax in 1980 when (along with 150 other writers) he cofounded the Regroupement des Écrivains pour le OUI, promoting the "yes" response in the Quebec referendum.

Throughout his political career, as throughout his medical practice, Ferron continued to write, in particular refining his skills as a raconteur and novelist. His first novel, *Cotnoir* (1962), translated by Pierre Cloutier as *Dr. Cotnoir* (1973), translated by Pierre Cloutier as *Dr. Cotnoir* (1973), drew on his own medical experiences (and on his fascination with a real Quebec doctor named Augustin Cotnoir), the narrative presenting a doctor engaged in a variously heroic and ignoble struggle with death and in a similarly ambivalent friendship with a mental patient named Emmanuel.

Ferron's next two novels (more accurately *nouvelles*) reflect his awakening political conscience. *La Nuit* (1965) focuses on a narrator-writer named François Ménard (a persona for Ferron), a character whose strange unity with his wife Marguerite not only deprives him of his very soul but also perpetuates his spiritless existence and launches him on a quest for his soul within a kind of annihilating suburbia. Ménard's relationship with Frank Archibald Campbell marks only one of many appearances throughout Ferron's work of a character named Frank (each of them an alter ego of the Montreal poet F. R. Scott, whom Ferron first encountered in the CCF), in this case a person whose death from eating poisoned quince jam finally allows Ménard to rediscover his soul. *Papa Boss* (1966) is a kind of morality narrative exploring the perverse Faustian relationship of a working-class woman and a plutocratic man-angel, Papa Boss, who exercises control over her that amounts to a type of demonic possession. Ferron revised both works (*La Nuit* in particular on the hard edge of his October Crisis experience) as part of the collection *Les Confitures de coings et autres textes* (1972), which Ray Ellenwood translated as *Quince Jam* in 1977. The concluding section of the 1972 revision, "Appendice aux Confitures de coings; ou le congédiement de Frank Archibald Campbell," offers an elucidating discussion of the author's quite agitated cultural and political stance at the time. A subsequent edition in 1977 enlarged the collection even further, adding Le *Journal des confitures de coings*.

In *La Charrette* (1968), translated by

Ellenwood as *The Cart* (1981), Ferron extends the theme (explored in each of his earlier novels) of the life-and-death marriage of self-sacrifice and self-destruction, in this case embodied in the character of a doctor who dies and experiences a resurrection and who undertakes a Dantesque journey through the underworld. In dedicating the book to his sister Thérèse, who had recently died, Ferron also acknowledged one of his most important inspirations, the figure of death which as a physician (and as a man who had suffered his first heart attack) he had dedicated himself to disfiguring.

The appearance of *Le Ciel de Québec* in 1969 marked a change in direction for Ferron as a novelist. Arguably his most ambitious novel, *Le Ciel de Québec*, which appeared in a 1984 translation by Ellenwood as *The Penniless Redeemer*, expands the concept of the frame story to suit the *nouvelle*, as Ferron recounts four narratives commemorating the centenary of the Patriote rebellions of 1837 and 1838. These historical events are seen from the vantage points of church and state, Quebecois and métis, and seen through the eyes of a cast of fictional and historical characters, ranging from Dr. Cotnoir (Augustine Cotnoir) and Frank-Anacharsis Scot (F. R. Scott) to Orpheus (Hector de Saint-Denys-Garneau) and Prometheus (Maurice Duplessis). Here is Ferron at his most allusive and erudite, like Virgil, carefully conducting his readers toward a peculiarly Quebecois heaven and introducing them to hosts of the most memorable and forgettable figures from contemporary Quebecois culture. Ferron's tendency to place historical figures in fictional situations (and thus literally to characterize them) is perhaps most graphically evident in his *conte*-like essay collection *Historiettes* (1969).

Of his other novels from the 1970s, *L'Amélanchier* (1970), translated by Raymond Y. Chamberlain as *The Juneberry Tree* (1975), stands out as his most lyrical and optimistic. The central metaphor of the juneberry tree (which because it is the first to bloom in the spring is also the first to sense the approach of winter) serves to highlight the psychological struggle of the heroine, Tinamer de Portanqueu, for self-perpetuation. As Tinamer concludes: "I sometimes feel that I am commingling with an intimate country which once existed outside of me but of which I am now the sole location, and that I am nothing now under the spread of the flowering Juneberries." Although here it finds a highly idiosyncratic expression, the idea of person intermingling with

Cover for the second edition of Ferron's novel that brings together four narratives commemorating the centenary of the 1837-1838 Patriote rebellions (courtesy of Kenneth Landry)

place, of Quebecois coalescing with Quebec, is pervasive in Ferron's fiction, sometimes taking the particular form (as in the case of the F. R. Scott persona) of the *anglais* becoming "Quebeckized." Even when, as in *Le Salut de l'Irlande* (1970), the setting moves outside Quebec or francophone Canada, the author's politics remain very much the same. That Ferron first published *Le Salut de l'Irlande* serially in 1966 and 1967 in *L'Information médicale et paramédicale,* and thereafter revised the novel only slightly, suggests something of the continuity of his ideas.

Similarly in *Le Saint-Elias* (1972), which Pierre Cloutier translated as *The Saint-Elias* (1975), the historical focus is on the archaic—a trading ship of nineteenth-century Quebec—but the fictional thrust is toward something new and dynamic: the contemporary Quebecois psyche and its neural links with the past. In *La Chaise du maréchal ferrant* (1972) Ferron takes "the blacksmith's chair" of *habitant Québec* and at once an-

chors it in the Gaspé, transforms it into a flying machine, and pilots it over the political terrains of Mackenzie King and Maurice Duplessis. Innovative and imaginative as these novels are, however, they do suffer from aesthetic unevenness, because Ferron seems much more intent on faithfully recounting his tales in the oral tradition than on turning them into marketable finished products.

Certainly his most refined novel of the 1970s is *Les Roses sauvages; petit roman suivi d'une lettre d'amour soigneusement présentée* (1971), translated by Betty Bednarski as *Wild Roses: A Story Followed by a Love Letter* (1976), a sensitive narrative about two generations. One is represented by the Baron, a businessman of the old order who, faced with the pressures of a province changing beyond his comprehension, eventually degenerates into insanity and suicide; the other is represented by his daughter, Rose-Aimée, who, as her name suggests, accepts the natural growth of Quebec and manages to adapt to her shifting situation. As a political allegory, the novel makes an intelligent comment on the difficult rite of passage through the Quiet Revolution. In 1972 *Les Roses sauvages* received the Prix France-Québec, and in the same year the Société Saint-Jean-Baptiste gave Ferron the Prix Duvernay in recognition of his entire *oeuvre.* In 1977 the government of Quebec awarded him the Prix David in similar recognition. As it happened, these prestigious awards served to cap the literary career that effectively began with the important prize of 1963.

After the publication of the essay collection *Historiettes* in 1969, Ferron devoted an increasing amount of his time to essay writing and to compiling the articles he had written over the preceding fifteen years. In *Du fond de mon arrière-cuisine* (1973), a book he dedicated to Quebecois essayist Pierre Vallières, Ferron explores some of his favorite subjects—literature, philosophy, history, and culture—and makes a number of aphoristic observations pertinent to his *oeuvre* and thinking. In "Le Verbe c'est fait chair—On manque de viande," for example, he notes: "Quand je parle ou j'écris, je ne dispose que d'un seul acteur. Ce visage nu, il se nomme JE, mais il s'affuble aussi de personnages, savoir le TU, le IL, le NOUS, le VOUS, le ILS. Cela me confirme dans ma solitude tout en témoignant de mon besoin d'en sortir. Je reste unique et pourtant je me multiplie pour me rendre compte de la diversité du monde" (When I speak or write, I use one actor only. This naked countenance, it is called I, but it has other guises too—YOU, HE, WE, THEY. That confirms me in my solitude, attesting at the same time to my desire to leave it. I remain unique and nevertheless I multiply myself to give an account of the world's diversity). Such was Ferron's authorial motivation and such were the alphabetic personae he assumed throughout his writing. His essays consistently reach out beyond their author, and his ideas collectively embrace an audience of human conditions.

A third essay collection was published in 1975, the two-volume *Escarmouches: La Longue Passe,* in which Ferron tiptoes along the razor-sharp argumentative edge that he meticulously honed during the 1960s. The articles and letters compiled in *Escarmouches* appeared initially in such establishment publications as *Le Devoir* and *Le Maclean* and in left-wing publications such as *Revue Socialiste* and *Situations.* His expression in these polemical forms is clever and his ideas are often edifying, providing some of the best examples of the satirical sense and social conscience that run throughout his work. Many of Ferron's publications remain to be collected from the many journals to which he contributed.

In the last two works published during his life, Ferron returned to fiction and to some of the themes that inspired him during his medical practice in the Gaspé and in Montreal and, in particular, to his habit of reciting catalogues and litanies of place names. The *nouvelle Gaspé-Mattempa* (1980), for example, takes readers on a whistle-stop tour through the Gaspé Peninsula and introduces them to Dr. Maski, a character who acts as a kind of foil to Dr. Ferron. The author continues to superimpose the names of places and characters in his last book, *Rosaire précédé de L'Exécution de Maski* (1981). In the opening section he vicariously documents his own demise and expands on his favorite theme of interdependent being, on the paradox of one autonomous soul depending on another merely for its precarious existence. As the narrator says of Maski: "Qui avait tenu la plume à peu près chaque jour durant trente ans, qui avait signé les livres? C'était moi et non Maski. J'avais besoin d'écrire pour vivre. L'exécution de Maski annonçait la mienne" (Who had taken up the pen nearly every day for thirty years, who had signed the books? It was I and not Maski. I needed to write in order to live. The execution of Maski announced my own).

In the sense that Maski is an extension of Ferron himself, both the literary and the physical "executions" of the story can be seen as exercises in authorial self-destruction, attempts to resolve the creative conflict between man and amanuensia. The psychological dimension is also important in *Rosaire,* the companion piece to *L'Exécution de Maski,* in which Ferron draws specifically on his experiences a decade earlier as a general practitioner working with psychiatric patients at Saint-Jean-de-Dieu hospital in Montreal. The work assumes the form of a medical journal or case history which in 1961 the narrator, also a doctor at Saint-Jean-de-Dieu, keeps on a psychiatric patient named Rosaire Gélineau, a plasterer whose menial job makes him feel redundant in his highly technological world. In a series of confidences and confessions by Rosaire about his life and family, Ferron expresses his own frank criticism of the medical profession and sketches a poignant cartoon of the working class of La Rive-Sud.

His return in these two stories to places of geographic, cultural, psychological, and linguistic intimacy is the most fitting conclusion to Ferron's *métier* and *oeuvre.* Even his last published words, "maudit fou," suggest the love and contempt he had for the world about and without him. A fitting testament to his literary life appeared shortly after his death from a heart attack in April 1985, *Le Choix de Jacques Ferron dans l'oeuvre de Jacques Ferron,* representing some of the author's most enduring writing: selections from *La Chaise du maréchal ferrant, Du fond de mon arrière-cuisine,* and *Les Confitures de coings.* Testament has now turned to testimony in a paean of criticism, both French and (increasingly) English.

Not only do Ferron's contributions to Quebecois literature point to his admirable involvements in medicine and politics but they also manage to reflect the cultural development of Quebec over the past forty years: from the clerical garrison through *La Révolution Tranquille,* and indeed to the twin towers in the fortress of sovereignty: the FLQ and the PQ. Ferron's influence and his memory have even presided over the Quebecois passage from referendum failure (1980) to constitutional accord (1987). In the second half of the twentieth century, Quebec has produced few writers who have voiced its concerns with the urgency and dynamism of Jacques Ferron and none who have articulated an *oeuvre* at once so idiosyncratic and so peculiar to his people and place. In all his accomplishments—writing, medicine, politics—Ferron proved himself a kind of intellectual *ferronier,* pounding out words and works and worlds that will doubtless stand the test of history, a history grounded in Quebec and in the Quebecois language and culture but worthy of being translated and transported and regrounded around the world.

Letters:

Jacques Ferron: Les Lettres aux journaux, edited by Pierre Cantin, Marie Ferron, and Paul Lewis (Montreal: VLB, 1985).

Interview:

Donald Smith, "Jacques Ferron: The Marvellous Folly of Writing," in his *Voices of Deliverance: Interviews with Quebec and Acadian Writers,* translated by Larry Shouldice (Toronto: Anansi, 1986), pp. 82-103.

Bibliography:

Pierre Cantin, *Jacques Ferron, polygraphe* (Montreal: Bellarmin, 1984).

References:

Alexandre L. Amprimoz, "Sémiotique de l'organisation textuelle d'un conte: 'Les Méchins' de Jacques Ferron," *Présence Francophone,* 23 (Autumn 1981): 131-141;

Betty Bednarski, "Jacques Ferron," in *Profiles in Canadian Literature,* volume 5, edited by Jeffrey M. Heath (Toronto: Dundurn, 1986), pp. 121-128;

Bednarski, "Jacques Ferron (1921-1985)," *Canadian Literature,* 107 (Winter 1985): 193-195;

Bednarski, "Reading Jacques Ferron," *Antigonish Review,* 61 (Spring 1985): 43-49;

Gérard Bessette, " 'Mélie et le boeuf ' de Jacques Ferron," *Modern Fiction Studies,* 22 (Winter 1976): 441-448;

Neil B. Bishop, "Structures idéologiques, spéciaux et temporelles dans 'Le Saint Elias' de Jacques Ferron," *Revue de l'Université d'Ottawa,* 54 (January-March 1984): 65-89;

Jean-Pierre Boucher, "Une Analyse de *La Barbe de François Hertel* de Jacque Ferron," *Voix et Images du Pays,* 9 (1975): 163-180;

Boucher, *Les 'Contes' de Jacques Ferron* (Montreal: L'Aurore, 1974);

Boucher, *Jacques Ferron au pays des amélanchiers* (Montreal: Presses de l'Université de Montréal, 1973);

Brick, special issue on Ferron, 16 (Fall 1982);

André Dallaire, "Le Fantastique Ferron," *Brèches,* no. 1 (1973): 29-42;

Jacques De Roussan, *Jacques Ferron: Quatre Itinéraires* (Quebec: Presses de l'Université du Québec, 1971);

Normand Doiron, "Bestiaire et carnaval dans la fiction ferronienne," *Canadian Literature,* 88 (Spring 1981): 20-30;

Danielle Dubois, "En quête de Ferron," *Voix et Images du Pays,* 6 (1973): 111-121;

Ray Ellenwood, "Death and Dr. Ferron," *Brick,* 24 (Spring 1985), pp. 6-9;

Ellenwood, "Morley Callaghan, Jacques Ferron, and the Dialectic of Good and Evil," in *The Callaghan Symposium,* edited by David Staines (Ottawa: University of Ottawa Press, 1981), pp. 37-46;

Etudes Françaises, special issue on Ferron, 12 (October 1976);

Jean-Cléo Godin, "Le Soleil des indépendances," *Etudes Françaises,* 4 (February 1968): 208-215;

Phillipe Haeck, "Perdre son corps: Une Méthodologie pour l'étude du 'corps romanesque': Une Lecture de *L'Amélanchier,*" *Présence Francophone,* 18 (Spring 1979): 127-133;

Patrick Imbert, "Antithèses et bouleversement culturel dans *La Nuit* de J. Ferron," *Revue du Pacifique,* 4 (Spring 1978): 68-81;

Maximilien Laroche, "Découpage et montage dans 'Le Petit Chaperon rouge' de Jacques Ferron," *Nord,* 7 (1977): 165-179;

Laroche, "Nouvelles Notes sur 'Le Petit Chaperon rouge' de Jacques Ferron," *Voix et Images du Pays,* 6 (1973), 103-110;

Michelle Lavoie, "Jacques Ferron: De l'amour du pays à la définition de la patrie," *Voix et Images du Pays,* 1 (February 1967): 83-98;

Lavoie, "Jacques Ferron ou le prestige du verbe," *Etudes Françaises,* 5 (February 1969): 185-193;

Pierre L'Hérault, "L'Acadie de Jacques Ferron," *La Revue de l'Université de Moncton,* 6 (May 1974): 72-74;

L'Hérault, *Jacques Ferron, cartographe de l'imaginaire* (Montreal: Presses de l'Université de Montréal, 1980);

L'Hérault, "Jacques Ferron et la question nationale," *Dérives,* nos. 14-15 (1978): 3-23;

Jean Marcel, *Jacques Ferron malgré lui* (Montreal: Editions du Jour, 1970); revised and enlarged as *Jacques Ferron malgré lui* (Montreal: Parti Pris, 1978);

Elaine F. Nardocchio, "Dimensions sociopolitiques dans *Les Grands Soleils* de Jacques Ferron," *Présence Francophone,* 22 (Spring 1981): 131-140;

Nardocchio, "*Les Grands Soleils* de Jacques Ferron

et la question du Québec," *Mosaic,* 14 (Summer 1981): 113-117;

Jean-Marcel Paquette, "Jacques Ferron ou le drame de la théâtralité," in *Le Théâtre Canadien-Français: Evolution, témoignages, bibliogaphie,* edited by Paul Wyczynski, Bernard Julien, and Hélène Beauchamp-Rank (Montreal: Fides, 1976), pp. 581-596;

Alain Pontant, "Jacques Ferron et ses *Grands Soleils,*" *Québec,* 68 (May 1968): 84-87;

Diane Potvin, introduction to *La Nuit de Jacques Ferron,* edited by Potvin (Montreal: Editions France-Québec / Paris: Fernand Nathan, 1979), pp. 5-17;

Maurice Rabotin, "La Langue et le style des *Contes* de Jacques Ferron," in *Mélanges littéraires publiés à l'occasion du 150e anniversaire de l'Université McGill de Montréal* (Montreal: Hurtubise HMH, 1971), pp. 147-156;

Guy Robert, "Jacques Ferron, l'ironie engagée," *Culture Vivant,* 24 (March 1973): 21-24;

Eileen Sartar, "The Uncertain Countries of Jacques Ferron and Mordecai Richler," *Canadian Fiction Magazine,* 13 (Summer 1974): 98-107;

Donald Smith, "Jacques Ferron ou la géographie d'un pays certain," *Journal of Canadian Fiction,* 25-26 (1979): 175-185;

Yves Taschereau, *Le Portuna: La Médecine dans l'oeuvre de Jacques Ferron* (Montreal: L'Aurore, 1975);

Lesley Van Wassenhoven, "L'Idéologie du texte et la subversion littéraire dans *Le Ciel de Québec* de Jacques Ferron," *Revue Frontenac,* 1 (1983): 41-60;

Voix et Images, special issue on Ferron, 8 (Spring 1983);

Jonathan M. Weiss, "La Préciosité dans le théâtre politique de Jacques Ferron," *Voix et Images,* 3 (September 1977): 127-146;

Mary Ziroff, *A Study Guide to Jacques Ferron's "Tales from the Uncertain Country"* (Toronto: Anansi, 1977).

Madeleine Gagnon

(27 July 1938-)

Wendy E. Waring

University of Toronto

BOOKS: *Les Morts-vivants* (Montreal: HMH, 1969);

Pour les femmes et tous les autres (Montreal: L'Aurore, 1974);

Portraits du voyage, by Gagnon, Jean-Marc Piotte, and Patrick Straram le Bison ravi (Montreal: L'Aurore, 1974);

Poélitique, Les Herbes Rouges, 26 (February 1975);

La Venue à l'écriture, by Gagnon, Hélène Cixous, and Annie Leclerc (Paris: Union Générale d'Editions, 1977);

Retailles. Complaintes politiques, by Gagnon and Denise Boucher (Montreal: Etincelle, 1977);

Antre, Les Herbes Rouges, 65-66 (July-August 1978);

Lueur. Roman archéologique (Montreal: VLB, 1979);

Au coeur de la lettre. Poésie (Montreal: VLB, 1981);

Autographie 1. Fictions 1970-1980 (Montreal: VLB, 1982);

Pensées du poème. Poesie (Montreal: VLB, 1983);

La Lettre infinie. Récit (Montreal: VLB, 1984);

Les Fleurs du Catalpa (Montreal: VLB, 1986);

L'Infante immémoriale. Poesie (Trois-Rivières, Quebec: Ecrits des Forges/Cesson, France: La Table Rase, 1986);

Au pays des gouttes (Montreal: Editions Paulines, 1986);

Les Samedis fantastiques (Montreal: Editions Paulines, 1986).

PERIODICAL PUBLICATIONS: "*Angéline de Montbrun*: le mensonge historique et la subversion de la métaphore blanche," *Voix et Images du Pays*, 5 (1972): 57-68;

"Productions culturelles et lutte de classes," *Socialisme Québécois*, no. 24 (1974): 63-77;

"La Critique d'André Brochu ou la Mise en crise d'une littérature," *Livres et Auteurs Québécois* (1974): 192-196;

"La Femme et le langage: sa fonction comme parole et comme manque," *La Barre du Jour*, 50 (Winter 1975): 45-57;

" 'Essayer de saisir cet instant entre raison et folie, cette lutte, moment decisif . . . '

(Emma Santos)," *Chroniques*, 1 (January 1975): 38-42;

"Libération de la femme et lutte de classes," by Gagnon and Thérèse Arbic, *Chroniques*, 2 (February 1975): 2-7;

"Entretien. *Dora* et *Portraits du soleil de* Hélène Cixous," by Gagnon, Philippe Haeck, and Patrick Straram le Bison ravi, *Chroniques*, 2 (February 1975): 16-25;

"Les Communistes américaines et la lutte des femmes," *Chroniques*, 2 (February 1975): 34-36;

"Les Ratés du système: l'asile, la prison," *Chroniques*, 3 (March 1975): 37-41; 4 (April 1975): 29-33;

"Elle est objet du sujet elle, ou l'histoire de l'Autre," *Le Devoir*, 10 May 1975, p. 19;

"L'Avortement: encore une affaire de classes," *Chroniques*, 5 (May 1975): 26-29;

"Le Journal *ASTEUR;* un exemple d'écriture militante," *Chroniques*, 6-7 (June-July 1975): 122-126;

"Pourquoi, pour qui, comment écrire?," *Chroniques*, 6-7 (June-July 1975): 122-126;

"Notes critiques sur 'Le drame de l'enseignement du français' [de Lysiane Gagnon]. II.," *Chroniques*, 8-9 (August-September 1975): 126-131;

"Entre folie et vérité," *Chroniques*, 10 (October 1975): 37-42; 11 (November 1975): 36-40; 12 (December 1975): 32-36;

"Sur la langue," *Chroniques*, 12 (December 1975): 15-18;

"*Stratégie*: un exemple de dogmatisme," *Chroniques*, 13 (January 1976): 20-43;

"Une Rencontre différente des autres," *Chroniques*, 13 (January 1976): 59-62;

"Histoire d'O," *Chroniques*, 14 (February 1976): 56-61;

"Si elle se mettait à parler," *Chroniques*, 15 (March 1976): 33-38;

"D'une nef à l'autre," *Chroniques*, 16 (April 1976): 30-37;

"Ecriture/Parole. Atelier animé par Madeleine

photograph by Kèro

Madeleine Gagnon

Gagnon," *Chroniques*, 17 (May 1976): 8-25;

"Un Après-midi, à Villetaneuse, le 1er mai 1976," *Chroniques*, 18-19 (June-July 1976): 3-5;

"La Femme et l'écriture. Actes de la Rencontre québécoise internationale des écrivains," *Liberté*, 106-107 (July-October 1976): 249-254;

"Le Viol," *Chroniques*, 22 (October 1976): 66-75;

"Pour les femmes et tous les autres," *Change. Souverain Québec*, 30-31 (March 1977): 136-139;

"Des mots pleins la bouche," *La Barre du Jour*, 56-57 (May-August 1977): 139-147;

"La Mort du texte en moi, maintenant le lieu de sa lecture," *Chroniques*, 29-32 (Fall 1977-Winter 1978): 210-215;

"Lueur (Pré-texte)," *Interprétation*, 21 (Spring 1978): 69-70;

"Dire ces femmes d'où je viens," *Le Magazine Littéraire*, 134 (March 1978): 94-96;

"Femmes du Québec, un mouvement et des écritures," by Gagnon and Mireille Lanctot, *Le Magazine Littéraire*, 134 (March 1978): 97-99;

"Elle m'a parlé de son sang . . . ," *Sorcières* (September 1978);

"*Une Mémoire dechirée* de Thérèse Renaud et *Une voix pour Odile* de France Théoret," *Voix et Images*, 4 (September 1978): 143-146;

"Quand le pouvoir patriarcal s'en prend aux fées," *Le Devoir*, 8 December 1978, p. 5;

"L'Infante immémoriale," *Possibles*, 4 (Fall 1979): 83-92;

"Ecriture. Sorcellerie. Féminité," *Etudes Littéraires*, 12 (December 1979): 357-361;

"La Tradition féminine en littérature," *Revue de l'Université d'Ottawa*, 50 (January-March 1980): 28-29;

"Lecture de *Naissances. De l'écriture québécoise*," *Voix et Images*, 6 (Spring 1981): 393-396;

"L'Ecriture malgré tout," *Dérives*, no. 33 (1982): 5-12;

"L'Etrange figure du lent destin des choses," *La Nouvelle Barre du Jour*, 122-123 (February 1983): 129-133;

"Le Camping aux trésors," *Vidéo-Presse*, 15 (September 1985): 52-55;

"L'Agate du Finistère," *Vidéo-Presse*, 15 (October 1985): 52-55;

"Le Drame de Sancho," *Vidéo-Presse*, 15 (November 1985): 52-55;

"Le Diamant perdu," *Vidéo-Presse*, 15 (December 1985): 52-55.

Madeleine Gagnon was born in 1938 to Jean-Baptiste and Jeanne Beaulieu Gagnon at Amqui, Quebec. One of ten children, she grew up in the countryside of the Gaspé region of Quebec. She received her B.A. in literature from the Université Saint-Joseph du Nouveau-Brunswick, her M.A. in philosophy from the Université de Montréal, and her doctorate in literature from the Université de Nice in France. Married early in her life, Gagnon divorced after her first book, which she signed with her married name, Madeleine Gagnon-Mahoney. She currently lives in Montreal with her two children, Charles and Christophe, and teaches literature at the Université de Québec à Montréal.

Although Gagnon is recognized chiefly for her poetry, she has successfully explored a number of different genres, beginning with the publication of her first work, *Les Morts-vivants* (1969), a collection of short stories, through her political articles in *Chroniques*, to her recent volume of poetry, *Les Fleurs du Catalpa* (1986). The variety of her writing styles reflects in part the political turmoil of the period in which she began to have her works published. During the 1970s, she was an active member of the Union des Ecrivains Québécois and a member of the editorial collective for *Chroniques* (1974-1976). Her more "militant" texts, such as *Retailles* (1977) or *Pour les femmes et tous les autres* (1974), and her articles in *Chroniques* (1974, 1975) bear witness to her *engagement* in many of the struggles for political liberation then current: the burgeoning trade-union movement, the emergence of radical feminism, the struggle for linguistic freedom in Quebec.

This "quiet revolution" was not, however, the sole motivation for the multiplicity of her writing styles. Gagnon's texts outline a concerted effort to explode the boundaries of genre, to recognize the textual conjunctions of theory and fiction, of prose and poetry, of autobiography and history. Her best-known work, the "archaeological" novel *Lueur* (1979), is a blend of theory and autobiography written in language that floats between prose and poetry. It tells of a feminine exploration that searches for an origin, the origin of language, and of personal history. Similarly, in the collaborative work *La Venue à l'écriture* (1977), she describes the discovery of her own voice, as well as the discovery by women in the 1970s of their own expressive possibilities. In two of her latest volumes, *Les Fleurs du Catalpa* and *L'Infante immémoriale. Poesie* (1986), a blending of haiku prose poems, intimate journal entries, and theoretical reflections elaborates this same textual approach.

Her work, although intensely personal and intimate for the most part, nonetheless recognizes in a number of ways the influences of writers around her. Many of her works have been written in collaboration with other writers: *Portraits du voyage* (1974), with Quebecois writers Jean-Marc Piotte and Patrick Straram le Bison ravi, *La Venue à l'écriture* (1977), with French authors Annie Leclerc and Hélène Cixous, and *Retailles*, with Quebecois playwright Denise Boucher.

In books like *Retailles* (1977) or *Pour les femmes et tous les autres* (1974), her use of collage acknowledges debts to the voices and texts from which she draws inspiration. She mixes her own reflections with citations from other authors. In addition to well-known international figures such as Marguerite Duras, Paul Claudel, Maurice Blanchot, and Gabriel García Márquez, she is fond of integrating the work of writers from the Quebecois community (Philippe Haeck, Claude Gauvreau) to signpost her textual affiliation.

As did many Quebecois writers during the 1970s, Gagnon used the Montreal dialect *joual* in her work, but her everyday Quebecois voices are, for the most part, those of women. Gagnon juxtaposes reflections on politics or prose poems on the act of reading with these voices of everyday life to create a textual counterpoint. In some instances, she has used ad copy from popular magazines to orchestrate harmony, and sometimes dissonance, in her pieces. The fragmentation and ambiguity of pronoun reference in her work also adds to the impression of a polyvocal text and develops poetically Gagnon's continuing theoretical focus on the dissolution of the modern subject.

Early in the 1980s, Gagnon took pains to put distance between her present writing projects and her earlier, more militant texts. In an inter-

La création poétique, disait Charles Mauron, est chose difficile car "elle exige que l'esprit morde sur deux étrangetés — celle du mythe intérieur, inconsciente, celle de l'objet extérieur, inconnaissable" (Mallarmé par lui-même, p. 136). Ainsi en est-il de la création amoureuse au point que l'écriture de l'amour et l'amour de l'écriture, tout en demeurant chacune, activité inexplicable, ne peuvent pourtant se connaître l'une sans l'autre.

Le mythe intérieur, première étrangeté, est un jardin de lettres amoureuses, indéchiffrables pulsions pré-alphabétiques mais pourtant lettres que l'amant livre à l'aimé dans la parole amoureuse. Et cette parole est reçue par l'aimé, second étrangeté objective, comme un poème. Tous les amoureux de la terre, de tout temps, sont des poètes: des scripteurs de lettres à la fois mystérieuses et lumineuses. Comme ces premiers gestes de la mère ou du père, gravés amoureusement sur le corps de l'enfant, ne s'expliquent pas par quelque science ou ne se racontent pas dans une limpide prose intrigante et soutenue: ces gestes, pulsions de lettres, se captent fugacement, parfois, au détour d'une émotion, par bribes fulgurantes quand le corps, à l'aide des lettres, se met en musique.

Manuscript page (by permission of the author)

view which appeared in *Voix et Images* in 1982, she describes how, like Pasolini, she had to find courage to leave behind those writings which she felt had been co-opted by a discourse of power. Her later writing no longer takes part in a "feminist realism," but rather searches for the traces of an unwritten female language. Increasingly in her later texts, such as *Antre* (1978) or *Lueur* (1979), Gagnon turns to a psychoanalytic approach in literature, drawing out her relationships to such French feminists as Cixous, Annie Leclerc, Michèle Montrelay, and Luce Irigaray. Gagnon finds that the inscription of hysteria and history on the female body becomes the source of a feminine language heretofore marginalized. In what might be called a psychoanalytical version of "the personal is political," Gagnon works with corporal symptoms of hysteria that constitute a sign system exploitable in texts.

Her interest here accounts for the thematic and linguistic fascination in her writing with the relationship between mother and daughter and her concerted efforts to imagine a world outside of the Oedipal relation. The prominence of metaphors of fluidity, of fissures and gaps, and of sewing and quilting, harken to this preoccupation with an "écriture féminine," as in *Antre*: "Un pré de blé. En plein milieu de la forêt touffue, un pré de blé. Elle est allongée de tout son long, dedans, une femme, comme endormie, la tête sur une ardoise plate ou c'est écrit, hiéroglyphes. Des lettres sont gravées dont elle ne comprend ni la disposition ni le sens. De son index, elle balaie la poussière de blé sur hiéroglyphes. Elle souffle sur l'ardoise. Emergent des mots signifiants jamais appris nulle part. Ce sont des mots de tous les jours" (A field of wheat. Right in the middle of the thick forest, a field of wheat. Stretched out full-length, within, a woman, as if asleep, her head on a flat slate on which are written hieroglyphs. Letters are engraved of which she understands neither the order nor the meaning. With her index finger she sweeps away the wheat dust on the hieroglyphs. She blows on the slate. Meaningful words emerge never learned anywhere. Everyday words).

Although her most recent publications have been volumes of poetry, the appearance in *Vidéo-Presse* of several short stories indicates a return to the genre with which she had begun her published fiction. Gagnon, whose *Autographie 1* was published in 1982, is presently working on the second and third volumes in this series of retrospective collections of her writing from 1970-1980. Her writing, as well as her teaching, lectures, and writing workshops continue to multiply her many critical and literary contributions to the vibrant life of Quebec letters.

Reference:

Voix et Images, special issue on Gagnon, 8 (Fall 1982).

Gary Geddes

(9 June 1940-   )

Laurie Ricou
University of British Columbia

BOOKS: *Poems* (Waterloo: Waterloo Lutheran University, 1971);
Rivers Inlet (Vancouver: Talonbooks, 1971);
Letter of the Master of Horse (Ottawa: Oberon, 1973);
Snakeroot (Vancouver: Talonbooks, 1973);
War & Other Measures (Toronto: Anansi, 1976);
Conrad's Later Novels (Montreal: McGill-Queen's University Press, 1980);
The Acid Test (Winnipeg: Turnstone, 1981);
Les maudits Anglais, by Geddes and members of the Theatre Passe Muraille (Toronto: Playwrights Canada, 1984);
The Terracotta Army (Ottawa: Oberon, 1984);
Changes of State (Moose Jaw, Saskatchewan: Coteau Books, 1986);
The Unsettling of the West (Ottawa: Oberon, 1986);
Hong Kong Poems (Ottawa: Oberon, 1987).

PLAY PRODUCTIONS: *Les maudits Anglais,* Montreal, Theatre Passe Muraille at Théâtre d'Aujourd'hui, September 1978;
Hong Kong, Winnipeg, University of Winnipeg Theatre Department, 21 November 1986.

RADIO: "War & Other Measures," *Anthology,* CBC, August 1976;
"The Inheritors," *Time for Verse,* BBC, November 1983;
"The Terracotta Army," *Anthology,* CBC, August 1985; *Third Programme,* BBC, 1987; with other poems, *Saturday Spotlight,* CBC, October 1986.

OTHER: *20th-Century Poetry & Poetics,* edited by Geddes (Toronto: Oxford University Press, 1969; revised and enlarged, 1973, 1985);
15 Canadian Poets, edited by Geddes and Phyllis Bruce (Toronto: Oxford University Press, 1970); revised and enlarged as *15 Canadian Poets Plus 5* (Toronto: Oxford University Press, 1978);
Heart of Darkness and other stories by Joseph Conrad, edited by Geddes (Don Mills, Ontario: Nelson, 1971);

photograph by c. j. sweet

Skookum Wawa: Writings of the Canadian Northwest, edited by Geddes (Toronto: Oxford University Press, 1975);
Divided We Stand, edited by Geddes (Toronto: PMA, 1977);
Chinada: Memoirs of the Gang of Seven, edited by Geddes (Dunvegan, Ontario: Quadrant, 1983);
The Inner Ear: An Anthology of New Poets, edited

by Geddes (Dunvegan, Ontario: Quadrant, 1983);

"Dennis Lee," "Stephen Scobie," "John Newlove," and "Phyllis Webb," in *The Oxford Companion to Canadian Literature,* edited by William Toye (Toronto: Oxford University Press, 1983), pp. 442-443, 558-559, 739-740, 825;

I Didn't Notice the Mountain Growing Dark, poems of Li Pai and Tu Fu, translated by Geddes and George Liang (Dunvegan, Ontario: Cormorant Books, 1986);

Vancouver: Soul of a City, edited by Geddes (Vancouver: Douglas & McIntyre, 1986).

PERIODICAL PUBLICATIONS: "Conrad and the Fine Art of Understanding," *Dalhousie Review,* 47 (Winter 1967-1968): 492-503;

"Piper of Many Tunes: Duncan Campbell Scott," *Canadian Literature,* 37 (Summer 1968): 15-27;

"The Structure of Sympathy: Conrad and the Chance that Wasn't," *English Literature in Translation,* 12, no. 4 (1969): 175-188;

"A Cursed and Singular Blessing," *Canadian Literature,* 54 (Autumn 1972): 27-36;

[Poems / Poèmes], poems with French translations, *Ellipse,* no. 32 (1984): 48-85;

"Going the Distance," *Open Letter,* sixth series, 2/3 (Summer / Fall 1985): 167-176.

Gary Geddes's poetry focuses on marginal figures in society, especially those who are caught in an ethical bind. Geddes is interested in people who are pulled between an instinctive sense of what is eternally, morally right and a desire, which has not quite surfaced, to say to hell with it all and to ignore any responsibility for human beings who have ignored their responsibilities to them. This is the concern which defines Geddes as a political poet. He is political not so much because he addresses issues of current public-policy debate or because he adopts modish causes, but because his characters are involved, or are implicated almost in spite of themselves, in considering their responsibility to their community of fellow humans and in discovering the lines of power and obligation in communities as large as a nation or as small as a classroom. As this description implies, Geddes's poetry is more concerned with subject than with language. Certainly a Geddes book is more memorable for its people, and for their stories, than for its cleverly sustained metaphors, or its witty wordplay, or its pithily quotable lines. Which is

not to say that Geddes is not careful about language, only that his care is directed toward shaping story and meaning.

Geddes's social themes and storytelling poems have their basis in poor, working-class origins which he admits to sometimes exaggerating. He was born in Vancouver, 9 June 1940 to Laurie James and Irene Turner Geddes. His father worked as a carpenter and shipwright at British Columbia Marine and North Van Shipyards, while his mother did promotional work in local department stores. Wartime separation of his parents after his father joined the Royal Canadian Navy led to divorce and then to the eventual remarriage of both parents. His mother died in 1947, a year after her marriage to Jim Frieson. Geddes's father married Margaret Killian (née Peichl), whose first husband had been killed in action, and Geddes, with his older brother and father, moved to Gainsborough, Saskatchewan, and then, out of financial necessity, to his stepmother's parents' farm near Yorkton. In 1952 his father returned to the West Coast to fish commercially at Rivers Inlet; Geddes joined him and completed his public school education in Vancouver, graduating from King Edward High School. Some of these early years were spent in an apartment above a store on Commercial Drive in Vancouver's East End.

From 1958 to 1962 Geddes attended the University of British Columbia, studying for a B.A. (1962) in English and philosophy. He taught high school for a year at Vanada on Texada Island and then married Norman Fugler, a nurse, in 1963. The next year they spent in England, where Geddes took a diploma in education at the University of Reading. The marriage lasted about three years; the couple had one daughter, Jennifer Leslie. In 1964 Geddes began study at the University of Toronto, graduating with an M.A. in English (1966) and a Ph.D. (1975).

During the years at University of Toronto, Geddes began to contribute poems to journals and to compile such teaching anthologies as *20th-Century Poetry & Poetics* (1969) and *15 Canadian Poets* (1970). He launched, with Hugo McPherson, the Studies in Canadian Literature series, which eventually resulted in fifteen monographs from three different publishers. These activities might be thought tangential to an account of a poet's career, but they demonstrate an essential missionary and entrepreneurial dimension to Geddes's political interests. For twenty-five years he has been as energetically committed to ensuring that other Canadian writers are read and understood as he has been to developing his own writing. His founding of the subscription presses Quadrant Editions (1980-1983) and Cormorant Books (1984- ; devoted mainly to poetry and ethnic materials) demonstrates in the 1980s his continuing sense of cultural vacuums and how to fill them and ways to make Canadian writing available to the public.

The first significant encouragement to a career in poetry was Geddes's winning of the University of Toronto's E.J. Pratt Medal and prize (1969) for an early version of *Letter of the Master of Horse,* a spare book-length poem in which the master of horse on a Spanish expedition to the New World is imagined writing home to his sister. His story centers on the ship becalmed and on having to force the horses over the side to save water. Amidst the agony of the horses' helpless deaths lies Geddes's typical fascination with the dilemma of the man subject to the authority of king and captain, wondering desperately, confusedly, rhetorically (there is no answer): "what is the shape of freedom/after all?" The poem was published after several revisions by Oberon Press in 1973.

Letter of the Master of Horse established Geddes's reputation for telling a story in the voice of an observer who fears being implicated as a participant. Several other books appeared in the early 1970s while Geddes was at first traveling in Europe and later teaching at Carleton University and at the University of Victoria: a chapbook of apprentice work titled *Poems* (1971); *Rivers Inlet* (1971), a series of four brief meditations on one of his West Coast homes, interpreted in the language of fishing and of mapping a geography where rivers and ocean intermingle; and *Snakeroot* (1973), something of a companion volume to *Rivers Inlet,* which recalls in more humorous and diverse lyrics the landscape and especially the rituals of the poet's years spent growing up in Saskatchewan.

In 1971, after having spent most of four years with Phyllis Bruce with whom he collaborated on several projects, Geddes met and married Jan Cox (née Macht), who was born in Battleford, Saskatchewan, and raised in Ocean Falls and Victoria. A daughter, Bronwen Claire, was born in 1975. After leaving the University of Victoria in 1974, Geddes free-lanced for a year, then was writer in residence and part-time teacher at the University of Alberta. In 1978 he took up his present teaching job at Concordia Uni-

Dust jacket for Geddes's second book of poetry, a series of four brief meditations on one of his West Coast homes

versity and settled on a farm in Dunvegan, Ontario.

In 1976 his *War & Other Measures* appeared, a work that has proved to be at the center of Geddes's poetic method and concern. The book is a sequence of dream-memory lyrics in the voice of a man who resembles Paul Joseph Chartier, the strange figure who died in the men's washroom of the House of Commons in May 1966 when a bomb he was carrying exploded. In this book the relative flatness of Geddes's diction often works well to reinforce his theme of the banality and torment of a life lived in the midst of war (the stories begin with experiences in World War II, but suggest many kinds of wars). Chartier becomes a type of the Canadian in the 1970s, someone trying to relate to a community in which, as a fighter, he can "have been intimate / only with strangers." Chartier's particular dilemma as an outcast Quebecois, who must live his life in a language other than his own, is one of Geddes's most noticeable national themes, one prominent in his dramatic farce *Les maudits Anglais* (1984) and in several of the poems in *The Acid Test* (1981), winner of the National Poetry Prize from the Canadian Authors' Association.

In 1977 Geddes made a trip to Hong Kong. This first personal contact with China was extended in 1981 by his participation, with six other Canadian writers, in an official exchange to the People's Republic of China (see the anthology *Chinada: Memoirs of the Gang of Seven*, 1983) and by a second tour, at the invitation of the Chinese Writers' Association, in the summer of 1985. Many of the best poems in *Changes of State* (1986) develop the encounter between the Western artist and Chinese art forms. Particularly memorable is "The Uses of Poetry," which develops the anecdote of a man carving at the Daxing Ivory Factory into a manifesto for the leisure and miniaturist exactness of Chinese art in Geddes's own poetry. In "To the Women of the Fo Shan Silk Commune" his politics is typically subtle, as his appreciation of the subtlety of ancient craft is very political.

Another result of his encounters with China is *I Didn't Notice the Mountain Growing Dark* (1986), collaborative translations with George Liang, of the classic Chinese poets Li Pai and Tu Fu. The generalities, abstractions, and rhetorical questions of these translations do not entirely harmonize with Geddes's poetic strengths, which, he admits in the foreword, lie more in "narratives of separation and war or in the lyrics of departure and loss." Nonetheless, the exercise of translating from the Chinese, which Geddes says began in the mid 1970s, contributed imagery and elements of form to *The Terracotta Army* and *Hong Kong Poems*.

Geddes's finest book since *War & Other Measures*, *The Terracotta Army*, appeared in 1984. In this work Geddes extends his talent for sequential dramatic monologues by creating the voices of some of the 8000 life-size sculpted soldiers and horses who were constructed in the third century B.C. as a posthumous bodyguard for the first emperor of China. Each military figure comments on himself as a model for a pottery replica, on his own modeling for the sculptor, and on his sense of the validity of the resulting clay figure. Geddes makes shrewd use of the couplet as a stanza to emphasize the riddling which is implicated in this form, and, he suggests, in Chinese poetry. The book is a compelling series of takes on unknown artists, on their politics, and on the politics of war. *The Terracotta Army* employs with judicious effectiveness the self-reflexive fashion of so much writing in the 1980s. The Minister of War comments on the other artist (not sculptor, but poet) who is giving him voice, and a paradoxical mimicry, of "hav[ing] twice as much to answer for." Like *Changes of State*, with its frequent puns, joking allusions, and carnivalesque metaphors, *The Terracotta Army* gives quiet evidence through-

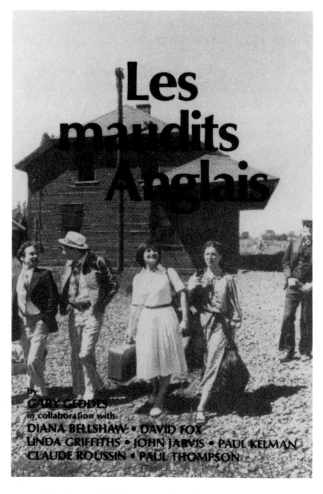

Cover for the published script of Geddes's 1978 collaboration with members of Theatre Passe Muraille. According to Geddes's introduction, "It isn't a great play, but it is good entertainment and a bold, even audacious, theatrical coup—a Quebec play written by Anglophones and played in French, that dared to take on the question of separatism and French nationalism, with some insight and a lot of humour."

out of a poetic maturing, of a long-standing allegiance to a poetry of political nuance and shadow extended and sharpened by a slightly more explicit interest in the plasticity of the poet's medium. The volume won first prize that year in the Americas Division of the British Airways Commonwealth Poetry Prize.

In fiction, rather curiously given its more likely use of representational language, Geddes is less of a political writer. In a collection of short stories, *The Unsettling of the West* (1986), the most political story, "The Accounting," about the displacement of Japanese-Canadians, is among the weakest. In prose, a lack of adaptability in language is evident, whereas in *The Terracotta Army*, and still more so in *Hong Kong Poems* (1987), the poet becomes more skilled at tailoring his language(s) and forms to particular subject and character.

Hong Kong Poems is a confirmation of this tendency, as it sustains Geddes's concern for the ethics of war, for his country's collective psyche, and for his interest in Canada's Asian ties. The book brings together the "meagre voices / and chance fragments" of the Canadian troops who were sent, futilely and unreasonably, to defend Hong Kong in 1941. Again Geddes tries the difficult juggling of what he describes as "fine discriminations of language" with the tedious monologues he gives to (or records from) the soldiers and veterans. The notable difference in this poem is that Geddes the writer is a much more obvious presence, especially in prose vignettes which tell the poet's own story as it runs tangentially to the stories of history. Typically, the primary force of the book is in its discovery (and the writerly self-consciousness intensifies it) of a hidden and uncomfortably black communal history. *Hong Kong Poems*, like the strongest of Geddes's work, contains the "desperation so quietly profound" which he salutes in the poem "Philip Larkin" from *Changes of State*. Philip Larkin's ethical subtlety provides a useful definition of Geddes's aspiration. Another definition of his best work is the principle he enunciates in his book of translations: "Bringing into your midst through the medium of your own language what is best from other cultures is an important activity. It enriches; it also teaches humility."

References:

Donald R. Bartlett, "Gary Geddes' *War and Other Measures:* An Analysis," *Canadian Poetry*, 8 (Spring / Summer 1981): 64-73;

Jay Johnson, " 'Où en est la coeur de l'homme?': la poésie de Gary Geddes," *Ellipse*, no. 32 (1984): 86-95.

Roland Giguère

(4 May 1929-   )

Jacqueline Viswanathan
Simon Fraser University

BOOKS: *Faire maître* (Montreal: Erta, 1949);

Trois Pas (Montreal: Erta, 1950);

Les Nuits abat-jour (Montreal: Erta, 1950);

Midi perdu (Montreal: Erta, 1951);

Yeux fixes, ou l'Ebullition de l'intérieur (Montreal: Erta, 1951);

Images apprivoisées (Montreal: Erta, 1953);

Les Armes blanches (Montreal: Erta, 1954); translated in part by Jean de Beaupré and Gael Turnbull as *Eight Poems from "Les Armes blanches"* (Toronto: Contact, 1955);

Le Défaut des ruines est d'avoir des habitants (Montreal: Erta, 1957);

Adorable Femme des neiges (Aix-en-Provence: Erta, 1959);

L'Age de la parole: poèmes 1949-1960 (Montreal: Editions de l'Hexagone, 1965);

Pouvoir du noir (Montreal: Ministère des Affaires Culturelles, Musée d'Art Contemporain, 1966);

Naturellement (Montreal: Erta, 1968);

La Main au feu, 1949-1968 (Montreal: Editions de l'Hexagone, 1973);

La Sérigraphie, à la calle (Montreal: Editions Format, 1973);

Abécédaire (Montreal: Erta, 1975);

J'imagine (Montreal: Erta, 1976);

Miror and Letters to an Escapee, translated by Sheila Fischman (Erin, Ontario: Press Porcépic, 1977);

Forêt vierge folle (Montreal: Editions de l'Hexagone, 1978);

10 Cartes postales (Montreal: Aubes, 1981);

A l'orée de l'oeil (Montreal: Noroît, 1981);

Les sorciers de l'île d'Orléans (Montreal: Loto-Québec, 1985).

OTHER: *Twelve Modern French Canadian Poets*, French texts with English translations by G. R. Roy, includes poems by Giguère (Toronto: Ryerson, 1958);

A. J. M. Smith, ed., *The Oxford Book of Canadian Verse*, includes poems in French by Giguère (Toronto & New York: Oxford University Press, 1960);

Guy Sylvestre and H. Gordon Green, eds., *Un Siècle de littérature canadienne. A Century of Canadian Literature*, includes poems by Giguère (Montreal: HMH / Toronto: Ryerson, 1967);

John Glassco, ed., *The Poetry of French Canada in Translation*, includes poems by Giguère (Toronto: Oxford University Press, 1970).

PERIODICAL PUBLICATION: "Life Outfaced," "Go on Living," and "Beginning to Live," poems by Giguère, translated by John Thompson, *Ellipse*, 2 (Winter 1970): 11, 13, 15, 17, 21.

Roland Giguère, the son of Maurice and Jeanne Bourgoin Giguère, was born in Montreal on 4 May 1929. After graduation from secondary school in 1947, he began his study of the graphic arts. In 1949, to publish poetry and prints by Quebec writers and artists, he founded Editions Erta in Montreal. The value and significance of Giguère's own poetic work has been widely recognized only since the publication of retrospective volumes which span his writings from 1949 to 1978. Until then, Giguère, who at Erta was his own printer and publisher, had circulated his poems in artistically superb but not widely available limited editions. With the first retrospective volume, *L'Age de la parole*, published by Hexagone in 1965, many Quebec readers discovered an exhilarating and original poetic adventure. With courage and audacity, Giguère had quietly practiced a poetry which explored the unknown regions of inner and outer space, which uncompromisingly aimed at changing readers' perceptions of themselves, their language, and the world.

A parallel reading of *L'Age de la parole* (1965), *La Main au feu* (1973), and *Forêt vierge folle* (1978), which collect Giguère's most important poems to date, gives a broad perspective on his artistic achievement. In his poetry Giguère pur-

photograph by Kèro

Roland Giguère

sues a single aim: poetry is the privileged instrument through which one may achieve a fullness of life, mind, and body which he calls "le total." Different stages in this relentless search more or less correspond to different periods in Giguère's poetry. The first group of poems ("Midi perdu," in *L'Age de la parole*; "Miror," "Lettres à l'évadé," and "La Grande Nuit," in *La Main au feu*) express a darkness of despair, a feeling of alienation which echoes that of Hector de Saint-Denys Garneau and the early works of Anne Hébert. The exasperation of suffering coming from the destruction of the self must precede the next phase, which is one of total rebellion, expressed in a series of violent and ebullient poems, first collected in *Yeux fixes* (1951), *Les Armes blanches* (1954), and in the sections entitled "Lieux

exemplaires" and "En pays perdu" in *Le Défaut des ruines est d'avoir des habitants* (1957). These majestic songs of apocalyptic destruction announce the time of rebirth after a total conflagration of the old world. Fires and volcanoes burn in most of the poems of this group, as in "Le Cri," included in *La Main au feu*:

> L'éruption sera flambante, fumante,
> partout, par couples, debout,
> les amants s'embraseront
> comme les dernières torches de l'humanité.

> (The eruption will be flaming and smoking /
> everywhere, in couples, erect, / lovers will burn /
> like the last torches of mankind.)

It is in this paradox of creative destruction that

Cover design for Giguère's Les Armes blanches, *a collection of eleven poems and six drawings published in 1954*
(courtesy of Kenneth Landry)

Giguère's verse is thematically closest to surrealist poetry. In 1959, during a stay of several years in France, Giguère published a volume of contemplative love poems, *Adorable Femme des neiges*, a glowing testimonal to the regenerating power of love and woman. The stark simplicity of these poems contrasts with the exuberance of the earlier works. Such sobriety also characterizes the later volumes *Pouvoir du noir* (1966) and *Naturellement* (1968); in both the tone of appeasement of *Adorable Femme des neiges* and the earlier images of destruction are present. Giguère's poetry of bold exploration leads him through a wide variety of poetic forms, from the harmonious, well-balanced progession of free-verse poems to the more abrupt but striking rhythms of poetic prose, from verses reminiscent of Paul Eluard to those which suggest an affinity with Henri Michaux. Some of the coherence and continuity of Giguère's poems comes from his use of sound games, alliterations and homophonies, and word games based on puns and synonyms often beyond the traditional bounds of the poetic lexicon. Such games release the power of language to reach into the irrational. In this sense, and not as a blind mechanical production, Giguère practices "l'écriture automatique" of the surrealists. "Roses et ronces," included in *L'Age de la parole*, is one of the most effective and, because of its heavy dependence on alliteration, most untranslatable examples:

> rosaces les roses les roses et les ronces
> les rouges et les noires les roses les roses
> les roseaux les rameaux les ronces
> les rameaux les roseaux les roses[.]

Giguère's ties with the surrealist movement were strengthened during his stays in France in 1954 and from 1957 to 1963. His second sojourn in Paris was made possible by a Canada Council Grant. It was then that he became a member of a surrealist group named Phases. He also met André Breton. Giguère's strongest tie to the movement is his belief that surrealism is a way of thinking, feeling, and acting with the purpose of deepening man's awareness of himself and the world.

Poetry is only one among many instruments which can be used to pursue this objective; painting is another. Giguère the graphic artist is inseparable from Giguère the poet. A graduate of Montreal Ecole des Arts Graphiques and the Ecole Estienne in Paris, Giguère, as director of the printing and publishing studio Erta, has produced many superb artistic editions. His volumes of original poems are all accompanied by his own drawings and etchings. His artistic work has been exhibited in Quebec, Montreal, and Paris. À

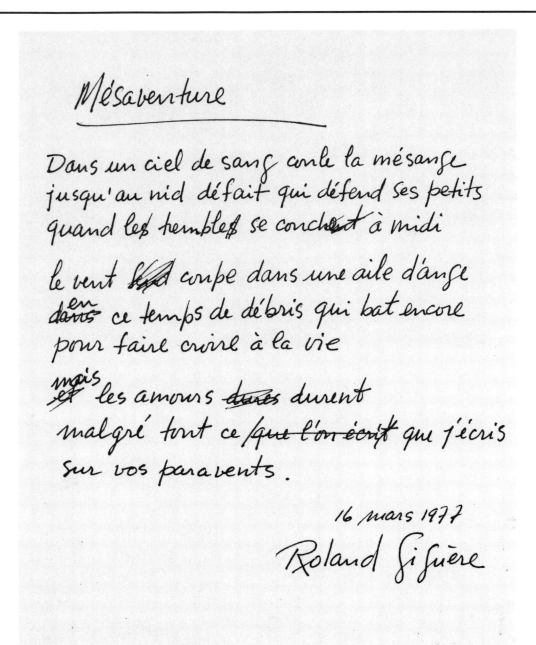

Manuscript for a poem by Giguère (by permission of the author)

l'orée de l'oeil (1981) is a volume of fifty drawings by Giguère with a text of presentation by his friend Gilles Hénault.

Giguère found his poetic voice early in his career and his later works do not show significant evolution. In a 1984 interview published in *Voix et Images*, Giguère states that he does not believe in a constant and systematic search for novelty—in his words, "un renouvellement continuel et systématique." In the French-Canadian society of Giguère's youth the search for liberation and the

rebellion against social constraints had special significance. The oppressive, narrow-minded 1950s are usually designated by Quebec historians as the era of "La grande noirceur" or "The Dark Ages." Giguère's reminiscences, published in 1968 in *La Barre du Jour*, describe the period well: "Je me souviens des années cinquante comme d'une période d'effervescence extraordinaire. Il y avait quelque chose de clandestin dans les activités pratiquées par quelques poètes isolés. Nous étions comme des taupes creusant un tunnel vers la lumière. Là est sans doute la raison du ton prémonitoire et dramatique des poèmes que j'écrivis alors. Sans public, sans éditeur, sans rien d'autre que notre jeune rébellion, nous devions tout faire et nous l'avons fait" (I remember the fifties as an extraordinary period of effervescence. There was something clandestine about the activities carried out by a few isolated poets. We were like moles digging a tunnel toward the light. This may be the reason for the dramatic tone of premonition of the poems I wrote then. With no public, no publisher, without anything else but our young rebellion, we had to do everything and we did).

Giguère's three retrospective volumes have been favorably received. *L'Age de la parole* earned him the Prix France-Canada, the poetry prize of the Concours Littéraires du Québec, and the Grand Prix Littéraire de la Ville de Montréal. In 1974, the year after *La Main au feu* appeared, he refused a Governor General's Award for political reasons. Special issues of two influential journals, *La Barre du Jour* and *Voix et Images*, have been devoted to his work, further testifying to his importance as one of those Quebec artists who patiently and courageously worked toward the cultural upheaval that shook Quebec during the Quiet Revolution.

References:

Roland Bourneuf, "Roland Giguère," *Europe*, nos. 478-479 (February-March 1969): 157-163;

Connaissance de Giguère, special issue of *La Barre du Jour*, nos. 11-13 (December 1967-May 1968);

Dossier sur l'oeuvre de Giguère, special issue of *Voix et Images*, 9 (Winter 1984);

Maximilien Laroche, *Deux études sur la poésie et l'idéologie québécoises* (Quebec: Institut Supérieur des Sciences Humaines, Université Laval, 1975);

Gilles Marcotte, "Roland Giguère," in his *Une Littérature qui se fait* (Montreal: HMH, 1966), pp. 298-307;

Axel Maugey, "Roland Giguère," in his *Poésie et société au Québec (1937-1970)* (Quebec: Presses de l'Université Laval, 1972), pp. 145-164.

Dave Godfrey
(9 August 1938-   )

Peter Buitenhuis
Simon Fraser University

BOOKS: *Death Goes Better with Coca-Cola* (Toronto: Anansi, 1967; revised, Erin, Ontario: Press Porcépic, 1973);

The New Ancestors (Toronto & Chicago: New Press, 1970);

I Ching Kanada (Erin, Ontario: Press Porcépic, 1976);

Dark Must Yield (Erin, Ontario: Press Porcépic, 1978);

The Elements of CAL: The How-to Book on Computer-Aided Learning, by Godfrey and Sharon Sterling (Victoria: Press Porcépic, 1982; Reston, Virginia: Reston Publishing, 1982).

OTHER: *Man Deserves Man: CUSO in Developing Countries*, edited with contributions by Godfrey and Bill McWhinney (Toronto: Ryerson, 1968);

New Canadian Writing, 1968: Stories by David Lewis Stein, Clark Blaise, and Dave Godfrey (Toronto: Clarke, Irwin, 1968);

Gordon to Watkins to You, Documentary: The Battle for Control of Our Economy, edited by Godfrey and Mel Watkins (Toronto: New Press, 1970);

Read Canadian: A Book about Canadian Books, edited by Robert Fulford, Godfrey, and Abraham Rotstein (Toronto: James Lewis & Samuels, 1972);

Gutenberg Two: the New Electronics and Social Change, edited with contributions by Godfrey and Douglas Parkhill (Toronto & Victoria: Press Porcépic, 1979; revised, 1980, 1982, 1985);

The Telidon Book: Designing and Using Videotex Systems, edited by Godfrey and Ernest Chang (Victoria: Press Porcépic, 1981; Reston, Virginia: Reston Publishing, 1981);

Computer-aided Learning Using the NATAL Language, edited by Godfrey and Jack Brahan (Victoria: Press Porcépic, 1984);

Harold Adams Innis, *Empire and Communications*, edited with introduction and afterword by Godfrey (Victoria: Press Porcépic, 1986).

Dave Godfrey has been an active and influential force in Canadian writing, publishing, and cultural nationalism since 1967 when he returned to Canada from graduate study in the United States. His literary, teaching, and political activities have as their common goal creating those conditions under which the writer in Canada can best flourish.

Godfrey was born 9 August 1938 in Winnipeg, Manitoba. His father, Richmond Godfrey, was a lawyer, and his mother, Margaret, was a teacher. He married Ellen Swartz in 1963; they had three children, Jonathan Kofi, Rebecca, and Samuel. He received all his postsecondary education in the United States, earning a B.A. (1960), an M.F.A. in creative writing (1962), and a Ph.D. in English (1967) from the University of Iowa and an M.A. in English (1963) from Stanford University. He has taught at Trinity College of the University of Toronto and at York University and is now chairman of the Department of Creative Writing at the University of Victoria. A determining factor in his career was the period 1963 to 1965, which he spent with the Canadian University Service Overseas (an organization similar to the Peace Corps) as acting head of the Department of English at Adisadel College in Ghana, West Africa. Working in a former colony of the British gave him insights into the cultural colonialism of Canada.

After returning to Canada to live he founded the House of Anansi (named after the African spider god) in 1967 along with the Toronto poet Dennis Lee and stayed with that press until 1970. Anansi has concentrated on publishing works by new Canadian talents and has built up an enviable reputation. With James Bacque and Roy McSkimming, Godfrey founded New Press in Toronto in 1969, and in the early 1970s he founded and became the senior editor with the Press Porcépic in Erin, Ontario. As an editor he has played a significant role in the publication of books by many Canadian writers, including Dennis Lee, Eli Mandel, Michael Ondaatje, Joe

Rosenblatt, Robertson Davies, George Ryga, and others. Godfrey has also served as the fiction editor and member of the editorial board for the *Canadian Forum* and as a trustee of the British-based Books Canada. He was also the founding director of the Association for the Export of Canadian Books. More recently, he has become concerned about the immense changes that are taking place in publishing and education as a result of the computer industry. He has written extensively on the subject and is a member of the editorial board of *CIPS*, a magazine on microcomputers.

Godfrey's first collection of short stories, *Death Goes Better with Coca-Cola* (1967), reflects his experience and concerns as a youth and a student activist in the late 1950s and early 1960s. Several of the stories are about hunting and carry the imprint of Hemingway's influence; others have to do with the Vietnam war and the presence of American draft-dodgers in Canada; one is about an interracial marriage in Africa, but all deal in some way with the workings of human relationships. The epigraph of the book is drawn from the writings of Konrad Lorenz, the anthropologist who has been an important influence on Godfrey's thought. The epigraph reads, in part: "To kill a culture, it is often sufficient to bring it into contact with another, particularly if the latter is higher, or is at least considered as higher, as the culture of a conquering nation usually is." The quotation is from Lorenz's well-known book *On Aggression*. Aggression, against animals, other humans, and of one culture against another may be said to be what *Death Goes Better with Coca-Cola* is about.

The opening story, "Generation of Hunters," serves as a metaphor for the whole collection. It consists largely of a story told by an American marine in a bar in southern California. Recently back from Vietnam, he is assigned to an escort detail for the dead. He relates his story to the narrator, telling how, as a young boy with his father away fighting in World War II, he guarded his mother and sister from bears while they picked blueberries. When a she-bear and her two cubs came upon them he killed the two cubs and wounded the she-bear in the stomach. Instead of dispatching her with a fourth shot as she retreated, he held his fire, for his father had told him to conserve ammunition during wartime. When his father returned on leave the next day, they went on a week-long search for the bear's body. When they found her it was evident that

she had died in great agony. "Sometimes you have to waste something," his father says. It is not a long step from the blueberry patch to the Vietnam jungle. The implication of the story is that not enough Americans had learned the lesson that the marine's father had taught him when they came to fight the Vietcong.

Death Goes Better with Coca-Cola also includes "The Hard-Headed Collector," the story for which Godfrey won the University of Western Ontario's President's Medal for the best short story of 1967. This story cleverly juxtaposes a heroic journey by a group of Queen Charlotte Islanders across Canada with remarks made by the American industrialist Joseph H. Hirschorn on the occasion of the presentation of his art collection to the United States in 1966. Godfrey's story makes the point that Hirschorn had made much of his large fortune from his Canadian mining interests, especially uranium. In the writer's view, there is a clear relation between this resource exploitation and the exploitation of Canada's native peoples by American interests. The theme of the story is emphasized in the title of the collection: *Death Goes Better with Coca-Cola*.

Perhaps the most effective stories in the collection are not those with a political message but those which explore the nuances of human relationships, such as "In the Distant Guts of the Moment" and "On the River." The first concerns a young man and woman who sail (as they had often done in the past) to a secluded shore of a lake to make love and remember the past in the light of the changed circumstances of the present. The second is about a married couple. The wife, pregnant with the couple's second child, is in danger of miscarrying. Sertustrand, the husband, is having some problems adjusting to their changing circumstances and laments the loss of their former passionate selves. As the story proceeds, he gradually accepts the inevitability of change and realizes the need for adjustments and compromises. "He realized somehow," Godfrey writes near the close, "that what he had always desired had happened and that he had got, somehow, beyond certain desires which had blinded his early life."

In *Death Goes Better with Coca-Cola* there is ample evidence that Godfrey had paid close attention to Hemingway. The prose is usually spare and laconic, the conversations short and pointed. Meaning lies under the surface. In one of the stories, Godfrey uses an incident from Hemingway in which a frozen corpse is stacked until spring thaw as if it were a piece of cordwood. The influence of Hemingway is in tune with the quotation from Lorenz which prefaces the collection. *Death Goes Better with Coca-Cola* marked an impressive beginning for a young writer. The book received some good notices, as many reviewers recognized the arrival of a fresh talent.

In 1968 a book appeared which called attention to Godfrey as a writer of nonfiction concerned with sociopolitical problems. *Man Deserves Man: CUSO in Developing Countries*, edited by Godfrey and Bill McWhinney, is a collection of articles by young men and women who had served or were still serving with the Canadian University Service Overseas. Godfrey contributed an article about his experiences in Ghana in addition to editing many of the thirty articles, compiling statistics, and writing appendices. He also wrote the conclusion, "Doomsday Idealism," which is an interesting compendium of many of the ideas which inform his creative and critical thinking in subsequent years. He posits a new organization, CUSO TWO, as a solution to the staggering problems of the developing world, which the efforts of the CUSO volunteers, no matter how well-intentioned, had done so little to remedy.

Using again the Lorenz theory of aggression as the determining factor in human affairs, Godfrey asserts that the fundamental problem is how to control this aggression and channel it into creative behavior. He goes on to draw upon the writings of another anthropologist, Ruth Benedict, to point a way. From her research among numerous tribes, she concluded that the tribes which were most successful in their social relations were what she described as high-synergy groups, those in which the individual serves his own advantage and that of the tribe at the same time. The "rich" man was not the one with the large herds and many possessions, but the one who gave most away to family and friends. In low-synergy tribes the individual and the society work together to enable the rich man to keep and augment his riches, with resulting deprivation for many. The colonial situation, whether it be the cultural and economic colonialism of the United States in Canada or the colonial government of a French possession in Africa, is clearly an example of low-synergy. Nations, concludes Godfrey, should strive toward the ideal advanced by Tanzanian president Julius K. Nyerere in *Ujamaa* (1968)–that of a society in which all contribute to material wealth. The alternatives of militarism and imperialism will clearly not work.

As Godfrey points out, because of enormous technological advances made by the United States and the other industrialized nations it has become possible to render massive and effective aid to the underdeveloped nations through the use of computerized information retrieval systems or through atomic power, with its enormous potential to create energy for mechanized agriculture and for fertilizers. "Combine, somehow," Godfrey concludes, "inventiveness and vast amounts of cheap energy and the individual's desire to create social change and to share cultures; . . . find a structure of abundance, and our castle security and fertility might become as common as Okanagan Valley apples." In the light of recent history, Godfrey's expectations of social change and his optimism about nuclear power seem naive. But Godfrey is unusual among creative writers for his optimism and his belief in the possible benefits of technological change.

In his next book and first novel, *The New Ancestors* (1970), Godfrey explores in greater detail the meaning of his own African experience. The work is set in Lost Coast, a country similar to Ghana; a dictator, known as the Redeemer, rules; and revolt is seething beneath the surface. The country is going through the trauma of postcolonialism, in which, obscurely, the people are trying to find the new ancestors, who are in fact their own old tribal origins and gods. The major characters embody the political concerns of the novel. Michael Burdener, an Englishman left over from the colonial past, is married to a native woman, Ama Awotchi Burdener. She is in turn one of the mistresses of the Redeemer. First Samuels plots against the Redeemer and Gamaliel, who is the Redeemer's propaganda minister. Finally, there is Captain Rusk, who is probably a CIA agent. The novel charts the complex interweaving of the lives of these characters, often in a chaotic fashion, as each in turn becomes the focus of the narrative. At the end of the novel, First Samuels, Gamaliel, and Rusk are dead, by murder, and Burdener is on the point of being exiled.

The novel presents a rich and evocative tapestry of life on the African continent, a portrayal so rich in detail that it sometimes overshadows the drama and significance of events played out against this backdrop. At the end the reader is left uncertain about the meanings of all these events–which is perhaps one of Godfrey's intentions. The novel won the Governor General's Award for fiction in 1971.

Later jacket for Godfrey's first novel, set in Lost Coast, an African country resembling Ghana

Godfrey's next book, *Gordon to Watkins to You, Documentary: The Battle for Control of Our Economy* (1970), which he edited with University of Toronto economist Mel Watkins, is a collection of documents related to a battle involving Watkins and Walter Gordon, former finance minister in the Liberal government of Lester Pearson. Watkins, the economist Cy Gonick, and others sought to convince the Canadian people and government that it was essential to free the economy from American interests, who had invested billions of dollars in Canada which enabled them to drain the profits of Canadian enterprises in the form of dividends to American shareholders. At the same time American-dominated multinational corporations exerted undue influence on the Canadian government.

The issue was not simply one of nationalism but also one of socialism. Gordon believed that Canada could gain power over her economy by the acquisition of these companies, or by establish-

ing at least a controlling interest through a process of investment by Canadian capital. Watkins and his fellow socialists believed that the situation had gone too far for capitalist remedies and advocated that the government take over these companies and run them in the public interest. In order to achieve this end Watkins and his followers started the Waffle Group within the New Democratic Party. In a historic debate and vote in Winnipeg in 1969, the Wafflers lost on this issue. *Gordon to Watkins to You* provides a dramatic and succinct account of this question, which remains a vital one in Canadian politics. *Read Canadian: A Book about Canadian Books* (1972), edited by Godfrey with *Saturday Night* editor Robert Fulford and economist Abraham Rotstein, is another manifestation of Godfrey's cultural nationalism. It is a guide to Canadian culture by means of short essays and bibliographies dealing with Canadian history, economics and politics, society, literature and the arts, and the publishing industry. Useful at the time, it is now quite dated.

In *I Ching Kanada* (1976) Godfrey's career as a writer took a new turn. Based on the Chinese classic *I Ching*, the book is, in the words of its author, "a transformation of its meaning, a shaping to fit our own myth and experience in social ways." It is a particularly oblique and allusive collection of sixty-four one-page prose poems, influenced in form by the *Cantos* of Ezra Pound. The poems deal with different aspects of Canada's past and present: the myths and legends of the native peoples, the original settlement from the American colonies in the east, the western settlements, and the encroachment of American economic and cultural interests. In a "Note on the Text" at the end of the volume, Godfrey discusses the various myths that have shaped Canadian culture and which in turn have shaped his *I Ching*. He emphasizes that his book is a political statement, "a manual on how to run a revolution against Americanization without becoming Americanized." Some sections have an appealing simplicity and beauty; others are knotted and obscure, because the conventions of the Chinese form often seem to obfuscate the meaning of the Canadian experience. But the book is a fascinating experiment both in form and content.

Many of the stories in Godfrey's next book, *Dark Must Yield* (1978), are also experimental. Some include dream sequences or fantasies; most have an autobiographical basis and stress the need for a national consciousness. The central theme of the collection is expressed in the story

Cover for the 1976 volume of prose poems described by Godfrey as a "transformation" or "shaping" of the meaning of the I Ching *"to fit our own myth and experience in social ways"*

"East and / or West." The autobiographical narrator of the story writes: "In the sixties, Dennis Lee used to talk about breathing holes. Because what imperialism is about is pattern and what, for us, nationalism was about was always possibility and possibilities. But it was hard enough to do that at the centre, with all the advantages. So there were circles, like regionalism, like experimentalism, and you didn't deny them, but the battle defined itself in terms of the centre." The stories in this collection are mostly "breathing holes" about revolt, lost love, lost identity; many are experiments in language in form. Some work well, as, for example, "Newfoundland Night" and "East and / or West." Others are not so successful. Some of the best work in the collection, however, is in a more traditional vein, as in "River Two Blind Jacks," which was included in *Short Story International.*

In 1979 Godfrey turned back to the realm of public affairs with *Gutenberg Two,* a volume ed-

ited in collaboration with Douglas Parkhill. The book is a collection of essays and data about the revolution in communications. *Gutenberg Two,* Godfrey claims, is "a key to the technology of the new maze"–the marriage of computers with existing forms of communications such as the telephone and television. Godfrey and the other writers represented in the volume look forward to the time when most homes are hooked up through computers to massive data banks of information and entertainment. Newspapers, it is claimed, will be obsolete: the education structure will change; and the publishing industry will be transformed. The global village that Marshall McLuhan predicted in his 1962 book *The Gutenberg Galaxy* will become a reality. Godfrey contributes an introduction; an essay entitled "Survival of the Fastest," concerning the vulnerability of the various media to the new technology; an article, "No More Teachers Dirty Looks," on the vulnerability of education; and, finally, a piece entitled "Apples, Sorcerers, and Other Monsters," on the state of the art of home computers. Among the other articles is one by Alphonse Ouimet, former head of the Canadian Broadcasting Corporation, about the steps necessary to preserve Canada's cultural and communications independence in the face of the coming technological revolution. Both through government policy and private initiative, Canada is a leader in adaptation to the new communications technology. *Gutenberg Two* is a useful handbook of the best current thinking in the country on the topic.

Subsequent to *Gutenberg Two,* Godfrey has produced three more books about the new world of communications that the computer has made and an edition of Harold Adams Innis's seminal work on communication theory, *Empire and Communication* (1986). His aim in these recent works is both to instruct users of computers and to explain how the mechanism operates. *The Elements of CAL* (computer-assisted learning), a collaboration with Sharon Sterling published in 1982, is a basic guide for students in secondary schools and colleges investigating the possibilities for using computer programs to assist learning in a variety of fields. *The Telidon Book* (1981), edited by Godfrey and Ernest Chang, is a guide to a data transmission system which has many programs in color. This system has been developed largely in Canada and may become popular throughout the developed world. *Computer-aided Learning Using the NATAL Language* (1984), edited by Godfrey and Jack Brahan, introduces the NATAL system,

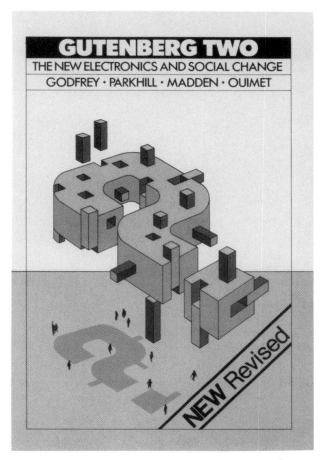

Cover for the 1985 revision of Godfrey's first collaborative work on the communications revolution

compares it to other CAL languages, and discusses its applications to military, industrial, and educational environments. The book includes a step-by-step tutorial system for learning NATAL.

Godfrey's most recent books show that he has kept moving with the times in his awareness of technology. As an artist he uses his ability to welcome and put to use new ideas. As a social commentator, he is highly sensitive to the role that the arts can play in social change. Underlying all his work is a passionate desire to make Canada culturally, politically, and economically independent. No small part of the credit for the movement toward these goals is due to his efforts in writing, publishing, editing, and crusading.

Interviews:

Graeme Gibson, "Dave Godfrey," *Eleven Canadian Novelists* (Toronto: Anansi, 1972), pp. 155-179;

Donald Cameron, "Dave Godfrey: Myth and Gardens," in his *Conversations with Canadian Writers,* volume 2 (Toronto: Macmillan, 1973), pp. 34-47;

Alan Twigg, "Dave Godfrey: 'I'm quite hopeful about the demise of some areas of publishing,'" *Quill & Quire,* 47 (April 1981): 16-17.

References:

Deane E. D. Downey, "The Canadian Identity and African Nationalism," *Canadian Literature,* 75 (Winter 1977): 15-26;

Robert A. Lecker, "Relocating *The New Ancestors,*" *Studies in Canadian Literature,* 2 (Winter 1977): 82-92;

Jane E. Leney, "In the Fifth City," *Canadian Literature,* 96 (Summer 1983): 72-80;

Robert W. Margeson, "A Preliminary Interpretation of *The New Ancestors,*" *Journal of Canadian Fiction,* 4, no. 1 (1975): 96-110;

John Moss, "The Voice of a Restless Dreamer: Godfrey's *The New Ancestors,*" in his *Sex and Violence in the Canadian Novel: The Ancestral Present* (Toronto: McClelland & Stewart, 1977), pp. 199-231;

William H. New, "Godfrey's Book of Changes," *Modern Fiction Studies,* 22 (Autumn 1976): 375-385;

New, "Godfrey's Uncollected Artist," *Ariel,* 4 (July 1973): 5-15;

Calvin L. Smiley, "Godfrey's Progress," *Canadian Literature,* 75 (Winter 1977): 27-40.

Kristjana Gunnars

(19 March 1948-   )

M. Travis Lane
University of New Brunswick

BOOKS: *One-Eyed Moon Maps* (Victoria: Press Porcépic, 1980);
Settlement Poems, 2 volumes (Winnipeg: Turnstone, 1980, 1981);
Wake-Pick Poems (Toronto: Anansi, 1981);
The Axe's Edge (Victoria: Press Porcépic, 1983);
The Night Workers of Ragnarök (Victoria: Press Porcépic, 1985).

OTHER: *Redhead the Whale and Other Icelandic Folktales,* translated by Helga Miller and George Hauser, edited with an introduction by Gunnars (Winnipeg: Queenston House, 1986);
"Avoidance and Confrontation" and "Essay Parcels from Andrew Suknaski," in *Trace,* edited by Birk Sproxton (Winnipeg: Turnstone, 1986).

TRANSLATIONS: D. Arnason and M. Clito, eds., *The Icelanders,* includes translations by Gunnars (Winnipeg: Turnstone, 1981);
Icelandic Writing Today, includes translations by Gunnars (Reykjavik: Summer, 1982);
Jars Balan, ed., *Identifications: Ethnicity and the Writer in Canada,* includes translations by Gunnars (Edmonton: Canadian Institute of Ukranian Studies, 1982);
Finnbogi Gudmundsson, *Stephan G. Stephansson: In Retrospect, Seven Essays,* translated by Gunnars (Reykjavik: Mal og Menning, 1982);
Lögberg Helmskringla, 95 (December 1981) and 96 (Fall 1983), includes translations by Gunnars.

PERIODICAL PUBLICATIONS: "Whale Constellations" (fragments), *Canadian Literature,* 90 (Autumn 1981) and *Ariel,* 17 (April 1986);
"Epistle of Wilderness," *Northward Journal,* 27 (Winter 1983);
"Reef," *Paunch,* 57-58 (Winter 1984);
"Mistaken Masters" (fragments), *Poetry Canada Review,* 6 (Spring 1985).

photograph by W. C. Christie

Kristjana Gunnars was born in 1948 in Reykjavik, Iceland, to Gunnar Bodvarsson and Tove Christensen. She has been a landed immigrant in Canada since 1969 and has a son, Eyvindur Kang, born in 1971. She was educated at Oregon State University (B.A. 1973), the University of Regina (M.A. 1978), and is currently working on a Ph.D. from the University of Manitoba. Although primarily known as a poet, she is also much respected for her work as translator and as researcher into the Nordic settlements in Canada and Greenland, and, especially, for her work on the poetry of the Icelandic-Canadian poet Stephan G. Stephansson (1853-1927).

Gunnars has also contributed numerous short stories, scholarly articles, and reviews to various periodicals. Her writing indicates two major concerns. The first is to affirm her Icelandic roots and to use the cultural and linguistic richness of her education to inform her poetic language, and, thus, indirectly, to enlarge the resources of Canadian English. The second is to bear witness to human experience, and, in particular, to humanity as part of nature, not as distinct from it.

The distinguishing characteristic of her first five books is their use of myth and folklore not as material for literary and decorative play but as a body of perception and experience out of which her imagined personae speak. In Gunnars's story "Crossroads" (in *The Axe's Edge*, 1983) the protagonist reads that someone who can lie all night at a crossroads staring at an axe's edge held over his head will have everything he wants to know about the past told him by his dead relatives. A similar desire to act as medium for the ancestral voices through a sort of self-hypnosis, a concentration on material from the world she wishes to reawaken, produces in Gunnars's writing a tone of internalized language and a tendency toward primitive reference (although aligned with contemporary data), a tone very far from the socialized, conversational language that colors most contemporary verse.

Gunnars's first poetry collection, *One-Eyed Moon Maps* (1980), is a cycle which explores the psychological and poetic values and the philosophic implications of two sets of esoteric knowledge: the ancient knowledge of runes and Nordic mythology and the new knowledge of the astronomer. For Gunnars, science does not (in Keats's phrase from "Lamia") "empty the haunted air" but rather nourishes the poetic imagination. The title of the cycle refers to Odin, the god who gave an eye for wisdom. His concentration, the one-eyed peering through a telescope, is paralleled with the poet's concentrative desire to fuse personal reminiscence and the arational material of legend.

Settlement Poems (1980, 1981) is a two-volume narrative cycle made up of the musings of characterized individuals, Icelandic settlers in the first hard years of their coming to Canada. Gunnars uses material from the daybooks of the historical settlers, whose lives she imagines with the help of her own knowledge of Icelandic culture. The cycle emphasizes the extreme hardships endured and the push toward madness such hardships at times entailed.

Wake-Pick Poems (1981) is a collection of three cycles. "Changeling Poems" depicts the gradual humanization of a child from birth to preadolescence. "Monkshood Poems" represents a young girl growing into an adult understanding. "Wake-Pick Poems" is spoken in the voice of a mature woman dedicated to her community. The pervading themes of all three cycles are the growing understanding of and acceptance of mortality as well as of human community. "Wake-Pick Poems" is sited in the preindustrial world; "Monkshood" represents contemporary life; "Changeling Poems" combines folkloric and science fiction elements. These cycles, like the earlier ones, are exotic in their rich use of folkloric materials: magic herbs, rituals, ghosts, and so forth.

Gunnars's most recent collection, *The Night Workers of Ragnarök* (1985), is less exotic. The book is a collection of cycles, none narrative, which variously explore the general themes of old world versus new world, nature versus technology, beauty versus desperation, and the ambiguous glory of human endeavor. The two "Milky Way Vegetation" cycles show Gunnars's astronomical and botanical interests but without the medievalism of the earlier cycles. "Stone Bridge Poems," "Bed of Opium," "North Country Wake," and "The Silent Hand" use the material of Gunnars's Icelandic past and her revisits home. The brief cycle "Wild Waters" represents a canoe trip in the Canadian North. The title cycle is largely concerned with the contemporary predicament of humankind, going about its daily life under the shadow of ecological and perhaps nuclear disaster. "Ragnarök" is the mythic end of the world in Nordic tradition.

Gunnars's verse is neither conventionally metrical in stanza patterns or even line lengths, nor is it free. Her preference for direct statement with few dependent clauses and for short words and strong stresses gives her lines a sense of measuredness at their most prosaic, but she also employs the stress patterns of Nordic verse and the normal iambics of modern English where her material calls for them.

Gunnars's excellence as a poet is in part due to her willingness to handle important

Cover for Gunnars's most recent poetry collection, eight cycles written from 1981 to 1985

themes. Her technical skill, the richness of her doubled linguistic heritage, and, above all, her choice of form significantly contribute to the profundity and significance of her verse. As form, the cycle seems to insist on a major theme. For the cycle (as Gunnars construes it) is a series of poems which are developmentally and thematically related to each other and controlled by the initiating idea. It is probable that Gunnars prefers the term *cycle* to the vaguer terms *long poem* or *sequence* in order to emphasize the coherence of her material and the fact that her cycles do have resolutions in the musical or emotional sense of the term. Often her cycles end in an affirmation of life and humane values, in a gesture made as if moving toward the future (not unlike the affirmations at the end of the long poems by Dorothy Livesay). Further, a cycle cannot be constructed as a rapid sequence of images, in the less concentrative manner of poets who do not trust their images to bear them long. Rather, the cycle insists

upon the exploration of the initiating impulse. Its revelations unfold gradually and build upon rather than abandon what has gone before.

One senses in all of Gunnars's poetry a conviction of the importance of that to which her language refers. She does not skim linguistic surfaces in search of puns and decorative amusements without reference to the darker connotations and ambivalences that her language expresses. The linguistic texture of her poetry is rich because life is rich, not vice versa. Humane values, especially the desire to give credit and expression to the courage and suffering of ordinary working women and men, figure strongly in Gunnars's work. But her social loyalties do not lead to facile judgment. Her workers are both noble and ignoble. The emphasis, even with all her folkloric material of rune and potion, is on realism.

Gunnars's work has something in common with much Latin American writing, which likewise uses folkloric fantasies as an integral part of experienced history. And her work reflects also the Western World's last two centuries interest in gods less fatigued by overuse than the classical or Judeo-Christian and, along with this, the appeal of the violence and morbidity of gods unrelated to church or social morality. The popularity of medieval fantasy, away from the intellectualized tepidities of urban life, parallels these preferences. Indeed, much of Gunnars's writing, in its use of nightmare and in its preference for a rural northern landscape with its primitive, even brutal, vitalities, reminds one strongly of the films of Ingmar Bergman.

But Gunnars is also one of the writers for whom a sense of contemporary ecological and political predicaments is organic to the poetic imagination, for whom the daily news is not irrelevant to poetry, and to whom the discoveries of science are not alien. The concentration with which she "listens" to the voices of ancestors and contemporaries prohibits nostalgia. Her habit of not letting one short poem "do" for a subject, but of working with the material, developing it into a cycle, gives a sense of thought experienced over a length of time, of thinking and rethinking. Her short stories, collected in *The Axe's Edge*, less developmental in their approach, are slices of life. Although well written, they have neither the intellectual depth nor the rhetorical eloquence of the poem cycles.

Most of the reviews of Gunnars's work are fairly brief. A majority praise her "heroic,"

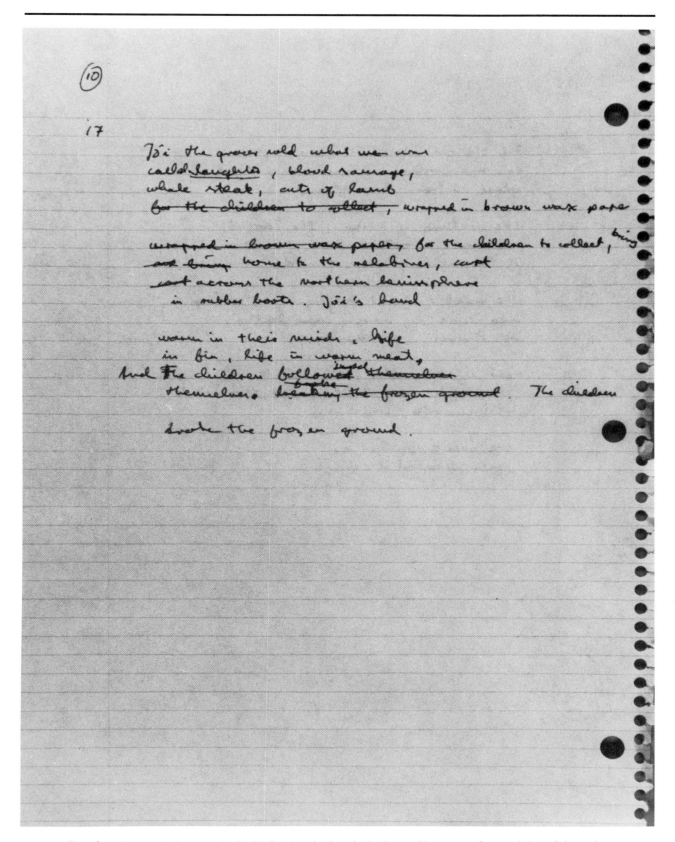

Page from Gunnars's "manuscript book" showing the first draft of one of her poems (by permission of the author)

"epic," or "mythological" style. The most interesting reviews are probably George Johnston's "Icelandic Rhythms" (*Canadian Literature,* Spring 1982) and M. Travis Lane's "Self Voyages" (*Canadian Literature,* Winter 1982), "Troll Turning: Poetic Voice in the Poetry of Kristjana Gunnars" (*Canadian Literature,* Summer 1985), and "Ground of Being" (*Canadian Literature,* Winter 1986).

In an interview with Jane Casey (*Contemporary Verse II,* September 1984), Gunnars speaks of her major concerns in poetry: "voice" and "ethical concern." She stresses the importance of letting the voice of the poem ring true to the narrator's personality: "There's a first person there, but it isn't me." Similarly, of her work as a translator, she says, "I read the poem over and over again until I have it in my bones, hear the voice, or until I feel the author is looking over my shoulder."

Writing is "ultimately an ethical concern," says Gunnars. It has, necessarily, political implications, although it "isn't the writer's job to speak in political terms." The writer can tell the truth about human circumstances and affirm humane values, life against death. Speaking of *Wake-Pick Poems,* as an example, Gunnars says that the book "was about an entrance into what I feel was a kind of post-confirmation world." At the end of the cycles the speaker "insists on going into the open death; the world, in other words. It seems to me," says Gunnars, "that we spend most of our energy just fighting through this jungle of death. So I think part of what I've been doing is trying to get back into an orientation where I can find some joy, happiness and grace."

Gunnars speaks of herself in the preface to *The Night Workers of Ragnarök* as wanting to register daily life, to depict emotions accurately, to tell truth "imbedded in place." For truth is not and cannot be abstract. In a sense we all lie at the crossroads of the past and the future and under the axe's edge. The concentration, the listening, the true report—are Gunnars's.

Robert Gurik

(16 November 1932-)

Jeannette Urbas
York University

BOOKS: *Spirales* (Montreal: Holt, Rinehart & Winston, 1966);

Hamlet, prince du Québec (Montreal: Editions de l'Homme, 1968); translated by Marc-F. Gélinas as *Hamlet, Prince of Quebec* (Toronto: Playwrights Co-op, 1981);

Le Pendu (Montreal: Lèméac, 1970); translated by Philip London and Laurence Bérard as *The Hanged Man* (Toronto: New Press, 1972);

A coeur ouvert (Montreal: Leméac, 1969);

Les Tas de sièges (Montreal: Leméac, 1971);

Api 2967; La Palissade (Montreal: Leméac, 1971); *Api 2967*, translated by Gélinas (Vancouver: Talonbooks, 1974);

Le Tabernacle à trois étages (Montreal: Leméac, 1972);

Le Procès de Jean-Baptiste M. (Montreal: Leméac, 1972); translated by Allan Van Meer as *The Trial of Jean-Baptiste M.* (Vancouver: Talonbooks, 1974);

Sept courtes pièces (Montreal: Leméac, 1974);

Allo . . . Police by Gurik and Jean-Pierre Morin (Montreal: Leméac, 1974);

Lénine (Montreal: Leméac, 1975);

Le Champion (Montreal: Leméac, 1977); translated by Van Meer as *The Champion* (Toronto: Playwrights Co-op, 1982);

La Baie des Jacques (Montreal: Leméac, 1978);

Jeune Délinquant (Montreal: Leméac, 1980).

PERIODICAL PUBLICATIONS: *Le Chant du poète, Cahiers de l'ACTA*, 2, no. 4 (1963): 13-27;

Les Louis d'Or, Théâtre Vivant, 1 (November 1966): 11-60.

MOTION PICTURE: *Les Vautours*, script and dialogue by Gurik, Jean-Claude Labrecque, 1975.

PLAY PRODUCTIONS: *Les Portes*, Montreal, Théâtre de la Place Ville Marie, March 1965;

Api or not Api, voilà la question, Montreal, Théâtre du Gésu, 1966; revised as *Api 2967*, Montreal, Egrégore, 1967;

Robert Gurik

Le Pendu, Montreal, Théâtre du Gésu, 24 March 1967;

Les Louis d'Or, Montreal, Expo 67, 1967;

Hamlet, prince du Québec, Montreal, L'Escale, 17 January 1968;

A coeur ouvert, Montreal, Théâtre de Quat' Sous, 1969;

Les Fourberies de Scapin, adapted from Molière's play, Ste-Thérèse, Quebec, Collège Lionel Groulx, 1970;

Echec à la reine, Chicoutimi, Quebec, 1971;

"Q", adaptation of Armand Gatti's play *Chant public devant deux chaises électriques*, Ste-Thérèse, Quebec, Collège Lionel Groulx, 1971;

101

Les Tas de sièges, Quebec City, Théâtre de Ste-Foy, 1972;

Le Procès de Jean-Baptiste M., Montreal, Théâtre du Nouveau-Monde, 12 October 1972;

Le Tabernacle à trois étages, Quebec City, Théâtre de Ste-Foy, 1973;

La Palissade, Saint-Jean, Quebec, Collège Militaire Saint-Jean, 1973;

Allo . . . Police, Beloeil, Quebec, Polyvalente de Beloeil, 1974;

Sept courtes pièces, Plessisville, Quebec, Polyvalente Plessisville, 1974;

La Baie des Jacques, Ste-Thérèse, Quebec, Collège Lionel Groulx, 1974;

Lénine, on tour, in Benin and Togo, Africa, Théâtre de L'Arc en Ciel, 1978;

Le Champion, Cotonou, Benin, Théâtre de L'Arc en Ciel, 1978.

Robert Gurik's plays are constant interrogations of society and the theater. He poses questions but does not give answers. According to Gurik in a 1978 interview with Adrien Gruslin: "mon théâtre pose des questions, analyse des problèmes, montre ce qui n'est pas évident. Je ne pense pas que le théâtre soit un objet pamphlétaire. Il est plutôt un révélateur, un déclencheur" (My theater raises questions, analyzes problems, reveals what is not immediately apparent. I do not think that the theater has the same objective as a pamphlet. Rather, it is a source of revelation, a setting in motion).

Gurik feels an affinity with the theater of Brecht both in its social concern and its tendency to question the validity of accepted values and ideas. This outlook contrasts with the Aristotelian view of theater which has catharsis as the desired result: the spectator feels emotional release and is no longer agitated by the problems he has seen on the stage. As Gurik told Gruslin: "La réalité, le journal sont pour moi des déclencheurs. Le point de départ d'une pièce est souvent un fait divers. J'exploite les faits de la société où je suis inclus comme témoin. Il se peut que demain survienne un fait que je ne peux passer sous silence de sorte que je vais tout arrêter pour écrire la pièce qu'il m'inspire" (Real life, newspapers are starting points for me. The source of a play is often a news item. I exploit the facts of a society in which I am included as a witness. It is possible that tomorrow something may happen which I cannot overlook in silence, so that I stop everything to write the play that it inspires). Gurik's emphasis is always on the sociological rather than on

the psychological and individual.

Of Hungarian parentage, Robert Gurik was born in 1932 in Paris to Maximilien and Hélène Davidovits Gyurik. After studies at the Collège Turgot, he came to Montreal in 1950 and graduated as an engineer from the Ecole Polytechnique in 1957. His debut as a playwright came about by chance. In 1963 his wife, Renée Noiseux, and a friend wrote a one-act play for a contest sponsored by ACTA (Association Canadienne du Théâtre Amateur). When asked for an opinion, Gurik commented that the play they had written was terrible. His wife challenged him to do better. The result was *Le Chant du poète* which won Gurik first prize in the contest. He had never written anything before except some poems. By 1972 he was able to leave engineering and devote himself exclusively to the theater. To date he has written more than twenty plays.

After *Le Chant du poète* came *Les Portes,* produced in 1965 but not published. The year 1966 saw production of *Api or not Api, voilà la question,* which was revised and staged in 1967 as *Api 2967.* The revised version had a strong impact on audiences in Montreal. Though on the surface the play is a futuristic fable, it deals with the problems of contemporary man in his search for happiness. One of its main themes is the signification of words in relation to the reality they represent. Like Adam and Eve, the two characters on stage eat a forbidden apple. Up to that point their existence, based solely on the instinct of preservation, has been a death in life. The apple represents the spirit of adventure, the way to rediscover some form of vitality.

In his very positive review of *Api 2967* in an April 1967 edition of *La Presse* Luc Perreault wrote: "Ce recours à un futur antérieur constitue à mon avis une trouvaille géniale: cerner l'homme d'aujourd'hui entre deux miroirs, celui du passé et celui du futur, c'est souligner doublement sa nature et montrer par quel genre d'angoisse il est déchiré. . . . J'ai ri aussi à cette pièce, car Gurik possède un humour très fin qui trahit toute une conception de la société dans laquelle il vit" (Resorting to an anterior future constitutes in my opinion an ingenious find: to hem the man of today in between two mirrors, one of the past and the other of the future, is to doubly underline his nature and show by what kind of anguish he is torn. . . . I also laughed watching this play, for Gurik possesses a very keen sense of humor which reveals a whole conception of the society in which he lives).

la personne entre dans la zone éclairée : c'est
Denise.

Denise (doucement)
.... excusez-moi...
Gardien (fort, agressif)
..... Qu'est-ce que vous voulez?...
Denise (calme, indifférente à l'humeur du gardien)
..... le bureau du Docteur Brunet.
Gardien (Il met sa main en cornet à l'oreille)
Quoi?
Denise (même ton, mais plus fort)
... le bureau du Docteur Brunet.
Gardien (Bêtement)
A cette heure-ci, tout est fermé.
Denise
Je l'ai (elle se reprend, plus fort)... Je l'ai appelé. J'ai
rendez-vous.
Le gardien regarde Denise qui lui sourit. Il hésite
, hausse les épaules, puis vérifie finalement son registre.
Gardien (sèchement)
C'est au quinzième. Chambre 1501
Denise va pour s'éloigner.
Gardien
Hé! ... il faut signer votre nom....
Il pousse vers elle un registre et un crayon. Elle
se penche pour écrire, voit l'article decoupé, le tourne
pour l'avoir en face d'elle. Elle lit le titre, puis écrit
son nom sur la première ligne. Le Gardien la
regardé faire.
Gardien (avec un sourire ambigüe)
.....(se referant à l'article) c'est du beau travail, hein?
... (il se saisit des ciseaux sur la table et donne
un coup avec son bras armé, en direction de Denise)... coiric!
et coiric! (sourire sadique) six comme ça

3

Page from the manuscript for Le Signe du cancer, *one of the plays included in Gurik's 1974 collection* Sept courtes pièces
(by permission of the author)

Other reviewers, while generally favorable, criticized some aspects of the play. In *Sept-Jours* (22 April 1967) Jacques Merles, for one, pointed out "une trop grande disparité" between the two parts of the play: "C'est le seul grief formulable à l'encontre de l'auteur qui fait preuve, parfois, avec humour, . . . d'un sens certain du théâtre" (It is the only reproach one can make when one finds an author who demonstrates, sometimes with humor, . . . a sure sense of theater).

The highly experimental parody *Les Louis d'Or* was performed in 1967 in Montreal as part of the Festival des Jeunes Compagnies at Expo. In the same centennial year *Le Pendu* swept the boards at the Dominion Drama Festival in St. John's, Newfoundland, after its initial success earlier that year in the Gesù auditorium in Montreal. It was performed again at Expo with the same cast that had appeared at St. John's.

In *Api 2967* Gurik utilized as symbol a mythic object, the apple; *Le Pendu* centers on a mythic Christ figure named Yonel. Yonel, who wants to save the world and improve humanity, is defeated by the greed and cynicism of those he hopes to save. In the end he is forced to sacrifice himself without accomplishing his goals. The fate of Yonel and his friends is determined by social conditions, poverty being a prime one. Yonel's visionary and magical approach to problems cannot perform the miracle he seeks and the play gives no solutions; ultimately every spectator has to decide for himself. The use of the two choruses; one of children, the other a single character known as the Singer, enables the spectator to keep a certain distance from the action and so better retain the faculty of making judgments. *Le Pendu*, named the best play at the Dominion Drama Festival, was published in French in 1970 and translated into English as *The Hanged Man* in 1972.

Hamlet, prince du Québec, performed in 1968 in Montreal at L'Escale, was enthusiastically received by the public. In this work Gurik remains faithful to Shakespeare's play while using the characters to make a satiric and political comment on Quebec-Canada relations. Each character represents a public figure or group: Hamlet stands for Quebec; Claudius for Anglo-Saxon power, which may be interpreted as a combination of American capitalism and Ontario bureaucracy; the Queen represents the Catholic Church; Polonius, Prime Minister Lester Pearson; Laertes, Pearson's successor, Pierre Elliott Trudeau; Ophelia, Jean Lesage, Liberal premier of Quebec in 1960 at the

start of the Quiet Revolution; Horatio, René Lévesque, head of the Parti Québécois founded in 1968, later elected premier in 1976. In his foreword to the 1968 published version (translated, 1981), Gurik states that "Hamlet c'est le Québec avec toutes ses hésitations, avec sa soif d'action et de liberté, corseté par cent ans d'inaction. Autour de lui se meuvent les masques des personnages qui conduisent sa destinée" (Hamlet is Quebec with all its hesitations, with its thirst for action and liberty, confined by one hundred years of passivity. Around him move the masks of the characters who control his destiny). In performance each character wears the mask appropriate to the political personage or group he represents. The play was prophetic in the roles it assigned to certain political figures who were just coming to the fore in 1968.

Of *Hamlet, prince du Québec* André Major wrote in *Le Devoir* (24 January 1968): "Rien, au théâtre, n'aura si férocement, si profondément, critiqué notre monde politique. . . . Si le théâtre est un art qui suppose la participation collective, eh bien, Gurik a écrit là une pièce de théâtre qui appartient, malgré son évidente nature politique, au grand théâtre" (Nothing, in the theater, has so fiercely, so profoundly, criticized our political world. . . . If theater is an art that supposes collective participation, well then, Gurik has written a play which belongs, despite its evidently political nature, to great theater). However, Jean Garon expressed serious reservations about Gurik's play in *Le Soleil* (30 January 1968): "Sans vouloir en aucune façon minimiser l'importance de cette nouvelle avenue ouverte à nos dramaturges, il ne faudrait pas qu'un souci d'appartenance nous fasse oublier le caractère tout temporaire d'une telle entreprise. . . . Que l'ironie puisse servir à une libération quelconque du Québécois n'est plus une vérité à prouver. . . . C'est ainsi que le *Hamlet* de Robert Gurik fait plus figure de chronique qu'autre chose" (Without desiring to minimize in any way the importance of this new avenue open to our dramatists, a concern for appurtenance should not make us forget the very temporary character of such an undertaking. . . . That irony may serve to bring about some kind of liberation for the Quebecois is no longer a truth that needs to be proved. . . . Thus Robert Gurik's *Hamlet* gives the impression of being a news report more than anything else).

A coeur ouvert, produced in Montreal in 1969, uses the metaphor of open-heart surgery to make a comment on the corruption of a society that exploits one group, in this case, laundry-men, to ensure longevity for those in power. In this play hearts are ruthlessly extracted from laundrymen to provide transplants for those who run the society, the executives, the administrators, the president. These hearts are stored in the Heart Bank. During the play the laundrymen are on the condemned list, obliged to "donate" hearts; the coalmen and the firemen have been temporarily withdrawn from the list but are in danger of being reinstated at any time.

The corruption of the regime is evident in a scene of debauchery involving the president and a secretary in which the president has a heart attack. Class friction (and contradiction) surfaces when the president dies after he rejects the heart of a coalwoman which has been given to him to save his life. The firemen, who foresee their future as new victims, overthrow the regime that tyrannizes them. However, they continue to use the slogans and practice the persecution of their oppressors. In the end a new revolt is simmering; one suspects it may have the same results.

Les Tas de sièges, published in 1971, consists of three one-act plays (*D'un séant à l'autre; J'écoute; Face à face*) written in response to the author's indignation and distress over the October Crisis. In 1972 *Le Procès de Jean-Baptiste M.* was performed at the Théâtre du Nouveau Monde in Montreal. This play, as the author points out in the foreword to the 1972 published version, is based on the premise that every worker at some time wishes for the death of his boss. Jean-Baptiste M. is an Everyman who is neither a revolutionary nor a political activist nor a visionary. The irony of the play comes from the fact that Jean-Baptiste M. wants to become an integral part of the multinational corporate society which his employer, the Dutron Company, represents. He believes in justice and accepts the slogans that promise advancement on the basis of merit and hard work. Finally, in frustration, he kills three of his bosses. In the foreword the playwright asks: "Par intérêt? par folie? par accident? ou incapable de résister à une provocation qui continue d'exister? Ou y-a-t-il une autre raison?" (Out of self-interest? madness? by accident? or is he unable to resist a form of provocation which continues to exist? Or is there another reason?) Gurik, typically, gives no answer in this play, which was translated into English in 1974 as *The Trial of Jean-Baptiste M.*

Two of Gurik's plays deal with famous personalities. *Lénine* was first performed in 1978 by the Théâtre de l'Arc en Ciel on an African tour. The play uses the image of a chess game to describe events leading to the Russian Revolution. This forms part one. Part two attempts to transfer the same image to the present in various parts of the world, without succeeding. The issues are not clearly focussed and the play, as a result, is confusing. However, *Lénine* received an enthusiastic reception when it was performed in Benin. *Le Champion* was also performed by the Théâtre de l'Arc en Ciel in 1978. It follows the career of prizefighter Cassius Clay/Muhammad Ali. Ali is a tragic hero in the playwright's eyes, a black man rebelling against the brutality and injustice of a racist society. But he is defeated by the same forces he sought to overcome.

Gurik has actively participated in the development of Quebec drama. In 1965, with four other writers, he founded the Centre d'Essai des Auteurs Dramatiques, an organization that has encouraged many young Quebec authors. He was also codirector and founder of the Théâtre de la Mandragore in Quebec. He is probably the Quebec playwright most produced outside of Canada. His plays have been performed in France, Italy, Belgium, Holland, and Benin.

Recently, for a variety of reasons, Gurik has concentrated on writing for television and radio rather than for the theater. With the collaboration of Jean-Paul Fugère he prepared *Jeune Délinquant*, a highly successful series of five one-hour programs on juvenile delinquency, televised in the fall of 1980. The same material is the basis of his volume of fiction with the same title, published in 1980. He has written one other novel, *Spirales*, published in 1966.

References:

Pierre-R. Desrosiers, "La Nouvelle Dramaturgie québécoise," *Culture Vivante*, no. 5 (1967): 71-77;

Entretien avec Robert Gurik, Marie-Francine Hébert et le Théâtre Parminou (Montreal: Centre d'Essai d'Auteurs Dramatiques, 1976);

Marc-F. Gélinas, "Orientations de la dramaturgie nouvelle," *Culture Vivante*, no. 9 (1968): 11-16;

Jean-Claude Germain, "Robert Gurik: l'auteur qui n'a rien à enseigner," *Digeste Eclair* (November 1968): 17-20;

Jean-Cléo Godin and Laurent Mailhot, "Le procès de (Jean-Baptiste) Gurik, ingénieur," in their *Le Théâtre québécois*, volume 2, *Nouveux auterus, autres spectacles* (Montreal: Hurtubise HMH, 1980), pp. 105-127.

Ray Guy

(22 April 1939-)

Allan Bevan
Dalhousie University

completed by

W. H. New
University of British Columbia

BOOKS: *You May Know Them as Sea Urchins, Ma'am,* edited by Eric Norman (Portugal Cove, Newfoundland: Breakwater Books, 1975; revised, 1985);
That Far Greater Bay, edited by Norman (Portugal Cove, Newfoundland: Breakwater Books, 1976; revised, 1985);
Outhouses of the East, by Guy and Sherman Hines (Halifax: West House, 1978);
Beneficial Vapours, edited by Norman (St. John's: Jesperson Press, 1981);
An Heroine for Our Time (St. John's: Harry Cuff Publications, 1983);
This Dear and Fine Country (St. John's: Breakwater Books, 1985).

PLAY PRODUCTION: *Young Triffie's Been Made Away With,* St. John's, Resource Centre for the Arts, 1985.

OTHER: "I Went Up Into a Dory," in *Baffles of Wind and Tide: An Anthology of Newfoundland Poetry, Prose and Drama,* edited by Clyde Rose (Portugal Cove, Newfoundland: Breakwater Books, 1973), pp. 31-34;
"No more 'round the mountain We'll be ridin' CN busses," in *The Blasty Bough,* edited by Rose (Portugal Cove, Newfoundland: Breakwater Books, 1976), pp. 2-15;
"What a Charm, What a Racket," in *Landings: A Newfoundland & Labrador Literature Anthology,* edited by Eric Norman and others (St. John's: Breakwater Books, 1984), pp. 17-23.

Ray Guy was born in Come-By-Chance, Newfoundland, on 22 April 1939, to George Hynes and Alice Louise Guy. He was raised in Arnold's Cove, Placentia Bay, where he went to school; his sketches describe his teachers—a range of people that sometimes seem like miserable sadistic mis-

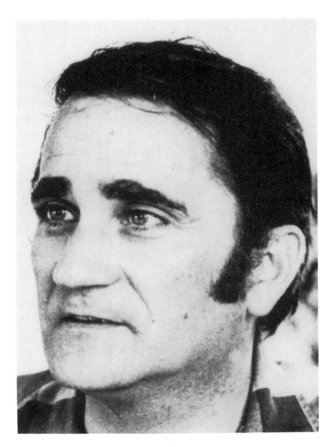

Ray Guy

fits but also include men and women who were inspiring and dedicated. After a year at Memorial University in St. John's in 1957, he moved to Toronto to study journalism at Ryerson Polytechnic Institute. After his graduation in 1963, he returned to St. John's to work for the *Evening Telegram.* His career with the newspaper lasted more or less regularly till 1975, the year he married Katherine Housser of Port Alberni, British Columbia; they have two daughters, Anne and Rachel.

Currently living in St. John's, Guy works as a freelance journalist, story-writer, and playwright; his work is published regularly in *Atlantic Insight, Newfoundland Quarterly, This Week*, and other Atlantic journals, and he has written for CBC radio and television. Among his television writings are the Old Skipper's monologues in a 1970s CBC program entitled *All Around the Circle* and some of the episodes of the later *Up at Ours* series, in which he also acted. Several monologues are soon to be collected into book form, and Guy has recently been turning his hand to stage drama as well. *Young Triffie's Been Made Away With* was produced by the Resource Centre for the Arts in St. John's in 1985 (and reviewed by Philip Hicks in the *Newfoundland Herald*, 27 April 1985); a play-in-progress has the working title "Against the Pricks."

Guy has several times been honored with Canadian national prizes, his sketches having been applauded from coast to coast for their wit and their trenchant social comment. Winner of the 1967 National Newspaper Award for Feature Writing (for "No more 'round the mountain We'll be ridin' CN busses," which appeared first in the *Evening Telegram*, 6 October 1967, and is anthologized in Clyde Rose's *The Blasty Bough*, 1976), he also won the Leacock Medal for Humour in 1977 and has twice won National Magazine Awards (1980, 1984) for humorous writing. In 1978 he collaborated with the photographer Sherman Hines on a witty book of local history, *Outhouses of the East. An Heroine for Our Time* (1983), written as though it were for children, is an illustrated fable about a giant one-ton child besieged by commercial interests, who later rises to fight crimes, and in *This Dear and Fine Country* (1985) Guy extends his skill with the anecdotal sketch.

"Putting out books this way [as collections of previously published material] is great fun," he writes in a preface to *That Far Greater Bay* (1976, revised 1985):

> It suits my disposition—which leans heavily, and wearily, toward inertia. Less couth persons would describe it as sloth.
>
> But flogging books in the manner which the modern marketplace seems to demand is a discomfort in the fundament.
>
> You are supposed to hop hell-west-and-crooked all over the countryside, sticking your mug on the television, quavering and warbling into radio microphones and sitting yourself down amongst optimistic heaps of your produce waiting for people

> to come along and ask you to scribble your name in one.
>
> It is a loathsome business.... But ... you can still get hooked on it.

This passage delights in its own technique, relaxing into the exaggerations of the Newfoundland vernacular, celebrating while seeming to diminish. Reversal is a characteristic rhetorical device in Guy's prose: "maybe for the sake of variety we shall Undercome," he writes sardonically in *That Far Greater Bay*. "In either case, we will go back and by this means we will have gone ahead." The exaggeration and the paradox leave no doubt about the political message. Recurrently Guy points to the disparities that continue to separate Newfoundland from the rest of Canada.

In 1949, when Joseph Smallwood led Newfoundland into the national union—thus becoming premier of the new province and "the only living Father of Confederation"—Newfoundlanders were not unanimous in their enthusiasm. Suspicion of the "mainland" remains strong. "But You Said We Won," a sketch from Guy's first book, *You May Know Them as Sea Urchins, Ma'am* (1975, revised 1985), is cast as a conversation, circa 1975, with "an older person who passed away in August, 1943." It closes with the older person, puzzled—not so much at the new Newfoundland, as poor as the old, but at the new attitude, which seems to consider life improved—emptily reiterating his surprise at the undefended surrender: "THERE WASN'T NO ONE KILLED?"

The flavor of Guy's work is most readily apparent in his sketches, many of which Eric Norman collected from the *Evening Telegram* columns to shape Guy's first two books, *You May Know Them as Sea Urchins, Ma'am* and *That Far Greater Bay*. In these sketches Guy addresses a variety of local political and social interests, records some personal memoirs, spoofs the literary and political establishments, punctures the aspirations of would-be historical greats, and generally runs verbal rings around pretension, which is what endears him to many readers and enrages a few others. *Beneficial Vapours*, which appeared in 1981, also edited by Norman, collects forty-three additional columns. This group is less disparate in subject though as satiric and whimsical in tone as the earlier sketches. These later columns—as illustrated by "What a Charm, What a Racket"—at once reach nostalgically back to the shared Newfoundland memory of a village ("Outharbour") history and ridicule the ways by which official-

*Cover for the second collection culled from Guy's columns for
the St. John's* Evening Telegram

dom and academia have attempted to categorize
and rearrange reality. Most particularly, Guy rev-
els in using language to expose the presumptuous-
ness of language in many people's mouths. The
result is a sophisticated naiveté, not at all unaware of the conscious mask:

> First thing you could hear in the morn-
> ings was a few woody sort of klunks and
> the punt oars where the fishermen were
> shoving off to their collars.
>
> Then you would hear the splashings
> where they were bailing her out with the pig-
> gin if it had rained the night before, and
> then you would hear a few "pffttttts" from
> the priming cup, a few backfires and then
> "chunk-chunk-chunk" right out through
> the harbour.
>
> Some people say it is "buck-buck-buck-
> buck" but I think that would be more like
> your Atlantic than your average Acadia.

Politicians come in for a hard time from
Guy, especially Joey Smallwood, "the Only Living
Father," "the Only Living Millstone," "the Birthday Boy Himself," "the Skipper." Guy writes that
the House of Commons during the question period is "too gruesome" to contemplate; those in politics are "decent, upright, honest persons whose
mothers always count the silverware after having
them to tea." While a number of the political columns are dated, those that make up "Guy's Encyclopedia of Juvenile Outharbor Delights" are not.
They sometimes appear maudlin in their nostalgia, until Guy offers one of his undercuts to
show that the delights were very often mixed
with real hardships and deprivations. "Winter
and the Outharbor Juvenile" describes the tropical heat of the kitchen with the stove "stoked to
the dampers, red enough to read fine print by,
with an iron kettle and so many iron boilers heav-
ing up steam by the wholesale" that "there you
had the Amazon jungle." This scene is in traumatic contrast to "the frost on the bedroom windows devil-deep. A wonder the flame in the
kerosene lamp didn't freeze." Guy then describes
the dash to the bedroom, after "a drop of
cocoa": "Off up the stairs with your beachrock in
tow. It might sound sissy but it was a matter of survival. A beachrock—or a brick in homes that
could afford one—heated in the oven and put
into two wool socks."

Guy, people-watcher and eavesdropper, has
a keen eye and a good ear. Some of his essays
deal with the meanings of words, the origins of
phrases, the strength that Newfoundlanders have
in their use of strong language. One piece describes poor John Lundrigan, M.P., the recipient
of Pierre Elliott Trudeau's remark in parliament
solemnly recorded in *Hansard* as "Fuddle
duddle." Lundrigan, Guy notes, was forced to accept Trudeau's words in silence, while "there sits
Pierre with a smirk on his face because he delivered himself of a little poo-poo." Newfoundlanders, writes Guy, "have the best coarse language in
North America, perhaps the world. Grade A Number One Choice. Top-notch certified cursers"
Given a chance Lundrigan could have displayed
the strength of this language. "It would take only
one simple sacred, riddlin', dyin', liftin' string of
oaths to wilt Pierre's daisy and dingle his dan-
gling participles."

The range of Guy's topics is immense. He
can be exaggeratedly alarmed by food fads and
possible health hazards or he can relive the horror of an encounter with rats, write about the

weather or about his health. Seemingly any subject can provide him the core of one of his columns. What makes his writing stand out is his verbal dexterity. He creates moods and situations and draws miniature character sketches with economy and skill. Above all Guy is a very funny man.

Reference:

Lisa de Leon, "Ray Guy," in her *Writers of Newfoundland and Labrador* (St. John's: Jesperson Press, 1985), pp. 285-294.

Robert Harlow
(19 November 1923-   )

Peter Buitenhuis
Simon Fraser University

BOOKS: *Royal Murdoch* (Toronto: Macmillan, 1962);

A Gift of Echoes (Toronto: Macmillan, 1965; New York: St. Martin's, 1966);

Scann (Port Clements, British Columbia: Sono Nis, 1972);

Making Arrangements (Toronto: McClelland & Stewart, 1978);

Paul Nolan (Toronto: McClelland & Stewart, 1983);

Felice: A Travelogue (Lantzville, British Columbia: Dolichan Books, 1985).

OTHER: J. Michael Yates, *Man in the Glass Octopus*, introduction by Harlow (Delta, British Columbia: Sono Nis, 1968);

Paul von Baich, *British Columbia,* introduction by Harlow (Toronto: Oxford University Press, 1979).

Robert Harlow is a novelist of British Columbia whose work comprises a significant survey of the province, from small town to big city and from the lives of working men to those of the rich. His most ambitious work to date has been a trilogy about a mythical town in northern British Columbia named Linden. His first three novels make up this trilogy, and the most important of them is the epical *Scann* (1972), which purports to survey the fifty-year history of the town.

There is little doubt that much of the material for this trilogy was derived from Harlow's years in Prince George, British Columbia, where he grew up. He was born in Prince Rupert, but

moved to Prince George in early childhood. His father, Roland Alden Harlow, was a roadmaster on the Canadian National Railway. His mother was Kathleen Isobel Grant Harlow, whose father was moderator of the Presbyterian Church of Canada in 1933. Robert Harlow has been married three times and has three children, Gretchen, Genevieve, and Kathleen.

During a stint in the Royal Canadian Air Force, he saw action in World War II as a bomber pilot and was awarded the Distinguished Flying Cross. He then went to the University of British Columbia, which granted him a B.A. in 1948. He then attended the writers' workshop at the University of Iowa and received an M.F.A. from Iowa in 1950. Harlow has called the writers' workshop "probably the most important postwar experience of my career." He joined the Canadian Broadcasting Corporation in 1951 and served as a public-affairs producer. In 1953 he became station manager of CBU in Vancouver and in 1954 director of radio for the British Columbia region. In 1965 he became head of the creative writing department at the University of British Columbia, the first such department in Canada. He held this position until 1977; since then he has continued to teach at UBC. As one former student put it, Harlow "has helped nearly a generation of prose writers sharpen their technical axes, to go after the literary timber in the CanLit woods."

While Harlow was a producer for CBC, he worked on *Portraits of British Columbia,* a series of

documentaries broadcast in 1952. The project took him to several northern British Columbia locations, including Prince Rupert, Prince George, and Williams Lake. In an interview for a 1975 issue of *Canadian Fiction Magazine* devoted to him, Harlow describes how, on the journey back to the region of his birth, he thought about ways in which he might turn the material to his own use as a writer. It occurred to him that the unifying theme in the history of the first settlers of the region "was the fact that they had white wives in London or Montreal and they had Indian wives out here."

The central fact of his first novel, *Royal Murdoch* (1962), is that the title character, the long-time mayor of Linden, has a white wife in the big house at one end of his ranch and an Indian wife in the cottage at the other end. Royal Murdoch is dying of cancer, and his children

come home to be at his bedside. The story concerns Murdoch's family and Roger, son of the Indian wife by a previous liaison, as they return to their past in the small British Columbia town. The novel is conventional in structure and characterization and has a vigorous story line, which is concluded by Royal's death after he has made his last campaign speech. The next novel in the trilogy, *A Gift of Echoes* (1965), is set in Onion Lake, a mill town a few miles distant from Linden. It is a yarn narrated in retrospect since the mill has burned and what remains is described in the first few pages as "a simple black scar between the railway and the shore." The point of view is that of John Grandy, a teacher who has returned to Onion Lake after drifting in Paris after World War II, searching for some kind of emotional reality. In this novel Harlow, who focuses on metaphysical themes, raises questions that the novel fails to answer, in part because the characters are not sufficiently developed to make their destinies meaningful.

The last novel in the trilogy, *Scann* (1972), is Harlow's longest and best-known book to date. It is also his most experimental and self-reflexive work. The narrator is Amory Scann, the editor of the *Linden Chronicle,* preparing the fiftieth anniversary issue of the paper which celebrates almost the entire history of the town. He has disappeared into a room in the Linden Hotel, telling everybody that he has left town, and sits down to write the narrative that is the novel, which is also an epic of the town, Scann's personal history, and the biography of one of the town's settlers, half-crazy David Thrain. The novel spans four generations and, in recounting Scann's World War II experiences, includes a generous slice of narrative about an incident on an RCAF airfield in England when Scann investigates a charge that an overzealous CO has sacrificed his men needlessly.

There are numerous shifts of time and place in *Scann,* but the time frame of the writing of the narrative is Easter weekend, and the structure is that of the Christian cycle of death and resurrection, although the cycle is ironically reversed, starting with the birth of David Thrain and ending with the death of Mary-Ann, the Indian who was the native wife of Royal Murdoch in the earlier novel. The novel owes a considerable debt to William Faulkner in its use of the Easter cycle, its intense regionalism, its stylistic experiments, and its obsessive characters.

The novel, with its many actions, characters,

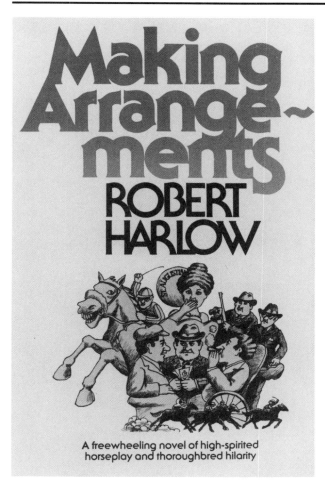

Dust jacket for Harlow's humorous novel about Vancouver race-track regulars who attempt to mastermind an impossible betting coup

hension. Most authors these days seem hardly capable of syntax, much less a sophisticated overview of modern fiction. One gets the impression that Scann reads very little." This smells, as the phrase goes, very much of the lamp.

In his next novel, *Making Arrangements* (1978), Harlow leaves the interior of British Columbia for the coast. *Making Arrangements* is set in the seedier parts of Vancouver, in an ambience not unlike that made familiar by Damon Runyon's *Guys and Dolls* (1931)–the world of the racetrack tout, the pimp, the whore, and the cop. The plot is a complicated one but basically involves a scheme by two of the characters who have been barred from the racetrack for shady practices. Their goal is to raise money to pull off a betting coup, both to reestablish their credit and to get even with the racetrack owner, Carson Noma. Through a series of farcical events the plan goes awry. The narrative is fast-paced and amusing, full of the lore and argot of the track. In form it is a return to a more conventional realism. The narrator, a legless hanger-on, remains constant and dependable.

Paul Nolan (1983) is another departure for Harlow. Its ambience is far removed from that of *Making Arrangements,* as the protagonist lives in an expensive house, with pool and gardens, overlooking the ocean from a hillside in West Vancouver. *Paul Nolan* is a finely written, complexly constructed novel, with frequent time shifts. It is told from the point of view of the eponymous hero, a successful businessman with a beautiful wife, Katherine, two grown children, and a restlessness that drives him to promiscuous sexuality.

As the story unfolds, with flashbacks to his childhood, young manhood, an almost terminal bout with cancer, and other incidents, the reader comes to understand Paul's essential selfishness and exploitative sensuality. Although he is highly aware, intelligent, and energetic, he is at heart shallow, unconnected, and cruel. His life, outwardly rich and complete, is a shambles, and he seems scarcely aware of the hurt and loss he leaves behind him. He even betrays his best friend, a diplomat he has known since they were both students at the University of British Columbia. The novel concludes with a party at Paul's house, arranged by Katherine to show off the work of a young sculptor. The party ends with Katherine, finally pushed beyond her limits, throwing Paul out of the house and telling him never to return.

Paul Nolan is a novel about hedonism, about

and incidents, has a ramshackle air that sometimes baffles the reader. It is held together by the unlovely character of Scann, who is a coward, voyeur, fool, clown, adulterer, adventurer, and truth seeker. The novel deals robustly with sexuality, drunkenness, scandal, murder, and other violence; it is, in short, full of life and vitality, even to excess. At the same time there is a self-consciousness about the narrative that reveals that Harlow has spent much of his time reading and teaching fiction as well as writing it. Commenting on the novel which Scann is writing, an editorial voice states late in the novel: "The whole story is in jeopardy, as is the novella form itself, the very form he is here trying to master. . . . How our poor authors can embark on the perilous seas of genre and sub-genre without once cocking an eye at the British and American weathermen-critics who have gone before and charted the voyage properly, is beyond compre-

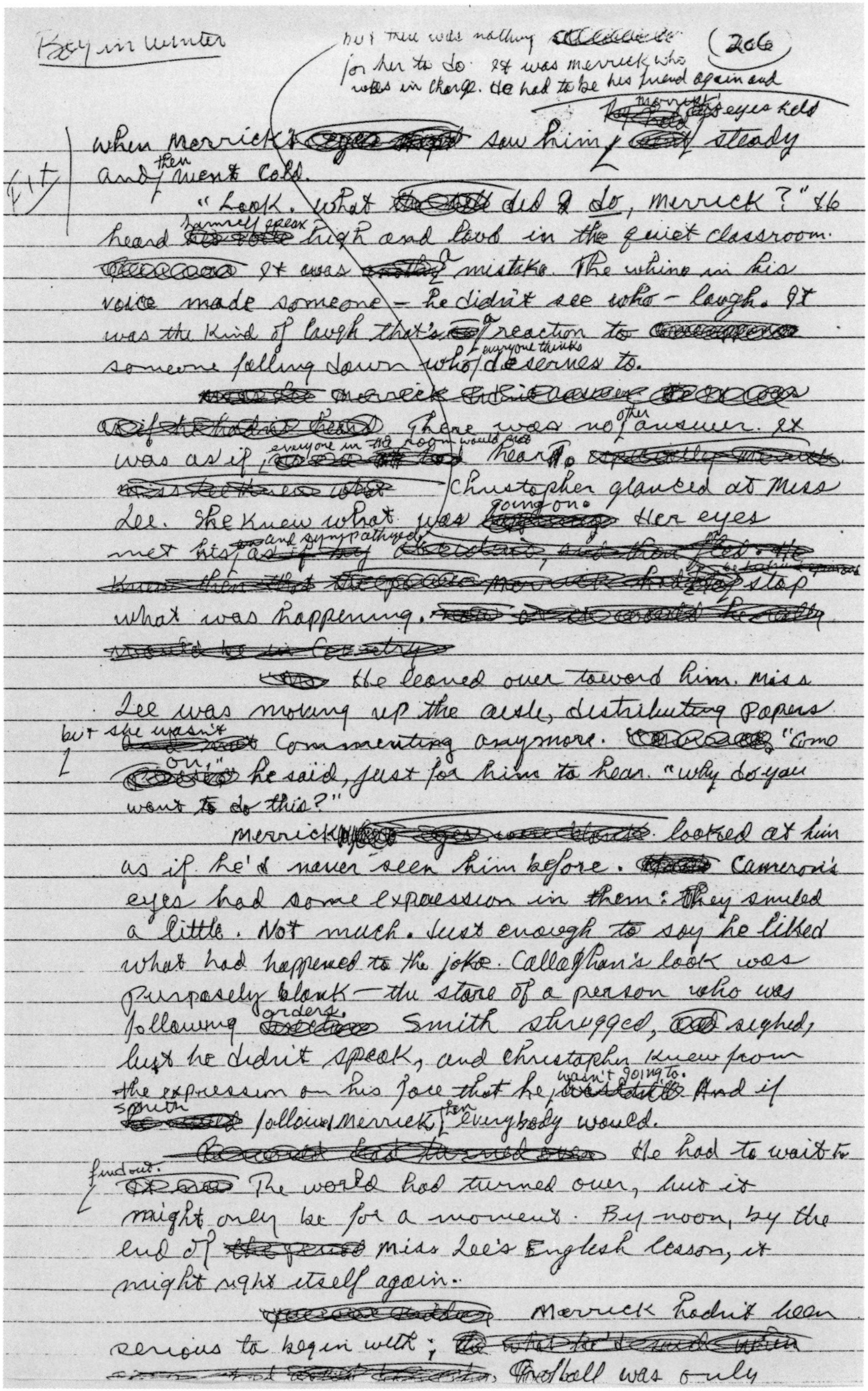

Boy in Winter

(206)

but there was nothing for her to do. It was merrick who was in charge. He had to be his friend again and

when merrick saw him, his eyes held steady and then went cold.

"Look. What did I do, merrick?" He heard himself speak high and loud in the quiet classroom. It was a mistake. The whine in his voice made someone — he didn't see who — laugh. It was the kind of laugh that's a reaction to someone falling down who everyone thinks deserves to.

There was no other answer. It was as if everyone in the room would first hear

Christopher glanced at Miss Lee. She knew what was going on. Her eyes met his as if they and sympathized stop what was happening.

He leaned over toward him. Miss Lee was moving up the aisle, distributing papers but she wasn't commenting anymore. "Come on," he said, just for him to hear. "Why do you want to do this?"

Merrick looked at him as if he'd never seen him before. Cameron's eyes had some expression in them: they smiled a little. Not much. Just enough to say he liked what had happened to the joke. Callaghan's look was purposely blank — the stare of a person who was following orders. Smith shrugged, sighed, but he didn't speak, and Christopher knew from the expression on his face that he wasn't going to. And if smith followed Merrick, then everybody would.

He had to wait to find out. The world had turned over, but it might only be for a moment. By noon, by the end of miss Lee's English lesson, it might right itself again.

Merrick hadn't been serious to begin with; football was only

Page from the manuscript for a forthcoming novel (by permission of the author)

entering middle age, about outward success and inner failure. It is a deeply felt work, whose authenticity is strengthened by the skillfully depicted landscapes of Vancouver and West Vancouver.

Harlow's 1985 novel, *Felice: A Travelogue*, begins and ends in Vancouver but is mostly set in contemporary Poland. Felice, the wife of a prosperous dentist, is recovering from a major cancer operation when the novel opens, and her husband suggests that they take a trip through Europe, beginning in Poland, where they can stay with an old friend who is now in the Canadian diplomatic service in Warsaw.

It is the Poland of the communist dictatorship and of Lech Walesa. The diplomat takes them to Auschwitz where Felice encounters a strange, intense woman whom she had met on the ship coming over. The woman had been a prisoner in the camp, survived by becoming a mistress to one of the guards, and later married him and immigrated to Canada. In talking with Felice she forces her to experience the horror of Auschwitz. Then, without warning, she stabs herself, falls on Felice, and dies. Immediately before encountering Felice, she had stabbed her husband in one of the camp huts.

Felice, who cannot shake the image of the camp and the murder-suicide from her mind, goes to the city of Warsaw by herself, is followed by the secret police and arrested, questioned, and beaten before being released. She is in such a state of shock that when she returns to Vancouver with her husband, she cannot return to her former safe bourgeois life. She knows too much about the modern world—a world of violence, totalitarianism, and fear.

Felice: A Travelogue is a complex, moving, and powerful novel about Poland's past and present history, about oppression and brutalization, and about the place of women in contemporary Canadian culture. It is Harlow's most impressive novel to date.

Robert Harlow's works are hard to classify. Each novel has marked a new departure; he is a risk taker, and some of the risks have paid off better than others. It is difficult to understand, however, why this novelist, who has ventured into so many areas of experience and who has written so well, has generated little critical attention. As *Paul Nolan* and *Felice* show, his work continues to grow in power and perception.

References:

Canadian Fiction Magazine, Special Robert Harlow issue, 19 (Autumn 1975);

John Harris, "Arrangements Unmade," *Journal of Canadian Fiction*, no. 31-32 (1981): 248-251;

John Moss, "Violence and the Moral Vision," in his *Sex and Violence in the Canadian Novel: The Ancestral Present* (Toronto: McClelland & Stewart, 1977), pp. 232-254.

David Helwig

(5 April 1938-   )

Tom Marshall
Queen's University

BOOKS: *Figures in a Landscape* (Ottawa: Oberon, 1967);

The Sign of the Gunman (Ottawa: Oberon, 1969);

The Streets of Summer (Ottawa: Oberon, 1969);

The Day Before Tomorrow (Ottawa: Oberon, 1971); republished as *Message from a Spy* (Don Mills, Ontario: Paperjacks, 1975);

The Best Name of Silence (Ottawa: Oberon, 1972);

A Book about Billie, by Billie Miller as told to Helwig (Ottawa: Oberon, 1972);

Atlantic Crossings (Ottawa: Oberon, 1974);

The Glass Knight (Ottawa: Oberon, 1976);

Jennifer (Ottawa: Oberon, 1979; New York: Beaufort Books, 1983);

A Book of the Hours (Ottawa: Oberon, 1979);

The King's Evil (Ottawa: Oberon, 1981; New York: Beaufort Books, 1984);

It Is Always Summer (Toronto: Stoddart, 1982; New York: Beaufort Books, 1982);

The Rain Falls Like Rain (Ottawa: Oberon, 1982);

A Sound Like Laughter (Toronto: Stoddart, 1983; New York: Beaufort Books, 1983);

Catchpenny Poems (Ottawa: Oberon, 1983);

The Only Son (Toronto: Stoddart, 1984; New York: Beaufort Books, 1984);

The Bishop (Markham, Ontario, New York & London: Penguin, 1986).

OTHER: *Fourteen Stories High*, edited by Helwig and Tom Marshall (Ottawa: Oberon, 1967);

New Canadian Stories, annual volumes, edited by Helwig and Joan Harcourt (Ottawa: Oberon, 1972-1975);

The Human Elements: Critical Essays, first and second series, edited by Helwig (Ottawa: Oberon, 1978, 1981);

Love and Money, edited by Helwig (Ottawa: Oberon, 1980);

Coming Attractions, annual volumes, edited by Helwig and Martin (Ottawa: Oberon, 1983-1985);

Best Canadian Stories, annual volumes, edited by Helwig and Sandra Martin (Ottawa: Oberon, 1983-1986).

Poet and novelist David Helwig is a notable member of the generation of talented and prolific writers who came to prominence in Canada in the 1960s and 1970s. Like his more famous fellow graduate of the University of Toronto, Margaret Atwood, he has turned his hand to various kinds of writing: poems, short stories, plays, novels, radio and television scripts, reviews, and even an unpublished libretto for an opera. If some of his books are more successful and memorable than others, all are well crafted.

An only child, Helwig was born in Toronto

and lived in Hamilton for a time before his parents, William Gordon and Ivy Lorraine Abbott Helwig, settled at Niagara-on-the-Lake in 1948. For generations many of his father's family were German cabinetmakers; his mother's were English paperhangers and painters. His father worked at the De Havilland aircraft plant and then made office furniture until he opened an antique business at Niagara. Helwig attended the University of Toronto (B.A., 1960) at the same time as fellow writers Margaret Atwood, Dennis Lee, Henry Beissel, David Lewis Stein, and John Robert Colombo; in 1959 he married Nancy Keeling. In 1962 he completed an M.A. at the University of Liverpool. Here his daughter Maggie, now a published poet, was born in 1961; a second daughter, Kate, was born in Kingston, Ontario, in 1964.

From 1962 to 1974 Helwig worked as a professor of English at Queen's University. He was also, with Michael Ondaatje, Tom Marshall, and Douglas Barbour, one of the editors of the magazine *Quarry*. He is a determined and energetic person, always inventing new projects, some of which turn into books. Possessed of a powerful bass voice (though he is not a large person), he sings with the Pro Arte Singers of Kingston.

In the 1960s Helwig's poems and stories were widely published in Canadian periodicals. His first book, *Figures in a Landscape* (1967), which included poems and plays, the most substantial of which is *The Coming of Winter,* produced in 1967 and featuring his wife Nancy in a leading role. This volume received generally enthusiastic reviews, as did the short-story collection *The Streets of Summer* (1969) and his first novel, *The Day Before Tomorrow* (1971). All of his books have been concerned with the joys and woes of domestic life, the loneliness of the individual and the difficulties of human relationship, but the most impressive work has a political and historical dimension as well.

Outstanding among Helwig's stories is the novella "The Streets of Summer." It concerns a love triangle: the sober graduate student John, who wants to learn how to be truly young; the emotionally wounded Sonya, who needs to feel that every man loves her though she cannot love in return; the despairing suicidal actor Matt. Each character is shaped by the horror of much contemporary history.

The Day Before Tomorrow is a less successful attempt to deal with social and political themes. Two brothers, one a diplomat turned spy and the

Cover for Helwig's first book, a collection of poems and plays published in 1967

other a student activist, are the focus for an extended consideration of what kind of political action might prove meaningful. The exploration of the character of the disturbed spy is the most successful and interesting aspect of the novel.

Helwig's finest poem is the four-part *Atlantic Crossings* (1974), which concerns four voyagers to the new world: those of St. Brendan, a slave trader, Christopher Columbus, and the Norse. The first three parts examine the religious and the commercial imperialism that were epitomized by Columbus. The fourth part of this poetic symphony has a female narrator, a Norsewoman who espouses a saner life of communion with the ever self-renewing land. The poem contains some of Helwig's most vividly effective writing.

From 1974 to 1976 Helwig worked for director John Hirsch as literary manager of the Cana-

*

Henry waited impatiently for night, when they would leave him alone in the darkness. They thought there something ominous, something dangerous about leaving him in the night, but he frightened of nothing. Everything that could frighten him already happened long ago.

Rose come to say goodbye to him before she home. Her squat, powerful figure a pleasure to him; he have the illusion, that many have that she cold in control; he understand how easily touched she she in love with him, in some distant, harmless way, and Henry not discourage. Love came in many forms and he had learned how few of these should be avoided. He took no pride in her feeling. It sprang from no virtue in him, and it was impersonal, really, power exercising itself because he close and tried to encourage love of all sorts. Rose had never told him her story, and yet he knew somehow that there one, a left hanging, a half-tragedy, something uncompleted that would never find a terrestrial resolution, like a melody that has been interrupted on a an echo of always there. Dear Rose. He would never know her story now unless the dead allowed such secrets; but it hardly mattered. He could hear the echo in her voice. There something in the touch of her hands that told him all he need to know. In her impatience. The Bible box she rushed to make over a weekend, in a wood she didn't like, because she had some urgent loving need to have it completed and in his hand. When love gripped her, she was shaken too deeply to have any control. Dear Rose, he would say to her if he had a voice, I have loved you very much for the gusty weather of your attack on the world.

Page from the revised typescript for Helwig's most recent novel, The Bishop, *about a religious man's review of his life from his deathbed*

116

dian Broadcasting Corporation's television-drama department; he was also story editor for the crime series *Sidestreet*. From 1976 to 1980, when he resigned his academic post, he taught part-time at Queen's. In these years he produced another volume of poems, *A Book of the Hours* (1979), and the first two novels of a quartet, *The Glass Knight* (1976) and *Jennifer* (1979).

The Glass Knight is narrow in scope but effective; it provides a close-up view of the intense but mutually destructive love affair of a fortyish man and a neurotic young girl. *Jennifer* is a searching examination of the life of a socially concerned Canadian woman in the 1960s and 1970s. *A Sound Like Laughter* (1983), Helwig's first comic work, and the more lyrical *It Is Always Summer* (1982), which are meant to be read in this order, complete the quartet of interrelated "Kingston novels" and greatly broaden its scope. Taken together, the four novels, with their overlapping stories and shared cast of characters, provide an impressive panorama of contemporary life in this unique eastern Ontario city. Indeed, the Kingston quartet is Helwig's most substantial achievement in fiction to date. It employs a symbolic pattern of the four seasons and the four elements—fire, water, earth, and air—to suggest what Diana Brydon has called "the spiritual weather" of this time and place.

Two other novels, *The King's Evil* (1981), a bizarre excursion into madness and vision, and *The*

Only Son (1984), a sober study of class divisions and their destructive effect on a sensitive man's life, display Helwig's versatility. His selected poems, *The Rain Falls Like Rain* (1982), has confirmed his achievement as a poet. A further sequence, *Catchpenny Poems* (1983), won the CBC's literary prize for that year.

Helwig's latest novel, *The Bishop* (1986), was published internationally by Penguin. This vivid and intense account of a religious man's reliving his experience as he lies dying will perhaps win the author a larger readership, though his work is already widely respected by readers and critics. A steady and prolific writer, he is at his best when portraying individuals within a social-historical context.

References:

Diana Brydon, "David Helwig's Kingston Novels: This Random Dance of Atoms," in *Present Tense*, edited by John Moss (Toronto: NC Press, 1985), pp. 112-121;

D. G. Jones, "David Helwig's New Timber: Notes on The Best Name of Silence," *Queen's Quarterly*, 81, no. 2 (1974): 202-214;

Tom Marshall, *Harsh and Lovely Land* (Vancouver: University of British Columbia Press, 1979), pp. 162-170;

Jon Pearce, ed., *Twelve Voices: Interviews with Canadian Poets* (Ottawa: Borealis, 1981), pp. 25-41.

Daryl Hine
(24 February 1936-   )

Laurie Ricou
University of British Columbia

SELECTED BOOKS: *Five Poems* (Toronto: Emblem Books, 1955);

The Carnal and the Crane (Toronto: Contact, 1957);

The Devil's Picture Book (London & New York: Abelard-Schuman, 1961);

The Prince of Darkness & Co. (London & New York: Abelard-Schuman, 1961);

Polish Subtitles: Impressions from a Journey (London & New York: Abelard-Schuman, 1962);

The Wooden Horse (New York: Atheneum, 1965);

Minutes (New York: Atheneum, 1968);

In and Out (Chicago: Privately printed, 1975);

Resident Alien (New York: Atheneum, 1975);

Daylight Saving (New York: Atheneum, 1978);

Selected Poems (Toronto: Oxford University Press, 1980; New York: Atheneum, 1981);

Academic Festival Overtures (New York: Atheneum, 1985).

OTHER: *The Homeric Hymns and The Battle of the Frogs and the Mice*, translated by Hine (New York: Atheneum, 1972);

The Poetry Anthology 1912-1977: Sixty-five Years of America's Most Distinguished Verse Magazine, edited by Hine and Joseph Parisi (Boston: Houghton Mifflin, 1978);

Theocritus: Idylls and Epigrams, translated with an introduction and epilogue by Hine (New York: Atheneum, 1982).

When "a bee for beauty boomed behind the grove" in Daryl Hine's first small book of poems, it might have been buzzing with the poet's own enthusiasm. Certainly Hine is the most elegant artificer among contemporary Canadian poets, yet most readers and critics find the beauty booms so loudly that they can detect little experience or meaning beyond. So Hine has remained in Canada, if not largely in his adopted United States, a poet treated with awe but with little interest.

Hine, the son of Robert Fraser and Elsie James Hine, was born in 1936 in New Westminster, British Columbia. His early life is remembered in *In and Out* (1975), a privately printed confessional novel in verse, as friendless and boring–until he discovered Latin. His most recent book, *Academic Festival Overtures* (1985), expands on this earlier autobiographical work, seeming to fuse the intimate detail of Proust's *A la recherche du temps perdu* with the metrical meditations of Wordsworth's *Prelude* in a twelve-part anti-epic account of Hine's British Columbia youth and especially of the experiences and discoveries of his thirteenth year.

At age eighteen Hine had *Five Poems* (1955) published and began to study at McGill. Before he graduated with a B.A. in classics in 1958, *The Carnal and the Crane* (1957) had appeared in the McGill Poetry Series, edited by Louis Dudek. The book is dedicated to Jay Macpherson, a poet whose austere technical brilliance and mythic echoes he shares. Northrop Frye discussed the mythic allusions of *The Carnal and the Crane* in a 1957 issue of *University of Toronto Quarterly*, noting the "inequalities" of Hine's expression but forecasting much: "I doubt if any Canadian poet has potentially greater talents than Mr. Hine."

After graduation Hine spent four years in Europe, living mainly in France. During a short trip to Poland in the fall of 1961 Hine worked editing English subtitles for a Polish film. His impressions, recorded in the punningly named *Polish Subtitles* (1962), are memorable for the slightly acerbic generalizations: "Poland is adorned by the jewels that she does not wear." "Places have this power," Hine writes near the end of the book, "more than persons or events, to focus our feelings and nebulous thoughts; it is a property of places to be haunted."

The poems of this period, published in *The Devil's Picture Book* (1961), are, however, strikingly and peculiarly placeless. There is neither identifiable location, nor person, nor event: "harmonious ambiguities in a swarm / burrow at the fulcrum of his speech." There is a slight loosening to simpler forms here and there–the repetitions in "The Black Swan," the short stanzas in "Under the Hill"–yet intricate rhyme and dense al-

Daryl Hine

lusiveness rule. Clever allusiveness also rules in Hine's solitary novel, *The Prince of Darkness & Co.* (1961); "the novel he wrote about Robert Graves," Richard Howard complains in *Alone with America* (1980), "cuts much too close to biography to be satire, and the whine of harpies' wings drowns out the laughs." It is a very talky, cerebral novel in which Hine, characteristically, often seems—in the charm of Phillip Sparrow's "spiritual obliquity" or in the aphorism "symmetry was the innermost secret of his art"—to be wittily describing himself.

In 1962 Hine returned to the United States and worked briefly in New York as a free-lance poetry editor. Soon he moved to the University of Chicago where he studied for an M.A. (1965) and Ph.D. (1967) in comparative literature (his doctoral dissertation was on the Latin poetry of George Buchanan, the sixteenth-century Scottish humanist). He became editor of the prestigious *Poetry* in 1968 and continued there for a decade.

The return to North America and his subsequent teaching at several universities (principally the University of Chicago) coincide with a further, slight relaxing of Hine's commitment to pre-Romantic poetic forms. *The Wooden Horse* (1965) combines the tours de force of wit and prosody with an anecdotal note. The blend is particularly evident in "Plain Fare," whose narrative, described in a subtitle as "Night thoughts on crossing the continent by bus," is occasionally almost documentary: "Sometime before dawn another stop, for breakfast– / Country ham / And eggs."

Minutes (1968) continues the trend with travelogue poems that seemed absent from his earlier works. The fascinating poem "Terminal Conversation" clearly roots its metaphysical speculations in identifiable experience "in a great railway station /after midnight." Several of these poems–"Lovers of the River," "Among Islands," "Point Grey,"–return for their setting to the Canadian west coast where Hine was born.

The title of Hine's next collection of poems, *Resident Alien* (1975), which so cleverly summarizes the poet's stance and reputation, comes from the almost chatty "A B.C. Diary," an occasional poem in rhymed couplets written for a friend's wedding. "Later," he notes wryly, "confronted by the paradox of free / verse, I trade my meaning for a rhyme." Whatever the loosening of Hine's verse in the 1970s (and in *Resident Alien* his linguistic play is much more likely to begin with the poetry of the cliché and the colloquial), the witty formalist remains in the foreground, rhyme before meaning. "Hine's stylistic predicament in the world of poetry," noted Barry Cameron in a 1976 review for *Canadian Literature*, "is also one of being a resident alien. . . . His need to distance life through his art . . . is even more urgent here than in the earlier poems."

In *Daylight Saving* (1978) the erudition is again more balanced by the commonplace. But, as John Fuller, reviewing this volume for the *Times Literary Supplement*, shrewdly observed, "his commonest device is to bring the world of the senses and the world of grammar into metaphorical conjunction." This typical device puts the emphasis on relationships among words rather than on feelings; the reader is likely to shelve the poems under esoterica. Hine himself provides one persuasive context for modifying this classification in *Theocritus: Idylls and Epigrams* (1982), which, in addition to the entertaining combination of gossipy tone and sensory extravagance in the poet's translations, provides in the introduc-

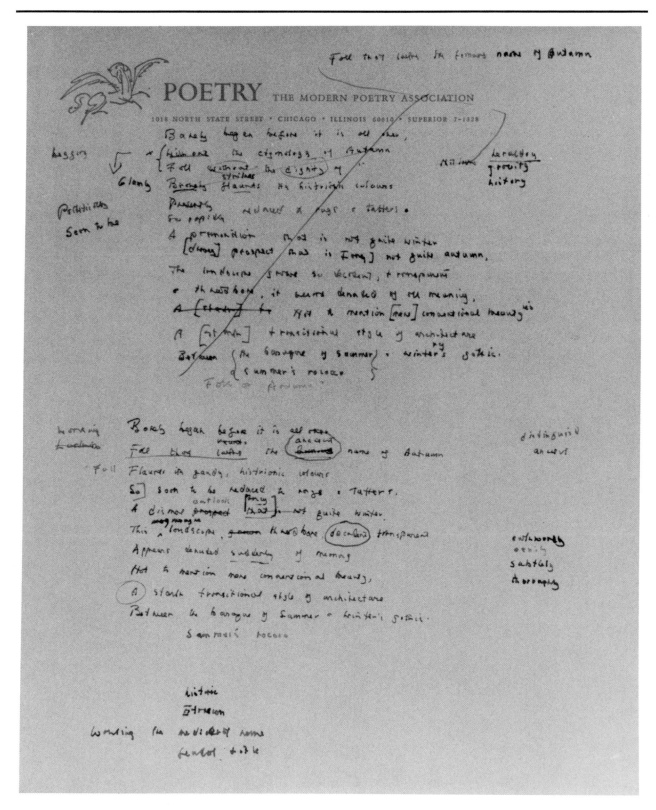

Draft—"far from final," in Hine's words—for a recent poem (by permission of the author)

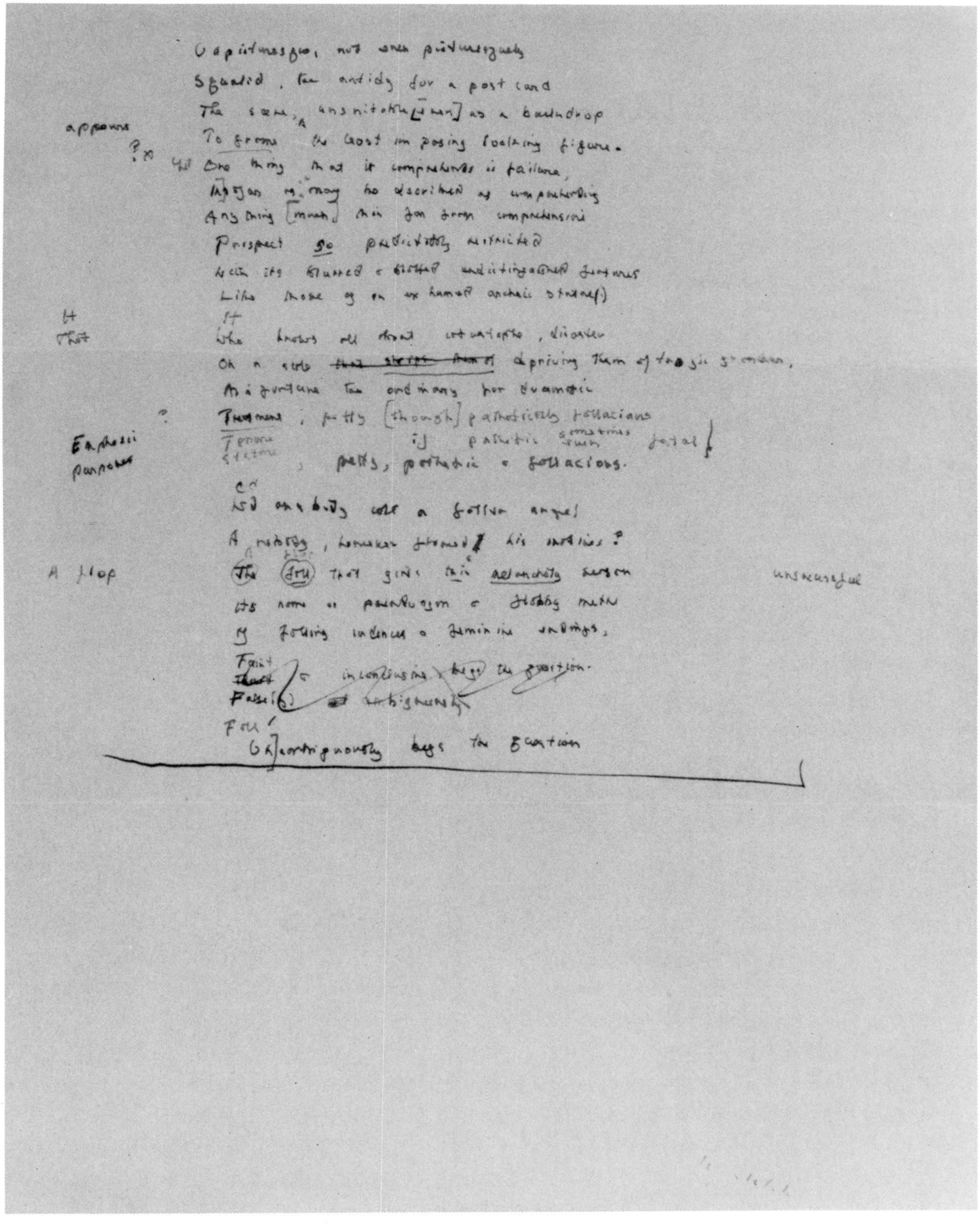

tion and in the long letter to Theocritus which is the book's epilogue an extended apologia for his own poetics. Hine makes an eloquent case for "the first academic poet," whose strengths are "a curious and not always decorous erudition; ostentatious verbal ingenuity . . . ; a certain detachment or dryness of tone . . . ; a fondness . . . for the gnomic or sententious statement of which the poem is the ostensible if ironic illustration; shameless artifice . . . ; and more than a craftsman's interest in form."

Hine's Theocritus, however, is not widely read. Evidently only a massive change in taste, for which Hine's own *Selected Poems* (1980) makes one of the few audible arguments, would make Hine other than a resident alien among Canadian poets. George Woodcock's remark in a 1981 review of *Selected Poems* for *Saturday Night* is to the point: "For any reader not professionally concerned with the craft of verse, Hine's manner will always seem too detached, his vision of existence too rarefied, and his forms and diction too conservative. Yet no poet can read him and recognize his consummate skill without admiration and even a little envy."

Reference:

Richard Howard, "Daryl Hine," in his *Alone with America: Essays on the Art of Poetry in the United States Since 1950* (New York: Atheneum, 1980), pp. 209-221.

Jack Hodgins

(3 October 1938-   )

David L. Jeffrey
University of Ottawa

BOOKS: *Spit Delaney's Island: Selected Stories* (Toronto: Macmillan, 1976);

The Invention of the World: A Novel (Toronto: Macmillan, 1977; New York: Harcourt, Brace, Jovanovich, 1978);

The Resurrection of Joseph Bourne (Toronto: Macmillan, 1979);

The Barclay Family Theatre (Toronto: Macmillan, 1981);

Beginnings—Samplings from a Long Apprenticeship: Novels Which Were Imagined, Written, Rewritten, and Then Submitted and Rejected, Abandoned, and Supplanted (Toronto: Grand Union Press, 1983);

The Honorary Patron (Toronto: McClelland & Stewart, 1987).

OTHER: *Voice and Vision*, edited by Hodgins and W. H. New (Toronto: McClelland & Stewart, 1972);

The Frontier Experience, edited by Hodgins (Toronto: Macmillan, 1975);

The West Coast Experience (Toronto: Macmillan, 1976);

Teaching Short Fiction, edited by Hodgins and Bruce Nesbitt (Vancouver: Commcept, 1977).

Jack Hodgins is one of the most important talents to emerge in English-Canadian fiction in the decade of the 1970s. Especially since his receiving a Governor General's Award for *The Resurrection of Joseph Bourne* in 1980, his work has been accorded significant national and international acclaim. In laudatory reviews Hodgins has been regularly, if perhaps somewhat inaccurately, described as a practitioner of "magic realism" and considered a Canadian counterpart to Gabriel García Márquez.

Hodgins was born to Stanley Hodgins, a logger, and Reta Blakely Hodgins on a small landholding in the Comox Valley of Vancouver Island. Since his marriage in 1960, he, his wife Diane Child Hodgins, and their three children have lived for the most part in or near the Vancou-

Jack Hodgins (photograph by Elaine Briere)

ver Island logging community of Nanaimo, where, from 1961 to 1979, he was a high-school teacher. After two years as writer in residence at the University of Ottawa, he returned to the West Coast; he now lives in Victoria and teaches creative writing at the University of Victoria.

He wrote his first story, a murder mystery, as a boy of about nine and persuaded a babysitter to type it for him. When she had finished, he took the pages and sewed them into a book. In the late 1950s, he left Vancouver Island to pursue a degree in English literature and education at the University of British Columbia, which awarded him a B. Ed., in 1961. At UBC he studied creative writing under poet and Chaucerian scholar Earle Birney, who encouraged him to continue his writing. Nevertheless, it was not until Hodgins had endured eight discouraging years of rejection slips that he sold his first short story, "Every Day of His Life," published in the *Northwest Review* in February 1968.

Hodgins has spoken candidly of the modern authors who have interested him. From his university years he cites William Faulkner, John

Steinbeck, and Joseph Conrad (he claims to read *Lord Jim* each year); from the 1960s he adds Flannery O'Connor, Margaret Laurence, and Malcolm Lowry; from the early 1970s, he names Frank O'Connor (whom Hodgins "discovered" while traveling in Ireland in 1973), John Gardiner, Wright Morris, and John Fowles; his most recent favorites include García Márquez, Jorge Amado, John Nichols, and, among Canadian writers, Robert Kroetsch and Rudy Wiebe. From this special convocation (underwritten by Hodgins's affection for earlier British authors Chaucer, Swift, and Fielding) certain patterns of interest emerge.

Because the center of Hodgins's geographical world is his native Vancouver Island and because the grotesque extravagance of his characters seems tied to that place, it is tempting to treat Hodgins as a regional writer. But, like other Canadian writers of his generation (Wiebe, Kroetsch, Marie-Claire Blais, Roch Carrier) Hodgins might better be called a subcultural writer. While the regional writer's work makes of his locale a microcosm of the world at large, the subcultural writer expresses, in addition, his community's prepossessing sense of contest with the outside world and strives to articulate, as the adolescent heroine of Hodgins's *The Invention of the World* puts it, their essential "difference." The motive of the subcultural writer has been shaped by the wider struggle around him for differentiation.

If Hodgins is more accessible than many Canadian subcultural writers, it is partly because of the particular subcultural proclamation he makes; the Vancouver Island he portrays is an extravagant paradigm, a sort of historical cartoon by which a much wider contemporary psychosis may be dramatized. The Island as Hodgins depicts it is not so much a state of nature or of civilization as it is a modern and especially North American state of mind. It is a kind of reserve of lost causes, misty nostalgia for Europe thoroughly mixed up with innumerable backyard versions of the American dream; it is a place where history seems condensed and motives and patterns are made more visible by the force of particular extremes. What Hodgins writes about is the Island Mind itself, its bizarre dreams, its truncated perspectives on the world, its frenetic ambivalence about history, its flight from the world, and, above all, its unending pursuit of the private mythology. But what he mirrors is the frustrated questioning of a whole frontierless continent now increasingly turned in upon itself and unable to discern where mythology stops and "reality" begins. "Where is the dividing line?," asks Spit Delaney, the "separated" man in *Spit Delaney's Island* (1976), Hodgins's first volume of stories, when he is suddenly forced to experience his separateness without discovering its meaning.

As far west as the traveler can go, on the last beach, Delaney stands in confusion, and Hodgins's readers with him. For the real division is within, the boundary reached not the real border at all; separation occurs as often as not because one is standing on the line itself, unable to cross over, to recover the meaning of history or interpret life. Like other characters in an apocalyptic age, Hodgins's personalities look for a conclusion they can believe in, some dream which can put time and the world back together. Unable to find what they seek outside themselves, many of them, each in his or her peculiar way, are driven to invent private worlds, islands, islands within islands, islands in the mind.

The real problem for Hodgins's characters is reality in the larger sense; it is not in the singularity of the self, but in the mutuality of personal realities that this theme is forged. The line between reality and mythology is, he argues, impossible to determine from within a solipsism. If one could construe it in a more complete and yet practical way, as that same line between Self and Other, then, he suggests, certain "real" frontiers might perhaps be recognized and mutually crossed.

In "Three Women of the Country," from *Spit Delaney's Island,* one of Hodgins's observer-characters exclaims of a neighbor woman careening toward her in panicked distress, "My God, if you could only see yourself." Hodgins portrays voyeuristic moderns who see little of what they look at. In his stories the initiation to adult life is not, for example, the cliché of sexual initiation, but rather an initiation into interpersonal reality, into awareness and understanding of another's point of view.

Hodgins's sense of the "real" reveals the continuing impact of his early intensive reading of Plato and, in the early 1960s, of Mary Baker Eddy. If he himself avoids the precise formulation of his Mr. Porter in "Three Women of the Country"–that "every human being is a spiritually perfect idea" reflecting the image of God–or of the similar teaching of Webster Traherne's Old Man in "At the Foot of the Hill, Birdie's School," he translates the general precept, protesting that to realize the self one must first love creation, love others. The trip to Eden (or Vancouver Is-

Dust jacket for Hodgins's 1981 story collection featuring the seven Barclay sisters, characters introduced in his first book, Spit Delaney's Island

land) is not likely, otherwise, ever to be quite the voyage of discovery the pilgrim has in mind.

Hodgins's novel *The Invention of the World* (1977) makes this central point dramatically. Though *The Invention of the World* is a novel, it is developed almost as if it were a collection of short stories. What makes the novel formally different from *Spit Delaney's Island* is the degree to which, to apply Hodgins's term, the stories "overlap" to portray the "reality" of a single community. The novel has no single narrator; instead the action is filtered through the worlds of several minor as well as major characters. The plurality of voices and perspectives is, in fact, a deliberate statement from Hodgins about the nature of a larger community of experience, its communicability, and the possibility of any comprehensive overview. The most important characteristic of a subcultural novel, Hodgins has said, is that it can be communal, a voice for community.

In *The Invention of the World* the foreground

story is a quixotic romance between Maggie, a kind of logging-camp mamma, and Wade, a jaded tourist-trapper who has built a phony "historical" fort. The background story of Donal Keneally and his Revelations Colony of Truth relates to the history of Vancouver Island (as did the short stories in *Spit Delaney's Island*), recalling Brother Twelve, "Canada's False Prophet" as his biographer called him, a crackpot religious colonist who claimed to be waiting for the end of the world with his band of willing slaves on Valdes Island, killing or copulating as he chose among his "subjects." In *The Invention of the World* the mythic roots of Vancouver Island are traced to Keneally, an Irish grotesque who is rumored to have been fathered on an idiot girl by a great black bull. The Taurus-Europa myth takes a new shape and is but the beginning of a comparably bizarre "fallen" history. The offspring comes to Vancouver Island, conquers everything from loggers to the wife of the mayor of Victoria, leaves the city in a shambles, and then goes back to Ireland to hypnotize his whole village into following him to the promised Eden. On his way, he swindles his disciples out of money and personal integrity alike, and, through their subjection, builds his own island kingdom. Though larger-than-life, Keneally is a manically successful *ubermensch* who preaches that the only reality is material and the only god the man who can master it, namely himself. He is a "god-man," an incarnation of material egocentrism so perverse as to horrify.

It is Hodgins's point that between the manic and the much more plausible egocentrism of his more mundane characters—even Spit Delaney—there is only the thinnest and most confusing of distinctions, that between manipulative advocacy and unacknowledged reflex. Both create "island history"; each pursues a private mythology; each is a manifestation of the island mind. All face, therefore, the same peril and have the same need for crossing the "reality line," for making choices which involve communal values.

Hodgins shows subculture that cannot do without religious phenomena, whether of the Brother Twelve sort, or, as Keneally's last wife puts it, "some sort of magic," the electrical gadget, the Second Coming, a world government that would solve everything, science, medicine, sensitivity training—whatever faith or antifaith structure might be imagined. What animates all of these options for Hodgins's characters is that they offer some sense of personal control, some defense against confusing, insecure times.

Among his books, *The Invention of the World* particularly bears the stamp of literature written for an apocalyptic age and culture, one which is afraid that the end might well come upon it before there can be any real sense of personal conclusion. Hodgins's novel records, therefore, the yearning for a sense of story with conclusive personal meaning and defense of that meaning, no matter how elaborate that protection might be. It records also the desire to flee history, the script already written, and to become the author of one's own mythology, to escape creation for invention.

In Hodgins's view, however, nobody ever really invents a successful private mythology, and nobody owns the "real" story—not even his own. What is the real story? Where is it written? Where can it be read? These are questions with which Hodgins prods his readers at every step in *The Invention of the World*. Becker, the tape recording documentary narrator, explicitly disclaims possession. Yet he offers hints concerning the relationship between story and life, creation and creativity. Picking up a Bible, Becker reflects on Creation: "A strange story, he said, if you'd read it. It has two beginnings. The first, a single chapter, would have us all made in the image of God, perfect spiritual creatures. Then someone else came along, started it all over again, and had us all made out of clay. The rest of the story shows a lot of people trying to get back to that first beginning, back before the mist and the clay. You get all the way up to nearly the end of the book before you meet the man who knows how to manage it."

Hodgins's third book, *The Resurrection of Joseph Bourne* (1979), like his earlier work, occupies psychological territory between ironic extremes—the tranquil island seascape of the novel's setting, Port Annie, and the Hogarthian richness and Swiftean proportions of the action that takes place there. In a variety of ways *The Resurrection of Joseph Bourne* bears overtly the imprint of eighteenth-century style.

To begin with, Hodgins models chapter titles, rubrics, and much in his narrative style on eighteenth-century fiction. The book is divided into three large "chapters" or sections. The last and key phrase of the first elaborate section title is "The Ragged Green Edge of the World," suggesting, in the context of Hodgins's first novel, man's fallen Eden and also Hodgins's "dividing line," both a perilous habitation and perhaps a point of prospect. The prospect is announced in key phrases of the other two chapter titles: "The

Old Man and His Deeds" and "The New Man." The vocabulary is biblical (St. Paul) and Christian, and Hodgins's rendition of his themes is evocative of the themes of eighteenth-century novels such as *Tom Jones* and *Joseph Andrews*, no less in matter than in mode of presentation. *The Resurrection of Joseph Bourne* portrays a contest between charity and cupidity, inviting a pursuit of love which could lead to understanding, cartooning some pitfalls along the way, and warning of the distractions and distortions of affectation. (As with Fielding, the affectations of Hodgins's characters usually proceed from vanity or hypocrisy, and are the source of the "truly ridiculous" in Hodgins's aesthetic.)

When a stunningly beautiful sea nymph (always suggestively, never explicitly described) is washed up miraculously onto the grubby streets of Port Annie, her presence as she walks through the town provokes a litter of responses and interpretations which tell the reader far more about the observers than the observed. The lady herself remains ineffable, a mystery. Hodgins's other characters are extravagant, but for the most part imaginable up-islanders. Moreover, their particular manifestations of general cultural narcissism create, even in a Hogarthian overdrawing, paradigms for a much wider experience of life. The sea nymph, the first mysterious stranger who comes to the island town, is a catalyst, the embodiment of a force which can best be understood in terms of what happens to those who encounter her beauty. Principally, the residents of Port Annie are induced to recapitulate their own and the town's history, almost inadvertently, as a result of trying to understand the lady who seems almost without history. It is the essence of the book's irony that in trying to interpret her the people of Port Annie are the ones who are interpreted.

In Hodgins's world (as in Chaucer's or St. Augustine's), people interpret according to who they are, which is to say, according to what and how they love. Charity or cupidity thus become key elements of distinction in moral life. Evil—even in the form of petty sin—creates distortions, and in those who succumb to it wholly (such as merchant Jeremy Fell and his wife Cyn, proprietress of the Museum of Evil) the full effects of the Fall are an active hostility to truth, miracle, and joy. Ultimately it is the title character Joseph Bourne, who carries the higher quality of unselfish love to the citizens of Port Annie, becoming as he does "the salvation of the whole town." The

poet refuses to be what the citizens would first make of him; a newly acknowledged legislator of the world. To the disappointment of many he becomes a neighbor, a bearer of grace and love to those whose squalor least anticipates it.

One of the problems Hodgins wrestles with in this multilayered, complexly textured book is the modern world's lack of belief and the absence of forms—literary or otherwise—that can represent or promote an understanding of belief. In the first few pages the boarded-up church in Port Annie emerges as a symbol for modern rejection of one form. But this rejection is paralleled by another loss, one which deeply affects the novelist—the fact that there seem to be no options left for the creation of belief in modern fiction itself. Two questions are central. Can there be a myth which is true? If so, how can it be written down?

Bowman the teacher has turned to reading poems and heroic romances because in them "hoping was not considered to be a crime." This sentence, the last of section two, marks the point at which Hodgins asks his readers to imagine that there may be aspects of a realistic life other than despair and negation. The title of section three more or less maps novel territory: "Of the Battle of Life and Death in its New Disguise; of Mrs. Barnstone's Ambitious Epic Poem and the promised descent of Fat Annie (God of this World) at last, with Calamities Following, or, THE NEW MAN." Port Annie is shown to be our world, a world looking for deliverance. Unfortunately, what offers itself as the redemptive spirit of the age is a slick and seductive antagonist. The town is infiltrated by another mysterious stranger—this time much more like the one in Twain's book of that title. Damon West is a real estate agent who wants to "develop" the town's potential, even at the cost of bulldozing the landscape and ousting residents to do it. The contemporary "war" is symbolized in *The Resurrection of Joseph Bourne* by an explicit battle between "real" estate and spiritual estate. Damon West's attempt to convert the townspeople comes in the ramshackle church, informally deconsecrated, where he offers them a "hymn to the praise of the future, . . . a psalm to the glories of progress"—another, less happy eighteenth-century legacy. The verbs are *seize, get, take:* what is celebrated by Damon West is the spirit of cupidity. There have apparently been Scripture verses painted on the church wall. One reads "For he that loveth not his brother abideth in death." Mayor Weins puts over it his poster

"Grab your chance, don't think too small; the Future's coming, with fortunes for all." Another verse–"For whatsoever is born of God overcometh the world"–disappears beneath "When opportunity knocks on your door will you answer the call, or hide your head in the sands of lethargy?" In the coming order Mammon replaces not only God, but neighbor and the world as well.

Even though Hodgins offers these several "keys" to our understanding, his central message parallels that of Bourne to Port Annie. That is, despite the fact that this is a richly literary novel, with overtones of Fielding, Milton (*The Resurrection of Joseph Bourne* is a kind of *Paradise Regained* to the *Paradise Lost* in *The Invention of the World*), Twain, Swift, Tolstoy, Chaucer, and the Bible, Hodgins does not depend upon the modern reader's acquiescence to credal or dogmatic forms for understanding which he knows will likely have long been discarded by many. As Bourne admits, "the old metaphors for eternity don't work any more." In consequence, Bourne puts it, "if symbols don't work–and what else can a poet use? Then eternity can only be expressed by implication, by the way we live our lives." In *The Resurrection of Joseph Bourne* Hodgins also suggests some answers concerning the modern novel and a form for belief. The hypothesis is a "comic-epic-poem-in-prose" which Fielding could have liked, not only because of its hilarity and sense of worldly affectation, but also because it points congenially beyond, by a charitable vision, to realities we may not yet have envisioned.

Hodgins's second collection of short stories, *The Barclay Family Theatre* (1981), reveals an author who continues to adopt a Chaucerian posture. The book invites comparisons, both in style and subject matter, with *Spit Delaney's Island*. What is notably different here is that *The Barclay Family Theatre* is more laboriously contrived to appear as a unified volume. Whereas in *Spit Delaney's Island* the first and last chapters stand as bookends to a shelf of wildly discoordinate intimations of Vancouver Island life, in this more recent collection Hodgins tries to tie his stories in one way or another to the already inchoate lives of a group of seven sisters whom he introduces as characters in *Spit Delaney's Island*. Introduced all together only in the last story, these sisters take a major role in only half of the stories. Two of the pieces are written in the first person and concern themselves with a harried nephew of the sisters who desires to become a novelist in order to obtain some measure of revenge for their domi-

nation. The others have much more remote connections. On balance, *The Barclay Family Theatre* is less weighty than *Spit Delaney's Island*, in part because of tone. *The Barclay Family Theatre* is dominated by madcap and farcical burlesque. This aspect of Hodgins's style is most fully realized in "Ladies and Gentlemen, the Fabulous Barclay Sisters" (last in the volume), in "The Concert Stages of Europe" (first in the volume, and a brilliant petit-point), and in "The Sumo Revisions" (the volume's longest story).

Hodgins's choice of the theater metaphor for his title and several of the stories highlights his interest in the stage in a curious way. The theatrical encounters he imagines–a child's unsuccessful piano recital, a failed politician's grotesquely unsuccessful attempts to identify with sumo wrestling or Japanese theater, a young boy's discovery of how to upstage his mad aunts' melodrama–are concerned with the potential of theatrical situations for embarrassment. Young Barclay Desmond's tutelage in the title story has been at the hands of experts in the art of manipulation and mockery. "Cheeky Mabel," who imitates local eccentrics just well enough "that every person there except the mimicked one knew who you meant," offers, in the last story, a kind of coda for the potential of theatricality to invade privacy. This sister's view of art is as mockery, making fools of people while appearing to be innocent. In the first and last stories, Barclay Desmond's boyish concern is to avoid being mocked or manipulated. Closest in voice (we suspect) to the author, the boy is presented in "Ladies and Gentlemen, the Fabulous Barclay Sisters" as graduating from the sisters' school for small scandal, having progressed from embarrassed tutelage to the privileges of successful tricksterism.

It is significant that Desmond's achievement is then at the expense of his mother and her sisters. Hodgins is one of many male Canadian writers whose works are shadowed by dominating, upstaging women, and it is conceivable that his identification with young Barclay Desmond has several levels of intonation. But it is not in the stories specifically about the Barclay sisters that the central values of *The Barclay Family Theatre* are most successfully realized; it is those stories which are directly concerned with the artist as artist. In this book, much more evidently introspective and self-preoccupied than any of Hodgins's previous works, there is an insistent turning toward the larger question of art–its purpose, its val-

shining you don't feel the cold."
He would not see her again. Suddenly this mattered to him.
They were saying goodbye, and yet did not either of them know
how. Perhaps it didn't matter to her, having lived without sight
of him all these years. What did she want with a brother? It
shouldn't matter to him either, yet he felt this cold horror. He
should never have come here, to manufacture this artificial
family sorrow out of something he had not had any interest in
before.

She dropped her hands to her lap and studied him openly,
narrowing her eyes. "And what about her? Is she really going to
let you run off a second time without making you pay for the
first? I don't believe it." She pushed herself up from the bed
and began a search of the room, overturning cushions, looking
inside the closet, even lifting one end of the oval braided rug
on the floor. "I wouldn't breathe free until my plane had left
the ground if I was you." She lifted the pillows on her bed. No
sweater. "Of course they may be glad to see the end of you. There
are some of us -- and I'm certain your Elizabeth is one -- who
have felt ourselves more present because of your absence -- if
that makes any sense."

What did she mean? That his absence had been more than mere
absence, had been a sort of negative space that gave more
definition to their positive? It was not something he could
afford to think about -- not now.

"You fill up, and overflow, and cast some of us into shadow.
Well you do! In my own case, I feel more than in shadow, I feel
totally obscured. And I haven't even been in your company for
more than a minute or so since you arrived! Is it terrible of me
to be saying this?"

He had no answer for her. He would prefer to think she was
merely rambling, without any real understanding of what she said.
"Are you comfortable here, Tessie? Do they treat you well?"

She stopped in mid-stride in her search for the sweater and
tilted her head to look at him sideways in that same coy way of
the other night, her thick short fingers fumbling at her smiling
lips. "WHy? You want to move in here with me?" She rolled her
eyes about. "Or do you want to put your name in for my bed for
after I'm gone? Heeeee!"

"I am simply concerned for your comfort. All those years you
had a home of your own. Then, when you needed it, Father made
certain you were left the little house, the shack. This room --
is it big enough for you?"

Her expression went fierce. "You think you're never gonna
need to move in to one of these places? You just wait! Aggie
must be out there now, she's probably fretting and pacing and
getting one of her tummy aches thinking I'm not coming. Of course
it would kill her to knock on my door and ask! She would rather
suffer, that one. A bloody martyr. SHe can't bear to face life
without me beside her but she would rather die than come right
out and ask. ISn't it fun to be old, Charles? I bet you can
hardly wait until it's your turn!" She pounced on the magazine
stack behind him and tossed them aside. The sweater was hiding
beneath, and was quickly put on. "The shack?"

"The little house where we were children. Where you lived

3

Page from an early draft of Hodgins's 1987 novel, The Honorary Patron *(by permission of the author)*

ues, its methods, and above all its effect upon those closest to its making.

The first of the stories about art is entitled "More Than Conquerors" and deals with three families, each of which lives on one level of a three-level seaside Vancouver Island house. On the top level, with his wife, lives an elderly Finnish immigrant, a painter just about to open a life-restrospective exhibition in Nanaimo. On the middle level is a couple whose only daughter's body lies in a local funeral home. The mother has announced to the neighbors that after three days the child will come back to life. The lowest level houses the most appealingly presented couple—an earthy, appetitive, bankrupted contractor and his worldly-wise wife, Gladdy Roote. The artist presents his work to an audience he knows will misunderstand; like the couple who hope for their daughter's resurrection, most of the townspeople expect from an artist an irrefragible sign, a kind of visible miracle. When it does not come, only the downstairs "realists" are able to live untouched by what must in their world appear as the vain promises of art and wishful thinking. As for the artist who has banked his whole career on the probity of a place small enough to "identify with," he is left with the dismal apprehension that he may have, in attempting to serve his audience, overestimated them and betrayed himself. In this story the audience speaks too, in the interior monologue of the painter, and what it seems to ask for is not to be embarrassed. The islanders' demand is for "an artist who was normal, who wouldn't try to cheat, who wouldn't be tempted to make a fool of you." Hodgins portrays the artist as caught between fidelity to his art and complicity with the artless expectations of his "consumers."

The second story which deals with the artist's predicament is "The Leper's Squint." It is a fine piece, among Hodgins's best, and stands out in this volume. In it an older Desmond has gone to Ireland with his family in hope of gaining the advantages of a "separate place" in which to write. What he discovers is a whole world of attractive alienations, like those of his own island in many respects and radically different in others. Ireland offers a milieu in which the writer comes to understand himself as an outsider looking in into privacies and intimacies he cannot hope to invade without impropriety, if not actual trespass. The title image is inspired by a small opening in stone through which lepers were allowed to view the Mass in a medieval church. Desmond imag-

ines himself such a squinter, huddled far back in the hospice of the unclean. When an Irish writer (an attractive woman) tries to introduce him to various features of the cultural landscape, especially those intimate to a writer's fancy, he finds himself in instinctive flight. When he is confronted with an intrusive pretense to intimacy, he withdraws to a longed-for world of words, there building, as with stones, a close with only a squint from which to see safely into dramas in which he would rather not take on a role himself.

Although *The Barclay Family Theatre* is perhaps excessively preoccupied with introspection, it is the frankly introspective stories which seem to go deepest. The farcical tales seem almost without centering by contrast, as though burlesque itself is their subject and not merely one among many styles. To Hodgins's credit, it must be said that this book is an eloquent witness to his own awareness of the artist's dilemma. Hodgins is talented, yet he knows talent by itself will not achieve what he wants. He puts the warning to himself in the mouth of Eleanor Barclay, whose response to an identification of talent in her nephew is to say, "Talent? . . . You've got to know how to control it." At its most personal level, *The Barclay Family Theatre* is a kind of author's examination of conscience. Though not Hodgins's best work, it represents a turning point, a gathering of perspectives and new focus in his development as a writer.

The shape of Hodgins's ongoing career is impossible to predict with precision. Yet two books, *Beginnings*, a series of reflections, fragments, and works-in-progress published in 1983, and the novel *The Honorary Patron* (1987), offer some sense of his direction. For some years Hodgins has also been working on a novel entitled "The Master of Happy Endings." The central character ia a quixotic one-legged ex-logger named Topolski—a fine example of Hodgins's self-confessed love for the "obsessed" and larger-than-life character.

In this novel Hodgins highlights the altruism and idealism of an unlikely hero, someone whose fondest imagination is the reuniting of families and the healing of communities, but whose own talents for such an enterprise seem hopelessly oblique to the task, In the author's own summary: "The main concern of the novel is with the way people fight to preserve what they have and the way people learn . . . to find other things that are important. It's a love story. A middle-aged love story being told by this one-legged logger who fancies himself a servant of love." It is perhaps enough to say of Hodgins in this novel that his own fancies as a writer are not so different from those of his characters and that, like Chaucer, he imagines himself in relationship to his readers as a kind of "servant of the servants of love."

Interviews:

Geoff Hancock, "An Interview with Jack Hodgins," *Canadian Fiction Magazine,* no. 32/33 (1979-1980): 33-63;

J. R. (Tim) Struthers, "Thinking about Eternity," *Essays on Canadian Writing,* 20 (Winter 1980-1981): 126-133;

Alan Twigg, "Jack Hodgins," in his *For Openers: Interviews with Canadian Writers* (Madeira Park, British Columbia: Harbour, 1981), pp. 14-21;

Peter O'Brien, "An Interview with Jack Hodgins," *Rubicon,* 1 (Spring 1983): 35-71.

Reference:

David Lyle Jeffery, *Jack Hodgins; The Writer and His Work* (Toronto: ECW, 1987).

Margaret Hollingsworth
(5 June 1940-   )

Cynthia Diane Zimmerman
York University

BOOKS: *Alli Alli Oh* (Toronto: Playwrights Co-op, 1979);

Mother Country (Toronto: Playwrights Canada, 1980);

Ever Loving (Toronto: Playwrights Canada, 1981);

Operators / Bushed: Two Plays by Margaret Hollingsworth (Toronto: Playwrights Canada, 1981);

Islands (Toronto: Playwrights Canada, 1983);

Willful Acts (Toronto: Coach House Press, 1985)— includes *The Apple in the Eye, Diving, Islands, Ever Loving,* and *War Babies.*

PLAY PRODUCTIONS: *Bushed,* Vancouver, New Play Centre at Vancouver Playhouse II, March 1973;

Operators, Vancouver, New Play Centre at Vancouver East Cultural Centre, 27 April 1974;

Alli Alli Oh, Toronto, Redlight Theatre, 24 February 1977; revised Vancouver, New Play Centre, 12 May 1977;

Mother Country, Toronto, Tarragon Theatre, 21 February 1980;

Ever Loving, Victoria, Belfry Theatre, 13 November 1980;

Islands, Vancouver, New Play Centre, 23 February 1983;

Diving, Vancouver, Waterfront Theatre, March 1983;

The Apple in the Eye, Vancouver, Women and Words Conference, Summer 1983;

War Babies, Victoria, Belfry Theatre, 5 January 1984;

It's Only Hot for Two Months in Kapuskasing, Toronto, Theatre Centre, 4 June 1985.

RADIO: *Join me in Mandalay,* CBC, 29 October 1973;

Prairie Drive, CBC, 1 December 1974;

War Games, CBC, 28 October 1979;

Responsible Party, CBC, 17 February 1985;

Woman on the Wire, CBC, January 1986.

OTHER: *Operators* [original version], in *West Coast Plays,* edited by C. Brissenden (Vancouver: New Play Centre /Fineglow Plays, 1975), pp. 99-135;

"Tulips," in *1983: Best Canadian Stories,* edited by David Helwig and Sandra Martin (Ottawa: Oberon, 1983), pp. 25-35.

PERIODICAL PUBLICATIONS: "English Speaking Aliens," *Room of One's Own,* 9 (February 1984): 19-37;

"Of Shoes and Ships," *Writing,* 9 (Spring 1984): 30-35;

"Widecombe Fair," *Room of One's Own*, 9 (August 1984): 44-57;

"Cubbing," *Canadian Fiction Magazine*, 52 (February 1985): 26-32;

"Why We Don't Write," *Canadian Theatre Review*, 43 (Summer 1985): 21-27;

"Smiling Underwater," *Canadian Fiction Magazine*, 56 (February 1986): 89-95;

"The Day I Killed The Pope," *Writing*, 17 (Winter 1986): 3-7.

In 1973 Margaret Hollingsworth had her first play staged in Canada by Vancouver's New Play Centre, a group which, since its inception in 1970, has had as its mandate the fostering of original scripts by local playwrights. Although she has created almost a dozen scripts since then, it is only recently that her work is being mounted by mainstream theaters. As she understands it, the

difficulty for artistic directors has been that her work does not come easily off the page–while rooted in practical realism, it has a surreal quality.

Born in Sheffield, England, the only child of George and Nellie Potts Hollingsworth, Margaret Hollingsworth grew up in London and took her training as a librarian at Loughborough College. She traveled and worked in Italy and Japan before immigrating to Canada in 1968. Arriving in Canada, she settled at Thunder Bay, Ontario, and spent four years there as chief librarian of the city's public library. In 1972 she received her bachelor of arts degree in psychology from Thunder Bay's Lakehead University and moved to Vancouver. There she worked on a master of fine arts degree in theater and creative writing at the University of British Columbia, completing it in 1974. The next five years she spent on Galiano Island working as an editor and free-lance journalist before going to Nelson, British Columbia, for two years of teaching writing at David Thompson University Centre. In the fall of 1983 she moved to Toronto, where she currently resides. She spent the winter of 1985 as writer in residence at Concordia University in Montreal and the summer of 1986 as writer in residence with the Stratford Festival Theatre. As well as writing for the stage, she has written radio and television plays and short stories.

Hollingsworth's first plays produced in Canada, the one-acts *Bushed* (1973) and *Operators* (1974), were born of her experiences living in northern Ontario. "[They] grew out of watching people . . . sitting around in laundromats, or outside various cultural centres like the Finnish Hall and the Ukrainian Hall. . . . I tried to get into their heads." *Bushed* is set in a run-down laundromat. Two men, retired immigrant workers, reminisce and fantasize while, in the background, a group of women do their laundry in a slow, rhythmic fashion. The women have work and community; they are part of the natural order of things. Excluded, the men just sit. Used up by the Canadian wilderness, exhausted, they are outsiders in every way. Isolation and loneliness are central to *Operators* as well. In this play Jerri, a young woman who has just started working the factory night shift, is the intruder into a relationship of many years between two older women. Jerri's neurotic chatter, her probing questions, and the intensity of her presence serve as catalysts to a crisis for the others. Whether these friends are bonded by boredom, as Jerri accuses, or whether this interlude of interrogation and confession will lead to a deeper, more honest relationship, the portrait remains a bleak one. A similarly bleak outlook is found in *Alli Alli Oh*, commissioned and produced in 1977 by the now-defunct feminist Redlight Theatre, and its sequel, *Islands*, produced at Vancouver's New Play Centre in 1983.

A powerful play, *Alli Alli Oh* is set in an isolated farmhouse on an island in British Columbia. Muriel, a competent matter-of-fact person, brought Alli here a year ago to be her partner and helpmate. Now she needs Alli's assistance birthing a cow in difficulty, but Alli is disintegrating herself. In long monologues Alli speaks of her painful marriage and separation, her timely rescue from the mental institution by Muriel, and her present turmoil. Unable to stand the tension, Alli suddenly runs outside with a carving knife. Soon after, at the end of the play, Alli telephones the hospital to say she is returning, that she's been "cowed." *Islands* shifts the focus to Muriel. A more straightforwardly realistic piece than *Alli Alli Oh*—Alli's compulsive talking and the pervasive animal imagery give a surreal quality to the earlier work—*Islands* presents Alli's return to the farm six months later. The animals are gone and Muriel has committed herself to self-reliance and solitude. Alli's unexpected arrival coincides with a visit by Muriel's mother, a self-righteous, judgmental woman who hopes to make the island her home. Alli also wants to "come home" and claims that her mind was not lost but only in temporary "cold storage." At play's end, Muriel, unable to tolerate the proximity of either of these demanding, manipulative women, is confirmed in the necessity of her own isolation.

The island image, with its associations to struggle for independence and the experience of deprivation, recurs in Hollingsworth's first full-length play, *Mother Country*. A play about culture and country, about belonging and home, its occasion is a reunion of mother and daughters to celebrate the sixty-fifth birthday of the mother, Janet. The island home, shaped to resemble a ship's captain's cabin, is virtually a little England with Janet as the ruling monarch. The prevailing metaphor is that of a crippling connection which is as handicapping for Janet's daughters as it is for expatriates. First produced at Toronto's Tarragon Theatre in 1980, *Mother Country* drew the criticism that Janet's malevolence and her power were too extreme to be credible. Although Hollingsworth did not intend the work to be strictly realistic, as the stage directions indicate,

Cover for Hollingsworth's 1985 collection that includes The Apple in the Eye, Diving, Islands, Ever Loving, *and* War Babies

psychological realities are perhaps portrayed too literally.

In her second full-length play, *Ever Loving*, produced in 1980 at the Belfry Theatre, Victoria, the immigrant's sense of dislocation is presented through the story of three European war brides. In this, her most-produced play, the disjunction for her characters between the lives they imagine and the realities they experience is skillfully rendered. The script makes frequent leaps in time and location as Hollingsworth interweaves popular songs from the periods she covers with scenes showing the evolution of the three relationships. The play traces the initial courtships of the three couples, the wives' journey to Canada to be reunited with their husbands, and their lives together until 1970.

Willful Acts, a collection of five of Hollingsworth's plays published in 1985, makes clear that her interest in the inner experience, often viewed from multiple perspectives, and her

The Green Line.

TAD	FINALLY Karim brought me a water melon..when? Time passes so quickly. It was ripe...as he gave it to me it slipped out of my grasp and split open HE INDICATES THE FLOOR
KELLY	Too bad.
TAD	we laughed. The skin was oiled you see... the oil from his rifle had seeped...red pulp.. juice everywhere. Schplat. PAUSE You say that your Canadian river is green. here we have a red river. Baal's river- they still call it that. The Phoenician god Baal was killed in a cave above the river. It runs through a canyon. One of the most beautiful canyons in the world they say...how would we know, you and I? We are merely scientists. But even I can see that it is beautiful, and i have no eye for beauty. It is was beautiful. Vinyards, orchards, small, white, neat houses terraced right down to the water, brown terraced and at the top-violet. A trick of the light you see. 1 often went there-oh many years ago, when I first came to this country. I was helping to reconstruct an old Cistercian abbey nearby-unique. A masterpiece of building- it took us five years. I understand it was one of the first casualties...
KELLY	There's not much left.
TAD	Whenever I would go to the river I would sit by the water in the hope that it would turn red before my eyes. PAUSE In the evening, when the sun set, the whole valley turned red. Deep, blood red. That was always the same. And once a year they said, the river ran red with the blood of Baal. For one full day, red, right out to where it joined the sea. And the sea turned red. That's what they believed. But they left us no records. we can only surmise. The gods are everywhere- in the air, the hills, the water. PAUSE something happened to one of the-blood would flow... After. Blood would flow.
KELLY	TURNS AWAY FROM HIM
TAD	And every year women shaved their heads on the day the river turned red.
KELLY	LOOKS AT HIM, ALARMED

Page from the revised typescript for a play-in-progress (by permission of the author)

presentation of that experience in a nonlinear, nonsequential, and often surreal style, has not abated. The one-acts *The Apple in the Eye* and *Diving* (both produced in Vancouver in 1983) have a connection to *Alli Alli Oh*: the heroines enter their own mental landscapes while increasingly withdrawing from the real world. *War Babies*, produced at the Belfry Theatre in 1984, is a play-within-a-play: Esme, pregnant at forty-two, writes a play about her future relationship with her war-correspondent husband. In it their own war games and survival strategies contaminate their life together and ensure the worst possible outcome. The issues and impact of war are also central to Hollingsworth's play-in-progress, commissioned by the Stratford Festival. The title, "The Green Line," refers to the border between the Christian and Muslim sectors of Beirut. The play focuses closely on two characters caught in the excruciating dilemmas of a war-torn country.

Margaret Hollingsworth's work shows her continuing desire to give the audience access to the mental life of her characters, to make visible the conflict between psychological realities and external ones. But in her most recent plays, the sense of marginality experienced by the immigrant or outsider in search of a home seems to have given way to the portrayal of characters actively involved in defining the home they are in.

While still focusing on the lives of women, still experimenting with episodic structure and with moving from one level of experience to another, Hollingsworth's latest plays—*War Babies*, for example—and the radio plays *Responsible Party* (1985) and *Woman on the Wire* (1986) indicate that her concerns are becoming more political, more socially conscious. Her most recent completed play, a farce entitled "Marked for Marriage," is scheduled for production in January 1988 by Alberta Theatre Projects. Her short-story collection "Smiling Under Water" has been accepted for publication by Collins.

References:

Rita Fraticelli, "Readings in Review: *Willful Acts*," *Canadian Theatre Review*, 47 (Summer 1986): 149-151;

Jon Kaplan, "Double Dose of Hollingsworth," *Now*, 5 (9-15 January 1986): 9;

Anne Saddlemayer, "Introduction" to Hollingsworth's *Willful Acts* (Toronto: Coach House Press, 1985), pp. 9-15;

Cynthia Zimmerman, "Margaret Hollingsworth," in *The Work: Conversations with English-Canadian Playwrights*, by Zimmerman and Robert Wallace (Toronto: Coach House Press, 1982), pp. 90-101.

Harold Horwood
(2 November 1923-)

Allan Bevan
Dalhousie University

completed by

W. H. New
University of British Columbia

BOOKS: *Tomorrow Will Be Sunday* (Toronto & Garden City: Doubleday, 1966);

The Foxes of Beachy Cove (Toronto & Garden City: Doubleday, 1967);

Newfoundland (Toronto: Macmillan, 1969; New York: St. Martin's, 1969);

White Eskimo: A Novel of Labrador (Toronto & Garden City: Doubleday, 1972);

Death on the Ice, by Cassie Brown with the assistance of Horwood (Toronto & Garden City: Doubleday, 1972);

Beyond the Road: Portraits and Visions of Newfoundlanders, photos by Stephen Taylor (Toronto: Van Nostrand Reinhold, 1976);

Bartlett, The Great Canadian Explorer (Toronto & Garden City: Doubleday, 1977; revised, 1980);

The Colonial Dream 1497-1760 (Toronto: Natural Science of Canada/McClelland & Stewart, 1978);

Only the Gods Speak (St. John's: Breakwater Books, 1979);

A History of Canada (Greenwich, Connecticut: Bison Books, 1983);

Pirates and Outlaws of Canada, 1610-1932, by Horwood and Edward Butts (Toronto & Garden City: Doubleday, 1984);

A History of the Newfoundland Ranger Force (St. John's: Breakwater Books, 1986);

Corner Brook—A Social History of a Paper Town (St. John's: Breakwater Books, 1986);

Historic Newfoundland (Toronto: Oxford University Press, 1986);

Remembering Summer (Halifax: Pottersfield Press, 1987);

Dancing on the Shore (Toronto: McClelland & Stewart, forthcoming 1987);

Bandits and Privateers: Canada in the Age of Gunpowder, by Horwood and Butts (Toronto & Garden City: Doubleday, forthcoming 1987).

OTHER: *Voices Underground,* edited by Horwood (Toronto: New Press, 1972);

Tales of the Labrador Indians, edited by Horwood (St. John's: Harry Cuff Publications, 1981).

Harold Horwood's writing at its best reflects the life and history of Newfoundland which he obviously knows well and loves deeply. In journalism, essays, fiction, travel, and biography and as editor of a volume of poetry, Horwood gives his readers an insight into Newfoundland's past (by Canadian standards a very long past) and present. Works such as his 1976 travel book, *Beyond the Road,* or Cassie Brown's 1972 account of the heroes of the sea, *Death on the Ice,* written with Horwood's assistance, testify to his commitment to Atlantic Canada and its way of life. Horwood's own passionate belief in the possibility of heroism, in a number of different manifestations of the heroic, permeates his writing. As he said in a 1973 interview with Donald Cameron in *Conversations with Canadian Novelists,* "A person who is worth writing about needs to be an extraordinary person, someone larger than life."

Harold Andrew Horwood was born on 2 November 1923 in St. John's, Newfoundland, the son of Andrew and Vina Maidment Horwood. Andrew Horwood was the author of a book of poetry and a volume entitled *Newfoundland Ships and Men,* and Andrew Horwood's father, Capt. John Horwood, published several historical articles. In 1946 Harold Horwood, with his brother Charles, founded the literary journal *Protocol.* In the same year he became involved in the labor movement as an organizer for the Newfoundland Federation of Labour; in 1948 he served as an orga-

Harold Horwood

nizer for the Canadian Congress of Labour. He worked with Joey Smallwood on the campaign that brought Newfoundland into Canada in 1949. Following confederation he represented the District of Labrador in the legislature until he resigned from the Liberal party in 1952.

He joined the New Democratic party but was an unsuccessful candidate in the riding of Trinity-Conception. His next work was as a journalist with the St. John's *Evening Telegram* until 1958, during which time he wrote what he calls "a fighting, campaigning, crusading column–an opposition column." As a free-lance writer his "income fell to almost zero for a couple of years, and then gradually . . . picked up, bit by bit." He was managing editor of the St. John's *Examiner*, 1960-1961, and associate editor of the *Evening Telegram* from 1968 to 1970. He has taught creative writing at Memorial University and the University of Western Ontario and has been writer in residence at Western Ontario (1976-1977) and Waterloo (1980-1982). He was awarded the Order of Canada in 1980 "for contributions to Ca-

nadian literature"; in 1981 he served as president of the Writers' Union of Canada, of which he was a founding member. He now lives in Annapolis Royal, Nova Scotia, with his wife, the former Cornelia Lindsmith.

Calling himself a "radical" in the personal note that accompanies the entry on him in *Canada Writes!* (the 1977 directory of the Writers' Union of Canada), Horwood goes on to attack "the dehumanized school system, . . . dehumanized industry, . . . [and] organized medicine" and to praise "pioneer arts." "Most of my close friends are children. The rest are writers." In all three of his novels–*Tomorrow Will Be Sunday* (1966), *White Eskimo* (1972), and *Remembering Summer* (1987)–Horwood is on the side of those who rebel against society. As he said in his conversation with Cameron, "I don't think anybody is worth a damn in any field of endeavour unless he profoundly dissents. We're living in a society in which the Establishment, which includes all the people who control the society, is still nineteenth-century and they're still thinking in nineteenth-century terms. And unless you dissent from this, you're nowhere." In *Tomorrow Will Be Sunday* the world of the outport Caplin Blight is dominated by the church and its primitive Christianity emphasizing the dangers of the flesh. By having Pastor Tishrite "deflower" young Sister Bertha Penchley and his successor Brother John McKim seduce Eli Pallisher into a homosexual relationship, Horwood emphasizes the corruption of the establishment. The novel's three central figures–Christopher Simms, Virginia Marks, and Eli Pallisher–are all young and intelligent rebels against the unreasoning restrictions of the community. Chris (the Christ figure) returns to teach, which he does with great success through love and understanding. He is loved by (and loves) both Virginia, the rebellious, free-spirited, and beautiful daughter of the local merchant and Eli, his brightest student, one destined to make his mark in the world. Although the central plot and the main characters are not always convincing, the novel comes to life through the descriptions of the hard life in the outports. Most readers would agree with Horwood's comment that "I think I managed to capture the essential nature of Newfoundland outports."

In *White Eskimo* the chief representatives of the establishment are the Reverend Manfred Kosh, who disrupts the Inuit way of life by demanding their attendance at church for Christmas and Easter; and Dr. William Tocsin (a thin disguise for the English physician and missionary Dr. Wilfred Grenfell), who also exerts power over the natives for his own selfish purposes. In contrast, the White Eskimo Gillingham uses his personal magnetism and his amazing strength and agility to lead the Inuit back to their roots. Nootka, the young Eskimo who had learned so much from the White Spirit Gillingham, sums it up: "He showed us how to shake off the past that had been inflicted upon us, the two hundred years of the scientific myth and the Christian superstition and the trappings of colonialism." Horwood is not naive about the power of one individual against the establishment, however. After Gillingham's disappearance into the interior, his young wife Nasha "started walking over the hill . . . to visit the mission church and to pray." This novel is full of lively descriptions of hunting, fishing, travel, and survival in the rugged grandeur of Labrador; the history of the Labrador fur trade is also sketched to show the rapacity and shortsightedness of some of the early traders, especially the Moravians. The White Eskimo Gillingham is of epic dimensions, physically and otherwise. He arrives mysteriously and disappears again into the unknown. In Horwood's words, "The book is consciously into the mythological in the sense that it goes back to the old hero epic. . . . It incidentally recounts the social history of Labrador, but this simply comes in as background. And it's a deliberate revolt against the anti-hero. Gillingham is a *real* hero." The novel has a rather awkward narrative technique, with a Conradian group aboard a little ship chugging up the Labrador Coast and talking of many things until they focus on Gillingham. The main storyteller knows all the central characters, admires Gillingham without reservation, and damns his enemies; then another narrator takes over and discloses that Gillingham had murdered his blood brother Abel. It is never known for certain why Abel died, or who shot him, but the evidence does point to the "*real* hero." Unfortunately, the characters for the most part remain abstractions, representatives of the author's thesis about the good life—for the natives at least.

In *Remembering Summer* Horwood shifts his ground somewhat, although the protagonist of this, his most recently published novel, is Eli Pallisher from *Tomorrow Will Be Sunday*. Set in Newfoundland, *Remembering Summer* examines the counterculture of the late 1960s and early 1970s—"a time when millions believed in miracles that soon empire would be no more, and the lion

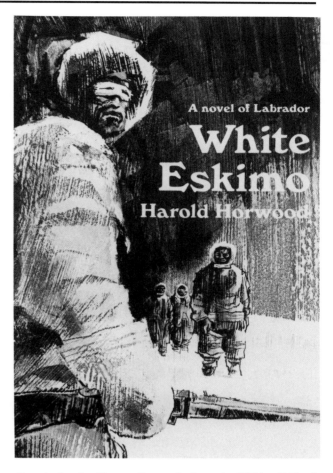

Dust jacket for Horwood's novel about the "White Eskimo" Esau Gillingham and his sojourn among the Inuit. "This book is fiction with a backbone of history," Horwood writes in the preface. "The places are real places. . . . Gillingham himself was a real man, much like the one here described."

and the wolf would cease." The novel reveals both the idealistic aspirations and the naivete of some of the people involved. After the fact much of the naivete is apparent, as is the violence of the era (whether in politics or protest) and the openness of many of the one-time protesters to the selfish banalities of a later time.

Horwood's *The Foxes of Beachy Cove* (1967), which has been compared to Thoreau's *Walden*, is full of detailed information on the animals and birds of Newfoundland. In this book Horwood emerges as a patient, keen, and sympathetic observer of the natural world who portrays modern man (the establishment again?) as the most destructive of all creatures. In *Newfoundland* (1969), part of the Traveller's Canada series, Horwood takes readers on a tour of a world he knows and loves. As he travels to various places, he gives the background of exploration, comments on the vari-

Page from "Dancing on the Shore" – in process.   Harold Horwood

Willet   (1)

I have seen the willets dancing in the springtime on the ~~Fundy~~ shore,

dancing not only on the short salt grass that is covered monthly

by the tide, but dancing in air like butterflies or salamanders

wrapped in flame. This three-dimensional dance, a spiral reaching

toward the sky, expands and replicates the helix that is at the ~~very root~~ core of

life--the double spiral of the chromosome, the protean spirals of

the albuminoids, the simplicity and perfection of the circle with

the added dimensions of motion and time, the elements that make of

all perfection a transience, a flowering and a becoming.

Such is the dance of these feathered spirits; they move in rhythmic

measures ~~beside~~ through radiance that glimmers the ~~light that dances~~ from the waves, as ~~double~~ how planets

might move, each orbiting the other about ~~a common~~ their common centre, then rise

quiver at perihilion

like twirling smoke, still orbiting, and ~~xxxxxxxxxxxxxxxxxxxxxxxxxx~~

before returning to the earth to complete the dance with intertwined

circles once more, a quadrilateral symmetry, adorned at both ends with

~~xxxxxxxxxxxxxxxxxxxxxxxxxxxxxxxxxxxxxxx~~ simple but decorative

motifs, like a minuet or scherzo.

For a long time this boldly-patterned shorebird, ~~a little~~ slightly larger than a

wealthy

pigeon, was almost extinct in eastern North America. The/gunners of

the club - owners of the Atlantic

the 19th century, some of whom killed thousands of shorebirds in a

the

single day for sport, came close to destroying willet. ~~as~~ they succeeded

in destroying

destroyed the ~~xxxxxxxxxx~~ Eskimo curlew. Mass ~~killing~~ slaughter for sport ceased

to be respectable just in time to save the willet, which has been

slowly reoccupying its former range. ~~and now nests as far north as~~

~~southern Nova Scotia.~~ ~~xxxxxxxxxxxxxxxxxx~~ Today it nests once

more along the shores of Annapolis Basin, as it did in early Acadian

the tenants of   of

times, each pair ~~occupying~~ a patch of salt marsh or a clearing in the

Page from the revised typescript for Horwood's forthcoming book Dancing on the Shore *(by permission of the author)*

ous peoples who have contributed to the past and present, and gives effective descriptions of the different parts of Newfoundland. In the 1977 biography, *Bartlett, The Great Canadian Explorer* (revised, 1980), Horwood's subject is a real hero, "a true Victorian," Newfoundlander Robert Bartlett, the courageous, enterprising Arctic explorer who was with Robert Peary and Vilhjalmur Stefansson and others on some of their voyages. Horwood has edited a collection of Nascapee legends for a juvenile audience, *Tales of the Labrador Indians* (1981), and his *Pirates and Outlaws of Canada, 1610-1932* (a collaboration with Edward Butts published in 1984) is a work of wide appeal. He has also written works of history and social history, short stories (a collection, *Only the Gods Speak*, was published in 1979), magazine articles, television and radio scripts, book re-

views, and newspaper features. Two books are forthcoming in 1987, *Dancing on the Shore* and *Bandits and Privateers*—the latter, Horwood's second collaboration with Edward Butts. In *White Eskimo* the character who represents Horwood is one of the passengers aboard the *Kyle*; he describes himself as a "feature writer on tour" who "prowled the ship from stern to stern." Horwood has "prowled" Newfoundland, and his writing provides the reader with a comprehensive account of one of the most interesting parts of Canada.

Reference:

Donald Cameron, "Harold Horwood: The Senior Freak of Newfoundland," in his *Conversations with Canadian Novelists*, volume 1 (Toronto: Macmillan, 1973), pp. 65-80.

Claude Jasmin

(10 November 1930-   )

Valerie Raoul
University of British Columbia

BOOKS: *La Corde au cou* (Montreal: Cercle du Livre de France, 1960);

Délivrez-nous du mal (Montreal: Editions à la Page, 1961; revised, Montreal: Editions internationales Stanké, 1980);

Ethel et le terroriste (Montreal: Déom, 1964; translated by David S. Walker as *Ethel and the Terrorist* (Montreal: Harvest House, 1965);

Blues pour un homme averti (Ottawa: Parti Pris, 1964);

Et puis tout est silence (Montreal: Editions de l'Homme, 1965); translated by David Lobdell as *The Rest is Silence* (Ottawa: Oberon, 1981);

Pleure pas, Germaine! (Montreal: Parti Pris, 1965);

Les Coeurs empaillés (Montreal: Parti Pris, 1967);

Les Artisans créateurs (Montreal: Lideac, 1967);

Rimbaud, mon beau salaud! (Montreal: Editions du Jour, 1969);

Tuez le veau gras (Montreal: Leméac, 1970);

Jasmin par Jasmin (Montreal: Claude Langevin, 1970);

L'Outaragasipi (Montreal: Actuelle, 1971);

C'est toujours la même histoire (Montreal: Leméac, 1972);

La Petite Patrie (Montreal: La Presse, 1972);

Pointe-Calumet boogie-woogie (Montreal: La Presse, 1973);

Sainte-Adèle-la-vaisselle (Montreal: La Presse, 1974);

Danielle, ça va marcher! (Montreal: Stanké, 1975);

Revoir Ethel (Montreal: Stanké, 1976);

Le Loup de Brunswick City (Montreal: Leméac, 1976);

Feu à volonté (Montreal: Leméac, 1976);

Feu sur la télévision (Montreal: Leméac, 1977);

Le Veau dort (Montreal: Leméac, 1979);

La Sablière (Montreal: Leméac, 1979); translated by Lobdell as *Mario* (Ottawa: Oberon, 1985);

Les Contes du Sommet-Bleu (Montreal: Québécor, 1980);

Claude Jasmin (photograph by Kèro)

L'Armoire de Pantagruel (Montreal: Leméac, 1982);

Maman-Paris, Maman-La France (Montreal: Leméac, 1982);

Deux mâts, une galère, by Jasmin and Edouard Jasmin (Montreal: Leméac, 1983);

Le Crucifié du Sommet-Bleu (Montreal: Leméac, 1984);

L'Etat-macquereau, l'état-maffia (Montreal: Leméac, 1984);

Une Duchesse à Ogunquit (Montreal: Leméac, 1985);

Des Cons qui s'adorent (Montreal: Leméac, 1985);

Alice vous fait dire bon soir (Montreal: Leméac, 1986).

PLAY PRODUCTIONS: *La Nourelle Gigue,* Dominion Drama Festival, 1952;

Le Veau dort, Dominion Drama Festival, 1963.

MOTION PICTURE: *Délivrez-nous du mal,* screenplay by Jasmin, 1969.

TELEVISION: *La Rue de la Liberté,* Radio-Canada, 1960;

La Mort dans l'âme, Radio-Canada, 1962;

Blues pour un homme averti, Radio-Canada, 1964;

Les Mains vides, Radio-Canada, 1964;

Tuez le veau gras, Radio-Canada, 1966;

Un Chemin de Croix dans le métro, Radio-Canada, 1968;

C'est toujours la même histoire, Radio-Canada, 1970;

La Petite Patrie, Radio-Canada, 1974-1976;

Pointe-Calumet, boogie-woogie, Radio-Canada, 1980-1981;

Procès devant juge seul, Radio-Canada, 1983;

Nous sommes tous des orphelius, Radio-Canada, 1987.

OTHER: Robert Roussil, *Manifeste,* edited by Jasmin (Montreal: Editions du Jour, 1965);

Une Saison en studio, edited by Jasmin (Montreal: Guérin, 1987).

PERIODICAL PUBLICATION: *La Mort dans l'âme: Télethéâtre, Voix et Images du Pays*, 4 (1971): 134-174.

Claude Jasmin, in his mid-fifties, has produced over thirty books in the last twenty-five years. He is one of the most prolific and popular writers in Quebec, and though not always praised by critics, he has built up a large and faithful body of readers, many of them attracted to his works by the adaptation of some of them for television.

Jasmin grew up in a modest French and Italian district of Montreal (Rue Saint-Denis near Jean-Talon) and spent summer holidays at Pointe-Calumet on the Lac des Deux Montagnes. These settings of his childhood are evoked in his autobiographical writings and also appear in many of his works of fiction. His father, Edouard Jasmin, an importer of Oriental goods turned restaurant keeper, was an amateur artist and ceramist. Jasmin abandoned his classical studies at the Collège André Grasset to follow in his father's footsteps, completing technical training in pottery and ceramics at the Ecole du Meuble (in 1951). He worked for a year as a teacher of ceramics at the Sainte-Adèle Art Centre (1951-1952) and subsequently for three years as a specialized instructor in arts and crafts for the Montreal Recreational Service. In 1956 he became a designer and decorator for Radio-Canada Television, a position which he held for over twenty years. From 1959 to 1961 he gave ceramics classes for working women, sponsored by their union.

His interest in the plastic arts did not prevent Jasmin from beginning at an early age to experiment with different forms of writing, although he experienced difficulties with spelling and grammar as a student. Fascinated by Pirandello and Brecht, he wrote a play, "Dans de beaux draps" in 1955. It was not performed until 1963, when it was staged at the Dominion Drama Festival under the title *Le Veau dort*. His first novel, *Et puis tout est silence*, was written in 1959. Although it almost won the annual competition of the Cercle du Livre de France and was published in *Ecrits du Canada Français*, it passed largely unnoticed until its 1965 publication in book form by Editions de l'Homme. Twenty years later it appeared in an English translation by David Lobdell, under the title *The Rest is Silence*. Jasmin's second novel, *La Corde au cou*, succeeded in winning the coveted prize in 1960. Both these early novels received mixed receptions. In the first the anonymous narrator is lying trapped by debris in the ruins of a stage he was constructing for an experimental summer theater in the Richelieu valley. He relives his childhood (which closely resembles Jasmin's) before being murdered by a harmonica-playing derelict who resents finding this intruder in his habitual refuge.

A strike at Radio-Canada gave Jasmin time to finish *La Corde au cou* and involved him in the social and political ferment which followed the death of Maurice Duplessis in 1959. In his second novel Jasmin expresses the bitterness felt by many Quebecois during the Duplessis years through the person of a murderer on the run. His evocation of a criminal mentality was convincing enough to prompt one critic to inquire whether he was an ex-convict. The violence of the events and the style were interpreted as a revolt against Americanization and materialism by Gérald Godin, who pointed out that this novel appeared in the same year as Jean-Paul Desbiens's *Les Insolences du Frère Untel* (*Le Nouvelliste*, 3 December 1960).

La Corde au cou enjoyed a *succès de scandale*. *Délivrez-nous du mal* (1961), Jasmin's third novel, shocked for a different reason. In it the author dared to depict two homosexuals, André Dastous (the wealthy narrator) and Georges Langis, whose relationship somewhat resembles the real-life relationship of the French poets, Verlaine and Rimbaud. Apart from facing the ambivalent reactions of some homosexuals (was he ridiculing them? one of them?), Jasmin had difficulty in finding a publisher for the book, which nevertheless received good reviews and was reedited in 1980.

In 1961 Jasmin embarked on a further parallel career in journalism, becoming art critic for *La Presse*, a position he held until 1966. From 1953 to 1966 he also taught the history of modern art at the Institut des Arts Appliqués (formerly Ecole du Meuble). From 1961 to 1966 he abandoned novel-writing in favor of composing dramatic texts for television. Of the dozen which he wrote in this period five were performed. These texts were published in the review of the Collège Saint-Ignace (April 1967), accompanied by a preface in which Jasmin comments on the contribution of television at this time to the "prise de conscience" of a Quebec identity. One of the plays, *Blues pour un homme averti*, was published by Parti Pris in 1964, another, *Tuez le veau gras* by Leméac in 1970. In 1963 Jasmin had triumphed in live theater with his play, *Le Veau dort*,

Cover, with illustration by Gilles Séguin, for a pocket edition of Jasmin's second novel, winner of the 1960 Prix du Cercle du Livre de France

which won first prize at the Dominion Drama Festival. In 1969 another television play, *Un Chemin de Croix dans le métro*, was awarded the Wilderness-Anik prize in Toronto. He was also working then on the screenplay for *Délivrez-nous du mal*.

The ceramist-teacher-journalist-playwright had returned to the novel, however, with *Ethel et le terroriste* (1964), considered by some critics his best work of fiction, winner of the Prix-France Québec in 1965, and one of the few to be translated into English (*Ethel and the Terrorist*, 1965). In it Paul, a young F.L.Q. (Front de Libération du Québec) terrorist, flees to New York City with his Jewish girlfriend, Ethel, wondering whether the bomb he placed in a Montreal post office has killed anyone. The narration is divided into short passages with titles and follows closely Paul and Ethel's itinerary and events which befall them in New York. There the help of a black sympathizer, Slide, cannot save Paul from the clutches

of either the R.C.M.P. or his former friends in the "movement." Forced to place another bomb, at the risk of losing Ethel, Paul prepares to leave once more for Montreal and finds Ethel waiting for him in the car. According to Jasmin, he wanted this novel to be a love story, above all, but critical reaction was affected more by his treatment of the terrorist mentality and his attribution of anti-Semitism to the Quebec independence movement.

His fifth novel, *Pleure pas, Germaine!* (1965), became equally controversial, because of the author's choice of the Montreal working-class slang *joual* as the medium of narration. The story is told through the eyes of Gilles Bédard, a minimally educated, unemployed father of a large family, bent on leaving the metropolis for a better life in Gaspésie. Once more the novel develops around a journey, from Montreal to Bonaventure. The element of crime is also present again, since Gilles is in fact in pursuit of his oldest daughter's supposed murderer rather than in search of work. For the first time Jasmin depicts a nonintellectual hero and the life of a family. Germaine, the mother (the author's mother's maiden name was Germaine Lefebvre), is a memorable character. The book would certainly have received a warmer critical reception, had it not become associated almost exclusively with the controversy over the literary use of *joual*.

Jasmin abandoned the novel once more for several years after the disappointing response to *Pleure pas, Germaine!* in favor of essays (collected in *Les Artisans créateurs*, 1967) and short stories. *Les Coeurs empaillés* (1967) is a volume of ten stories, involving nine women and one transvestite. It illustrates the precision of décor, time and place in Jasmin's narration, the importance he attributes to sex and violence in the lives of "ordinary" people, and his ability to retain his reader's attention. *Rimbaud, mon beau salaud!* (1969) is a completely different type of text, closer to poetry, intermingling autobiography with biography, reflection on creative writing with its practice, in an imaginary dialogue with Rimbaud, one of Jasmin's favorite role models. In *Jasmin par Jasmin* (1970) he deals directly with himself, rather than a double, reviewing his early experiences in the literary world, classifying reactions to his books and ˆcounterattacking those critics by whom he felt mistreated.

L'Outaragasipi (1971) represents another new departure, since it is an account of the early history of L'Assomption, near Montreal, based on considerable research, intertwined with contemporary nationalist politics and issues of the Women's Liberation Movement. Like several of Jasmin's works, it is an inextricable combination of autobiography, political pamphlet, novel, and poem. The television drama *C'est toujours la même histoire*, produced in 1970 and published in 1972, also represents an attack on the surviving values of the Duplessis régime. The doomed love affair between a Jewish-American draft dodger and the daughter of a bourgeois family in Percé results in the death of the young man, David Kaufman, and the shameful submission of the girl to pressure from her family.

Between 1972 and 1974 Jasmin produced three volumes of memoirs covering his childhood in Montreal (*La Petite Patrie*), his adolescent summers at the Lac des Deux Montagnes (*Pointe-Calumet boogie-woogie*, 1973), and his first experiences as an underemployed artist (*Sainte-Adèle-la-vaisselle*, 1974). In the first part of the trilogy the atmosphere of the pre-World War II years is recreated through the eyes of the child that he was. The second focuses on the awakening of his interest in the opposite sex and his experiences at the Collège André Grasset. The third evokes his disagreements with his parents over religion and life-style, his initial faith in artistic activity, and his painful acceptance of adulthood. The sexual frustration which dominates the last account ends with an epilogue revealing that only one year after the period Jasmin recalls here, he became the father of a daughter. *La Petite Patrie* was presented by Radio-Canada as a televised serial (1974-1976) with great success. The sequel, *Pointe-Calumet boogie-woogie*, was adapted for broadcast in 1980-1981. Several of Jasmin's novels have also been adapted into films (*La Corde au cou, Délivrez-nous du mal, Pleure pas, Germaine!*).

Jasmin has stated that he would have liked to be a filmmaker. Two of his works of fiction (*Revoir Ethel* and *Le Loup de Brunswick City*, both published in 1976) read almost like scenarios. In *Revoir Ethel* the hero of *Ethel et le terroriste* makes another journey south to the States after his release from several years in prison for his previous activities. He is now convinced that personal happiness and love for a woman are goals more valid than political revolution. He is accompanied by Patrick, a Breton who resembles Paul as he was and is planning to plant a nuclear device at the Montreal Olympics, and Walter, a francophile American homosexual. Paul, who now calls himself Germain,

is in search of Ethel, who has married a black man and become a widow. His quest leads him south to the home of Walter, who becomes reconciled with his past, back to New York, and once more to Montreal, where he betrays Patrick and is finally reunited with Ethel.

Like most of *Revoir Ethel*, *Le Loup de Brunswick City* takes place in the United States. It is based on the (true?) story of a two-year-old boy of Quebecois origin, Louis Laberge, who is lost in the forest and becomes the leader of a wolf pack. He is twelve when he is finally captured, having terrorized the citizens of Brunswick City. Reunited with his parents, he becomes educated and apparently normal. His plans to study veterinary medicine and his relationship with his girlfriend come to an abrupt end, however, when, having decided to abandon an attempt to return to the woods, he is run over by a car and dies howling. The short, dated entries mark a modest experiment with chronology. The identity crisis of the protagonist has been interpreted as a parable of that of Quebec as an anomaly in North America. The novel, like *Revoir Ethel*, is based on the interplay of personal and political destiny, of individual crisis and the desire to share life with an ideal other. The threat of sudden death, violence, or capture lurks in the background.

Jasmin maintained his journalistic activities throughout the 1970s and was responsible for a daily column in the *Journal de Montréal* from 1971 to 1974. His major articles have been collected and published in two volumes, *Feu à volonté* (1976), and *Feu sur la télévision* (1977). He has been frequently engaged in polemical exchanges, and the appearance of his inquiry into the life of the notorious Danielle Ouimet (*Danielle, ça va marcher!*, 1975), sparked off a particularly vehement attack from Victor-Lévy Beaulieu, to which Jasmin replied, as is his custom, by a letter to the editor of *Le Devoir*.

His novel of 1979, *La Sablière*, received a mixed reception, much as his earlier ones had. In this novel Jasmin again evokes the world of childhood in a mixture of fantasy and realistic detail. The setting is Pointe-Calumet, the main characters are Clovis, aged fifteen and preparing to face the adult world, and his retarded younger brother, Mario. Although Clovis sees death as preferable to lifetime captivity for his brother, the potentially violent conclusion does not come about, and this novel is one of the few by Jasmin to have a "happy ending." While some critics admired the skill with which the author recalls an

Covers for a paperback edition of Jasmin's novel about an FLQ terrorist who flees from Montreal to New York with his girlfriend, Ethel

era and a child's attitude to life, others reproached Jasmin for continuing to reproduce the same novel in yet another guise. In 1980 the National Film Board was working on a film version of *La Sablière*, directed by Jean Baudin and released in 1984 under the title *Mario*. *La Sablière* (translated by David Lodbell in 1985 as *Mario*) won the Prix France-Canada in 1980; the same year Jasmin was honored by the Saint-Jean Baptiste Society with the Prix Duvernay for his literary work.

Since then he has become a full-time writer. He has produced several books since 1980. *Les Contes du Sommet-Bleu* (1980) is a new departure: a collection of eight stories for children illustrated by the author. In *L'Armoire de Pantagruel* (1982) he returns to the backdrop of postwar Montreal, but this time to show its sordid side. The narrative vacillates between *joual* and well-

turned *monologue intérieur*, as a detective called Dick Mars attempts to solve six murders in three hours. The mystery-thriller atmosphere and suspense also dominate *Le Crucifié du Sommet-Bleu* (1984) and *Une Duchesse à Ogunquit* (1985). The first relates a confrontation between developers and an ecology group whose leader is crucified. The second involves the search by two policemen for a missing Radio-Québec script. In 1983 Jasmin coauthored a book entitled *Deux mâts, une galère* with his father, Edouard Jasmin. This work, in large part a tribute to the elder Jasmin, is illustrated with photographs.

Jasmin's most ambitious work of fiction in recent years is undoubtedly *Maman-Paris, Maman-La France* (1982), which received a relatively warm critical reception. Clément Jobin, an ex-Christian Brother, accompanies his wife to France on a trip which she has won in an amateur photography contest. During their twenty-three-day stay he sends twenty-three letters to his mother. The letters contain not only reflections on France but also many satirical references to well-known literary figures of Quebec, thinly disguised. This novel is less violent than most of his others, extolling more feminine values and ending on a positive note. In the mid-1980s Claude Jasmin continues to write. He has not renounced the attempt to persuade critics in Quebec to take his work more seriously. The size of his output and his popularity with readers make his writing worthy of attention.

Interviews:

Jean Basile, "Claude Jasmin dénonce tout," *Le Devoir*, 1 October 1961;

Joseph Costisella, "Entretien avec Claude Jasmin," *Le Droit*, 14 October 1961;

Gilles Marcotte, "Claude Jasmin, entre le cinéma et la littérature," *La Presse*, 7 April 1962;

Gaston Saint-Pierre, "Ethel. . . . .Racisme contre la révolution," *Le Devoir*, 11 April 1964;

Gérald Godin, "On est les poubelles de la littérature," *Le Magazine Maclean* (June 1964);

Godin, "Le joual politique," *Parti Pris*, 7 (March 1965);

Jean Boyer, "Je crois au théâtre comme à une religion," *L'Action*, 30 November 1966;

Renaude Lapointe, "Cessons nos jasminades," *La Presse*, 21 December 1968;

André Major, "Bonjour Claude Jasmin," *Le Devoir*, 19 April 1969;

Jacques Thériault, "Quand Claude Jasmin dansait le boogie-woogie!," *Le Devoir*, 1 December 1973;

Réginald Martel, "Claude Jasmin: écrire pour être lu," *La Presse*, 21 February 1976;

Jean Royer, "Claude Jasmin. Ecrivain populaire," *Le Devoir*, 15 September 1979.

References:

David J. Bond, "Claude Jasmin's Fictional World," *International Fiction Review*, 3 (July 1976): 113-119;

Robert Dickson, "*L'Armoire de Pantagruel, Maman-Paris, Maman-La France,*" *Livres et Auteurs Québécois* (1982): 60-62;

Richard Dubois, "*Une Duchesse à Ogunquit,*" *Lettres Québécoises*, 40 (Fall 1985): 78;

Jean Ethier-Blais, "Les Romans de l'année," *University of Toronto Quarterly*, 35, no. 4 (1965-1966): 509-523;

François Gallays, "Claude Jasmin et le retour à l'innocence," *Livres et Auteurs Canadiens* (1967): 191-197;

Pierre de Grandpré, "Notre génération 'beat,' " in his *Dix ans de vie littéraire au Canada français* (Montreal: Beauchemin, 1966), pp. 184-195;

André Lamarre, "Les Contes du Sommet Bleu," *Livres et Auteurs Québécois* (1980): 235-236;

Suzanne Lamy, "Claude Jasmin, de la ferveur à l'inquiétude," *Voix et Images du Pays*, 4 (1971): 115-134;

Victor Lévy-Beaulieu, "Jasmin pour l'argent," *Le Devoir*, 27 March 1976;

Pierre L'Hérault, "La Sablière," *Livres et Auteurs Québècois* (1979): 52-54;

Clément Lockquell, "Dans les romans de Claude Jasmin, la ville innombrable," *La Presse*, 3 April 1965;

Robert Major, "Espace et mouvement dans l'oeuvre de Claude Jasmin," *Revue de l'Université d'Ottawa*, 46 (April-June 1976): 153-168;

Gilles Marcotte, "L'Aventure romanesque de Claude Jasmin," in his *Littérature canadienne-française* (Montreal: Presses de l'Université de Montreal, 1969);

Robert Mélançon, "*La Sablière*, un roman de l'enfance," *Le Devoir*, 15 September 1979;

Jean-Marie Poupart, "The Apprenticeship of Claude Jasmin," *Le Devoir*, 21 December 1974;

André Renaud, "Jasmin," *Livres et Auteurs Québécois* (1970): 161-162;

François Richard, "Deux livres de Claude Jasmin," *Le Devoir*, 22 January 1977;

Paul-Emile Roy, "L'Univers romanesque de Claude Jasmin," *Lectures*, 11 (December 1964): 87-89;

Ben-Zion Shek, *Social Realism in the French-Canadian Novel* (Montreal: Harvest House, 1977), pp. 245-257;

Adrien Thério, "*Le Crucifié du Sommet Bleu,*" *Lettres Québécoises*, 37 (Spring 1985): 75;

Thério, "Lettre ouverte à Claude Jasmin," *Livres et Auteurs Québécois* (1972): 62-64;

Régis Tremblay, "L'Enfance pénible de Claude Jasmin," *Le Soleil*, 11 October 1979;

Mireille Trudeau, *Claude Jasmin* (Montreal: Fides, 1973);

Clodius Willis, "Claude Jasmin: *Pleure pas, Germaine!*, French Review, 49 (December 1975): 299.

Basil H. Johnston

(13 July 1929-   )

S. Penny Petrone
Lakehead University

BOOKS: *Ojibway Heritage* (Toronto: McClelland & Stewart, 1976; New York: Columbia University, 1976);

Moose Meat & Wild Rice (Toronto: McClelland & Stewart, 1978);

How the Birds Got Their Colours (Toronto: Kids Can Press, 1978);

Ojibway Language Course Outline (Ottawa: Ministry of Indian and Northern Affairs, 1978);

Ojibway Language Lexicon for Beginners (Ottawa: Ministry of Indian and Northern Affairs, 1978);

Tales the Elders Told: Ojibway Legends (Toronto: Royal Ontario Museum, 1981);

Ojibway Ceremonies (Toronto: McClelland & Stewart, 1982).

OTHER: "Bread Before Books or Books Before Bread," in *The Only Good Indian: Essays by Canadian Indians,* edited by Waubageshig (Toronto: New Press, 1970), pp. 126-141;

"The Indian Heritage of Ontario," in *Travel Ontario* (Toronto: New Press, 1971);

"The Nootka, Nomads of the Shield, Hunters of the Plains," in *Teachers' Manual for History Series* (Toronto: Ginn, 1972);

"Indians, Metis and Eskimos," in *Read Canadian: A Book about Canadian Books,* edited by Robert Fulford and others (Toronto: Lewis & Samuel, 1972), pp. 168-174;

"The Smoking of the Peace Pipe or Calumet" and "To a Deer Slain by a Hunter," in *Starting Points in Reading,* compiled by Gladys Whyte and Jesse Shular (Toronto: Ginn, 1974), pp. 164-168 and 169;

"Glossary of Indian Tribal Names," in *The Dictionary of Canadian Biography,* edited by F. G. Halpenny, volume 3 (Toronto: University of Toronto Press, 1974), pp. xxxi-xlii;

"The Cultural and Ethical Aspects of Archeology in Canada: an Indian Point of View," in *Symposium on New Perspectives in Canadian Archeology,* edited by A. G. McKay (Ottawa: Royal Society of Canada, 1976), pp. 173-175;

"The Sacred Earth," in *Canada: Discovering Our Heritage* (Toronto: Ginn, 1977), pp. 2-25;

A View of Life, issue of *Tawow* edited by Johnston, 6, no. 1 (1978);

"A Man Named Weendigo," in *Windigo: An Anthology of Fact and Fantastic Fiction,* edited by John Robert Colombo (Saskatoon: Western Producer Prairie Books, 1982), pp. 201-203;

"Ojibway and French Plant Names," in *Flowers of the Wild,* edited by Ziles Zichman and James Hodgins (Toronto: Oxford University Press, 1982), pp. 259-267;

"Cowboys and Indians," in *First People, First Voices,* edited by Penny Petrone (Toronto: University of Toronto Press, 1983), pp. 182-188;

"Creation," in *Contexts: Anthology Three,* edited by Clayton Graves (Toronto: Nelson, 1984), p. 162.

PERIODICAL PUBLICATIONS: "Indian History Must be Taught," *Educational Courier,* 41 (March 1971);

"The Four Hundred Year Winter," *Educational Courier,* 41 (January 1972): 16-20;

"Is There a Place for Us on This Blanket," *Educational Courier,* 44 (March 1974): 20-22;

"The Robin," *Toronto Native Times,* 5, no. 7 (1974): 10-11;

"Zhomin and Mandamin," *Toronto Native Times,* 5, no. 11 (1974): 11-12;

"Tikinaugun," *Toronto Native Times,* 5, no. 11 (1974): 9-10;

"Our Brother, the Deer, Part I," *Toronto Native Times,* 5, no. 3 (1974): 10-11;

"Our Brother, the Deer, Part II," *Toronto Native Times,* 5, no. 4, (1974): 10-12;

"The Path of Souls," *Toronto Native Times,* 5, no. 8 (1974): 11-12;

"The Grandchildren," *Tawow,* 4, no. 1 (1974): 31-34;

"Supp-Kay–Shee, (Netmaker or Spider)," *Toronto Native Times,* 6, no. 4 (1975): 9;

Basil H. Johnston

"Forget the Totem Poles," *Educational Courier*, 45 (May 1975): 34-36;

"The Heart Berry," *Toronto Native Times*, 6, no. 2 (1975): 11;

"To a Friend in an Old Age Home," *Toronto Native Times*, 6, no. 2 (1975): 11;

"The Miracle," *Tawow*, 4, no. 4 (1975): 18-19;

"The Kiss and the Moonshine," *Tawow*, 4, no. 4 (1975): 21;

"Yellow Cloud's Battle with the Car," *Tawow*, 4, no. 4 (1975): 22-23;

"Father's Mighty Heave," *Tawow*, 4, no. 4 (1975): 25;

"Zhomin and Mandamin," *Native American Prose and Poetry* (Fall 1975): 5-8;

"Four Cree Legends, The Path of Souls—the Milky Way; Zhomin and Mandamin; The Man, the Snake, and the Fox; 'Tiki–Naugin'– the Cradle Board," *Canadian Fiction Magazine*, translation issue, no. 20a (Spring 1976): 6-20;

"The Path of Souls—The Milky Way," *Tawow*, 6, no. 1 (1978): 28-32;

"History of the Ojibway People," *Tawow*, 6, no. 1 (1978): 5-7;

"Hah–Mah–Tsa," *Tawow*, 6, no. 1 (1978): 8-12;

"The Vision," *Tawow*, 6, no. 1 (1978): 14-15;

"The Maple Sugar Festival, as told by Jim Skye to Basil H. Johnston," *Tawow*, 6, no. 1 (1978): 16-20;

"The Ceremony of Peace Pipe Smoking," *Tawow*, 6, no. 1 (1978): 22-23;

"He Knows Lots, Him!" *Ontario Indian*, 3 (May 1980);

"Cpl. Shamus McNut," *Ontario Indian*, 3 (June 1980);

"Divine Revenge," *Ontario Indian*, 3 (September 1980): 33-36;

"Where's Simon," *Ontario Indian*, 3 (December 1980): 40-45;

"My Rope," *Ontario Indian*, 4 (February 1981): 57;

"Batman and Robin," *Ontario Indian*, 4 (March 1981): 22-24;

"Stealing the Strap," *Ontario Indian*, 4 (May 1981): 32-36;

"Everybody Gotta Drink It," *Ontario Indian*, 4 (June 1981): 23-25;

"Don't Let Little Things Bug You," *Ontario Indian*, 4 (July 1981): 22-25, 50-51;

"Cowboys and Indians," *Ontario Indian*, 4 (August 1981): 26-29, 58-59;

"Tired Chickens," *Ontario Indian*, 4 (October 1981): 26-29;

"Social Graces," *Ontario Indian*, 4 (November / December 1981): 24-29;

"How Bats Came to Be—an Ojibway Legend," *Rotunda*, 14, no. 4 (1981 / 82): 4-6;

"The Bean Rebellion," *Ontario Indian*, 5 (January 1982): 18-22;

"Cattle Drive, Indian Style," *Ontario Indian*, 5 (March 1982): 18-21, 54-55;

"Only An Indian Can," *Ontario Indian*, 5 (April 1982): 28-29, 42-43, 45, 47;

"Escape from Spanish River," *Ontario Indian*, 5 (May 1982): 30-33, 56-57;

"Culture Shock," *Ontario Indian*, 5 (June 1982): 14-15, 55-57;

"Don Need Good Uniforms, Us," *Ontario Indian*, 5 (July 1982): 14-15, 63-65;

"Spanish," *Ontario Indian*, 5 (August 1982): 18-27;

"Great Spirit," *Ontario Indian*, 5 (September 1982): 22-26, 59-61;

"Nanabush," *CCL: a Journal of Criticism & Review*, no. 31 / 32 (1983): 41-45;

"Running Like a Charm," *Sweetgrass*, 1 (May / June 1984): 21, 28, 44;

"The Man Who Helped Santa Claus," *Globe and Mail* (24 December 1984);

"Mercy Killing," *Whetstone* (Spring 1985): 58-60.

Basil H. Johnston writes about his people— the Ojibway—their traditions, customs, and rela-

Dust jacket for Johnston's 1981 retelling of nine traditional Ojibway tales. According to Johnston's introduction, "if these stories do no more than give some idea of the scope of the Ojibway imagination, and perhaps bring a smile, they will have fulfilled their purpose."

tionships with the white man on and off the reserve. His writings, whether short stories, poems, retellings of traditional legends, or historical and critical essays, articulate the feelings of a Canadian Indian author who wishes to set the record straight and to preserve aspects of a culture which is facing assimilation into the mainstream. Johnston achieves these goals through quiet dignity, wit, and humor. His short stories abound in jovial banter for, in the bewilderment of the complexity and acquisitiveness of modern technological society, laughter helps to wipe out hard feelings and misunderstandings and to lighten the load of failure and disappointment. His sense of humor reflects the Ojibway's sociability and recreation. And humor, sometimes wry and subtle, sometimes mischievously funny, plays an important role in Johnston's writings.

The son of Rufus and Mary Lafreniere Johnston, Basil H. Johnston was born on the Parry Island Indian Reserve in Ontario on 13 July 1929. A member of the Cape Croker Indian

Reserve, he received his elementary education there and his secondary education at the Spanish Indian Residential School, from which he graduated in 1950. Later he studied at Loyola College, Montreal, and graduated cum laude in 1954. He attended the Ontario College of Education and received his high school assistant's certificate in 1962.

His early career spanned a variety of occupations. From 1943 to 1946 he was employed in hunting, fishing, trapping, and farming. During the summers of 1947 to 1954, he worked in the lumbering and mining industries. From 1955 to 1961 he was employed by the Toronto Board of Trade. From 1962 to 1969 he taught history at Earl Haig Secondary School in North York, and in 1969, encouraged by his friend Dr. E. S. Rogers of the Department of Ethnology at the Royal Ontario Museum in Toronto, he joined the museum to initiate a program of Indian history studies. During the summers of 1970 and 1971 he taught courses for teachers of Indian children at Trent University in Peterborough.

Johnston is currently employed by the ethnology department of the Royal Ontario Museum. He is vice-chairman of the Ontario Geographic Names Board and serves on the Canadian Council for Native Business. He has also been a consultant on native studies for the Ontario Ministry of Education. Since 1959 he has been married to the former Lucie B. Desroches and they have three children, Miriam, Elizabeth, and Geoffrey.

Johnston is a prodigious writer, and his many short stories, essays, articles, and poems have regularly appeared in such native newspapers and periodicals as the *Toronto Native Times, Tawow,* and *Ontario Indian,* as well as in journals such as the *Educational Courier.* In 1976 he won the Fels Award of the Coordinating Council of Literary Magazines, New York. His books attest to the beauty and wisdom of his Ojibway inheritance. In his first book, *Ojibway Heritage* (1976), Johnston relates a considerable body of his tribe's mythology in order to reveal the Ojibway understanding, insights, and attitudes toward life and human conduct and to show the universality of the basic ideas underpinning the myths.

Johnston's most popular book, *Moose Meat & Wild Rice,* published in 1978, is a collection of twenty-two short stories set on a modern fictional reserve, Moose Meat Point near Blunder Bay. Arranged in four parts ("The Resourcefulness of the Moose Point Ojibway"; "Christianity, Religion and Worship at Moose Meat Point"; "Getting Along and Ahead Outside the Reserve"; and "With Housing, Education, and Business . . . Poof!"), these stories based in fact portray contemporary Indians and cross-cultural relations with gentle satire that cuts both ways. Although the reserve Moose Meat Point has been deemed a creation worthy of comparison with Stephen Leacock's Mariposa and Charlie Farquharson's Parry Sound, one critic "found the stories only mildly amusing and was deeply offended by the stereotypes (both red and white) that they perpetu-

ate." But, as Johnston has noted on several occasions, the limitations of translation and the printed word are barriers to a full exposition of Ojibway humor.

Johnston's next book, *Tales the Elders Told* (1981), which has been translated into German, includes nine stories of how the world developed and how various creatures, including butterflies, bats, spiders, dogs, and fireflies, came to be. Before Johnston committed these tales to print, they had been transmitted by storytellers from one generation to the next. Johnston's most recent book, *Ojibway Ceremonies* (1982), gives the reader information about Ojibway folklore and the ceremonies which embody their religious beliefs and social customs—their spiritual rites of passage; vision journeys; healing rituals; codes of warfare; naming, drum, and marriage ceremonies along with their prescribed songs, prayers, and invocations. And because Johnston's tone is personal, the book reads more easily than an ethnologist's report.

The Ojibway language is one of Johnston's central preoccupations. In 1978, for the Ministry of Indian and Northern Affairs, he produced the *Ojibway Language Course Outline* and the *Ojibway Language Lexicon.* His translations reveal a native sensitivity to both English and Ojibway. Because of this proficiency, he is much sought after as a translator. In his efforts to encourage young Ojibway to learn the language, Johnston offers an Ojibway language course on tape.

Johnston is, first and foremost, a storyteller in the tradition of his ancestors. His style is remarkable for its linguistic exuberance, dramatic flair, and energetic affirmation of life. His works constitute an impressive testimony to the richness and diversity of the cultural heritage of Canada's Ojibway people. They also reveal Johnston's ability to nurture, renew, and share it with native and nonnative readers alike.

Marie Laberge

(29 November 1950-   )

Brian Pocknell
McMaster University

BOOKS: *Profession: je l'aime* (Montreal: Centre d'Essai des Auteurs Dramatiques, 1978);

Le Banc (Montreal: Centre d'Essai des Auteurs Dramatiques, 1981);

C'était avant la guerre à l'Anse à Gilles (Montreal: VLB, 1981);

Ils étaient venus pour . . . (Montreal: VLB, 1981);

Avec l'hiver qui s'en vient (Montreal: VLB, 1981);

Jocelyne Trudelle trouvée morte dans ses larmes (Montreal: VLB, 1983);

Le Bourreau (Montreal: Centre d'Essai des Auteurs Dramatiques, 1983);

Au bord de la nuit (Montreal: Centre d'Essai des Auteurs Dramatiques, 1983);

Deux Tangos pour toute une vie (Montreal: VLB, 1985);

L'Homme gris, Eva et Evelyne (Montreal: VLB, 1986);

Oublier (Montreal: Centre d'Essai des Auteurs Dramatiques, 1986);

Aurélie, ma soeur (Montreal: Centre d'Essai des Auteurs Dramatiques, 1987);

Le Night Cap Bar (Montreal: VLB, 1987).

PLAY PRODUCTIONS: *Profession: je l'aime*, Quebec, Théâtre du Vieux Québec, 10 January 1979;

T'sé veux dire and *On a ben failli s' comprendre*, Montreal, Café-Théâtre du Quartier Latin, 10 January 1980;

Avec l'hiver qui s'en vient, Quebec, Théâtre du Vieux Québec, 3 September 1980;

C'était avant la guerre à l'Anse à Gilles, Montreal, Salle Fred Barry, 15 January 1981;

Ils étaient venus pour . . . Quebec, Théâtre du Bois de Coulonge, 31 July 1981;

Le Banc, Quebec, Théâtre du Petit Champlain, 1 March 1983;

L'Homme gris, Montreal, Salle Fred Barry, 13 September 1984;

Deux Tangos pour toute une vie, Quebec, Théâtre du Petit Champlain, 6 November 1984;

Jocelyne Trudelle trouvée morte dans ses larmes, Quebec, L'Implanthéâtre, 8 October 1986;

Le Night Cap Bar, Montreal, La Licorne, 3 April 1987.

PERIODICAL PUBLICATIONS: "Autoportrait," *Québec-Français*, 44 (December 1981): 32-33;

"Entrevue avec Jean Guy," *Jeu*, 25 (1982): 133-146;

"Pourquoi j'écris pour le théâtre," *Etudes Littéraires*, 18 (Winter 1985): 213-222;

"Cher Rainer Maria Rilke," *Jeu*, 40 (1986): 52-54;

"On ne peut pas fausser son écriture: entretien avec Jacques de Decker," *Jeu*, 40 (1986): 211-218.

Marie Laberge belongs to a new generation of Quebec dramatists. The author of some seventeen plays, twelve of which have been produced in theaters in Quebec and sometimes elsewhere, she has also written a novel and taught classes in theater studies at the university level. She is an accomplished actress; she has directed several stage works, and for three years she was an administrator of the Théâtre du Trident, the foremost repertory company in Quebec City. An active member of the dynamic Centre d'Essai des Auteurs Dramatiques, she has been an important figure in Quebec theater since 1982, the year in which she received a Governor General's Award for *C'était avant la guerre à l'Anse à Gilles*, probably the best known of her plays.

Laberge's works reflect her undeniable concern with the place of women in society, yet they are far removed from thesis plays. Her portrayal of everyday life is a complex one; the characters she creates are multidimensional. Her keen sense of observation is apparent over a wide range of material, from portrayals of the essential moments in the life and death of a community to scenes depicting humorous aspects of human behavior, wherein women may be more often her targets than men. Her most striking quality, however, is her ability to convey the tension and anguish of her characters' personal lives as she explores the psychological stress to which they are subjected; the result is a sequence of tightly knit

photograph by Louis Ducharme

dramatic conflicts, which can be seen in most of her more recent plays.

Marie Laberge was born in Quebec on 29 November 1950, the daughter of Paul-André and Rita Ménard Laberge. Her father was a teacher of French, Latin, and Greek; he later moved to Laval University where he eventually became secretary-general of the university. Marie Laberge was one of eight children. Her early childhood years were spent at the Village de l'Ancienne-Lorette in the country, a few miles from the city of her birth, where her father held the office of secretary-treasurer of the municipality. The death of her brother at the age of eight when she was five years old left an indelible impression on her and her family; in several of her major plays she returns to the subject of death, and its presence permeates at least one of them.

The family returned to Quebec City when Laberge was twelve; there she continued her education, entering the Collège des Jésuites when she was sixteen, one of the first girls to be admitted to what had been an exclusively male institution.

In an interview in *Jeu* in 1981 she recalled the cultural shock and the disappointment she experienced at this school; she felt that she was not being taken seriously by the boys around her, that her opinions were of no account. It was then that she turned to the theater, attracted by its lively, free atmosphere. Initially, she helped with costumes, makeup and scenery; she did not act, and in fact still clung to the idea that she might fulfill her childhood ambition of becoming a dancer. She joined the Troupe des Treize when she enrolled at Laval University, where she spent two years. She studied a variety of subjects, including theater and journalism, but she said later that what she really learned was self-reliance and personal responsibility, lessons that she has passed on to some of her dramatic characters. For the next three years she studied at the Conservatoire d'Art Dramatique de Québec. The experience was a demanding one for her, emotionally and artistically, and she sometimes thought she would not persist; many of her fellow students did not. She persevered, however, because she had realized by this time that she wanted to have a career in the theater. She completed her professional training, and thereafter, for several years, she worked with modern dance at Danse-Partout. In 1977 she embarked on her career while she was still in her hometown, but she moved to Montreal, where she still lives, in the fall of 1981 in order to be closer to the heart of theater activity in the province.

Laberge acted in the early stages of her career more than she has in recent years. She has some fourteen roles to her credit, some of them in radio plays. She was Masha in Chekhov's *The Seagull*, Lucy and the balladeer in Brecht's *The Threepenny Opera*, and Pauline in Garneau's *Quatre à Quatre*, all at the Théâtre du Trident. She played Petra in Fassbinder's *Les Larmes amères de Petra von Kant*, Marianna in her own *C'était avant la guerre à l'Anse à Gilles*, and Suzanne in her *Deux Tangos pour toute une vie*.

As a director she has been responsible for twelve productions; at the University of Quebec at Chicoutimi she staged seven works by playwrights ranging from Euripides and Brecht to Tremblay and Arrabal. She often directs her own

Laberge as Marianna and Andrée Samson as Rosalie in a 1982 production of C'était avant la guerre à l'Anse à Gilles, *the play that won the Governor General's Award for French-language drama in 1982 (photograph by Patrick Bergé)*

plays for their first performances, the most recent being *Jocelyne Trudelle trouvée morte dans ses larmes* in the fall of 1986. Her professional insights into the demands of acting help her as a director to communicate with her cast; her experience as both actor and director can be seen to work to her advantage as a playwright.

Laberge has been writing since the age of ten when she composed stories to read to her sister Francine, sensitively agreeing to substitute happy endings for the sad ones to comply with her sibling's preferences. Her work as a dramatist dates from her student days at Laval University, but she counts as her first play *Eva et Evelyne*, written in 1977.

This short work presents two sisters in their sixties who have spent their lives performing the duties expected of them by dominant parents. Now alone, they confess their regret at never having known love; each relates the moment that most closely resembles that experience: for one, the rapid kiss on the cheek from an awkward boy, inappropriately named Roméo, who later apologized; for the other, the more confident sex-

ual approach of a traveling salesman who never returned, doubtless having changed his territory. A gentle humor pervades this work; both characters emerge as victims of a way of life that has relegated them to secondary roles, half suppressing their identities, as the similarity in their names may indicate. Yet they speak without bitterness, with only some sense of loss for the life that has passed them by.

Eva et Evelyne was staged in 1979 with other short works under the collective heading of *Profession: je l'aime*. The title work shows three women in relation to the men in their lives, men who remain invisible but whose wishes nevertheless determine the behavior of the women who suppress their own feelings to accommodate them. *T'sé veux dire* and *On a ben failli s' comprendre*, written about the same time as the plays of *Profession: je l'aime*, depict in a series of short scenes the social and sexual mores of a group of young people, inarticulate and inept in their strategies yet eager to conform, to preserve their image. These early works indicate Laberge's talent for expressing the difficulties of human relationships, those between the sexes and between parents and children. The Quebecois French that Laberge uses in her plays roots her characters unmistakably in their sociocultural context, so that they become metonymical figures, typical of their milieu, expressing the frustrations of many of their counterparts in society.

In the fall of 1980 there followed a successful staging of *Avec l'hiver qui s'en vient* by the Commune à Marie, a women's theater group in Quebec. It shows the home life of Cécile and Maurice. Maurice is suffering from postretirement depression. In an aphasic withdrawal from his family, he expresses his feelings only when he can recall, in an acting area reserved for recreating the past, a childhood memory of his sincere emotional ties to an aunt. Maurice's excursions into the past fall into sharp contrast with the current domestic situation played out before us, in which Cécile, frustrated and cheated by the conventional structures that have bound her, now rebels. The pent-up tensions, the product of years of noncommunication, give the play strong dramatic qualities which admirably express in a manner which resembles that of Michel Tremblay the solitude and the neuroses marriage can bring about.

Laberge returns to the study of depression in other works, but her next play, *C'était avant la guerre à l'Anse à Gilles*, produced in 1981, follows quite different lines. In 1936 the young widow Marianna, a laundress, dreams of moving away from the narrow community of l'Anse à Gilles; the sight of the ocean-going liner passing down the St. Lawrence nearby tempts her strongly. She has her friends: Honoré, her admirer, who is kind, affectionate, and attentive; and Rosalie, a young orphan girl employed as a servant in a local rich home. There is Aunt Mina also; she proclaims testily her old-style ideas on woman's role as man's mate; she is guided by the local priest in all matters and favors reactionary politics. This ready acceptance of a status quo conflicts with Honoré's broader and freer views and with Marianna's concept of an emancipated future role for women. When Rosalie is sexually assaulted by her sanctimonious and hypocritical employer, she seeks refuge with Marianna. Marianna realizes that Rosalie's account of the incident will never be believed here, and Honoré's arrival with a report of a theft and a servant's running off confirms this. The incident is a catalyst. Marianna asserts her independence; she rejects the traditional view of woman encapsulated

in a passage from Louis Hémon's *Maria Chapdelaine* (1914) quoted on stage. Tired of the past, rebelling against the codes that regulate daily life in l'Anse à Gilles, she will take Rosalie away with her, hoping to find a freer atmosphere where "silence and prayers do not rule." The play shows Laberge's talent for using the material resources of the stage to the full extent. Marianna's kitchen may denote her immediate function of self-employed laundress and baker of pies for Honoré and others, but beyond that it connotes the traditional domain of the woman. Marianna is trapped between this space and the passing days, cleverly indicated by the changing design on the sheets hanging as backdrop to the set. When Marianna introduces her new acquisition, a radio set, into this kitchen, the confused noises it emits soon turn to music from a world outside. The network of signs produces a message that change is imminent in time and space. The impact of the play was considerable; it achieved success outside Quebec too, playing to full houses and critical acclaim in Toronto. The Governor General's Award for 1981 was a recognition of an outstanding achievement for a dramatist who, at thirty, was already one of Quebec's most promising writers.

The same year saw the opening of *Ils étaient venus pour . . .*, which is Laberge's most Brechtian effort to date. It was written for a workshop production at the University of Quebec at Chicoutimi and involves some forty-three roles. It depicts the life and death of the community of Val-Jalbert, created near Chicoutimi to operate a mill. The play moves through a series of tableaux, with monologues, songs, and extracts from actual speeches and documents that helped to determine events. The manner of the work, sometimes reminiscent of Jacques Ferron's *Les Grands Soleils* (published in 1958) and Carol Bolt's "docudrama" *Buffalo Jump* (1972), is vigorous but less satisfying than Laberge's more usual intimate style. The work was selected for performance in France, in Angoulême, the town twinned with Chicoutimi, although it is not easy to imagine how this provincial town in the heart of Poitou could be truly receptive to the difficulties of the vocabulary of the Quebecois-French text.

After the 1983 production of *Le Banc*, an engaging play that unfolds around a park bench where different characters come and go in turn, Laberge was able to stage two new works in 1984. *Deux Tangos pour toute une vie* was produced by the Commune à Marie with Laberge playing

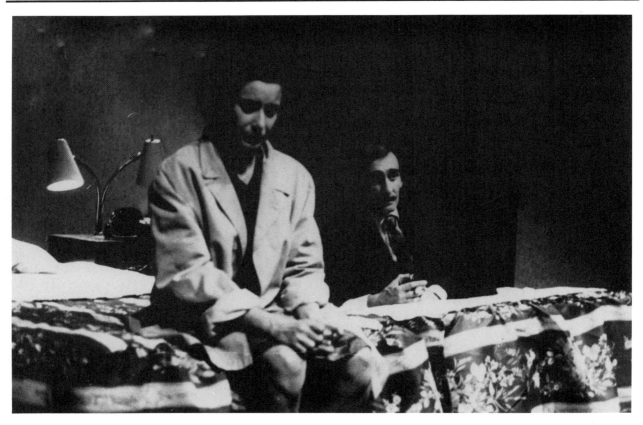

Marie Michaud as Christine and Yvon Leroux as Roland in the 1984 Montreal production of L'Homme gris
(photograph by Carl Sévigny). Laberge's play was also staged in
Belgium and France.

the leading role. Suzanne is a young nurse, on leave of absence from her job because of depression. Her husband Pierre is not unsympathetic, yet he is dull and unimaginative, functioning on a different emotional level from her, locked in a routine of suburban living and everyday preoccupations. Fresh glimpses of Suzanne appear in her scenes with her mother, Martine; their relationship is strong, contrasting the attitudes of two generations. For Martine, Suzanne should seek the traditional solution to her malaise in motherhood, like her other daughter. Yet one of the main currents in this play is Suzanne's attempt to avoid the role of mother-wife-victim; her depression is a form of revolt. When Gilles comes on the scene, Suzanne finds in him an attractive alternative to Pierre. The tango they dance is a sensuous mixture of strong rhythmic harmony and willing sexual complicity, a form of metadiscourse that operates at a level different from that of their verbal exchanges and far removed from Pierre. This triangle is unlike its trite version in the commercial theater, however; it entails considerable anguish and has no exit; Gilles

has a child, Suzanne has Pierre. The play's epilogue, with Suzanne pregnant listening to a second tango on a child's music box, is perhaps a necessary bathos, yet Suzanne attains a degree of poignancy, in the way of Chekhov's Masha, left with her dull schoolmaster husband after Colonel Vershinin's departure.

Laberge's other 1984 production, *L'Homme gris*, after a somewhat slow start in Montreal in which at least one critic was urging the public to hurry to fill the theater, has become one of her most successful works, having already played in Belgium and France, with a second run of 120 performances in Paris at the Petit Marigny on the Champs-Elysées, a theater founded by Jean-Louis Barrault in 1954 for significant works that broke new ground. It is being translated into English and Dutch, and *L'Avant-Scène*, the French theater-text series, chose this play for a special number which provided its readers with the original Quebecois text and Jacques de Decker's standard French version. The dramatist agreed to this "translation" being used in France, preferring to have her work directly understood by her French audiences to the alternative, having them kept at a distance, perhaps distracted by the unfamiliar, exotic ring of the Quebecois.

The play shows Roland, arriving at a motel with his daughter Christine, whom he has rescued from the hands of a brutal husband. This pause in their homeward journey during a rainstorm offers him the chance to expound on the father-daughter relationship, revealing more than he realizes as the gin he is drinking takes effect. The audience penetrates the tension between the two, assessing the reasons for Christine's accepting her husband's violence, her anorexia, her profound silence, all signs of her being a victim of the covert aggressiveness of her father who has denied her an existence in her own right. Her ultimate reaction, recourse to bloody violence, is a desperate attempt to protest the psychological repression that has crippled her since childhood. The action moves to this climax through his torrent of words which clashes with her unspoken inner torment. The production at Bobigny, in the Paris suburbs, in the hands of Gabriel Garran, a director formed in the Vieux Colombier tradition, was acclaimed by the French critics in publications ranging from *Le Figaro* to *L'Humanité,* and the performances, particularly that of Claude Piéplu, who had just won the critics' prize for acting, were universally praised. More than one journal perceived a parallel between this play and Sartre's *Huis Clos,* for *L'Homme gris* offers another example of Laberge's ingenious use of space to heighten the dramatic tension. The claustrophobic confinement in the motel room during the storm brings an intensification to the father-daughter relationship, their final moment being the result of the psychological pressures that the spatial construction of the play accentuates, from the noise of the storm outside to the violent colors of the bedspreads and carpets.

In 1986, while *L'Homme gris* was enjoying a second run in Paris, Laberge, in Quebec, directed the first stage production of a play written six years earlier, *Jocelyne Trudelle trouvée morte dans ses larmes.* This is in some ways the most compelling of her plays, a contemplation of the threshold between life and death, a study of profound loneliness and rejection in an indifferent world. Set in a hospital, the production showed three levels of acting area: a waiting room facing the audience "like a pointing figure," according to *Le Soleil's* critic Jean Saint-Hilaire; above, an area with a hospital bed; and uppermost, at right, in a

Micheline Bernard as Carole (seated) and Johanne Doucet as Jocelyne in the 1986 production of Jocelyn Trudelle trouvée morte dans ses larmes, *directed by Laberge (photograph by Richard Lamontagne)*

"twilight zone," in death, there is the pianist whose music accompanies Jocelyne's songs. Jocelyne has shot herself, deliberately; she lies comatose in bed; her spirit, freely moving on stage, reacts to the discourse of others. Two nurses, one for day, one for night, act as commentators, sometimes as a simple form of chorus, providing continuity and measuring the duration of this crucial moment in Jocelyne's existence. The dominant question of Jocelyne's survival lingers throughout the play, creating a certain suspense, modified in the light of the picture that emerges. In her solitude and sadness, Jocelyne has little reason to cling to life. In turn, the mother, shocked and ineffectual, the father, conventional, embarrassed, and dismissive of the stress that inspired Jocelyne's act, and the lover of one night, Ric, inept and uncomprehending, offer inadequate reasons for Jocelyne to survive. Her only friend, Carole, a foil for each of the others, is repelled by all of them. Jocelyne decides to move into the area of death in a penultimate song that mirrors her situation, the music providing a level of communication beyond the dialogue. The initial question now answered, Carole joins Jocelyne in death, her own suicide reaffirming Jocelyne's gesture. The intense pathos that builds toward the end of the play is assuaged in the last song, where both girls are invisible, the stage empty apart from the nurse-chorus changing the vacant bed, a final statement of the emotional vacuum in which Jocelyne lived.

Jocelyne Trudelle trouvée morte dans ses larmes shows Laberge at her most powerful. Not only does she organize the acting space so that the life-death axis is a constant basis of the action but she suggests a color coding for the costuming, with Jocelyne in blue, the color of the death area, and a color that reappears in different nuances in other costumes, a technique reminiscent of the early Maeterlinck in *Pelléas et Mélisande* (1892), allowing the dramatist to address the audience nonverbally. Her use of music, for Jocelyne never speaks, is part of the metadiscourse that space and color constitute; it reminds us that she wrote recently that music is superior to words to give access to a "specific dramatic world."

Few writers in Quebec theater today can match Marie Laberge's skill in analyzing human emotions. Her perception of the familiar subjects of interpersonal relationships and the stress of living, taken from everyday life, gives them a new vitality. Hers is a sincere, penetrating involvement with her characters, one of the reasons that caricature never threatens to distort her compositions. The effect is telling; audiences can scarcely fail to recognize the echoes she awakens within themselves. She has already achieved much. Her talents must be counted among the great assets of the francophone theater today.

References:

Hélène de Billy, "Marie Laberge: tout un métier que de dramatiser," *Châtelaine*, 22 (October 1981): 180-186;

Gilbert David and Pierre Lavoie, "Marie Laberge," *Jeu*, 21 (1981): 51-63;

André Dionne, "Marie Laberge," *Lettres Québécoises*, 25 (Spring 1982): 62-66;

Paul Lefebvre, "Marie Laberge," *Le Devoir*, 11 October 1986, C8;

Jean Saint-Hilaire, "La *Jocelyne Trudelle* de Marie Laberge," *Le Soleil*, 10 October 1986, C2.

Michèle Lalonde
(28 July 1937-   )

Richard Giguère
Université de Sherbrooke

BOOKS: *Songe de la fiancée détruite* (Montreal: Editions d'Orphée, 1958);
Geôles (Montreal: Editions d'Orphée, 1959);
Terre des hommes. Poème pour deux récitants (Montreal: Editions du Jour, 1967);
Dernier recours de Baptiste à Catherine (Montreal: Leméac, 1977);
Défense et illustration de la langue québécoise suivi de prose et poèmes (Paris: Seghers/Laffont, 1979);
Portée disparue (Outremont, Quebec: Les Compagnons du Lion d'Or, 1979);
Métaphore pour un nouveau monde (Montreal: Editions de l'Hexagone/Change Errant, 1980);
Cause commune: manifeste pour une internationale des petites cultures, by Lalonde and Denis Monière (Montreal: Editions de l'Hexagone, 1981);
Petit testament (Outremont, Quebec: Les Compagnons du Lion d'Or, 1981).

PLAY PRODUCTIONS: *Ankrania ou celui qui crie,* Montreal, Le Proscenium at the Festival d'Art Dramatique de l'Ouest du Québec, 6 March 1957;
Dernier recours de Baptiste à Catherine, Montreal, Théâtre d'Aujourd'hui, 22 September 1977.

PERIODICAL PUBLICATION: "Speak White" and other poems, French texts with English translations, *Ellipse,* 3 (Spring 1970).

Michèle Lalonde is one of the poets of the Hexagone generation. Although she has been a poet since she first began to write, her poetry has perceptibly evolved from the obscure works written toward the end of the 1950s to the poems of commitment of the 1960s and 1970s. Over the years she has become an essayist and has contributed articles to leftist reviews; besides writing plays, radio scripts, film commentaries, and screenplays, she has also acted as an organizer of poetry readings. During the 1970s she was active on literary, intellectual, artistic, and sociopolitical fronts simultaneously.

It was not her academic background, however, which prepared her for her career as a writer. After taking a degree in philosophy at the University of Montreal in 1959, she continued her research at Harvard in 1960 and also in Baltimore (1962-1963) and in London (1963-1964). She was the author of several programs on philosophers and thinkers—from Plato and Descartes to Schopenhauer and Russell—which were broadcast by Radio-Canada in 1964, and in 1965, at the University of Montreal, she began studies for a doctorate which she never completed. Along with these academic pursuits, she began to write poetry, and in 1958 there appeared her *Songe de la fiancée détruite,* a poem composed for radio, which in May of that year had been produced for Radio-Canada by Jean-Guy Pilon with a musical score by Ginette Martenot. The next year her publisher, Editions d'Orphée, brought out *Geôles,* a collection of twenty of her poems written between 1955 and 1957.

Lalonde's contribution to literary and cultural reviews began with *Situations,* a magazine cofounded in 1959 by the poet Maurice Beaulieu (and also published by Editions d'Orphée). It was while she was a member of an editorial committee composed of young writers, artists, and intellectuals that her first essays were published, and at the beginning of the 1960s she was one of the most active contributors to the review *Liberté,* which first appeared in 1959. From 1960 to 1962 she served as secretary to the editor and in 1963 and 1964 was a member of the editorial committee with Hexagone authors Jean-Guy Pilon, Fernand Ouellette, and Jacques Godbout, writing columns, feature articles, and book reviews. Ten years later, while a member of the editorial committee (1973-1974) of the review *Maintenant* (which was published from 1962 to 1974), she wrote for this magazine her most incisive essays on the dispute over language and on the question of nationalism in Quebec.

Songe de la fiancée détruite deals with the conscience of the individual, his innermost thoughts,

Michèle Lalonde (photograph by Kèro)

while the broad themes of this polyphonic poem are solitude and the inability of human beings to communicate. This poem and the collection which followed it bear the imprint of the literary influences which marked the poet's early efforts—Hector de Saint-Denys Garneau, Alain Grandbois, and Anne Hébert. During an interview with D. G. Jones in 1970 Lalonde spoke of the "nightmarish climate" of *Geôles* with its voids and chasms, its cries, its hatred and anger, its violence and destruction. Most of the poems in the collection—"le Silence effrité," "leur Solitude," "Ils sont un grand cri," and "le Jour halluciné," for example—are superior, as far as form goes, to *Songe de la fiancée détruite*, but in both works Lalonde writes in the poetic tradition of solitude and deprivation, of exile and alienation.

The period of change in Lalonde's concept of poetry and in her writings may be assigned to the middle 1960s. With the publication of *Terre des hommes. Poème pour deux récitants* (1967), her poetry was no longer addressed to a small number of readers but to the general public, to a mass of spectators. This radical transformation coincided with the nationalistic awakening of the Quiet Revolution in Quebec during the years from 1960 to 1966. In this context, the Quebecois poet sought to draw closer to her public and to their social and political preoccupations, a rapprochement which, in the case of Lalonde's work resulted in a passing from the abstruse to an openness toward the outside world, from the private to the public and to the group, from the abstract or distant to a concrete commitment in literature. "True poetry," she told Jones in 1970, "is the opposite of abstruseness; it is the fulness of meaning with all its vitality and diversity." With music by André Prévost, Lalonde's "symphonic fresco" *Terre des*

Cover showing music written by André Prévost for Lalonde's "symphonic fresco," performed as part of the inaugural ceremonies at Montreal's Expo 67 (courtesy of Kenneth Landry)

hommes was performed at Montreal's Place des Arts, 29 April 1967, as part of the inaugural ceremonies for Expo 67.

Lalonde's preoccupations with nationalism were present in her poetry of the early 1960s, even though they did not fully emerge until the end of the decade and the first years of the 1970s. In March 1970 she participated in the Nuit de poésie in Montreal, declaring her commitments in "Panneaux-réclame" and "Speak White." "Speak White"–which for many writers, both francophone and anglophone, came to typify the cultural anger in Quebec during the 1970s–ironically draws upon an English-language phrase borrowed from the American Civil Rights Movement to attack anglophone cultural presumptiveness in Quebec. In D.G. Jones's translation, the poem reads in part:

> Speak white
> it is so lovely to listen to you
> ....
>
> We are a rude and stammering people
> but we are not deaf to the genius of a lan-

guage
speak with the accent of Milton and Byron
    and Shelley and Keats
speak white
and please excuse us if in return
we've only our rough ancestral songs
and the chagrin of Nelligan
....
Speak white
feel at home with your words
we are a bitter people
but we'd never reproach a soul
for having a monopoly
on how to improve one's speech
....
Speak white
tell us again about freedom and democracy
We know that liberty is a Black word
as misery is Black
....
We know now
that we are not alone.

At the beginning of the 1970s, the time of the October Crisis and the War Measures Act in Quebec, Lalonde also wrote "Outrage au tribunal" and "la Prise de parole" and took part in a performance entitled *Poèmes et chansons de la résistance,* championing the cause of people she saw as Quebec political prisoners. Lalonde also regularly gave college and university poetry recitals with the guitarist-composer Jean-François Garneau. Since 1957 she had been a member of the organizing committee of the first "rencontres" of Canadian writers and subsequently took an active part in the yearly meetings which, from 1968 to 1971, were known as *rencontres des écrivains.* She continued to have poems and essays published in *Liberté,* to take part in symposia, round tables, and poetry readings, and to participate in the Rencontre Québécoise Internationale des Ecrivains (1972, 1974, 1976, and 1978), as the annual writers' gathering finally came to be called.

As far as her poetry is concerned, the years from 1965 to 1975 were unquestionably Lalonde's most productive. Her most important poems of this period were brought together in the book entitled *Défense et illustration de la langue québécoise suivi de prose et poèmes,* published in France in 1979. In the section of this collection entitled "Poésie intervenante" appear the most telling *poèmes-affiches* and dramatic texts, while in "Prose intervenante" are grouped the essays, lectures, manifestoes, and documents bearing on the question of language and politics, on the commitment of intellectuals and writers, and on feminism and the condition of women in Quebec.

During the last ten years, Lalonde has multiplied her activities both in Quebec and abroad. She likes to work with other writers, intellectuals, and artists in the United States, France, and Canada, looking for new means of expression the more directly and effectively to reach her target, the public. In this context Lalonde collaborated on a film about La Nuit de poésie, and in the summer of 1980 she visited France with six other Quebecois poets.

In 1977 the author of *Ankrania ou celui qui crie* (1957) returned to the theater with *Dernier recours de Baptiste à Catherine*. Two new volumes of poetry—*Portée disparue* and *Métaphore pour un nouveau monde*—appeared in 1979 and 1980. *Petit testament* and *Cause commune*, a collaboration with Denis Monière, were published in 1981. Both are manifestoes, the former more literary, the latter more political. A passage from *Petit testament* suggests the flavor of the work: "J'écrivais autrefois dans un style plus pur. Des phrases sans lourdeur et magnifiquement détachées du réel. Soustraites à la loi de l'attraction terrestre, sans gravité en somme, les syllabes flottaient. J'aimais les voir s'élever, successivement belles et de forme bien ronde, au bout de la pipette en verre stérilisé qu'on appelle Esthétique et qu'on m'avait prêtée." (I used to write in a purer style. In weightless sentences, magnificently cut off from reality. Removed from the laws of terrestrial attraction—without gravity—syllables floated. I liked to see them rise, beautiful and well-rounded, in succession, at the mouth of a pipette in a sterilized glass called Aesthetics, which had been loaned to me). Lalonde's concern is repeatedly with the consequentiality of language: of words, even syllables, and of naming.

As early as 1959 the French poet Pierre Emmanuel made complimentary remarks about the author of *Songe de la fiancée détruite* and *Geôles*. *Terre des hommes* has likewise received praise not only from literary critics but also from critics of art and music. In 1970 the review *Ellipse* published the first translation of Lalonde's poems and of D. G. Jones's interview with her, thus introducing her works to readers in English Canada and the United States. French reviews and newspapers warmly praised the selection of her writings which appeared in *Défense et illustration de la langue québécoise*. This chorus of praise set off in the review *Liberté* a war of words between the Quebecois critic François Hébert and

Michèle Lalonde   Denis Monière

CAUSE COMMUNE

manifeste
pour une
internationale des petites cultures

L'HEXAGONE

Cover for one of Lalonde's 1981 manifestos

the French writer Jean-Pierre Faye (who had written the preface to the collection) dealing with the content, the quality, and the scope of her work. As if to give its imprimatur to Michèle Lalonde and her endeavor to speak directly to the Quebecois collectivity, the Société Saint-Jean Baptiste awarded her in 1980 the Prix Duvernay in recognition of her accomplishments. In 1982 she was elected president of FIDELF, the International Federation of Francophone Writers.

References:
Guy de Bosschère, "Michèle Lalonde et la francophonie," *Agecop liaison*, 62 (November-December 1981);
Jean-Pierre Faye, "La défense de Michèle Lalonde. . . ," *Liberté*, 129 (May-June 1980): 91-97;
François Hébert, "Polémique—Des dazibaos à Outremont?," *Liberté*, 127 (January-February 1980): 95-99;
D. G. Jones, "An Interview with Michèle Lalonde," *Ellipse*, 3 (Spring 1970): 33-41.

Betty Lambert

(23 August 1933-4 November 1983)

Ann Messenger
Simon Fraser University

BOOKS: Song of the Serpent (Toronto: Playwrights Co-op, 1973);

Sqrieux-de-Dieu (Toronto: Playwrights Co-op, 1975);

Clouds of Glory (Toronto: Playwrights Canada, 1979);

Crossings (Vancouver: Pulp Press, 1979); republished as *Bring Down the Sun* (New York: Viking, 1980);

Jennie's Story (Toronto: Playwrights Canada, 1982);

Three Radio Plays, edited by Malcolm Page, *West Coast Review*, 19 (January 1985)—comprises *Grasshopper Hill, Falconer's Island*, and *The Best Room in the House.*

PLAY PRODUCTIONS: *Song of the Serpent*, Vancouver, Holiday Theatre, 1958:

The Riddle Machine, Vancouver, Holiday Theatre, February 1966;

The Visitor, Vancouver, Stage 2, April 1969;

Once Burnt, Twice Shy, Vancouver, New Play Centre, November 1972;

Sqrieux-de-Dieu, Vancouver, Vancouver East Cultural Centre, 20 August 1975;

Clouds of Glory, Vancouver, Vancouver East Cultural Centre, May 1979;

Jennie's Story, Saskatoon, Canadian Theatre Today Conference, October 1981;

Under the Skin, Vancouver, Waterfront Theatre, November 1985.

TELEVISION: *This Side of Tomorrow*, CBC, 1962;
Prescription for Love, CTV, 1966;
The Infinite Worlds of Maybe, CBC, January 1977.

RADIO: *Death Watch*, CBC, 1959;
The Best Room in the House, Wednesday Night, CBC, December 1959;
The Good of The Sun, CBC, 1960;
The Summer People, CBC, 1961;
Falconer's Island, Midweek Theatre, CBC, March 1966;

*bibliography rearranged by *DLB* staff to conform to *DLB* format

The Encircling Island, Sunday Stage, CBC, March 1972;

Grasshopper Hill, Festival Theatre, CBC, March 1979.

OTHER: "The Pony," in *New Voices: Canadian University Writing of 1956*, edited by Earle Burney and others, foreword by Joseph McCulley (Toronto & Vancouver: Dent, 1956), pp. 33-42;

The Riddle Machine, in *Contemporary Children's Theater*, edited by Betty Jean Lifton (New York: Avon, 1974), pp. 377-438;

"The Last Dinner," in *Elbow Room*, edited by Linda Field and Mary Beth Knechtel (Vancouver: Pulp Press, 1979), pp. 185-225.

PERIODICAL PUBLICATIONS: *The Good of the Sun, West Coast Review*, 10, no. 1 (June 1975): 3-18;

"On Writing Plays for Children: Or, You Can't See the Audience from the Trapeze," *Canadian Children's Literature*, no. 8/9 (1977): 27-29;

"Guilt," *West Coast Review*, 13, no. 2 (October 1978): 3-15.

Betty Lambert, who wrote in several genres, is best known as a dramatist. Born in Calgary, Alberta, in 1933, she was the oldest of Christopher and Bessie Cooper Lee's three daughters. As Elizabeth Minnie Lee, she grew up in Calgary, graduating from high school in 1951; she soon moved to Vancouver where she graduated from the University of British Columbia in 1957. Before she joined the English Department at Simon Fraser University as an instructor and charter member of that new university in 1965, she had taken a year of graduate work at the University of British Columbia, married Frank Lambert (1952), given birth to a daughter, divorced (1962), and held a variety of odd jobs, besides doing free-lance writing for the CBC. She had been writing poems and stories as well as radio material since her Calgary days. When she died in 1983 in Burnaby, British Columbia, she was an associate professor specializing in teaching drama, and she had over seventy plays for stage, radio, and television, as well as both long and short fiction, to her credit.

Only a small fraction of Lambert's work is in print. It is to be hoped that more will be published when her papers, which include many manuscripts, are sorted and studied, and that a full bibliography of her work will be compiled. Until then no comprehensive assessment or complete bibliography of her work can be made. However, even considering only the few published pieces which are readily available and one recently performed unpublished play, one can describe her central concerns and offer some idea of the quality and the power of her writing.

Lambert was most centrally concerned with the ancient dualism of body and mind and the conflicting demands of flesh, intellect, morality, individual selfhood, and freedom. She focused especially on women, for whom the needs of the mind are threatened, undermined, sometimes denied by their dependence on men for the needs of the body, all within a social context that itself represses or disapproves of and thus warps female sexuality and often represses or disapproves of and warps female mind as well. These concerns are present throughout her work. "The Pony," one of her first stories, published in *New Voices* in 1956, tells of a young farm girl's yearning for a wild, violent, slightly older boy. When the boy offers to take her to the movies if she will let him ride her new mare, it appears that the yearning will be satisfied. But he has been killing trapped gophers, and the blood on his hands terrifies the horse. About to dismount, the girl suddenly understands the greed in the boy's eyes—the lust for dominance—and, kicking aside his bloodstained hand, she rides her mare away from him, leaving the conflict between fear and longing essentially unresolved. The violence is both physical and psychological in two early radio plays, *The Best Room in the House* (produced in 1959) and *Falconer's Island* (1966), rather sinister dramas in which ineffectual young wives gradually supplant the older housekeepers into whose territory their husbands have brought them, as the older women themselves had supplanted their rivals. Society's repressive sexual mores warp and victimize all these women in turn. These early works were still timely when they were first published in the January 1985 issue of *West Coast Review.*

Lambert often creates intellectual, highly "civilized" female characters who are brought to fuller femaleness and fuller humanity, by their relationships with earthier characters, usually male. In the radio play *The Good of the Sun* (produced in 1960 and published in *West Coast Review* in 1975), a refined, virginal young wife accompanies her older, lower-class husband to Mexico where he regains his health and where she is renewed by her relationship with her husband's Mexican doctor and her volunteer work in his clinic. In the short story "Guilt," another *West Coast Review* publication (1978), a conventionally "good" wife breaks with her selfish, manipulative husband; she takes a job teaching English in a prison and blossoms in the atmosphere created by the semiliterate, violent, sexually overpowering men. In another story, "The Last Dinner," published in *Elbow Room* (1979), a young woman writer is painfully but fruitfully entangled with a family dominated by a classic Jewish mother. In both the radio play *Grasshopper Hill* (1979) and *Crossings* (1979), her one published novel, an intellectual woman is intensely involved with a man who abuses her physically and emotionally yet satisfies not only her body but also something in her spirit; despite the suffering and the inevitable ending of the relationships, these are both love stories. The violence, the sexuality, the crudeness, potentially destructive, are primarily constructive and fulfilling for the women in these works. Lambert seems to be saying that a woman is truly alive only when she accepts in herself and in all of humanity the impulses that her culture suppresses and denies.

The stage play *Sqrieux-de-Dieu*, produced and published in 1975, presents the conflict of mind and body and the potential constructiveness of violence more lightly. On the surface, it is a witty comedy of manners about a West Vancouver housewife longing for freedom, a successful career woman longing for maternity, and their man, but it is rooted in the myth of bacchic destruction and renewal: the man, whose "vital fluids . . . are on vacation. . . . In Hawaii," replaces his rebellious wife with his frustrated mistress, but as the play ends he is about to be "regenerated," perhaps violently, by a dangerous young virgin; and Gramma, the wife's mother who acts as chorus and talks like an eccentric but harmless senior citizen, also suggests violence—she killed her husband years ago on a sunny spring morning because he had grown impotent with age. The fates

Cover for Lambert's only published novel

ted forced sterilization of the supposedly mentally or morally unfit, laws not repealed until 1971 (Alberta) and 1973 (British Columbia). In this play Jennie's mother, a weak and conventional woman, is persuaded to allow her slightly unusual daughter to be sterilized, persuaded by the local priest who employs the young Jennie as both housekeeper and mistress. Jennie discovers the truth about her operation only when her subsequent marriage proves barren. Her suicide is her revenge. Finally, *Under the Skin,* performed in 1985 shortly after Lambert's death, is based on an actual case of sexual slavery: a man abducts a teenage girl who lives nearby and hides her in a concealed cellar in his workshop for many months; his wife tries to comfort the bereaved mother, her best friend, but when she becomes aware that her husband is the abductor, she slowly gathers the courage to call the police. The abducted girl never appears in the play. The mother's grief is profound; the psychopath is shown in all his ordinariness and extraordinariness. But the central figure is his wife, a woman torn between her dependence on her man and her socially conditioned sense of a wife's role on the one hand and, on the other, her own independent moral judgment. Her judgment wins the painful struggle, but just barely.

Lambert's children's plays deal with similar themes, though the sexuality is somewhat less obvious. *Song of the Serpent,* performed in 1958 and published in 1973, takes up freedom and slavery, pride and prejudice, in a historical context. *The Riddle Machine,* produced in 1966, shows the conflict between authority and individuality in a futuristic fantasy; this play was included in Betty Jean Lifton's 1974 anthology, *Contemporary Children's Theater.* Lambert never condescends or preaches to children, as she never sweetens or simplifies for adults her sense of the unresolvable conflict at the heart of the human condition. Her vision takes many forms, some darker and some lighter: her work includes some juvenile verse; adaptations for radio of Shaw (*The Doctor's Dilemma, The Devil's Disciple*), Chekhov (*The Sea Gull, The Three Sisters*), Henry James (*The Portrait of a Lady*), and Michael Innes (*Hamlet, Revenge!*); original mystery plays; plays in verse; musical comedies; and broadcast talks. *Crossings* stirred much controversy: Mark Abley called it "tedious" and "offensive," and some feminists agreed, but Jane Rule found it "an hilarious, reprehensible, moving book, brilliantly written." Lambert's radio and television writing was a valuable contribution to

of the wife and mistress are more equivocal: apparently they will gain, respectively, the freedom and the maternity they crave, but such resolutions are temporary, perhaps illusory, because in the cycles of life there are no final endings.

Violence is more destructive than constructive in Lambert's last three plays. Her work is always political in the broadest sense, but these plays address issues and events which are quite specifically political. *Clouds of Glory,* a reaction to the invocation of the War Measures Act in 1970, produced and published in 1979, embodies Canada's philosophical problem of individual freedom in conflict with political authority in a plot about student radicals and faculty infighting at "your Basic Instant University." The dialogue and situations are funny and ironic, but at the end there is a corpse on the floor and the philosophical problem remains unsolved. *Jennie's Story,* produced in 1981 and published the following year, expresses outrage at the laws which permit-

CBC's programming. Her major stage plays have succeeded in festivals and regular seasons alike. *Sqrieux-de-Dieu* has been particularly popular, praised by critics as "clever" and as "literate and incisive, . . . screamingly funny." Her works show that she was still growing in awareness and in-

sight when she died.

Reference:

Ann Messenger, "Betty Lambert's *Sqrieux-de-Dieu,*" *Canadian Literature*, 85 (Summer 1980): 166-170.

M. Travis Lane
(23 September 1934-   )

W. H. New
University of British Columbia

BOOKS: *An Inch or So of Garden* (Fredericton: University of New Brunswick, 1969);

Poems 1968-1972 (Fredericton: Fiddlehead, 1973);

Homecomings: Narrative Poems (Fredericton: Fiddlehead, 1977);

Divinations, and Shorter Poems, 1973-1978 (Fredericton: Fiddlehead, 1980).

OTHER: "To Stretch However Little," in *Reflections On A Hill Behind A Town*, edited by Robert Gibbs, published as *Fiddlehead,* 125 (Spring 1980): 136-146.

M. Travis Lane was born Millicent Travis in San Antonio, Texas, the daughter of Elsie Ward Travis and William Livingston Travis, a colonel in the United States Air Force. The family left San Antonio within the year. "I have no hometown," the poet has written; air force duties required the family to continue to move, sometimes almost yearly, from station to station. Her education was also gathered in various places. Ultimately she went on to specialize in English literature at university, taking a B.A. at Vassar (1956), an M.A. at Cornell (1957), a Ph.D. at Cornell (1967). It was at Vassar that she often used the name Travis; she now no longer uses Millicent.

She met her husband, the critic Lauriat Lane, Jr., at Cornell, where he taught; they moved to New Brunswick in 1960, had two children (Hannah Marguerite Lane and Lauriat Lane III), and became Canadian citizens in 1973.

Travis Lane is currently an honorary research associate at the University of New Brunswick in Fredericton and since 1970 has been a "resident book reviewer" for the *Fiddlehead.* She is the author of critical articles on a number of Canadian and West Indian poets (Robert Gibbs, Ralph Gustafson, Alfred Goldsworthy Bailey, Kristjana Gunnars, Derek Walcott, and others) and on the art of the long poem; her academic studies have been published in such journals as *Fiddlehead, Ariel, Canadian Literature, Studies in Canadian Literature,* and *University of Toronto Quarterly.*

On the editorial board of *Vassar Review* while she was at college, she had some of her earliest poetry published during her university years (as in the Cornell English Department publication *Five Poets: Cornell, 1960*). Her first book, however, was *An Inch or So of Garden* (1969), a thirty-page chapbook collecting poems from Cornell and Vassar publications and from such journals as *Fiddlehead* and *Canadian Forum.* One of the poems here ("The Apollonian Whale") was later set to music by Humphrey Searle and was also included in Greg Gatenby's 1980 anthology *Whales Art.* For the most part, these early poems are experiments in voice–the vernacular often at odds with forms of closure–all influenced by her training in English literature. There are kennings, Eliotian contrivances, hints of Hopkins and Walcott, and strong echoes of the Elizabethan lyricists. Formal rhyme is common, occasionally used ironically, as in the opening stanza of "The Zebra": "The Zebra to his betters/is unexpected joy,/implying neither half nor one/nor permanent alloy." The ironic distance does not last, however, and the poem closes in open moral: "His bars beyond our bars suggest/a freedom further, mind at rest." Yet such an orderly conclusion remains for the most part out of reach. In the book as a whole, the images recurrently tell of darkness unalleviated by light, of the beckoning chaos of Arctic, the whale-storm sea. The predominant mode, moreover, is interrogative. "I'm hard to read./As a light?" one poem queries. Other questions follow: "will I yes or will I no?"; "Where was our scented mansion?"; "Where do the fields of wheaten grace/And the olive quiet grow?"; "Are the world's roots safe in the turtle-backed tombs/in the timeless hill?" The questions can be simple, single-lined—"Father?"—or complex and acutely personal, as in "Jonah's Song": "Under the whale of Earth I hide me/. . . who will spit back Millicent?/. . . I have/no words."

The quest for a personal idiom continues through the books of the next two decades—already more confident, more secure in rhythm and image, by the time of *Poems 1968-1972* (1973) and extended in the meditative lyrics and longer poems of *Homecomings: Narrative Poems* (1977), *Divinations, and Shorter Poems* (1980), and the periodical poems that are the promise of a fifth volume to come. The lyrics primarily saw first publication in journals, Lane's reputation growing first in the Maritimes (*Antigonish Review, Dalhousie Review*) and then expanding across Canada (with publications in *CVII, Waves, Arc,* among others). Her poem "The Bomber Pilot" (addressed to her father) won *Northern Light*'s 1975 prize for best poem by a new contributor; in 1980 *Divinations* won the Pat Lowther Prize, awarded by the League of Canadian Poets. In *Poems 1968-1972* imitative echoes have turned into deliberate allusions—to Dylan Thomas, Andrew Marvell, Christopher Okigbo—or into this direct address to Derek Walcott: "Poet of our passaging, in you we are 'half-home.' " "Tom Fool" recurs as a "character" in these poems, held over from the first book, but the later lyrics are attitudinally more settled. The sea, "tolling, indefinitely," is no longer such a threat. The poetic persona now takes more delight in uncertainty; she receives chaos with chagrin but not despair, as in a punning poem about a nuisance of a cat, an existential feline perhaps, intruding on poetic composition, advising "iamb, anapest, catastrophe." The poet recognizes the line between aspiration and accomplishment: "The Past is Never Irrelevant" muses one title, the double negative a

sign of a celebration of individuality by means of a withdrawal from a set of received norms, both poetic and social. References to Canadian history and details of local observation ("Dominion Day," "kinnikinnick") begin to appear in the poetry as the writer puts down roots in a new country. Proverbs are reversed; puns are common. Yet most typically, the poems flower associatively—from single images, from observations of character. The processes of revelation are more central to the poems than are any messages about society or self. Understanding, if not order, remains of consequence to her.

"My self is for God. Nor do I suppose that I or anyone knows the inner self of others," Lane emphasizes in her essay "To Stretch However Little" (1980); the declared intent of her poetry is not to display ego or restructure society but to re-create a complex association of idea, situation, and mood "in musically cadenced verse." That which does not depart from the received culture will win immediate fame, she avers; her "more ambitious" desire is to stretch the imagination a little, to reach not for the immediate and "general" but for the "eternal." Her Christian allusions ("Day so pure/even a breath is eucharist") and associative processes of image-making have led some reviewers to liken her to Margaret Avison and Marianne Moore. Other reviews (favorable, though brief and few) have stressed her control over craft, as do those by Michael Hurley in *Canadian Literature* (Summer 1981) and Michael Hornyansky in *University of Toronto Quarterly* (Summer 1978).

The shorter poems from the middle 1970s make Lane's Christian assertions both more overt and more cryptic. Such poems as "The Unproved Glory" and "If That Mocking Bird Don't Sing" muse their way through apothegm and anecdote to statements of complicated belief: "The unproved glory itches us"; "And yet these sureties occur. The sense of self/like a wet transience englobes/a moment, opals it, spins out,/becomes en-angelled, Alled—/and so saints speak. . . ." The quest into the unknown is not unacquainted with politics and person, nor does it always take explicitly Christian form. Allusions to African politics and Amerindian culture (often through other writers: Wole Soyinka, Susan Musgrave, Emily Carr) invite the presence of different mysteries. "Zunoqua" (whose title is a reference to Nootka myth) closes with a striking reversal of Christian emblem: " 'Mother of darkness, serpent-crowned,/ totem to all I labour for,/your tree hands hug-

Early draft for "Our Young Deacon" (by permission of the author). A revised version of this poem appeared in the spring 1985 issue of New Quarterly.

ging their silences!' " But it is the ordinary and familiar that calls forth most difficulty ("How to uphold the usual? To say Look, Look,/how this is lovely? Ah, for the disappointed tongue/tolling the day call . . . "). The problem is one (as an essay by Emily Carr once put it) of "fresh seeing." "On These Bare Rocks" shows that the rhythms of exact local speech can conjure the familiar: "Codsweep and kelp. On these bare rocks/a cold light flattens out all deeps. . . . /The lighthouse cliff's an island,/basalt, black, milk-veined./It fists the choppy waters of the bay,/the fog-iced oily Quoddy, with its horn." The assonance, the alliteration, the vowel sequences, the compounded images (landscape, body, myth), the adjectival rhythm, the metaphoric verbs: all these techniques turn simple observation into a conscious act of composition. Behind this act lies a belief in an associative connection between sound, cadence, sensibility, and understanding.

The five longer poems of *Homecomings* and the three-part title poem of *Divinations, and Shorter Poems* extend the poet's meditative range. Recurrently, Lane's theme is that of fulfillment, whether by aesthetic insight, religious inspiration, or the heroism of action or survival. Emily Carr, William Blake, Penelope: all are models of a kind. "Divinations" follows a *Divine Comedy* pattern, its inferno the scream of an adolescent girl in the Catskills, its purgatorio the unsentimental, moving, documentary journal of a nurse's visits to an Indian reserve in New Brunswick, its paradiso a punning, allusive, singing testament to the power of religious vision in the art of the streets. The main poems of *Homecomings* also characteristically take fragmented form–more "monody" than "monologue," notes reviewer Guy Hamel (*Fiddlehead,* Fall 1977)–though "Bushed, a pastoral" is a minidrama, involving a lost couple, a mountie, a French-speaking moon, and an Indian spirit of the seasons named Ed Bear, who resists the idea that anyone can ever be really lost

in nature. "Daughters" is a woman's lament at her husband's funeral and, at the same time, a testament to life, to the changes that distinguish one generation from another. These disparate identities have in the persona's life allowed her to break away from the "art form" of Presbyterianism that her mother "enjoyed" and yet to hold back from her daughter-in-law's unnostalgic rituals of efficiency. Hence at the funeral one form of separation weighs against another, loss against gain. To link glory with distress in this reflection on heritage is not an unfamiliar poetic theme; Lane does not challenge tradition so much as she extends it, reinvesting the vernacular present with the complex vitalities of a continuing civilization.

The "narrative" of these longer works exists not in plot but in the record of psychological process. "Homecoming," for example, conveys the musings of Penelope in an Ithaca shaded like New Brunswick, one (in the author's words) "with moose among the olive trees." Over the seasons of two years (a truncated twenty), Penelope grieves, rebels, blames, waits. She lives the life of Everywoman (curtailed, free). Central to the whole is the distinction between nullity and pregnancy: the waiting for a something that too often translates into nothingness, the cycles of repetition being intrinsically different from the cycles of return. "Nothing returns that I recognize/but time," she hears herself saying; "The sea-dyke hardens against the sea." But that is not the end. As in other poems by Lane, it is an interim conclusion only, one seeking fulfillment but now resisting closure, one waiting for the further transformations of faith and art.

References:
Guy Hamel, Review of *Divinations, Fiddlehead,* 128 (Winter 1981): 97-101;
Hamel, Review of *Homecomings, Fiddlehead,* 115 (Fall 1977): 133-136.

André Langevin
(11 July 1927-   )

V. A. Harger-Grinling
Memorial University of Newfoundland

BOOKS: *Evadé de la nuit* (Montreal: Cercle du Livre de France, 1951);

Poussière sur la ville (Montreal: Cercle du Livre de France, 1953); translated by John Latrobe and Robert Gottlieb as *Dust over the City* (Toronto: McClelland & Stuart, 1955; New York: Putnam's, 1955);

Le Temps des hommes (Montreal: Cercle du Livre de France, 1956);

L'Oeil du peuple (Montreal: Cercle du Livre de France, 1958);

L'Elan d'Amérique (Montreal: Cercle du Livre de France, 1972);

Une Chaîne dans le parc (Montreal: Cercle du Livre de France, 1974); translated by Alan Brown as *Orphan Street* (Toronto: McClelland & Stewart, 1976; Philadelphia: Lippincott, 1976).

PLAY PRODUCTIONS: *Une Nuit d'amour*, Montreal, Théâtre du Nouveau Monde, 1954;

L'Oeil du peuple, Montreal, Théâtre du Nouveau Monde, 1 November 1957.

RADIO: *Une Neige en octobre*, Les Beaux Dimanches, Radio-Canada, 19 October 1968;

Les Semelles du vent, Les Beaux Dimanches, Radio-Canada, 5 November 1968.

André Langevin (photograph by Kèro)

André Langevin is a major twentieth-century Canadian writer. A Quebec author, he expresses in his works, particularly in his five novels, the solitude, despair, and search for identity which are universal themes of modern occidental literature. These themes can be specifically related to the political situation of French Canada and to the author's personal life.

Langevin's first published works were a trilogy of novels which appeared in quick succession— *Evadé de la nuit* (1951), *Poussière sur la ville* (1953), *Le Temps des Hommes* (1956)—and a largely unsuccessful play *L'Oeil du peuple* published in 1958. Almost fifteen years of nearly total silence followed before Langevin's next novel, *L'Elan d'Amérique*,

appeared in 1972. It received Le Grand Prix de la Ville de Montréal in 1973 and distinguished its author as something of a literary phenomenon. This work, which Jean Ethier-Blais described in *Le Devoir* as "un livre qui pleure sur notre destin," differs in style from Langevin's preceding works but is remarkably innovative for an author who, in 1972, could no longer be considered a writer of the younger generation. Beneath the vigorous modern style of this book, one which is in every sense a *nouveau roman*, the reader discerns not only the differences between this work and those of the trilogy but also the continuity of this novel with all the author's other writings. A second "new novel," entitled *Une Chaîne dans le parc* (1974), followed two years later. It, too, was accepted with acclaim. First published in Montreal, *Une Chaîne dans le parc* (translated as *Orphan Street*, 1976), was subsequently brought out by Editions Julliard in Paris–an indication of the author's achievement and of a certain international recognition.

Langevin, the son of Raoul and Brigide Gravel Langevin, was born in Montreal on 11 July 1927. Precise details of his childhood and adolescence are hard to come by, for Langevin dislikes interviews, but the salient biographical facts are those which complement his fiction. Orphaned at an early age, he spent seven years of his life in an orphanage which he described as a "mélange de prison et d'asile." He was educated in the *collège classique* system of Quebec, completing his education at the Collège de Montréal. After trying his hand at several odd jobs–clerk, farm boy, and tavern worker, among others–he became a messenger for the prominent Quebec newspaper *Le Devoir*. His next position was as journalist with the same newspaper, for which he produced ninety-seven articles within two years. Although he was in charge of the literary section of *Le Devoir,* he also wrote political and social articles for *La Liberté, Le Nouveau Journal,* and *Le Magazine Maclean.* Transferring to the newspaper *Le Temps* in 1947, again in charge of the literary section, in one year alone he produced another forty-seven articles.

In 1948 he began his long association with Radio-Canada, where he still works. He continued contributing articles to various journals, reviews, and newspapers, winning the Prix Liberté for his journalism in 1967. As for his novels, in 1951, consequent to the publication of his first novel, *Evadé de la nuit,* he was awarded the Prix du Cercle du Livre de France; in 1953 he received the same award for *Poussière sur la ville* which was hailed by critics as one of the best novels of the 1950s.

The following year he made his first foray into the theater with his historical romance *Une Nuit d'amour,* produced at Montreal's Théâtre du Nouveau Monde. The play, set in eighteenth-century Acadia after the takeover of the colony by the English, had a moderately successful run. The text, however, was not published and, unfortunately, there is no extant version.

In 1958 Langevin received first prize in the dramatic competition organized by the Théâtre du Nouveau Monde. The award was for his second dramatic work, *L'Oeil du peuple,* produced in Montreal in November 1957 and subsequently in Sherbrooke in 1967. The play is quite different in subject matter from his first attempt at theater. Basically a satire on municipal politics, on Quebec premier Maurice Duplessis, and the cor-

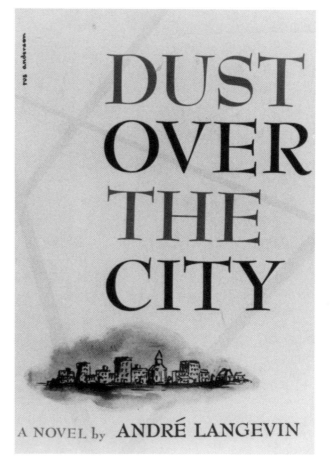

Dust jacket for the first English translation of a work by Langevin. Dust over the City (Poussière sur la ville) *was Langevin's second novel and, like his first, winner of the Prix du Cercle du Livre de France.*

ruption of his régime, it was not received with enthusiasm by the public or the critics.

After these two attempts at theater Langevin wrote dramatic pieces for the radio. Radio-Canada, the Canadian Broadcasting Company's French network, presented two works by Langevin within the framework of their series *Les Beaux Dimanches.* The first of these was *Une Neige en octobre,* broadcast 19 October 1968, followed by *Les Semelles du vent,* aired on 5 November 1972.

It was the arrival in Quebec after World War II of the works of the French existentialists Sartre and Camus that clarified for Langevin his own philosophy of life, one based on a concept of the absurd. It is these two writers who have most profoundly marked Langevin's works and, in particular, his early trilogy. In spite of the sixteen-year gap between the author's third novel and his fourth his existential vision of the world stands almost unchanged throughout his works,

works which are not limited to depiction of the individual but which go beyond the particular to the national and, finally, the universal. The influence of Sartre and Camus on Langevin is not merely literary; it also adds universal dimension to a profoundly expressed individual and very personal pessimism regarding the state of man.

In Langevin's every work the main character makes a vain attempt to replace a lost element of his own existence–personified and symbolized usually in the missing father–and experiences the need to recover this loss in the lives of others whom he sees as reflections of himself. The result is inevitably failure, a failure which contains all the fatal elements of classical tragedy. Langevin's characters are flawed and doomed by their hubris, expressed in their belief that they can help others. The result is their own destruction and a fall from grace in which they are accompanied by those they would save.

When the novels are considered individually there is both continuity and evolution in the philosophy of the novelist. *Evadé de la nuit* recounts the attempt of a young man, Jean Cherteffe (who often seems a mouthpiece for his creator), to create a paternal figure from a man who would prefer to abrogate all responsibility toward his own dying child and, by extension, to the human race. This putative father chooses suicide rather than assume the role forced upon him. His failure is transferred to the personal failure of the protagonist who also kills himself, leaving behind an infant son presumably doomed to repeat the infernal cycle of his father's life. There is a certain lack of maturity in this first novel, evident in part in the extraordinary number of deaths–ten in all–at which the reader can only register disbelief.

Evadé de la nuit was followed by *Poussière sur la ville* (translated as *Dust over the City*, 1955), a novel which can be interpreted on a humanistic or a political level. The Quebec critic Jean Ethier-Blais has suggested that the novel is a symbolic depiction of the province's infamous 1949 Asbestos strike. The plot concerns a young physician, Alain Dubois, struggling against his personal destiny. Like Camus's Sisyphus, he fights continuously to find meaning in an absurd world and to help others in their combat with the absurd. The principal female character, Madeleine Dubois, is to a large extent a complement to her husband's half-formed character, a part of his life which is lacking but one which will escape his possession. As a physician Dubois is able to extend his humani-

tarianism beyond the limited range of Jean Cherteffe but with equal lack of success. The characters of *Poussière sur la ville* are more fully developed than those in *Evadé de la nuit*. In his figure of cuckold Dubois is particularly memorable, for Langevin's portrayal places him on the plane of a tragic hero, bringing him close to Meursault of Camus's *L'Etranger* or to the doctor in the same author's *La Peste*.

Third in the trilogy, *Le Temps des hommes* (whose title refers to the Book of Job) is set in the wild regions of northern Quebec, traditionally a man's territory. The defrocked priest Dupas, like Dubois a would-be saver of men, has tried to go beyond the ecclesiastical bounds of his calling and to reach out to men, refusing God. Like the protagonists of Langevin's earlier novels, he succeeds only in destroying those he would save. The fates seem to mock him when, after he unsuccessfully attempts to save a murderer's soul, the killer dies in a banal accident. The only resolution for Dupas is suicide.

L'Elan d'Amérique, Langevin's first novel after the trilogy, seems on the surface, radically different from his novels of the 1950s not only in style but also in scope. The single male protagonist and the interior monologue have given way to two protagonists, a man and woman named Antoine and Claire, whose parallel or at times interwoven streams of consciousness express a desperate sense of fatality, tragic misunderstanding, and lack of communication. While the protagonists share many traits with their predecessors, neither of them is attempting to save others. It is their own identities which are at stake. Madeleine Dubois of *Poussière dans la ville*, refusing all involvement with others, is the closest to Claire and Antoine. The protagonists of *L'Elan d'Amérique* are orphans. Survival not in the face of absurdity but in the modern decadent Western world is what concerns them. The novel's title has more than one meaning–as do all Langevin's titles–referring both to the *élan*, moose or American elk, and to the *élan vital*, or vital force, of America. The failure of the protagonists to reconcile their pasts with the present and the future and their total inability to recognize in themselves or in others their weakness or flaws is an extension of the problems that plague earlier protagonists.

Langevin's latest novel, *Une Chaîne dans le parc*, depicts a young orphan who experiences love, hate, death, and deception to arrive at a recognition of the impossibility of any reconciliation with the world exterior to himself. Passing from in-

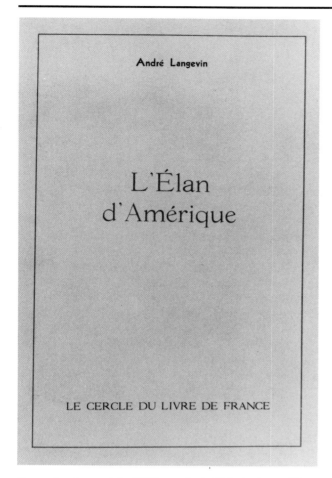

André Langevin

L'Élan
d'Amérique

LE CERCLE DU LIVRE DE FRANCE

Cover for Langevin's 1972 novel, published almost fifteen years after his preceding book. L'Elan d'Amérique *won the Grand Prix de la Ville de Montréal.*

stitution to institution he completes a full circle, and though he is seemingly a deviation from the preceding protagonists, he is nevertheless acutely aware of the futility of his existence, another Langevin protagonist deformed by his solitude.

Though on a symbolic level all of Langevin's novels reflect the author's view of the condition of Quebec, the *québécité* of his fiction is most fully appreciated in the light of his nonfiction writings. In many of these articles the themes of death, failure, and orphanhood found in the novels are discussed as relevant to Quebec. Langevin's criticism of Canadian intellectuals and writers, of their superficiality and that of the whole of North American society, is similarly a

concern that surfaces in the essays and as well as in the novels, both of which are written in an almost classic French. In his *Une Littérature qui se fait* (revised edition, 1968), Gilles Marcotte has said of Langevin's writing, "Elle est remarquablement écrite dans une langue ferme et variée qui a peu d'égales dans nos lettres." He is one of those modern Quebec writers who has refused to use *joual* or the popular language of Quebec in his novels, dismissing its employ in literature as a form of trickery and thus remaining faithful to an ideal of language as he has to his philosophy of life.

References:

Alexandre L. Amprimoz, *"Poussière sur la ville:* vers une sémiotique des gestes," *Présence Francophone: Revue Littéraire,* 14 (Spring 1977): 97-104;

Gérard Bessette, *"L'Elan d'Amérique* dans l'oeuvre d'André Langevin," in his *Trois romanciers québécois* (Montreal: Editions du Jour, 1973);

Jo-Anne Elder, "The Temptation of Despair—A Study of the Quebec Novelist André Langevin," *Canadian Literature,* 101 (Summer 1984): 121-124;

Virginia Harger-Grinling, "Le Personnage en arrange chez Hébert et Langevin," *Canadian Studies,* 21 (December 1986): 293-297;

Harger-Grinling and R. Hodgson, *"L'Elan d'Amérique:* silence articulate," *Comparison,* 12 (Spring 1981): 3-14;

Pierre Hébert, "Le discours immédiat: essai de modèle et lecture de *Poussière sur la ville* d'André Langevin," *Présence Francophone: Revue Littéraire,* 14 (Spring 1977): 105-119;

Gilles Marcotte, "L'Oeuvre romanesque d'André Langevin," in his *Une Littérature qui se fait,* revised edition (Montreal: HMH, 1968);

Gabrielle Pascal, *La Quête de l'identité chez André Langevin* (Montreal: Aquila, 1976);

Anthony Purdy, "Stopping the Kaleidoscope: The Logic of Life and the Logic of Story in André Langevin's *Poussière sur la ville,"* *Dalhousie French Studies,* 8 (1985): 78-102;

Paul Socken, "Alain Dubois's Commitment: A Reading of *Poussière sur la ville,"* *International Fiction Review,* 4 (January 1977): 174-177.

Gilbert La Rocque

(29 April 1943-26 November 1984)

Patricia Merivale
University of British Columbia

BOOKS: *Le Nombril* (Montreal: Editions du Jour, 1970);

Corridors (Montreal: Editions du Jour, 1971);

Après la boue (Montreal: Editions du Jour, 1972);

Serge d'entre les morts (Montreal: VLB, 1976);

Le Refuge: théâtre (Montreal: VLB, 1979);

Les Masques (Montreal: Québec/Amérique, 1980); translated by Leonard W. Sugden as *The Masks* (Montreal: Québec/Amérique, forthcoming);

Le Passager (Montreal: Québec/Amérique, 1984).

TELEVISION: *Le Refuge,* for *Scénario,* Radio-Canada, 4 half-hour installments, 4, 11, 18, and 25 November 1977.

Gilbert La Rocque, son of Charles-Edouard La Rocque and Lucie Savard La Rocque, was born in Rosemont, Quebec, studied at the Ecole Brébeuf, moved to Montréal-Nord at the age of eleven, took five years of the *cours classique,* then went to work at a series of more or less menial and, for him, disagreeable jobs—tinsmith, like his father, construction worker, bank employee, city clerk—which he was finally able to give up when he entered publishing in 1970. By this time La Rocque had already begun the writing of the six novels, published over the next fourteen years, which are his chief claim to fame as a Quebec writer. He became editor in chief of Editions de l'Homme in 1972 and a founding member of VLB Editeur in 1975, but he moved to the post of literary director at Editions de l'Aurore in that year and became literary director at Québec/Amérique in 1978, founding the distinguished series Littérature d'Amérique in which fifty titles appeared over the next six years.

Meanwhile, La Rocque also wrote numerous articles, published chiefly in *Québec-Amérique,* the information magazine of the press. In 1982, having won both the Prix Canada-Suisse and the Grand Prix du *Journal de Montréal* for his novel *Les Masques* (which was also short-listed for a Governor General's Award and the Prix France-Québec), he was elected Grand Montréalais de l'Avenir for his contributions to Quebec literature. He died suddenly, of a cerebral hemorrhage, on 26 November 1984, shortly after the publication of his sixth novel, *Le Passager.* He is survived by his widow, Murielle Ross, a daughter, Catherine, and a son, Sébastien.

The numerous tributes that followed La Rocque's death laid stress not only on his writing but also on his notable contributions as an editor to the encouragement of younger writers. They alluded also to the literary polemics that resulted from embroilment in an obscure literary quarrel with the critic Reginald Martel, occasioned at least in part by La Rocque's sensitivity to the supposed critical neglect or undervaluing of his own work.

While La Rocque has often been compared to Faulkner, and once or twice to Proust, one of his closest affinities is with French novelist Louis-Ferdinand Céline, all of whose works, Donald Smith reports, La Rocque "read regularly." There is a remarkable and rather Célinean consistency in the morbid intensity of La Rocque's vision, in his narrow repertory of almost entirely negative sensory impressions, in the run-on breathlessness of his underpunctuated interior monologues, and in the capacity of both author and characters for hatreds that must be largely self-hatreds.

Five of La Rocque's six novels deploy and redeploy the same thematic plot elements: in each a hero tries to fight free of his obsession with a series of childhood traumas, among which the (accidental?) drowning of a young child is frequent. Both the interleaved childhood recollections of the central consciousness and the adult's struggles with those recollections partake of the mud, the stink, the decay, the grinding poverties of material life and of the interpersonal relationships of the claustrophobic families which, in Balzacian fashion, grow out of and correspond to those poverties. This at times monotonous pattern encourages the notion, shared by some of his critics

Gilbert La Rocque (photograph by Kèro)

with the author himself, that all of La Rocque's books are, as it were, parts of one huge work.

His third novel, *Après la boue* (1972), and his fifth, *Les Masques* (1980), vary this pattern. The former does so by switching from the solely masculine consciousness of the other five to the use of a surprisingly successful feminine voice. Gaby's three adult traumas, a connubial rape, a self-inflicted abortion, and an attack upon her blind old father, are all connected to the inevitable series of childhood sufferings, yet, unusual for La Rocque, the sequence leads to a moderately successful therapy, an acceptance of herself, and some prospect of a new life. *Les Masques* is the only other novel by La Rocque that has any hint of a concluding affirmation, and it is one almost wholly undermined by the damply existential logic of the writer-protagonist, who has been recounting, in some of the best Quebec prose ever written, his tripartite obsession with "fêtes, masques, et mort," social masks, foul, muddy rivers, and the skull beneath the skin, all exemplified in the brilliant Proustian pastiche of the concluding set piece, the family festival by the dank river of his son's drowning. *Les Masques* is certainly La Rocque's masterpiece: it concentrates quintessentially all the elements of the Larocquian universe, as seen in his first novel *Le Nombril* (1970), and the 1979 play *Le Refuge*, adapted from it; in *Corridors* (1971), with its shadowy, mildly Aquinian, subplot involving the FLQ (Front de Libération du Québec); in *Serge d'entre les morts* (1976); and in *Le Passager* (1984). *Serge d'entre les morts* is remarkable for playing the role, unique in Quebec literature, of being appropriated into another writer's book; it provides, in huge hunks, the *mise en abyme* in Gérard Bessette's academic novel, *Le Semestre*, in which La Rocque's text, the subject of study, radiates outward into the lives of professor and students alike.

If *Après la boue* gives a sense of what La Rocque might have accomplished had he made more often the imaginative effort to create a character a bit different from the (presumably at least somewhat autobiographical) Larocquian hero, *Le Passager*, while gloomily interesting (in its fictionalizing of the literary feud with Martel) as a roman à clef, is a falling away from the triumph of *Les Masques*; at best it offers tantalizing clues to what La Rocque might have gone on to write, rather than a significant development of his basic pattern.

Donald Smith's excellent bibliography in *Gilbert La Rocque: l'écriture du rêve* (1985) outlines the very considerable extent of La Rocque's unpublished works and manuscripts, so it is quite possible that the presently available corpus (plus the English translation of *Les Masques* scheduled to appear shortly), is not all that we are to hear from this remarkable Quebec writer.

Interview:

Donald Smith, "Gilbert La Rocque," in his *L'Ecrivain devant son oeuvre* (Montreal: Québec/Amérique, 1983), pp. 293-311; Smith's book, translated by Larry Shouldice as *Voices of Deliverance* (Toronto: Anansi, 1986), includes an updated version of the interview, pp. 297-315.

Bibliography:

Donald Smith, Bibliography of La Rocque, in his *Gilbert La Rocque: l'écriture du rêve*, by Smith and others (Montreal: Québec/Amérique, 1985), pp. 123-138.

References:

Mary Jane Edwards, "Gilbert La Rocque," *Canadian Literature*, 106 (Winter 1985): 182-184;

Gilbert La Rocque: le voyage au bout de la vie, special issue of *Québec-Amérique* (February 1985);

"Hommage á un grand écrivain," *Le Devoir*, 1 December 1984, p. 25;

Patricia Merivale, "Black Lyricist," *Canadian Literature*, 112 (Spring 1987): 124-126;

Merivale, "Foul-Weather Pastorals," *Canadian Literature*, 96 (Spring 1983): 147-149;

Donald Smith and others, *Gilbert La Rocque: l'écriture du rêve* (Montreal: Québec/Amérique, 1985).

Félix Leclerc
(2 August 1914-   )

Paul Socken
University of Waterloo

BOOKS: *Adagio* (Montreal: Fides, 1943);
Allegro (Montreal: Fides, 1944); translated by Linda Hutcheon (Toronto: McClelland & Stewart, 1974);
Andante, illustrated by Nicole Benoît (Montreal: Fides, 1944);
Pieds nus dans l'aube (Montreal: Fides, 1946);
Dialogues d'hommes et de bêtes (Montreal: Fides, 1949);
Les Chansons de Félix Leclerc-Le Canadien (Paris: Raoul Breton, 1950);
Théâtre de village (Montreal & Paris: Fides, 1951);
Le Hamac dans les voiles (Montreal: Fides, 1951);
Moi, mes souliers. Journal d'un lièvre à deux pattes (Paris: Amiot-Dumont, 1955);
Le Fou de l'île (Paris: Denoël, 1958); translated by Philip Stratford as *The Madman, the Kite & the Island* (Ottawa: Oberon, 1976);
Douze chansons nouvelles (Montreal: Archambault, 1958);
Le P'tit Bonheur; Sonnez les Matines (Montreal: Beauchemin, 1959);
Le Calepin d'un flâneur (Montreal & Paris: Fides, 1961);
L'Auberge des morts subites (Montreal: Beauchemin, 1964);
Chansons pour tes yeux (Paris: Robert Laffont, 1968);
Cent chansons (Montreal: Fides, 1970);
Carcajou ou le diable des bois (Montreal: Editions du Jour/Paris: Robert Laffont, 1973);
L'Ancêtre (Châteauguay, Quebec: Nantel, 1974);
Bonjour de l'île (Châteauguay, Quebec: Nantel, 1975);
Qui est le père? (Montreal: Leméac, 1977);
Un Matin (Lacolle, Quebec: Nantel, 1977);
Le Petit Livre bleu de Félix; ou, Nouveau calepin du même flâneur (Montreal: Nouvelles Editions de l'Arc, 1978);
Le Tour de l'île, illustrated by Gilles Tibo (Montreal: Editions la Courte Echelle, 1980);
Le Choix de Félix Leclerc dans l'oeuvre de Félix Leclerc (Charlesbourg, Quebec: Presses Laurentiennes, 1983);

Rêves à vendre ou Troisième du même flaneur (Montreal: Nouvelles Editions de l'Arc, 1984).

PLAY PRODUCTIONS: *Maluron*, Montreal, Compagnons de Notre Dame Théâtre du Gesù, March 1947;
Le P'tit Bonheur, Montreal, Compagnic VLM at Théâtre du Gesù, 23 October 1948;
Caverne des splendeurs, Montreal, Théâtre du Gesù, Autumn 1949;
Voyages de noces, Montreal, Théâtre du Gesù, 1949;
La Petite Misère, Montreal, Société VLM at the salle du Gesù, 13 April 1950;
Cantique, Sudbury, Ontario, Festival-concours, 1953;
Sonnez les Matines, Montreal, Théâtre du Rideau Vert, 16 February 1956;
L'Auberge des morts subites, Montreal, Théâtre Québec at Théâtre du Gesù, 24 January 1963;
Les Temples, Montreal, Comédie Canadienne, 10 January 1966;
P'tit bonheur à trois, Montreal, Théâtre de l'Egrégore, 17 February 1966;
L'Eau qui coule, troupe des Gestaux, Spectacle du Vieux Québec, 28 June 1968;
Qui est le père?, Saint-Pierre (Ile d'Orléans), Quebec, Théâtre Le Galendor, 7 August 1973.

Félix Leclerc was born to Leo and Fabiola Parrot Leclerc at La Tuque, a small rural Quebec community, on the eve of World War I, 2 August 1914. The sixth of eleven children, he attributes his musical gift and love of life to his mother's influence and to the atmosphere she created at home where, he recalls, the members of the family sang more than they spoke. His childhood life is lovingly recreated in his autobiographical works and in the numerous interviews he has given.

He left home at the age of fourteen to study in Ottawa and it was at the University of Ottawa, at the age of eighteen, that he first began

Félix Leclerc, Vaudreuil, Quebec, 1960s (photograph by Kèro)

to compose songs. Those songs were the seeds of what later became the short stories, poetry, novels, and plays of one of Quebec's most widely read and acclaimed literary craftsmen. Because of the depression, his family could not afford to send him back to university, and so he returned to their farm near the Cap-de-la-Madeleine.

On a trip to Quebec City with his godfather in 1934, Leclerc astounded himself by getting a job as a radio announcer, a position that he kept for three years. During that period, he acquainted himself with the artistic world and began playing the guitar, which was to become his constant companion. After a short period back on the family farm, he accepted an offer to join a new radio station in Trois-Rivières. He worked there for two and a half years, making the acquaintance of novelist Yves Thériault and writing radio sketches.

In 1939 Leclerc moved on to Radio-Canada in Montreal where he sang his first song in public ("Notre Sentier"), began acting, and devoted himself wholeheartedly to his writing. A few brief periods in other occupations—mortician's assistant, for one—only confirmed him in his chosen path. By 1941 he had established a solid reputation as a writer and had worked with some of the finest artistic talent of the day, including Guy Mauffette, a prominent director at Radio-Canada. The following year, he married Andrée Vien, a public relations employee at Radio-Canada. In 1943 Leclerc visited the Laurentian Mountains where he met Albert Tessier who, impressed with Leclerc's work, encouraged him to have his writing published. That year his collection of stories, *Adagio*, appeared, a volume that, for the first time in the history of Canadian publishing, sold 4,000 copies in less than a month. It was named book-of-the-month by Institut de la Nouvelle-France. The following year, Leclerc produced both *Allegro*, a series of fables, and a volume of poetry, *Andante*. The celebrated novelist André Langevin called *Andante* a "hymn to life."

In fact the three volumes, taken together, constitute Leclerc's ethical framework and philosophical weltanschauung. "The burden of Leclerc's religious message," writes Elizabeth Jones in the introduction to Linda Hutcheon's translation of *Allegro*, "is one of acceptance of pain, loss and death as being all part of God's plan; . . . renunciation . . . unquestioning respect for authority . . . and complete obedience to 'the old law of hope, work, sacrifice and praying for daily bread.'"

To this summary one might add the theme of universal brotherhood. Humility and submission, for Leclerc, do not exclude an excitement about life that finds its expression in a confidence in human solidarity. God's presence is everywhere felt and celebrated. Life, in particular rural life, is a symphony composed by the Creator.

The birth of Leclerc's son Martin in 1945 was followed the next year by the death of the author's mother. During that period, one of melancholia, he wrote a short novel, *Le Fou de l'île*, which did not appear in print until 1958, and *Pieds nus dans l'aube* (1946), an autobiographical novel based on his early life and written in a vivid and lively style.

Philip Stratford, who translated *Le Fou de l'île* as *The Madman, the Kite & the Island* in 1976, called this novel a masterpiece, and Jean-Noël Samson, editor of *Félix Leclerc* (1967) in the Fides series Dossier de documentation sur la littérature canadienne-française, states that the work has been unjustifiably ignored. Part of a long-standing literary tradition that includes, among many other works, French Canada's *Le Survenant* (1945) by Germaine Guèvremont, Leclerc's novel deals with a stranger, an outsider, whose brief sojourn in a small, traditional community profoundly influences its people. The novel is an allegory of the quest for happiness on this earth. As Samson puts it, one sees Leclerc in "ce fou aux prises avec l'angoisse d'exister, hanté par le souvenir d'un paradis perdu, et qui poursuit une recherche passionnée du bonheur dans un monde qui en a perdu jusqu'à la saveur et la signification" (this madman grappling with the anguish of existence, haunted by the memory of a paradise lost, and who passionately searches for happiness in a world that has lost flavor and meaning).

In 1947 Leclerc began his long association with the theater with the writing of *Maluron*, produced at Montreal's Théâtre du Gesù. In a note on the program he urged the creation of a truly Canadian theater that would reflect national preoccupations in a Canadian style. For him, theater is "le pain du peuple." "Servons le pays," he exhorts his fellow dramatists, and great art will be created in the process: "Les chefs d'oeuvre viendront par surcroît."

In 1949 Leclerc helped found the VLM theater (Vien, Leclerc, Maufette) in Vaudureil. The same year saw the publication of *Dialogues d'hommes et de bêtes*, a collection of thirteen stories. In 1950 the French impresario Jacques Canetti heard Leclerc perform in Montreal and asked him to come to Paris. Once in France, Leclerc was hailed as a fresh, new talent by Maurice Chevalier. Jacques Brel, whose career had also been launched by Canetti, wrote: "Grâce à Félix Leclerc, Paris a découvert dans son coeur l'amour du Canada." In fact, Brel credits Leclerc with pointing him in the direction of the chanson: "Leclerc m'ayant ouvert la voie, je l'ai suivi. C'est par lui que la chanson m'a été révélée."

His initial success was consolidated by a two-year engagement at the Trois-Baudets theater in Paris. Working with André Grassi and a twenty-eight-piece orchestra, he began making records. One of them, *Moi, mes souliers* earned the 1951 Grand Prix du Disque, given by the Académie Charles-Cros, the first of three such awards for Leclerc. Before returning home in 1953, Leclerc toured France, other European countries, and Africa, drawing large and enthusiastic crowds. Leclerc says of his popularity in France that he was fortunate to have arrived there after the war, during what he considered to be a period of chaos: "La chanson française était merveilleuse mais d'un pessimisme morbide. La grande Piaf traduisait l'angoisse des gens avec ses chansons qui parlaient de foule en panique et d'amours impossibles. Moi . . . j'arrivais maladroitement avec ma guitare sèche . . . et mes chansons de grands espaces qui résonnaient à leurs oreilles comme une terre promise" (The French *chanson* was marvelous but morbidly pessimistic. The great Piaf translated the anguish of the people with songs that spoke of crowds in panic and impossible loves. I . . . arrived clumsily with my simple guitar . . . and my songs of great spaces that resounded in the ears like a promised land).

At home in Quebec, Leclerc wrote for the stage and for television and gave concerts throughout the province. During the late 1950s and the early 1960s his work continued unabated, resulting in widespread popularity. The year 1955 saw publication of *Moi, mes souliers. Journal d'un lièvre à deux pattes,* a volume of memoirs devoted to Leclerc's years as actor, playwright, writer, singer. In 1963 twenty of thirty-four classical colleges in Quebec voted him the most important French-Canadian writer.

Le Calepin d'un flâneur, published in 1961, is a collection of pithy reflections and meditations. The topics range from relationships between men and women to the differences between city and country to human nature in general. The feeling expressed, not new but refreshingly rendered, is that humanity is trapped by its own conventions and that only the privileged few—the poets, the "flâneurs" (loafers)—are free.

In 1963 Leclerc returned to the theater with his production of *L'Auberge des morts subites.* In the preface to the published version of the play (1964), the author pronounces himself in quintessentially Leclerc fashion: he is both French-Canadian and Catholic, which are to him two warm garments needed in his harsh land. He may stain them, he may even alter them slightly, he declares, but they fit. The following year, his *Le P'tit Bonheur,* first performed in 1948, was revived. Composed of twelve "sanyètes" (playlets), its presentation varied widely, depending on the material drawn upon for each occasion. The play was performed sixty times in the province and was subsidized by the government to allow it to be seen in Paris. The year 1966 saw production of *Les Temples,* which dealt with the theme of silence, the absence of communication, and the resultant lack of understanding between people.

In the 1970s Leclerc became identified with the independentist movement and took a political stance, citing Solzhenitsyn's remark about artists who withdraw to their ivory towers taking the risk of abandoning the world to madmen. The politicized Leclerc has called his fellow Quebeckers excellent losers and laid blame squarely on the shoulders of his compatriots: "L'ennemi n'est pas l'Anglais, c'est nous, les désunis, les divisés qui n'arrivons pas à faire un tout." One of his later plays *Qui est le père?*, produced in 1973 and published in 1977, embodies the question of Quebec nationalism: "C'était cette histoire d'enfant qui naît et dont plusieurs pères réclament la paternité: allégorie d'une situation historique vécue tous les jours. Le Québécois et sa province,

les richesses de cette province qui couche avec tout le monde et abandonne des plumes aux Anglais, aux Américains, aux plus offrants . . ." (It was the story of the infant born and claimed by several fathers: allegory of a historical situation lived every day. The Quebecois and his province, the riches of this province that lies down with everyone and sells out to the English, to the Americans, to those who offer the most . . .).

In 1976 Leclerc won the Prix Calixa-Lavallée, awarded by the Société Saint-Jean-Baptiste, for his role in the creation and artistic nourishment of the French-Canadian chansonnier tradition. On 25 January 1980 Leclerc was honored with a medal offered by the Mouvement National des Québécois during a "Journée Félix" held throughout Quebec. Taken as a whole, the works of Félix Leclerc reflect, in a popular form, the concerns of Quebec's major writers, both traditional and modern. The quest for fraternity and communication can be seen in Gabrielle Roy, the fierce independence and love of the land in Félix-Antoine Savard, for example, and the belief in the role of the artist in Hector de Saint-Denys Garneau, among others. The phenomenon which is Leclerc springs from the very soil of Quebec: "Leclerc's songs are just a flower at the tip of a branch," Philip Stratford contends in his introduction to *The Madman, the Kite and the Island.* "Behind them stretches a vigorous and creative life deeply rooted in Quebec but little known outside it." Christian Larsen, in *Chansonniers du Québec* (1964) states that if Leclerc did not invent the Canadian chanson, he prepared the way for its acceptance by creating a climate and a market for it. Gilles Vigneault is only one of a host of chansonniers who have followed in his footsteps.

The value of Leclerc's achievement, however, has been hotly contested. In fact, on the subject of his aesthetic contribution, evaluation has been greatly polarized. It has signaled one of the liveliest debates in the history of contemporary French-Canadian letters, with Leclerc's defenders as complimentary as his attackers have been vituperative. In the delicately worded assessment of one commentator, "Félix Leclerc a cette qualité de ne pas laisser indifférent."

If Leclerc's place in French-Canadian literature cannot yet be defined with certainty, one fact must be acknowledged: his long career has spanned the most vitally creative phase of French Canada, and his work reflects that period. Whether he is extolling the virtues of rural life and voicing the traditionalist's faith in church values, or whether he takes a more militantly nationalistic stand, as he has done in recent years, Leclerc has embodied and expressed, perhaps more than any other single artist, Quebec's complex evolution.

Interviews:

J. Richer, "Etre Canadien Français et être Catholique: deux vêtements chauds bien à moi . . . ," *Actualité* (January 1963): 16-17;

Q. Saint-Pierre, "Conversation avec notre barde national, le toujours jeune Félix Leclerc," *Le Devoir,* 20 June 1964.

References:

Luc Bérimont, *Félix Leclerc* (Paris: Seghers/ Montreal: Fides, 1964);

Jacques Bertin, *Félix Leclerc Le Roi Heureux* (N.p.: Arlea, 1987);

Jean-Claude Le Pennec, *L'Univers poétique de Félix Leclerc* (Montreal: Fides, 1967);

Jean-Noël Samson, ed., *Félix Leclerc* (Montreal: Fides, 1967).

Jack Ludwig

(30 August 1922-   )

Hallvard Dahlie
University of Calgary

BOOKS: *Recent American Novelists* (Minneapolis: University of Minnesota Press, 1962);

Confusions (Toronto: McClelland & Stewart Limited, 1963; Greenwich, Connecticut: New York Graphic Society, 1963; London: Secker & Warburg, 1963);

Requiem for Bibul (Agincourt, Ontario: Book Society, 1967; Toronto & Vancouver: Clarke, Irwin, 1967);

Above Ground (Boston & Toronto: Little, Brown, 1968; Toronto: McClelland & Stewart, 1974);

Hockey Night in Moscow (Toronto: McClelland & Stewart, 1972); enlarged as *The Great Hockey Thaw, or, The Russians are Here!* (Garden City: Doubleday, 1974);

A Woman of Her Age (Toronto: McClelland & Stewart, 1973);

Five-Ring Circus: The Montreal Olympics (Toronto & Garden City: Doubleday, 1976);

Games of Fear and Winning: Sports with an Inside View (Toronto & Garden City: Doubleday, 1976);

The Great American Spectaculars: The Kentucky Derby, Mardi Gras, and Other Days of Celebration (Garden City: Doubleday, 1976).

OTHER: *Stories: British and American,* edited by Ludwig and W. Richard Poirier (Boston: Houghton Mifflin, 1953);

Soundings: New Canadian Poets, edited by Ludwig and Andy Wainwright (Toronto: Anansi, 1970).

Jack Ludwig enjoys a reputation as a writer of vitality and versatility: as novelist, short-story writer, essayist, literary critic, journalist, sports writer, television writer, and editor, he has over the past two decades established himself as something of a literary phenomenon in both Canada and the United States. He belongs to the Canadian literary scene by virtue of his birth, early life, and education, to the American through three decades of residence and teaching in the United States, and to the North American Jewish literary tradition on the basis of his major fictional concerns and characterizations.

Born in Winnipeg to Misha and Fanny Dolgin Ludwig, he received his public and university education in that city, graduating with a B.A. from the University of Manitoba in 1944. He married Leya Lauer of Edmonton in 1946 (they have two children) and subsequently attended the University of California, Los Angeles, where he earned his Ph.D. in 1953. Since the late 1940s he has been involved in academic life, teaching at Williams College, Bard College, the University of Minnesota, Harvard, and, since 1961, at the State University of New York at Stony Brook. He

Jack Ludwig, early 1960s (photograph by Joseph Zimbrolt)

served as writer-in-residence at the University of Toronto in 1968-1969, and in 1970 he was an associate at the Stratford Shakespeare Festival in Stratford, Ontario.

Ludwig's fiction very much reflects the versatility of his life and academic career, and in some respects the title of his first novel, *Confusions* (1963), can stand as a description of his aesthetic and metaphysical vision. He is very broadly in the realistic tradition, but his prevailing satire renders his fictional worlds at times more surrealistic than realistic. Ludwig's incisive wit and his ability to cut through the hypocrisy and pretense of his worlds are his strong features, but a problem that recurs for the reader is to find a character drawn with sufficient compassion against whom he can measure the shortcomings that Ludwig quite appropriately brings into focus. To be totally effective, satire should emerge from within a world that the writer not only understands but at heart is sympathetic to, as is the case, for example, with Sinclair Lewis or Robertson Davies. Ludwig's posture of detachment from the worlds he depicts relegates his fiction at times closer to artifice than to art, with his protagonists emerging as caricatures rather than credible representatives of a confused world.

In his first novel, as the title suggests, Ludwig examines the components of a world of confusion—moral, racial, sexual, academic—through a schizophrenic protagonist, Joe Galsky/ Joseph Gillis, who is both Roxbury Jew and Harvard intellectual. The structural pattern of duality thus established at the outset is intelligently conceived, but in its execution it is more successful in superficially exposing academic and social hypocrisy than in seriously exploring the dilemmas of identity which this elaborate pattern might lead one to expect. The two identities serve as both escape and protection: Galsky suggests chaos, freedom, uninhibited behavior, while Gillis (the name inscribed in Latin on his Harvard degree) evokes decorum, ritual, and restrictions. "Superegos of Galsky, unite," the protagonist implores at one point, "you have nothing to lose but Gillis." The sentence is fairly typical of Ludwig's style. Academic wordplay, in-jokes, witty allusions, double entendres—these elements constitute the basis of Ludwig's prose, and their brilliance can be offset by tedium and predictability.

The other structural pattern in *Confusions* is more successful—the obligatory journey of the picaresque hero from obscurity to prominence and eventually to self-knowledge. Galsky's passage from Roxbury to Harvard to California's Royce College has the trappings of the mythic about it, but Ludwig's conception of this pattern does not distinguish clearly enough among these three worlds. That Galsky/Gillis comes to self-knowledge of sorts in California is only in part dictated by his growing realization that he has all along been involved in a phony game; his epiphany is mainly another extravagant joke, without the attendant moral growth which defines the genuine moment of revelation.

The problems that confront Ludwig in *Confusions* are modified in his second novel, a tripartite work set in Winnipeg, Los Angeles, and New York. *Above Ground* (1968), like its predecessor, exploits the elements of moral and metaphysical confusion, but this time with a protagonist who has no problem with knowing who he is. Joshua equates being with sensual gratification, an obsession that achieves some credibility when one

Dust jacket for Ludwig's first novel, portraying the morally, racially, and sexually confusing world of a schizophrenic protagonist

takes into account the fear of dying he experienced as a child hospitalized first for a tonsillectomy and shortly after for a broken hip. It is during his hospitalization that he first experiences both the fact of death and awareness of the delights of the flesh. He remains in a sense metaphorically crippled all his life, suspended between life and death, and his compulsive sexual conquests reflect a kind of Marvellian awareness that "above ground" is indeed the only place where one can embrace.

Ludwig's narrative style here matches the psychological frenzy that characterizes Joshua: abruptness, sudden transitions, montage effects, unannounced shifts in scene and character–all these devices give the novel an agitated quality. Again, as in *Confusions*, the element of compassion is missing, and the result is caricature and distortion; Alvira, Nina, Mavra, Zora, among others, all give themselves willingly to Joshua without the slightest hesitation or scruples, but they fail

to achieve either realistic or allegorical dimensions.

In his third novel, Ludwig achieves his greatest character triumph in Doba Goffman, a woman he had first created in a 1959 story published in the *Tamarack Review*. Taking the same title as that story, *A Woman of Her Age* (1973) depicts through a twelve-part multicharacter structure the experiences and visions that have shaped Doba's moral and psychological growth. Like Galsky/Gillis, Doba is a split character: now an eighty-five-year-old rich Westmount lady, she nevertheless retains her early radical leanings–she once saw herself as the Rosa Luxemburg of Montreal–and regularly has her chauffeur drive her through the slums of St. Lawrence Main, to keep in touch, as it were, with the real world.

Unlike many of Ludwig's earlier characters, Doba is compassionately drawn, and she emerges ultimately as a proud and almost tragic figure. She is preeminently alone in her world: one son dead, another in his sixties still engaged in rape fantasies, a daughter-in-law trying, like Joshua, both to escape and to reaffirm herself in sexuality. But because she radiates love and strength, and because she, almost alone of Ludwig's characters, has matured emotionally, she has ceased living on borrowed credit, finding sustenance instead in the dilemmas of daily experience. Furthermore, she sustains the half dozen other characters of the novel, though with some of them it is doubtful how they will fare once she is gone–and the dramatic strength here resides in the fact that what is depicted is not merely one day in the life of Doba Goffman, but the last day of her life.

Ludwig won many awards for his early work–the Atlantic First Award for fiction in 1960, the Longview Foundation (fiction) Award in 1960, the Martha Foley Best American Short Story Award in 1961, and O. Henry awards in 1961 and 1965. But the critical reception of his three novels has been less generous, supporting the view that he has not achieved the stature that these early recognitions suggested he would, though the critics themselves are not in agreement as to the relative merits of each novel.

Ludwig is often measured in terms of comparison to such other North American Jewish novelists as Mordecai Richler and Philip Roth, and in this respect two of his early critics in Canada see him as inferior to Richler. John Carroll, in the Autumn 1963 issue of *Tamarack Review*, describes *Confusions* as a shallow exposé of the academic world, a novel that fails in terms of both character-

Dust jacket for Ludwig's 1968 novel set in Winnipeg, Los Angeles, and New York

ization and style. "The worst quality in the novel," he writes, "is a constant straining to be witty, touching, allusive, profound in every paragraph." And Warren Tallman, in the Winter 1964 number of *Canadian Literature,* suggests that Ludwig is not sufficiently involved with his subject, seeing his performance "minimized to a steady stream of facetious wit that is light, and light again, and light again, ad tedium." Dave Godfrey, on the other hand, reviewing *Above Ground* for *Tamarack Review* in 1968, has some reservations about Ludwig's style but feels that this novel marks him as "twice the novelist that Roth is. . . . It kicks him up there among the ones who change and do not simply add on."

Ludwig's third novel comes off better among the critics, except for a very negative, sarcastic review in *Canadian Literature,* Summer 1974, by Phyllis Grosskurth, who charges Ludwig with triteness and superficiality. Most other critics focus on Ludwig's use of his early short story as the basis of *A Woman of Her Age,* finding the transformation from genre to genre only a qualified success, though they tend to praise the novel's central character. In *Tamarack Review* for November 1973, Ivon Owen regrets that Ludwig did not make this novel a sequel to the story

rather than a "rewrite" but describes the book as "a fine piece of work, much better than Ludwig's other two published novels. . . . This novel has all the vigour and most of the comedy of its source, with richer variety of character and incident." Arguing somewhat confusingly that the novel's "greatest strength" and its "greatest weakness" is "its pace," Michael Smith, reviewing for *Books in Canada,* January-February 1974, sees the movement from short story to novel as a risky but on the whole a successful process. "Against what seem to be pretty stiff odds," he states, "Jack Ludwig has retreaded an 11-year-old short story, set in an already overworked locale and built around a character who sometimes comes dangerously close to caricature, into a tight and raunchy new short novel."

On the whole it seems that Ludwig has not been as successful with the novel as he has been with the short story, and he has made his mark, too, in his controversial nonfiction books about the sports worlds that he knows intimately. What is missing in his full-length fiction are a sustained compassion and a consistent point of view; where incisive wit and brilliant exposé will satisfy journalistic requirements and the conventions of the shorter sketch, they are not in themselves sufficient for novels of the first order. "His problem," writes Lila Stonehewer in a 1966 article for *Canadian Literature,* "is how to sustain a heightened prose style without becoming tiresome, how to achieve variety without bathos." That he has not written any full-length fiction since the early 1970s suggests that he has not yet discovered a novelistic voice or style that totally satisfies him, and for the moment, therefore, his significance in both the Canadian and the American literary community is not as pronounced as it was during the early years of his career.

Interviews:

Donald Cameron, "Jack Ludwig: Sleeping is a Criminal Activity," in his *Conversations with Canadian Novelists,* part one (Toronto: Macmillan, 1973), pp. 116-129;

Graeme Gibson, "Jack Ludwig," in his *Eleven Canadian Novelists* (Toronto: Anansi, 1973), pp. 209-235;

John Parr, "Jack Ludwig," in his *Speaking of Winnipeg* (Winnipeg: Queenston House, 1974), pp. 96-107.

References:

Frank Davey, "Jack Ludwig," in his *From There to Here: A Guide to English-Canadian Literature Since 1960* (Erin, Ontario: Press Porcépic, 1974), pp. 173-176;

Esther James, "Ludwig's *Confusions,*" *Canadian Literature,* 40 (Spring 1969): 49-53;

Lila Stonehewer, "The Anatomy of Confusion," *Canadian Literature,* 29 (Summer 1966): 34-42.

Alistair MacLeod

(20 July 1936-   )

James Doyle
Wilfrid Laurier University

BOOKS: *The Lost Salt Gift of Blood* (Toronto: McClelland & Stewart, 1976);

As Birds Bring Forth the Sun and Other Stories (Toronto: McClelland & Stewart, 1986).

PLAY PRODUCTIONS: *The Lost Salt Gift of Blood*, Mulgrave Road Co-op Theatre Company, tour of twenty Maritime communities, October-November 1982;

The Boat, Mulgrave Road Co-op Theatre Company, tour of Maritimes, Spring 1983; Canadian National Tour, Summer-Fall 1983; tour of England and Scotland, Spring 1984.

PERIODICAL PUBLICATIONS: "Two Graves in Late November," *Antigonish Review*, 2 (Spring 1971): 19;

"Just Passing Through," *Dalhousie Review*, 51 (Spring 1971): 92;

"Generation Gap," *Quarry*, 23 (Spring 1974): 55-56;

"In the Summertime," *Canadian Forum*, 58 (February 1979): 36;

"On Hearing of the Death of Alden Nowlan, Early in the Morning, June 28, 1983," *Antigonish Review*, 57 (Spring 1984): 12;

"The Road to Rhu and Cairn an' Dorin," *Antigonish Review*, 61 (Spring 1985): 7.

Alistair MacLeod is the most important chronicler in fiction of the landscape and folkways of Cape Breton to appear on the Canadian literary scene in recent years. Although his creative output is small, consisting of only two thin volumes of short stories and about a dozen poems published in various periodicals, he has earned the respect of critics and editors in both Canada and the United States, especially for his mastery of the short-story form. His work has been repeatedly selected for anthologies and annual collections of outstanding stories; he has been the recipient of several arts grants, prizes, and honorable mentions; he has been a popular visiting reader and lecturer at universities and schools across Canada. In 1984-1985 he was selected as the Canadian participant in a Canada-Scotland writers-in-residence exchange program.

This most regionally loyal of Maritime writers was born in North Battleford, Saskatchewan, to Alexander and Christena MacLellan MacLeod, two sixth-generation Cape Bretoners who had moved west to escape the economic problems of Depression-era Nova Scotia. After five years in Saskatchewan and five in the coal-mining regions of Alberta, the MacLeods moved back to the family farm in their native Inverness County, Nova Scotia. Here in the small communities of Inverness and Dunvegan, Alistair MacLeod completed elementary and high school. In 1956 he earned a certificate from the Nova Scotia Teachers' College of Truro and began a one-year term as a schoolteacher on Port Hood Island, off Cape Breton. In 1957 he entered St. Francis-Xavier University in Antigonish and graduated with a B.A. and B.Ed. in 1960. Instead of continuing as a schoolteacher, however, he enrolled as a graduate student at the University of New Brunswick, where he completed an M.A. in 1961, with a thesis on the Canadian short story of the 1930s.

MacLeod was meanwhile writing fiction and poetry and had a story, "The Greater Good," published in the New Brunswick magazine *Intervales* in 1961. But he continued to devote his energies to an academic career, serving as an English instructor at the Nova Scotia Teachers' College from 1961 to 1963 and enrolling as a Ph.D. candidate at the University of Notre Dame, in Indiana. His main scholarly interests were in English Victorian literature and the short-story genre, interests which he combined in a dissertation, completed in 1968, on the editorial and authorial revisions of Thomas Hardy's *A Group of Noble Dames*. In 1966 he joined the English Department of the University of Indiana at Bloomington. In 1969 he moved to the University of Windsor, where he continues as a professor of English and creative writing and has served as fiction editor of the *University of Windsor Review* since 1973. Since the

photograph by Wallace Ellison

late 1960s he has maintained a slow but steady output of stories and poems, which have appeared in literary periodicals such as the *Atlantic Advocate, Fiddlehead*, the *Antigonish Review*, the *Tamarack Review*, and *Quarry*. Seven of his stories were collected in *The Lost Salt Gift of Blood* (1976), and seven more appeared in *As Birds Bring Forth the Sun and Other Stories* (1986). MacLeod is married to a native of Cape Breton, Anita MacLellan, and the couple has six children.

MacLeod's two books have met with almost unanimous praise from fellow writers as well as critics. Hugh MacLennan described *The Lost Salt Gift of Blood* as "the best pure writing ever to appear in Canadian fiction"; and the *Atlantic Provinces Book Review* (May-June 1986) greeted his long-awaited second volume of stories with a glowing full-page article, comparing the author's achievement to that of D. H. Lawrence. A concise demonstration of the esteem afforded MacLeod's work is provided by the literary fortunes of his first short story to reach an international audi-

ence. "The Boat" appeared in the *Massachusetts Review* in 1968. It was selected for *Best American Short Stories* of 1969 and for the roll of honor of the *Yearbook of the American Short Story*. Since 1968 it has appeared in ten different anthologies, in the United States and Canada, and in 1983 was adapted for the stage and produced by a touring company across Canada and in England and Scotland. Other stories have likewise been repeatedly anthologized, dramatized, and broadcast. MacLeod has been associated for several years with the summer program of the Banff School of Fine Arts as an administrator and teacher and has lectured and read his work at universities, high schools, and libraries across Canada. In 1984-1985 he served as Canadian representative in a Canada-Scotland writer-in-residence exchange program and gave numerous public lectures and readings throughout Great Britain.

Most of MacLeod's few published poems involve memorable, if sometimes prosaic, renderings of crucial emotional experiences, usually set against a backdrop of maritime landscape and seasonal change. But it is in his short stories that he has most successfully re-created the scenery and human drama of his native region. In theme and purpose his stories fall roughly into two categories. Several are variations on the time-tested motif of the initiation of the child or young man into the knowledge of tragedy or of the vanity of human aspirations. Other works, such as "The Boat" and "Road to Rankin's Point," trace a pattern of exile and return in the lives of Cape Bretoners, who yearn to escape their bleak and exhausted country but find themselves irresistibly drawn back, either in actuality or imagination. Frequently, MacLeod's stories reflect elements of both the initiation and exile/return motifs. Virtually all his stories are devoted to the exposition and dramatization of the folkways, socioeconomic realities, and relationships of family and community in Cape Breton.

Like all good regional writers, MacLeod seeks to highlight what is universal in human experience; but his stories are nonetheless important as documentary records of an exotic way of life. Ethnic writing has always been an important element in Canadian literature, but in modern writing this tradition has referred primarily to communities deriving from late-nineteenth- and early-twentieth-century continental European migrations. Writers of British descent usually write about a vaguely homogeneous or international anglophone culture or define cultural identity rather narrowly in terms of place. MacLeod has been eager to show the historical as well as the geographical ties of his Maritime characters and to reveal their strong links—including the links of language—to the past. Many of his stories are about the Highland Scots people of Cape Breton who have preserved the highland traditions and Gaelic language for almost two hundred years.

Thus MacLeod's stories can be seen as variations on a theme that has been identified as characteristic of much Canadian literature: the struggle for survival. For many of his characters, this struggle is often a tense and destructive force. On the one hand is the urge to escape the poverty and cultural introversion of a dying society; on the other is the love of the land and community and the desire to preserve old traditions and attachments. MacLeod's Cape Bretoners often find themselves in a state of unresolved suspension, imprisoned psychologically in their region and their past, even as they move physically out toward the world beyond. The young man in "The Vastness

Cover for a 1987 paperback edition of MacLeod's most recent book, a collection of seven stories set in the coal-mining country and farming communities of Canada's east coast

of the Dark" coolly prepares to leave home for good on his eighteenth birthday. But the words of his miner grandfather ring in his ears as he hitchhikes westward: "Once you drink underground water, you will always come back to drink some more." And in a carload of migrant Nova Scotians hurtling toward vague opportunities and temporary destinations, he discovers once again the dark atmosphere of compulsion and tragedy that has held his people to the land for generations. In "The Return," the drama of inevitability is presented ritualistically, as an old miner introduces his city-bred grandson to the "underground water" that is his inheritance. In "The Closing Down of Summer" a mine worker in early middle age pauses to reflect on the violent and often tragic life to which he has succeeded and recognizes that his acceptance of this life has been an acceptance of the pervasiveness and inevitability of death. A similar point is made, somewhat more sentimentally, in "The Road to Rankin's Point," where a terminally ill young man returns to his grandmother's farm in an effort to fulfill her futile yearning for the reunion of her dispersed family and the preservation of their traditional way of life.

As many of his titles suggest—"In the Fall," "Second Spring," "To Everything There is a Season"—MacLeod is fascinated by the cycle of nature, especially as it is reflected in the harsh contrasts, cold sterility, and brilliant revitalizations of his rural Cape Breton. The exile's return to his native land is in some sense a movement toward death, MacLeod implies, and "should we be drawn by death, we might well meet our own" ("Winter Dog"). Winter and death are frequently associated in the stories, in the familiar domestic situation of exiled sons and daughters called home to a deathbed or a funeral, in a boy's desperate attempt to get back home from a reckless expedition on the pack ice ("Winter Dog"), or in a marathon auto trip through a snowstorm to get home for Christmas ("To Everything There is a Season"). But winter and death always imply spring and revival. MacLeod is not interested, however, in dramatizing a joyous revival, such as that of a Christian resurrection. Rather he uses the seasonal inevitability as a lesson in reconciliation and acceptance. The individual who refuses to come to grips with the conditions of his own life is denying his own identity, his own humanity, his participation in the fixed principles of life itself.

Like other regional writers, such as William Faulkner or Thomas Hardy, MacLeod strives for impressions of interconnectedness and cohesiveness by means of subplots, parallel plots, and at times a seemingly aimless discursiveness which takes a story through several permutations of character, incident, and theme. "This has been the telling of a story about a story," says the narrator of "Vision," the concluding tale of *As Birds Bring Forth the Sun;* "but like most stories it has spun off into others and relied on others and perhaps no story ever really stands alone." MacLeod is fascinated by the origins, development, and moral implications of the process of narrative creation, as well as the relevance of this process to the surviv-

al of ethnic identity. He is interested in folktales and songs and in the aging generations who attempt to preserve such traditions. "The Tuning of Perfection" is a celebration of such attempts and a dramatization of the tensions between the modern world and older ways of life. Turning in upon folkways, turning back to the past are seen as sources of strength which are frequently unacknowledged or despised but which are nonetheless essential to the survival not only of regional communities but also of the human race itself.

The fiction writer occupies a similar essential role in the drama of survival. The folkloric elements, as well as discursive narrative and interior rumination, are the vital means of exploring and preserving an image of life that relatively few people may have experienced in its specific detail but that is universal in its implications. "We are aware that some beliefs are what others would dismiss as garbage," says one of MacLeod's narrators. "We are aware that there are men who believe the earth is flat and that birds bring forth the sun." MacLeod is talking here not about ignorance, or superstition, but the creative power of belief—a power that underlies communal ties, love, creativity, life itself. MacLeod is a subtle, economical, forceful writer, whose small but important output must not be overlooked.

References:

Harold Barratt, "Writing in Cape Breton: A Critical Introduction," *Essays on Canadian Writing,* 31 (Summer 1985): 175-191;

Mark Fortier, "Alistair MacLeod" (interview), *Books in Canada,* 15 (August-September 1986): 38-40;

Jack Hodgins, "Home is the Haunter," *Books in Canada,* 15 (August-September 1986): 12-13;

Ken MacKinnon, "Alistair MacLeod's Fiction: Long Homeward Journey from Exile," *Atlantic Provinces Book Review,* 13 (May-June 1986): 3;

Colin Nicholson, "Signatures of Time: Alistair MacLeod & his Short Stories," *Canadian Literature,* 107 (Winter 1985): 90-101;

Simone Vauthier, "Notes sur l'emploi du présent dans 'The Road to Rankin's Point' d'Alistair MacLeod," *Ranam,* 16 (1983): 143-158.

Louise Maheux-Forcier
(9 June 1929-   )

Valerie Raoul
University of British Columbia

BOOKS: *Amadou* (Montreal: Cercle du Livre de France, 1963);
L'Ile joyeuse (Montreal: Cercle du Livre de France, 1964);
Une Forêt pour Zoé (Montreal: Cercle du Livre de France, 1969); translated by David Lodbell as *A Forest for Zoe* (Ottawa: Oberon, 1986);
Paroles et musiques (Montreal: Cercle du Livre de France, 1973);
Neige et palmiers; Le Violoncelle (Montreal: Cercle du Livre de France, 1974);
Un Arbre chargé d'oiseaux: téléthéâtre, précéde de Journal de la maison d'Irène (Ottawa: Editions de l'Université d'Ottawa, 1976);
Le Coeur étoilé; Chrysanthème et de Miroir de nuit (Montreal: Cercle du Livre de France, 1977);
Appassionata (Montreal: Cercle du Livre de France, 1978);
En toutes lettres (Montreal: Pierre Tisseyre, 1980); translated by David Lobdell as *Letter by Letter* (Ottawa: Oberon, 1982);
Arioso; Le Papier d'Arménie (Montreal: Pierre Tisseyre, 1981);
Un Parc en automne (Montreal: Cercle du Livre de France, 1982);
Le Sablier. Journal intime 1981-1984 (Montreal: Pierre Tisseyre/Cercle du Livre de France, 1984);
Le Piano rouge; Comme un oiseau (Montreal: Cercle du Livre de France, 1985).

PLAY PRODUCTION: *Un Parc en automne*, Montreal, Café de la Place, 3 November 1982.

TELEVISION: *Un Arbre chargé d'oiseaux, Les Beaux Dimanches*, Radio-Canada, 1975;
Le Manuscrit, Les Beaux Dimanches, Radio-Canada, 1977;
Arioso, Les Beaux Dimanches, Radio-Canada, 1982;
Le Piano rouge, Les Beaux Dimanches, Radio-Canada, 1985;
Un Parc en automne, Les Beaux Dimanches, Radio-Canada, 1985.

Louise Maheux-Forcier (photograph by Kèro)

RADIO: *Neiges et palmiers*, Radio-Canada, 1970;
Une Forêt pour Zoé, Radio-Canada, 1972;
La Phrase qui ne sera pas écrite, Radio-Canada, 1973;
Le Violoncelle, Radio-Canada, 1973;
"Huberdeau," *Un Ecrivain et son pays*, Radio-Canada, 1975;
Miroir de nuit, Radio-Canada, 1976;
"La Grèce," *Du monde entier au coeur du monde*, Radio-Canada, 1976;
Chrysanthème, Radio-Canada, 1976;
Les Jumeaux, Radio-Canada, 1979;
La Modification, Radio-Canada, 1979;
Le Papier d'Arménie, Radio-Canada, 1979;
Un Parc en automne, Radio-Canada, 1981;
Comme un oiseau, Radio-Canada, 1982;
"Journal intime" [fifteen episodes], *Auteurs de notre temps*, Radio-Canada, 1982-1985;

Le Rendez-vous de minuit, Radio-Canada, 1982;
Eleven portraits of contemporary writers, *Auteurs de notre temps*, Radio-Canada, 1983.

PERIODICAL PUBLICATIONS: "Triptyque," *Écrits du Canada Français*, 20 (1965): 177-191; "Poétique," *Le Devoir*, 30 October 1965.

Louise Maheux-Forcier is among the best-known writers of her generation in Quebec and has been at times among the most controversial. She was born in Montreal in 1929, the daughter of Louis-Alfred Maheux, a banker, and his wife Cécile Giguère Maheux. On completing high school at the Ecole Supérieure Sainte-Croix in 1946, she began advanced studies in music at the Quebec Conservatoire de Musique et d'Art Dramatique, where she remained until 1951. She obtained a teaching certificate at the Académie de Musique du Québec before leaving Canada for Paris in 1952. There, supported by a scholarship from Quebec, she trained under the direction of Yves Nat at the Paris conservatoire and as a pianist, participated in the Concours du Prix d'Europe. On her return to Quebec she studied art history at the University of Montreal, and in 1955 she married Marcel Forcier, an interior designer who had also been a student in Paris. In 1959 she visited Europe again. It was at this time that she decided to abandon her musical career in favor of writing–partly, as she admitted in a 1963 interview with Solange Chalvin, because of stage fright. Her early training in music has left many traces in her written works.

Maheux-Forcier's first work, *Amadou*, was published in 1963. The critical reception of this novel was mixed, but it won the Prix du Cercle du Livre de France. For its treatment of love between two women, it was condemned in Catholic circles by such critics as Clément Lockquell, writing for *Le Soleil*, and Paul Gay, who, in a review for *Lectures*, called it "des fleurs sur du fumier"–flowers on a dunghill. Monique Bosco, in *Le Magazine McLean*, and Gilles Marcotte, in *La Presse*, berated it on more aesthetic grounds, while others recognized the remarkable stylistic qualities evident in this first work.

Amadou deals with the relationship between two couples, Nathalie, a young Quebecois pianist, Julien, an artist, Robert, a bohemian friend of Julien's, and Robert's mistress, Sylvia, who fascinates Nathalie. In the course of the novel Nathalie, who is haunted by memories of a lesbian relationship with her childhood friend,

Anne, becomes fascinated with Sylvia, has an affair with Robert that arouses Julien's jealousy, and eventually agrees to marry Julien. When Julien finds some love letters that Sylvia has written inviting Nathalie to join her and Robert in a ménage à trois, Nathalie attempts to poison him and plans to set fire to the house with herself in it.

In *Amadou* Maheux-Forcier's sober but poetic style and the force of her imagery are already apparent, in spite of the many reflections on art and life which disrupt the narration and have generally been seen as a defect. The author acknowledged the influence of her own travels in Europe–especially the "La volupté Mediterranéenne" she had discovered in Greece. She also attributed some aspects of the novel to the influence of her husband and his critical reading of her manuscript. The novel ends with a message from Julien asserting that a "vie saine et normale" is preferable, leaving the overall judgment of sexual deviation in doubt.

Amadou is the first of a trilogy of novels concerned with similar themes. The second, *L'Ile joyeuse* (1964), is like its predecessor, a first-person narration by a young female character, in this instance, Isabelle, who is torn between the alcoholic Stéphane and Stéphane's wife, Julie. Julie, like Sylvia in *Amadou*, sees the ideal couple as open to a third person. The book is structured like a concerto, using counterpoint and, as in *Amadou*, the puritanical mother as one source of the heroine's problems is another theme developed.

The third part of the trilogy, *Une Forêt pour Zoé* (1969), is considered by several critics to be the most successful. It won a Governor General's Award in 1970. The central character, Thérèse, is haunted by a childhood friend, Zoé, and lives in a world which vacillates between dream and reality. She attempts to escape from her obsession and from her past by writing a novel, rejecting her education and the idea of the traditional couple in favor of an ideal love between women. In this novel subtle, impressionistic imagery conveys a more explicit eroticism. Writing for *La Presse* in January 1970, Reginald Martel summarized the overall effect as "de la sobriété dans l'excès." Jean-Guy Blondin's 1971 article "Aux sources de la rêverie poétique chez Louise Maheux-Forcier" compares the three novels.

Since 1970 Maheux-Forcier has become as well known for her radio and television work for Radio-Canada as for her fiction. One of her first texts for radio was a 1972 adaptation of *Une Forêt pour Zoé*. Of the many other dramatic works broadcast from 1970 to 1983, several have been published in book form: *Neige et palmiers* and *Le Violoncelle* (1974), *Le Coeur étoilé, Chrysanthème,* and *Miroir de nuit* (1977), *Le Papier d'Arménie* (1981), *Un Parc en automne* (1982). *Arioso* (1981) and *Le Piano rouge* (1985) are among Maheux-Forcier's television dramas which are available in print. *Un Arbre chargé d'oiseaux* (1975) was also shown in France, Switzerland, and Belgium as Quebec's entry in the competition for the Louis-Philippe Kammans prize. *Arioso* was at first refused for the series *Les Beaux Dimanches* because of its treatment of lesbianism, and when it finally was shown in 1982 it created a considerable controversy, one recorded in *Le Devoir*, 2, 13 and 20 February, and *La Presse*, 2 and 23 February.

Un Parc en automne, written for radio in 1981, was successfully staged in Montreal at the Café de la Place the following year. Produced, as were Maheux-Forcier's television dramas, by Jean Faucher, the stage play featured Françoise Faucher and Guy Próvost in the leading roles as a man and a woman who meet again after thirty years, in an old folks' home. The play was adapted for television in 1985.

Some of Maheux-Forcier's work for radio has been overtly autobiographical in nature: "Huberdeau" (1975) was part of the series *Un Ecrivain et son pays* and deals with her attitude to Quebec; "La Grèce" (1976), her contribution to a series entitled *Du monde entier au coeur du monde*, speaks of the fascination Greece has exerted on her. From 1982 to 1985 parts of her diary were read by Françoise Faucher in a series of fifteen episodes produced by André Major and Yves Lapierre for the program *Auteurs de notre temps*. These texts, which reveal much about the author's personality and tastes as well as her views on a variety of topics, were published in 1984 as *Le Sablier. Journal intime 1981-1984*. In 1983 she provided eleven portraits of contemporary foreign writers for *Auteurs de notre temps*.

During this productive period Maheux-Forcier did not abandon narrative fiction. She published two further novels, *Paroles et musiques* (1973) and *Appassionata* (1978). In the first a woman dying of cancer confides in a female friend (her last love?), recalling her childhood and adolescence in the Quebec of myth and taboos. In a 1982 interview with Jean Royer published in *Le Devoir*, the author has depicted writing as the only defense against death, and this novel is a projection of that premise. Some hope is also placed, however, in the power of love; in the same interview, Maheux-Forcier maintains that love alone is not absurd.

In *Appassionata* one of her concerns is, again, love between women. The book begins with a letter (signed L. M.-F.) to the editor, in which the author-narrator questions the value of writing. She claims the manuscript to be the text of a long letter attributed to her friend, Renée, who has committed suicide, and addressed by her to another woman, Amélie. This work, even more freely "poetic" than the preceding ones, prompted one critic–Gabrielle Pascal in *Livres et Auteurs Québécois*–to wonder if it marks the beginning of a new cycle in which the novelistic elements will become increasingly marginal. Already in her "Poetique," published in 1965 in *Le Devoir*, Maheux-Forcier had claimed that "Roman-poème," in the tradition of Virginia Woolf, was the only label she would accept for her novels.

The one work by Maheux-Forcier available in English translation is written in a very different vein from the novels. *En toutes lettres*, published in 1980 and translated by David Lobdell as *Letter by Letter* in 1982, is composed of twenty-five short stories or vignettes characterized by irony and humor, qualities apparent in the diary but generally sparse in the novels before *Appassionata*. There is one vignette titled for each letter of the alphabet except *C* ("Les Billets de Clara" does double duty), although the sketches are not presented in alphabetical order. The tone is conversational, the style more familiar and colloquial than in her other works. Striking images and plays on words abound. Several texts are hardly narrative in form ("Les Yeux," "Le Poème," "Fantoches," and "Zoé"). The whole collection is a virtuoso performance, making fun not only of everyday life and human foibles but also of literary figures and sexual relationships.

One story, "L'Interview," attacks journalists who insist on searching for links between an author's life and his or her work. Maheux-Forcier has herself not been forthcoming in discussing autobiographical elements in her writing. Her main purpose in giving interviews has been to reject association with feminist or lesbian movements or schools of thought. She has also remained resolutely apolitical on the "national" question. This refusal to commit herself and the difficulty of categorizing her works are part of the reason for the lack of critical attention paid to the novels and dramatic works of this widely recognized writer. Her work tends to fall between the traditions of the old guard (purity of language, emphasis on style, aestheticism, bourgeois heroines reacting against their past) and those of the new (experimentation with language, questioning of sexual identity and roles, iconoclasm): she is consequently neglected by academic critics interested in one or the other. Yet her strengths are precisely in this ambivalence, as Madeleine Ouellette-Michalska has pointed out in a 1980 article for *Le Devoir*.

Jean Ethier-Blais has called her books, "passionnés et sages" and compared her to Colette. Louise Maheux-Forcier is certainly a strong presence on the literary scene in Quebec. She has written for numerous reviews, including *Ecrits du Canada Français, Liberté, La Nouvelle Barre du Jour, Bulletin du Centre de Recherches de Civilisation Canadienne-Française, Diapason, La Voix des Poètes,* and *L'Ingénu*. She is a member of many writers' associations, including the Union des Ecrivains Québécois, the Société des Ecrivains Canadiens, and the P.E.N. Club, and has been a member of several literary juries. She became a member of the French-Canadian Academy in 1982 and a fellow of the Royal Society of Canada in 1985. The ceremony for her reception into the Society took the form of a dramatic dialogue between herself and her sponsor, Jean-Guy Pilon.

Maheux-Forcier's manuscripts are deposited at the archives of the University of Ottawa, where she worked at the Research Centre for French-Canadian Civilization in 1972-1973 and was writer in residence in 1979. Among contemporary Quebecois writers she is one of those whose work deserves further study and detailed analysis.

Interviews:

Solange Chalvin, "Le Plus Récent Auteur Canadien, Louise Maheux-Forcier, nous raconte sa douceur de vivre," *Le Devoir*, 26 October 1963, p. 42;

David Lonergan, "Louise Maheux-Forcier: Je suis obsédé par mon enfance," *Québec-Presse*, 1 March 1970, p. 17;

Reginald Martel, "Louise Maheux-Forcier: Lutter contre la mort," *La Presse*, 28 March 1970, p. 33;

Jean Royer, "Louise Maheux-Forcier: Seul l'amour n'est pas absurde," *Le Devoir*, 30 January 1982, p. 15.

References:

Jacques Allard, *"Paroles et musiques,"* *Livres et Auteurs Québécois* (1973): 46-48;

Jean-Guy Blondin, "Aux sources de la rêverie poétique chez Louise Maheux-Forcier," *Livres et Auteurs Québécois* (1971): 295-304;

Monique Bosco, "*Amadou* de Louise Maheux-Forcier, un roman qui me scandalise," *Le Magazine McLean*, 3 (December 1963): 91;

André Brochu, "*Amadou* ou les cercles du mal," *Parti Pris*, 1 (January 1964): 58-60;

Léonce Cantin, "L'Ile joyeuse de Louise Maheux-Forcier," *Livres et Auteurs Québécois* (1964): 21-22;

Paulette Collet, "La Notion du bien et du mal chez Louise Maheux-Forcier," *Présence Francophone* (Spring 1976): 113-122;

Hélène Dorion, "Louise Maheux-Forcier. *Un Parc en automne*," *Livres et Auteurs Québécois* (1981): 180-181;

Jean Ethier-Blais, "*Amadou*," *University of Toronto Quarterly*, 33 (July 1964): 511-513;

Ethier-Blais, "Louise Maheux-Forcier. Une Oeuvre lente, mesurée, mais non sans profusion," *Le Devoir*, 31 January 1970, p.13;

François Hébert, "Louise Maheux-Forcier, *Le Sablier. Journal intime*," *Le Devoir*, 15 December 1984, p. 27;

Naim Kattan, "*Amadou*," *Tamarack Review*, 30 (Winter 1964): 48-52;

Suzanne Lamy, "Louise Maheux-Forcier. *Un Arbre chargé d'oiseaux, téléthéâtre*, précédé du *Journal de la maison d'Irène*," *Livres et Auteurs Québécois* (1976): 184-186;

Clément Lockquell, "Le Prix du Cercle du Livre de France: *Amadou* de Louise Maheux-Forcier," *Le Soleil*, 19 October 1963, p. 12;

Pierre Longtin, "*Amadou*. Le roman de l'enfance," *Lettres et Ecritures*, 1 (April 1964): 14-17;

Gilles Marcotte, "Les Iles de l'enfance, les Amériques de l'avenir," *La Presse*, 13 February 1965, p. 6;

Jean Ménard, "*Amadou*. Le Roman de l'enfant," *Livres et Auteurs Canadiens* (1963): 22-24;

Madeleine Ouellette-Michalska, "Louise Maheux-Forcier ou le charme discret de l'ironie," *Le Devoir*, 27 December 1980, p. 17;

Gabrielle Pascal, "Louise Maheux-Forcier." *Appassionata*," *Livres et Auteurs Québécois*, (1978): 60-61;

André Renaud, "Les confidences de Louise Maheux-Forcier," *Lettres Québécoises*, 37 (Spring 1985): 58-59;

Marie-Josée Rinfret, "*Le Piano rouge* de Louise

Maheux-Forcier," *Lettres Québécoises*, 38 (Summer 1985): 75;

Normand Rousseau, "La Poétique de l'espace dans *Une Forêt pour Zoé*," *Journal of Canadian Fiction*, no. 25-26 (1979): 212-226;

Guy Sylvestre, "*L'Ile joyeuse* de Louise Maheux-Forcier," *Le Devoir*, 6 February 1965, p. 13;

Louise Trudel, "*Amadou* de Louise Maheux-Forcier," *Incidences*, 5 (April 1964) 53-56;

Paul Wyczynski, "Vers le roman-poème," *Incidences*, 8 (May 1965): 31-38;

Wyczynski, "*Une Forêt pour Zoé*," *Livres et Auteurs Québécois* (1969): 15-17.

Papers:

Maheux-Forcier's papers are at the University of Ottawa archives.

Antonine Maillet
(10 May 1929-   )

Larry Shouldice
Université de Sherbrooke

BOOKS: *Pointe-aux-coques* (Montreal & Paris: Fides, 1958);

On a mangé la dune (Montreal: Beauchemin, 1962);

Les Crasseux (Toronto: Holt, Rinehart & Winston, 1968);

Rabelais et les traditions populaires en Acadie (Quebec: Presses de l'Université Laval, 1971);

La Sagouine (Montreal: Leméac, 1971); translated by Luis de Céspedes (Toronto: Simon & Pierre, 1979);

Don l'Orignal (Montreal: Leméac, 1972); translated by Barbara Godard as *The Tale of Don l'Orignal* (Toronto: Clarke, Irwin, 1978);

Par derrière chez mon père (Montreal: Leméac, 1972);

L'Acadie pour quasiment rien, by Maillet and Rita Scalabrini (Montreal: Leméac, 1973);

Gapi et Sullivan (Montreal: Leméac, 1973); translated by Céspedes as *Gapi and Sullivan* (Toronto: Simon & Pierre, 1986);

Mariaagélas (Montreal: Leméac, 1973); translated by Ben-Zion Shek as *Mariaagelas: Maria, Daughter of Gelas* (Toronto: Simon & Pierre, 1986);

Emmanuel à Joseph à Dâvit (Montreal: Leméac, 1975);

Evangéline Deusse (Montreal: Leméac, 1975); translated by Céspedes (Toronto: Simon & Pierre, 1986);

Gapi (Montreal: Leméac, 1976);

Les Cordes-de-bois (Montreal: Leméac, 1977);

La Veuve enragée (Montreal: Leméac, 1977);

Le Bourgeois Gentleman (Montreal: Leméac, 1978);

Pélagie-la-Charrette (Montreal: Leméac, 1979), translated by Philip Stratford as *Pélagie: The Return to a Homeland* (Toronto & Garden City: Doubleday, 1982; London: Calder, 1982);

Cent ans dans les bois (Montreal: Leméac, 1981); republished as *La Gribouille* (Paris: Grasset, 1982);

Christophe Cartier de la Noisette dit Nounours (Paris: Hachette/Montreal: Leméac, 1981); translated by Wayne Grady as *Christopher Cartier of Hazelnut, Also Known as Bear* (Toronto: Methuen, 1984);

La Contrebandière (Montreal: Leméac, 1981);

Les Drolatiques, Horrifiques et Epouvantables Aventures de Panurge, ami de Pantagruel, d'après Rabelais (Montreal: Leméac, 1983);

Les Acadiens, piétons de l'Atlantique, by Maillet and others (Paris: ACE, 1984);

Crache à pic (Montreal: Leméac, 1984), translated by Stratford as *The Devil Is Loose!* (Toronto: Lester & Orpen Dennys, 1986);

Garrochés en paradis (Montreal: Leméac, 1986);

Le Huitième Jour (Montreal: Leméac, 1986).

PLAY PRODUCTIONS: *Entr'Acte*, Dominion Drama Festival, 1957;

Poire-Acre, Dominion Drama Festival, 1958;

Bulles de Savon, Moncton, 1959;

Antonine Maillet (photograph by Kèro)

Les Jeux d'enfants sont faits, Dominion Drama Festival, 1960;

La Sagouine, Montreal, Theatre du Rideau Vert, 1972;

Mariaàgélas, Montreal, Théâtre du Rideau Vert, 1973; revised as *La Contrebandière,* Montreal, Théâtre du Rideau Vert, 1981;

Les Crasseux, Montreal, Compagnie Jean Duceppe, 1974;

Evangéline Deusse, Montreal, Théâtre du Rideau Vert, 1976;

Gapi, Montreal, Théâtre du Rideau Vert, 1976;

La Veuve enragée, Montreal, Théâtre du Rideau Vert, 1977;

Emmanuel à Joseph à Dâvit, Montreal, Théâtre du Rideau Vert, 1978;

Le Bourgeois Gentleman, Montreal, Théâtre du Rideau Vert, 1978;

Panurge, Montreal, Théâtre du Rideau Vert, 1983;

Garrochés en paradis, Montreal, Théâtre du Rideau Vert, 1986.

TELEVISION: *La Sagouine,* CBC, January-February, 1975.

RADIO: *La Sagouine,* Radio-Canada, 1970-1971.

PERIODICAL PUBLICATION: "Aunt Evangeline's Treasure," *Saturday Night,* 102 (January 1987): 50-52.

Since 1755, when the British army expelled and dispersed the French-speaking population from what is now the Canadian province of Nova Scotia, Acadia has existed only in history—and in the imagination of a few "Acadien" (Acadian or Cajun) communities in largely rural areas of New Brunswick and Louisiana. After more than two centuries of isolation and assimilation, recent years have seen a resurgence of the culture of this once-forgotten people. The outstanding figure in this Acadian renaissance is no doubt Antonine Maillet, a former village schoolmistress who in less than a decade has emerged as one of Canada's best-known writers. Growing international recognition of her work, which is profoundly Acadian in both subject and expression, culminated with her being awarded France's prestigious Prix Goncourt in 1979.

Antonine Maillet was born and raised in the village of Bouctouche, New Brunswick, the daughter of two schoolteachers, Léonide and Virginie Cormier Maillet. Receiving her secondary and collegial education at various religious schools, she early showed signs of literary interests, producing her first dramatic "sketches" for her family. Over the next few years, alternating between teaching and studying, she obtained a B.A. (1950) and M.A. (1959) from the Collège Saint-Joseph de Memramcook. Her master's thesis was on Gabrielle Roy. While she was at the university, her early plays, *Entr'Acte* and *Poire-Acre* (which remain unpublished), were performed locally in Moncton; the latter went on to win first prize in the Dominion Drama Festival. In 1962 Maillet earned a *licence ès lettres* from the University of Montreal and spent several years doing research in Paris, working for Radio-Canada, and teaching at various universities. In 1970 she was granted a doctorate from Laval University; her dissertation entitled *Rabelais et les traditions populaires en Acadia* was published in 1971 after Maillet had studied with the distinguished folklorist Luc Lacourcière. While the influence of Rabelais shows up most directly in her 1983 play *Les Drolatiques, Horrifiques et Epouvantables Aventures de Panurge, ami de Pantagruel, d'après Rabelais,* her fiction and drama have continually employed an earthy Rabelaisian humor to expose the dimensions of exploitation in Acadia. Always the earthy, ordinary characters, for all their apparent powerlessness, are the embodiments of folk wisdom. The powerful, by contrast, and the discreet, are exposed as shallow.

Since her first novel in 1958, Maillet has had more than some twenty works published. In the course of her career she has been awarded a number of literary prizes that include the Prix Champlain for *Pointe-aux-coques* (1958), a Governor-General's Award for *Don l'Orignal* (1972), the Grand Prix de la Ville de Montréal for *Mariaagélas* (1973), and the Prix Goncourt for *Pélagie-la-Charrette* (1979). In addition to being given honorary degrees by sixteen Canadian universities, Maillet has been made a companion of the Order of Canada and is a member of the Académie Canadienne-Française and the Royal Society of Canada.

Virtually all of Maillet's writings are intimately related to Acadia. Many of her novels and plays have interconnected characters and share the same general setting—an imaginary space reminiscent of her native village of Bouctouche. Her language, too, is distinctly Acadian: a blend of French, sixteenth-century provincial French dialects, and the accent and intonation peculiar to her area; it is a language, she says, "distorted by the climate and sharpened by the sea." In "Aunt Evangeline's Treasure" Maillet tells of her Aunt Evangeline's command over a language that her aunt scarcely knew she possessed:

> What . . . I could have told her, was that between the time of Rabelais, who made use in his books of a vocabulary of 100,000 words, and Racine, who only a century later had to make do with 5,000 words, the French language had been "purified" by a succession of grammarians intent on weeding out their cultural garden. And what happened to those 95,000 expurgated and forgotten words?
>
> They're right here in Acadia, Aunt Evangeline, tucked away in your own unconscious, ancestral memory.
>
> And what is more, this language. . . is still alive in us. . . .

In a similar way, Maillet's humor, subjects, themes, and even many of her narrative techniques are often derived from the history, traditions, and folklore of Acadia.

Antonine Maillet is foremost a "conteuse" or storyteller; in Acadian speech she is a "radoteuse," a person with a gift for talking. Her

early works, *Pointe-aux-coques* (1958), a chronicle of village life, and *On a mangé la dune* (1962), a series of children's tales, originally attracted little attention. However, the publication of Maillet's play *La Sagouine* in 1971 was a huge success, and the stage performance, at Montreal's Théâtre du Rideau Vert in 1972 with Viola Léger as "The Slattern" won both popular and critical acclaim. The play, which originated as a sixteen-part series for Radio-Canada, was widely performed throughout Canada and also in Paris and went on to become a television series which made "La Sagouine" a familiar character to millions in French Canada.

La Sagouine (translated into English in 1979) is a series of sixteen monologues by a seventy-two-year-old charlady who tells her story—and presents her opinions—as she scrubs the floor. A former prostitute and now the wife of Gapi, an Acadian fisherman, she creates a compelling and forceful presence as she muses on subjects ranging from politics and philosophy to the moon landing. Combining tremendous naiveté with a deep folk wisdom, she is a tissue of contradictions: humble and irreverent, humorous and embittered, contemplative but uninformed, angry yet resigned, and passive but vaguely rebellious.

The story is told of a reception at Moncton University, during which Viola Léger appeared unannounced, cleaning floors in a corner of the salon, and startled unsuspecting guests as she stopped her work and began railing in Acadian French against some of La Sagouine's favorite targets. In any case, a strange intimacy between actor and audience is developed during the play; as the monologues continue, La Sagouine becomes increasingly believable both as a rather bizarre individual and as a powerful spokesperson for the views and concerns of her people. In distinct contrast to Longfellow's romanticized heroine, La Sagouine is a kind of anti-Evangeline: a passionate and unforgettable symbol of the harsh realities of everyday life in Acadia.

As is the case with her play *Les Crasseux* (1968), much of Maillet's theater and fiction published in the 1970s presents an Acadian world sharply divided against itself. On the one hand are such "establishment" figures as the mayoress and the barber, and on the other a motley collection of characters from "en-bas," the wrong side of the tracks: Noume, Citrouille, La Sainte, La Cruche, and so on. The recurring struggles and intrigues of one group against the other set the action for a series of plays (published in Montreal by Leméac): *Gapi et Sullivan* (1973; translated in

Viola Léger in the role of Maillet's La Sagouine, a seventy-two-year-old Acadian charwoman with opinions on subjects ranging from politics and philosophy to the moon landing (Guy Dubois-Photographe Montréal)

Cover for the 1979 English translation of Maillet's sixteen monologues performed by Léger in 1972 at Montreal's Théâtre du Rideau Vert

1986) *Mariaagélas* (adapted in 1974 from the 1973 novel of the same title and published in 1981 as *La Contrebandière*); *Emmanuel à Joseph à Dâvit* (1975); *Evangéline Deusse* (1975; translated, 1986); *Gapi* (1976); and *La Veuve enragée* (1977). Full of picturesque—and picaresque—characters, with echoes of Homer, Rabelais, Balzac, and Faulkner, these are lively and engaging dramas whose thrust may be alternately nostalgic, narrative, allegorical, social, political, or any combination of these.

Maillet's prose works of the same period share many of these characteristics—and several of the same characters. *Par derrière chez mon père* (1972) is a book of tales, while *L'Acadie pour quasiment rien* (1973), a collaboration with Rita Scalabrini, is described as a humorous tourist guide to Acadia. *Don l'Orignal* (1972; translated, 1978), *Mariaagélas* (1973; translated 1986), and *Les Cordes-de-bois* (1977) are novels in which the lit-

tle guys continue to battle the big shots and the forces of hypocrisy, prudery, poverty, and prohibition. Extravagant characterizations, dynamic and sometimes surrealistic narration, a liberal use of stereotype and grotesque—all combine to produce fast-moving novels in which a mixture of fantasy, folklore, and hard-hitting action intensifies the storytelling.

Le Bourgeois Gentleman (1978) is Maillet's first play set outside Acadia. In it she recounts the laughable attempts of a Montreal manufacturer in the 1940s to achieve an upward social mobility commensurate with his newly won wealth. Since the elite to which he aspires happens to be English-speaking, and he French, the plot is compounded by a great deal of farce, linguistic humor, and social satire that provide a contemporary version of Molière's classic *Le Bourgeois Gentilhomme*. Critical reaction to the play, as indeed to almost all of Maillet's work in the late

1970s, was generally very favorable, although some critics complained of what they saw as the increasing predictability of her writing.

Such complaints ceased abruptly in 1979 with the publication of *Pélagie-la-Charrette* (translated as *Pélagie: The Return to a Homeland*, 1982). Hailed as a masterpiece, it tells of the quest of its heroine who, after being expelled from her homeland and spending fifteen years in brutal labor on a Georgia plantation, sets out with her cart and oxen one morning in 1770, determined to regain "l'Acadie" some two thousand miles to the north. Accompanied by various children, by Bélonie, a hundred-year-old storyteller, and by several others, Pélagie pushes on despite seemingly endless obstacles: heat, cold, forest, swamp, skirmishes with Indians, Charleston slave merchants, hostile Bostonians, and so on. Not even the constant presence of death, whose black cart Bélonie sees just behind their own, can dissuade them. After ten years of arduous travels and perilous adventures–in which Pélagie is given occasional help by Beausoleil-Broussard, her seafaring lover–the group, which now numbers some thirty families or "clans" and assorted hangers-on (including an escaped black slave who has been given an Acadian name), finally reaches the Tantramar (Tintamarre) Marshes on the Acadian coast. Her mission fulfilled, and home at last, Pélagie dies on native soil.

Although it is a historical novel, based partially on fact, *Pélagie-la-Charrette* is also very much an Acadian epic with strong overtones of myth, fable, biblical allegory, and the traditional folktale. The narration moves between intense lyricism and surrealistic adventure, unconventional romance, and relentless messianism. Characters who at one level seem grotesquely superhuman gradually emerge as deeply convincing representatives of the Acadians and their bravery, tenacity, forbearance, and sense of humor. Setting her story against the backdrop of an entire continent at a time of great political significance (Pélagie, for instance, passes through Philadelphia in July of 1776), Maillet re-creates the history and mythology of her people, and almost in passing articulates much of the cultural distinctiveness that has made their survival possible.

A sequel to *Pélagie, Cent ans dans les bois* (1981) was less enthusiastically received, partly because it seemed to be more consciously contrived. It intertwines two stories: one is an oral tale, involving a quest for treasure and the surprising conclusion that the city of Philadelphia belongs to the

Dust jacket for Philip Stratford's translation of Pélagie-la-Charrette, *Maillet's novel about an eighteenth-century Acadian woman's ten-year journey from Georgia to her native land*

Acadians; the second is a written tale, one sent from Pélagie's descendant, Pélagie-la-Gribouille (the "scribbler"), to her daughter's suitor in an attempt to dissuade the young people from marrying. The problem is that he is a sailor, and she (like other Acadians, after the "Great Unsettlement" of the British expulsion) is determined to keep her culture rooted in the earth. The whole narrative is set about 1880–one hundred years after Pélagie-la-Charrette had led the exiles home–when the Acadians who had hidden in the woods for a century, avoiding one kind of exile only to suffer another, emerge to claim their heritage. Ultimately the sailor gives up the sea to claim his sweetheart, and thus the novel closes having demonstrated a variety of ways to keep history alive.

Maillet has observed that her works are not to be confined by the label "regional." Acadia for her is not only a particular society but also the world in microcosm. *Evangéline Deusse* makes the

Page from the manuscript for a novel-in-progress (by permission of the author)

point that the Acadians' exile has its parallels in other cultural wanderings: that of the Jews, for example. But the more successful of the works of the 1980s, whatever the parallels that formally shape them, insist on their Acadian roots. In "Aunt Evangeline's Treasure," the author traces her interest in Acadian stories to her own family's store of legends: "I've scoured the four horizons and rummaged through the sand and the dunes and the seaweed, and I've yet to find a treasure more precious than the one I found buried under my feet. . . . It was a treasure that ten generations of my ancestors had jealously guarded, and which, unknown to her, Aunt Evangeline [in story, speech, and attitude] had delivered to me. . . ."

Maillet's *Christophe Cartier de la Noisette dit Nounours* (1981) is a whimsical children's story about a teddy bear ("nounours") with the names of two intrepid explorers Columbus and Cartier, who emerges by the seaside to tell of his dream life (hibernation), of legends, and of myths. Bearlogical–in that he contravenes human logic–he tells of epic battles over hazelnuts and other grand events. But, in small, he, too, reenacts the Acadian survival legend, and his seaside tales at once revive and rejuvenate the aging narrator. This work was translated in 1984 under the title *Christopher Cartier of Hazelnut, Also Known as Bear*.

In *Crache à pic* (1984; translated as *The Devil Is Loose!*, 1986), Maillet returns to the sea (and, as with *Mariaàgélas*, to the world of smuggling), once again seeking structural parallels for the Expulsion; she finds them both in sacred and in secular events–in the expulsion from Eden and in the years of Prohibition that followed the passing of the Volstead Act in the American Congress. Set in the twentieth-century present, the novel nonetheless employs (thus keeps alive) the extravagant adventures of legendary romance. The title character, Crache à Pic, is the female commander of a schooner who sets sail in order to bring drink to the people and set injustices aright. Her crew is made up of neighbors and friends; her opponents are both the Coast Guard and the wicked bootlegger (the pirate captain, so to speak) who, but for Crache à Pic, would rule the seas. Once again an Acadian woman takes on the giants and wins, the absurdity of the tale's exaggerations serving here to remind that laughter is a restorative reaction to threats of confinement, deracination, and defeat.

Maillet's most recent books are the novel *Le Huitième Jour* (1986), a combination of picaresque

and litany that recounts what happens after the "eighth day" of creation begins, and *Garrochés en paradis* (1986), the published version of a play that premiered in October 1986 at Le Théâtre du Rideau Vert, with La Sagouine, Mariaàgélas, and other familiar figures among the characters. Despite the success of Maillet's several latest works, many readers still regard *Pélagie-la-Charrette* as the high point to date of Maillet's career as a writer. In it the reader finds her characteristic mastery of language, whether French, Acadian, or a mixture of the two. It exemplifies, too, her abundant sense of humor, her wit and gift for anecdote, her ability to spin a good tale. The vitality and deep humanity of Antonine Maillet are also apparent, as are the themes that run throughout her writing: the courage, cunning, and ultimate triumph of the disadvantaged; the richness and relevance of Acadia's cultural heritage; the importance of fidelity, individuality, and creative energy; and, most of all, the celebration of her people and their particularities.

References:

"Antonine Maillet and the Modern Epic," special section of *Quebec Studies*, 4 (1986): 220-336;

K. J. Crecelius, "L'Histoire et son double dans *Pélagie-la-Charrette*," *Studies in Canadian Literature*, 6, no. 2 (1981): 211-220;

James De Finney, "Antonine Maillet: un example de réception littéraire régionale," *Revue d'Histoire Littéraire du Québec et du Canada Français*, 12 (Summer-Fall 1986): 17-33;

Bruno Drolet, *Entre dune et aboiteaux . . . un peuple. Etude critique des oeuvres d'Antonine Maillet* (Montreal: Fides, 1975);

Jean-Cléo Godin, "L'Evangéline selon Antonine," in *Théâtre Québécois II*, edited by Godin and Laurent Mailhot (Montreal: HMH, 1980), pp. 147-164;

Michèle Lacombe, "Breaking the Silence of Centuries," *Canadian Theatre Review*, no. 46 (1986): 58-64;

René Le Blanc, "L'Oralité du style dans les romans d'Antonine Maillet," *Revue d'Histoire Littéraire du Québec et du Canada Français*, 12 (Summer-Fall 1986): 35-49;

Le Blanc, ed., *Derrière la Charrette de Pélagie: lecture analytique du roman d'Antonine Maillet, "Pélagie-la-charrette"* (Pointe de l'Eglise, Nova Scotia: Presses de l'Universitè Sainte-Anne, 1984);

Raymond Leblanc, "Lire Antonine Maillet de

Pointe-aux-Coques à *La Sagouine*," *Revue de Université de Moncton* (May 1974): 57-68;

Marguerite Maillet, *Histoire de la littérature acadienne. De rêve en rêve* (Moncton: Editions d'Acadie, 1983);

André Major, "Entretien avec Antonine Maillet," *Ecrits du Canada Français*, no. 36 (1973): 9-26;

Ben-Zion Shek, "Antonine Maillet: A Writer's Itinerary," *Acadiensis*, 12 (Spring 1983): 171-180;

Donald Smith, "Antonine Maillet: Acadia, Land of Tales and Cunning," in his *Voices of Deliverance: Interviews with Quebec & Acadian Writers*, translated by Larry Shouldice (Toronto & Buffalo: Anansi, 1986), pp. 243-268;

Smith, "Maillet & the Prix Goncourt," *Canadian Literature*, 88 (Spring 1981): 157-161;

Renate Usmiani, "Recycling An Archetype: The Anti-Evangelines," *Canadian Theatre Review*, no. 46 (1986): 65-71.

André Major

(22 April 1942-   )

Ginette Michaud

Université du Québec à Montréal and *Université de Montréal*

BOOKS: *Le Froid se meurt. Poèmes* (Montreal: Editions Atys, 1961);

Holocauste à 2 voix (Montreal: Editions Atys, 1961);

Nouvelles, by Major, Jacques Brault, and André Brochu (Montreal: A.G.E.U.M., 1963);

Le Pays, by Major, Paul Chamberland, Ghislain Côté, Nicole Drassel, and Michel Garneau (Montreal: Déom, 1963);

Le Cabochon. Roman pour adolescents (Montreal: Parti Pris, 1964);

La Chair de poule. Nouvelles (Montreal: Parti Pris, 1965);

Le Vent du diable. Roman (Montreal: Editions du Jour, 1968);

Félix-Antoine Savard (Montreal & Paris: Fides, (1968; revised, 1970);

Poèmes pour durer (Montreal: Editions du Songe, 1969);

Le Désir, suivi de Le Perdant (Montreal: Leméac, 1973);

L'Epouvantail. Roman (Montreal: Editions du Jour, 1974); translated by Sheila Fischman as *The Scarecrows of Saint-Emmanuel* (Toronto: McClelland & Stewart, 1977);

L'Epidémie. Roman (Montreal: Editions du Jour, 1975); translated by Mark Czarnecki as *Inspector Therrien* (Victoria & Toronto: Press Porcépic, 1980);

Une Soirée en octobre (Montreal: Leméac, 1975);

Les Rescapés. Roman (Montreal: Quinze, 1976); translated by David Lobdell as *Man on the Run* (Montreal: Quadrant, 1984);

La Folle d'Elvis. Nouvelles (Montreal: Québec/ Amérique, 1981); translated by David Lobdell as *Hooked on Elvis* (Montreal: Quadrant, 1983);

L'Hiver au coeur (Montreal: XYZ, 1987).

PLAY PRODUCTION: *Une Soirée en octobre*, Magdalen Islands, Quebec, Théâtre Populaire du Québec, 10 September 1975.

TELEVISION: *Doux-Sauvage*, *Les Beaux Dimanches*, Radio-Canada, 7 January 1968.

RADIO: *Inutilement tragique* and *Le Grand Personnage*, *Les Muses s'amusent*, Radio-Canada, 14 July 1969;

"Le Coeur net," *L'Atelier des inédits*, CBF-FM, 30 May 1972;

La Dalle-des-Morts, adapted by Major from Félix-Antoine Savard's play, *Sur toutes les scènes du monde*, CBF-FM, 12 March 1973;

"Préface pour la radio," CBF-FM, 25 February 1985.

OTHER: Jacques Godbout and John Robert Colombo, eds., *Poésie/Poetry 64*, includes poems by Major (Montreal: Editions du Jour/ Toronto: Ryerson, 1963);

"Notes sur une façon de voir," in *Littérature du Québec*, edited by Robert Guy, volume 1 (Montreal: Déom, 1964);

Jacques Renaud, *Le Cassé*, includes "Entre cassés," preface by Major (Montreal: Parti Pris, 1964), pp. 9-11;

"Notes sur une façon de voir," in *Littérature du Québec*, edited by Robert Guy, volume 1, second edition (Montreal: Déom, 1970);

Berthelot Brunet, *Histoire de la littérature canadienne-française suivi de Portraits d'écrivains*, preface by Major (Montreal: HMH, 1970);

Marcel Dubé, *Médée*, preface by Major (Montreal: Leméac, 1973);

Dominique de Pasquale, *Oui, chef, suivi de L'Arme au poing, ou Larme à l'oeil*, preface Major (Montreal: Leméac, 1973);

"Avant-propos," "Pierre Vadeboncoeur, un socialiste de condition bourgeoise," and "Vivre autrement (en marge d' *Indépendances*)", in *Un Homme libre: Pierre Vadeboncoeur* (Montreal: Un Leméac, 1974), pp. 7, 9-18, 56-60;

"Thief of Bonsecours Market," in *Stories from Quebec*, translated and edited by Philip Stratford (Toronto, New York, Cincinnati, London & Melbourne: Van Nostrand Reinhold, 1974), pp. 153-160;

"En finir avec la survivance," in *Interventions— Octobre* (Montreal: Quinze, 1975), pp. 43-50;

Prefatory note and "Le Cas douteux," in *Fuites et poursuites* (Montreal: Quinze, 1982);

"C'est moi maintenant qui attends . . . ," in *Dix contes fantastiques* (Montreal: Quinze, 1983), pp. 151-164;

Claude Janelle, *Les Editions du Jour. Une Génération d'écrivains*, preface by Major (Montreal: HMH, 1983);

"La grande nuit blanche," in *Aimer* (Montreal: Quinze, 1986), pp. 7-22.

PERIODICAL PUBLICATIONS: "Une erreur. Nouvelle," *Liberté*, 28 (July-August 1963): 297-299;

"Le second mari. Nouvelle," *Châtelaine*, 4 (November 1963): 34-35, 62, 64, 66-67;

"Nouvelles. I. Modern Style. II. Hiverner?," *Parti Pris*, 1 (December 1963): 38-42;

"Comme une petite boue humaine. Nouvelle," *Parti Pris*, 1 (February 1964): 40-42;

"Rafales. Nouvelle," *Châtelaine*, 5 (November 1964): 24-25, 79-83;

"La Semaine dernière pas loin du pont. Nouvelle," *Parti Pris*, 2 (November 1964): 37-42;

"Un Déménagement," *Parti Pris*, 2 (December 1964): 48-50;

"Poésie?," *Ecrits du Canada Français*, 18 (1964): 87-118;

"Le Premier Pas. Nouvelle," *Châtelaine*, 6 (April 1965): 32-33, 57-58, 60-61;

"Mémoires d'un jeune canoque," *L'Action Nationale*, 55 (October 1965): 245-249; 55 (November 1965): 369-377; 55 (December 1965): 496-502; 55 (January 1966): 622-632; 55 (February 1966): 746-751; 55 (March 1966): 869-875; 55 (April 1966): 986-991; 55 (May-June 1966): 1155-1159;

"L'Ile du silence," *Europe*, 47 (February-March 1969): 111-117;

"La Rage au coeur. Nouvelle," *Châtelaine*, 11 (November 1970): 30-31, 60, 62, 64-65;

"Pour une pensée québécoise," *Voix et Images du Pays*, 1 (1970);

"Le Journal d'un collectionneur de frissons," *Voix et Images du Pays*, 3 (1970): 213-242;

"Entretien avec Antonine Maillet," *Ecrits du Canada Français*, 36 (1973): 9-38;

"Pour une lecture des oeuvres québécoises," *Québec Français*, 16 (November 1974): 20-21;

"Langagement (1960-1975)," *Voix et Images*, 1 (September 1975): 120-125;

"Journal d'un hypnotisé," *Liberté*, 19 (May-June 1977): 73-77;

"L'horrible, le savoureux quotidien," *la Nouvelle Barre du Jour*, 68-69 (September 1978): 33-36;

"L'Influence d'un rêve," *Québec Français*, 42 (May 1981): 52-53;

"Petite Histoire d'une obsession," *Canadian Literature*, 100 (Spring 1984): 207-211.

By turns polemicist, literary critic, poet, novelist, essayist, and dramatist, André Major is a Quebec writer who has practiced nearly every literary form, including the television play. If this many-sidedness has made Major of special interest, so too has his intellectual journey, which has made him representative of a certain type of youth during the Quiet Revolution of the 1960s. It is, however, for his work in fiction—notably his celebrated series Histoires de déserteurs—that Major is best known.

Major, the son of Arthur Major, a teacher, and his wife, the former Anna Sharp, was born in Montreal in April 1942. He was educated at

André Major (photograph by Kèro)

the Collège de Montréal until he was dismissed for having published and distributed a Socialist, independentist journal entitled *Liberté Etudiante*. With hindsight, one might say, a little mischievously perhaps, that this episode prefigured his entry onto the Quebec literary scene. He subsequently graduated from the Institut Arbique in 1960, spent the next year at the Collège Valéry in Montreal, and began his career working for the publisher Editions du Jour, the Montreal news-

paper *Le Devoir*, and the University of Montreal information department. Faithful to the political and social commitments he began with, Major later became part of the group that founded and edited *Parti Pris*, the literary and political review that was, during the 1960s, the major ideological forum for Quebec intellectuals. "Laïcisme, indépendance, socialisme"–lay attitudes, independence, socialism–so went their slogan as the first bombs of the FLQ (Front de Libération du

Québec) were beginning to burst. The *Parti Pris* writers considered that they took upon themselves the collective destiny of their people and that it was their function to carry into literature the war of decolonization by putting the colonized and his impoverished language, the Montreal sociolect *joual*, into the center of action.

It was in this context that Major produced in 1964 his first important work, a "novel for adolescents" according to the author, entitled *Le Cabochon*. He had already published in 1961 two pamphlets of poetry, *Le Froid se meurt* and *Holocauste à 2 voix*, both concerned with the theme of the land; they had received a quiet, but favorable welcome from the critics, and Gilles Hénault had recognized in Major a gifted prose writer. By the time *Le Cabochon* appeared Major had also written, in collaboration with Jacques Brault and André Brochu, a volume of short stories, *Nouvelles* (1963). The tone (direct, violent, rebellious) and themes (denunciation of the family and society, protest, scarcely veiled autobiography) that dominate Major's stories in this volume are ones he was later to develop and amplify.

In the early 1960s Major believed that literature was linked to history. Accordingly, he reacted against what he saw as the deficient realism of traditional literary form, and he undertook to deconstruct this realist illusion—the characteristics of which were impersonal narration, narrative coherence, meaningful details, and a false objectivity that stood for reality. In the novel that he says he wrote for adolescents but which is more the novel of adolescence itself, Major recounts the escapades of his hero, Antoine, who is expelled from the college where he is studying, finds work in a bakery, then loses his job, leaves his parents' house, heads north, tries to write, and finally returns to the fold, where it seems that he accepts conformity. More than a reformulation of the parable of the prodigal son, Major provides here a convincing version of the theme of alienation through the *cabochon*'s aborted revolt against all institutions and generally accepted ideas. (A "cabochon," in popular idiom, is a stubborn person, someone with a hard head.) In the novel Major makes constant reference to a precise social context, that of Montreal East, at the same time as he examines the global politics of colonialism through Antoine, the "colonized" character. To emphasize the struggle further, Major, in the manner of other *Parti Pris* writers, uses *joual*, making this language the major sign of the disintegrated culture of the colonized (Antoine's language has

lost its integrity, been destroyed), as well as an instrument of vindication.

In 1965 Major produced a collection of stories entitled *La Chair de poule* in which one finds the same buffeting sensibility, the same hazing tenderness, the same rough nervousness as in *Le Cabochon*. The stories all have urban settings: they are tied to concrete historical situations, those in which the proletarian/colonized, those problematic, unruly, and unsatisfied heroes, those "cassés," or broken ones, to use the phrase of another *Parti Pris* writer, Jacques Renaud, always struggle. Major here reinforces his vision of the Quebec family (which he judges conformist and passive) in the same way as he does the image of an alienated society; and he sets up in *La Chair de poule*, as in *Le Cabochon*, a confrontation with a dispossessed brother. But whereas the narrative of *Le Cabochon* remains linear throughout, Major gives further development in these stories to his concern for fictional form, and, in order to convey better the lives of these crushed characters, he produces stories that are themselves fractured, dislocated, again using *joual*, a language that is constantly at odds with conventional literary language, reaching for its own limit.

One of the techniques that he uses to break up his stories consists of addressing himself directly to the reader, to abuse him (since, paradoxically, the reader of this "proletarian" literature is himself bourgeois) or to make him his accomplice. Broken rhythms, authorial intrusions, tension among diverse fictional techniques (monologues, descriptions, dialogues) which are inclined to dissolve into each other: these are some of the characteristics of these violent, provocative stories. The dividing line between fiction and autobiography, between social testimony and intimate journal, is not clear here. With its many contradictory tensions, this jagged writing (all the more effective because the lyricism is held in check) shows a constant uneasiness about its own form: as Lise Gauvin has noted judiciously, "ni distance, ni identification, mais l'un et l'autre à la fois, en même temps, pêle-mêle, tel est l'insoustenable rapport qu'entretient l'écrivain avec son sujet" (neither distance from it nor identification with it, but both at once, at the same time, pell-mell: such is the unbearable rapport that keeps the author with his subject).

Meanwhile, Major left *Parti Pris* in 1964. After this period of intense commitment (both political and literary) and after these first prose works, Major secluded himself for a while. He did not, however, stop his work as a journalist for the principal papers (*La Presse, Le Devoir, Le Petit Journal*), and he wrote reviews (for such publications as *L'Action Nationale* and *Liberté*) in which he turned his attention to foreign literatures. As a critic, he reviewed mainly works in translation.

Several years after leaving *Parti Pris*, Major produced another novel, *Le Vent du diable* (1968), which seems at first a return to more traditional content and structure. Albert-le-Calme is torn between his pregnant wife Marie-Ange (spirit, virtue, patience), who is associated with the town, and La Verte (desire, passion, eroticism), who lives on the mountain. Suddenly the "vent du diable" starts to blow, the sensual, liberating wind, which disturbs everything, which blows away all the irrational fears that hinder living. Albert leaves Marie-Ange for La Verte, tears her away from Tom the madman with whom she lives, and brings her back in an ambiguous dénouement to live with him in town. About love and hate, and perhaps symbolically alluding to the author's desire for the rebirth of Quebec, *Le Vent du diable* is lyrical in tone, which is unusual in Major's work. Although he produced a collection of verse, *Poèmes pour durer*, in 1969, Major said he got rid of his aspirations to poetry in *Le Vent du diable*, a novel which evinces the influence of French writer Jean Giono, or closer to home, of Major's compatriots Yves Thériault and especially Félix-Antoine Savard to whom Major devoted an enthusiastic essay in 1968. The story of *Le Vent du diable* is followed by an epilogue in the form of a notebook, "Le Carnet bleu," in which the author, identifying himself with Albert, takes up in his own voice the fictional narrative he had begun in the voice of another. This passion for autobiography constitutes an especially noteworthy aspect of Major's work. Using it more or less adroitly in his early work, it is in his later Histoires de déserteurs series that Major achieves the optimal effect, transposing things remembered and things true-to-life until the landscapes of experience and imagination blend.

After a six-year pause in writing fiction, from 1968 to 1974, Major began to produce his "déserteurs" chronicle, a trilogy: *L'Epouvantail* (1974; translated as *The Scarecrows of Saint-Emmanuel*, 1977); *L'Epidémie* (1975; translated as *Inspector Therrien*, 1980); and *Les Rescapés* (1976; translated as *Man on the Run*, 1984). Related to this trilogy, Majors suggests, are two other texts: *Une Soirée en octobre* (1975) and "Le Journal d'un collectionneur de frissons" (published in 1970 in

Cover for Mark Czarnecki's translation of L'Epidémie, *the second novel in Major's "Histoires de déserteurs" trilogy*

the periodical *Voix et Images du Pays*). These "Histoires de déserteurs" are generally considered to be mature works, and they were received favorably by the critics. In 1977 Major received a Governor General's Award for *Les Rescapés*.

Through the turbulent lives of the various characters, Momo and Gigi, Inspector Therrien and Emérence, through a climate of violence, Major symbolically treats life in Quebec during the 1970s in the aftermath of the October Crisis. Though he does not refer explicitly to these political events, it is clear that they work continually through the chronicle and that they inform Major's minute and, in some respects, sociological examination of a little world in decay, a world where time seems suspended and events ahistorical.

At first glance *L'Epouvantail* is a detective story: the prostitute and barmaid Gigi (former friend of Momo, the "hero") has been stabbed, and Inspector Therrien goes looking for her murderer (one suspects Momo) all the way to Saint-Emmanuel where he has taken refuge. Quickly the police enquiry turns into a sociological quest: the reader will never know who has killed Gigi, but he learns much about the personal problems, the brutal relationships that bind together and divide the "habitants" of this disquieting village, and about their dispossession. Using flashbacks (one of them, for example, involves a sexual meeting between Gigi and Momo in a wheat field, beside crossed scarecrows) and a dense style which aims at achieving a "*réel*" beyond reality, Major produces an oppressive story. Some characters, scarcely sketched, like the defrocked priest Saint-Pierre or Momo's brother Calixa, remain in the shadows; others return like survivors in the other parts of the chronicle.

In *L'Epidémie* the returning characters acquire dimension and complexity, including Inspector Therrien, now retired; the hotelkeeper, Jérôme, and his wife, Emérence; and Momo, who is imprisoned, then a fugitive. In *L'Epidémie* (the title evokes Camus's *La Peste*), in *L'Epouvantail*, one can distinguish two movements: the first part centers on a single point of view, alternating between Momo's and Therrien's, but in the second there is no center, and all the characters are equally important, requiring each in turn the attention of the reader. These characters are all phantoms haunted by fear, death, and the flesh; survivors with no present to live in; deserters on the run, as powerless to live as to die. But as François Ricard has observed in a 1975 review for *Liberté*, the true protagonist of the book is the village of Saint-Emmanuel itself: "C'est lui, en effet, qui exerce dans le récit l'action la plus puissante, d'autant plus efficace qu'elle se fait toujours diffuse, insidieuse, aussi subtile mais en même temps aussi concrète qui l'air et que le temps, aussi maléfique qu'un sortilège auquel nul se soustrait, en un mot: 'épidémique'" (It is that, in effect, which causes the most powerful action in the story, all the more effective because it is always diffuse, insidious, subtle, but at the same time as concrete as the air and the weather, as harmful as a spell that no one can remove, in a word, "epidemic").

Between the second and third volumes of the trilogy, Major's play, *Une Soirée en octobre*, was published in 1975. In the drama the author assembles, in a small country hotel, various characters from *L'Epidémie*: the hotelkeeper Jérôme, now deputy mayor, his striptease-artist sister-in-law Cherry, a habitué of the hotel bar named Phil,

and a stranger (terrorist?) called Antoine. Fear, lies, impotence, reprieve: the world of this dead-end society is familiar to Major's readers, for it strongly resembles the world that took shape in the novels. The play, a commissioned work, makes reference to the events of October 1970, but they are relegated to the background; it received mixed reviews at the time of its 1975 stage production by the Théâtre Populaire du Québec.

In *Les Rescapés*, Major pursues further his exploration of this decaying traditional society; it does not matter much what events actually happen—Momo's escape, Jérôme's social rise, and so on—for in the village where everything has already taken place, it is now a dead time. From this point on, everything is held in suspense: the deserters, who have in turn been deserted, remain in this "desert," unable to leave. Contaminated by the place and existing in moral isolation, the inhabitants of the village, despite their claim on "tradition," are without lineage, without a real claim on the past—except (and it is a diffuse connection) for the brothers Momo and Calixa, whose mother was Indian. Major includes at the end of *Les Rescapés* a list of all the characters in the trilogy, thus conferring upon them a quasi-historical status. Reinforcing the illusion of documentary realism, he also provides a topograhic map of the region in which the place names take on the names of the novel's characters, a vivid representation of the way the village has swallowed its inhabitants.

Major's work, and particularly his trilogy, compels recognition as a body of work marking the 1970s and provides a vivid and imaginative representation of Quebec society. In recent years Major has produced a new collection of short stories, *La Folle d'Elvis* (1981; translated as *Hooked on Elvis*, 1983), in which he returns to themes he developed more than fifteen years earlier in *La Chair de poule*. Major has also produced a journal, or rather an autobiographical chronicle, in *Liberté*: "Journal d'un hypnotisé" (1977). Although it is impossible to predict what turn Major's work will take in the future, it is plausible to think that he will pursue further his interest in the border territory between fiction and autobiography. The critical acclaim given his novels and the numerous republications and the translations of his work indicate that there is a lively interest in his solidly crafted prose. Major's writing displays a dense and rich imagination which analyzes particular sociopolitical events in Quebec while proposing an interpretation, a *reading*, of these events at the same time.

Interviews:

Jacques Pelletier, "Allez au bout de moi-même," *Le Carabin* (October 1967): 6-7;

Raymond Plante,"Entretien avec André Major," *Voix et Images du Pays*, 8 (1974): 217-231;

Léonce Cantin and André Gaulin,"Entrevue avec André Major," *Québec Français*, 42 (May 1981): 43-47;

Pelletier and André Vanasse, with the collaboration of Henri-Paul Jacques, "L'Ecriture, ultime recours: une entrevue avec André Major," *Voix et Images*, 10 (Spring 1985): 13-21.

References:

Aurélien Boivin, "Bibliographie," *Voix et Images*, 10 (Spring 1985): 70-89;

André Brochu,"*l'Epouvantail*, d'André Major," *Livres et Auteurs Québécois* (1974): 23-26;

"Dossier: André Major," *Québec Français*, 42 (May 1981): 43-54;

"Dossier André Major," *Voix et Images*, 10 (Spring 1985): 5-89;

Lise Gauvin, *Parti pris littéraire* (Montreal: Presses de l'Université de Montréal, 1975), pp. 128-133;

Gauvin, "Les Romans de Parti Pris, ou le difficile accès à la parole," *Voix et Images du Pays*, 7 (1973): 95-100;

Gauvin, "Une Ville en mode mineur: considérations sur Montréal dans le roman récent," *Possibles*, 3 (Autumn 1978): 17-21;

Robert Major, *Parti pris: idéologies et littérature* (Montreal: Hurtubise HMH, 1979);

Jacques Pelletier, "André Major, écrivain et Québécois," *Voix et Images du Pays*, 3 (1970): 27-63;

Pelletier, "André Major et langagement. *Les Histoires de déserteurs*," *Canadian Literature*, 88 (Spring 1981): 61-70;

Pelletier, "Où va André Major? Remarques sur ses productions récentes," *Liberté*, 109 (January-February 1977): 58-66;

Michael A. Peterman, "Ordered Madness. André Major and Victor-Lévy Beaulieu," *Canadian Literature*, 88 (Spring 1981): 100-104;

François Ricard, "Roman d'hier, roman d'aujourd'hui (*l'Epidémie*, d'André Major)," *Liberté*, 17 (September-October 1975): 92-99.

Kevin Major

(12 September 1949-   )

J. Kieran Kealy
University of British Columbia

BOOKS: *Hold Fast* (Toronto & Vancouver: Clarke, Irwin, 1978; New York: Delacorte, 1980);

Far from Shore (Toronto & Vancouver: Clarke, Irwin, 1980; New York: Delacorte, 1981);

Thirty-six Exposures (New York: Delacorte, 1984).

OTHER: *Doryloads,* edited by Major (Portugal Cove, Newfoundland: Breakwater Books, 1974).

Kevin Major's impact on Canadian children's literature has frequently been compared to that of Judy Blume in the United States, both being among the first to present honest, realistic accounts of the problems of the modern adolescent. Not surprisingly, Major's frank approach to the juvenile novel has created a great deal of controversy. School boards in both Newfoundland and Ontario, for example, have steadfastly refused to put his novels on the list of books approved for classroom study and, in a celebrated incident in 1982, the chairman of the Rainy River Library Board in Ontario canceled a reading by Major because of the crude language of his novels. Such condemnations, though, are few; most critics of children's literature clearly regard Major as one of Canada's most promising talents.

Major was born on 12 September 1949 in Stephenville, Newfoundland, the youngest of the seven children of Edward Major, a fisherman, and his wife, Jessie Headge Major. Though interested in journalism in high school, Kevin Major turned to studying medicine and finally education while at Memorial University, graduating in 1972 with a bachelor of science degree. He accepted his first full-time teaching position later that year, an experience that led directly to his first publishing venture, a 1974 collection of Newfoundland writing and art titled *Doryloads,* edited by Major to help preserve a literature and culture that he found almost totally ignored in the schools.

Kevin Major (photograph by Don Hayes)

In 1976 Major decided to give up full-time teaching and concentrate on his writing career, supporting himself by periodic work as a supply teacher. Within months he completed his first novel, *Hold Fast,* which, after some revising, was published in 1978. The success of this first effort was resounding. Not only did it receive all three of the major Canadian awards for children's literature (the Canada Council Children's Literature Prize, the Canadian Library Association Book of the Year for Children Award, and the Ruth Schwartz Children's Book Award) but it was also included on the 1980 Hans Christian Andersen Honor List, thus making it one of the most acclaimed books in the history of Canadian children's literature.

Hold Fast traces the familiar story of the difficulties a parentless child faces when forced to adjust to a new environment. But Major's Michael of Marten, Newfoundland, is not another Anne of Green Gables. Rather, he is a troubled atomic-age adolescent, unable to deal with either his nascent sexuality or the transition from his small coastal hometown to the urban world of St. Albert. In his new world Michael's accent is ridiculed and his attempts to fit in both in his new town and at school are consistently frustrated by adults. Finally, he rebels, escaping from the city and returning to his wilderness where he defiantly asserts his individuality by surviving for three days in the bathroom of a campsite abandoned for the winter. But Michael's quest does not have a traditional happy ending, for though he finally returns to his beloved Marten, his accomplice on his odyssey, his cousin Curtis, must return home to confront his brutish father with no real assurance that anything will really change. Thus, though the problems considered in *Hold Fast* may be stereotypic, the characters are hardly those found in the traditional juvenile novel. Critics of *Hold Fast* have praised not only the realism of Major's characters but also the accurate portrayal of what is unique in Newfoundland, in particular its dialect and its sense of the past. As one reviewer wrote in an October 1978 article for *Saturday Night*: "You . . . find yourself wanting to see all of this, this grand and generous and overflowing heritage, set down. Major is one of those devoted to setting it down, before it disappears entirely. The fact that he has done so in a novel for adolescents, and enjoyed a certain modest success in the process, is in its small way an emblem of the beautiful thing that Canadian regional culture has become in the 1970s."

Far from Shore, Major's second novel, published in 1980, is an even more innovative and challenging examination of the difficulties of adolescence. Told from multiple perspectives, the narrative consists of interior monologues of the five main characters who recount the problems of Newfoundland's Slade family, particularly those of the oldest son, Christopher. The father, jobless, frequently drunk, is forced to move to Alberta to find work. The mother, tired of trying to keep her quarrelsome family together, is on the verge of having an affair with her employer. Chris's life is a series of adolescent tragedies: he breaks up with his girlfriend, fails grade ten, is un-

Dust jacket for Major's first novel, winner of Canada's three most prestigious awards for children's literature

able to get a job, and takes up with a gang of older youths who eventually get him into trouble with the law. And yet somehow, despite all adversity and with the somewhat convenient support of a newfound girlfriend, Chris survives. But again, as in *Hold Fast*, there is no assurance that all will end well. Although the father and the mother are together again at the end, the father still has no job and, as Chris's final words suggest, if he does not find one, things could get "loused up here again." Though some critics question the overall success of Major's narrative style in *Far from Shore*, Silver Donald Cameron in his March 1981 review for *Atlantic Insight* provides perhaps the best summary of critical response when he suggests that though this book "is less perfect than his first, it is because he has set himself a much more difficult challenge." Cameron adds that he suspects that very few youthful readers "will care about such quibbles," for they will find "very few books anywhere which speak to their condition with such candor and understanding."

Far from Shore won the Canadian Young Adult Book Award and was named Best Book of the Year by *School Library Journal.*

The third of Major's juvenile novels, *Thirty-six Exposures*, published in 1984, is his most ambitious book and also his most controversial. The subject is again the maturation of a Newfoundland teenager, in this case a poet-photographer named Lorne about to graduate from high school and wondering what he is to do with his life. Yet, rather than simply tell Lorne's story or even present it from multiple viewpoints, Major chooses to present thirty-six verbal snapshots. The result is a kind of puzzle that the reader must put together, a blurry scene that must be put into focus. For many critics, the complexity of the style was too demanding for an adolescent readership. Even more disturbing was the language of the characters and the frankness with which the book deals with sex. Paul Kropp suggests in a November 1984 review for *Quill and Quire* that the book may be testing the limits of the adolescent novel and that it is unlikely to find "a place in our schools." More significant, however, Kropp questions the somewhat contrived and, he feels, unnecessary tragedy that concludes the novel. But there are others who consider Major's third book his finest. In fact, in an *Atlantic Insight* review for November 1984, Lorri Neilsen confidently calls *Thirty-six Exposures* "the best Canadian portrait ever drawn of seventeen-going-on-adult."

Major now lives in Sandy Cove, Newfoundland, with his wife Anne Crawford Major (they married in 1981) and their sons, Luke and Duncan. His fourth novel, "Dear Bruce Springsteen," will be published in the fall of 1987, and he is presently working on a fifth novel that promises to add another chapter to his continuing portrayal of contemporary Newfoundland life. As he writes in his introduction to his earliest book, *Doryloads*, it is only "when we understand where we have come from and what our present way of life is like, that we can think wisely about what we want our futures to be."

Jovette Marchessault

(9 February 1938-   )

Kathleen L. Kellett
University of Toronto

BOOKS: *Comme une enfant de la terre/I: Le crachat solaire* (Montreal: Leméac, 1975);
La Mère des herbes (Montreal: Quinze, 1980);
Tryptique lesbien (Montreal: Editions de la Pleine Lune, 1980); translated by Yvonne M. Klein as *Lesbian Triptych* (Toronto: Women's Press, 1985);
La Saga des poules mouillées (Montreal: Editions de la Pleine Lune, 1981); translated by Linda Gaboriau as *Saga of the Wet Hens: A Play* (Vancouver: Talonbooks, 1983);
La Terre est trop courte, Violette Leduc (Montreal: Editions de la Pleine Lune, 1982);
Lettre de Californie (Montreal: Nouvelle Optique, 1982);
Alice & Gertrude, Natalie & Renée et ce cher Ernest (Montreal: Editions de la Pleine Lune, 1984);
Anaïs, dans la queue de la comète (Montreal: Editions de la Pleine Lune, 1985).

PLAY PRODUCTIONS: *Les Vaches de nuit*, included in the collective feminist production *Célébrations*, Montreal, Théâtre du Nouveau Monde, 5 March 1979; translated by Yvonne M. Klein as *Night Cows*, New York, Women's Salon, Fall 1979;
La Saga des poules mouillées, Montreal, Théâtre du Nouveau Monde, 24 April 1981; translated by Linda Gaboriau as *Saga of the Wet Hens*, Toronto, Tarragon Theatre, 18 February 1982;
La Terre est trop courte, Violette Leduc, Montreal, Théâtre Expérimental des Femmes, 5 November 1981; translated by Suzanne de Lotbinière Harwood as *The Edge of the Earth is Too Near, Violette Leduc*, New York, Ubu Repertory Theatre, 16 October 1984; Toronto, Nighwood Theatre, May 1986;
Les Faiseuses d'anges, Montreal, Café-Théâtre L'Ex-Tasse, 20 November 1981;
Alice & Gertrude, Natalie & Renée et ce cher Ernest, Montreal, Atelier Continu, October 1984;
Anaïs, dans la queue de la comète, Montreal, Théâtre de Quat'Sous, September and October 1985.

PERIODICAL PUBLICATION: "Alice and Gertrude and Natalie and René [sic] and dear Ernest," translated by Basil Kingstone, *Canadian Fiction Magazine*, no. 47 (1983): pp. 58-64.

Jovette Marchessault, a self-taught artist and writer, is well known for her work as a painter, sculptor, novelist, and playwright. Born in Montreal in 1938 to working-class parents, Alice Bertrand and Roger Marchessault, she spent her childhood in Montreal and in the nearby countryside, as she recounts in her autobiographical novels *Comme une enfant de la terre* (1975) and *La Mère des herbes* (1980). In the latter she describes the traumatic move from the countryside to one of the poorer quarters of Montreal, where she attended school until the age of thirteen when she quit in order to work. From her first job at a diaper service she went on to work in the textile industry and then to a series of jobs. At the age of thirty-one, with the death of her grandmother Louisa Marchessault, she gave up employment at the Grolier encyclopedia company–transposed in *La Mère des herbes* as Groslôt–to devote herself to creative expression. As she explained in a 1981 interview with Julie Stanton for *Châtelaine* magazine, her grandmother, by her own tremendous creativity, had provided Marchessault with an alibi, allowing her to suppress her desire to create.

Frustrated in her early attempts at writing, Marchessault turned to painting and sculpture and gave her first solo exhibition in 1970 at the Maison des Arts La Sauvegarde in Montreal. Other exhibitions in North America and in Paris and Brussels followed. In 1974 she again turned to writing, drawing on details of her own life, particularly her travels in Mexico, the United States, and Canada, to produce *Comme une enfant de la terre* which won the Prix France-Quebec in 1976. This lyric novel begins and ends with the narrator's birth as she descends from the sky like "un crachat solaire" to become "une enfant de la

Jovette Marchessault [signature]

terre." It includes twelve cantos in which the author speaks, often polemically, of America's history and landscape, Quebec society, the urban landscape of Montreal, her personal history, and that of her parents and grandparents, with emphasis on her American-Indian heritage.

La Mère des herbes is a more typical autobiographical novel, relating the author's life up until the death of her grandmother, all the while affirming Marchessault's rejection of what she refers to as "l'Enorme-normal." Marchessault's condemnation of the patriarchal order, whether manifested by the physical abuse of young girls by their fathers or by certain aspects of Catholic doctrine, is a dominant theme here. She contrasts a misogynous Christian order with the celestial order of the Great Mother, the expression "la mère ·des herbes" being her grandmother's name for the moon.

This criticism of the Catholic church is taken up again in *Tryptique lesbien* (1980; translated as *Lesbian Triptych*, 1985) composed of three monologues in which Marchessault affirms herself as a lesbian feminist. Describing the attempt of society, in particular the Catholic church, to coerce lesbians to conform to the heterosexual norm, in "Chronique lesbienne du moyen-âge québécois" Marchessault relates her own develop-

ment as a lesbian. The second part of the triptych, "Les Vaches de nuit," which has been performed in Montreal, New York, Toronto, and Vancouver, is an imaginative celebration of women, using the metaphor of women as nurturing cows who meet at night with sister animals in the Milky Way to remember the prephallocratic order. In the final part, "Les Faiseuses d'ange," which was staged in Montreal in 1981, the author presents a pro-choice view of abortion as a way in which women can oppose the social pressure that ties them to the biological function of reproduction.

Marchessault has become increasingly involved in the theater since the performance of *Les Vaches de nuit* by Pol Pelletier in 1979 at the Théâtre du Nouveau Monde in Montreal as part of *Celebrations*, a feminist stage production conceived by Marchessault and the Quebec feminist Nicole Brossard. In *La Saga des poules mouillées* (published in 1981; translated as *Saga of the Wet Hens: A Play*, 1983) and in later plays, Marchessault makes use of details from the lives of women writers. Produced in Montreal in 1979 and in English in Toronto the following year, *La Saga des poules mouillées* stages an imagined encounter of four major Quebec writers, Laure Conan (Félicité Angers), Anne Hébert, Germaine

Covers for the published version of Marchessault's play about French author Violette Leduc. First produced in Montreal in 1981, the play was also staged in New York under the title The Edge of the Earth is Too Near, Violette Leduc.

Covers for Marchessault's 1984 play portraying a Paris rendezvous of five literati: (left to right) Reneé Vivien, Natalie Barney, Alice B. Toklas, Ernest Hemingway, and Gertrude Stein

Guèvremont, and Gabrielle Roy, who participate in a lively, often humorous discussion of the problems of censorship and self-censorship faced by women writers in Quebec. Marchessault's next play, *La Terre est trop courte, Violette Leduc* (published in 1982), depicts the French author Violette Leduc as a rather pitiful figure who nonetheless had the courage to write openly about her unconventional sexuality and faced censorship for having done so. At times this play seems to be a collage, as Marchessault borrows passages from the works of Leduc, notably *La Bâtarde* (1964), and sets them in a new context to give the spectator insight into the character of Violette Leduc. In 1981 the play was produced in Montreal; three years later an English translation, *The Edge of the Earth is Too Near, Violette Leduc*, was staged in New York.

Marchessault continues to celebrate women in *Lettre de Californie* (1982), a volume which includes a poem in homage to the radical American feminist Meridel Le Sueur as well as ten biographical pieces on women who were "semeuses d'oxygène" (sowers of oxygen), including the medieval French poet Christine de Pisan, the British feminist Emmeline Pankhurst, and the American feminist Susan B. Anthony.

Performed in Montreal and published in 1984, the play *Alice & Gertrude, Natalie & Renée et ce cher Ernest* presents the four lesbian literary figures, Alice B. Toklas, Gertrude Stein, Natalie Barney, and Renée Vivien, and gives a sympathetic portrait of Ernest Hemingway. Using her customary technique of doubling up roles, Marchessault has Hemingway also play the role of his own father in a discussion with his mother, played by Gertrude Stein. In this way Hemingway's debt to his mother, who gave up her singing career for the conventional role of wife and mother, is superimposed on his debt to Stein for her advice on writing.

Anaïs, dans la queue de la comète, produced and published in 1985, criticizes the notion of women's self-sacrifice, a positive value in the patriarchal order. Here the writer Anaïs Nin refuses the self-effacing altruism that had governed her mother's life, affirming her ego by writing her diaries and having them published, and by "stealing" time from the work traditionally done by women for men in order to do her own. This play was awarded the Prix du *Journal de Montreal* in 1986.

It is perhaps only a small step from Marchessault's autobiographical novels to the fictional biography of her plays, as she admits to identifying deeply with women such as Laure Conan and Violette Leduc. Like her grandmother, Marchessault follows the feminine tradition of transmitting knowledge from generation to generation, but her intention is the specifically feminist one of providing an alternative history to that propagated by the patriarchy.

Bibliography:
Barbara Godard, "Bibliography," in Marchessault's *Lesbian Triptych*, translated by Yvonne M. Klein (Toronto: Women's Press, 1985), pp. 97-100.

Interviews:
Donald Smith, "Jovette Marchessault, de la femme tellurique à la démythification sociale," *Lettres Québécoises*, 27 (Fall 1982): 52-58;
Julie Stanton, "Pour Jovette Marchessault, ç'a été: 'Tu crées ou tu crèves,'" *Châtelaine*, 22 (June 1981): 110-114, 116, 118, 120.

References:
Linda Gaboriau, "Jovette Marchessault; A Luminous Wake in Space," *Canada Theatre Review*, 43 (Spring 1985): 91-99;
Barbara Godard, "Flying Away with Language," in Marchessault's *Lesbian Triptych*, translated by Yvonne M. Klein (Toronto: Women's Press, 1985), pp. 9-28;
Martha Rosenfeld, "The Development of a Lesbian Sensibility in the Work of Jovette Marchessault and Nicole Brossard," in *Traditionalism, Nationalism and Feminism: Women Writers of Quebec*, edited by Paula Gilbert Lewis (Westport, Conn.: Greenwood Press, 1985), pp. 227-239.

Daphne Marlatt

(11 July 1942-   )

Laurie Ricou
University of British Columbia

BOOKS: *Frames of a Story* (Toronto: Ryerson, 1968);

leaf leaf/s (Los Angeles: Black Sparrow, 1969);

Rings (Vancouver: Georgia Straight Writing Supplement, 1971);

Vancouver Poems (Toronto: Coach House Press, 1972);

Steveston, photographs by Robert Minden (Vancouver: Talonbooks, 1974; revised, Edmonton: Longspoon, 1984);

Our Lives (Carrboro, North Carolina: Truck Press, 1975; Lantzville, British Columbia: Oolichan Books, 1980);

The Story, She Said, British Columbia Monthly, 3 (December 1977);

Zócalo (Toronto: Coach House Press, 1977);

What Matters: Writing 1968-70 (Toronto: Coach House Press, 1980);

Selected Writing: Net Work (Vancouver & Los Angeles: Talonbooks, 1980);

Here & There (Lantzville, British Columbia: Island Writing Series, 1981);

How Hug a Stone (Winnipeg: Turnstone Press, 1983);

Touch to My Tongue (Edmonton: Longspoon, 1984);

Mauve, by Marlatt and Nicole Brossard (Montreal: nbj/Writing, 1985);

character, poems with translations by Brossard (Montreal: nbj/Writing, 1986).

OTHER: Raymond Souster, ed., *New Wave Canada: The New Explosion in Canadian Poetry*, includes poems by Marlatt (Toronto: Contact, 1966);

Steveston Recollected: A Japanese Canadian History, edited by Marlatt and Mayo Koizumi (Victoria: Provincial Archives of British Columbia, 1975);

Opening Doors: Vancouver's East End, edited by Marlatt and Carole Itter (Victoria: Provincial Archives of British Columbia, 1979);

Maxine Gadd, *Lost Language: Selected Poems*, edited by Marlatt and Ingrid Klassen (Toronto: Coach House Press, 1982);

In the Feminine: Proceeding of the Women and Words/ Les femmes et les mots Conference 1983, edited by Marlatt and Ann Dybikowski, Victoria Freeman, Barbara Pulling, and Betsy Warland (Edmonton: Longspoon, 1985).

PERIODICAL PUBLICATIONS: [Poems], *Origin*, third series 16 (January 1970): 1-39;

"In the Month of Hungry Ghosts," *Capilano Review*, nos. 16-17 (1979): 45-95.

Any biographical note on Daphne Marlatt seems especially slight because her published work gives so much of herself. Marlatt's reader will find not only the vital statistics, for example that her son Christopher Alan (Kit) was born 3 May 1969, but also the movements of her mind and body responding: the anticipation of pregnancy, the medical confirmation, the fears of miscarriage, the push to give birth. Marlatt's writing is an intimate autobiography, a life *as* it is being written, "a minute and painstaking examination," Frank Davey summarizes in *From There to Here* (1974), "of the processes of perception and of the moment-by-moment contents of consciousness." The aspiration behind Marlatt's painstaking, she writes in *What Matters* (1980), is phenomenology: "to catch the web of experience itself, not as thought (pursuit of an idea) which tends to shortcut sensory input, but the interplay of sensory being-in-a-place & thoughts about (connections with memory or surmise)."

Marlatt's devotion to this interplay has its origin in the early 1960s when she became closely associated with the famous little magazine *Tish*, in its second series, and thus with Black Mountain poetics and the particulars of a West Coast locale. Marlatt had lived in Vancouver since age nine, but she was born Daphne Buckle, in Melbourne, Australia. From age three to nine she lived in Penang, a Malaysian island in the Indian Ocean. (Her "re-entry" into Penang during a 1976 trip she shares with readers in "In the Month of Hungry Ghosts," *Capilano Review*, 1979.) After a few

photograph by Tim Hellum

Daphne Marlatt

months in England, her parents, Arthur (an accountant) and Edrys Lupprian Buckle, moved the family to North Vancouver in 1951.

Following graduation from the University of British Columbia (B.A., 1964), Marlatt began to move around the continent with her husband Gordon Alan Marlatt, a clinical psychologist. Marlatt's early magazine publications quickly established her as an important innovator: Raymond Souster included fifteen of her poems in *New Wave Canada* (1966), his pivotal anthology of "the most exciting, germinative poetry written by Canadians in the last hundred years." The Marlatts moved to Bloomington, Indiana, after a summer in Spain. There Marlatt began to write *Frames of a Story* (1968), the "shadow play of my mind" on Hans Christian Andersen's fairy tale of the Snow Queen. In "Perceiving It as It Stands," a 1978 article in *Canadian Literature*, Robert Lecker describes the use of fairy tale as framework for the poet's own story: "Marlatt has every right to join Kay and Gerda in flight, for their predicament, and the development of their story,

serve as a metaphor for the problems of growth encountered by a poet struggling to break away from the frames imposed by established word patterns and the falsities implied by a world view which categorizes experience, storytelling it in standardized form, as if the motion of living was always the same, always sane."

Frames of a Story alternates short-line poems with the proselike line necessary to story. Her next book, *leaf leaf/s* (1969), is made entirely of severely pared short-line poems in which, whatever the heightening of visual and aural perception, the poet is oblique and at her most obscure. Marlatt takes a firm step here toward letting the language itself become an active creator of the poem; yet the form is not finally congenial, and all her later books are dominated, as she writes in *What Matters*, by "poems [which] run on like prose—the ongoing line gives a larger context while the short lines tend to stress the words in isolation."

At Indiana University Marlatt received an M.A. in 1968; after a short stay in the Napa Valley, during her husband's internship, in the fall

*Cover for the collection of poems by Marlatt and photographs by Robert
Minden celebrating the fishing village of Steveston,
British Columbia*

of 1968 she returned to Vancouver where she
taught English at Capilano Community College
and began work on poems about Vancouver. She
continued work on those poems in 1969 in Wiscon-
sin, but when her marriage ended in late 1970
she returned permanently to Vancouver with her
son. This double return home, and her evolving
poetics, are movingly recorded through journal
and poems in the 1980 volume *What Matters*, a
book which incorporates *Rings* (1971), Marlatt's articulation of being a mother. *What Matters* also records the evolution of *Vancouver Poems* (1972): the
"lush sensuality," "the refreshing waywardness
. . . of skid row drunks," the "lst human recognitions of the place, Kwakiutl, Salish," which give
those poems some of their multiple layers.

The publication of *Steveston* (1974), a collection of photos by Robert Minden and poems by
Marlatt recording her "finding" of that fishing village at the mouth of the Fraser, secured Marlatt's
national reputation, at least among enthusiasts of
experimental writing. Drawing on her work on
an oral-history project, published as *Steveston Recol-

lected* (1975), Marlatt's major work shows, according to Fred Wah in the introduction to Marlatt's
Selected Writing: Net Work (1980), new "confidence
and authority." The flow of town and history, of
the Japanese people and the cannery, especially
of the river and language, are more securely
rooted in place and concentrated in the writing
consciousness than in any other of her books.

Our Lives (1975) explores the "organic implo-
sions of relationships" within an experiment in
communal living in the summer and winter of
1972. *Zócalo* (1977) was, until "Ana Historic"
(forthcoming), the closest Marlatt had come to
writing a novel, a meditation on the camera eye
to which nothing is foreign, by a consciousness
which feels very foreign in Mexico. R. H.
Ramsey, reviewing the novel in the *Canadian
Forum* (June-July 1978), might be speaking of
the general reader's reaction to all Marlatt's elliptical prose poetry: "Much of the novel is concerned more with general atmosphere and mood
than with exposition; consequently, much remains unexplained."

10

& we were raised on them. raised to be faithful, & self-effacing, & patient --
"what every girl should know." embroidering in the castle window waiting for
destiny to turn up. good girls, i.e. princesses, don't get into trouble --
they endure it.

you're forgetting something, Annie T. you're forgetting how you loved to be
a star. that was third person, seeing your name up in lights, heroine of your
own tale. you weren't exactly waiting.

i remember. but then something changed. you stopped telling them, or told
me to stop telling them. "are you telling stories again?" as if stories were
always lies. as if they don't have their own truth, in all the turns & twists.
(caught in the labyrinth between your repainted walls, you turned tale & fled.)

it was you who changed. you grew up. you learned the difference between story
& history, & then you scorned my bedtime tales.

i learned that history is his, the tale of his exploits embroidered against the
backdrop of trees. she holds in her anonymous hands, lovingly. so many claims to
fame. so many ordinary men turned into heroes. (& the ordinary women with them
erased, de-faced from pages & pages of 'fact'.) city fathers (where are the city
mothers?) bragging about the birth they've engineered, building a city out of
so many shacks that would be someplace when it grew up. The Western Terminus
of the Transcontinental, steel Straits of Anian, Gateway to the East: all these
capital letters to announce the fact of their being present.

"I had 400 men working..."
"I built the two and one half miles from Hastings to Hastings Sawmill..."
"I hauled logs with oxen down Gore Avenue..."

"I...built VANCOUVER'S FIRST CITY HALL..."

all these numbers & place names, as if they conveyed the _feel_ of it (they
don't)--what it was like to be here, in the beginning. Hastings Mill,
small settlement with its camp & store & school surrounded by stumps, saw-
dust, slash burning. connected by a trail along the shoreline to its
nearest neighbour, Gastown of saloons & how did it go? "three hotels:
Deighton's, Sunnyside, & Joe Mannion's; one grocery store and Chinese
wash house and lock-up." the rudiments of civilization on a diminutive
scale from pleasure to punishment, embryo of a city. & over the split shake

Page from the revised typescript for Marlatt's novel-in-progress "Ana Historic" (by permission of the author)

From 1973 to 1976 Marlatt taught English at Capilano Community College, and from 1977 to 1981 edited, with Paul de Barros in Seattle, *periodics*, a magazine devoted to prose and its theory. The end of *periodics* and the appearance of *Selected Writing: Net Work* (1980) mark a subtle turning point in Marlatt's work. Her interest in literary theory shifted to more specifically feminist concerns, and the wider public anticipated by Talonbooks's selection of her writing was realized because both small formal changes in her poetry and a growing sympathy for semiotic theory in the general literary culture made Marlatt's work more accessible. Through the journal *Tessera* and the collective Women and Words (originating in the conference of that title, Vancouver, 1983), Marlatt began to associate with Quebec feminist writers, most notably Nicole Brossard and Louky Bersianik. This association reinforced a longstanding French/English interchange in her language and encouraged polyphonic texts.

How Hug a Stone (1983), for example, which traces Marlatt's 1981 journey to England with her son, uses apparent transcriptions of voices recorded on her son's tape recorder to incorporate the unique speech patterns of the many people she met. The form of travel journal, which shapes almost all Marlatt's books, is made more explicit, as if to acknowledge how central the travel diary has been historically to women's writing: sections are numbered, maps are provided, and cryptic journal entries frame the poems. The use of italics makes her familiar etymological journeying more obvious and easier to follow. *Touch to My Tongue* (1984)–accessible in a different way–creates an audience within a community increasingly interested in theory by combining poems, which appear to be prose pieces, with an essay, "musing with mothertongue," which could be a poem. The lines between what Marlatt calls "essay-ing" and poem-ing blur and disappear. But at the same time the book comes closer to the traditional lyric than most of her earlier work: once-open parentheses are closed and purely incantatory repetition is more evident. As a feminist and lesbian exploration of the erotics of language, the book is indebted to many theorists, especially to Julia Kristeva and Hélène Cixous. In Marlatt's words, it "redefine[s]" and "signals us beyond limits in a new tongue our connection runs along." As such it looks forward to "Ana Historic," her novel-in-progress in which she speaks in the new tongue

of the forgotten or silent writing women of Vancouver's past and future.

Interviews:
David Arnason, Dennis Cooley, and Robert Enright, "There's This and This Connexion," *CVII*, 3 (Spring 1977): 28-33;

George Bowering, "Given This Body," *Open Letter*, fourth series 3 (Spring 1979): 32-88;

Ellea Wright, "Text and Tissue: Body Language," with Betsy Warland, *Broadside: A Feminist Review*, 6 (December 1984-January 1985): 4-5;

Janice Williamson, "Speaking In and of Each Other," with Warland, *Fuse*, 8 (February-March 1985).

References:
Douglas Barbour, "The Phenomenological I: Daphne Marlatt's *Steveston*," in *Figures in a Ground: Canadian Essays on Modern Literature in Honour of Sheila Watson*, edited by Diane Bessai and David Jackel (Saskatoon: Western Producer Prairie Books, 1978), pp. 174-188;

Christina Cole, "Daphne Marlatt as Penelope Weaver of Words: A Feminist Reading of *Steveston*," *Open Letter*, sixth series 1 (Spring 1985);

Frank Davey, "Daphne Marlatt," in his *From There to Here* (Erin, Ontario: Press Porcèpic, 1974), pp. 193-197;

Barbara Godard, " 'Body I': Daphne Marlatt's Feminist Poetics," *American Review of Canadian Studies*, 16 (Winter 1985);

Robert Lecker, "Perceiving It as It Stands: Daphne Marlatt's Poetry," *Canadian Literature*, 76 (Spring 1978): 56-67;

John Bentley Mays, "Ariadne: Prolegomenon to the Poetry of Daphne Marlatt," *Open Letter*, third series 3 (Fall 1975): 5-33;

Roy Miki, "The Lang Poem: The Cosmology of the Long Poem in Contemporary Canadian Poetry," *Open Letter*, sixth series 2-3 (Summer-Fall, 1985): 71-90;

Jack Silver, "Moving into Winter: A Study of Daphne Marlatt's *Our Lives*," *Open Letter*, third series 3 (Spring 1978): 89-103;

Fred Wah, "Introduction" to Marlatt's *Selected Writing: Net Work* (Vancouver & Los Angeles: Talonbooks, 1980), pp. 7-21;

Janice Williamson, "Citing Resistance: Vision, Space, Authority and Transgression in Canadian Women's Poetry," Ph.D. dissertation, York University, 1987.

Tom Marshall
(9 April 1938-   )

Peter Stevens
University of Windsor

BOOKS: *The Silences of Fire* (Toronto & London: Macmillan, 1969; London: Macmillan, 1969);
The Psychic Mariner: A Reading of the Poems of D. H. Lawrence (New York: Viking, 1970; London: Heinemann, 1970);
Magic Water (Kingston: Quarry, 1971);
The Earth-Book (Ottawa: Oberon, 1974);
The White City (Ottawa: Oberon, 1976);
Rosemary Goal (Ottawa: Oberon, 1978);
Harsh and Lovely Land: The Major Canadian Poets and the Making of a Canadian Tradition (Vancouver: University of British Columbia Press, 1979);
The Elements (Ottawa: Oberon, 1980);
Playing with Fire (Ottawa: Oberon, 1984);
Dance of the Particles (Kingston: Quarry, 1984);
Glass Houses (Ottawa: Oberon, 1985);
Adele at the End of the Day (Toronto: Macmillan, 1987).

OTHER: *The Beast with Three Backs,* includes poems by Marshall (Kingston: Quarry, 1965);
A. M. Klein, edited with a postscript by Marshall, (Toronto: Ryerson, 1970);
Fourteen Stories High, edited by Marshall and David Helwig (Ottawa: Oberon, 1971).

In an unassuming way Tom Marshall has established a quiet but firm presence in contemporary Canadian literature. His poetry is meditative, sometimes calmly ironic at his own expense, yet moving to a clearly articulated sense of self and place, patriotic without being jingoistic. In the same way his criticism, while avoiding the overly polemical, persuasively expresses perceptive insight into individual authors, together with a well-conceived appreciation of an author's place not only within the native tradition but also within the larger scheme of literature.

Thomas Archibald Marshall, the son of Douglas Woodworth and Helen Kennedy Marshall, was born in Niagara Falls, Ontario, "that roaring border outpost of vulgarity," as he has de-

scribed it. He spent some of his childhood in the United States—mostly in Joplin, Missouri, and Memphis, Tennessee—as his father, a chemical engineer, worked on scientific projects there during World War II.

In 1961 he received his B.A. in history and in 1965 his M.A. in English, both from Queen's University, Kingston, a city in which he still resides and which with its environs figures constantly in his writing. In his first year of teaching at Queen's he had his first small collection of poems published in a volume entitled *The Beast with Three Backs* (1965), which also contained verse by Tom Eadie and Colin Norman. The press which published this book was an outgrowth of the poetry magazine *Quarry* which, beginning in the 1960s, has established itself as a publication responsive to a wide variety of trends in poetry. Marshall was associated with the magazine as an editor and was one of a group of Kingston poets connected with the magazine (including, among others, Michael Ondaatje, Douglas Barbour, Stuart McKinnon, and David Helwig) who later developed their own presences in the field of contemporary Canadian poetry.

Marshall has remained in Kingston and taught at Queen's since 1964, although he has spent some time in Europe, including a stay in London (1966-1968) for study toward his Ph.D. which he never completed. Those graduate studies, however, led to the publication of his thoroughgoing reading of D. H. Lawrence's poetry, *The Psychic Mariner* (1970), a book that attempts to trace the development of Lawrence's characteristic poetic methods and the way in which the poet reached a maturity of vision and technique.

Marshall's own poetry has developed as a kind of continuing poetic sequence cohering around the general theme of the four elements. Each of his first four volumes is devoted to one of the elements respectively, and the books have since been revised and reedited for publication as *The Elements* (1980), one long poetic sequence.

The four books show a gradual maturing of style, beginning with *The Silences of Fire* (1969), which generally expresses Marshall's sense of man in his own lost space, searching for some central firmness, often falling away or teetering on the edge of darkness. The poems are rigorously clipped and formal, though occasionally the stiffness is undercut by a slightly self-mocking diffidence and cynicism.

Magic Water (1971) shows a loosening of language and form, though the poet has the annoying habit of passing off as poems anecdotal fragments about friends and fellow writers. While there is more flexibility of style in this book, Marshall still clings to some traditional framework. "Islands," the poem from which Marshall takes his title *Magic Water*, is a sort of sonnet sequence: each poem is a loose fourteen-line poem, and the sequence itself is fourteen poems long, echoing the major formal divisions of a sonnet, as the first eight poems pose certain problems with some resolutions in the closing six poems.

Dust jacket for the volume Marshall calls his "book of air," fourth in the series that he revised as The Elements *(1980)*

The third book in the series, *The Earth-Book* (1974), picks up some Lawrentian notions in a desire to establish some sense of the sublimity, together with both awe and dread, that can pervade earthly existence. Unfortunately, Marshall tries to capture this sense in some quasi-dramatic longer poems and sequences, but his style is more suited to the lyric glimpse, the teasing out of particulars with the tone of dread being mirrored by a neurotically comic self-mockery.

The White City (1976) contains highly charged evocations of Canadian place, in particular, of small country places in Ontario, including his own Kingston, although there are poems centering on his travels as well. Again Marshall attempts the large statement in one long sequence in an effort to define Canadianness. But such a vision comes through more clearly at the close of the book where the poems tend to focus on Canadian history, eventually zeroing in on the city of

10.

afternoon's drinking ~~would~~ *will* not be too obvious. He ~~was~~ *feels* just tipsy enough to be friendly, energetic, charming in company.

What to wear to this arty affair? He consider~~ed~~ *s* his meagre wardrobe. Something casual but smart, he suppose~~d~~ *s*; but that ha~~d~~ *s* never quite been his style. He settle~~d~~ *s* on corduroy pants and jacket with an open shirt. Casual, but not as sloppy on the one hand or as bizarre and flashy on the other as he ~~thought~~ *thinks* some of Rosemary's artist friends ~~would~~ *will* be.

He ~~could~~ *can* walk to the gallery which ~~was~~ *is* on one of those streets whose names he ~~could~~ *can* never remember just north of Yorkville. Would it be gauche to arrive *can* at the beginning?

He ~~had~~ *has* another drink, to kill time.

Walking along Lowther to Avenue Road and Yorkville he observe~~d~~ *s* how pleasant Toronto ~~was~~ *is* in spring. The trees ~~were~~ *are* just beginning to bud, *and* the air seem~~ed~~ *s* marginally less dirty than before, though there ~~was~~ *is* dust enough everywhere too. *Spring dust, he sighs.*

Harold crosse~~d~~ *s* Avenue Road to Yorkville Avenue.

~~Now~~ *Here* he mingle~~d~~ *s* with the crowd that attend~~ed~~ *s* upon the fashionable shops and outdoor coffee places. The sun ~~was~~ *is* shining on the glass and brick and cars and tables and people. On the just and the unjust.

He turne~~d~~ *s* left and walk~~ed~~ *s* one block north to the gallery that Rosemary's dealer, Maud Pollen, ha~~d~~ *s* owned for some ten years. Pollen Gallery ha~~d~~ *s* acquired a considerable reputation in that time, and Rosemary ha~~d~~ *s* become one of its several "star" painters. "I'm busy as a bee," Maud ~~was~~ *is* fond of ~~saying~~ *announcing* as her promotion of her favourites ~~grew~~ *grows* ever more active. Often, in past years when he ha~~d~~ *s* sometimes accompanied Rosemary to Toronto, Maud ~~would~~ *has* whisk~~ed~~ them off for a pleasant beer in the old Pilot Tavern where so many artists ~~had~~ *have* "hung out".

It ~~was~~ *is* five-thirty. Was that still too early to arrive? Bravely Harold soldier~~ed~~ *s* on and enter~~ed~~ *s* the gallery.

Page from the revised typescript for Marshall's 1985 story collection, Glass Houses *(by permission of the author)*

Kingston. What emerges is a sense of being Canadian very much in keeping with the tone of Marshall's own poetry: gently aloof, somewhat lacking in dynamic commitment, yet with a desire to transcend common reality in order to find peace through the aching possibilities of love.

His revisions and condensation of these books into one collection, *The Elements* (1980), have in general managed to delineate these themes and clarify his poetic gifts. His most recent collections of poetry also show his continuing interest in the themes and modes already established. The very title of one collection *Playing with Fire* (1984) connects it with his meditations on the four elements, and *Dance of the Particles* (1984) contains two quietly dramatic but still essentially lyrical longer poems.

Marshall's notion of being Canadian within his own place and yet acknowledging a greater outer reality is the base of his studies in Canadian poetry. His work on A. M. Klein (he wrote a master's thesis on Klein and edited the critical collection *A. M. Klein* in 1970) shows an appreciation of Klein's immersion in his Jewish past and Zionist present, and his full-length study of Canadian poetry, *Harsh and Lovely Land* (1979), avoids reading Canadian literature in dogmatically nationalist terms, accepting the fact that Canadians are somewhat fluid in their outlines and so produce a literature constantly shifting in its frames of reference.

One of the points he makes in his book on Canadian verse is that quite a number of contemporary poets have turned to fiction to the enhancement of both genres. Marshall himself has written two novels and a collection of short stories. *Rosemary Goal*, a quietly comic work which expresses an intricate dance of sexual manners mirrored at times in the fictional writing of one of the principal characters of Marshall's novel and projecting a subjective view of "reality" through passages from that same character's diary. On the whole, however, the novel is slight with no firm engagement with the characters who too often seem to be manipulated merely to

fit the measures of a dance of changing partners. In fact, a journal entry in which the fictional fiction writer describes his own first novel might well summarize Marshall's novel: "a deliberately somewhat grotesque, somewhat surreal cartoon-show of a book."

The five stories in *Glass Houses* (1985)—which appeared first in such journals as *Canadian Forum* and *Journal of Canadian Fiction*, and which include the enigmatic fable "The Story of T."—demonstrate Marshall's abilities as a social mannerist, aware of the bitter predicaments of contemporary relationships and also of the potential for comedy. These stories tend mostly to express the inherent sadness of human relationships and an attendant sense of loss as the characters ruminate on the past, their failures, and their missed opportunities. His second novel, *Adele at the End of the Day* (1987), is concerned with this same sense of loss, although the title character, a woman in her seventies, does take some delight in her past. She is perturbed in the present by her relative failure with her adopted son who devotes much energy to analyzing his mistakes and debating the ambiguities of his character. In *Adele at the End of the Day* the tone is quiet, somewhat lyrical, as the chapters focus alternately on the voice and character of each of these two principal characters. The narrative lines converge at the end in somewhat contrived melodrama, though on the whole the two characters are presented in a convincing way.

Tom Marshall has shown a refreshing willingness to attempt different genres. Yet despite his accomplishments in fiction, it is his poetic voice which seems to remain his true voice, meeting the challenge of form and language in the most consistently engaging way.

References:

Stan Dragland, "Tom Marshall's *The White City*," *Essays on Canadian Writing*, no. 12 (1978): 192-203;

Jon Pearce, ed., *Twelve Voices: Interviews with Canadian Poets* (Ottawa: Borealis, 1980), pp. 76-93.

Claire Martin
(18 April 1914-   )

Lorraine Weir
University of British Columbia

BOOKS: *Avec ou sans amour* (Montreal: Cercle du Livre de France, 1958);

Doux-amer (Montreal: Cercle du Livre de France, 1960); translated by David Lobdell as *Best Man* (Ottawa: Oberon, 1983);

Quand j'aurai payé ton visage (Montreal: Cercle du Livre de France, 1962); translated by Lodbell as *The Legacy* (Ottawa: Oberon, 1986);

Dans un gant de fer (Montreal: Cercle du Livre de France, 1965); translated by Philip Stratford with *La Joue droite* as *In an Iron Glove* (Toronto: Ryerson Press, 1968); Stratford's translation republished separately as *In an Iron Glove: An Autobiography* (Montreal: Harvest House, 1975);

La Joue droite (Montreal: Cercle du Livre de France, 1966); translated by Philip Stratford with *Dans un gant de fer* as *In an Iron Glove* (1968); Stratford's translation republished separately as *The Right Cheek: An Autobiography* (Montreal: Harvest House, 1975);

Les Morts (Montreal: Cercle du Livre de France, 1970);

"Moi, je n'étais qu'espoir" (Montreal: Cercle du Livre de France, 1972);

La Petite Fille lit (Ottawa: Editions de l'Universitè d'Ottawa, 1973).

PLAY PRODUCTION: *"Moi, je n' étais qu' espoir,"* Montréal, Théâtre du Rideau Vert, 1972.

TRANSLATIONS: Markoosie, *Harpoon of the Hunter,* translated as *Le Harpon du Chasseur* (Montreal: Cercle du Livre de France, 1971);

Pitseolak, *Pictures Out of My Life,* translated as *Le Livre d'images de ma vie* (Montreal: Cercle du Livre de France, 1972);

Margaret Laurence, *The Stone Angel,* translated as *L'Ange de Pierre* (Montreal: Cercle du Livre de France, 1976);

Robert Thomas Allen, *The Violin,* translated as *Le*

Claire Martin, 1940s (courtesy of Kenneth Landry)

Violon (Montreal: Cercle du Livre de France, 1976);

Robertson Davies, *The Manticore* translated as *Le Lion avait un visage d'homme* (Montreal: P. Tisseyre, 1978);

Davies, *World of Wonders,* translated as *Le Monde des Merveilles* (Montreal: Cercle du Livre de France, 1979);

Clark Blaise, *Tribal Justice,* translated as *La Justice tribale* (Montreal: P. Tisseyre, 1985).

Claire Martin's pseudonym itself proclaims two elements central to her work and its place in the history of French-Canadian literature. Asserting the continuity of the female line through her use of her mother's maiden name Martin, she also signals her commitment to the exploration of the varieties of women's experience within a male-dominated culture. As she writes in her 1966 volume of memoirs, *La Joue droite,* her interest is in the possibilities of women's lives beyond the traditional rhythm of "yearly maternities, sleepless nights and dreary days, nursing children, washing, cooking, finished off with eclampsia or puerperal fever." She has made a significant contribution to French-Canadian literature through her willingness to move beyond the conservative stereotypes of Catholic Quebec in order to investigate the meaning of love, whether in terms of familial bondage or of erotic and emotional involvement.

On 18 April 1914 Claire Martin was born in Quebec to Ovila Montreuil, a civil engineer, and his wife, Alice Martin Montreuil. Martin studied with the Ursulines in Quebec and with the Soeurs de la Congrégation de Notre-Dame in Beauport. She worked as a radio announcer first with station CKCV in Quebec and later with Radio-Canada in Montreal. On 13 August 1945 she married Roland Faucher, a chemist, and they lived in Ottawa until 1972. Her first book, *Avec ou sans amour*, was published in 1958, and in the course of the next two decades she won a number of awards including the Prix du Cercle du Livre de France (1958), for *Avec ou sans amour;* the Prix de la Province de Québec (1965) and the Prix France-Québec (1965), both for *Dans un gant de fer;* and a Governor General's Award (1967), for *La Joue droite*. From 1963 to 1965 she was president of the Société des Ecrivains Canadiens-français and in 1970-1971 Martin served as president of the jury for the Governor General's awards. After her husband's retirement, Martin moved with him to France and lived in Cabris in the Maritime Alps from 1972 to 1982 when they returned to Canada and took up residence in Quebec City, where her husband died on 30 November 1986. In 1973 she spent a term as writer in residence at the University of Ottawa and also devoted herself to the translation of English versions of Inuit narratives as well as of fiction by Robertson Davies and Margaret Laurence, among others.

Martin's first book, the collection of short stories entitled *Avec ou sans amour*, is a series of experiments with tightly controlled form and style. For the most part brief and ironic, these stories reveal Martin's insight into the predicaments of love from a woman's point of view. Those who demand "realism" have been dissatisfied not only with Martin's short stories but also with her novels. As Maurice Blain has summed up these objections in his essay "Comment fille inconstante devient femme fidèle" collected in Gilles Marcotte's *Présence de la critique* (1966), "Roman

Cover for the 1967 paperback edition of Martin's first novel, a lyrical account of ten years in the life of an editor in love with one of his authors (courtesy of Kenneth Landry)

immoral, diront les moralistes, qui va de l'inconstance un peu cynique a la fidélité un peu durable. Roman invraisemblable, diront les psychologues"; however, as Blain himself concludes, a novel like Martin's *Quand j'aurai payé ton visage* (1962) is a "Roman de l'intelligence du coeur."

Martin is a moralist who is less concerned with plot and character development than with the elucidation of a situation, a moment, a problem which becomes representative of a life. This metonymic mode is obvious in Martin's second book, *Doux-amer* (1960), in which her use of lyrical first-person narration focuses the novel on ten years in the life of the narrator, an editor, and on his relationship with Gabrielle Lubin whose first book he has edited. A retrospective and frequently elegiac view of Lubin's relationship with the narrator's rival, Michel Bullard, her marriage to Bullard, and the return to the editor in the end, *Doux-amer* is structured in terms of two narratives set within the frame of the editor's

Markoosie

Le harpon du chasseur

roman

Traduit de l'anglais par
Claire Martin

LE CERCLE DU LIVRE DE FRANCE LTÉE

Cover for Martin's translation of the English version of an Inuit novel

story itself. *Doux-amer* was translated into English as *Best Man* in 1983.

Taken a step further in her next novel, *Quand j'aurai payé ton visage* (1962), this technique of narrative doubling produces two narrators, Catherine Lange and Robert Ferny, and two parallel narratives of ten chapters each. These narratives are, in turn, separated by the narrative of Robert's mother, Jeanne Ferny, which is set between them. A retrospective narrative like *Doux-amer*, this novel presents three monologues on essentially the same event: the marriage of Catherine and Bruno Ferny, Catherine's love for her husband's brother, Robert, and her leaving of Bruno to live with Robert. Martin's working title for the first draft of the novel summarized these relationships: "Triangles pour un quatuor."

Equally difficult relationships form the subject of Martin's two volumes of memoirs, *Dans un gant de fer* (1965) and *La Joue droite*. Both volumes of this autobiography were published in English translation in one volume under the title *In an*

Iron Glove (1968); separately published translations appeared in 1975. Essentially the record of Martin's survival in the house of a tyrannical father, these memoirs powerfully evoke the Jansenist-Catholic ethos of Quebec before the social transformation heralded by the Quiet Revolution. In her presentation of her mother's tragic life, Martin clearly demonstrates the extent to which both physical and emotional violence were directed particularly against women and from which individuals seldom—and only at great cost to themselves—managed to escape. The depth of female bonding which also emerges at times under such conditions is shown by Martin in her depiction of her maternal grandmother to whom she was devoted and to whom she attributes her love of the French language.

Like Anne Hébert, her great contemporary, Martin has resisted the political pressure toward incorporation of *joual* (colloquial Quebecois French) and toward an Americanized French into her work. Her syntax remains traditional and her lexicon that of the French Academy, choices which made her work suspect during the 1970s and which have distanced her from the climate of vigorous stylistic experimentation characteristic of contemporary Quebecois writing. Her 1970 novel, *Les Morts*, and its stage adaptation, *"Moi, je n'étais qu'espoir,"* produced at Montreal's Théâtre du Rideau Vert and published in 1972, aroused a good deal of opposition from those committed to the view that the primary function of a writer in Quebec is to explore the circumstances of contemporary Quebecois life using the language of the majority. Martin has, however, resolutely refused to participate in this transformation, seeing the movement away from the language and intellectual traditions of the mother country as cultural folly.

Regarded by many as her finest novel, *Les Morts* has been classified by Martin as a "roman-essai," an intricately structured analysis of love which may be seen as the counterpart to her memoirs. Another retrospective narrative in the first person, this novel presents its narrator as a writer in search of the meaning of past loves and of love itself, struggling in elegantly taut prose to disentangle the erotic from the conventionally romantic, the body of the other from her own longing, the experience of love from the saying of words which nourish—perhaps invent—love.

With the exception of *La Petite Fille lit* (1973), a brief narrative composed as a literary exercise in fulfilment of her term as writer in residence at the University of Ottawa in 1972, Martin has not written a work of fiction since *Les Morts*. Alienated from the stylistic experimentation and commitment to feminist theorizing about writing which characterizes the work of such contemporary Quebecois novelists as Nicole Brossard and Louky Bersianik, Martin's work is now set firmly in the middle distance by contemporary Quebecois critics. It is ironic that, perhaps in part because her work has not been well served by English translators, being blunted and deprived of much of its feminist anger in the process, her writing has not yet found the place of honor in English Canada which it may yet achieve.

References:

Maurice Blain, "Comment fille inconstante devient femme fidèle," in *Présence de la critique*, edited by Gilles Marcotte (Ottawa: HMH, 1966), pp. 167-169;

Françoise Iqbal and Gilles Dorion, "Claire Martin: Une interview," *Canadian Literature*, 82 (Autumn 1979): 59-77;

Françoise Kaye, "Claire Martin ou le 'je' aboli," *Incidences*, 4 (May-December 1980): 49-58;

Suzanne Paradis, *Femme fictive, femme réelle* (Quebec: Garneau, 1966);

Jeannette Urbas, *From 'Thirty Acres' to Modern Times* (Toronto: McGraw-Hill Ryerson, 1976);

Annick Vanbrugghe, "De la tentation de la lucidité à l'amour dépoetisé: *Avec ou sans amour* de Claire Martin," *Livres et Auteurs Québécois* (1969): 223-226;

Robert Vigneault, *Claire Martin: son oeuvre, les réactions de la critique* (Montreal: Pierre Tisseyre, 1975).

Seymour Mayne

(18 May 1944-   )

David Staines
University of Ottawa

BOOKS: *That Monocycle the Moon* (Montreal: Privately printed, 1964);

Tiptoeing on the Mount (Montreal: McGill Poetry Series, 1965; revised, Montreal: Catapult, 1965);

From the Portals of Mouseholes (Vancouver: Very Stone House, 1966);

Manimals (Vancouver: Very Stone House, 1969);

Mouth (Kingston, Ontario: Quarry, 1970);

For Stems of Light (Vernon, British Columbia: Very Stone House, 1971; revised, Ottawa: Mosaic Press/Valley Editions, 1974);

Face (Burnaby, British Columbia: Blackfish Press, 1971);

Name (Erin, Ontario: Press Porcépic, 1975; revised, Oakville, Ontario: Mosaic Press/Valley Editions, 1976);

Diasporas (Oakville, Ontario: Mosaic Press/Valley Editions, 1977);

The Impossible Promised Land: Poems New and Selected (Oakville, Ontario: Mosaic Press/Valley Editions, 1981);

Children of Abel (Oakville, Ontario: Mosaic Press/Valley Editions, 1986).

OTHER: *Collected Poems of Red Lane*, edited by Mayne and Patrick Lane (Vancouver: Very Stone House, 1968);

Forty Women Poets of Canada, edited by Mayne and Dorothy Livesay (Montreal: Ingluvin, 1971);

Engagements: The Prose of Irving Layton, edited by Mayne (Toronto: McClelland & Stewart, 1972);

Jerzy Harasymowicz, *Genealogy of Instruments*, translated from the Polish by Mayne and Catherine Leach (Ottawa: Mosaic Press/Valley Editions, 1974);

The A. M. Klein Symposium, edited and with an introduction by Mayne (Ottawa: University of Ottawa Press, 1975);

Irving Layton: The Poet and His Critics, edited and with an introduction by Mayne (Toronto: McGraw-Hill Ryerson, 1978);

Abraham Sutzkever, *Burnt Pearls: Ghetto Poems of*

photograph by Sharon Katz

Abraham Sutzkever, translated from the Yiddish by Mayne (Oakville, Ontario: Mosaic Press/Valley Editions, 1981);

Rachel Korn, *Generations: Selected Poems of Rachel Korn*, edited by Mayne (Oakville, Ontario: Mosaic Press/Valley Editions, 1982);

Essential Words: An Anthology of Jewish Canadian Poetry, edited, with an introduction, by Mayne (Ottawa: Oberon, 1985).

PERIODICAL PUBLICATIONS: "Irving Layton: A Bibliography-in-Progress, 1931-1971," *West Coast Review* (January 1973): 23-32;

"A Dialogue on A. M. Klein," by Mayne and M. W. Steinberg, *Jewish Dialog* (Passover 1973): 10-16;

"A Conversation with Patrick Anderson," *Inscape*, 11 (Fall 1974): 46-79;

"Other Montrealers," *Canadian Literature*, 64 (Spring 1975): 98-101.

"Jewish Canadian poets on the whole are recognizable by their emphasis on the human dimension, the translation of the experience of the immigrant and the outsider, the finding of joy in the face of adversity, the linking with tradition and the concern with history in its widest sense," Seymour Mayne writes in his historical introduction to *Essential Words: An Anthology of Jewish Canadian Poetry* (1985), referring explicitly to Jewish-Canadian poets yet providing an accurate commentary on his own poetry. These poets, he continues, "strive for the essential words that echo more than the individual's need. They move to enter a communal language, to find the words that speak to and for the community, whether they relate to the everyday or the eternal. Their words draw in their contemporaries, while invoking the presence of ancestors and tradition."

The eldest of two sons of Henry and Doris Minkin Mayne, Seymour Mayne was born on 18 May 1944 in the predominantly Jewish district of Cartier in Montreal and grew up in the same neighborhood. From an early age he was a member of the Jewish Public Library, which was a major influence on his artistic formation. The library was a center for the revered of Montreal's Yiddish community, including the poet and man-of-letters Melech Ravitch, to whom Mayne pays tribute in a poem collected in *The Impossible Promised Land* (1981):

Dust jacket designed by Sharon Katz for Mayne's 1981 poetry collection

Who can forget your dignified manner,
your cane and soft smile
and the words you offered
a bristling and critical youth
that spring day both of us stood
before the larger-than-life
painting of the barricade–
Warsaw Ghetto tableau
at the Jewish Public Library?

About what continually corrodes
you spoke: 'Never succumb to cynicism–
if you're a poet, you can't be a cynic.'
Bearing yourself with the etiquette
of the lyrical and innocent
you found a way in wanderings,
Authentic words and poems,
testimonies dot that map,
the continent of Yiddish
blood soaked and staining
the blotter of Europe forever–

Such writers as Ravitch guided Mayne's reading

and thinking in his early years.

In 1961 Mayne entered McGill University to pursue an honors degree in English. In his first year he became so actively involved with *Forge*, the student literary magazine that had begun two decades earlier with the participation of Louis Dudek and Irving Layton, that he became its poetry editor. As an undergraduate he studied with Dudek and Hugh MacLennan and attended poetry classes conducted by Irving Layton at Montreal's other English university, Sir George Williams (now Concordia). Each spring he submitted a manuscript of poetry to Dudek and Layton, the two figures who still dominated the Montreal poetry scene. Dudek imposed on Mayne's verse the rigors of his stylistic concerns and demands, while Layton focused on the thematic content.

Dudek and Layton, Mayne recalled in a 1980 interview with Kathleen C. Moore published in *Athanor*, "did help the younger writers to clarify their own views and poetics. And we became more independent, in fact—that is, those few of us who survived what Louis ironically calls the victimization by the lyric muse. The Montreal writers didn't hang around in packs or gaggles, as, for example, the Tish group and their acolytes. In Montreal we maintained a sense of allegiance to a shared poetics, but we didn't fall in at the sound of a bugle. Nor did we backslap each other in reviews and articles. There was a sense of healthy criticism and awareness in the air."

During his Montreal years Mayne began to have his poetry published: in the McGill student magazines, in a variety of little magazines, and in such national periodicals as the *Canadian Forum*. His first collections, *That Monocycle the Moon* (1964), which won the Chester Macnaghten Prize in Creative Writing from McGill University, and *Tiptoeing on the Mount* (1965), are lighthearted explorations of human passion and sensuality. Layton's presence is evident in the interest in the sensual dimensions of man's nature, while Dudek's influence is perceptible in the carefully executed formal verse patterns.

Upon graduation in 1965 Mayne traveled to the University of British Columbia, intending to study with Earle Birney. The latter, however, left the Vancouver campus that summer. Mayne obtained his master's degree in English from U.B.C. in 1966; his thesis, a collection of some of his previously published poetry, was supervised by Dorothy Livesay. For his Ph.D., which he received in 1972 from the same university, he wrote a dissertation on Irving Layton and the Montreal poets under the supervision of Donald G. Stephens.

The poetry of Mayne's Vancouver years marks a deepening awareness of the human condition. In *Mouth* (1970) he begins to examine the body in mystical rather than merely sensual terminology. Partly foreshadowed in *From the Portals of Mouseholes* (1966), his interest in the world beyond the physical and his commitment to a more profound exploration of man in his relationship not simply to himself but increasingly to those around him already suggest the distinctive Jewish voice that characterizes his later verse.

A lecturer in the Department of English, University of British Columbia, for the fall term of 1972, Mayne accepted an appointment as lecturer in the Department of English at the University of Ottawa for the winter term of the same academic year. Since that time Ottawa and its university have been his home. He became assistant professor of English in 1973, associate professor

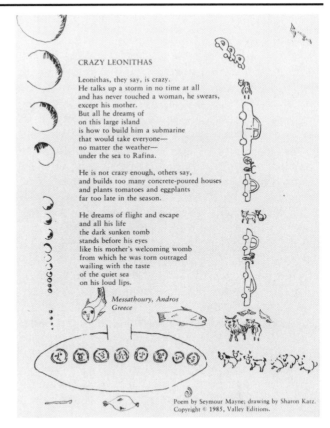

Broadside published by the press Mayne helped found in 1974 (by permission of the author)

in 1978, and full professor in 1985. He has taken leaves of absence to accept invitations to serve as visiting professor at Hebrew University of Jerusalem (1979-1980; 1983-1984) and at Concordia University (1982-1983).

Name (1975), which received the J. I. Segal Prize in English-French Literature and the York University Poetry Workshop Award, begins Mayne's exploration of his Jewish heritage, and such exploration coincides with a new interest in social issues. Society, for him, remains humanity itself rather than its institutions, and social polemics find little place in his essentially humane vision. The sexuality and self-absorption of his early romantic poetry are now replaced by pain and melancholy about human transience and mortality.

Diasporas (1977), *The Impossible Promised Land: Poems New and Selected* (1981), and *Children of Abel* (1986) reveal the secure voice of a mature poet conscious of his Jewish heritage and his poetic calling. The "arrogance, the callousness of early manhood" (to quote Mayne's words from the poem "Steve") have disappeared in a poetic vi-

XIX *Getting into Line*

Everything itches hiding ~~from the crystallizing~~ *wary of the crystalline*
cold.

Only the eyes in the deepfreeze of the wolf's
hour ~~unblinkered~~ stand their own and refuse to smart.

. . .

Codes of grief, the trees, dark sky, will not
yield. It's that shattering star giving the false
impression of pulsing that needs the shock of a comet's
tail to get it into line.

Lines whip the eyes, sentences spastic and
flailing, jealous of the syntax of wholeness.

Draft for "Getting into Line," a prose poem from the sequence "Simple Ceremony" published in Children of Abel, *1986 (by permission of the author)*

sion that bears little resemblance to the witty celebratory verse of his early years. A bleak, even pessimistic, vision of life permeates his powerful verse, yet Mayne finds hope in his steadfast commitment to his Jewish traditions and in man's awareness and acceptance of the cyclic pattern of life. He looks to Judaism, as in *Children of Abel's* "Yom Kippur," not only to recapture the beauty and the pain of its history but also to place himself and his contemporaries within a continuum that offers meaning amid the flux of life:

> Of course it should rain on a day of fasting and atonement. The drops cleave to the circling leaves, wait awhile, and slide over towards the oblivion of lawn and pocked earthbeds.

> And tug us back to beginnings.

Mayne is the direct literary descendant of A. M. Klein, the disciplined control of his verse reminiscent of Klein's poetry and the increasing emphasis on Jewish characters, idiom, and traditions reminiscent of Klein's early writings. As tribute to Klein, Mayne organized the University of Ottawa's A. M. Klein Symposium in May 1974, the first reassessment of Klein's literary stature, and edited the proceedings as *The A. M. Klein Symposium* (1975). His early indebtedness to Layton is acknowledged by two volumes he edited, *Engagements: The Prose of Irving Layton* (1972) and *Irving Layton: The Poet and His Critics* (1978).

During his Montreal years Mayne was one of the editors of *Cataract* and later of *Catapult*. When he moved to Vancouver, he was dismayed at the American influence on the West-Coast literary scene. Not alone in his desire to counter the Tish group's power over British Columbian poets, he founded, along with Jim Brown, Bill Bissett, and Patrick Lane, the publishing firm of Very Stone House in 1966. The committed quartet discovered a printer who would extend credit to them, and, using Mayne's graduate fellowship as collateral, they produced pamphlets and small books. Whereas Very Stone House fostered the presence of eastern writings in the west, Mayne became, in 1971, one of the founders of Ingluvin Publications in Montreal, formed to introduce western writers to eastern audiences. In 1974 he helped start another press, Mosaic Press/Valley Editions, to publish new writers and those whose works had fallen into neglect. Mayne has also translated poetry from Polish, Russian, and Yiddish, and his own poetry has been translated into French, Hebrew, and Spanish.

Writing of the Jewish-Canadian poets of his generation in the introduction to *Essential Words*, Mayne concludes that they "are not concerned with style or poetic experimentation for its own sake. Nor do they simply emphasize statement or message. The balance of the private and public elements—almost a continuous touchstone of Canadian poetry—informs the work of these younger poets." Mayne himself balances the private and the public and not only in his verse. His sensitive poetry stands alongside his many contributions to Canadian culture as critic, editor, publisher, and translator.

References:

Aviva Layton, "Small Press Ties that Bind," *Quill & Quire*, 44 (December 1978): 17-18;

Kathleen C. Moore, "Signature Marks and Burnt Pearls: An Interview with Seymour Mayne," *Athanor*, 1 (December 1980): 6-23;

John Oughton, "After the Holocaust," *Books in Canada*, 11 (March 1982): 15-16.

David McFadden
(11 October 1940-   )

James Doyle
Wilfrid Laurier University

BOOKS: *The Poem Poem* (Kitchener, Ontario: Weed/Flower Press, 1967);

The Saladmaker (Montreal: Imago, 1968; revised, Montreal & New York: Cross Country, 1977);

Letters from the Earth to the Earth (Toronto: Coach House Press, 1968);

The Great Canadian Sonnet (2 volumes, Toronto: Coach House Press, 1970; 1 volume, Toronto: Coach House Press, 1974);

Poems Worth Knowing (Toronto: Coach House Press, 1971);

The Ova Yogas (Toronto: Weed / Flower Press, 1972);

Intense Pleasure (Toronto: McClelland & Stewart, 1972);

A Knight in Dried Plums (Toronto: McClelland & Stewart, 1975);

The Poet's Progress (Toronto: Coach House Press, 1977);

I Don't Know (Montreal: Véhicule, 1978);

On the Road Again (Toronto: McClelland & Stewart, 1978);

A New Romance (Montreal & New York: Cross Country, 1979);

A Trip around Lake Erie (Toronto: Coach House Press, 1980);

A Trip around Lake Huron (Toronto: Coach House Press, 1980);

My Body Was Eaten by Dogs: Selected Poems of David McFadden, edited by George Bowering (Toronto: McClelland & Stewart, 1981);

Three Stories and Ten Poems (Toronto: Prototype, 1982);

Country of the Open Heart (Edmonton: Longspoon, 1982);

A Pair of Baby Lambs (Toronto: Front Press, 1983);

Animal Spirits: Stories to Live By (Toronto: Coach House Press, 1983);

The Art of Darkness (Toronto: McClelland & Stewart, 1984);

Canadian Sunset (Windsor: Black Moss Press, 1986).

David McFadden (photograph by Lesley Harper)

MOTION PICTURE: *A Trip Around Lake Ontario*, script by McFadden, Great Lakes Films, 1987.

OTHER: "The Twilight of Self-Consciousness," in *The Human Elements: Critical Essays*, first series, edited by David Helwig (Ottawa: Oberon, 1978), pp. 78-96.

PERIODICAL PUBLICATIONS: "Here Are Some More Snaps," *Fiddlehead*, 87 (November-December 1970): 6-14;

"The Sick-Bed of the Heart: A Day in the Life of a Writer," *Quill & Quire*, 49 (June 1983): 28.

Among modern Canadian writers David McFadden, poet, novelist, short-story writer, essayist, and journalist, is one of the most adept at the exposition of the heroic and ironic elements of commonplace human experience. As might be expected of a writer who finds profundity in small things, his more distant literary antecedents are romantic: his favorite poet is William Blake, and he has been an enthusiastic reader of Walt Whitman; he follows in the footsteps of such twentieth-century disciples of Blake and Whitman as William Carlos Williams, Allen Ginsberg, and Jack Kerouac. His Canadian literary associations have included the West Coast *Tish* writers who introduced projectivist and other postmodern American literary movements to Canada. In spite of his admiration for American literary traditions, he is very consciously a Canadian writer and has tried to bridge the gap between a new localism and a broader sense of nationalism—through both his widely dispersed literary associations and his attempts to absorb his travel experience into his writing. McFadden has been prolific, producing sixteen books of poetry and four books of fiction in the past twenty years. The quality of his writing has been uneven, but the best of his work indicates that he is one of the most talented authors to emerge in Canadian literature in the 1970s and 1980s.

David William McFadden was born in Hamilton, Ontario, to William and Elizabeth Pidgeon McFadden. After completing high school, he worked at various jobs in and around Hamilton. In 1962 he went to work as a proofreader for the Hamilton *Spectator*; he became a reporter in 1970, at which job he continued until 1976. He had been an inveterate writer from his early years and claims to have written a complete novel while he was still in high school; but, as he states in his introduction to *Poems Worth Knowing* (1971), "I first started writing poems seriously in January, 1960." His first publications were in Canadian little magazines, especially the local Hamilton periodical *Mountain*, which McFadden originated and edited from 1960 to 1963. Throughout the 1960s, while continuing his newspaper work, he had poems published in a variety of Canadian little magazines, including *Quarry*, *Fiddlehead*, *Weed*, *Talon*, and others. In the late 1960s he produced three books of poems: *The Poem Poem* (1967), *The Saladmaker* (1968), and *Letters from the Earth to the Earth* (1968).

In 1963 McFadden married Joan Pearce of Hamilton (they were divorced in 1979); their two daughters, Alison and Jennifer, were born in 1964 and 1968. In these early years of his marriage McFadden began the practice, which he continued through several of his books, of featuring in his work his wife and children, their family pets, their friends, their house and car, and all the minutiae of daily experience in an urban home. This fabric of immediate experience is usually related to the poet's creative processes, and ultimately to the forces, creative and other, governing the whole of human and cosmic activity. McFadden's conception of the purpose and nature of poetry parallels his perception of the purpose and nature of life as a whole and is essentially simple: the only genuine and lasting force is creative energy, and the thrust of all energy is toward perfection.

The Poem Poem, a continuous work published in a twenty-seven-page chapbook, is McFadden's solipsistic analysis of his own processes of poetic composition, which he parallels with an allusive account of his wife's pregnancy and the birth of their first child. It is a good first effort, but the echoes of William Carlos Williams's *Paterson* are, perhaps, too prominent. In *The Saladmaker*, a collection of short lyrics, McFadden makes considerable progress toward finding his own distinctive voice and form. The influence of Williams and imagism is still evident, but the poet is scrutinizing his immediate environment with greater care, fitting words to images with more consistent success, and evolving a more regular, almost iambic line. In *Letters from the Earth to the Earth*, the poet's personality and vision emerge more clearly than in the earlier poems. The volume is illustrated with snapshots of his wife, children, and other relatives, but these adjuncts are almost irrelevant to the author's exuberant self-centeredness, evident, for example, in "A Spring of Poems":

Me with my enormous dream
of flooding the world with poems
the whole race praising itself
through my pink flesh ecstasy.

While continuing to work for the Hamilton newspaper, McFadden received a Canada Council grant and wrote regularly for various little magazines. In 1970 he produced his first novel, *The Great Canadian Sonnet*, presented in the form of a "Big Little Book," illustrated by his friend, London (Ontario) artist Greg Curnoe. The work is the anecdotal story of an obvious alter ego of the author, thirty-three-year-old Ricky Wayne, of

Covers for the one-volume edition of McFadden's first novel, a picaresque narrative about thirty-three-year-old Ricky Wayne of Hamilton, Ontario, who sets out in pursuit of "human perfection"

Hamilton, who sets out in pursuit of "human perfection" amid the detritus of modern North American junk culture. The narrative of his conversations and adventures is picaresque, satirical, sometimes absurdist, and frequently obscure. But, in the end, the protagonist recognizes that the imagination must learn to accept conditions of the material world before there can be hope of fulfilling moral visions.

Throughout the early 1970s, McFadden continued experimenting with an idiosyncratic kind of fiction through short stories published in various little magazines. Eleven of these stories he eventually collected in *Animal Spirits: Stories to Live By* (1983). Also illustrated by Greg Curnoe, *Animal Spirits* was in format the antithesis of *The Great Canadian Sonnet*, made to look like an oversize, large-print children's book. The stories, often cryptic and inconclusive, seem to be attempts to render impressions of the absurdity, mystery, and terror of modern life.

At the same time, McFadden continued his prolific production of poems in periodicals. In 1976 he gave up journalism to launch out as a freelance writer. This new departure was marked by the autobiographical long poem, *The Poet's Prog-*

ress (1977), which describes in Whitmanesque language the poet's "falling awake" to a new stage of his life when his newly discovered poetic sensibility grapples with "his inability to understand / the Cosmos, a blade of grass." Like Ricky Wayne of *The Great Canadian Sonnet*, the poet progresses toward an acceptance of "everything."

From December 1978 to April 1979, McFadden was a writer in residence at Simon Fraser University, which was the beginning of a five-year sojourn in British Columbia. After his year at Simon Fraser, he was appointed a creative-writing instructor with the Kootenay School of Writing at the David Thompson University Centre in Nelson, a position he held until 1983. In 1980 he was the founding editor of a new periodical, *Writing*.

On the West Coast McFadden wrote poems about his new environment, but he continued to be mainly preoccupied with his native Ontario. It was during these years that he wrote his two most popular books, his comic travelogue novels *A Trip around Lake Erie* and *A Trip around Lake Huron* (both published in 1980). The first two volumes of a projected series on all the great lakes, these books are McFadden's most successful ven-

Cover for the 1984 collection poet Dennis Lee described as McFadden's "extraordinary new music—reflective, muscular, improvisatory. Here the planet earth, the kitchen sink, dreams of apocalypse/redemption cohabit remarkably."

tures into satirical fiction. Unlike *The Great Canadian Sonnet*, the "trip around" volumes are told in a straightforward, deceptively simple language, by a carefully created and totally convincing narrator, ostensibly the author himself. "Dave McFadden" is a good-natured typical tourist and conscientious (if occasionally mischievous) husband and father, by turns naive, intolerant, openminded, patient, and indignant in his encounters with modern Americans and Canadians and the icons of their leisure culture.

In 1981 the British Columbia poet and novelist George Bowering edited a volume of selected poems by McFadden, *My Body Was Eaten by Dogs*. Drawn from at least six different volumes, this collection is an excellent overview of McFadden's work of the 1960s and 1970s. It includes several of his best comic poems, such as "A Typical Canadian Family Visits Disney World," which introduces the main characters of the "trip around"

books. The collection also shows his preoccupation with dream and nightmare, in which life experiences appear as frantic animated cartoons, or commonplace moments are disrupted by intrusions of panic or bemused incredulity.

McFadden's most recent poetry, typified by *The Art of Darkness* (1984), reveals a continuation of his exuberant exploitation of the autobiographical mode, as well as his sense of incongruity and absurdity, and his confidence in the ultimate possibilities of the human psyche. But as the title suggests, there is a bit more solemnity, an awareness of the ominous sides of experience, than formerly. If "The Cow That Swam Lake Ontario" is a delightful fable of determination and idealism, there are also certain "poisonous poems," as McFadden calls them in his preface, dealing with murder, suicide, disfigurement, and other manifestations of human cruelty and grotesqueness. "Analysis of these poems is strictly forbidden," the author jokes in his preface; but the reader must be forgiven for seeing in the volume a search for a point of equilibrium between the reassuring and the horrifying, an attempt to navigate the obscurity of life with creative energy and skill.

The same tendencies continue to be evident in his fiction. His most recent novel, *Canadian Sunset* (1986), interweaves wild farce and gruesome tragedy, in which commonplace experiences build to bizarre climaxes and grotesque elements conversely seem familiar and trivial. The episodic narrative (much of it previously published as short stories in periodicals) is connected by the peregrinations and comments of an eccentric narrator, Walter J. Littlewood, an incongruous combination of armaments salesman and poet, who presumably incorporates both the creative and destructive impulses of modern society. A somewhat enigmatic but occasionally funny book, *Canadian Sunset* seems partly an experiment in offbeat humor and perhaps a foray into "magic realism."

In 1983 McFadden returned to his home province to become writer in residence for a year at the University of Western Ontario. He also became a contributing editor to the publishers' trade periodical *Quill & Quire*, writing for the next two years a regular column of interviews and opinion entitled "Writer's Block," in which he displayed his considerable talents as a journalist. Since 1984 McFadden has continued his career as a free-lance writer and teacher, serving as a creative-writing instructor in various high schools and, in the summer of 1985, as the first writer in residence of the Metropolitan Toronto Public Library.

In recent years McFadden has been the recipient of two senior Canada Council fellowships, the National Magazine Award, and a Governor General's Award nomination. Three plays based on his poems were produced in Toronto in 1977-1978, 1982 and 1983; three of his works of fiction have been adapted as short films.

With his genial but intellectually provocative voice, McFadden has demonstrated the accessibility of poetry and the flexibility of traditional literary forms. His writing is by turns impish and solemn, colloquial and cryptic, at times providing snapshotlike pictures of a familiar world of domestic and social experience and at times revealing dark or bizarre levels of perception and meditation lying beneath the surface of the conscious mind.

References:

Frank Davey, *From There to Here: A Guide to English-Canadian Literature Since 1960* (Erin: Press Porcépic, 1974), pp. 182-185;

Gary Draper, "David McFadden" [interview], *Books in Canada*, 13 (October 1984): 29-31;

Brian Fawcett, "McFadden's Dilemma," *Books in Canada* (March 1987): 3-5;

Ronald Kiverago, "Local Poet Deserves Attention: The Poetics of David McFadden," *Open Letter*, third series 5 (Summer 1976): 16-26.

Florence McNeil
(8 May 1937-)

Laurie Ricou
University of British Columbia

BOOKS: *A Silent Green Sky* (Vancouver: Klanak, 1967);

Walhachin (Fredericton: Fiddlehead, 1972);

The Rim of the Park (Port Clements, British Columbia: Sono Nis, 1972);

Emily (Toronto: Clarke, Irwin, 1975);

Ghost Towns (Toronto: McClelland & Stewart, 1975);

A Balancing Act (Toronto: McClelland & Stewart, 1979);

Miss P. and Me (Toronto: Clarke, Irwin, 1982);

The Overlanders (Saskatoon: Thistledown, 1982);

All Kinds of Magic (Vancouver: Douglas & McIntyre, 1984);

Barkerville (Saskatoon: Thistledown, 1984).

RADIO: *Barkerville*, CBC, 13 December 1980.

OTHER: Fred Candelaria, ed., *New West Coast: 72 Contemporary British Columbia Poets. New Poems with Personal Commentaries and Autobiographical Sketches*, includes poems by McNeil (Vancouver: Intermedia, 1977);

When Is a Poem: Creative Ideas for Teaching Poetry Collected from Canadian Poets, edited with contributions by McNeil (Toronto: League of Canadian Poets, 1980);

Here Is a Poem: An Anthology of Canadian Poetry, edited by McNeil (Toronto: League of Canadian Poets, 1983).

No Canadian poet, not even P. K. Page, has focused as steadily as Florence McNeil on the intersection of the visual and verbal. In the anthology *New West Coast* (1977) she wrote: "I've always been interested in the differences: representation of the thing and the thing itself and the various shades of truth in what is perceived. So I use movies, photographs, television, paintings as source material." This interest in thing and representation of thing is realized in poetry which consistently combines graphic precision and fine verbal shading.

The storytelling tradition which McNeil's father shared with his Outer Hebridean ancestors provided a childhood which McNeil remembers

as rich with vivid verbal pictures. Born to John and Jean Gillies McNeil, and raised in North Burnaby, close to ocean, forest, and mountain, McNeil studied at the University of British Columbia, receiving a B.A. in 1960. She spent the next year at the University of Alberta, where she met Eli Mandel and Rudy Wiebe, whom she recalls reading from an early novel in one of her creative-writing classes. After intermittent high-school teaching, she returned to U.B.C. where she studied with Earle Birney and received an M.A. in English and creative writing in 1965. That year she won the Macmillan of Canada Prize for Poetry and began to teach English at Western Washington State College in Bellingham.

McNeil's first book is the published version of the poems which she submitted as her M.A. thesis. Elegantly and sensitively designed by Takao Tanabe, *A Silent Green Sky* (1967) is a delight to

the eye. McNeil describes objects and places—a parking lot in fog, a hospital corridor, a ferry, "four green shoots climbing out / of the edges of the trash can"—with, as her publisher enthuses in a foreword, "depth of observation and acute microscopic perception." McNeil anticipates her later work by frequent use of metaphors from the visual arts: in "Interior August," for example, "beach people . . . [are] stranger than / parchment figures glazed on a Chinese screen," the sky is "like a bar-room nude," and the branches overhead are a "sweeping fresco." Implicit in these examples, however, is the most persistent criticism reviewers have made: as Peter Stevens wrote in *Canadian Forum* (November 1968), this poem is "a catalogue of images quite precise in themselves, but giving a generally exaggerated tone because of an over-use of similes."

In 1968 McNeil left Bellingham for the University of Calgary, where she taught until 1973. The poetry written during this period is strongly influenced by nostalgia for the West Coast. *Walhachin* (1972), prompted by driving past the small community on many trips between Calgary and Vancouver, shows two significant developments in the poet's work: the attempt at an integrated suite of poems and at using the voice of a historical figure. McNeil describes the poem as "the imagined monologue of an Englishwoman in Walhachin," a town settled by English colonists in 1907. In twenty-two parts the poem describes a seven-year attempt to irrigate the desert and establish a town; McNeil fixes on the trees, and their analogy with the speaker's poems, which define the community's dream. *The Overlanders* (1982) is a later attempt at a similar serial poem, in which a pregnant woman, solitary among a group of male fortune-hunters en route to the Cariboo gold fields, dreams (concealing her pregnancy, she is "secretly fertile") of a "magic carpet" and a clear image of her self.

The Rim of the Park, which appeared the same year as *Walhachin*, is a more random collection of poems, loosely organized along biographical lines. A "didactic / prairie winter" is recalled in "Afterthought," followed by a series of poems on the scenes and personalities of Halfmoon Bay, where McNeil has a vacation home on the ocean. Her fine evocations of landscape are here extended by an increasing interest in the way humans represent their world. In the title poem a companion is a camera: "I'm on fire in your eight millimeter / eyes," the poet complains. The metaphors of the earlier volume lead to poems

```
                    reading
Allan Steart sits at his window
in his green eyeshade
looking over the treetops
that slope downwards like
a green ski slope
to the ocean with its fisboats
slpashed by a clear-wind green sun
and the mountains blown sky high
are tinted snapshots   in the clear day
His world is split into two halves
the preface   a summer when his eyes were full
his body perfect as the
ads for muscle tone he cut from magazines
and ever afterward
when the green fingers of gas
touched his lungs   rushed
and the magazine ad was trampled
in the slime of the trench

and the magazine body crupled
into the slime of a trench
he wakes still his hands impaled
on a wet pillow
even now   another war later
when his war has been rationalized into
a set of leater volumes
with the backs   with their spines broken
mould eating the golden words names
and through
he sees now through a split screen
on one side out of reach
the perfect gren clarity of
of words and line —
on the other below his eyes
the words that rush and bumble
that fuse into small repetivite explosion
that even his glasses   the eyeshade
the brightest light
cannot control.
```

```
ALLAN
Tim Stewart sits at his window
with his book   in his green eyeshade
with the words that fade like
spots on a bleached out sheet
lookig over the treetops
ghat slant downwards like
a green ski slope
to the ocean with its fishboats
splashed by a green sun
and the mountains blown sky high
tinted shanpshots   in the clear day
His world is split into two halves
the preface   a summer when his eyes were whole
his body pefect as the
ads for muscle tone he cut from amagazines
And ever afterward
after the green fingers of gas
rushed his lungs
And the magazine ad was trampled
in the slime of the trench

And still
wars later
he wakes  his hands impaled
on a wet pillow
even now  his eyes eeing only liquid blurs
even now
when his war has been rationalized into a
hundred leather volumes
with their spines split
moulding eating the golden names
even now
that they have all become myths split
he sees only through a split screen
on one side out of reach
the perfect green clarity
of word and line
on the other below his eyes
the words that rush and tumble
that fuse into small repetitive explosions
that even the eyeshade —
the brightest light
cannot control.
```

```
                ALLAN STEWART

Allan Stewart sits at his window
in his green eyeshade  with his book
with the words that fade like
spots on a bleached out sheet
looking over the treetops
that slant downwards like
a green ski slope
to the ocean with its fishboats
splashed by a green sun
and the mountains blown sky high
tinted snapshots  in the clear day
His world is split into two halves
the preface  a summer when his eyes were whole
his body perfect as the
ads for muscle tone he cut from magazines
And ever afterward
after the green fingers of gas
rushed his lungs
And the magazine ad was trampled
in the slime of the trench

And still
wars later
he wakes  his hands impaled
in a wet pillow
his eyes liquid blurs
even now
when his war has been rationalized into a
hundred leather volumes
with their spines split
mould eating the golden names
even now
when they have all become myths
he sees only through a split screen
on one side
the perfect green clarity
of form and line
on the other before his eyes
the words that rush and tumble
that fuse into small repetitive explosions
that even the greenest flare of light
cannot control.
```

Drafts for a poem by McNeil that was pubished in the summer 1983 issue of Canadian Literature *(by permission of the author)*

about photographs and movies, and about remembering: in "Silents" "tom mix / and ws hart" are "pure / pantomimes / of an age / chased out of / existence."

In *Emily* (1975) McNeil secures her great talent for the poetic interpretation of painting with an ideal subject—the West Coast painter Emily Carr—who is a lyrical, energetic writer: "I who wrestle with words / as with paint / wanting to catch the cobalt sky / and let it trickle / through black and white type / force veridian (forests) through the / swirl of a sentence." The economical focus on Carr's eccentricity and "wild canvasses," the shadow of Carr's biography, make this McNeil's most satisfying book. As Jean Wilson wrote simply in a review for *Canadian Literature* (Winter 1977), "The spirit of Emily Carr is in this book, not any easy thing to capture."

Ghost Towns, also published in 1975, is a more general collection combining the interest in history and art found in *Walhachin* and *Emily*. Here the focus on the visual artifact—not only photograph and movie, painting and television show, but magazine advertisement or illustration from a Dickens novel—becomes so pervasive that the "typical" McNeil poem is identifiable. "It is close to being a formula," wrote Dorothy Livesay when reviewing this volume for *Canadian Literature* (Winter 1976). McNeil begins with an image by which a culture expresses its perception, finds the right verbal and metaphorical means for presenting it with great clarity, and then pushes the limits of both word and visual representation to extend her own seeing of the world.

Having discovered her forte—the anecdotal poems often flounder by comparison—McNeil began *A Balancing Act* (1979) with a suite of poems on specific paintings and on painterly schools and movements. At their best these can serve as a genuinely novel guide to seeing what is usually unnoticed: "A Paul Klee Cat" could be a brilliant program note to a gallery showing. *Barkerville* (1984) gives similar prominence to the visual: it is designed as an album of archival photographs elaborated by verbal portraits of the characters who peopled the Cariboo mining boomtown in the last thirty years of the nineteenth century. McNeil's extensive use of a range of prose and dramatic forms is a formal recognition of the problematics of relating verbal grammars to camera-eye framing.

Perhaps the descriptive lucidity and immediacy of McNeil's poetry has created a sense that her poetry is excessively simple. Her suggestions of the many dimensions inherent in the two-dimensional have elicited surprisingly little critical interest. But new work in different genres may change that: in 1980 she wrote a radio play about Barkerville. Most interestingly, she has turned to writing juvenile novels: *Miss P. and Me* (1982) is a puberty-blues novel about a thirteen-year-old dreaming of becoming a writer, and *All Kinds of Magic* (1984) is a mystery thriller set in the interior of British Columbia, which has been the literary landscape she prefers. In one sense these novels for young people seem an appropriate direction: as in *Alice in Wonderland*, one of her favorite books, McNeil has always combined a childlike directness and a magical intelligence.

References:

Sean Ryan, "Florence McNeil and Pat Lowther," *Canadian Literature*, 74 (Autumn 1977): 21-29;

Christopher Wiseman, "Reticence and Emergence: The Poetry of Florence McNeil," *CVII*, 4 (Spring 1979): 36-40.

George McWhirter

(26 September 1939-   )

Andrew Parkin
University of British Columbia

BOOKS: *Catalan Poems* (Ottawa: Oberon, 1971);
Bodyworks (Ottawa: Oberon, 1974);
Bloodlight for Malachi McNair (Vancouver & San Francisco: Kanchenjunga Press, 1974);
Queen of the Sea (Ottawa: Oberon, 1976);
Twenty-Five (Fredericton: Fiddlehead, 1978);
Ties (Toronto: League of Canadian Poets, 1980);
The Island Man (Ottawa: Oberon, 1981);
God's Eye (Ottawa: Oberon, 1981);
Coming to Grips with Lucy (Ottawa: Oberon, 1982);
Fire Before Dark (Ottawa: Oberon, 1983);
Paula Lake (Ottawa: Oberon, 1984);
Cage (Ottawa: Oberon, 1987).

RADIO: *Suspension*, CBC, 1969;
The House on the Water, CBC, 1981;
The Listeners, CBC, 1981.

OTHER: *The Selected Poems of José Emilio Pacheco*, edited by McWhirter, translated by McWhirter and others (New York: New Directions, 1987).

PERIODICAL PUBLICATIONS: "Writing: A Home for Exile," *Canadian Journal of Irish Studies*, 3 (December 1977): 2-11;
"Five Ulster Poets: The Martyrdoms of Modesty," *Canadian Journal of Irish Studies*, 4 (December 1978): 56-61;
"Somewhere between the Blockhouse and the Cliff Face: A Response to Line and Line Break in a Poem," *Epoch*, 29 (Winter 1980): 205;
"The Second Coming: Hard Men Fermenters, Catalysts," *Helix*, 9/10 (October 1981): 103-108.

Don MacGregor Photography Ltd. Vancouver

George McWhirter

George McWhirter is best known for his poetry, although he has also written short stories and novels. His radio plays betoken an interest in broadcast literature, and McWhirter, who has been a frequent contributor to radio poetry readings, as well as a radio interviewer and interviewee, has had stories broadcast in addition to his plays. His publications, the first of them contributions to journals, have been appearing steadily since the late 1960s. In the early 1980s he produced at least a book a year, besides his articles and reviews. However, although he shared the Commonwealth Poetry Prize with Chinua Achebe in 1972, he has yet to achieve widespread public acclaim.

McWhirter was born in Belfast, Northern Ireland, in 1939 to James and Margaret McConnell McWhirter. His father was a fitter in a shipyard. Since most of the family has earned a living by shipbuilding, it would have been natural for George McWhirter to follow suit; at the age of seven, though, he passed the entrance examination for the Belfast Model Boys' School and went from there to Grosvenor High School, Springfield Road. McWhirter's education enabled him to secure a place at the Queen's University, Belfast, to read honors English in a group which also included Seamus Deane and Seamus Heaney, both of whom later became prominent poets and critics in Ireland. After graduating with a B.A. in English in 1961, McWhirter completed a teaching diploma. He spent three years teaching and then went to Spain where he taught at Barcelona's Berlitz school and at the university, thus building on the Spanish he had learned as a schoolboy and taken as a subsidiary subject at the university. While he was in Europe, he had the experiences which led to his writing of *Catalan Poems* (1971), the volume for which he won the Commonwealth Poetry Prize. Immigrating to Canada in 1966, McWhirter taught school for two years in Port Alberni, British Columbia, a place which formed the background of his later books *Coming to Grips with Lucy* (1982) and *Paula Lake* (1984). He moved in 1968 to Vancouver where he now heads the Department of Creative Writing at the University of British Columbia and lives with his wife, Angela Coid McWhirter, and their children, Liam and Grania.

Catalan Poems is a series that works backward from a death bed to a marriage bed, with continuity provided by frequent glimpses of Eduardo and Señora Valls, figures who give human interest to a volume marked by a sometimes obtrusively fancy linguistic footwork. This oblique, obscure quality is McWhirter's main flaw in *Catalan Poems*, as in his other early work. Frank Davey, reviewing McWhirter's first volume for *Canadian Literature* (Winter 1973), detected an anachronistic modernism in the poems, but the best qualities of McWhirter's writing are here as well: the unexpected word or image; a wit that is verbal tied to a surreal angle of vision; a sensitivity to the ordinary work of obscure yet significant people.

His concern with an unusual way of seeing things is worked out most fully in *Bodyworks* (1974), a collection of short fiction criticized by most reviewers for its obscurity. Here the askew angle of vision provides a glimpse into another world. This world, an island of gray drizzle, is called Sarne and allows of strange metaphysical speculation, surreal curiosities of vision, and the evolution of human swimmers toward the aquatic feats of the first merman.

Cover for McWhirter's first collection of verse, co-winner of the Commonwealth Poetry Prize in 1972

In the long sequence of poems *Queen of the Sea* (1976) McWhirter focuses on the Belfast of the shipyards that built the *Titanic* and the *Reina del Mar*. He constructs in experiments of form, such as "Keel," appropriate shapes by the way in which his poems are arranged on the page, but he also includes poems that are more formally conventional. The result is a strong book, sensitive to the hardiness and earthy courage of his people. He trusts and celebrates the work they do, using the vocabulary of shipbuilding to achieve a steely power in densely textured verse with images that startle and make us see anew. McWhirter is at his best in the poems that describe jobs and scenes of the shipyard in short, sometimes alliterative lines that make use of internal rhyme.

McWhirter's interest in Hispanic cultures, evident in *Catalan Poems,* is applied to Mexico in *Twenty-Five* (1978), a book of twenty-nine poems

And Back, Still By Early Morning

The mist, dog's breath. Tap those unexpected
Samovars, the colour of tea brews from the branches ——— this
Of the willow trees anything to your taste the sun
On the well-muzzled ground; Tendrils of recreated
Scent/inching up from the trees droppings /Amber eyes
Peak out to watch the heart's hawk,
Always returning to her hand. Home, God

God you're not sudden, too savage with her any more.

Through the shallow, bed warmed air
The body beats back indoors: — "mouth open", the doors
To the dovecot jammed with feathers Some sway
And float the words. He has armed us at each other
— Man and Woman, did Our separate instincts /home
Perfectly

The mist, dog's breath. Tap these unexpected
Samovars; the colour of tea brews from the branches
Of the willow trees, At this time of year, Everything
To your taste The sun Everything to your taste the sun
On the well muzzled

Notebook draft for one of the poems collected in McWhirter's 1983 volume Fire Before Dark *(by permission of the author)*

using free verse reminiscent of William Carlos Williams, the prose poem, and the form of the nursery rhyme. In this volume McWhirter explores Mexican experience, especially village life, and finds in its Catholicism one of his recurring themes. Critics have found his work since *Twenty-Five* that of a generally assured writer. As Paul Roberts put it in *Quill and Quire* (January 1982), McWhirter has the "ability to make the ordinary numinous" and so create "art at its most sublime."

His radio plays *The House on the Water* and *The Listeners*, both aired in 1981, reveal a humorous side to this writer. *The Island Man*, a book of poems published the same year and praised for its eloquent treatment of the immigrant theme, deals with Spanish explorers of West Coast islands as well as with the life lived there now, blending McWhirter's Canadian experience and his interest in Hispanic themes. But Ireland, too, is an island; and in this book of assured and mature verse McWhirter's use of the metaphor also accommodates his roots. The same year saw the publication of *God's Eye*, a book of stories set in Mexico, and in 1982 McWhirter produced *Coming to Grips with Lucy*, stories which demonstrate his ability to render the adventures and perceptions of childhood without sentimentality. "The Followers," arguably his best short story to date, is in this volume.

Fire Before Dark (1983) is an accomplished book of poems drawing on his familiar themes, but not discovering new directions; this McWhirter does in the novella *Paula Lake* (1984). It is a tense, haunting account of the abduction of a Japanese boy by a disturbed young man whose life is, in a way, saved by the crime and its victim. McWhirter explores the urban and wilderness mentalities, maleness, ambition, and sexuality in this exciting book. His latest work, a novel published in 1987 and again drawing on Mexico, is about Catholicism, power, bureaucracy, and pre-Christian beliefs and habits. It features magic, miracle, and the cages we build for ourselves, as its title, *Cage*, suggests. It is organized in "eclogues" rather than chapters, perhaps an allusion to its being a version of pastoral. Eclogues eight to thirteen, featuring the fat, lecherous, and seismic Turcomano, first appeared in *Canadian Fiction Magazine*, number 55. McWhirter's writing deserves wider recognition; the April 1987 publication of *Cage* (Oberon Press) and of his edition of verse by the Mexican poet José Emilio Pacheco (New Directions) should enhance his reputation.

Robert Melançon
(12 May 1947-   )

Philip Stratford
Université de Montréal

BOOKS: *Inscriptions* (Montreal: L'Obsidienne, 1978);
Peinture aveugle (Montreal: VLB, 1979); bilingual edition, revised by Melançon and translated by Philip Stratford as *Blind Painting* (Montreal: Véhicule, 1985);
Territoire (Montreal: VLB, 1981).

OTHER: *Paul-Marie Lapointe*, edited by Melançon (Paris: Seghers, 1987).

PERIODICAL PUBLICATIONS: "Le Pétrarquisme travesti de Sigognes," *Etudes Françaises*, 13 (April 1977): 71-88;
"Qu'est-ce que la littérature québécoise," *Revue des Sciences Humaines*, 173 (January-March 1979): 7-24;
"The Question of the Book," *World Literature Today*, 56 (Spring 1982): 231-239;
"Un Chapitre de suggestions sur la poésie," *Liberté*, 150 (December 1983): 58-69;
"Eloge de la solitude," *Liberté,* 164 (April 1986): 61-77.

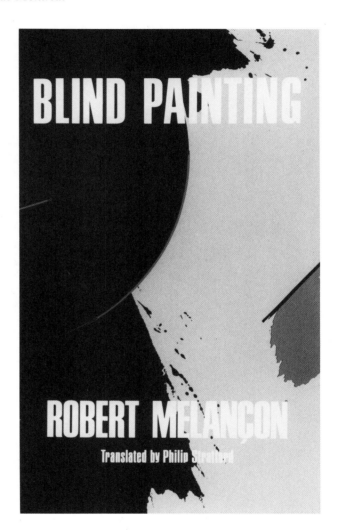

Cover for the 1985 bilingual edition of Melançon's second poetry collection, Peinture aveugle. *As Melançon explains in his preface, he revised nearly every poem from the earlier book so extensively that the 1985 volume is really a new collection.*

Robert Melançon was born in Montreal on 12 May 1947. His father, Horace Melançon, was a notary; his mother, Madeleine Beaulieu Melançon, raised seven children of whom Robert was the sixth. He was educated at local schools and did his undergraduate work in the French department at the Université de Montréal where he began his career as a published writer with some translations of poems by Earle Birney and articles. In September 1969 he married Charlotte Côté and the couple went to France where they studied literature at the Université François Rabelais in Tours. Melançon received his M.A. in 1970 and his doctorate in 1972 for a thesis on French baroque poetry. On his return to Canada he joined the French department at the Université de Montréal where he has taught since, becoming full professor in 1984.

Besides fulfilling the usual professional functions (for example, he was president of the Canadian Society of Renaissance Studies 1984-1986), he has been closely associated with several important Quebecois literary reviews, particularly *Etudes Françaises* (from 1974 to 1982) and *Liberté* (1977-1985). For three years (1977-1980) he wrote a bimonthly "poetry chronicle" for Quebec's leading newspaper *Le Devoir* and since

Robert Melançon (photograph by Kèro)

1986 he has been doing the same thing for the Radio-Canada program *En Toutes Lettres*. In his reviewing, besides dealing with works on his Renaissance specialization, he has concentrated on Quebec writers, principally poets; but he is also at home in contemporary literature of all kinds with special interests in French authors Michel Butor and Francis Ponge and English-Canadian poets A. M. Klein and Earle Birney.

Melançon's poetic production is small but of high quality. He has produced four books of poetry of which *Peinture aveugle* (1979), a collection of fifty poems, is to date the most considerable. His first, *Inscriptions* (1978), is a limited deluxe edition of nine haiku on seasonal subjects dedicated to the memory of seventeenth-century Japanese poet Matsuo Bashō and accompanied by engravings by Gisèle Verreault. *Territoire* (1981) is a long poem, at least for Melançon, that celebrates literally nothing: winter, the nudity of trees, the lack of light, the eradicating whiteness of the snow, the blankness of the writer's page, and the coldness of his heart. In its reductionist style and sentiment it stakes out a naked territory, one which—to borrow Leonard Cohen's words—is "clean and empty, a place to begin from, a particular place."

In *Peinture aveugle* (1979) Melançon occupies that terrain with a suite of poems developing to the rhythm of the seasons, almost abstractly delineating day, night, dawn, dusk, snow, rain, art, love, city streets, and countryside. The poems are painterly, sometimes even cubist, their subdued use of detail and color more Braque than Picasso.

They are not autobiographical or anecdotal in any way although they do deal directly and intimately with universal themes and emotions (love, loss, the ephemeral quality of life, the nature of poetry, and so on), as well as recording in the clearest and simplest language shifts of light, movements of mood, changes of climate. Over half of the poems share common titles: a dozen interspersed throughout the book under the name "Blind Painting" treat the anomalies of the creative act (the title is drawn from an observation by Leonardo da Vinci: "If one may call painting 'mute poetry' the painter can give the name 'blind painting' to the poet's art"). Another interrupted sequence, "At . . . 'The Small Orchard,' " evokes a private place; a third interleaved series comprises love poems. These variations on a restricted number of themes give continuity to the book, as does the quiet passion of the tone, the purity of the diction, and the Renaissance resonance of some of the imagery. In their poise, melodiousness, and modesty these poems achieve a classic, timeless quality.

Peinture aveugle won the 1979 Governor General's Award for poetry in French. It was translated as *Blind Painting* by Philip Stratford in 1985, and during the process Melançon rewrote nearly every poem, so that Véhicule Press's edition with French and English texts appearing on facing pages could really be titled "Blind Painting II."

As a critic Melançon is as precise as he is a poet. He gives a graduate course in "The Physics of Poetry" and handles aesthetic questions with scientific rigor. In the long introduction to *Paul-Marie Lapointe* (1987), a selection of poems by a fellow Quebecois edited by Melançon, he expresses his shared and uncompromising belief in the importance of poetry and quotes the German romantic Novalis who described poetry as "absolute reality." This is the tenor of his own artistic credo.

Since 1981 Melançon has done more and more translating. He has not only tackled challenging poets but he also writes penetratingly about the art of translation, as he does about his poetic practice. He has completed a translation of a volume of selected poems by Earle Birney and, together with his wife who is also a translator (she is preparing a French edition of Emily Dickinson's poems), is working on a translation of A. M. Klein's novel *The Second Scroll*. Melançon has spoken of every poet as being a translator, as "one who seeks with great difficulty to find words to transpose with the least inaccuracy possible the very things that words, perhaps, can never capture." It is certain that this new interest in translation will continue to enrich his poetry.

John Metcalf

(12 November 1938-)

Barry Cameron
University of New Brunswick

BOOKS: *New Canadian Writing, 1969: Stories by John Metcalf, D. O. Spettigue and C. J. Newman* (Toronto: Clarke, Irwin, 1969);

The Lady Who Sold Furniture (Toronto: Clarke, Irwin, 1970);

Going Down Slow (Toronto: McClelland & Stewart, 1972);

The Teeth of My Father (Ottawa: Oberon, 1975);

Dreams Surround Us, by Metcalf and John Newlove (Delta, Ontario: Privately printed, 1977);

Girl in Gingham (Ottawa: Oberon, 1978); republished as *Private Parts: A Memoir* (Scarborough, Ontario: New American Library, 1980);

General Ludd (Downsview, Ontario: ECW, 1980);

Selected Stories (Toronto: McClelland & Stewart, 1982);

Kicking Against the Pricks (Downsview, Ontario: ECW, 1982);

Adult Entertainment (Toronto: Macmillan, 1986).

OTHER: *Sixteen by Twelve: Short Stories by Canadian Writers,* edited with contributions by Metcalf (Toronto: Ryerson, 1970);

The Narrative Voice: Short Stories and Reflections by Canadian Authors, edited by Metcalf (Toronto & New York: McGraw-Hill Ryerson, 1972);

Kaleidoscope: Canadian Stories, edited by Metcalf (Toronto: Van Nostrand Reinhold, 1972);

Here and Now: Best Canadian Stories, edited by Metcalf and Clark Blaise, includes contributions by Metcalf (Ottawa: Oberon, 1977);

Stories Plus: Canadian Stories with Author's Commentaries, edited with contributions by Metcalf (Toronto: McGraw-Hill Ryerson, 1979);

Making It New, edited with contributions by Metcalf (Toronto: Methuen, 1982);

The Bumper Book, edited with contributions by Metcalf (Downsview, Ontario: ECW, 1986);

"Robert standing," in *Canadian Short Fiction,* edited by W. H. New (Scarborough, Ontario: Prentice-Hall, 1986), pp. 443-450.

PERIODICAL PUBLICATIONS: "Playground," *Queen's Quarterly,* 85 (Spring 1978): 17-31;

"The Curate's Egg," *Essays on Canadian Writing,* 30 (Winter 1984-1985): 35-59;

"Paintings About Painting: Notes Towards An Essay on Tony Calzetta," *Malahat Review,* 70 (March 1985): 81-97.

Although he has produced two fairly well-received novels, John Metcalf, perhaps more than any other contemporary Canadian writers, is closely identified with the short story and its extended form, the novella. In the latter, his only peer in Canadian writing is Mavis Gallant. He is also unquestionably one of the best satiric and comic writers in the country. As Keith Garebian has said, "Metcalf uses fiction's mirrors like an expert, showing an age its own grimaces, gapes, and follies with witty grace."

Born in Carlisle, England, to a clergyman, Thomas Metcalf, and his wife, Gladys Moore Metcalf, a teacher, John Metcalf came to Canada in 1962, two years after graduation with a B.A. from the University of Bristol. He began to write fiction by entering a CBC short-story contest. Shortly thereafter, at the prompting of Canadian poet Earl Birney, eight of Metcalf's stories were accepted by *Prism International,* the Vancouver-based small magazine, and since then Metcalf has considered himself a professional writer. In addition to editing and compiling anthologies to help support himself financially, Metcalf has taught English and creative writing intermittently–either as an instructor or writer in residence–at various high schools, colleges, and universities in Canada, mainly in the Montreal area, where he founded the Montreal Storytellers, a performance group of writers involving himself, Clark Blaise, and Hugh Hood. These writers have all reflected on the experience of working with the group and of taking short fiction directly to audiences in J. R. (Tim) Struthers's collection *The Montreal Storytellers* (1985). Metcalf, who married Myrna Teitelbaum in 1975, now makes his home in Ottawa.

Metcalf's best stories are approximations of poetry. These stories ask to be taken as perceptions of "inscape": a moment of epiphany in which form is realized and textured surface becomes profundity. The rhythmic unit of a Metcalf story is the word, particularly the verb and the adjective, and, despite Metcalf's expertise in using first-person narration, the focus most frequently is that of a limited or controlled third-person point of view in which the center of consciousness is apparent first-person perception but the voice is the narrator's, a narrative strategy thus providing Metcalf with a firm sense of control and a flexible rhetorical space.

Most of Metcalf's stories in *New Canadian Writing, 1969,* a volume which also included works by D. O. Spettigue and C. J. Newman, and

in *The Lady Who Sold Furniture* (1970) are about children, adolescents, or youth and the process of growing up. Metcalf explores such themes as the dialectical relationship between the past and the present, innocence and experience, the child and the adult, the individual and society and its institutions, order and chaos, structure and freedom, the pastoral and the urban, the natural or organic and the mechanistic or technological, and the real and the fantastic. Metcalf captures the feel and texture of childhood perception in these early stories, in which the child's confrontation with nature is both exciting and fearful–always disturbing. "The Lady Who Sold Furniture," a novella, deals implicitly with many of these themes, particularly innocence or naiveté in confrontation with experience or sophistication, as David, a young university graduate, is forced to face the conflicting moral values exemplified in Jeanne, his older lover, the lady who sells other people's furniture illegally. The humorous and the somber, the absurd and the pathetic, the satiric and the sentimental, are mingled in this story, as they often are in Metcalf's fiction, and it is a good example of his skill with dialogue, the idiom and rhythms of speech, which is a foregrounded narrative mode in his fiction.

For Metcalf, the novel is a loose, accommodating form in contrast to the short story and the novella. Set in Montreal, *Going Down Slow* (1972), his first novel, is on the surface a comic assault on the puerility of secondary education, but Metcalf's account of the young teacher's capitulation to an absurd system is really witnessing a story about integrity, corruption, and compromise, a story, in fact, about psychological death. The schoolteacher, David, like his two best friends, Garry and Jim, finally does sell out and, as a result, is symbolically poisoned. Despite the brilliant comic set pieces in the novel–the novel's real strength, in which character moves toward caricature or grotesque and satire drifts toward farce–the story line is conventional, one more instance of another young man who compromises.

The stories in *The Teeth of My Father* (1975) are among Metcalf's best, particularly the first five, beginning with "The Strange Aberration of Mr. Ken Smythe" and ending with "The Years in Exile," which form a self-contained sequence. These stories show Metcalf moving firmly into Canadian-set material, and all five are concerned in different ways with different aspects of the same dilemma: the plight of the artist in terms of either the relationship between the artist and soci-

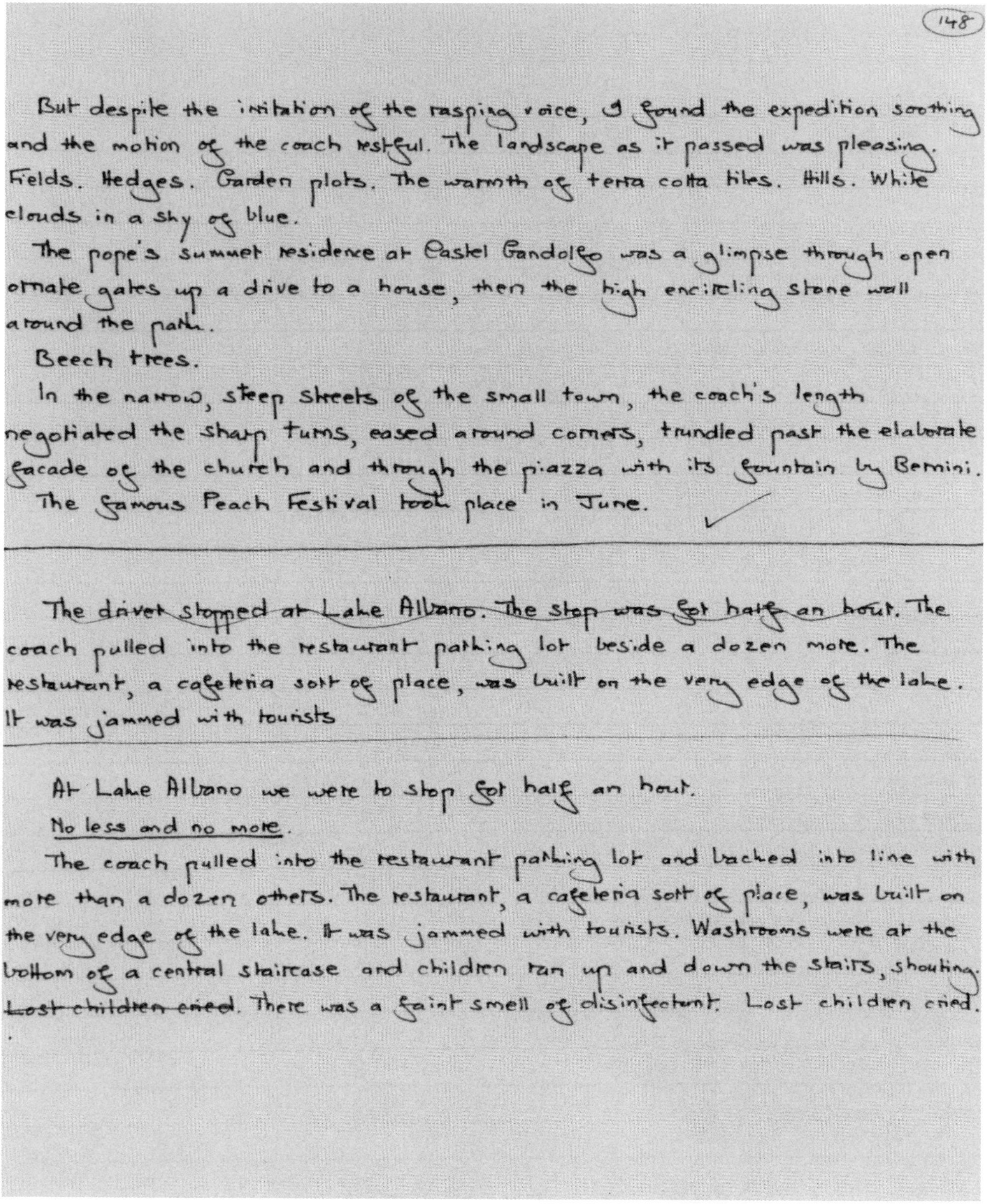

(148)

But despite the irritation of the rasping voice, I found the expedition soothing and the motion of the coach restful. The landscape as it passed was pleasing. Fields. Hedges. Garden plots. The warmth of terra cotta tiles. Hills. White clouds in a sky of blue.

The pope's summer residence at Castel Gandolfo was a glimpse through open ornate gates up a drive to a house, then the high encircling stone wall around the path.

Beech trees.

In the narrow, steep streets of the small town, the coach's length negotiated the sharp turns, eased around corners, trundled past the elaborate facade of the church and through the piazza with its fountain by Bernini.

The famous Peach Festival took place in June. ✓

___

The driver stopped at Lake Albano. The stop was for half an hour. The coach pulled into the restaurant parking lot beside a dozen more. The restaurant, a cafeteria sort of place, was built on the very edge of the lake. It was jammed with tourists

___

At Lake Albano we were to stop for half an hour.

No less and no more.

The coach pulled into the restaurant parking lot and backed into line with more than a dozen others. The restaurant, a cafeteria sort of place, was built on the very edge of the lake. It was jammed with tourists. Washrooms were at the bottom of a central staircase and children ran up and down the stairs, shouting. Lost children cried. There was a faint smell of disinfectant. Lost children cried.

Manuscript page (by permission of the author)

ety or the relationship between the artist's execution of his craft and his own personal life. A 1986 collection, *Adult Entertainment,* extends these themes, gathering five stories, including "Single Gents Only."

For Metcalf, the novella has the tautness and challenges of construction of the short story, but, like the novel, it also allows for expansion and a degree of license. *Girl in Gingham* (1978) contains two novellas. The first, "Private Parts," is a richly metaphoric first-person study by one T. D. Moore, a minor Canadian writer, of the sexual and spiritual drama of his childhood and adolescence. Structurally, there are two "private parts," the first a chronological account of the narrator's sense of displaced "self" in artistic, social, and sexual terms; the second, essentially a depressive meditation on the meaning of the chronicle for the narrator. Humor and pathos are fused in this, perhaps Metcalf's best, story, as they are in "Girl in Gingham," the title piece, which traces Peter Thornton's ironic search for the ideal through a computer-dating service, revolving thematically around the motive for "inventing" people, shaping them to fit the contours of one's needs and desires, and "inventing" or allowing oneself to be "invented."

Even more loosely structured than *Going Down Slow,* Metcalf's second novel, *General Ludd* (1980), concerns the war of one man–Jim Wells, writer in residence at a Montreal university– against the new technology of "communications" and all that it implies. It is also a devastating satiric attack on the mores of postsecondary education and the Canadian cultural scene in general. *General Ludd,* like Metcalf's earlier novel, demonstrates his skill in creating comic set pieces and memorable grotesques.

Witty, acidic, above all provocative, *Kicking Against the Pricks* (1982), a collection of eight essays and an interview with Metcalf on Canadian writing and his difficulties as a writer in Canada, is designed less to persuade than to disturb, to unsettle, the Canadian literary community with its laying bare of the nation's cultural and educational inadequacies. *The Bumper Book* (1986), a collection of poems, comments, and essays edited with contributions by Metcalf, continues his barbed, personal attacks on Canadian literary practice and on what he sees as Canadian literary pretensions.

Although Metcalf's canon is not large, the richness and craftsmanship of his work, especially the short stories and novellas, suggest that

Cover for a paperback edition of Metcalf's second novel, about one man's war against the new communications technology

on qualitative grounds, as many of his fellow Canadian writers and an increasing number of critics recognize, Metcalf is one of Canada's important fiction writers. Robert Lecker, for instance, comparing him to A. J. M. Smith, says that he has "influenced the literary values of a generation," and Kent Thompson, Canadian dramatist and short-story writer, has written that Metcalf "knows the aethetics of his craft, and that, besides making him a very good writer, is very important to a number of us. He is an artistic conscience; he is the preventor of shoddy work. And that is very important to the development of the short story in this country, in this language."

References:
Barry Cameron, "An Approximation of Poetry:

The Short Stories of John Metcalf," *Studies in Canadian Literature,* 2 (Winter 1977): 17-35;

Cameron, "Invention in *Girl in Gingham,*" *Fiddlehead,* 114 (Summer 1977): 120-129;

Cameron, *John Metcalf* (Boston: G. K. Hall, 1986);

Cameron, "The Practice of the Craft: A Conversation with John Metcalf," *Queen's Quarterly,* 82 (Autumn 1975): 402-424;

Keith Garebian, *"General Ludd:* A Satire on Decadence," *Canadian Literature,* 101 (Summer 1984): 43-55;

Robert Lecker, *On the Line: Readings in the Short Fiction of Clark Blaise, John Metcalf, and Hugh Hood* (Toronto: ECW, 1982);

Malahat Review, special issue on Metcalf, 70 (March 1985);

Douglas Rollins, *John Metcalf* (Toronto: ECW, 1985);

J. R. (Tim) Struthers, ed., *The Montreal Storytellers: Memoirs, Photographs, Critical Essays* (Montreal: Véhicule, 1985);

Kent Thompson, "John Metcalf: A Profile," *Fiddlehead,* 114 (Summer 1977): 57-63.

Gaston Miron
(8 January 1928-   )

Cécile Cloutier-Wojciechowska
University of Toronto

BOOKS: *Deux Sangs,* by Miron and Olivier Marchand (Montreal: Editions de l'Hexagone, 1953);

L'Homme rapaillé (Montreal: Presses de l'Université de Montréal, 1970);

Courtepointes (Ottawa: Editions de l'Université d'Ottawa, 1975);

The Agonized Life: Poems and Prose, edited and translated by Marc Plourde (Montreal: Torchy Wharf Press, 1980);

L'Homme rapaillé / Embers and Earth: Selected Poems, bilingual edition, translated by D. G. Jones and Marc Plourde (Montreal: Guernica, 1984).

Miron the Magnificent, as Jacques Brault has called him, may be considered the pivot of Quebec poetry. He has absorbed the work of his precursors into his own; he has served as a catalyst to others through his numerous activities; and he has taken the theory of language as one of his central concerns.

Born to Charles-Auguste (a carpenter) and Jeanne Michaudville Miron in Saint-Agathe-des-Monts in January 1928, he attended primary school there at the *collège* run by the brothers of the Sacred Heart and then took further schooling (with the same order) in Granby, where he

lived from 1941 (the year his father died) to 1946. Moving to Montreal in 1947, he undertook various jobs but settled increasingly on a life as a writer, producing poetry and a miscellany of poetry and prose (*L'Homme rapaillé,* which won the Prix de la Revue *Etudes Françaises* and the Prix France-Canada in 1970 and the Grand Prix de la Ville de Montréal in 1971) and becoming highly influential, both for his poetry and for his involvement in Quebec's political life.

Miron is at the heart of Quebec poetry because he has read it and because, with all his being, he carries it forward. At the core of Miron the poet, the editor, and the poetically and socially committed man is, perhaps above all, Miron the reader. It is therefore important to appreciate the reading he did in Canadian literature during his impressionable adolescence and youth. Miron has been known to give an astonishingly precise analysis of his reading, noting with scientific exactitude even the editions he used and the year he read each work in question.

First of all, from age fourteen to eighteen, he was interested in Octave Crémazie, Louis Fréchette, William Chapman, and Frère Marie-Victorin and was impressed by their sense of the French heritage. But he was particularly influenced by Pamphile Lemay, "un gars qui m'a

Gaston Miron (photograph by Kèro)

marqué parce qu'il référait à la partie intime, au Québec rural, parce qu'il avait la nostalgie de la perte de la France comme Nérée Beauchemin, un gars qu'il sentait concret, près de nous" (a man who has impressed me because he referred to the intimate, to rural Québec, because he felt nostalgic over losing France, like Nérée Beauchemin, a man whom he felt to be concrete, close to us). Then, at age sixteen, Miron came under the influence of Alfred Des Rochers. In 1947, soon after leaving school in Granby, he read at the same time both Des Rochers's *A l'Ombre de l'Orford* (1929) and a Chez Valiquette edition of Baudelaire. He admired the epic aspect of Des Rochers: "Je l'ai moi aussi, ce côté épique qui vient du dedans" (I also have it, this epic impulse which comes from within). And he was attracted by Des Rochers's realism: "Il venait dans ma lignée d'appartenance. J'ai toujours voulu une démarche totalisante. Je cherchais toutes les dimensions dans mon poème, qui ne doit pas

être seulement lyrique mais venir aussi d'un processus historique" (We belonged to the same lineage. I have always wanted an all-encompassing procedure. I sought to include all dimensions in my poetry, which should not only be lyrical but also relate to a historical process). He deeply admired the sense of the land in Des Rochers.

During the same period he read Emile Nelligan who, he admits, disappointed him somewhat: "J'étais déjà très nationaliste alors et l'angélisme de Nelligan m'irritait" (I was already very nationalist then and the angelic aspect of Nelligan irritated me). He believes that he lived more or less two lives then, reading, as he did, many modern French writers simultaneously: Péguy, Claudel, Hugo, Corneille (whom he read with enthusiasm), Mallarmé, Saint-Exupéry, Lautréamont, Corbière, Laforgue, and later the surrealists Char, Eluard, Desnos, Apollinaire, and Cendrars.

In 1947 he enrolled at the Faculty of Social

Sciences of the University of Montreal and there made the significant acquaintance of Gilles Carle and Olivier Marchand. In 1949 he joined the Ordre du Bon Temps (a young people's French folk-dance group) and met Ambroise Lafortune and Louis Portugais. He read socially oriented authors and has noted as especially strong the influence of Emmanuel Mounier. In 1949 he also heard Olivier Marchand speak about Hector de Saint-Denys-Garneau. He read him but admits that he did not understand him then.

In 1950 he read, by accident, that "gars capital qui m'a fait trouver ma voie" (fantastic man who has made me find my way)–Gilles Hénault. He discovered Hénault through some poems that had been published in a journal in the late 1940s and later observed that Hénault had grasped modernism: "Il a le sens de la modernité."

Then he had his epiphany. Miron read *La Quête de la joie* (1933) by Patrice de la Tour du Pin. He was impressed by the following sentence: "Tous les pays qui n'ont pas de légendes sont condamnes à mourir de froid" (All countries which do not have legends of their own are condemned to die of cold). The next day, Miron recalls, he understood Eluard. This was in 1951. He read Alain Grandbors's *Les Iles de la Nuit* (1944) and found it extraordinary, "une tentation, un monde qui fascinait." It was this universe, this atmosphere, which prepared Miron for the adventure of 1953, when he, Carle, Marchand, and others founded the publishing house Editions de l'Hexagone, which has directly influenced the course of poetry in modern Quebec. Miron's social and political interests continued to grow, and he claims to have been enormously influenced in his thinking by periodical commentary and by everyday events. These influences reveal themselves in *Deux Sangs*, a collaboration with Marchand published in 1953, and in the poetic cycles "La Marche à l'Amour," "La Vie agonique," and "La Batêche," which appeared in *Le Nouveau Journal* and in *Liberté* in 1962 and 1963.

In the mid 1950s two poets helped sharpen his thought and confirm his intuitions: André Frénaud and Aimé Césaire (André Langevin compared Miron to the latter at the publication of "La Batêche": "Tu écris comme lui!"). But Miron hastens to add that personal meetings rather than poetic influences were more important; among the poetic influences was his reading in 1958 of Jean-Aubert Loranger–that "ancêtre" of Saint-Denys Garneau with whom he felt no kinship.

He admits that his technique was mostly shaped by the surrealists. But the Ordre du Bon Temps sent him quickly back to the people. "De lui, me vient la vision totalisante du pays. Pourtant, je ne me sens pas en rupture avec eux, même si je me situe à leur opposé. J'emploie le mot Canada jusqu'en 1960. Ensuite, je parle de Québec, 'ma terre amande.' Je corrige le mot Canada. Dans 'La Vie agonique,' je dévoile notre aliénation. Puis je lis Sartre et je connais Paris où je vais parce que j'ai des choses à dire aux français" (From them, I receive the all-encompassing vision of the land. However, I do not feel that I have separated myself from the surrealists, even if I understand myself as being in opposition to them. I used the word Canada till 1960. After, I speak of Quebec, "my almond land." I correct the word "Canada." In "La Vie agonique," I expose our alienation. Then I read Sartre and got to know Paris, where I went because I had things to say to the French).

Miron lived in Paris for almost two years in 1959 and 1960 and studied graphic arts at l'Ecole Estienne. When he returned from France, he became the center of the Montreal poetry circle. His activities in and through the publications of Editions de l'Hexagone have become increasingly important since that time. He continued to participate in poets' meetings which took place first at the Maison Montmorency and then for many years in North Montreal. He played an important role in the journal *Liberté* and perhaps an even more important one in the magazine *Parti Pris* and in the literary and social movement that developed from it. He worked as a poetic journalist and represented Quebec for many years at the book fair in Frankfurt and at other international gatherings. He became writer in residence at the University of Ottawa (1971) and professor at the University of Sherbrooke (1971-1972); he gave numerous readings and lectures, took part in many radio broadcasts, and often appeared on television. He also played an important role in the organization of the formidable *salons du livre* in Montreal and won the Canada-Belgium Prize in 1972. Much to his distress, he added to his celebrity when he was arrested during the October Crisis in 1970 and a campaign started on his behalf. On that occasion a special issue of *La Barre du Jour* was dedicated to him. In many ways, he represents for an entire generation a model in thought, in writing, and in living.

His role as a center, a pivot, a hinge, has been enhanced through his reflections and pro-

Cover for Miron's first book, a collaboration with Olivier Marchand and the first title published by Les Editions de l'Hexagone, founded in 1953 by Miron, Marchand, and Gilles Carle

nouncements on the subject of language. Jean Marcel, in *Le Joual de Troie*, (1973) writes that "bien qu'il ait étudié la linguistique avec Chomsky, Guillaume, etc., le plus grand linguiste qu'il connaisse, c'est Gaston Miron" (although he has studied linguistics with Chomsky, Guillaume, etc., Gaston Miron is the greatest linguist he knows). In this sense, Miron follows the tradition of Félix-Antoine Savard, another humanist who spent a great part of his life in silence and contemplation in order to reflect with tenderness on the language of his country, on his complicities with the adjective, his friendships with etymology, his mysterious handshakes with nouns and verbs. Miron is profoundly affected by his language, and in this preoccupation he reflects all Quebec poets. A syntactic error wounds him; an anglicism is a burn. He discusses language with passion in an interview he granted to the journal *Maintenant*. Miron feels like a stranger in his own language, he says, which he perceives as a servile copy of English; he quotes numerous instances of

traffic signs like "Go on green," translated as "Passez au vert," or "Cars with exact change only," translated into "French" as "Automobiles avec monnaie exacte seulement." If one does not read English, one cannot understand this so-called French. And Miron notes, "Je ne sais plus dans ce bilinguisme instantané, colonial, reconnaître mes signes. Cette coupure, ce fait de devenir étranger à sa propre langue sans s'en apercevoir, c'est une forme d'aliénation linguistique qui reflète et renvoie à une aliénation plus globale qui est le fait de l'homme canadien-français, puis québécois, dans sa société, par rapport à sa culture et à l'exercice de ses pouvoirs politiques et économiques" (I no longer recognize in this instantaneous colonial bilingualism my own signs. This separation, this fact of becoming a stranger in one's own language without noticing it, is a form of linguistic alienation which reflects, and derives from, a more global alienation. This is the actual situation of the French-Canadian, the Quebecois, in his society).

He perceives the language to be in a state of "diglossie" and adds that one should not say "cheval" or "joual" but "horse." The language of the colonizer will adhere to the language of Quebec and finally destroy it. According to Miron, there is only one solution to this situation, and that is an urgently required decolonization, "Il faut changer la situation globale qui conditionne la langue: l'apprentissage, et la pratique doivent devenir des motivations profondes. La langue va fonctionner de par son propre système de signes, son propre code et dans l'inter-influence et les échanges que les langues exercent entre elles. Elle va vivre comme homogènes les éléments hétérogènes dans ses propres structures" (We must change the overall situation which conditions the language: linguistic apprenticeship and practice must become deeply felt motivations. Language will function through its own system of signs, its own code, and by influencing and exchanging with other languages. In its proper structures, heterogeneous elements of language will be activated as homogeneous ones). According to Miron, language will survive if it is needed. Miron formulates the political problem of "québécois" as a linguistic problem by saying, "Qu'on dise *un âbe, un âbre*, ou *un ârbre*, aussi long temps qu'on ne dit pas *tree*, on parle québécois." (One may say *âbe, un âbre*, or *un ârbre*; as long as one does not say 'tree,' one speaks *québécois*). And he adds that no matter how appealing a work of art may be, it will not be able to help develop a common language if it is based upon *aesthetic* criteria and grafted on to the structures of a *literary* language.

But perhaps even more than as a poetic catalyst and theoretician of a Quebec language, Miron is the pivot of Quebec poetry as an affective force. Indeed, even if there are some Quebec poets who have not read *L'Homme rapaillé* and *Courtepointes* (1975), there are few who have not heard Miron speak, on one occasion or another, at the Carré Saint-Louis at the corner of Sainte-Catherine, at Chez Déom, or in a café on the rue Saint-Denis. For Miron's speech is warm and "coeurue," to use the expression of the Renaissance. "Je suis un oral; je suis un verbal," he frequently asserts. He is oral, verbal, at the same time priest, oracle, and troubadour; he celebrates his people, suffers, and loves them. In order to understand his "québécitude," one must have heard him sing Quebec folksongs or appreciated the depth of his commitment to tradition. For this man of lectures and quotations, who often forgets that what he cites is less interesting than what he says, does sense constantly in himself a North American need for tradition. Telling, or writing, of his condition as a Quebecois–of the human condition–he reveals the links he has with the past and makes the past available to his audience as well. One senses that deep inside this inveterate Montrealer, this man living in a world of pavements, there are still the wheat fields and the sweet pine trees of his northern mountains. For Miron is both an image of Quebec man and a magus for modern times.

References:

Jacques Brault, *Miron le magnifique* (Montreal: Presses de l'Université de Montreal, 1966);

Paul Chamberland, "Fondation du territoire," *Parti Pris*, 4 (May-August 1967): 11-42;

Document Miron, special issue of *La Barre du Jour* (October 1970);

Thérèse Fabi, "Miron le libérateur; étude lexicale de trois poèmes de 'La Vie agonique,'" *L'Action nationale*, 44, no. 2 (1974): 179-192;

Gilles Marcotte, "La Poésie," *Etudes françaises*, 7 (February 1971): 103-114;

Axel Maugey, "Gaston Miron," in his *Poésie et Société au Québec (1937-1970)* (Quebec: Presses de l'Université Laval, 1972), pp. 171-183;

Cécile Pelosse, "L'Homme rapaillé," *Livres et auteurs Québécois* (1970): 102-118.

Ken Mitchell

(13 December 1940-   )

Neil Besner
Mount Royal College

BOOKS: *Wandering Rafferty* (Toronto: Macmillan, 1972);

Heroes (Toronto: Playwrights Co-op, 1973);

This Train (Toronto: Playwrights Co-op, 1973);

The Meadowlark Connection: A Saskatchewan Thriller (Regina: Pile of Bones, 1975);

Cruel Tears, by Mitchell and Humphrey and the Dumptrucks (Regina: Pile of Bones, 1976);

Everybody Gets Something Here (Toronto: Macmillan, 1977);

Davin: The Politician (Edmonton: NeWest Press, 1979);

The Con Man (Vancouver & Los Angeles: Talonbooks, 1979);

The Great Cultural Revolution (Toronto: Playwrights Canada, 1980);

Sinclair Ross: A Reader's Guide (Moose Jaw, Saskatchewan: Coteau Books, 1981);

Chatauqua Girl (Toronto: Playwrights Canada, 1982);

Ken Mitchell Country, edited by Robert Currie (Moose Jaw, Saskatchewan: Coteau Books, 1984);

Gone the Burning Sun (Toronto: Playwrights Canada, 1985);

Through the Nan Da Gate (Saskatoon: Thistledown Press, 1986).

PLAY PRODUCTIONS: *Heroes*, Centre Bilingue, University of Saskatchewan, August 1971;

Pleasant Street, Saskatoon, 25th Street Theatre, 1972;

This Train, Toronto, Tarragon Theatre, March 1973;

Cruel Tears, music by Humphrey and the Dumptrucks, Saskatoon, Persephone Theatre, 15 March 1975;

Showdown at Sand Valley, Regina, Merely Players, Summer 1975;

Genesis, by Mitchell and Douglas Hicton, Saskatchewan, Merely Players, 1975;

The Medicine Line, Moose Jaw, Saskatchewan, Moose Jaw Community Players, 1976;

Ken Mitchell (photograph by Bruce Pendlebury)

Davin: The Politician, Regina, Globe Theatre, 10 January 1978;

The Shipbuilder, Regina, University of Regina, 29 March 1978;

The Great Cultural Revolution, Vancouver, Arts Club Theatre, 22 November 1979;

Chatauqua Girl, Vancouver, Carousel Theatre, 1 February 1982;

Spirit of Saskatoon, Saskatoon, Saskatoon Multicultural Society, 1982;

Year of the Moose (with Geoff Ursell and Barbara Sapergia), Moose Jaw, Peacock Players, 1982;

Laffin' Jack Rivers Show, by Mitchell and Michael Taylor, Saskatoon, Saskatchewan, 25th Street Theatre, 24 March 1983;

Gone the Burning Sun, Guelph, Ontario, Guelph Spring Festival, May 1984;

The Plainsman, Saskatoon, 25th Street Theatre, November 1985;

Tommy, Stoughton, Saskatchewan, Stoughton Arts Centre, 11 July 1986;

Melody Farm, Saskatoon, 25th Street Theatre, 6 February 1987.

MOTION PICTURES: *Striker,* screenplay by Mitchell, National Film Board of Canada, 1977;

The Hounds of Notre Dame, screenplay by Mitchell, Père Productions, 1980;

The Shipbuilder, screenplay by Mitchell, National Film Board of Canada, 1985;

St. Laurent, screenplay by Mitchell, National Film Board of Canada, 1985.

TELEVISION: *The Train,* CBC, 1977;

The Front Line, CBC, 1985;

Moose Jaw, CBC, 1985.

RADIO: *Sand Valley Centennial,* CBC, 1967;

A Very Loving Person, CBC, 1967;

Showdown at Sand Valley, CBC, 1969;

The Medicine Line, CBC, 1970;

The Meadowlark Caper, CBC, 1971;

The Bald Eagle, CBC, 1976;

Cruel Tears, with Humphrey and the Dumptrucks, CBC, 1976;

The Shipbuilder, BBC, 1980; CBC, 1982;

The Promised Land, BBC, 1981; CBC, 1983;

The Heavenly Kingdom, CBC, 1984.

OTHER: *Horizon: Writings of the Canadian Prairies,* edited by Mitchell (Toronto: Oxford University Press, 1977).

PERIODICAL PUBLICATION: "The Importance of Being Norman," *Foothills,* 2 (Winter 1986): 6-8.

Since the beginning of his multifaceted and prolific career as a playwright, novelist, short-story writer, teacher, editor, actor, and critic, Mitchell's major contributions to Canadian writing have been in drama. Mitchell has continuously experimented with dramatic form and his plays have often explored the ambiguous characteristics of the modern hero in one of his many guises as rebel, cartoon figure, politician, everyman, madman, or martyr. At the center of many of Mitchell's best plays stands a complex figure with an extraordinary vision who is either revered by a whole culture—like Bethune in *Gone*

the Burning Sun— or cast out by his community—like Jaanus in *The Shipbuilder*. Mitchell's protagonists are at once attractive by virtue of their common touch—Nicholas Davin's blarney in *Davin: The Politician,* the verve of Johnny Roychuck, Ukrainian truck driver, hard-drinking lover, and latter-day Othello in *Cruel Tears*— and, despite their raw energy, flawed characters, prey to tragic or comic misperceptions of their conditions.

Although Mitchell's plays and fiction have ranged as widely in setting as they have in theme and form, the Canadian prairie and, in Mitchell's words from the preface to *Horizon: Writings of the Canadian Prairies* (1977), "the emotions evoked by its infinity of earth and sky, by its solitude and separateness and harsh climate," have formed his most powerful imaginative ground. The prairie ethos has also informed another essential element in Mitchell's work: a regional voice and vision firmly rooted in a populist conception of art. Commenting in a 1978 interview with M. T. Kelly on his purpose in compiling *Horizon,* Mitchell remarks: "There is a real regional identity in the West, as important as Quebec's, but it has never been defined. I tried to do that." Mitchell calls himself "a popularist by nature," remarking that "most of the writing that I do in any form, wants a general audience, a wide audience rather than a literary audience or a specific audience of one kind or another."

Kenneth Ronald Mitchell was born in Moose Jaw, Saskatchewan, to farmers Colin McIntyre and Eileen Reid Howe Mitchell. Mitchell's partly Irish ancestry emerges in various forms in his work, most memorably in his best and most anthologized short story, "The Great Electrical Revolution," an uproarious tale of an Irish family's immigration to Moose Jaw, where the grandfather cunningly combats the forces of the Moose Jaw Light and Power Company with some creative rewiring of his appliances. Another recurring element in Mitchell's vision of immigrants' first experiences of the prairies finds one of its most comic expressions in the grandfather's first encounter with the landscape. Returning to town from a trip in a rented Democrat to inspect his homestead, Grandfather "burst back into the room, his eyes wild and his face pale and quivering":

"Sweet Jesus Christ!" he shouted at them. "There's just too damn much of it out there." He ran around the room several times, knocking against the walls and moaning, "Miles and miles of nothing but miles and miles!" He collapsed onto one of the beds, and lay staring at the ceiling.

"It'ud drive us witless in a week!"

In an interview with Robert Wallace published in Wallace and Cynthia Zimmerman's *The Work* (1982), Mitchell has remarked that "growing up in the Prairies and gaining a perception of the world through this particular landscape has been very important to my development as a writer for the stage. In a general way, I think that Prairie people and Prairie writers take a vaster view of things." Conversely, in Mitchell's work newcomers to the prairie often experience an amplified sense of their own insignificance in relation to a vast and impersonal landscape.

Mitchell spent his elementary and high-school years in Moose Jaw. In a typically wry revelation, he credits his early experience in school with nurturing what became a vital gift with language: "I went to school on South Hill, where to survive you either had to be the biggest, meanest kid around–or else the most dazzling liar (i.e., storyteller) in the school. I was small for my age and learned early how to develop verbal skills."

Apocryphal or not, this recollection underscores Mitchell's lifelong attraction to the oral and communal nature of the dramatist's and storyteller's arts. An accomplished actor and a compelling reader of his own work, with some fifteen roles to his credit on radio, stage, and screen, to date Mitchell has given over 100 readings throughout Canada and in Mexico, the United States, Germany, Great Britain, and China.

In 1961 Mitchell traveled to England and married Betty Gail Grimm in Toronto before returning to attend the University of Saskatchewan, Regina campus (later the University of Regina). Mitchell's first two children, Kevin Edward and James Alexander, were born while he worked toward his B.A., which he received in 1965. Mitchell's first marriage was unsuccessful; in June 1965 he married Linda McLarty, and his third son, Colin Paul, was born in 1968. Mitchell earned his M.A. in English in 1967, with a thesis on William Faulkner's narrative techniques. That same year, he joined the university English department and has taught there since that time, with interruptions to take up positions as writer in residence, visiting professor, and instructor at the University of Victoria, British Columbia (1975-1976), the Banff School of Fine Arts

(1977, 1978, 1980), the universities of Edinburgh and Stirling (1979-1980), and the University of Nanjing, China (1980-1981). Mitchell also served as director of creative writing at the Saskatchewan Summer School of the Arts from 1970 to 1975. His 1986 book, *Through the Nan Da Gate*, is a compilation of photographs and lyric impressions that derives from his year in China, and which forms as a whole a poetic narrative.

Mitchell began writing radio and stage plays while at university. His first major success was his cutting parody, *Heroes*, which won the first prize in the Ottawa Little Theatre Play Competition of 1971, was produced in England at the University of Surrey in 1972, and has since had more than fifty productions in the United States, Canada, Germany, New Zealand, Turkey, and Scotland. In Mitchell's debunking of the "heroes"–Superman and the Lone Ranger–their roles as leading lights are upstaged by Lois Lane and Tonto, respectively, who have become more fashionable in the late 1960s and early 1970s, when women's and Native Americans' stock is booming.

Mitchell's first novel, *Wandering Rafferty*, was also published in 1972. Although it has a somewhat contrived narrative framework (Rafferty's adventures are narrated in part by an omniscient narrator, in part by his admirer Archie Payne, typesetter and would-be left-wing revolutionary), the novel offers an engaging and rollicking portrait of Rafferty, a learned hobo who rings changes on the quest theme as he roams across western Canada, selling subscriptions to *Mother Goose*, keeping the taverns in business, and careening in and out of Archie Payne's life.

Commenting on fiction, Mitchell told Robert Wallace "in writing fiction or poetry, the writer is quite isolated . . . . The playwright's function is an architectural one, almost like a sculptor working with his material, not so much as a writer whose job is to go away into a garret and write words in that isolated and private way." Indeed, Mitchell has always emphasized the communal or social element in writing for the theater, and his own fiction sometimes seems more vivid when read aloud: Mitchell first read his 1975 novel, *The Meadowlark Connection*, to an audience convened in Regina's Museum of Natural History. This spoof on bumbling RCMP operations against nefarious drug dealers in small prairie towns is engaging, but it does not succeed as powerfully as many of Mitchell's plays, in which he is able to give fuller expression to his vision of art as a communal, often political performance for a wide audience.

Dust jacket for Mitchell's novel about a learned hobo who wanders western Canada selling subscriptions to Mother Goose *magazine*

In 1972 Mitchell, divorced for some time from his second wife, married Zaharoula Rammogiannis; their son, Andrew Kenneth, was born in 1977, the year which saw the publication of *Horizon: Canadian Writings of the Prairies; Everybody Gets Something Here,* a collection of short stories; and the trade edition of one of Mitchell's most celebrated plays, the "country opera" *Cruel Tears,* written in collaboration with the rock group Humphrey and the Dumptrucks. In *Cruel Tears,* many of Mitchell's influences, aims, and experiments in theater powerfully converge; the play draws on *Othello* for plot; on Brecht's *Three-penny Opera* for some of the political and social commentary; on country western music for lyrics in order to appeal to a large audience; and on the image of the jealous truckdriver for its grounding in a contemporary working-class framework. The play opened at Saskatchewan's Persephone Theatre on 15 July 1975 and subsequently enjoyed popular success in a cross-Canada tour. Criti-

cal reception, Mitchell recalls, was mixed: "We kept warning people . . . , *don't* have an attitude in coming to this. Just experience it and make up your mind. Don't think of it as an opera. Don't think of it as a country and western music show. Don't think of it as a play. Just try to resist categories. Well, of course, the various reviewers began moralizing about whether it could be one or the other, whether it should be called this or that. It was ridiculous."

The late 1970s and early 1980s was a time of personal tragedy for Mitchell as his wife was fatally stricken with cancer. These years also marked a major shift in perspective and direction in Mitchell's art; although he continued to write drama set mainly on the prairies (*The Shipbuilder,* produced in 1978 and filmed in 1985, and *Davin: The Politician,* produced in 1978 and published in 1979) and another novel (*The Con Man,* 1979), he also spent a year in China. Mitchell's fascination with Eastern culture and politics (and in what he calls "Transpacific Art–a synthesis of Western and Eastern modes") was first evidenced in his 1979 production, *The Great Cultural Revolution,* which derives in part from *Hai Jui's Dismissal.* This play by Wu Han, Mitchell remarked in an interview with Alan Twigg published in *For Openers* (1981), "ignited the Great Proletarian Cultural Revolution in China." Mitchell considers his play to be an exploration of "the dominant role or influence of culture in political movements. You can see that clearly in China. The Cultural Revolution was very important in deciding whether art was for the people or for the elite. So my play is not so much about China as about the relationship between art–specifically theatre– and politics. It's a question which should engage us here in Canada."

The fullest, latest, and most personal integration of Mitchell's strong interest in China with his continuing exploration of heroism emerges in his 1984 play about surgeon, inventor, and political activist, Norman Bethune, *Gone the Burning Sun,* which premiered in Ontario at the Guelph Spring Festival in May of that year. Mitchell had wanted to write a play about Bethune–"one of the great heroes of our time"–for years, when he discovered in Scotland in 1980 that he and Bethune shared common ancestors, the Beaton clan that lived in the Hebrides during the Middle Ages. In China, where, in the 1930s Bethune fought with Communist forces against invaders from Japan, Mitchell was further inspired by people who claimed to notice "a remarkable physical resemblance" between Mitchell and Bethune and by peasants in remote areas who thought, in Mitchell's words, that he "*was* Bethune, somehow come back to life." Mitchell completed the play in 1983 and took it on an unsponsored tour in China that summer. He then introduced David Liang's music for the *pipa*– a Chinese instrument similar to the lute–and several international folk songs into the text. Revered, misunderstood, fatally proud, sainted, martyred, passionately political, and devoted to the preservation of human

life, Mitchell's Bethune provides him with the ideal figure to sustain an exploration of the hero in all his complexity and contradiction.

On 13 August 1983 Mitchell married Jeanne Shami, who is also a professor of English at the University of Regina; their daughter, Julia Yvonne, was born a year and a day later. In 1985 Mitchell was made an honorary professor at the Centre for Canadian Studies in Chongqing; in the fall of 1986 the family returned to China, where both parents taught for a year.

Mitchell's plays and fiction have been anthologized in Europe, Asia, and North America, and he continues to lecture at schools, libraries, conferences, and institutions on several continents, although he has always devoted most of his time in this context to appearances in Saskatchewan. He continues to write: his latest play, *Melody Farm,* explores the lives of four mentally handicapped men living in a group home. The play opened at Saskatoon's 25th Street Theatre in February 1987.

What specific direction Mitchell's work will take is difficult to predict. But the strong body of drama he has already developed speaks clearly out of its several particular regions–on the western Canadian prairie, on a widening world stage, and in the popular, passionate, personal and political idiom many have come to recognize as Mitchell's own dramatic voice.

Interviews:

M. T. Kelly, "Ken Mitchell's Progress as a Writer, From *Cruel Tears* to Thoughts on *Booze,*" *Books in Canada,* 7 (May 1978): 40;

Alan Twigg, "Ken Mitchell: Prairies," in his *For Openers: Conversations With 24 Canadian Writers* (Madeira Park, British Columbia: Harbour, 1981), pp. 163-173;

Robert Wallace, "Ken Mitchell," in *The Work: Conversations with English-Canadian Playwrights,* by Wallace and Cynthia Zimmerman (Toronto: Coach House Press, 1982), pp. 143-155.

Pierre Morency
(8 May 1942-   )

Kenneth W. Meadwell
University of Winnipeg

BOOKS: *Poèmes de la froide merveille de vivre* (Quebec: Editions de l'Arc, 1967);
Poèmes de la vie déliée (Quebec: Editions de l'Arc, 1968);
Au nord constamment de l'amour suivi de Poèmes de la froide merveille de vivre (Quebec: Editions de l'Arc, 1970);
Poèmes by Morency and Pierre Bertrand (Saint-Constant, Quebec: Passe-partout, 1970);
Les Appels anonymes (Quebec: Inédits, 1971);
Lieu de naissance (Montreal: Leméac, 1973);
Charbonneau et le chef, translated and adapted by Morency and Paul Hébert from the play by John Thomas McDonough (Montreal: Leméac, 1974);
Marlot dans les merveilles (Montreal: Leméac, 1975);
Le Temps des oiseaux (Quebec: André Dupuis, 1975);
Les Passeuses (Montreal: Leméac, 1976);
Tournebire et le Malin Frigo; Les Ecoles de Bon Bazou (Montreal: Leméac, 1978);
Torrentiel (Montreal: Editions de l'Hexagone, 1978);
Effets personnels (Montreal: Editions Le Tournepierre, 1986).

photograph by Anne-Marie Guérineau

Poet and playwright, Pierre Morency demonstrates a profound need for introspection, a need which he satisfies in sounding the depths of that which is initially unknown to man. His works are a stage upon which the secrets of life are revealed in their simplest form; he focuses on the passage of time which reveals man's mortality, and, more important, on man's eagerness to experience new sensations and renew knowledge. Born to Louis and Laurette Crousset Morency in Lauzon, Quebec, in 1942, Morency received a traditional education at the Collège de Lévis and obtained a *licence ès lettres* (1966) at Université Laval in Quebec City. It was at this institution, as Morency recalls, that he hoped to become a writer by pursuing his interests in literature, linguistics, philology, and French language studies.

Upon graduating, and after having taught literature at Université Laval, he discovered such poets as Gaston Miron and Paul Chamberland, fig-ureheads of engaged and national poetry of the 1960's. Despite this revelation of social consciousness transposed in literature, Morency remained refreshingly nonpartisan in his writings and chose rather to evoke with concise simplicity experiences of a universal nature. He was awarded the Prix Du Maurier (1968) for *Poèmes de la froide merveille de vivre,* as well as the Prix Claude-Sernet (1976) for his poetry. In addition to his literary works, Morency is well-known for his career as broadcaster with Radio-Canada,

Draft for one of the prose poems included in Morency's 1986 volume Effets personnels *(by permission of the author)*

Canada's national French-language radio network and for his achievements as a radio and record producer. His endeavors in the area of radio programming have earned him the Prix du Court Métrage (1976) and the Prix de l'Institut Canadien (1979).

Morency's first collection of poetry, *Poèmes de la froide merveille de vivre* (1967), expresses his need for a spontaneous and unaffected love, a feeling of unity with nature, the force which inspires images of birds, light, and water while at the same time suggesting those of heavy silence or alienating coldness. Morency continues to develop images and themes related to love in *Poèmes de la vie déliée* (1968), but does so in a surrealistic mode which, at times, communicates both extreme sensuality as well as a certain suffering experienced in the framework of a relationship that demands sharing. *Au nord constamment de l'amour*, Morency's 1970 collection, continues to evoke the poet's conception of love and of liberation in nature.

Effets personnels (1986), a collection of prose poems, reveals Morency's encyclopedic vocabulary, through movements of exaltation and uncertainty which bring the poet closer to the object of his thoughts: "Je ne parle pas. J'écris la saveur des premiers répertoires et dans le même souffle la plus dure flèche du carquois. J'écris le claquement des canifs, l'escadrille qui fauche, j'écris un petit torse d'avenir, une poitrine consumée" (I don't speak. I write the flavor of the first gatherings and in the same breath the strongest arrow in the quiver. I write the snapping of penknives, the squadron's strafing, I write a small torso of future, a chest consumed in flames). The freedom of movement in this collection reflects Morency's essential optimism, his belief that life is reinvented at each moment of one's existence, that the glory of nature is merely one manifestation of life's pulsation. It is precisely the dynamic process of both writing and living that is the heart of *Effets personnels*. In Morency's words, "les poèmes les plus lumineux s'accomodent très bien des lointains obscurs"–the hermetic in poetry comes often from that which is at the center of one's life and which is admitted through writing. Lyrical, yet not uniquely introspective, this collection demonstrates Morency's all-encompassing poetic vision; through his poetry he succeeds in transposing in images his desire to sound the depths of the here and now without, however, death being absent from his vision.

Morency's play *Les Passeuses* (1976) is written in the most colloquial of Quebecois French; although its humor might seem to hide the author's more serious side, the theme of old age, depicted in the play through the characters of Castor, Zime, and Pica, is one treated with insight and Morency's characteristic gentleness. As in *Effets personnels*, death is present in *Les Passeuses*. In the latter work it takes the form of an anemic taxidermist named Camard. The three male characters, retired and living in a home for the aged, demonstrate a naive and unpretentious appreciation of their lives. Old age is merely the beginning of life according to Castor, one of the more memorable characters of *Les Passeuses*. A former well-digger–like Morency's father and grandfather–Castor embodies a realistic outlook tempered by a poetic vision.

Reality and fantasy combine in this play to suggest the ineffable beauty of existence which might at times pass unperceived. Castor, whose name means "beaver" and who says to Zime "Don't you think I know what water is all about? I've lived all my life in it!," is drawn into the sea by Camard on a beach in the Virgin Islands. Although Castor dies, he reappears to voice his belief that death is the equivalent of birth, that old age and childhood are not dissimilar, and, moreover, that hope is the mediator between man and his potential.

Morency has said that there exists a painful contradiction within himself. While cultivating the ephemeral or penetrating the pulsation he senses behind each facade, he experiences a rare joy. Although he is a private individual, Morency feels compelled to share his discoveries by transmitting them in his writing, for it is the poet within him he feels, who reveals the unity of existence, since he has come to perceive the center of his own life. Morency's poetry, in particular, bears eloquent testimony to his commitment to literature which is a means by which man can better know himself as well as the often extraordinary world that surrounds him. Explorer and innovator, Pierre Morency has successfully eluded literary canons in order to create his own doctrine: *nosce te ipsum*, know thyself.

References:

Nord, special issue on Monrency (Summer 1972);

Donald Smith, "Entrevue: Pierre Morency, poète et dramaturge," *Lettres Québécoises* (November 1978): 39-47.

Erin Mouré
(17 April 1955-)

Andrew Parkin
University of British Columbia

BOOKS: *Empire, York Street* (Toronto: Anansi, 1979);
The Whisky Vigil (Madeira Park, British Columbia: Harbour, 1981);
Wanted Alive (Toronto: Anansi, 1983);
Domestic Fuel (Toronto: Anansi, 1985).

PERIODICAL PUBLICATIONS: "Poetics," *Quarry*, 32 (Autumn 1983): 80;
"I'll Start Out By Talking," *Poetry Canada Review*, 7 (Winter 1985-1986): 13.

Erin Mouré, born in Calgary on 17 April 1955, is the daughter of William Benedict Mouré, a customs broker, and Mary Irene Grendys Mouré, a nurse. She spent her early years in Calgary, where her mother taught her to read when she was four. At the age of six or seven she began writing and making her own books by sewing together pages made from grocery bags. In adolescence she read Irving Layton's *A Red Carpet for the Sun* (1959) and Al Purdy's *The Cariboo Horses* (1965). These and other Canadian books discovered in her formative years stimulated her attempts at writing. Raised a Catholic, Mouré sees herself as following a specifically Canadian tradition of writing, but also as reaching beyond her prairie background to more universal concerns. She took only two years of formal postsecondary education, and since then her working life has been mainly devoted to her job at VIA Rail Canada. She lived in Vancouver, where she took classes at the University of British Columbia, visited Europe, and she now resides in Montreal. Mouré's abiding concern as a poet is to preserve a living speech that clearly expresses common humanity without evasions of experience.

Her first book, *Empire, York Street* (1979), introduced to Canadian readers a twenty-three-year-old of remarkable promise whose poems give a distinct impression of contemporary Canadian speech and experience. Places, people, and the body's sensations are important in their own

right. Humanity, like the passengers from a late train at dawn on Christmas day, "are all / of the same flawed struggle." The great events and characters of Catholic tradition (the apocalypse, Christ, the Madonna, virgin birth) appear repeated in everyday life so as to bring out the significance of the ordinary and to point out that the existence of the ordinary is itself a miracle. Mouré's verse favors the short free-verse line, sparsely punctuated, sometimes using gaps instead of commas, and abbreviating such words as "with" and "without" to "w/" and "w/o." This device, like Mouré's use of the lower case personal pronoun "i," adds to the feeling of the poetry as dashed down on a pad in the middle of some lurching night shift on the railway for which she works: "i stand / alone in the shrunken coat / of my skin, map future / escape thru ribs & tendons." The true modernity here is not in modish spelling and capitalization but in the sensibility, anxiety, and optimism of this young woman's struggle to articulate her experience. The promise of this volume is in the sureness with which Mouré handles the free-form lyric, the mature range of her subject matter, and her laconic humor. Poems of personal life and the family mix unexpectedly with others—the compassionate and perceptive "Warsaw, 1929" or the deeply humane political poem: "for Rudolf Hess, on his 80th birthday (1974)," which in its way gives voice to "six million cries walled / inside your skull." There is little experiment with different kinds of expression in this volume, but there are many compelling poems on the order of "trusting the song," "Allegiance," and the pungent series "Riel: In the Season of his Birth."

Mouré's next volume, *The Whisky Vigil*, appeared in 1981. This volume of some sixteen poems opens with the image of Vancouver as the end of the line, an edge from which people fall. The poems are the scattered images of a fall into alcoholism and despair. They form in collage a portrait of the Speaker: a drunken woman and the fractured selves she bears within her in an un-

Self-portrait

holy marriage, that of Mrs. Jekyll and Mr. Hyde. But, as "Snowbound" makes clear, the Speaker is also gripped by fear of being "dry" as a writer: "I can't wring any more sense out of the words / is what it is / What it is is that I can't go on." The divorce of "Divorce From You" suggests, though, release from alcoholism, although its temptations are still fully acknowledged in the contrast between the empty room of the heart and the warmth of the Legion bar.

Two years after publication of *The Whisky Vigil*, Mouré produced *Wanted Alive* (1983), a volume containing five poems from the 1981 volume with sixty-six others. Here the railway provides a stock of new images and material that focuses the poet's attention more sharply on people, and the energetic lyrical sequence "Seven Rail Poems" contains some of Mouré's best sustained writing to date: "Saw-tooth trees glancing thru their huddled argument / Their song without name" or the engineer, seeing a loose rail, "pulled emergency, & the rail hit- / twisted up thru the train into the sky, & back down / thru

the train again like a stitch." *Wanted Alive* also shows a growing awareness of the possibilities of forms. Lines are stronger and less arbitrary than in some of her earlier work. "White Rabbit," for example, explores the effects of syntactically closing or leaving lines open at the end, of using verse paragraphs, closed or open-ended, and of deliberately avoiding closure at the end, so as to leave the poem hanging, like the rabbit.

Using the conventions of free linear verse Mouré's lines sometimes slacken to become disguised prose, sometimes overwritten. In her most successful work, Mouré avoids that danger, but it can dog her work even in her recent volume, *Domestic Fuel* (1985). In "Five Miles From Detonation" the immense horror of nuclear bombardment is inadequately described as "predicament": "I am one survivor / who would envy the dead / In the midst of nuclear predicament, not / its aftermath-." Mouré is better when she uses the harsh imagery of the modern world to render the violence in personal relationships, as in "Fusillade" or "Sowing," in which each line is

THE
~~THE COAT~~ HOLY MOTHER CHURCH   THE BEAUTY OF FURS

At lunch with the girls, the younger ones are talking about furs, & what looks good
with certain hair colours. Red fox looks no good with my hair, says one. White fox
looks snobbish, *its* beautiful but snobbish, says another one. They talk about the
pronunciation of coyote. I think of my brother catching muskrat. I think of
pushing the drown-set into the weeds, the freezing water of the Elbow, the brown
banks & snow we lived with, soft smell of aspen buds not yet coming out on the
trees, & us in our nylon coats in the backyards of Elbow Park Estates, pratically
downtown, trapping. *Coy-oh-tes*, the women say. In some places they say *Ky-oot*
or *Ky-oh!* I say, thinking *of their* moan in darkness, ~~heard from~~ the ~~trees~~ *the actual*
~~sound of the sky~~ where my brother now lives, ~~losing the trap of the city~~. & me
caught in the drown-set deeply, ~~my breath held~~ ~~snuffling up to those brown reeds~~
& then it comes. They are talking about the beauty of furs, and how so-and-so's
family is in the business. I remember, I say, I remember my mother had a muskrat
coat, & when she wore it & you grabbed her too hard by the arm, ~~hunks of fur come~~ *pulled came*
out. Eileen, ~~about 15 years old~~, starts to laugh, & puts her hand on my shoulder,
laughing. We both start laughing. I start to explain to her that it was old; my
mother wore it to church on Sunday & got upset if we grabbed her arm. We're
laughing so hard, now the young ones are looking at us, together we are laughing.
in our house there was a beaver coat like that Eileen said, then suddenly we are
crying, crying for ~~those fur coats~~ & the pride of our mothers, our mothers' pride,
the smell of the ~~fur~~ coat at church on Sunday, smell of the river, & us so small, *our hair wet* ~~still~~,
kneeling in that smell beside our mothers*x*
       & fur

                       of coyote calling
            their voice ~~the sound of the sky~~ .

       my breath snuffled for years

(*later you realize it is a poem about being born*

④ 14 Jan 87

Draft for a prose poem (by permission of the author)

clear and honest, brutally sustaining her tone. Mouré is a poet who has come a long way in a short time. She offers some surprises; her work is not merely predictable. She has achieved an authentic voice, earthy and strong, one of the strongest voices in her generation of Canadian poets.

References:

Peter O'Brien, Interview with Erin Mouré, *Rubicon*, 3 (Summer 1984): 24-25.

Bharati Mukherjee

(27 July 1940-)

Ann Mandel
Glendon College

BOOKS: *The Tiger's Daughter* (Boston: Houghton Mifflin, 1972; London: Chatto & Windus, 1973);

Wife (Boston: Houghton Mifflin, 1975);

Days and Nights in Calcutta, by Mukherjee and Clark Blaise (Garden City: Doubleday, 1977; revised and enlarged, Markham, Ontario: Viking-Penguin, 1986);

Darkness (Markham, Ontario, Harmondsworth, United Kingdom & New York: Penguin, 1985);

The Sorrow and the Terror: The Haunting Legacy of the Air India Tragedy, by Mukherjee and Blaise (Markham, Ontario: Viking, 1987).

PERIODICAL PUBLICATIONS: "Response: American Fiction," *Salmagundi,* 50-51 (Fall 1980-Winter 1981): 151-171;

"An Invisible Woman," *Saturday Night,* 96 (March 1981): 36-40;

"A Conversation with V. S. Naipaul," by Mukherjee and Robert Boyers, 54 (Fall 1981): 4-22.

Bharati Mukherjee (photograph by Stephani Karakas)

In the tradition of novels in English about India, Bharati Mukherjee's novels carry a special weight. Unlike E. M. Forster, Paul Scott, and J. G. Farrell, she writes as a novelist who grew up in Calcutta, knows Indian, and especially Bengali, culture intimately, and brings to her books this personal insight as it has been modified and refocused by many years of living in North America.

Whether she is writing about Indians living in India or in North America, she adds to the authority of her background an acute sense of the violence and chaos, however restrained, which can lie beneath the surface of a society, old or new, or of a person. Traditions can serve to prevent the victory of violent acts; they can also precipitate violence by their very restrictiveness.

Bharati Mukherjee was born in Calcutta, the daughter of Sudhir Lal Mukherjee, a Brahmin pharmaceutical chemist, and his wife, Bina Barrejee Mukherjee. She spent her first eight years as part of a large extended family. Shortly after India gained independence, for two and a half years she lived with her parents and two sisters in London, England, where she became fluent in English. In 1951 the family returned to Calcutta, after a period in Basel, Switzerland, and Mukherjee attended the English-speaking Loreto Convent School. Her father operated a factory which resembled the one run by Tara Banerjee's father in Mukherjee's first novel, *The Tiger's Daughter,* and her family's prosperity gave them protection from the poverty of Calcutta's streets. Mukherjee took a B.A. in honors English at the University of Calcutta in 1959 and an M.A. in English and ancient Indian culture at the University of Baroda in 1961.

As her sisters had done, Mukherjee went to the United States to study, going with a P.E.O. International Peace Scholarship to the University of Iowa's Writers' Workshop. At Iowa she received an M.F.A. and met Clark Blaise, a novelist, whom she married, North American-style, one lunch hour in September 1963. The couple has two sons, Bart and Bernard (the younger son is named after their friend, the novelist Bernard Malamud). In 1966 they moved to Montreal, where Mukherjee became a lecturer in English at McGill. In 1969 the University of Iowa awarded her a Ph.D. Mukherjee and Blaise subsequently moved to Toronto and in 1980 returned to the United States, though they both still hold Canadian citizenship. She has taught at University of Iowa and Skidmore College and is currently professor of English at Queens College, New York.

The Tiger's Daughter (1972) was begun during the Thanksgiving vacation of 1969 and completed in 1971. The novel concerns the return to India of Tara Banerjee Cartwright, a Brahmin woman who, like Mukherjee, comes from a prosperous Calcutta family, has gone to an American university, and married a North American. As a sheltered, convent-educated girl, Tara suffers the shock of sudden immersion in a new and alien world when she comes to the United States. Returning to Calcutta seven years later, she again suffers shock when she sees her family, her class, and her culture from a new perspective. After

the student riots and street murders of New York, home at first seems part of the safe, Victorian society she remembers, protected by walls, locks, and rituals from everything disturbing and "vulgar." Yet the friends who copy Tara's American speech tell her of strikes and riots, of factory seiges by "left-of leftist" workers, of the real threat of class warfare. The novel closes with Tara trapped in a car in the middle of a riot, watching one of her Brahmin friends, who is making a futile heroic attempt to save an old man, being killed by the mob.

Tara is treated from a distance by Mukherjee. A sensitive though passive woman, Tara's responses to events around her are recorded with irony and sometimes humor. One reviewer, for the *New York Review of Books* (9 May 1972), termed Mukherjee's first novel "acutely observed," while another, in *Best Sellers* (1 February 1972), described it as "freshly complex and enlightening."

In 1973 Mukherjee went to India during a sabbatical. She records in *Days and Nights in Calcutta,* a 1977 volume written in collaboration with her husband, and later revised and extended after a return visit, that in Calcutta "quite by accident, I heard the question that shaped my second novel: *What do Bengali girls do, between the ages of eighteen and twenty-one. . . ?" Wife,* published in 1975, concerns the arranged marriage and immigration to New York of Dimple Dasgupta, a young middle-class woman who has been raised to think of marriage as the only "real life" a woman can have. Husbands are "like gods with excellent managerial capacities," and wives must emulate the legendary Sita, who walked through fire to please her husband. But in America, Dimple's husband, Amit, shrinks into an ineffectual, unimaginative man. Dimple, who rebelled in India to the extent of secretly aborting a pregnancy, is terrified by the violence of New York streets. She spends hours alone in her apartment watching television, sleeping, or adding grotesque methods of suicide to a lengthening list until she feels herself edge into madness. While her husband eats Wheaties, Dimple stabs him repeatedly in the neck: "Women on television got away with murder."

In this novel Mukherjee analyzes the violence that can grow in an individual trained to passivity and self-denial. Dimple's madness mirrors the society outside the apartment walls; her desperate act comes to seem the only act of assertion she can make. Though the story Mukherjee tells in *Wife* is indeed grim, the novel has some comic elements, often based on cultural misunderstandings. These are better integrated than those in her previous book, and Mukherjee is less detached from her central character and more in command of tone. Many critics admired the style but resisted the book's political message. A finalist for a Governor General's Award, *Wife* was not widely distributed in Canada until it was republished by Penguin in 1987, by which time Mukherjee's subsequent publications had raised her literary and public profile.

Before leaving for India in 1973, Mukherjee and her husband conceived the idea of keeping separate journals during their trip, to be published later in a joint volume. They continued to work on these journals during a second stay in India in 1976 and 1977, when Mukherjee was director of the Shastri Institute in New Delhi. The result was *Days and Nights in Calcutta* (1977), the contrasting accounts of their responses to India as a Canadian who married into India and as a returned Indian who had married out of it. Mukherjee's section concentrates especially on the lives of the women with whom she had gone to school, now middle-class wives with a variety of frustrations and defenses.

The book as a whole is a well-written study of a society and of the strains of a cross-cultural marriage. The two halves of the journal often overlap and often unexpectedly enter into dialogue with each other. Blaise sometimes feels the outsider; so does Mukherjee, made aware by her friends of the "strangeness" of her marriage. Sometimes, too, over questions of politics, family, uncertainty, and security, the two authors read Indian culture in different ways.

In 1981 Mukherjee's "An Invisible Woman" was published in the Canadian magazine *Saturday Night*. An angry article about racial prejudice in Canada, it provides an explanation for Mukherjee and Blaise's return to the United States in 1980, rejecting the Canadian concept of "multiculturalism" and asserting that she finds greater freedom in the U.S.A. Encounters with prejudice serve as the basis for several of the angry short stories in her 1985 book, *Darkness,* a collection of twelve stories, most of them involving Indians in North America, and influenced to some degree by Malamud, to whom the book is dedicated. All but four were written, the author says in the introduction, "in a three-month burst of energy in the spring of 1984, in Atlanta, Georgia." Mukherjee, who became a Canadian citizen

Cover for Mukherjee's story collection dedicated to Bernard Malamud

in 1972, compares her experience of "expatriation" in Canada with her new status as an immigrant in the United States, though she now sees her Indianness as "a metaphor," a way seeing the world. Her own description of these stories as works about "broken identities and discarded languages" is accurate enough. They also continue her exploration of the violence that can erupt when a sense of identity, in a society or an individual, is shattered, when language, communication, fails.

Mukherjee's control of tone and event in these stories is much surer than in the novels, and her language is both more energetic and more subtle. Two of the stories have won major Canadian journalism awards, and the book has been well-received in Canada and the United States, though some Canadian reviewers have been distressed by what they regard as

Mukherjee's attempt to deny the existence of racial prejudice in the States.

By 1987 her attitude to Canada had somewhat modified. But the underlying dissatisfaction with Canadian cultural policy continues to inform her writing, showing up particularly in *The Sorrow and the Terror* (1987), an analysis of the causes and the "legacy" of the Air India crash on 23 June 1985, off the coast of Ireland. The book, which she coauthored with Blaise, investigates the reasons that led to the crash, in which several hundred Canadian citizens, most of Indian origin, were killed. Racism, prejudice, and the ethnic estrangements born of multicultural policy figure among them, the authors write; they also inquire into other cultural issues: the Khalistani independence movement, Sikh rivalries, tensions between Sikh and Hindu, terrorist bombings, naiveté, incompetence, and CIA involvement. Particularly moving are the portraits of those who died and of the other victims, those who still remember the dead and who now ask both for justice and for honor.

This request for recognition—the desire to be "visible" in honorable ways, to be recognized as person rather than as ethnic stereotype—characterizes much of Mukherjee's writing. Her characters sometimes cry out to be seen for who they really are; and sometimes, weak or tired, they surrender to taking on the identity of the "type" that others see them to be. In neither position can they lead satisfying lives, and Mukherjee dramatizes their conflicts. Currently she is completing a new volume of short stories on immigrant themes and a Marquezian political novel.

Ruth Nichols
(14 March 1948-)

J. Kieran Kealy
University of British Columbia

BOOKS: *A Walk out of the World* (Toronto: Longman, 1969; New York: Harcourt, Brace & World, 1969);
Ceremony of Innocence (London: Faber, 1969);
The Marrow of the World (Toronto: Macmillan, 1972; New York: Atheneum, 1972);
Song of the Pearl (Toronto: Macmillan, 1976; New York: Atheneum, 1976);
The Left-Handed Spirit (Toronto: Macmillan, 1978; New York: Atheneum, 1978).

PERIODICAL PUBLICATIONS: "Fantasy and Escapism," *Canadian Children's Literature*, 4 (1976): 20-27;
"Fantasy: the Interior Universe," *Proceedings of the Fifth Annual Conference of the Children's Literature Association* (March 1978): 41-47.

One of Canada's most celebrated fantasists, Ruth Nichols admits that she always knew she would be a writer. As a child she wrote numerous long narratives, and in 1962, the year her parents, Edward and Ruby Smith Nichols, moved the family from her birthplace, Toronto, to Vancouver, she won the grand prize in the Shankar International Literary Contest for Children for a novelette about the childhood imprisonment of Catherine de' Medici. In 1969 she graduated from the University of British Columbia with an honors degree in religious studies. During her student years in Vancouver, she composed her first two books, both of which focus on the kind of heroine who dominates her subsequent fiction: the brilliant girl/woman who is desperately trying to integrate the many fragments of her identity.

Ceremony of Innocence (1969), composed first but published a few months later than *A Walk out of the World*, is a realistic portrait of the maturation of Marjorie Baldwin. While accompanying her father, a prominent archaeologist, on a summer dig, Marjorie discovers him having sexual relations with one of his students. Feeling betrayed by a father she adores, she wishes him dead, and when he suddenly dies soon thereafter, she assumes that she is somehow responsible. Finally, however, through the loving intercession of two of her father's former associates, Neil and Catherine, Marjorie is able to confront and exorcise the specter of her dead father and face reality. Though most critics and, in fact, Nichols herself, do not consider *Ceremony of Innocence* an artistically successful book, Canadian critic George Woodcock, in his review in *Canadian Literature* (Summer 1971), calls it "a work of remarkable intelligence, sensibility and formal power."

A Walk out of the World (1969), for which Nichols wrote the first draft when she was eighteen, presents two troubled adolescents, Judith and Tobit, who escape their confining urban world simply by leaving it and walking into the world of fantasy. Here they find the space and opportunity to grow, becoming, almost immediately, significant figures in a cosmic battle between good and evil which pits the house of the children's true ancestors against the evil usurper Hagérrak. Though the story is clearly indebted to the fantasies of J.R.R. Tolkien and L.M. Boston, the final confrontation between good and evil is unusual, for Judith does not defeat Hagérrak in some epic battle; instead, she destroys him by forcing him to face his totally meaningless existence, thereby causing his suicide.

Critics praised the uniqueness, maturity, and integrity of this youthful fantasy. Ruth Hill Viguers's review in the *Horn Book Magazine* (August 1969) reflects the opinion of most: "The atmosphere is like that of no other fantasy; the unique details are crystal clear and belong only to the worlds of Tobit and Judith. The writing is disciplined and beautiful; the story exciting and triumphant."

In 1969 Nichols became a doctoral candidate at McMaster University; she received her M.A. in 1972 and Ph.D. in 1977, writing her dissertation on twentieth-century British novelist and poet Charles Williams. In September 1974 she married William Norman Houston. During this period Nichols wrote three books, each of which clearly asserts her belief that her primary purpose as a writer is to reaffirm, in an often nihilistic world, the need for hope and love.

In *The Marrow of the World* (1972), winner of the Canadian Library Association Book of the Year for Children Award in 1973, Nichols presents a heroine, Linda, who must confront not only the evil around her, but also the potential evil within her own half-human, half-witch self. Though the novel begins as a conventional otherworld adventure, the true quest takes place in Linda's mind: not only must she conquer her evil half-sister, Ygerna, the witch who sends her and her cousin Philip on the search for the sacred marrow which provides the framework for the novel, but she must also confront her fear that she is inherently and essentially evil. Philip's physical defeat of Ygerna, in fact, foreshadows Linda's greater triumph when she discovers that her shedding of a single tear conclusively proves her true humanity. Unlike *A Walk out of the World*, in which the protagonists return to the real world rather unwillingly, Linda's return to her family is the final proof that she is, in fact, free of fear and doubt and can rightfully assume her role in this world.

Critical response to *The Marrow of the World* featured praise, once again, for Nichols's approach to fantasy. Frances Frazer, in her review in *Canadian Literature* (Autumn 1974), comments particularly on Nichols's adeptness "at conveying nuances of mood that contribute psychological credibility to the incredible." Sheila Egoff, in her discussion of Nichols in *The Republic of Childhood* (1975), states: "She comes closer than anyone who has written fantasy in Canada to creating a believable 'sub-world' or 'secondary world' in the great tradition of fantasy."

In *Song of the Pearl* (1976), Nichols rejects the confines of Tolkienian fantasy with its journeys to other worlds and focuses instead on Margaret Redmond's exploration of her own fragmented self. She is the pearl of the title and, as such, she must delve into the many layers of her identity and discover the grain, the essence of her being. The story begins as the embittered Margaret, obsessed by her hatred for an uncle she seduced into raping her, dies. Upon her death, she is transported to a mysterious island where she meets Paul, an Oriental who forces Margaret to face herself and finally learn to grow. Margaret's growth involves a series of confrontations with her former selves who, in earlier lives, were consumed by hatred as she has been in her most recent incarnation. Finally she confronts Tirigan, a Sumerian overlord, and learns that it is his dying curse against his murderers that has dominated her life in all of her many incarnations. Understanding the source of her hatred, Margaret can now forgive her uncle, thus exorcising the emotion that has consumed her for thousands of years. Finally free, she returns to the

Editions of three of Nichols's books for young adults

pilgrimage of life; the novel that began with the heroine's death fittingly ends with her birth.

Song of the Pearl received mixed reviews, as many critics found both the prose and the plot too complex for youthful readers. Particularly irritating for many was the question of Margaret's complicity in the rape that initiates her quest. Phyllis Yaffe, for example, in *In Review: Canadian Books for Children* (Winter 1977), pointedly asks: "Must the victim remain guilty? Can we recommend books which propagate this myth? I think not. No matter what cleansing pilgrimage the author creates, the girl's guilt remains with the reader." She concludes: "Definitely not recommended for children." In contrast, Anthony Appenzell, in his review in *Canadian Literature* (Spring 1977), praises the psychological depth of the novel, suggesting that "the triumph of *Song of the Pearl* is the sense of concrete experience that is given to the world of death."

Though Nichols has asserted that her fifth novel, *The Left-Handed Spirit* (1978), is a continuation of the story of Paul (a minor character in *Song of the Pearl*) and Margaret, the form is quite different from that of the 1976 novel. More a historical novel or romance than a fantasy, this narrative presents a fictional biography in which Mariana, a Roman seer, describes her abduction by Paulus, a Chinese ambassador to Rome, and her subsequent journey to the land of his family. Though the journey does force Mariana to come to terms with both her powers and her growing love for Paulus, the story's main focus is not on any psychological journey but on the meticulously described physical one. As in the case of *Song of the Pearl*, critics have severely questioned the unnecessary complexity of *The Left-Handed Spirit*. In the words of one reviewer, it is "slow-moving and often too cryptic to understand, . . . a serious book which makes demands to which only the most mature readers are likely to respond." Aeron Rowland's review in *Books in Canada* (February 1979) goes so far as to suggest that Nichols has no clear audience in mind: "she tends to patronize her adult readers, while writing beyond the scope of most children."

Not surprisingly perhaps, Nichols's present interest appears to be in reaching an adult readership. Now living in Ottawa, she is working on historical novels, the first to be set in Renaissance Poland.

Interviews:

"Ruth Nichols: An Interview," *Children's Literature Association Newsletter*, 2 (Summer 1977): 1-4;

Jon Stott, "An Interview with Ruth Nichols," *Canadian Children's Literature*, 12 (1978): 5-19.

References:

Sheila Egoff, *The Republic of Childhood* (Toronto: Oxford University Press, 1975), pp. 76-79;

Adrienne E. Hass, "Ruth Nichols: 'The True and the Good,'" *Children's Literature Association Newsletter*, 2 (Autumn 1977): 1, 10-11.

Papers:

Nichols's manuscripts and notes are at Mills Memorial Library, McMaster University, Hamilton, Ontario.

Michael Ondaatje
(12 September 1943-   )

Ann Mandel
Glendon College

BOOKS: *The Dainty Monsters* (Toronto: Coach House Press, 1967);

The Man with Seven Toes (Toronto: Coach House Press, 1969);

Leonard Cohen (Toronto: McClelland & Stewart, 1970);

The Collected Works of Billy the Kid: Left Handed Poems (New York: Norton, 1970; Toronto: Anansi, 1970; London: Boyars, 1980);

Rat Jelly (Toronto: Coach House Press, 1973);

Coming Through Slaughter (Toronto: Anansi, 1976; New York: Norton, 1976; London: Boyars, 1979);

Elimination Dance (Ilderton, Ontario: Nairn, 1979);

There's a Trick with a Knife I'm Learning to Do (New York: Norton, 1979; Toronto: McClelland & Stewart, 1979; London: Boyars, 1980);

Claude Glass (Toronto: Coach House Press Manuscript Editions, 1979);

Running in the Family (New York: Norton, 1982; Toronto: McClelland & Stewart, 1982; London: Gollancz, 1983);

Tin Roof (Lantzville, British Columbia: Island Writing Series, 1982);

Secular Love (Toronto: Coach House Press, 1984);

In the Skin of a Lion (Toronto: McClelland & Stewart, 1987; London: Secker & Warburg, 1987; New York: Knopf, 1987).

PLAY PRODUCTIONS: *The Man with Seven Toes*, dramatic reading, Vancouver, Gallimaufry Repertory Theatre, 1968;

The Collected Works of Billy the Kid, dramatic reading, Toronto, St. Lawrence Centre, 23 April 1971; script version, Stratford, Ontario, Stratford Festival Theatre, Summer 1973; revised, Toronto, Toronto Free Theatre, 22 October 1974;

Coming Through Slaughter, Toronto, Theatre Passe Muraille, January 1980.

MOTION PICTURES: *Sons of Captain Poetry*, directed by Ondaatje, Mongrel Films, 1970;

Carry On Crime and Punishment, directed and

Michael Ondaatje (photograph by Rolf Kaufman)

filmed by Ondaatje, Mongrel Films, 1972;

The Clinton Special, directed by Ondaatje, Mongrel Films, 1972.

OTHER: "The Barn," in *The Story So Far*, volume one, edited by George Bowering (Toronto & Detroit: Coach House Press, 1971), pp. 26-27;

The Broken Ark: A Book of Beasts, edited by Ondaatje (Ottawa: Oberon, 1971);

Personal Fictions: Stories by Munro, Wiebe, Thomas & Blaise, edited by Ondaatje (Toronto: Oxford University Press, 1977);

"Garcia Márquez and The Bus to Aracataca," in *Figures in a Ground: Canadian Essays on Modern Literature Collected in Honor of Sheila Watson*, edited by Diane Bessai and David Jackel

(Saskatoon: Western Producer Prairie Books, 1978), pp. 19-31;

The Long Poem Anthology, edited with an introduction by Ondaatje (Toronto: Coach House Press, 1979);

A Book of Beasts, edited by Ondaatje (Ottawa: Oberon, 1979);

"The Scratch, Women Like You, & Jaffna Afternoons," in *Interchange: A Symposium on Regionalism, Internationalism, and Ethnicity in Literature* (Honolulu: InterArts Hawaii, 1980); pp. 27-34;

"Cut Down the Middle," in *Tasks of Passion: Dennis Lee at Midcareer,* edited by Karen Mulhallen (Toronto: Descant Editions, 1982), pp. 20-21.

PERIODICAL PUBLICATIONS: "Little Magazines/small presses, 1969," *artscanada,* 26 (August 1969): 17-18;

"O'Hagan's Rough-Edged Chronicle," *Canadian Literature,* 61 (Summer 1974): 24-31;

"Austin," *Periodics,* 1 (Spring 1977): 44-46;

"Lunch Conversation," *Periodics,* 5 (Spring 1979): 29-31;

The William Dawe Badlands Expedition 1916, Descant, 42 (Fall 1983);

"Wordsworth in the Tropics," *Descant,* 44-45 (Spring-Summer 1984): 175.

Winner of two Governor General's awards for poetry, Michael Ondaatje is one of the most brilliant and acclaimed of that impressive group of Canadian poets who first published in the 1960s, a group that includes Margaret Atwood, Gwen MacEwen, and B. P. Nichol. Ondaatje's widely praised books range from collections of tightly crafted lyrics to a narrative mixing poetry, prose, and fictional documentary, and a novel of lyric intensity. Using myth, legend, and anecdote drawn from the Wild West, the jazz world, film, and newspapers, his books have had wide popular appeal while at the same time occasioning considerable analysis by critics in Canada and elsewhere. The world of his poems has been called "surreal, absurd, inchoate, dynamic," "a dark, chaotic, but life-giving universe," and "the dangerous cognitive region which lies between reportage and myth."

Philip Michael Ondaatje was born in Colombo, Ceylon (now Sri Lanka), to Philip Mervyn and Enid Gratiaen Ondaatje. His paternal grandfather was a wealthy tea planter with a family estate in Kegalle. Ondaatje remembers "a great childhood" filled with aunts, uncles, many houses, and, judging from the stories he recounts in his autobiographical *Running in the Family* (1982), gossip and eccentricity. In his poem "Light" he tells of his grandmother "who went to a dance in a muslin dress / with fireflies captured and embedded in the cloth," and in "Letters & Other World" he speaks lovingly of his father's life as a "terrifying comedy" of alcohol and outrageous acts. In Colombo Ondaatje attended St. Thomas College. His parents separated in 1948, and in 1952 Ondaatje followed his mother, brother, and sister to London, England, where he attended Dulwich College. Dissatisfied eventually with the English school system which kept him trying "O" levels in maths when he wanted to study English, he immigrated to Canada at the age of nineteen, joining his brother Christopher already living in Montreal.

He entered Bishop's University, Lennoxville, majoring in English and history. It was there, finally able to concentrate on English literature and influenced by a teacher, Arthur Motyer, who "aroused an enthusiasm for literature," that Ondaatje began to write. It was there, too, that simultaneously with his reading of Browning, Eliot, Yeats, and younger modern poets, he came in contact with contemporary Canadian poets, notably D. G. Jones. It was his sense that Canada had "no big history," no weighty literary tradition, which freed Ondaatje to try to write.

A concluding year at the University of Toronto, at the end of which Ondaatje earned his B.A., brought him into contact with poet Raymond Souster, who included Ondaatje's work in his important anthology of young poets, *New Wave Canada* (1966). When Ondaatje won the university's Epstein Award for Poetry poet Wayne Clifford brought him to the attention of Coach House press. Coach House, a small but influential publisher of finely designed books, offered to publish one of Ondaatje's manuscripts, and though he refused then, it was with Coach House that his first collection, *The Dainty Monsters,* was published in 1967. From 1965 to 1967 he completed an M.A. at Queen's University, with a thesis on Edwin Muir ("because there was very little stuff written on him"), edited a university magazine, the *Mitre,* and wrote many of the poems included in his first book.

In 1964 Ondaatje married Kim Jones, an artist, and two children (Quentin and Griffin, for whom Dennis Lee wrote a children's poem) were born in the next two years. His wife had four children by a previous marriage, and the daily life of family and friends provided subject matter for many poems in his first book and in the 1973 volume *Rat Jelly*.

The Dainty Monsters, its title taken from a poem by Baudelaire, is divided into two sections: "Over the Garden Wall," thirty-six lyrics in which this domestic world collides with, or is transformed into, an exotic, violent, disorienting vision: and "Troy Town," nine poems centered on mythic and historical figures such as Lilith, Philoctetes, and Elizabeth I. The first section, with its plentiful animal imagery, concerns the "civilized magic" of family life. This magic can become extravagant: a dragon gets entangled in the badminton net, manticores clog Toronto sewers, a camel bites off a woman's left breast, pigs become poets, and strange, as yet unrecognized gods alter and reshape landscape, genetics, and the color and mood of a moment. Forces inside the body match forces outside it as all of the external world is involved in human visceral activity. Jungles and gorillas coexist with cocktails and cars, birds fly like watches, clocks swagger, zoo gibbons move like billiard balls, cars chomp on bushes with chrome teeth. Just as the natural world ranges from the domestic dog to the uncaged leopard, so each body or organism, animal or human, has the ability to hold within itself "rivers of collected suns, / jungles of force, coloured birds" as well as urges toward the suicidal refinement of overbreeding. As Sheila Watson has remarked in an article published in *Open Letter* (Winter 1974-1975), Ondaatje "is aware that all life maintains itself by functional specialization of some kind and as often as not loses itself for the same reason." Similarly, poetry is no absolute: it breaks the moment it seeks to record. It must, therefore, be sensitive above all to changes–to the altering moment, to the transforming imagination, and to the demands of an age when, as Ondaatje writes in *The Dainty Monsters*, "bombs are shaped like cedars." In some poems in the second section the poet imagines the characters of legendary figures: Prometheus in his martyred pain attracting mermaids at dusk, Lilith rioting with corrupted unicorns in Eden. Others are monologues in which historical characters–Helen, Elizabeth I– speak their lives and emotions. Formally these poems reflect Ondaatje's interest in longer discontinuous structures, but as far as subject matter is concerned, they represent a conclusion to one stage of his career. As Ondaatje recalls it, his friend the poet David McFadden

told him "no more Greek stuff," and he took that advice.

The Dainty Monsters, published in an edition of 500 copies, received more attention than most first books of poetry. Reviewers were especially impressed by Ondaatje's startling imagery. The volume is still in print, as are all his major books.

In *The Dainty Monsters* Ondaatje began his exploration of the intersection of animal, human, and machine worlds and of the intricate meshing of primitive, violent forces and ordered, exact responses. The book also, in direct references and in its imagery, suggests an interest in the visual arts, especially in the paintings of Henri Rousseau. Ondaatje's second book, *The Man with Seven Toes* (1969), had its origins in a series of drawings the Australian artist Sidney Nolan had done, based on the life of Mrs. Eliza Fraser, a Scottish lady who was shipwrecked off the Queensland coast, lived among aborigines, and was helped to civilization by an escaped convict to whom she promised freedom, then promptly threatened to betray. Ondaatje began with these drawings and Nolan's series of paintings of Ned Kelly, together with a sense of the Australian landscape as it is evoked in Alan Moorehead's books and a brief account of the Eliza Fraser story of Colin MacInnes. He began working on the poem in the fall of 1966, after spending a hot dusty summer working on a road gang–"the nearest thing to desert I could get"–and completed the poem about the time *The Dainty Monsters* was published. The book, a fine limited edition of 300 copies published by Coach House Press, appeared in 1969.

The Man with Seven Toes is Ondaatje's first major attempt at a long sequence, thirty-three short lyrics and a concluding ballad, prefaced by a striking reproduction of Canadian artist Jack Chambers's *Man and Dog* which visually suggests something of the loneliness, agony, and violent rich beauty in the poems. The woman of the poems is nameless, left in the desert by a departing train which hums "like a low bird." She comes across fantastically decorated aborigines, is raped, and escapes with Potter, the convict. Their trek takes them through swamp where teeth like "ideal knives" take off some of Potter's toes and snakes with "bracelets of teeth" hang in the leaves; they proceed into the hot plain, where Potter kills a sleeping wolf by biting open its vein. When they are found, the woman says only "god has saved me."

The poems move from a narrator's voice in and out of the minds of the convict and woman,

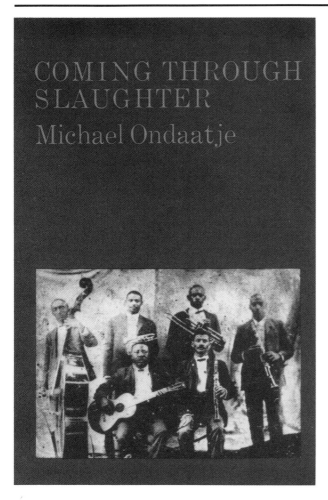

Dust jacket for Ondaatje's novel based on the life of New Orleans jazz musician Buddy Bolden

sometimes describing what happens, at others reflecting emotions. In the first poem she is merely a woman too tired to call after the receding train, but in the imagery of her responses to the rape, of the slaughter of animals, of the rape itself, the spilling of semen and blood are confused in ways that fuse terror, beauty, rich colors, sexuality, and death. And after her rescue, resting in the civilized Royal Hotel, she moves her hands over her body, "sensing herself like a map." While she sleeps, a bird is chopped up in a ceiling fan and scattered about the room. Her acceptance of violent death coincides with her acceptance of her sexual body, though she has rejected the moral dimension of her experience.

The poem conveys Ondaatje's acute awareness of song and the spoken voice. It has been performed as a dramatic reading for three speakers, first in Vancouver in 1968, then at Stratford in 1969. The second staging was directed by Paul Thompson in Toronto, with whom Ondaatje later worked on the 1971 adaptation and staging of *The Collected Works of Billy the Kid*, on the making of the 1972 film, *The Clinton Special*, and on the 1980 stage adaptation of *Coming Through Slaughter*.

In 1967 Ondaatje became an instructor in English at the University of Western Ontario in London. During the summer of 1968, while staying in Ganonoque, Ontario, he wrote *Leonard Cohen* (1970), a short critical study of the poet and novelist who had recently become known as a songwriter and performer. Ondaatje has said that Cohen was the most important influence on him as a young writer and on his generation, especially through the novel *The Favourite Game* (1963), which seemed refreshingly unelitist. Ondaatje's was the first book-length study of Cohen and remains an important work on that writer, though the book also illuminates Ondaatje and his work. He is clearly close to Cohen, sharing Cohen's love of the sensuous startling image, his understanding of the detached mind of the artist, of the authentic fakery of art, and, as Ondaatje writes of Cohen, of the necessity of promoting "our own private cells of anarchy."

Shortly after completing *The Man with Seven Toes*, Ondaatje, feeling dissatisfied with the form of that work, began to browse through Edmund Wilson's *Patriotic Gore* (1962) with the vague intention of writing a Civil War story or poem. Somehow deflected west, he wrote a few poems using the voice of Billy the Kid and, as he described it in a 1975 interview with Sam Solecki for *Rune*, "moved from these to being dissatisfied with the limits of lyric; so I moved to prose and interviews and so on." The legend of Billy merged with Ondaatje's memories of childhood cowboys-and-Indians games in Ceylon, and he wrote over a period of about two years, taking another year to edit and rearrange his materials. *The Collected Works of Billy the Kid: Left Handed Poems* appeared in 1970, designed by Coach House and published by House of Anansi, another small but important Canadian press.

Winner of the Governor General's Award for 1970, *The Collected Works of Billy the Kid* has become Ondaatje's most celebrated work, praised by critics and readers and roundly condemned—to his delight—by federal MPs for dealing with an *American* hero and outlaw. The familiar Wild West characters are in this volume—Billy the Kid, sheriff Pat Garrett, and other historical characters taken from Walter Burns's *The Saga of Billy the Kid* (1926)–but the focus is not on the historical outlaw nor on the Wild West motif. The book has been interpreted by some as a parable of the artist / outlaw, but Ondaatje has commented that though Billy may be on some instinctual level an artist, he did not intend to create a "portrait of the artist." Rather, the book continues thematically his exploration of the ambiguous and often paradoxical area between biology and mechanization, movement and stasis, chaotic life and the framed artistic moment. The artist in the book is not Billy but Ondaatje himself as writer, shaping and faking material, bringing into the poems some of his own experiences while at the same time standing apart, watching his characters feel and act, and, in the end, leaving them as he wakes in his hotel room alone.

The book includes poems, prose, photographs and other illustrations, interviews, and a comic-book legend. It begins with Billy's list of the dead, including his own death in the future at the hands of Pat Garrett. The narrative sections, funny, witty, full of strange stories, tell of such events as Garrett's gunning down Tom O'Folliard, Billy's pastoral sojourns on the Chisum ranch in Texas, his arrest, ride to trial and escape, Garrett's peculiar self-education in French and alcoholism, and finally Billy's murder. In the lyrics and especially in the frame of the story, Ondaatje's concerns become clear. Before the text, there is a framed blank square and a quotation from the great frontier photographer L. A. Huffman about the development of a technique which allowed him to take photographs of moving things from a moving horse. The book concludes with a small framed picture of Ondaatje, aged about six, wearing a cowboy outfit. The volume's subtitle, *Left Handed Poems*, refers to Billy's hands, small, smooth, white, and trained by finger exercises twelve hours a day, the hands of a murderer who is a courteous dandy, a gentle lover, a man sensitive to every nerve in his body, every sense extending to the whole sensual world: a man with "the range for everything." Pat Garrett, the lawman whose hands are scarred and burned, is a "sane assassin," an "academic murderer" who decided what is right and "forgot all morals." Garrett's morals are mechanical, insane in their neutrality. Billy reflects that he himself can watch "the stomach of clocks / shift their wheels and pins into each other / and emerge living, for hours," but insane images blossom in his own brain, and he knows that in

all ordered things, the course of the stars, "the clean speed of machines," "one altered move . . . will make them maniac." Awareness and exactitude imply stress; the frame holds within it the breaking moment. It is better to be in motion. Inside the small boy Michael Ondaatje are Garrett's and Billy's future legend; the three are held inside the book; the structure in its altering forms collects them all.

Canadian critics described *The Collected Works of Billy the Kid* as "one of the best books . . . in a long time," "profound in its dimensions," and praised the originality of the form. The critic for the *New York Times,* reviewing the American edition, published in 1970, called it "carefully crafted and thoroughly literate," though a "miniature." It has sold at least 20,500 copies in Canada and is currently in print in both Canada and the United States. In one American anthology, *Modernism in Literature* (1977), the entire book is republished in facsimile as an example of contemporary impressionism, literature which, through ambiguity, calls attention to itself as a conscious construct and insists on the relativity of experience.

The Collected Works of Billy the Kid evolved into a play, beginning with radio and stage readings. Ondaatje reshaped, cut, and added songs, and the play, in its present form, was first performed by the Toronto Free Theatre in October 1974, directed by Martin Kinch. It was performed at the Brooklyn Academy, New York, in October 1975 and continues to be presented in many countries.

Given the visual quality and inspiration of Ondaatje's work, it was natural for him to turn to film. One effort, using family and friends as cast, involves the dognapping of the family bassett hound, Wallace, and bears the title *Carry On Crime and Punishment* (1972). A more serious effort is a thirty-five-minute film, *Sons of Captain Poetry* (1970), on Canadian sound and concrete poet B. P. Nichol, made when *The Collected Works of Billy the Kid* was going to press. It is an entertaining and thoughtful introduction to the impulses behind sound and concrete poetry and an appreciative homage to a man from whom Ondaatje says he has learned much.

After finishing *The Dainty Monsters* and during the writing of his two subsequent books, Ondaatje continued to write short lyrics, collected in 1973 in *Rat Jelly*. Published by Coach House, the book has a stunning cover taken from a nursery school stained-glass window, depicting a pieman who clearly has sinister designs on Simple Simon. The book is divided into three sections, "Families," "Live Bait," and "White Dwarfs," which contain domestic poems, animal poems, and poems about art respectively. The first two sections continue the themes of the previous books, though the structure and line are generally more relaxed, the tone more humorous and casual. Ondaatje's genius for vivid images is here: his wife's ear is "a vast / musical instrument of flesh"; bats "organize the air / with thick blinks of travel"; a window "tries to split with cold," a moth in his pajamas is the poet's heart "breaking loose." Violent events explode into everyday life: "At night the gold and black slashed bees come / pluck my head away"; a woman's naked back during lovemaking is a wrecked aircraft scattered across sand; the fridge contains a live rat pie. In the second section the deaths of animals are related to man's hate for his own animality and mortality: men kill to "fool themselves alive." It is the third section of *Rat Jelly* which is perhaps the most interesting in that it contains several poems explicitly on art and the relationship of art to experience. In "King Kong meets Wallace Stevens" these two figures are humorously juxtaposed: Stevens all insurance and thought, Kong whose "mind is nowhere." As the poem develops, it is the poet who "is thinking chaos is thinking fences," whose blood is bellowing in his head. Ondaatje's constructed beast loose in the city is the poem as anarchic animal, fashioned in the poet's subversive imagination. The poem entitled "The gate in his head" contains lines which have often been cited as Ondaatje's clearest aesthetic statement. Looking at a blurred photograph of a gull, the poet writes:

> And this is all this writing should be then,
> The beautiful formed things caught at the
> > wrong moment
> so they are shapeless, awkward
> moving to the clear.

Certainly these lines reflect his wish to catch movement and to capture life without killing it, as clarity or the certainty of, say, Garrett's morals does. In "White Dwarfs," the concluding poem in the book, the poet speaks of his heroes as those who have "no social fuel," who die in "the ether peripheries," who are not easy to describe, existing in "the perfect white between the words." Silence is the perfect poetry, the silence of a star imploding after its brilliant parading in an unknown universe.

In 1971 Ondaatje left the University of Western Ontario ("they wanted me to do a Ph.D. and I didn't want to") and took an assistant professorship at Glendon College, Toronto. In a Toronto *Globe and Mail* interview in 1974, Ondaatje reported that he was working on a prose work about different characters in the 1930s. That work may yet see print, but the book which did appear in 1976 was *Coming Through Slaughter,* a novel about New Orleans jazz musician Buddy Bolden, a cornetist who went mad in 1907. The book, as Ondaatje disclosed in a 1977 interview for *Books in Canada,* was begun in London, triggered by a newspaper clipping describing "Buddy Bolden, who became a legend when he went berserk in a parade." Ondaatje worked on it for several years, especially during summers on the family farm near Verona, Ontario. In 1973, well after he had started on the book, Ondaatje went to Louisiana to do research and absorb the geography of Bolden's life. Very little is, in fact, known about Bolden: in the novel, on one page, Ondaatje lists the available facts. He used tapes of jazzmen remembering Bolden, books about New Orleans's Storyville district and the period, and the records of the hospital where Bolden lived, mad, until his death in 1931. But as in his work on Billy the Kid, Ondaatje's interest is not historical. He has altered dates, brought people together who never met, and polished facts "to suit the truth of fiction," as he comments in the book's acknowledgments. For him, "the facts start suggesting things, almost breed," and the landscape of the book is "a totally mental landscape . . . of names and rumours."

The book is in large part "a statement about the artist," Ondaatje noted in a 1980 interview published in *Eclipse,* though Bolden is an individual, not a generalized artist. It is, according to Ondaatje, "a very private book," in which an identification between author and character is made explicit in the text—"The photograph moves and becomes a mirror"—but it is also a controlled and impersonal creation, examining the tensions that exist among kinds of art, within certain artists, and within himself. By Ondaatje's account, one germ of *Coming Through Slaughter* was the tension he observed among some of the London, Ontario, painters who were his friends, especially between Greg Curnoe and Jack Chambers, one a "local" and the other a "classical" artist.

The book follows Bolden from New Orleans, where he barbers during the day, plays cornet at night, his two-year disappearance from family and the world of music, to his discovery by his policeman friend, Webb, his return to friends and music, and his explosion into madness. The structure is unchronological. The first section is mainly narrative, much of the second takes place in Bolden's mind, the third alternates interior monologue with narrative, and the final pages mix Bolden's thoughts in various mental hospitals with historical documentation, narrative, and explicit comments of the novelist. The book ends, as *The Collected Works of Billy the Kid* does, with the writer alone in a room: "Thirty-one years old. There are no prizes."

Bolden's relationship with Webb parallels structurally that of Billy and Garrett. Bolden's other relationships—with Nora, his wife, and with Robin Brewitt, the woman he comes to love during his retreat, with various other musicians, and especially with Bellocq, a photographer of Storyville's prostitutes—all develop aspects of Bolden as man and as musician. He is an "unprofessional" player, the loudest, the roughest, his music "immediate, dated in half an hour . . . showing all the possibilities in the middle of the story." His playing appears formless, but only because "he tore apart the plot" trying to describe something in a multitude of ways, the music a direct extension of his life. His life is haunted by fears of certainty: "He did nothing but leap into the mass of changes and explore them." Bolden is the totally social, unthinking, chaotic man and artist until he meets Bellocq, who introduces him to privacy, calculated art, the silence beyond the social world. Bellocq eventually commits suicide. After Webb "rescues" Bolden from his self-imposed absence from music, Bolden retreats to a cottage alone, and in his mental addresses to Webb, he meditates on his music and his life. He thinks about the temptation to silence and about the music of John Robichaux, whose formal complete structures "dominated . . . audiences," a tyranny Bolden loathes. Instead, he wants audiences to "come in where they pleased and leave when they pleased and somehow hear the germs of the start and all the possible endings. . . ." In his silence Bolden grows theoretical, and, returning to the "20th century game of fame," he brings self-consciousness into his uncertainties. He compares himself, needing and loathing an audience, with the sad transient mattress prostitutes, selling a wrecked talent. On his fifth morning home, playing in a parade, he sees a woman strut into the procession, and he begins to play for, at, her: she becomes all audiences, all the youth, energy, sexu-

ality he once had, all women, all pure cold art: "this is what I wanted, always, loss of privacy in the playing. . . ." He "overblows" his cornet, hemorrhages, and collapses, his goal realized, for he has utterly become his music. Bolden is released into madness and a calm serenity. In the passage in which Ondaatje connects himself to Bolden, he suggests that the temptations of silence, madness, and death have also been his, and, by implication, that Bolden's art, aesthetics, and tensions are his, too.

During the writing of *Coming Through Slaughter*, Ondaatje directed and edited a film about Theatre Passe Muraille's play *The Farm Show*, an actor-generated theater presentation based on the actors' experiences in a farming community. Ondaatje's interest in his film *The Clinton Special* is the play's merging of document, local gossip, and re-creation of these materials, a process which continues to hold his attention.

At the close of 1976 Ondaatje went to India for a Commonwealth Literature conference, the closest he had been to his birthplace in twenty-four years. On sabbatical in January 1978, he traveled to Sri Lanka for a five-month visit with his sister and relatives. The closing section of *There's a Trick with a Knife I'm Learning to Do* (his 1979 volume of selected poems covering the years 1963 to 1978 that won the Governor General's Award for poetry in 1980) contains new poems, some of which are based on this trip. Others further his concern with local history, and there are a few poems which develop his sense of the seductive, silent moon-world of night.

The final poem takes up his family history, a subject that Ondaatje continued to explore in his next book. He began a journal during his first trip to Sri Lanka and continued it while he was there, recording family stories he barely remembered. By the time he spent a second period in Sri Lanka in 1979 and 1980, he had become deeply involved in the lives and stories of his family history, a history he had ignored for years. *Running in the Family*, which he has refused to consign to any one genre—"the book," he claims, "is not a history but a portrait or 'gesture' "—furthers Ondaatje's experimentation in writing along the borders that separate history, story, and myth. At the same time it is an autobiographical quest, through memory and the tangled scandals and legends of family and a lost colonial world, for parents and the origins of his imagination.

Sri Lanka, fabled and invaded by Portuguese, Dutch, and English as Serendip, Taprobane, and Ceylon, peopled by a mix of Sinhalese, Tamil, and European, provides the tropical setting in which Ondaatje writes and records the memories and gossip of aunts, family friends, sisters and brothers, the history of his parents' courtship and divorce, the antic acts of his grandmother, Lalla, and the doings, "so whimsical, so busy," of earlier generations of Ceylonese society. History is shaped by conversation, anecdote, judgment, by its usefulness as family backdrop and to retelling the family's stories. Combining fiction, fact, poetry, and photographs, Ondaatje evokes the jungles, natural and social, in which his earliest memories grew. His father, an outrageous alcoholic whom he never knew as an adult, especially haunts his son's story. "I think all of our lives have been shaped by what went on before us," writes Ondaatje. Nevertheless, in imagination resides the power to bestow a countering magic on the past, which the writer uses to grant his flower-stealing grandmother the kind of death she always wanted. The book was praised by critics as much for its recreation of a particular society as for its stylistic exploration of the relationship between history and the poetic imagination.

Ondaatje spent the summer of 1979 teaching at the University of Hawaii. In 1980, as he continued his writing about his Sri Lankan family, his Canadian family situation changed radically when he separated from his wife and began to live with Linda Spalding. In *Secular Love* (1984), a collection of lyrics and lyric sequences, the pain of the marriage breakup and the sensual and emotional growth of new love make their way into the poems. One of the book's four sections, "Claude Glass," was published in 1979 as one of Coach House's manuscript editions. The book as a whole explores various landscapes: nighttime, moonlit, and rain-filled natural landscapes, the landscapes of love, a lover, a new life, and language. Like Billy the Kid with "the range for everything" and Bolden exploring chaos and change, the poet wants to know and see completely everything in his altering, altered life, from the "tiny leather toes" of geckos to the "scarred / skin boat" of another's body to "the syllables / in a loon sentence" signaling the lost and found moments which trace and locate a life. Again merging autobiography and poetics, the writer looks for a language which, like the love he seeks, names but does not dominate, which connects but does not control.

Dust jacket for the work Ondaatje describes as his "first formal novel"

In June 1981 Ondaatje went to Australia as winner of the Canada-Australia Exchange award. He continues to be interested in theater and film and has written a screenplay for Robert Kroetsch's 1975 novel *Badlands* which remains unproduced. Experimentation with the long poem has resulted in "Elimination Dance," a potentially endless comic poem taking off from a highschool dance ritual. One (unpublished) "elimination" is "All those bad poets who claim me as an early influence." He has worked for some years as an editor at Coach House, seeing through the press a number of important Canadian books; his own involvement in the design and production of his books is, by his own admission, obsessive.

He is now a professor at Glendon College, where he teaches Canadian and American literatures, contemporary literature in translation, and creative writing. In February and March of 1986 he spent four weeks teaching and lecturing at universities in Rome and Turin. In 1987 a novel that he had been working on for over three years was published in Canada, the United Kingdom, and the United States. Called *In the Skin of a Lion*, it draws its title from the *Epic of Gilgamesh:* "The joyful will stoop with sorrow, and when you have gone to the earth I will let my hair grow long for your sake, I will wander through the wilderness in the skin of a lion." According to Ondaatje in a 1987 *Quill and Quire* interview with Barbara Turner, it is his "first formal novel." Dealing with many of the social issues that most concern him— the "gulf between rich and poor, the conditions of the labour force, racism . . . in Canada"–the novel provides a historical glimpse of Toronto in the early years of the twentieth century. "I suddenly thought," says the author of the process of composing the book, "of a vista of Upper America where you had five or six people interweaving and treading . . . but somehow connected at certain times." The narrator of the novel not only tells his own story but also observes the lives of others: the immigrant workers who (without speaking the language of the community) build a bridge, the Bloor Street Viaduct, and the powerful Ambrose Small and his sometime lover Clara. What the narrator learns about life, he says, he learns in these years of tension: years of construction that placed the lives of the powerless in danger, years when the powerful were nonetheless susceptible to forces beyond their control. The historical millionaire Andrew Small disappeared at the height of his power in 1919 and was never found. The novel uses this event and the fictional lives of the years leading up to it to question the disparities between the character of life lived and the official versions of recorded history and culture.

Though Ondaatje is always insistent about the help he has received from other writers and friends, he is clearly an original writer, and his work has been received with enthusiasm by both scholars and general audiences. His importance lies, precisely, in his ability to combine a private, highly charged, sometimes dark vision with witty linguistic leaps and welcoming humor.

Interviews:

"Interview with Michael Ondaatje," *Manna*, 1 (March 1972): 19-22;

Sam Solecki, "An Interview with Michael Ondaatje," *Rune*, 2 (Spring 1975): 39-54;

"Billy, Buddy, and Michael," *Books in Canada*, 6 (June-July 1977): 9-10, 12-13;

"Moving to the Clear: An Interview," in *Twelve Voices: Interviews with Canadian Poets*, edited by Jon Pearce (Ottawa: Borealis, 1980), pp. 130-143;

Barbara Turner, "In the Skin of Michael Ondaatje: Giving Voice to a Social Conscience," *Quill and Quire* (May 1987): 21-22.

References:

Frank Davey, *From There to Here: A Guide to English-Canadian Literature Since 1960* (Erin, Ontario: Press Porcépic, 1974), pp. 222-227;

Gary Geddes and Phyllis Bruce, eds., *15 Canadian Poets Plus 5* (Toronto: Oxford University Press, 1978), pp. 402-403;

Smaro Kamboureli, "The Poetics of Geography in Michael Ondaatje's *Coming Through Slaughter*," *Descant*, 42 (Fall 1983): 112-126;

Dennis Lee, *Savage Fields: An Essay in Literature and Cosmology* (Toronto: Anansi, 1977), pp. 14-49, 115-116;

Leslie Mundwiler, *Michael Ondaatje: Word, Image, Imagination* (Vancouver: Talonbooks, 1984);

Stephen Scobie, "*Coming Through Slaughter*," *Essays in Canadian Writing*, 2 (Fall 1978): 5-23;

Scobie, "His Legend a Jungle Sleep," *Canadian Literature*, 76 (Spring 1978): 6-21;

Scobie, "Two Authors in Search of a Character," *Canadian Literature*, 54 (Autumn 1972): 37-55;

Sam Solecki, "Making and Destroying," *Essays in Canadian Writing*, 2 (Fall 1978): 24-47;

Solecki, "Michael Ondaatje," *Descant*, 42 (Fall 1983): 77-88;

Solecki, "Nets and Chaos," *Studies in Canadian Literature*, 2 (Winter 1977): 36-48;

Sheila Watson, "Michael Ondaatje: The Mechanization of Death," *Open Letter*, 3:1 (Winter 1974-1975): 158-166.

Papers:

Most of Ondaatje's papers are at the National Archives in Ottawa. An unpublished typescript for *The Collected Works of Billy the Kid*, revised as of 1 July 1975, is in the Theatre Department of the Metropolitan Toronto Library. There are letters from Ondaatje in the Earle Birney, A. J. M. Smith, and Raymond Souster collections at the Thomas Fisher Rare Book Library, University of Toronto.

Fernand Ouellette
(24 September 1930-   )

Paul Matthew St. Pierre
University of British Columbia

and

Evelyne Voldeng
Carleton University

BOOKS: *Ces anges de sang* (Montreal: Editions de l'Hexagone, 1955);

Séquences de l'aile (Montreal: Editions de l'Hexagone, 1958);

Le Soleil sous la mort (Montreal: Editions de l'Hexagone, 1965);

Edgard Varèse (Paris: Seghers/Montreal: HMH, 1966); translated by Derek Coltman (New York: Orion Press, 1968; London: Calder & Boyars, 1973);

Dans le sombre (Montreal: Editions de l'Hexagone, 1967);

Les Actes retrouvés (Montreal: HMH, 1970);

Poésie: Poèmes, 1953-1971; suivi de Le Poème et le poétique (Montreal: Editions de l'Hexagone, 1972);

Depuis Novalis, errance et gloses (Montreal: HMH, 1973);

Journal dénoué (Montreal: Presses de l'Université de Montréal, 1974);

Errances (Montreal: Editions Bourguignon, 1975);

Ici, ailleurs, la lumière (Montreal: Editions de l'Hexagone, 1977);

Tu regardais intensément Geneviève (Montreal: Quinze, 1978);

Ecrire en notre temps (Montreal: HMH, 1979);

A découvert (Sainte-Foy, Quebec: Editions Parallèles, 1979);

La Mort vive (Montreal: Quinze, 1980);

En la nuit, la mer: Poèmes 1972-1980 (Montreal: Editions de l'Hexagone, 1981);

Eveils (Outremont, Quebec: Obsidienne, 1982);

Lucie, ou un midi en novembre (Montreal: Boréal Express, 1985);

Les Heures (Montreal: Editions de l'Hexagone, 1987).

RADIO: "Lautréamont, ou le détour de Maldoror," CBF/Radio-Canada, November 1955;

"Maxime Gorki," *Chacun sa verité*, CBF/Radio-Canada, 4 December 1956;

"T. S. Eliot," *Poésie étrangère*, CBF/Radio-Canada, 26 March 1957;

"Pablo Neruda," *Poésie étrangère*, CBF/Radio-Canada, 21 May 1957;

"Blaise Cendrars," *Chacun sa vérité*, CBF/Radio-Canada, 28 January 1958;

"Poésie à quatre voix," *Chacun sa vérité*, CBF/Radio-Canada, 9 December 1958;

Collaborations diverses, by Ouellette and Jean-Guy Pilon, CBF/Radio-Canada, 1959-1961;

Les Créateurs du XXe siècle, by Ouellette and Gilbert Picard, CBF/Radio-Canada, 5 January 1961-29 June 1962;

"Visages du romantisme allemand," *Documents*, CBF/Radio-Canada, 18 April 1969;

"Marc Chagall," *Documents*, CBF/Radio-Canada, 6 November 1973;

"Prefaces pour la radio," CBF/Radio-Canada, 24 December 1984.

MOTION PICTURES: *Les Pèlerins*, commentary by Ouellette, National Film Board, 1958;

Angkor, parole d'un empire qui fut, commentary by Ouellette, National Film Board, 1961;

Armand Vaillancourt, commentary by Ouellette, National Film Board, 1964.

OTHER: "Citernes de soleil," "Sanglots d'ailes," "Banquise," and "Légende d'un monde vierge," French texts with translations, in *Twelve Modern French-Canadian Poets*, edited by G. R. Roy (Toronto: Ryerson, 1958), pp. 92-99;

Visages d'Edgard Varèse, edited by Ouellette (Montreal: Editions de l'Hexagone, 1959);

"Conque d'étoile," "Géants tristes," "Les Déserts de Varèse," "Le Mal de la paix," and "Etincelle," in *Poètes du Québec (1860-1968)*,

photograph by Kèro

edited by Jacques Cotnam (Montreal: Fides, 1969), pp. 184-188;

"Femme," translated by G. V. Downes as "Aubade"; "Psaumes pour abri I, II, III," translated by Downes as "Psalms for Shelter"; "50 Mégatonnes," translated by John Reeves as "50 Megatons"; "Communion," translated by F. R. Scott as "Communion"; "L'Ange," translated by Scott as "Angel"; and "Vers l'aube," translated by Scott as "Towards Dawn"; in *The Poetry of French Canada in Translation,* edited by John Glassco (Toronto: Oxford University Press, 1970), pp. 207-212;

"Note sur la poésie" and "Le Couple," in *How Do I Love Thee: Sixty Poets of Canada (and Quebec)*

Select and Introduce Their Favourite Poems from Their Own Work, translated by John Robert Colombo and Ben Shek, edited by Colombo (Edmonton: Hurtig, 1970), pp. 87-88;

"Alignements" and other poems, in *Anthology of Contemporary French Poetry,* edited and translated by Graham Dunstan Martin (Edinburgh: Edinburgh University Press, 1972) pp. 144-149;

Michel Salomon, *Mon calvaire roumain,* preface by Ouellette (Montreal: Editions de l'Homme, 1976).

PERIODICAL PUBLICATIONS:
POETRY
"Quinze Poèmes," *Etudes Françaises,* 3 (August 1967): 327-347;

"Femme" and "Et nous aimions," *Ellipse*, 1 (Fall 1969): 26-31;

"La Poésie dans ma vie" and "Dix-huit poèmes," *Ellipse*, 10 (1972): 10-69;

"Poèmes inédits," *Voix et Images*, 5 (Spring 1980): 497-513;

"Depuis la musique: sept poèmes," *Nota Beré* (Paris), 6 (Spring-Summer 1982): 161-167;

"Quatre poèmes," *Liberté*, 28 (August 1986).

NONFICTION

"Blaise Cendrars, ou l'homme aux deux pieds sur les pôles," *Liberté*, 1 (January-February 1959): 79-84; .

"André Jasmin, ou le pari de la sincérité," *Liberté*, 1 (January-February 1959); 347-355;

"La Désintegration d'un monde dementiel," *Liberté*, 2 (January-February 1960): 84-88;

"Il est d'étranges destin . . . ," *Liberté*, 2 (May-August 1960): 149-153;

"Aspects de Tagore," *Liberté*, 3 (January-February 1961): 401-405;

"Violence, révolution et terrorisme," *Liberté*, 5 (May-June 1963): 222-234;

"La Tolérance est-elle un mythe?," *Liberté*, 6 (January-February 1964): 9-29;

"La Lutte des langues et la dualité du langage," *Liberté*, 6 (March-April 1964): 87-113;

"Sören Kierkegaard, le passionné," *Ecrits du Canada Français*, 20 (1965): 273-291;

"Hommage à Varèse," *Vie Musicale*, no. 2 (1965);

"Edgard Varèse," *Journal Musical Français*, 153 (January 1967): 38-41;

"Et le bilinguisme?," *Europe*, 47 (February-March 1969): 16-21;

"Le Temps des veilleurs," *Liberté*, 13 (January-February 1971): 112-113;

"Divagations sur l'essai," *Etudes Littéraires*, 1 (April 1972): 9-13;

"Poetry in My Life," translated by C. R. P. May, *Ellipse*, 10 (1972): 46-58;

"The Poem and the Poetic," translated by Larry Shouldice, *Ellipse*, 10 (1972): 59-61;

"Jean-Paul Jérôme, peintre de la relation," *Vie des Arts*, 79 (Summer 1975): 14-17;

"La Poésie en son lieu," *Liberté*, 17 (November-December 1975): 35-40;

"Depuis que le Parti québécois . . . ," *Liberté*, 19 (January-February 1977): 86-87;

"La Lumière sous l'abîme," *Voix et Images* 5 (Spring 1980): 483-495;

"La Condition parasitaire," *Liberté*, 22 (March-April 1980): 13-14;

"Patinir ou l'harmonie du monde," *Liberté*, 23 (March-April 1981): 48-52;

"Africa: L'Art tribal de la forêt vierge et de la savane," *Liberté*, 23 (March-April 1981): 152-154;

"Peinture: Qu'est-ce que le romantisme?," *Liberté*, 24 (March-April 1982): 68-79;

"Peinture japonaise," *Liberté*, 25 (February 1983): 109-117;

"Le Cubisme," *Liberté*, 25 (August 1983): 102-112;

"Piero di Cosimo ou la forêt sacrilège," *Liberté*, 25 (December 1983): 112-120;

"Connaître les autres au Québec," *Le Devoir*, 3 January 1984, p. 11;

"Varèse, l'exception," *Liberté*, 26 (April 1984): 55-67;

"Vermeer," *Liberté*, 26 (December 1984): 139-145.

Poet of passionate sensitivity, essayist of ranging depth, novelist of technical daring, artist-hero of contemporary Quebec, Fernand Ouellette is as closely associated with the review *Liberté* and with the publishing house Editions de l'Hexagone as he is with his published works. During the last two decades in particular, he has been increasingly influential, even beyond the scope of his art, in the quiet social and discordant political revolutions of his native Quebec and in identifying and contributing to a curiously Quebecois poetic, aesthetic, and identity. His decision to decline (on political and moral grounds) the Governor General's Award for nonfiction, offered to him for his 1970 essay collection *Les Actes retrouvés*, has marked the greatest stroke of his literary life and career. His declaration of *non serviam* distinguished him less as only the second French-Canadian writer to refuse the prestigious award–two years earlier Hubert Aquin had declined it for political reasons when it had been awarded for his novel *Trou de mémoir*–than as the first Quebecois artist to register a historically indelible protest against the events of the October Crisis and the implementation of the War Measures Act. From this moment on, virtually for the next fifteen years, no artist in Quebec could claim to be apolitical and no art could purport to be nonpolitical. Ouellette and Quebec had come of age together.

Born in 1930 to Montreal working-class parents, Cyrille and Gilberte Chalifour Ouellette, Fernand Ouellette recognized a religious vocation long before even suspecting his literary vocation, becoming one of the many Canadians who entertained or entered the priesthood during and following the years of World War II. He studied for four years as a minor seminarian at the

Collège Séraphique des Capucins in Ottawa, but left in 1947, shortly before entering the major seminary. Returning to Montreal, he enrolled in the University of Montreal and received a *licence ès sciences sociales* in 1952. His religious upbringing, however, had left its imprint on him indelibly. In 1951, engaged in what he called his quest for "angelism," he had an experience of profound mystical illumination, during which he felt reborn: spiritually, also artistically, and especially physically. It was through this naissance into spirit, love, and poetry that he was later to accept the concept of the real body of flesh and blood whose unreality had touched and wounded him when he was a seminarian. Despite the religious-secular academic dichotomy of his youth, Ouellette has gone on to strike a spiritual-sensual balance throughout his literary career. This balance first entered his life in 1955 through his marriage to Lisette Corbeil (who has inspired many of his love poems and to whom Ouellette dedicated his 1958 volume *Séquences de l'aile*) and his tenure at CBC's Radio-Canada as a text-writer (1955-1984), the proving ground for his literary vocation. His fully romantic attachment to his wife as a kind of Beatrice in a lived poetic and his rigorously practical commitment to the CBC (evident in his scripts on poetic traditions and trends and on a host of writers ranging from Joyce and Eliot to Tagore and Neruda) seemed to balance each other, somewhat as the seminary and the university had done earlier. This most important year of his life to date, 1955, also marked the first meeting of the Hexagone group and the publication of Ouellette's first collection of poems, *Ces anges de sang*. As the title (Angels of Blood or Angels of Flesh and Blood) indicates, these poems express the poet's struggle against the conventional dualism of mind and body. At the same time, they represent a bloody and violent rebirth (as in "blood angels" or "avenging angels") and a new dawn illuminated by a sun that is at once real and mystical. Ouellette writes of the need "to root the sun in his unconscious in order to believe in life." Whereas one of the first poems, "Citernes de soleil," stresses his "disincarnation," the last poem, "Légende d'un monde vierge," emphasizes his infinite need of air and space, and the collection as whole follows this progression from the despair of making the past not-have-been to the hope of making a world still-to-have-been, Ouellette relying on an inventive technical unity of sound and rhythm, of "sang" and "songes" and "sanglots," of "anges"

and "angoisse" and "louanges," all to give voice to a kind of false hope and to find his own true voice. The idea of a "monde vierge," full of hope, is as unrealizable as virginity is irrecoverable. Nevertheless, the idea persists in its naiveté, as it does in the open-ended conclusion that the youthful Ouellette has given the collection.

In his second book, *Séquences de l'aile* (1958), Ouellette not only glorifies space and the infinite of life and Man, but also lets himself bathe in a second sun: Woman. At this point in his career, he is still trying to achieve through love a Novalis-like fusion with the cosmos of light. Another source of fascination for the poet is the spatial and dissonant music of the Franco-American composer Edgard Varèse (1883-1965), whose exclusively percussive piece "Ionisation" inspired Ouellette to write the four-movement poem "Quatuor climatisé," the poet achieving his own percussive effect "à l'esprit d'Ionisation" through the juxtaposition of harsh and soft, hard and harmonious sounds: "panorama de claxons"; "croissance de corps nickels"; "café moka"; "Le choc des os calfeutre le frais champagne"; "Le temps s'élargit, la tête s'élargit. Mon oeil propulse des aigles!" Through this kind of alliterative dissonance, Ouellette infuses his structurally prosaic assertions with poetic cadenzas, giving them a necessary sense of sprung spontaneity.

In 1959 Ouellette and his contemporary and colleague Jean-Guy Pilon (along with other writers, including André Belleau, Jacques Godbout, Paul-Marie Lapointe, Gilles Hénault, Gaston Miron, Gilles Carle, Jean Filiatrault, and Michel van Schendel) started the bimonthly literary journal and review *Liberté,* which Pilon and van Schendel directed initially and which Ouellette has served as editor and (until the present day) as contributor of numerous articles, most notably "Le Temps des veilleurs" (*Liberté,* January-February 1971), in which he justifies his decision to decline the Governor General's Award. To the degree that *Liberté* has shadowed the politics of Quebec (becoming political during the Quiet Revolution of the 1960s and critical again during the Parti Québecois tenure of the 1970s), it can serve as an accurate barometer of Ouellette's own political and literary climates. During the 1960s *Liberté* was influential in organizing a number of international literary conferences, culminating in 1972 with Ouellette, Pilon, and Belleau setting up the annual Rencontre Québécoise Internationale des Ecrivains, one of Canada's leading symposia for writers.

La <u>Simonetta</u> de Piero di Cosimo

La ~~perle~~ pensive enserre   / pierre
cette femme à collier menaçant,
vipère vive ~~autour de l'ivoire.~~
La nuée s'épand,   si près de l'ivoire.
le soleil palpite
à l'odeur, à la mort secrète.

Sans le parfum de l'orient possible,
le nu du front et du buste,
étrangement allumé par l'ange
depuis la chevelure,
s'éteindrait la plaine du regard.

L'union sera noire
si la lumière se brouille...
Qui se souviendra, après la nuit,
qu'un tel être concentré
(pensée, beauté ascendante),
en tel lieu en tel refuge,
aspirait tout l'horizon.

                    Fernand Ouellette

Revised typescript for one of Ouellette's poems (by permission of the author)

Ouellette's association with L'Hexagone also was personally fruitful; in 1972 the organization published his watershed work *Poésie: Poèmes 1953-1971*, a retrospective (including revisions and some previously unpublished verse) of his first four volumes of poetry, featuring, in addition to *Ces anges de sang* and *Séquences de l'aile*, *Le Soleil sous la mort* (1965) and *Dans le sombre* (1967). In his two volumes from the 1960s, Ouellette reveals his burgeoning political awareness and a kind of malignant melancholy. Several events, personal and national, contributed to the shape of *Le Soleil sous la mort:* his break with institutional Catholicism, at one extreme, the Quiet Revolution and the FLQ (Front de Libération du Québec) events–the surge of history into everyday life– at the other. The poet himself has acknowledged the book's many subjects: "Woman, the quest for collective identity, cinema, war, birds, trees, in short, life." In "50 Mégatonnes," for example, the spiritual within him and the political outside him come absurdly together in a nuclear aftermath: "Le Christ en fusion/s'adosse à l'amour/ Tout lumière il abrase la mort" (Christ in fusion/leans against love/All in light he erodes death). However, in the concluding poem, "Naissance de la paix," Ouellette leans characteristically toward a hope beyond hope: "LA PAIX OUVRE SES PAUPIERES/ET LONGTEMPS FIXE LA MORT" (PEACE OPENS ITS EYELIDS/ AND STARES FOR A LONG TIME AT DEATH). Thus, he suggests, is mankind precariously situated. The poetic sequence of *Le Soleil sous la mort* reflects a tension between sorrow and happiness typical of a poet who, through sensuous and sensual metaphors alike, celebrates the body nurtured by solar joy. *Dans le sombre* offers a more singular vision, centered as it is upon one theme, the sexual life of a couple caught between eroticism and death, a theme that initially caused the poet some problems with censorship. Ouellette celebrates in turn his grasp on life through woman and the erotic power of love, and his strange and incomprehensible death wish. Carnal and spiritual love come together through highly poetic symbolism. Complementing profane poems such as "Débauche," "Volupté," "Extase," "Le Lit," and "Le Couple" are philosophical and theological poems like "L'Immortalité" and "Résurrection" and such youthfully idiosyncratic observations as "L'ange pénétra la pierre" (The angel penetrated the stone) and "Lointainement des soleils fusent et s'engloutissent" (In the distance suns are slowly

burning and swallowing themselves up). Even though Ouellette conjures up the kind of death that envelopes not only men's lives but also the very source of life itself, he does offer the sun as a symbolic shield or comfort, thus sustaining the illusion that the "sombre," or human element, is also a source of mundane illumination. Ouellette's most substantial addition in *Poésie* to his four volumes of poetry is his critical essay "Le Poème et le poétique," in which he offers a confessional poetic based on the interconnectedness of being: "Célébration de l'émergence du poétisable dans toute la vastitude de l'être, de la réalité dans tous ses phénomènes: l'être soleil, l'être pierre, l'être feu, l'être mer, l'être humain s'unifiant dans la relation sexuelle, l'être en propension vers les êtres, l'être déchiré par l'absurde: l'Etre" (Celebration of the emergence of the poetic in all the vastness of being, of reality in all its marvels: the being of sun, stone, fire, sea, the human being unifying itself in the sex act, being inclining toward beings, being rent by the absurd: Being). For *Poésie*, Ouellette was awarded the prestigious France-Canada award. He had received the Prix France-Québec earlier for his biography, *Edgard Varèse* (1966; translated, 1968), the culmination of nearly a decade of work distinguished by his editing *Visages d'Edgard Varèse* (1959) for the Hexagone group and his composing the address for a New York concert in honor of Varèse.

The 1960s were also for Ouellette a decade of intense personal and administrative activity. He traveled several times to Europe and to the United States, took part in several writers' conferences, and sat on a commission inquiring into the teaching of the arts in Quebec. And in 1972 the poet traveled and lectured in Israel. All these activities, prompting as they did observation, self-reflection, and journal-keeping, provided a common basis for three of Ouellette's most important works: his celebrated collection of essays *Les Actes retrouvés* (1970), for which he declined the Governor General's Award; his curiously original *Depuis Novalis, errance et gloses* (1973), revealing his deep interests in Friedrich von Hardenberg (Novalis) and in German romanticism and mystical illumination; and his highly regarded autobiographical account of the spiritual quest recounted earlier in his poetry, *Journal dénoué* (1974), for which he received the *Etudes Françaises* prize. In this personal memoir, the poet reveals the same kind of confessional attitude as in his 1972 *poétique*. In his words, "Parfois le ton est celui d'une confession, parfois

ICI, AILLEURS, LA LUMIÈRE

FERNAND OUELLETTE

L'HEXAGONE

Cover designed by Roland Giguère for Ouellette's 1977 poetry collection

celui d'un journal" (At times the tone is that of a confession, at times that of a diary). He accurately describes the autobiography as an "histoire intérieure" and throughout the work juxtaposes his introspective self and confessional revelations with an empirical perspective of dates, events, places, and names. The work is particularly informative about the two main spheres of his interiority: the circumstances surrounding the composition of his books (including bibliographical details) and the stories behind his correspondence with writers and artists around the world. Ouellette produced another collection of essays in 1979, *Ecrire en notre temps*, exploring the relation of writer and environment, and in particular the imbalance-in-balance of literary aesthetics and a seeming malevolent world.

Since 1975 Ouellette has written six books of poems: *Errances* (1975); *Ici, ailleurs, la lumière* (1977); *A découvert* (1979); *Eveils* (1982); *Les Heures* (1987); and *En la nuit, la mer: Poèmes 1972-1980* (1981), a retrospective consisting of verse from *Ici, ailleurs, la lumière* and *A découvert*, as well as the previously unpublished short poem-sequence "Départs" and the volume-length verse-

progression "En la nuit, la mer." In the 1981 collection, the verse of his early maturity, Ouellette is impressively spare, studied and controlled, giving up some of his early spontaneity for the sake of a finished product and repeatedly exploiting the kind of metaphor and paradox that thrive on opposition (rather than simply reconciling opposites), as in the phrases "des pierres de mémoire" (stones of memory) and "une résonance d'ici" (a resonance of here) and in the lines "La barque s'avance avec le noir/comme une pensée dans la laitance" (The boat moves forward with the dark/like a thought in soft roe) and "Dans une spirale / trace bleue,/tout autour la mort tourne" (In a spiraling/blue trail,/all around death turns). In his verse of the 1970's and early 1980s Ouellette has reached a height of his poetic achievement. But he has also gone on to explore the distant twin peak of prose fiction.

His passage from poetry to the novel is marked by a preoccupation with realistically depicting the human body degraded by age and illness. In Ouellette's first novel, *Tu regardais intensément Geneviève* (1978), the narrator–at once character and audience, a protagonist who, as the title itself suggests, addresses himself in the second person: "Tu arrivas à la maison très vite, encore tout possédé" (You arrived at the house very quickly, still in possession of yourself)–ponders his diary documenting the slow disintegration of his recent marriage, the breakdown resulting mainly from his own inability to commit himself to working with his wife toward reintegrating their shared lives. Stylistically, *Tu regardais intensément Geneviève* suggests more a departure from poetry than a poetic derivation. The novel's editor, François Ricard, rightly called it not "un roman poétique" (a poetic novel) but "une oeuvre d'un réalisme dur, pénétrant, presque intenable . . . " (a work of hard realism, penetrating, almost untenable . . .). Ouellette's second novel, *La Mort vive* (1980), a third-person narrative written partly in the first person as a diary, retraces the mystical quest of a painter who, unable to achieve on earth the perfect fusion of erotic love and art, walks knowingly into a white, fulgurating, hyperborean death. From the title on, Ouellette deliberately suspends his readers in the midst of ambivalence, making them uncertain whether Jean's death is an act of artistic fulfillment and physical transcendence or merely an empty suicide. At the end of the novel, a character gazes through a window at a full moon on a majestic winter night and wonders, uncovering layers of ambiguity, "Je ne sais pas si Jean voit cette lune comme nous, s'il la dessine?" (I don't know if Jean sees that moon as we do, if he draws it?) Even the closing punctuation carries the novel's multiple implications. These qualities of narrative openness and thematic and technical open-endedness are among the most important aspects of Ouellette's fiction, evident also in his third novel, *Lucie, ou un midi en novembre* (1985), which represents yet another quest for the invisible and indivisible, in the form of a conventional narrative interspersed 'with pages from Lucie's diary and excerpts from her correspondence. Somewhat like Jean, Lucie is an artist-quester, a sensuous, mystical painter obsessed with her magnum opus and with death, "her ultimate work of art" and necessary initiation into a world of light and beauty. Ouellette repeatedly designs a kind of untoward world of *towards*, of unbecoming life and coming death.

Documenting the years 1974 to 1980, and stratifying the realities of word, memory, and image, action, dialogue, and movement, the novel represents Quebec in one of the most dynamic periods of its history. Ouellette depicts the simultaneous comings of age of a heroine and of the persons, places, and times she frequents. Comprising one hundred very brief chapters, the narrative offers a kind of shattered-mirror view of an already fragmented world, the author exposing in each sliver of life a different existential sense or aesthetic sensibility. As the narrator confides at the beginning of the story: "(Lisant le journal de Lucie, comme je l'ai fait tant de fois, j'ai l'impression de tout revoir à travers ses yeux. A travers son langage même. A travers sa parole. Je l'entends en moi. Ou parfois je retrouve 'mes mots' dans son journal, mes propres tournures ... Nous avons été par instants tellement imprégnés l'un de l'autre. Il me sera souvent difficile de savoir *qui* écrit . . .)" ([Reading Lucie's journal, as I've done so many times, I have the impression of seeing everything again through her eyes. Through her language even. Through her speech. I hear her in me. Or sometimes I rediscover "my words" in her journal, my own turns of phrase . . . At times we had permeated each other so much. It's often difficult for me to know *who* is writing. . . .]) Ouellette explores this perceptual premise by harmonizing devices of epistolary verisimilitude with tactics of the *nouveau roman*. The result is a technically inventive, stylistically poetic, thematically ambitious novel that grabs us by the wrist and wrestles us through the vicissitudes

of personality to the point that we can almost echo the narrator's concluding remarks: "J'appelle la mort. J'appelle Lucie. Qui pourrais-je appeler? Qui m'écoute?" (I call death. I call Lucie. Whom could I call? Who is listening to me?). In this way Ouellette finally releases us from his grasp, letting us fall into precisely the ontological situation of the narrator, never knowing exactly if we dare to penetrate the fourth wall of rhetoric and answer the queries on which our lives depend. This emphasis on the continuum of questioning is the novel's most impressive thematic and technical accomplishment, suggesting something of the perpetuity of existence and the irresolution of art. *Lucie, ou un midi novembre* received the 1985 Governor General's Award for French-language fiction, a prize that at once honored an excellent novel and acknowledged the phenomenal changes that have occurred both in Quebec and in Ouellette himself since he declined a Governor General's Award fifteen years earlier. History has afforded him not just an opportunity to liberate his country through nonfiction but also a chance to contain it in fiction. Ouellette has proved himself worthy of both tasks.

Through poetry of consistent ingenuity, essays of challenging insight, and fiction of unassuming intelligence, through a poetic, an aesthetic, and an identity pulsating with the tensions of erotic love and ecstatic death, and through his unceasing poetic questioning of language, ideas, media, politics, history, and life itself, Fernand Ouellette has established himself among Quebec's foremost writers and ultimately as a kind of secular priest in a wilderness of words and doubt and delight.

References:

Noël Audet, "Bibliographie des oeuvres de Fernand Ouellette," *Voix et Images*, 5 (Spring 1980): 471-475;

Audet, "L'Irradiation poétique: Entretien avec Fernand Ouellette," *Voix et Images*, 5 (Spring 1980), 435-470;

Audet, "Structure poétique dans l'oeuvre de Fernand Ouellette, " *Voix et Images du Pays*, 3 (1970): 103-124;

Joseph Bonenfant, "Fernand Ouellette, or Poetry as a Search for Wholeness," translated by Jay Bochner, *Ellipse*, 10 (1972): 62-69;

Bonenfant, "Lecture structurale d'un poème de Fernand Ouellette," *La Barre de Jour*, 39-41 (Spring-Summer 1973): 4-25;

Bonenfant, "Principes d'unité dans l'oeuvre de

Fernand Ouellette," *Etudes Littéraires,* 3 (December 1972): 447-461;

Cécile Cloutier, "Fernand Ouellette," *Europe,* 47 (February-March 1969): 170-178;

Edwin Hamblet, "La Poésie québécoise," *Canadian Literature,* 76 (Spring 1977): 93-94;

Gérald Godet, "Le Corps vibrant du désir: Entretiens de Gérald Godet avec Fernand Ouellette," *Lettres Québécoises,* 44 (Winter 1986-1987): 16-21;

Laurent Mailhot, "De la province au pays (1948-1973)," in his *La Littérature québécoise* (Paris: Presses Universitaires de France, 1974), pp. 79-80, 119;

Paul Chanel Malenfant "La Lumière sous l'abîme: Fernand Ouellette," in his *La Partie et le tout: Lecture de Fernand Ouellette et Roland Giguère* (Quebec: Presses de l'Université Laval, 1983), pp. 29-218;

Gilles Marcotte, "Poésie pour nommer," in his *Le Temps des poètes: Description critique de la poésie actuelle au Canada français* (Montreal: HMH, 1969), pp. 151-158;

Robert Marteau, "Un Poète du Québec: Fernand Ouellette," *Esprit* (Paris), 6 (June 1973): 1286-1294;

Axel Maugey, "Etude thématique de l'oeuvre chez dix poètes," in his *Poésie et société au Québec, 1937-1970* (Quebec: Presses de l'Université Laval, 1972), pp. 220-226;

Pierre Nepveu, "Une Poétique de la tension: L'Oeuvre de Fernand Ouellette," in his *Les Mots à l'écoute: Poésie et silence chez Fernand Ouellette, Gaston Miron et Paul-Marie Lapointe* (Quebec: Presses de l'Université Laval, 1979), pp. 21-110;

Jacques Rancourt, "A la recherche de l'être profond: De la Nouvelle-France au Québec," in *La Poésie contemporaine française depuis 1945,* by Rancourt and others (Paris: Bordas, 1973), pp. 544-545, 584-588.

Alice Parizeau
(25 July 1930-   )

Allison Mitcham
Université de Moncton

SELECTED BOOKS: *Voyage en Pologne* (Montreal: Editions du Jour, 1962);

Fuir (Montreal: Déom, 1963);

Survivre (Montreal: Cercle du Livre de France, 1964);

Une Québécoise en Europe "rouge" (Montreal: Fides, 1965);

Rue Sherbrooke ouest (Montreal: Cercle du Livre de France, 1967);

L'Adolescent et la société, by Parizeau, Denis Szabo, and Denis Gagné (Brussels: Dessart, 1972);

Ces jeunes qui nous font peur, by Parizeau and Marc-André Delilse (Montreal: Ferron, 1974);

Les Militants (Montreal: Cercle du Livre de France, 1974);

L'Envers de l'enfance (Montreal: La Presse, 1976);

Le Traitement de la criminalité au Canada, by Parizeau and Szabo (Montreal: Presses de l'Université de Montréal, 1977); translated, revised, and edited by Dorothy Crelinsten as *The Canadian Criminal-Justice System* (Lexington, Massachusetts: Lexington Books, 1977);

Protection de l'enfant, éche? Famille, état de droits de l'enfance (Montreal: Presses de l'Université de Montreal, 1979); translated by Crelinsten as *Parenting and Delinquent Youth* (New York: Lexington Books, 1980);

Les Lilas fleurissent à Varsovie (Montreal: Pierre Tisseyre, 1981); translated by A. D. Martin-Sperry as *The Lilacs are Blooming in Warsaw* (New York: New American Library, 1985);

La Charge des sangliers (Montreal: Pierre Tisseyre, 1982);

Côte des neiges (Montreal: Pierre Tisseyre, 1983);

Ils se sont connus à Lwow (Montreal: Pierre Tisseyre, 1985).

PERIODICAL PUBLICATIONS: "Les Solitudes humaines," *Ecrits du Canada Français*, no. 12 (1962): 277-305;

"Demain," *Châtelaine*, 6 (February 1965): 24-25, 38-43;

"Une drôle de fille," *Châtelaine*, 6 (September

photograph by Kèro

1965): 34, 110-112, 114-116, 120-122, 124, 126;

"Elzéar Bédard, premier maire de Québec," *La Presse* (magazine supplement), 82 (5 March 1966): 14, 16-17;

"Gabrielle Roy, la grande romancière canadienne," *Châtelaine*, 7 (April 1966): 44-45, 118, 120-123, 137, 140;

"Le Musée du Québec, une véritable maison de la culture," *Vie des Arts*, no. 47 (1967): 34-39;

"Le Système canadien de probation," *Revue de Droit Pénal et de Criminologie*, nos. 6 & 7 (1970): 637-646.

Alice Parizeau's publications reflect her various careers as journalist, novelist, and lawyer, as

291

well as her preoccupation with three countries, Poland, where she was born and lived until 1945, France, where she lived and studied from 1945 to 1953, and Canada, where she has lived since 1955.

Because her experiences during her formative years were so different from those of most Canadians, it is hardly surprising that Parizeau does not fit neatly into the tradition of either Quebec or Canadian literature. Doubtless this has much to do with Parizeau's background. She was born Alice Poznanska, 25 July 1930, in Poland. Her father, Stanilaus Poznanski, was an industrialist, her mother, Bronislawa Poznanska, a concert pianist. She was, even as a seven-year-old child, involved in the Polish underground. A considerable portion of her childhood and adolescence was spent amid the horrors of wartime Europe and in the German concentration camp Bergen-Belsen. When liberated from the camp, she went to Paris where she pursued her studies, receiving a *baccalauréat ès lettres* in 1948 and a certificate in political science and a degree in law in 1953. It was about this time that her uncle, who was already established in Quebec, persuaded her to come to Canada, where she remained. Her publications began to appear several years later. In 1976 she married Jacques Parizeau, an outspoken, high-profile economist and politician, at one time Quebec's finance minister.

Representative of her career as journalist are her early travel books, *Voyage en Pologne* (1962) and *Une Québécoise en Europe "rouge"* (1965), as well as magazine articles on such diverse topics as the first mayor of Quebec, the Quebec museum, and the work of Gabrielle Roy. In *Une Québécoise en Europe "rouge"* Parizeau frequently compares life in Poland in the mid 1960s with life in Canada (specifically Quebec) during this era. In this book, as in several of her novels, Canada is identified as a kind of utopia—"un pays de cocagne," to use her phrase. Whereas *Voyage en Pologne* received mixed reviews, *Une Québécoise en Europe "rouge"* tended to be unfavorably received. Henri Dorion, professor at the Institute de Géographie at Université Laval, reviewing the book for *Livres et Auteurs Canadiens* in 1965, faulted it for incorrect information, excessive generalizations, and wrong comparisons. Dorion made these observations on the basis of his theoretical knowledge of Poland and his two-year sojourn there.

Of Parizeau's first four novels—*Fuir* (1963), *Survivre* (1964), *Rue Sherbrooke ouest* (1967), and

Les Militants (1974)—the first is set in France; the second, in Poland; the third, in Canada, with many flashbacks to Poland; the last, chiefly in Canada. These novels are conventional in form and tone. In *Fuir* the protagonist, Paule, who has been living in a provincial French town for the last ten years with her husband Henri, and their three sons, returns to Paris, where she had been a student some ten years earlier. On this short vacation, she visits the Sorbonne where she had studied law, and she also encounters a former close friend, Guy, who still loves her. Her Paris sojourn makes her question her own dull bourgeois existence and leads her eventually to take a job practicing law. Though all appears to go well for Paule at first, she learns that her husband, who is a notary, has been losing his clientele because they do not approve of his wife's working. The situation is complicated by the fact that Paule has implicated herself, because of her idealistic and somewhat naive intentions, in a scheme to free a falsely accused convicted murderer. Seeing no way out of the quagmire, Paule commits suicide by drowning herself in the Seine. Henri and the children leave for Canada.

Critics dealt harshly with *Fuir*, and one tends to agree with Léandre Bergeron's observation in *Livres et Auteurs Canadiens* (1963) that, if one judges by *Fuir*, the novel has not changed since Flaubert's time. Indeed the book which Paule reads with such absorption in the hotel room in Paris is *Madame Bovary*.

Survivre is exciting and well written, the sort of story of survival and subterfuge during the war in occupied Europe that has already been the subject of many books and movies, but it adds little to the genre. Yves, the protagonist, the son of a wealthy and privileged Polish industrialist, experiences most of the horrors which the Russians and the German Gestapo can provide, including the torture and death of his parents. Like Parizeau herself, Yves, who spends the final days of the war in a German prisoner-of-war camp, survives all these miseries.

Survivre is chiefly interesting as the antecedent of *Rue Sherbrooke ouest*, in which Yves is again a major character, this time an immigrant to Canada. This is Parizeau's best novel, though not the most popular with readers. In *Rue Sherbrooke ouest*, there are many good short scenes, some of them quite moving. The novel invites comparison with several significant Canadian novels which focus on the plight of the immigrant to Canada—books such as Henry Kreisel's *The Betrayal* (1964)

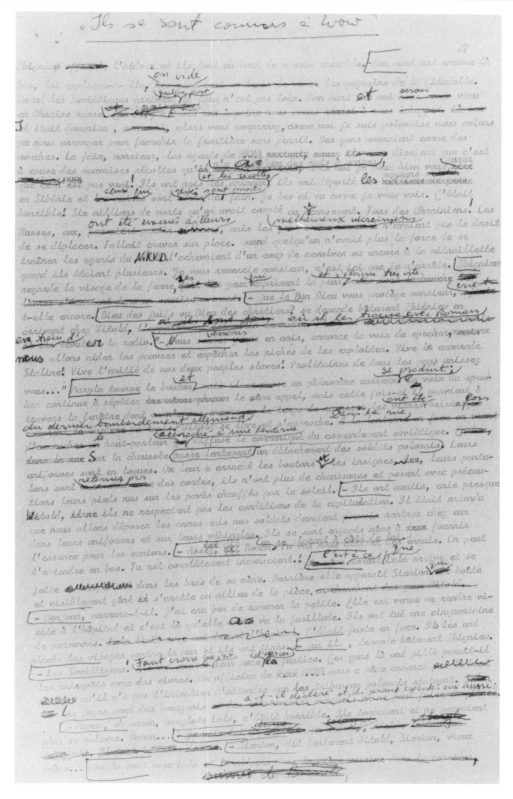

Page from the revised typescript for Ils se sont connus à Lwow, *Parizeau's 1985 novel about sociopolitical conditions in Poland and their effect on individual lives (by permission of the author)*

and Yves Thériault's *Amour au goût de mer* (1961) and *Aaron* (1954). Parizeau's next novel, *Les Militants* (1974), espouses the cause of Quebec nationalism, but it reads more like a *roman à thèse* than as a dramatization of real human situations.

In 1972 Parizeau was appointed Secretaire Générale du Centre International de Criminologie Comparée at the Université de Montréal. Many of her publications during the 1970s were related to her university position: books of a legal nature such as *Le Traitement de la criminalité au Canada* (1977), written in collaboration with Denis Szabo, and those with legal and sociological implications, such as *L'Envers de l'enfance* (1976), a volume examining case histories.

In Parizeau's most recent four novels, she turns again to narratives of her homeland. While she has not ignored her adopted country (especially in *Côte des neiges*, 1983), her primary concern in *Les Lilas fleurissent à Varsovie* (1981), its sequel *La Charge des sangliers* (1982), and *Ils se sont connus à Lwow* (1985) is the character of sociopolitical conditions in Poland and their effect upon individual lives. *Les Lilas fleurissent à Varsovie* attracted wide praise and many readers when it appeared, winning the Prix Européen for the best French novel of the year written by a writer whose first language is not French. When it appeared in English in 1985, translated by A. D. Martin-Sperry and published by New American Library, it again attracted an enthusiastic readership. (The book jacket carried encomia from Liv Ullmann—"A moving document"—and Eugene Ionesco—"One of the best novels I have had the pleasure of reading in many years.") The sense of the novel *as a document* is important. This novel, like Parizeau's other works, employs many conventional techniques of plotting and romantic characterization, yet it was read for its historicity. The popularity of the novel may well—in years when the Solidarity Movement was redefining Polish politics and preoccupying the world press—relate directly to its subject.

In a straightforward sequence of eleven chapters, *Les Lilas fleurissent à Varsovie* tells the intertwined stories of several characters—priest, medical student, young girl, wife torn between husband and lover—all of whom are pressured vengefully by the civil and military authorities. Picking up the stories in the aftermath of World War II, when the Polish fields were mined by the retreating armies, consequently maiming civilians as they tried to return to normal lives, the novel is most concerned with showing how a sequential set of pressures in Poland's modern history ultimately results in the cause of Solidarity. Resistance, says the book, is inevitable and an authoritarian regime always ultimately insecure. Despite the hopeful signs at the end of the book, which suggest the human capacity for survival and reconciliation against uneven odds, the pressures do not cease. "Life here in Poland," observes one character, "consists of never forgetting what's feasible and what isn't!" Other characters, however, continue to talk of uprising and dream of independence—which for Parizeau, of course, is a contemporary sociopolitical cause in Quebec as well as in Poland. It is possible to read the novel as an elaborate Quebecois allegory, therefore, but it nonetheless remains a romantic allegory, a popular fiction. The didactic method of Parizeau's stories, together with her style and conventional methods of characterization, continue to win her a readership; they also continue to place her on the margins of modern Quebecois literature.

Jean-Guy Pilon
(12 November 1930-   )

Jeannette Urbas
York University

BOOKS: *La Fiancée du matin* (Montreal: Editions Amicitia, 1953);

Les Cloîtres de l'été (Montreal: Editions de l'Hexagone, 1954);

L'Homme et le jour (Montreal: Editions de l'Hexagone, 1957);

La Mouette et le large (Montreal: Editions de l'Hexagone, 1960);

Recours au pays (Montreal: Editions de l'Hexagone, 1961);

Pour saluer une ville (Paris: Seghers/Montreal: HMH, 1963);

Solange (Montreal: Editions du Jour, 1966);

Comme eau retenue, poèmes 1954-1963 (Montreal: Editions de l'Hexagone, 1969);

Saisons pour la continuelle (Paris: Seghers, 1969);

Silences pour une souveraine (Ottawa: Editions de l'Université d'Ottawa, 1972);

Comme eau retenue, poèmes 1954-1977 (Montreal: Editions de l'Hexagone, 1986).

OTHER: *Poetry 62/Poésie 62*, edited by Pilon and Eli Mandel (Toronto: Ryerson, 1962);

Poèmes 70, edited by Pilon (Montreal: Editions de l'Hexagone, 1970);

Poèmes 71, edited by Pilon (Montreal: Editions de l'Hexagone, 1972).

PERIODICAL PUBLICATIONS: "Réflexions sur la poésie américaine," *Liberté,* 7 (July-August 1965): 390;

"Trois propositions," *Le Devoir,* 30 October 1965, p. 37;

"Appolinaire vu par 'Les Cahiers du Sud,' " *Le Devoir,* 9 June 1966, p. 6;

"Paris et le roman canadien," *Le Devoir,* 27 October 1966, p. 12;

"L'Anthologie de la poésie canadienne," *Le Devoir,* 19 December 1966, p. 11;

"Qu'est-ce que la poésie féminine?," *Le Devoir,* 24 December 1966, p. 10;

"Poésie," *Le Devoir,* 11 February 1967, p. 14;

"Une sorte de mythe," *Cité Libre,* 32 (Spring 1967): 79-80;

"Dix phrases pour Jérusalem," *Estuaire,* 6 (December 1977): 95-102.

As early as 1954 Jean-Guy Pilon defined his poetic goals as follows: "Notre vie à retenir, le poids de la mort à dépasser," holding on to life, overtaking the weight of death. His contribution to Quebec poetry has taken two forms: his own poetic production and the leadership he gave to two important literary groups, the young writers of Editions de l'Hexagone and those associated with the magazine *Liberté*. His activities, especially as a leader, have placed him in the center of contemporary poetic activity in Canada.

Born in 1930 to Arthur and Alida Besner Pilon, at Saint-Polycarpe, Quebec, Pilon studied law at the University of Montreal, from which he graduated in 1954. In 1959 he founded the magazine *Liberté* with some of his friends, including Jacques Godbout. He also became literary director of Editions de l'Hexagone where he began the series Les Matinaux. Since 1960 he has supervised literary broadcasts at Radio-Canada.

Pilon has initiated periodic meetings of poets and writers and has participated in a number of European poetry colloquies. In 1967 he was one of the principal organizers of an international gathering of poets at Expo in Montreal. In 1972 he founded La Rencontre Québécoise Internationale des Ecrivains. He has traveled widely, especially in France and Latin America. In 1967 he was elected a member of the Royal Society of Canada. In 1981 he became a member of the Académie Canadienne-française; he was chosen as president of the academy in 1982.

According to Pilon in *La Poésie canadienne-française,* volume four of *Archives des lettres canadiennes-françaises:* "Ma poésie n'a jamais été, je crois, intellectuelle. Je l'imagine toute simple, charnelle, à ras des mots et de la réalité. Des choses et des êtres. Un éclair tout autant sur soi-même que projeté hors de moi" (My poetry has never been, I think, intellectual. I imagine it to be very simple, sensual, close to the words and real-

Jean-Guy Pilon

ity it expresses. To things and people. A flash that illuminates me within as well as a projection outside myself). His themes are constant. He writes about nature and about man and society. The image of woman is everywhere present, in continual interaction with nature. He celebrates the joy and regeneration of love and accepts the existence of a divine order in the universe. His poetry does not seek the resolution of inner conflicts nor does it question the world. His style includes the regular verse of *Les Cloîtres de l'été* (1954); the lyric almost proselike flights characteristic of *Recours au pays* (1961); and the unadorned verse, stripped to essentials, of one of his later poems, "Dix phrases pour Jérusalem" (1977).

Pilon's verse has been influenced by his compatriot Alain Grandbois as well as by the French poet René Char, who wrote the preface for Pilon's second collection, *Les Cloîtres de l'été*, published one year after *La Fiancée du matin* (1953). *Les Cloîtres de l'été* consists of nineteen poems, untitled, notable for the simplicity and clarity of the language. The major theme is the opposition between life and death. The poet rejects the past

which he perceives as an absence of life, a source of shame, anger, and humiliation, to focus on the intensity of the present and turn with hope to the future. This theme of rupture with the past occurs frequently in the works of the poets of the Hexagone. The large number of religious terms in *Les Cloîtres l'été* reflects the influence of the Quebecois Catholicism on the poet who refuses to be bound by a narrow and stultifying view of religion.

Pilon's third book, *L'Homme et le jour* (1957), has as a primary theme the joy of paternity and the extension of being it represents, of existence beyond oneself. In *La Mouette et le large*, published in 1960, the child, growing in independence, has become the poet's friend, "Mon ami mon enfant," but he is still closer to the world of physical beauty–"la fraîcheur d'un caillou," "les jeux d'un oiseau"–than his father, who is bound by "la parole encombrante." The adult represents reason and intellect, the child emotion and spontaneity, "la vie inconsciente." In the same collection the poem "Incendie" points to the poet's growing love of *le pays*, Quebec, and the desire to rebuild it in a new image. He has grown tired of the

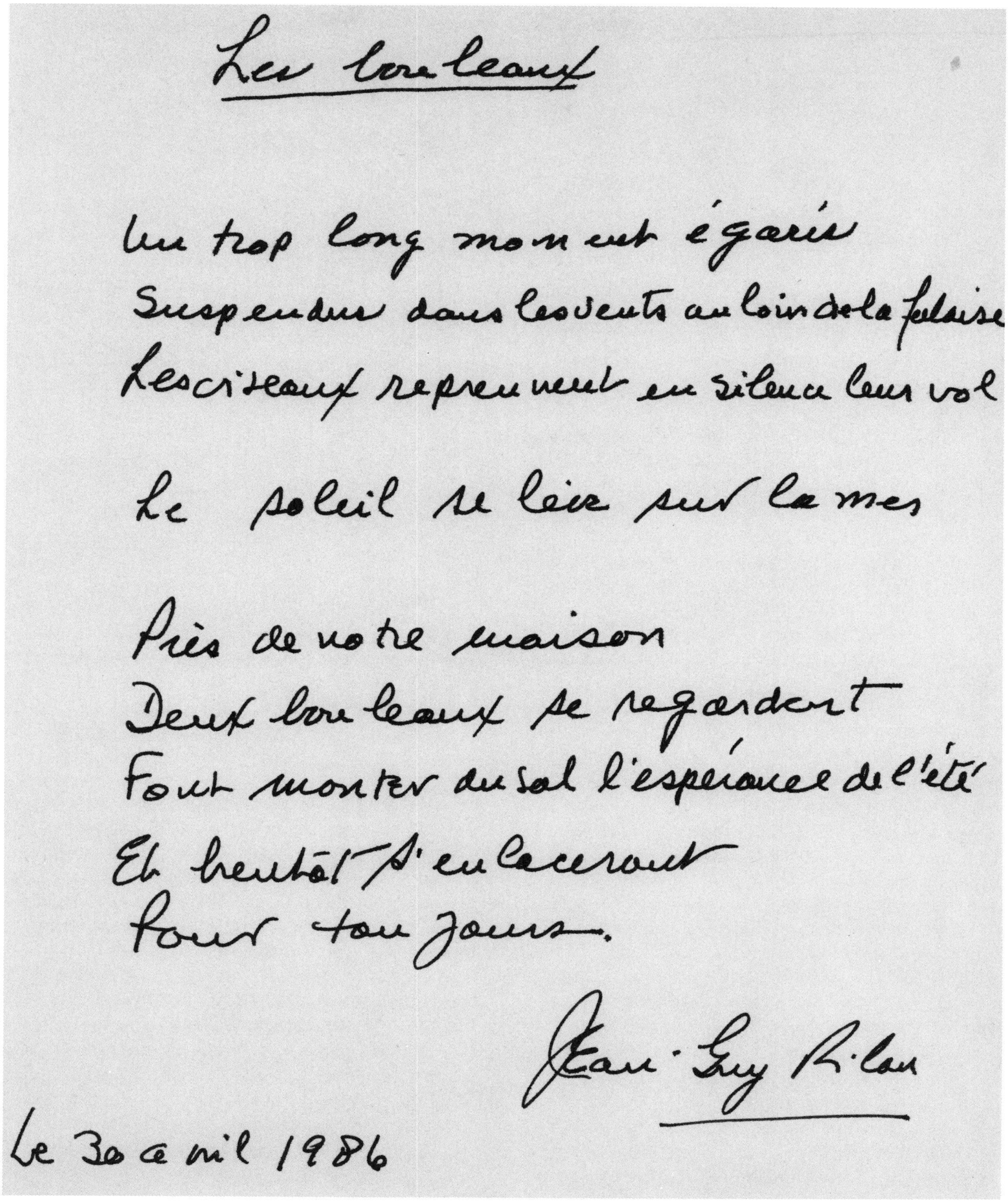

Les bouleaux

Un trop long moment égaré
Suspendu dans les vents au loin de la falaise
Les oiseaux reprennent en silence leur vol

Le soleil se lève sur la mer

Près de notre maison
Deux bouleaux se regardent
Font monter du sol l'espérance de l'été
Et bientôt s'enlaceront
Pour toujours.

Jean-Guy Pilon

Le 30 avril 1986

Fair copy of a poem by Pilon (by permission of the author)

search for exotic things—rare woods, delicate, fragile flowers—and rejects the past in order to start anew.

La Mouette et le large marks a turning point in Pilon's poetry as he moved from purely personal lyricism to ally himself with the collective needs of the Quebecois, which came to the fore in the 1960s, a period of ebullient nationalism and sociocultural struggle. In *Recours au pays*, published in 1961, Pilon's themes are those common to the poets of the 1960s in Quebec: love of country; rebuilding and rebirth; identification of the country with a beloved woman, possession of the one being also possession of the other; despair over the past and hope for the future; the power of language, naming, to overcome alienation and recreate reality. In *Le Temps des poètes* (1970) Gilles Marcotte, referring to "Poèmes pour maintenant" in the 1963 volume *Pour saluer une ville*, assesses Pilon's efforts: "Jean-Guy Pilon fera retentir des accents plus affirmatifs, mais décidément le clairon n'est pas son instrument. Les meilleurs, parmi ses poèmes patriotiques—employons cet adjectif, faute d'en trouver un moins éclatant—sont ceux qui, sur le mode mineur, demandent au pays de se conformer à l'image du bonheur, d'être le premier espace d'une liberté sans frontières. Cet immense pays qui est le sien, Pilon le voit comme un vide à remplir, comme un appel attendant réponse . . ." (Jean-Guy Pilon sounds more positive notes, but decidely the clarion is not his instrument. The best, among his patriotic poems—let us use this adjective for lack of finding a less ringing one—are those which, in the minor mode, ask the country to shape itself in the image of happiness, to be the first terrain of a liberty without frontiers. Pilon sees this immense country of his as an emptiness to be filled, a cry awaiting a response . . .).

In *Recours au pays*, *le pays* is equated with a woman, and the love for one mingles with the love for the other. Snow and ice imagery express rigidity and lack of promise in the past. The poet sees himself as a divided man, in conflict, pulled in different directions. "Nomme. . .," the poem that deals with the naming of things, is central to the collection. In the process of giving names to objects, to one's love and hatred, to the many facets of *le pays*, knowledge and understanding will come. The poet will no longer be a stranger to himself, to his own body, to his country. Language—"Naître à la parole," in Pilon's words—will conquer alienation.

The "Poèmes pour maintenant" of *Pour*

JEAN-GUY PILON • POUR SALUER UNE VILLE

seghers paris
h.m.h. montréal

Cover for one of Pilon's poetry volumes inspired by the nationalism and sociocultural struggle of 1960s Quebec

saluer une ville are in the same vein as those of *Recours au pays*, but to words and feelings action has been added: "Bâtir." In the poem "Je murmure. . .," which has appeared in anthologies both in French and in English translation, the poet begins by expressing his shame and the bitter humiliation of the past but moves out of anguish into "un jour de soleil et de grand vent" in the future: "Nous ouvrirons des bras nouveaux / Sur une terre habitable / Sans avoir honte d'en dire le nom / Qui ne sera plus murmuré / Mais proclamé" ("We shall open our arms again / On a habitable land / Without being ashamed to speak its name / Which will no longer be murmured / But proclaimed"; translation by Fred Cogswell in his *The Poetry of Modern Quebec*, 1976).

In 1969 Editions de l'Hexagone brought out *Comme eau retenue*, a collection of Pilon's poems published from 1954 to 1963 for which he won a Governor General's Award. Also in 1969 Pilon produced *Saisons pour la continuelle*. His next book, *Silences pour une souveraine*, with illustrations by Betty Idelson, appeared in 1972 and was not favourably received. In 1977 the manuscript of the poem "Dix phrases pour Jérusalem" was deposited in the Mishkenot Sha'ananim library in Jerusalem. The poem was published in the magazine *Estuaire* in December of the same year. In 1986 Editions de l'Hexagone published an enlarged edition of *Comme eau retenue*, which includes poems that first appeared from 1963 to 1977. In his introduction to the 1986 volume Roger Chamberland comments on the effectiveness of the title *Comme eau retenue* for Pilon's retrospective ensemble. Water conveys the idea of transparency, the essence of things, which takes form in words, and water that is restrained, held back in its course, produces a cascade of new poetic images.

In addition to the Governor General's Award, Pilon has won the Prix David for poetry (1956), the Prix Louise-Labé (Paris) and the Prix France-Canada (both in 1969), and the Prix Athanase-David (1984) for the entire body of his work. He has also published a novel, *Solange* (1966).

Although Pilon's books were published steadily in the 1950s and early 1960s, since 1963 his works have appeared less frequently. The diminution of his poetic output would indicate that the pressure of other responsibilities in the literary community leaves little time for writing poetry. While it is certain that his verse will continue to hold a place of importance in Quebec literature, it is possible that in the future his contributions will be measured more in terms of his work at Radio-Canada, in the publishing field, and as critic and surveyor of the literary scene.

References:

Jacques Blais, "Jean-Guy Pilon," *Europe,* no. 478-479 (February-March 1969): 163-169;

Axel Maugey, "Jean-Guy Pilon," in his *Poésie et Société au Québec (1937-1970)* (Quebec: Presses de l'Université Laval, 1972), pp. 164-171;

Michel van Schendel, "Cette poésie qu'on lit si peu," in *Présence de la Critique,* edited by Gilles Marcotte (Montreal: HMH, 1966), pp. 201-202.

Sharon Pollock
(19 April 1936-)

Paul Matthew St. Pierre
University of British Columbia

BOOKS: *Walsh* (Vancouver: Talonbooks, 1973; revised 1974);

The Komagata Maru Incident (Toronto: Playwrights Co-op, 1978);

Blood Relations and Other Plays (Edmonton: NeWest Press, 1981); includes *One Tiger to a Hill* and *Generations;*

Doc (Toronto: Playwrights Canada, 1986).

PLAY PRODUCTIONS: *A Compulsory Option*, Vancouver, New Play Centre, August 1972;

Walsh, Calgary, Theatre Calgary, 7 November 1973; revised, Stratford, Ontario, Third Stage at the Stratford Festival, Summer 1974;

New Canadians, Vancouver, Playhouse Holiday, 1973;

Superstition Throu' the Ages, Vancouver, Playhouse Holiday, 1973;

Wudjesay?, Vancouver, Playhouse Holiday, 1974;

The Happy Prince, Vancouver, Playhouse Theatre School, 1974;

The Rose and the Nightingale, Vancouver, Playhouse Theatre School, 1974;

Star-child, Vancouver, Playhouse Theatre School, 1974;

The Great Drag Race or Smoked, Choked and Croaked, British Columbia Christmas Seal Society commission for production in British Columbia secondary schools, 1974;

Lessons in Swizzlery, New Westminster, British Columbia, Caravan Theatre touring ensemble, 1974;

And Out Goes You, Vancouver, Vancouver Playhouse, March 1975;

The Komagata Maru Incident, Vancouver, Vancouver Playhouse at the Vancouver East Cultural Centre, 20 January 1976;

My Name Is Lisabeth, New Westminster, British Columbia, Douglas College, March 1976;

Tracings—The Fraser Story, by Pollock and others, Edmonton, Theatre Network, 1977;

The Wreck of the National Line Car, Calgary, Alberta Theatre Projects, 1978;

Chautauqua Spelt E-N-E-R-G-Y, Calgary, Alberta Theatre Projects, 1979;

Sharon Pollock

Mail vs. Female, Calgary, Lunchbox Theatre, March 1979;

One Tiger to a Hill, Edmonton, Citadel Theatre, February 1980; revised, Lennoxville, Quebec, Festival Lennoxville, Summer 1980; New York, Manhattan Theatre Club, November 1980;

Blood Relations, Edmonton, Theatre Three, 12 March 1980;

Generations, Calgary, Alberta Theatre Projects at Canmore Opera House, 28 October 1980;

Whiskey Six, Calgary, Theatre Calgary, 1983;

Doc, Calgary, Theatre Calgary, April 1984; revised, Toronto, Toronto Free Theatre, September 1984;
Family Trappings, Fredericton, Theatre New Brunswick, March 1986.

TELEVISION: *Portrait of a Pig,* CBC-Winnipeg, 1973;
The Larsens, CBC-Winnipeg, 1976;
Ransom, in the series *The Magic Lie,* CBC-Edmonton, 1976;
Country Joy, by Pollock and others, CBC-national network, 1979-1980.

RADIO: *A Split Second in the Life Of,* CBC, 22 November 1970;
31 for 2, CBC, 7 February 1971;
We to the Gods, CBC, 5 September 1971;
Walsh, CBC, 1974;
Generation, CBC, 10 December 1978;
Sweet Land of Liberty, CBC, 2 December 1979;
Intensive Care, CBC, 5 June 1983;
Whiskey Six, CBC, 22 October 1983;
One Tiger to a Hill, CBC, 8 December 1985.

Sharon Pollock is one of a growing number of Canadian writers who reach readers and audiences in imaginatively and strikingly unconventional manners. In her particular case, artistic diversity and originality have arisen out of a series of vocational contradictions. As a playwright, she has received greater critical recognition on the stage than in print, the majority of her plays having yet to find the publication, and the minority the production, they deserve. She has developed her craft as a writer through acting and through stagecraft, rather than through strictly literary and compositional means. She has reached even greater audiences on the radio (as with *Sweet Land of Liberty,* which received a 1980 ACTRA award for best radio drama) and through television (as with her writing for *Country Joy,* which received national exposure on the CBC in 1979-1980) than she has in the theater, the stage of her artistic success. At the beginning of her tenure in the theater and throughout the formative stages of her career, Pollock developed a subtle talent for dealing with historical subject matter through documentary techniques, yet in recent years she has addressed herself to more personal material through more intimate (and less intimidating) methods. As a writer she is prolific, as an author somewhat unprolific, partly because of the exigencies of publishing drama in Canada,

but mainly because she is a playwright with her mind's eye on the stage and only her natural eye on a first folio. In this respect she is more accurately a dramatist than a playwright, more a creator of drama than a maker of scripts.

Born in 1936 in Fredericton, New Brunswick, where her father, Everett Chalmers, was a physician and a politician, Mary Sharon Chalmers grew up in the Eastern townships of Quebec, returning to her birthplace for two productive years at the University of New Brunswick, where she distinguished herself mainly by setting in motion her career as an actor and a director and beginning her apprenticeship as a playwright. In Fredericton and later in Calgary (as a member of the semiprofessional Prairie Players, a touring company of MAC 14, the forerunner of Theatre Calgary), she enthusiastically participated in amateur theater. Her success in the theater is largely associated with the province of Alberta, where she has taught play writing and written plays at both the University of Alberta and the Banff School of Fine Arts. In 1954 she quit her program at U.N.B. to marry Ross Pollock, but, although they had five children together, the marriage eventually failed. Pollock moved to Calgary in 1971 and wrote her first play, *A Compulsory Option* (a two-act dark-comic farce about male cohabitation), which won her the 1971 Alberta Playwriting Competition and which was premiered in 1972 (and made available in script form the following year) by the New Play Centre of Vancouver. Upon this auspicious foundation, Pollock went on to develop her characteristic sardonic tones and historical foci, beginning with her second play, *Walsh,* written in 1972 and 1973 and produced on CBC radio in 1974. This two-act dramatic slice-of-history was premiered in 1973 by Theatre Calgary and produced in a revised version the following year by the Third Stage of the Stratford Festival. The play found its most prestigious audience in 1983 in a production at the National Arts Centre in Ottawa. Focusing on the dramatic setting and period of Chief Sitting Bull's four-year Canadian exile after the battle at Little Big Horn, the play helped to establish through public exposure and acceptance (specifically at Stratford) Pollock's concern with deeply Canadian historical incidents—especially with oppressed historical characters and characters oppressed by history itself. *Walsh,* in its original version, was published by Talonbooks of Vancouver in 1973. The revised version appeared in 1974.

Pollock has never lost her original flair for comic and light drama, however. In 1973 and 1974 she wrote a total of eight children's plays, most of them in cooperation with director Don Shipley of the Vancouver Theatre School and with the theater-in-education program of Playhouse Holiday, Vancouver. Following these fanciful and romantic works for elementary- and secondary-school children, she wrote a soberly contemporary two-act comedy satirizing partisan posturing and exchanges of power in the British Columbia political system. This play, *And Out Goes You*, was produced in 1975 at the Vancouver Playhouse by Christopher Newton, whom Pollock had met earlier at Theatre Calgary. Amid the vicissitudes of British Columbia politics, the play has managed to remain timely for over a decade.

In January 1976, at the Vancouver East Cultural Centre, the Playhouse's New Company produced one of Pollock's most strikingly original and historically perceptive plays, *The Komagata Maru Incident*, a long one-act drama holding up to ridicule the racist attitudes of the Canadian government and people toward a boatload of Sikh immigrants ultimately refused entry into Canada in 1914, despite the fact that, as British subjects, they were entitled to enter the country. Based on a historical incident, the play has grown in significance and recognition along with the growth of Vancouver's politically vocal and volatile Sikh community, and at its most recent production (at the Grand Theatre in London, Ontario, in April 1987), it assumed greater poignancy and perspicacity in the aftermath of the still unresolved 1985 terrorist bombing of an Air India plane carrying Indo-Canadians to India. But, topical as the play has turned out to be, it is even more important in that it marks Pollock's professional transition from an apprentice playwright to a kind of journeyman dramatist.

As her dramatic and literary skills were maturing during the 1970s, Pollock was also writing a series of thirty- and sixty-minute radio plays for regional and national broadcast by the Canadian Broadcasting Corporation (including for the CBC's national network: *A Split Second in the Life Of, 31 for 2, We to the Gods, Generation,* and *Sweet Land of Liberty*), as well as television scripts for CBC-Winnipeg (*Portrait of a Pig* and *The Larsens*), and CBC-Edmonton (*Ransom* and, with other writers, the *Country Joy* series).

The earliest indication of Pollock's professional maturity came in 1976 with the appearance of her first truly full-length play, *My Name*

Is Lisabeth (which would prove to be an early draft version of *Blood Relations*), produced at the New Westminster campus of Douglas College, with the playwright herself playing the title role of Lizzie Borden. In the same year Pollock returned briefly to Calgary, reestablishing her professional ties with Theatre Calgary and forming an important relationship with its artistic director, Rick McNair. From there she went on to Edmonton to become a visiting lecturer in the drama department at the University of Alberta (1976-1981), to the Banff School of Fine Arts to become leader of the Playwrights' Colony (1977-1979), to Calgary's Alberta Theatre Projects to become playwright in residence (1977-1979), to the National Theatre School in Ottawa to sit on the advisory committee (1979-1980), to the Canada Council to become chairman of the Arts Advisory Council (1978-1981), to Ottawa's National Arts Centre to become artist in residence (1981-1983). She subsequently renewed her association with Theatre Calgary and was the company's resident dramaturge and associate artistic director during the 1983-1984 season (in 1983 directing Joe Orton's play *What the Butler Saw*). She became Rick McNair's successor as artistic director (for just four months in 1984, after which she resigned over administrative differences). Pollock currently has a free-lance arrangement with Theatre Calgary. All these positions have helped to support her increasing writing for the stage, but more important they have motivated Pollock to assume a role of leadership in the dramatic and artistic communities of Western Canada.

One Tiger to a Hill, Blood Relations, and *Generations,* Pollock's full-length dramas following *My Name Is Lisabeth,* premiered in 1980 and were published collectively as *Blood Relations and Other Plays* in 1981, adding social and familial verisimilitude to the kind of historicity highlighted in *The Komagata Maru Incident.* Based on an actual hostage-taking incident at the British Columbia Penitentiary in 1975, in which a social worker was fatally shot by guards attempting to free her, *One Tiger to a Hill* is a biting indictment of prison brutality and a studied shriek for prison reform. The play was first performed in 1980 at Edmonton's Citadel Theatre, under the direction of Richard Ouzounian, and later that year at Festival Lennoxville and at New York's Manhattan Theatre Club. It is a study of character and especially of the distortions character undergoes through situation, as in the protagonist Dede Walker's climactic outpouring of love for her cap-

The Komagata Maru, a steamer carrying East Indian immigrants, sailed into Vancouver harbour in 1914. The months that followed were a nightmare of deprivation and suffering for its 376 passengers, who were refused entry by racist immigration officials.

THE KOMAGATA MARU INCIDENT is a dramatic depiction of this appalling event, and a kaleidoscope of scenes directed by a carnival barker traces the explosive prejudices of early Vancouver. The immigration official, his informers, brothel lover, and an East Indian woman representing the Komagata Maru victims all spin in and out of the spotlight.

THE KOMAGATA MARU INCIDENT is a brilliantly imaginative and searing portrayal of a shameful and hidden chapter in Canadian history.

Winner of the Governor General's Award for BLOOD RELATIONS in 1982, **Sharon Pollock** has written numerous plays for the stage, radio and TV. Her plays have been produced by theatres across Canada, including the Stratford Festival, The National Arts Centre, Edmonton's Citadel, Theatre Calgary and the Vancouver Playhouse. Pollock has been playwright-in-residence at the National Arts Centre and Alberta Theatre Projects as well as Artistic Director and Dramaturge at Theatre Calgary. She was head of the Banff Centre Playwrights Colony for four years.

Pollock's full-length plays include DOC, WALSH, A COMPULSORY OPTION, ONE TIGER TO A HILL, BLOOD RELATIONS, THE KOMAGATA MARU INCIDENT and WHISKEY SIX CADENZA. She has also written a number of children's plays. Sharon Pollock lives in Calgary.

Front cover photo: Veena Sood, Michael Ball, Guy Bannerman, Paddy Campanaro and John Hamelin in the 1979 Alberta Theatre Projects production of THE KOMAGATA MARU INCIDENT.

Front cover photo by Peter Gerrie
Cover design by Lisa Dimson

PLAYWRIGHTS CANADA $4.95

Covers for the 1985 edition of Pollock's long one-act drama first produced by the Vancouver Playhouse in January 1976

tor Tommy Paul, despite the state of terror into which he has forced her. In its treatment of characters in crisis and in its emphasis on emotional judgment, this play is among Pollock's most dramatic.

Her most acclaimed play, *Blood Relations*, had its premiere at Edmonton's Theatre Three in 1980, directed by Keith Digby. Drawing on events surrounding the historical Lizzie Borden and focusing on the rounds of doubt and speculation that have shadowed her alleged murder of her parents even to the present day, the play is an exercise in reenactment once removed, as an anonymous actress, a decade after the acquittal, elects to portray her friend Lizzie and, in a sense, to go through the motions of Lizzie's emotions. Pollock explores the ambivalence of empirical evidence and subjective testimony and of family and especially woman-to-woman relationships, in this case a relationship with lesbian implications. Lizzie herself acts as a kind of promptress to her actress friend, coaching her in her conjectural re-

enactments. The dream psychology of Lizzie's interactions with her parents, her brother and sister, and the lawyers for the defense, all through the mediation of the actress, conjures up a far more dramatic suspense than the suggested physicality of the ax murders themselves. This technical accomplishment, more than anything else, is the source of the play's triumph.

Blood Relations was the winner of the Governor General's Award for published drama in 1982, the first year drama was recognized on its own, in a category separate from poetry. The play was also the subject of controversy in 1982 and 1983, when Pollock sought an injunction against Calgary CTV affiliate station CFCN and $400,000 in compensation for damage to her literary reputation because of the station's decision to discard her television play and go ahead with a script of their own devising, a script which fell far short of her personal standards. The case that would have challenged Canada's archaic

1924 Copyright Act (which could not have ruled specifically on television transliteration) was, as it turned out, settled out of court, but it did draw much-needed attention to the issue of the extent of copyright and to the debate over the changing status of drama on stage, in print, and in the media, thus indirectly contributing to the Conservative government's decision in 1986 to give priority to drafting new copyright legislation. Pollock's involvement in this copyright case is indicative of her growing political awareness and of her interest in contemporary as well as historical issues of justice, morality, and human rights.

Generations, which was commissioned by Alberta Theatre Projects and premiered at Calgary's Canmore Opera House in 1980, focuses on the tensions that at once threaten to break a prairie family apart and manage to keep it together, albeit with lingering irony. Originally a 1978 CBC radio drama (titled simply *Generation*), the play is noteworthy for its crisp and casual dialogue. Even more important are its intense emphasis on family and its preoccupation with shared endurance–human tolerance and the ability to make a home in "THE LAND," which Pollock casts as a type of choral character of "omniscient presence and mythic proportion."

After completing her tenure as artist in residence at the National Arts Centre in Ottawa in 1983, Pollock returned to Calgary, first as dramaturge and assistant artistic director and subsequently as artistic director with Theatre Calgary. In *Whiskey Six,* she continued to explore her fascination with the idea of prairie community. First produced by Theatre Calgary in 1983 (and in the same year broadcast on the national network of the CBC), the play focuses on southern Alberta society during the period of prohibition and casts a somber light of verisimilitude on determined lives under the shadow of an arbitrary law. In her most recent play, *Doc,* Pollock reconciles the prototypes of the family and the archetypes of history by turning inward toward the autobiographical. Although she has publicly tried to reject the current critical opinion that the work is consistently autobiographical, *Doc* is in fact her most personal and confessional, and indeed her most ambitious, dramatic work to date. The play is situated around a confrontation between the title character, Ev (an aging doctor who has just received the honor of having a hospital named after him), and his daughter Catherine (a writer who holds her father responsible for serious family conflicts, and in particular for the suicide of his

mother and the suicidal degeneration of his relationship with his wife, Bob). In showing how Ev's dedication to his medical practice has taken precedence over his family responsibilities, Pollock develops the theme that even humanitarian efforts can lack the essence of humanity, but at the same time she casts Ev sympathetically, positing his persistent compunction over his mother's death as the very element that distorts his humanity. Even though Ev is clearly (if loosely) based on Pollock's own father, Dr. Everett Chalmers, who did in fact have a hospital named after him and whose wife seems to have committed suicide, the play as a whole remains an independently imaginative work.

In this, her most technically innovative play to date, Pollock seems to be interested as much in flexing the dramatic unities as in exploring lines of character. The drama takes place not only in the present moment and in the pasts of memory and flashback but also in the individual and collective reflections of the characters, the notion of shared thought blurring the outlines of Ev and Catherine and Bob and violating the very boundaries of being. Pollock exploits an interesting concept of ethereal setting, using the simple stage direction "shift" to announce changes in perceptual movement, in the ways in which her characters perceive the reality of surroundings and explore one another's present and former selves.

The character Katie, for example, is not just Catherine as a child, a kind of child-mother to the woman, but also an autonomous being, with her own stage presence, her own personality, her own mind. As Pollock points out in her opening stage directions, the characters are "able to speak across time." In addressing herself in this way to complex matters of conscience and consciousness, memory and remembrance, perception and perceptiveness, Pollock has produced drama that is emotionally stylized. She has managed to animate the simplest of conversational diction with poignantly expressionistic cadences, in particular in Ev's obsessive accounts of medical heroics, punctuated with ironic interjections of "I'm alright" (when clearly he is not). Throughout the play he grasps (yet fails to grasp) an unopened letter from his mother explaining her decision to commit suicide. This leitmotif helps to unify the play's fragmentary progression, but it is the subtle dramatic tension between Ev and Catherine that keeps the play grounded in the immediacy of the theater. For instance, when Catherine points out that she no longer wishes him to call

Pollock receiving a 1986 Governor General's Award for Doc *from Governor General Jeanne Sauvé (Canapress Photo Service, courtesy of The Canada Council)*

her Katie, Ev responds with characteristically maudlin indignation: "Oh, it's Catherine now, and you write Literature, don't you? And that means you can ignore your brother and your father and dump this Buchanan jerk and forget kids and family, but your father who gave his life to medicine because he believed in what he was doin' is an asshole!" This kind of undramatic dramatic writing sometimes seems little more than dead letters on the page, but in performance, in the mouths of the characters, it comes quite miraculously to life.

Doc was premiered in 1984 at Theatre Calgary and revised for a production later that year at the Toronto Free Theatre. In 1986 it was published by Playwrights Canada. In March of the same year, in her hometown of Fredericton, Pollock directed a Theatre New Brunswick production of a version of the play, under the title *Family Trappings*. This experience marked an important stage in her career, since, in returning to the place of her initial stage accomplishments with the touring company Prairie Players, Pollock

seems to have brought the first full circle of her career to its close.

In May 1987 she won the 1986 Governor General's Award for English-language drama for *Doc.* Receiving two such prestigious awards in five years seems to ensure that Pollock's theatrical work will be measured as much by official recognition and acknowledgment as by long lines at the box office and large television and radio audiences.

During the 1980s Pollock's radio drama has continued to air on the CBC. In 1983, for example, the national network produced (in addition to *Whiskey Six*) a new play titled *Intensive Care.* Enthusiastic public reaction to the CBC's national broadcast of *One Tiger to a Hill* in late 1985 led to a rebroadcast in early 1986. Pollock's mastery of colloquial idiom and cadence and her insight into historical tension and crisis seem to have earned her plays a natural (and permanent) radio audience.

Pollock's current project, a play with the working title "Egg," has been commissioned by

Theatre Calgary. Under its earlier title of "God's Not Finished with Us Yet," the play had been commissioned by the Vancouver Playhouse as part of the World Festival of Expo '86 in Vancouver, but when Pollock (collaborating with composer Bruce Ruddell) failed to complete the work to her satisfaction in time for its scheduled 20 June-5 July performances, the Playhouse production was cancelled. Theatre Calgary's production of "Egg" is expected to be substantially different in theme and style from the original version of the play, reflecting the playwright's growing concern with matters such as nuclear proliferation and defense spending, but at the same time offering what she has called "a somewhat comic treatment of a serious subject." The heroine of the play-in-progress is Martha, a woman savior whose salvific acts are inspired by madness, only to expire in madness. To Pollock the play is "about the contradiction between what appears to be an insane world—military and economically—and an individual who is deemed mad by society. The question is—who is mad?" The new play promises to augment the unprecedented theatrical success Pollock is currently winning in imaginative productions of *Doc* across Canada, from Calgary to Halifax.

Resident in Calgary since 1965, Pollock presently has a secure reputation as a dramatist with a peculiarly Western Canadian aesthetic perspective and theatrical following. Nevertheless, her dramatic interests are as expansive as her productions have been extensive and her writings prolific. Particularly in the years since the publication of *Blood Relations* and her reception of the Governor General's Award in 1982, she has won a formidable literary reputation. Her plays have been performed by every major theatrical company in Canada to the point that in the mid 1980s Pollock's plays are repertory standards to which artistic directors can confidently turn when they wish to balance Canadian content with popular appeal and artistic merit. Having recently turned fifty, Sharon Pollock herself is rapidly becoming a Canadian theatrical property, one of the most innovative and versatile dramatists in the nation.

Interview:

Robert Wallace, "Sharon Pollock," in *The Work: Conversations with English-Canadian Playwrights*, by Wallace and Cynthia Zimmerman (Toronto: Coach House Press, 1982), pp. 114-141.

References:

D. Balcon, "Question of Copyright: The Sharon Pollock Case," *Cinema Canada*, 102 (December 1983): 26-27;

Diane Bessai, Introduction to Pollock's *Blood Relations and Other Plays* (Edmonton: NeWest Press, 1981), pp. 7-9;

Brian Brennan, "Award Winning Playwright Still Feels Uneasy about Arts Awards," *Performing Arts*, 22, no. 4 (1980): 24;

"Canada's Playwrights Finding Their Place," *Canadian Theatre Review*, 34 (Spring 1982): 34-38;

A. Hustak, "Sharon Pollock's Triumph: A Hit for Theatre Calgary's New Boss," *Alberta Report* (30 April 1984): 54-55;

Hustak, "Very Dramatic Exit," *Alberta Report* (10 September 1984): 40-41;

M. Knelman, "Daddy Dearest: *Doc*," *Saturday Night*, 99 (October 1984): 73-74;

M. McKinley, "Sharon Pollock's *Blood Relations:* A T.V. Adaptation of Her Hit Play Enrages the Calgary Writer," *Alberta Report* (28 February 1983): 50;

Robert C. Nunn, "Performing Fact: Canadian Documentary," *Canadian Literature*, 103 (Winter 1984): 51-62;

Malcolm Page, "Sharon Pollock: Committed Playwright," *Canadian Drama*, 5 (Fall 1979): 104-111;

J. Webster, "Another Stage Triumph for Sharon," *Atlantic Advocate*, 64 (August 1974): 50.

Jacques Poulin

(23 September 1937-   )

Paul Matthew St. Pierre
University of British Columbia

and

Donald Smith
Carleton University

BOOKS: *Mon cheval pour un royaume* (Montreal: Editions du Jour, 1967); translated by Sheila Fischman as *My Horse for a Kingdom* in *The Jimmy Trilogy* (1979);

Jimmy (Montreal: Editions du Jour, 1969); translated in *The Jimmy Trilogy* (1979);

Le Coeur de la baleine bleue (Montreal: Editions du Jour, 1970); translated as *The Heart of the Blue Whale* in *The Jimmy Trilogy* (1979);

Faites de beaux rêves (Montreal: Actuelle, 1974);

Les Grandes Marées (Montreal: Leméac, 1978); translated by Fischman as *Spring Tides* (Toronto & Buffalo: Anansi, 1986);

The Jimmy Trilogy, translated by Fischman (Toronto: Anansi, 1979);

Volkswagen Blues (Montreal: Québec / Amérique, 1984).

TELEVISION: *Les Grandes Marées*, Radio-Canada, 29 November 1981.

Even with two of his six novels still to be translated into English, Jacques Poulin is the francophone Quebec writer with the greatest potential appeal to English-speaking audiences outside Quebec, not just in anglophone Canada but in the United States as well. The fluently bilingual novelist writes from a North American perspective and with a cosmopolitan awareness of pockets of French culture throughout the continent. Rather than restricting himself to *caractères québécois*, Poulin explores with a kind of aboriginal insight the four solitudes of French-English and Canada-United States. Although his favorite themes may appear to be typically *québécois*—politics and history, the beauty of Quebec City and the St. Lawrence River, and the Quebecker's mysterious attraction for the United States—his stylistic approach to these themes, based as it is on

Jacques Poulin (photograph by Kèro)

an engaging sense of humor and on a striking mixture of tenderness and revolt, is in fact atypical of other major novelists of the 1960s and 1970s. His style is more practical than polemical, his subject matter true more to the life that is than to the life that might be or might have been. His artistic vision is essentially comic, grounded in the humor of the present moment and in the irony of the ultimate moment of death. With scrupulous understatement and perfectionist exactitude,

307

Poulin has emerged as a master of fictional contrivance unsurpassed in his language, his province, his country, and his continent.

Jacques Poulin was born 23 September 1937 in Saint-Gédéon-de-Beauce, Quebec, the second child of Roger and Jeanne d'Arc Grondin Poulin. His father ran a general store, and the Poulin family of seven children enjoyed a certain affluence, Jacques Poulin himself becoming a skilled tennis player (at least on a neighbor's court). He received a classical education at the Séminaire de Saint-Georges (where he was a contemporary of Roch Carrier—and from which he was dismissed for giving mass wine to his classmates) and thereafter at the Séminaire de Saint-Nicolet, graduating with a *baccalauréat* degree in 1957. At Université Laval, Poulin studied literature and psychology in a bilingual arts program, receiving a *licence en orientation professionnelle* in 1960. He worked as a research assistant in the Department of Psychology at Laval (1960-1962) while studying for a *licence ès lettres* (which he received in 1964).

His literature and psychology specialities served him in two positions that were apprenticeships to a literary career and means to a literary living: from 1967 to 1970 Poulin worked as a counselor at Collège Notre-Dame-de-Bellevue in Quebec City, and from 1970 to 1973 he was a translator with the Government of Canada. Throughout his career he has supported himself by translating, most notably as a free-lancer for the *Dictionnaire biographique du Canada*. At the same time that he was distinguishing himself as a teacher, a civil servant, and an academic, Poulin was establishing himself as a novelist, having decided as early as 1965 to become a professional writer. He began to carry out his decision by publishing three novels from 1967 to 1970; that these novels form a tight trilogy emphasizes his opening achievement as *un écrivain*.

His first novel, *Mon cheval pour un royaume* (1967; translated by Sheila Fischman as *My Horse for a Kingdom* in *The Jimmy Trilogy*, 1979), is a poetic work inspired by the 1960s terrorist movement of the Front de Libération du Québec (FLQ) and comparable in its ironic and satirical tones and surrealistic and mythologic techniques to "romans de la violence" such as *Le Couteau sur la table* (1965) by Jacques Godbout and *Prochain épisode* (1965) by Hubert Aquin. Pierre Delisle, a young writer and the unfledged narrator of *Mon cheval pour un royaume*, relates the story of how he was injured in an FLQ bombing incident, all in a

confessional mode as part of his psychiatric treatment. For him, however, terrorism is more a means to self-awareness than deliberate political or therapeutic action. Before his injury, Pierre roams about Quebec City and marvels at the historic landmarks: Rue de la Fabrique (the artists' street), the Plains of Abraham, Place d'Armes, Parc Jeanne d'Arc, the Château Frontenac. Poulin describes these scenes in exacting detail, as if place is important precisely for the incidents that will take place there. The Château Frontenac and its *calèches* (horse-drawn carriages), in particular, are ironic symbols of the kingdom to be liberated by the bombing incident which both concludes and precedes the novel. In the inverted outcry of Richard III which gives the novel its title, we detect both the revolutionary struggle of the FLQ and the personal deformity of Pierre, a stone shattered in the explosion.

Pierre's attraction to the FLQ is a peculiarly instinctive element of his fascination with the grandeur which fills all things Quebecois: the historic beauty of Vieux Québec, the sensual beauty of his girlfriend Nathalie, the spiritual beauty of everything from flowers and fires to windows and beer glasses, even the metafictional beauty of his relationship to the psychoanalytic reader. In fact, as narrative, the novel is quite ambitious, Pierre addressing his reader directly in the second person. But whereas in the prologue he demands ironically, "Vous écrivez tout ce que je dis?" (Are you writing down everything I'm saying? [Fischman's translation]), in the epilogue he cries out in despair: "J'en arrive à me demander si vous existez vraiment. Vous ne dites jamais rien. Existez-vous réellement ou vous ai-je inventé comme je l'ai fait pour mon passé? Ou alors si vous existez, me suis-je inventé moi-même? Ne suis-je qu'un être inventé?" (It occurs to me to wonder if you really exist. You never say anything. Do you really exist or have I invented you as I invented my past? Or if you do exist, have I invented myself? Am I nothing but a creature of invention? [Fischman]).

Here the author takes the Platonic notion of the writer as the liar who tells the truth and renders it at once solipsistic and expressionistic. Poulin succeeds in transforming the rather unassuming Pierre into an archetypal figure whose youthful frustration and mature indecision represent the poignant feelings of many young Quebecois living in the troubled times of the quiet and not-so-*tranquille* revolutions of the 1960s. Likewise, the setting of Quebec City and the set of words describing it come to stand for the realm through which Quebecois move toward such ideals as independence, sovereignty association, special status, and distinct society. At the conclusion of *Mon cheval pour un royaume,* the reader finds himself echoing the narrator's questions, precisely because he feels unable to answer them.

Jimmy (1969), Poulin's second novel and the middle volume of his trilogy, is an extension of *Mon cheval pour un royaume.* The title character and narrator is an eleven-year-old boy who, like Pierre, is mesmerized by the poetic beauty of his surroundings. The narrators of both books are sensual individuals attempting to understand the world of adults, although Jimmy's struggle is not political. A disturbed child who lives in the isolation of a cottage built on piles above the St. Lawrence, Jimmy is confronted with an intellectual father, Papou, a literary critic (writing a book on Hemingway) and also a drunk; with a neurotic mother, Mamie, a tender woman unable to find the tenderness she needs to get over the loss of a son; and with a virtually human cat, Chanoine, that prowls through the novel like a lively chorus and a living leitmotiv. Recognizing his family's distress, Jimmy loses himself in a fantasy world of television celebrities and sports heroes (notably, Jimmy Clark the auto racer). He becomes obsessed with symbols of destruction, such as the cottage's rotting piles and the decaying fish washed up on the beach, representing the disintegration of the life around him.

Translated in 1979 as the title work of *The Jimmy Trilogy,* the novel offers a surrealistic vision of the breakup of the rigidly structured French-Canadian family, as Poulin addresses himself to one of the major themes of Quebecois literature of the 1950s and 1960s. By meticulously maintaining the point of view of a young narrator subsumed in the imagination, Poulin relinquishes his perspective on conventional reality and allows his novel to appear not only spontaneous but semiautomatic as well. To Poulin the semi-automatic cadences of a child's language are especially surreal, since they are free even of the random contrivance of fully automatic narration. This aspect of the *roman par hasard* is most graphically evident when the cottage finally collapses into the St. Lawrence, turns into a barge, and sails arklike downriver, Jimmy continuing to dream his dream of dreams, a pilot crying out over his short-wave radio: "BESOIN DE TENDRESSE, CROTTE DE CHAT! BESOIN DE TENDRESSE! Over." (REQUIRE ATTENTION, CATSHIT! RE-QUIRE ATTENTION! Over. [Fischman]). Although the story itself breaks off en route, the quest for tenderness ends in landfall, albeit more the sighting than the actual reaching of a land of love and attention.

The final volume of the trilogy, *Le Coeur de la baleine bleue* (1970; translated in *The Jimmy Trilogy* as *The Heart of the Blue Whale*) is, like the first volume, set in Vieux Québec. This time the young narrator is Noël, a transplant recipient who wakes up from his surgery to find he has the heart of a fifteen-year-old girl (Nathalie, who in *Mon cheval pour un royaume* commits suicide). The novel's postoperative perspective allows Poulin to explore less the medical problem of organ transplantation than the social problem of sexual prejudice arising out of male-female insensitivity. Can a man survive with the so-called core of female emotions, or will his virile body reject the female heart?

Poulin believes that beauty, whether expressed through language by a writer or appreciated passively by a reader or spectator, is one of the few cures for the many manifestations of heartlessness. *Un romancier en herbe,* Noël discovers upon returning home from the hospital and resuming his writing that his response to the world—indeed the world itself—has undergone a radical transformation. His marriage breaks down when his wife, Elise, suddenly leaves him for his friend Bill. After rejecting the temptation to give in to death, the young writer becomes an explorer in a newfound world of images and words, in particular as they are manifested in the mysterious character Charlie, "la baleine bleue" (or Blue Whale), who represents to Noël the donor of his new heart. Through his encounter with the Blue Whale, Noël enters into a kind of mythic existence, at once becoming a figure in his own story ("Petit à petit, j'entrais dans mon histoire") meeting with characters of his own creation and other characters from the trilogy. The conclusion of this final volume recalls the explosive end of the first book: "I get up with difficulty. I go to get Jimmy from the piano, I lay him down on the bed. Then I lift the lid of one of the boxes and take out a grenade. I remove the pin. I slip my hand, which is clutching the grenade, under my old grey sweater. I lie on my side, head bent, knees raised and my other hand between my legs. The nausea has passed and I feel well. There's a song in my head but I can't think of the title. No, it's more like the song of a bird. A bird that's been set free" (Fischman). In this way

Noël finally reconciles himself to the loss of his heart, a reconciliation that is at once animating and deathly. And in this way the canon of *Mon cheval pour un royaume*, *Jimmy*, and *Le Coeur de la baleine bleue* comes full circle.

Like those in the trilogy, the characters in *Faites de beaux rêves* (1974), a novel which won the Prix de La Presse, believe in the power of language, and in the ironic power of the irrational—in images, symbols, and myths—to give meaning to life, to make the "beaux rêves" of the title a goal worth pursuing. Here the subjects of dreams and the themes of the inner world (less concrete than Vieux Québec, a sensuous woman, and a decaying cottage) make up an ephemeral social pantheon of racing car ace (Jimmy Clark), hockey great (Maurice "the Rocket" Richard), movie star (Marlene Dietrich), and western hero (Buffalo Bill). Although the novel has numerous characters (the setting of the Grand Prix du Canada auto race at Mont-Tremblant overflows with spectators more down-to-earth, albeit no less illusory, than those in the celebrity pantheon), Poulin focuses on three young people attending the race: a mysterious woman named Limoilou ("Il était une fois une fille qui s'appelait Limoilou"), and two men she has befriended, Théo (a sports journalist) and his brother Amadou (an accountant). The novel takes the form of a sequence of closeups of the characters as they pursue their shifting relationships amid the constantly shifting images and sounds of the racing automobiles. So fluid is this world of mechanical motion and human movement that even authorial perception seems to fluctuate between the dream of heroism and victory and the reverie of revolutions per minute. Whereas the cars plot their single predetermined course on the track, the characters pursue various unplotted courses through life; their interaction at Mont-Tremblant has an intrinsic meaning but no meaning outside itself, in a larger scheme. In his conclusion to the novel Poulin simply reserves judgment and the characters go their ways, as in life, rather than forming the equilateral triangle of resolved fictional relationships. Ironically, this is Poulin's most finished novel in the sense that the incantatory *pouvoir* of words seems to end with the story's last statement: "Théo fit signe que non sans se retourner" (Without turning round, Théo shook his head). In *Faites de beaux rêves* the no-sign carries the ultimate signification of characters' words and the final significance of the narrative itself.

The protagonist of the 1978 novel *Les Grandes Marées* (translated in 1986 by Sheila Fischman as *Spring Tides*) is Teddy Bear, a translator of American comic strips whose anglicized name encodes his role as a "traducteur de bandes dessinées." He lives on a deserted island in the St. Lawrence River, in his twin effort to do his translations undisturbed and to write a definitive novel about French and American influences on the Quebecois mentality. In the course of his creational (writing), re-creational (translating), and recreational (playing tennis) activities, Teddy invents a woman out of dream and imagination (a woman of immaculate conception appropriately named Marie), much in he manner of earlier Poulin protagonists, and shares with her an idyllic life in a brave new cartoon-world. When his island is eventually invaded by friends and colleagues, Teddy realizes the impossibility of escaping from the real world.

Here Poulin offers a tentative answer to the central aesthetic question of whether fiction is in essence mimetic or nonmimetic, the author suggesting that, however wonderful the isolated island of fantasy might be, the ocean of reality will always crash ceaselessly onto its shores, plangently wearing away all its wonders. In a similar manner, the island of Quebec adrift in the sea of North America cannot exist on fantasy—whether it be the fantasy of political independence or that of cultural sovereignty—and as a result Quebec must step bravely into the waves.

Although *Les Grandes Marées* is more unabashedly humorous than *The Jimmy Trilogy* and *Faites de beaux rêves*, it does explore some of the same themes: the quest for tenderness, the daily process of death, and the conflict between creativity and responsibility. Poulin endeavors to expose technology as dangerous, seeing technology as a phenomenon that isolates and alienates mankind: Teddy has one machine, for instance, that can outserve him in tennis and another that threatens him with its superb translations. As in all his novels, Poulin has based his narrative technique on a broken chronology reminiscent of the *nouveau roman*. The novel features a sequence of tight structural and thematic units corresponding to the frames in a comic strip; the short episodic chapters are replete with daring turns of phrase and delightful typographic *coups d'oeil*, ranging from cartoons and sketches to recipes and math equations, from advertisements to questionnaires. The result is Poulin's most animated and engaging novel, the recipient of the 1978 Governor Gen-

13

— Ça me fait plaisir.

— On va aller prendre l'air quelques minutes et on va revenir pour visiter la bibliothèque, dit-il. ~~la fille.~~

~~Ils~~ Dehors, ~~ils~~

Ils sortirent du musée, et le chat ~~noin~~, qui s'était ~~aventuré~~ avait trouvé refuge sous le campeur, se précipita vers eux à toute allure. Ils marchèrent en silence jusqu'au ~~bord de la baie~~ à l'extrémité ~~point~~ qui s'avançait dans la baie. ~~où ils s'assirent sur la base~~

— Si mon frère était ici avec nous, dit l'homme, il nous ~~raconterait~~ expliquerait ce que Jacques Cartier a fait en arrivant dans la baie, combien il y avait de navires et ~~et~~ de marins, quel temps il faisait cette journée-là; il nous ~~dirait~~ montrerait l'endroit exact où ~~à quel endroit précis~~ il a jeté l'ancre et le rivage où il a débarqué, il nous ~~dirait~~ ~~où il~~ parlerait de la croix qu'il a plantée et ~~des~~ de la réaction des Indiens qui ~~étaient là~~ le regardaient faire, et il nous raconterait tout ça avec tellement de vie et de chaleur qu'on aurait tous les deux l'impression de voir la scène se dérouler devant nous.

La fille ne dit rien et ils contemplèrent en silence la grande baie dans laquelle ~~venaient se jeter trois rivières à saumons~~ qui avait abrité les navires du capitaine de Saint-Malo. la Dartmouth, la York et le Sorent-Jean.

Tout à coup, la fille dit qu'elle ~~avait~~ pensait à une idée.

— ~~Oui?~~ ~~fit l'homme.~~

— ~~Supposons~~ se dit-elle, ~~que~~ Théo a ~~utilisé~~ la technique de la photocopie ~~dit-elle~~

— Oui.

— ~~Il n'a~~ ~~Je me mets~~

— Mettez-vous à la place de Théo, dit-elle.

— Supposons Oui, dit l'homme

— Bon. Vous arrivez au musée, vous visitez et, pour une raison que j'ai du mal à comprendre, il vous prend l' vous avez envie d'envoyer une carte postale dont le texte serait le récit de Jacques Cartier que vous venez de lire dans la grande salle. Alors qu'est-ce que vous faites?

— J'achète une carte postale au comptoir.

Page from the manuscript for Poulin's novel Volkswagen Blues, *inspired by Jack Kerouac's* On the Road *(by permission of the author)*

eral's Award for French-language fiction and in 1981 the inspiration for a CBC television drama on Radio-Canada (starring Yvan Ponton as Teddy Bear and Béatrix Van Til as Marie).

Poulin's sixth and most recent novel, *Volkswagen Blues* (1984), both extends his interest in America and takes the author in new literary directions. Once again the fictional structure is that of a quest and the characters have quasi-imaginary existences, in this case the quest taking the narrator (an authorial persona ironically named Jack Waterman, as much for Jack Kerouac as for Jacques Poulin) and his Volkswagen minibus on a trip through the continental United States in search of his long-lost brother, Théo, who seems as much a hero of invention as a man of mere flesh and blood. In the company of a mysterious *métisse* known as Pitsémine and la Grande Sauterelle and a cat called Chop Suey (both of whom he picks up along the way), Jack explores much of the surrendered territory of New France and the abandoned trails of American pioneers. Through the eyes of a Quebecois artist and a dispossessed Indian, Poulin depicts the depressing environments of Detroit, Chicago, and Kansas City and the verdant landscapes of Oregon. Although the novel's inspiration is Kerouac's *On the Road,* its source is more accurately the year of research and the five years of writing (at a rate of one page per morning) that Poulin spent on his story and indeed the whole literary career that provides the backdrop to this self-portrait, ironically the first of Poulin's novels to be narrated in the third person.

The odyssey along the St. Lawrence, the Mississippi, and the Oregon Trail to San Francisco is essentially a quest for Quebecois identity, the novel a kind of French-language version of Frederick Philip Grove's *A Search for America* (1927) combined with his *In Search of Myself* (1946). Poulin's social allegory–Théo has become an American "bum," a cowboy who, not unlike Louis Hémon's Lorenzo Surprenant in *Maria Chapdelaine* (1916), is losing his language and his culture–goes far beyond the author's traditional themes. Despite their intimate relationship as travelers, Jack and Pitsémine simply part company at journey's end, he to return to Quebec, freed from his images of dispossession, she to remain in San Francisco, free to encounter another man. Upon entering the air terminal, Jack "souriait malgré tout à la pensée qu'il y avait, quelque part dans l'immensité de l'Amérique, un lieu secret où les dieux des Indiens et les autres dieux étaient rassemblés et tenaient conseil dans le but de veiller sur lui et d'éclairer sa route" (he smiled, despite everything, at the thought that somewhere in the immensity of America there was a secret place where the gods of the Indians and other gods were gathered and holding a council with the aim of keeping watch over him and lighting his way).

Poulin's implication is that the Quebecois quest through aboriginal America is an existential odyssey at once into island of oneself and into an island-nation of self. It is to these islands that Jack Waterman returns in the end. In discovering Théo he has uncovered, beyond a brother suffering from degenerative paralysis, an image of the divine everyman within himself and within all the *volks* of America. And that, Poulin rightly feels, is a subject worthy of the blues.

With its emphasis on childhood and initiation, innocence and tenderness, dream and fantasy, adventure and exploration, Poulin's fiction both lingers in the sunshine of comedy and malingers in the shadows of mimesis. In that they have yet to reach the age of unreason, his young first-person narrators demonstrate an enviable insouciance toward the perils of existence, and through his narrators Poulin acknowledges man's ardent psychic need to penetrate both the dream and the logic of childhood. In the dream sequence of his six novels, Poulin has in effect reinvented the ideas in which character and culture are grounded. As he himself has stated: "Je crois à la liberté la plus grande possible, au mélange des idées" (I believe in the greatest possible liberty, in the mingling of ideas). His recent fiction has offered a standing invitation to readers throughout North America to find the ground of their being in the tender kingdom of childhood.

Interviews:

Rachel Cloutier, Rodrique Gignac, Vincent Nadeau, and Richard Plamondon, "Entrevue avec Jacques Poulin," *Nord,* 2 (Winter 1972): 9-29;

Gilles Dorion and Cécile Dubé, "Jacques Poulin," *Québec Français,* 35 (May 1979): 33-35.

References:

Ivanhoé Beaulieu, "Petit collage (intime et fictif) au sujet d'un écrivain de Québec-la-Ville et où il est question de Guy Lafleur," *Nord,* 2 (Winter 1972): 71-72;

Nicole Beaulieu, "L'Ecrivain dans l'ombre," *L'Actualité,* 10 (April 1985): 73, 75, 77-78;

Paul-André Bourque, "L'Art de communiquer l'incommunicabilité," *Québec Français*, 29 (May 1976): 38-39;

Bourque, "La Fascination de l'enfance, de la tendresse et de la mort chez Jacques Poulin ou la recherche de l'androgynie absolue," *Nord*, 2 (Winter 1972): 74-92;

Roch Carrier, "Jacques Poulin, Toronto-Montréal," *Nord*, 2 (Winter 1972): 73;

Sylvie Choquette, "L'Archétype du temps circulaire chez Ernest Hemingway et Jacques Poulin," *Etudes Littéraires*, 8 (November 1975): 43-55;

Gilles Dorion, "La Littérature québécoise contemporaine, 1960-1977, II: Le Roman,"

Etudes Françaises, 13 (October 1977): 329-331;

Jacques Garneau, "*Le Coeur de la baleine bleue* ou le labyrinthe intérieur," *Nord*, 2 (Winter 1972): 59-68;

Jean-Cleo Godin, "Entre la pierre et l'extase," *Nord*, 2 (Winter 1972): 38-47;

François Ricard, "Jacques Poulin: Charlie Brown dans la Bible," *Liberté*, 20 (May-June 1978): 85-88;

Ricard, "Jacques Poulin: De la douceur à la mort," *Liberté*, 16 (September-December 1974): 97-105;

Jean Royer, "Jacques Poulin, romancier artisan," *Le Devoir*, 29 April 1978, p. 33.

Jacques Renaud

(10 November 1943-   )

Ronald Sutherland
Université de Sherbrooke

BOOKS: *Electrodes* (Montreal: Atys, 1962);

Le Cassé (Montreal: Parti Pris, 1964); translated by Gerald Robitaille as *Flat Broke and Beat* (Montreal: Bélier, 1964); French-language edition enlarged and republished as *Le Cassé et autres nouvelles, suivi de Le Journal du cassé* (Montreal: Parti Pris, 1977); translated by David Homel as *Broke City* (Montreal: Guernica, 1984);

En d'autres paysages (Montreal: Parti Pris, 1970);

Le Fond pur de l'errance irradie (Montreal: Parti Pris, 1975);

Le Cycle du scorpion (Montreal: Editions de la Lune Occidentale, 1979);

La Colombe et la brisure éternité (Montreal: Le Biocreux, 1979);

L'Inde et le Karma (Montreal: Editions du Transplutonien, 1979);

Clandestine(s) ou la tradition du couchant (Montreal: Le Biocreux, 1980);

D'ailies et d'Fles, by Renaud, Leonard Cohen, Claude Haeffely, and Michael Lachance (Montreal: Editions de la Marotte, 1980);

Arcane Seize, as Elie-Pierre Ysrael (Montreal: Editions de la Lune Occidentale, 1980);

La Ville: Venus et la Mélancolie (Montreal: Editions de La Lune Occidentale, 1981);

Par la Main du Soleil; Les Saisons du Saphir, as Ji R. (Montreal: Editions La Lune Occidentale, 1981);

La Nuit des Temps (Montreal: Editions de La Lune Occidentale et du Transplutonien, 1981).

OTHER: "The Coat-Rack," translated by Ronald Bates in *Stories from Québec*, edited by Philip Stratford (Toronto, New York, Cincinnati & London: Van Nostrand Reinhold, 1974).

PERIODICAL PUBLICATIONS: "And On Earth Peace," *Parti Pris*, 1 (April 1964): 25-39;

"Les Pieds sur la terre," *Passe-Partout*, 1 (March 1965): 4-5;

"Le Génoc," *Le Montréaliste*, 1 (March 1966): 31, 34, 39;

"Témoignages d'écrivains," *Etudes Françaises*, 3 (August 1967): 302-307;

Jacques Renaud (photograph by Kèro)

"Trois Zemmes et une Zamme," *Sexus,* 1 (August-
September 1976): 77-79;
"Der Fisch," *Brèves,* 24/25 (Spring 1987): 129-141.

Montreal-born Jacques Renaud burst upon
the literary scene of French-speaking Quebec at
the age of twenty-one. Two years earlier, in 1962,
his small book of poems, *Electrodes,* had been published without attracting much attention, but with
the novel *Le Cassé* (*cassé* means figuratively in Quebec French what *broke* means in English—without
money, down and out), he became the leading exponent of a new, scandalous, and significant phenomenon in Quebec literature—the *joual* syndrome.

The term *joual* has been used erroneously
and insultingly to signify the colloquial language
of French-speaking Quebeckers. The word itself
is a deformation of the standard French *cheval*
and can still be heard in rural areas of the province. Since Jean-Paul Desbiens, in his *Les Insolences du Frère Untel* (1960), gave the term
currency by employing it to attack the education
system and the resulting poor quality of spoken
French in Quebec, *joual* has taken on a specific
meaning. It does not refer to any of the dialects
of French spoken in Canada but rather to the tor-
tured slang of working-class, industrial areas of
Montreal. Desbiens characterized it as "the absence of language," and in recent years it has
begun to disappear.

The *joual* of Montreal developed when thousands of people from the farmlands, many of
whom had little or no formal education, moved
to the city in search of jobs. Factories were
mainly owned and operated by English-speaking
Canadians, with the result that the workers were
obliged to learn new vocabulary, mixing words
like "le foreman, le boss, la jobbe" or "l'overtime"
with their unsophisticated, rural French, adopt-
ing hybrid locutions such as *je bommais* (I was bum-
ming around), *Watchez le cop* or *hot dog stimé.*

Joual, therefore, symbolized the degradation
of working-class French Canadians in their own
homeland. As the Quiet Revolution, officially beginning with the election of Jean Lesage as provincial premier in 1960 under the slogan *Maîtres
chez nous,* gained momentum, and various movements for the separation of Quebec from Canada
emerged, French-speaking Quebeckers began a
process of self-assertion, rejecting the old survival
mechanism of "Christian resignation" and striv-
ing for renewed pride and dignity. Part of this
process was to drop the name *canadien-français,*
with its connotations of group inferiority, in
favor of *québécois.* Another part of the new nationalism was to draw attention to the dehumanizing
character of *joual.*

Jacques Renaud was not alone. Born and
raised in the working-class district of Rosemont
in the East End of Montreal, Renaud (after finishing high school) worked at manual jobs until
1965, when he became a reporter for *Métro-
Express.* He subsequently became a researcher for
Radio-Canada and began writing for several publications, including the magazine *Indépendance,*
founded by Pierre Bourgault and the official
organ of the separatist organization called Le
Rassemblement pour l'Indépendance Nationale
(R.I.N.). He also joined the young writers associated with the activist/socialist review *Parti Pris,* notably André Major, Laurent Girouard, Paul
Chamberland, and Gérald Godin. All of these writers were immersed in a variety of revolutionary
ideas, and all of them experimented with *joual* as
a means to shock readers into a consciousness of
the humiliating circumstances of the francophone Quebec working class. Renaud's *Le
Cassé,* however, undoubtedly had the greatest impact.

The novel is short, dense, hard-hitting and

Cover for the first English translation of Renaud's 1964 novel written in the Montreal sociolect joual

devastatingly accurate in its depiction of an unpleasant reality. Here, for instance, is protagonist Ti-Jean shouting at the man he finds in bed with Philomène, the girl he considers his mistress: "Ben, Yves, sor d'icitte crisse! T'as pas d'affaires à y poigner l'cul. C'est ma plote pour tout l'temps astheure! Mets-toé ben ça dans ton casse sale!" The reader unfamiliar with *joual* will find that even his *Nouveau Larousse Universel* does little to illuminate this passage, or indeed a good part of Renaud's novel.

Ti-Jean is a man reduced to the brute by the brutal conditions of his life. He knows only physical force and violence, which eventually he exercises in a senseless murder. He is surrounded by those who resemble him in one way or another, even though they may be from higher levels of society. At one point Philomène

becomes involved in a lesbian encounter with a university student, much to the amusement of Ti-Jean.

In his *Signets II* (1967) critic Jean Ethier-Blais has written that "*Le cassé* est plus qu'un cri; c'est un rugissement. Le 'portrait' est terrible, la déchéance absolue. . . . Le miroir est fidèle; c'est ainsi que parlent les humiliés et les offensés, c'est ainsi qu'à chaque ligne ils blasphèment." (*Le Cassé* is more than a cry: it is a roar. The "portrait" is terrifying, the decadence absolute. . . . The mirror is faithful; this is the way the humiliated and offended speak, the way they curse with each statement.)

After publishing *Le Cassé*, Renaud worked in advertising for a few months, then for Radio-Canada. He received a bursary to travel in Europe, returning to Montreal in 1968. His second novel, *En d'autres paysages*, published in 1970, is a mixture of reality, fantasy, and lyricism quite remote from the stark crudity of his first novel. Later works, often concerned with cabalistic doctrine, have been experimental and have not achieved the impact of *Le Cassé*. Renaud is the father of three children and lives in Montreal with his common-law wife.

In the years since 1960 French Canada may well have evolved more than during the previous 350 years. The reasons are many, including political change, extensive modification of the education system, advances in technology, increased communication, and the heightening of national consciousness by a veritable explosion of activity in the arts and literature. Distinctive Canadian French has become a legitimate and effective vehicle of literary expression recognized internationally. Jacques Renaud's *Le Cassé* may already be something of a linguistic curiosity, but it remains one of the important elements in the creation of the dynamic and viable culture of contemporary French Canada.

References:

Robert Barberis, *De la clique des Simard à Paul Desrochers en passant par le joual* (Montreal: Editions Québécoises, 1973), pp. 30-82;

Norman Cloutier, "Le Scandale du joual," *Le Magazine Maclean*, 6 (February 1966);

Jean Ethier-Blais, *Signets II* (Montreal: Cercle du Livre de France, 1967), pp. 239-245;

Robert Major, *Parti pris: idéologies et littérature* (Montreal: HMH, 1979).

Jane Rule

(28 March 1931-)

Constance Rooke
University of Victoria

BOOKS: *The Desert of the Heart* (Toronto: Macmillan, 1964; London: Secker & Warburg, 1964; Cleveland: World, 1965);

This Is Not For You (New York: McCall, 1970; Toronto: Doubleday, 1970);

Against the Season (New York: McCall, 1971; Toronto: Doubleday, 1971; London: Davies, 1972);

Theme for Diverse Instruments (Vancouver: Talonbooks, 1975);

Lesbian Images (Garden City: Doubleday, 1975; Markham, Ontario: Simon & Schuster of Canada; London: Davies, 1976);

The Young in One Another's Arms (Garden City: Doubleday, 1977; Toronto: Totem, 1978);

Contract with the World (New York: Harcourt Brace Jovanovich, 1980);

Outlander: Stories and Essays (Tallahassee: Naiad Press, 1981);

Inland Passage and Other Stories (Toronto: Lester & Orpen Dennys, 1985; Tallahassee: Naiad Press, 1985);

A Hot-Eyed Moderate (Tallahassee: Naiad Press, 1985; Toronto: Lester & Orpen Dennys, 1986).

PERIODICAL PUBLICATIONS: "Life, Liberty and the Pursuit of Normalcy: The Novels of Margaret Atwood," *Malahat Review*, 41 (January 1977): 42-49.

"Inside the Easter Egg," *Room of One's Own*, 9 (June 1984): 41-45.

photograph by Dave Morgan

Jane Rule

Jane Rule writes disciplined, tightly organized, nonautobiographical novels which are concerned much more with character and theme than with plot. Her novels are intellectual, though not very difficult; they are also passionate and tender and optimistic. Rule's characters are typically people who have left behind certain conventions of social grouping and behavior or who are tempted to do so. The challenge they face is one of "voluntary human relationships," in which they must invent new and variable guidelines for communal life. The author's respect and sympathy for her characters, in particular for their growth and freedom, are strongly felt throughout. Herself a lesbian, Rule always includes at least one lesbian relationship in each of her novels. A particularly attractive feature of Rule's fiction is that such relationships never overshadow her portrayals of characters who do not submit to definition by a single factor such as sexual orientation. Rule's style is clear and unmannered, but rather complex. Dialogue accounts for much of her novels, and she is particularly interested in tonalities or the interplay of voices; the analogy Rule uses to describe this interest is that of chamber music.

Jane Rule was born on 28 March 1931, in Plainfield, New Jersey. She was a middle child, whose parents, Arthur Rule, a businessman, and Jane Packer Rule, moved the family around a good deal in the United States. She received a B.A. in English from Mills College in California (1952) and was an occasional student at University College, London, England, and at Stanford University. After two years teaching English at Concord Academy in Concord, Massachusetts, she moved to Canada in 1956 and later became a Canadian citizen. For twenty years she worked intermittently as a teacher in the English and creative writing departments at the University of British Columbia in Vancouver. She now lives on Galiano Island.

Her first book, *The Desert of the Heart* (1964), focuses on the hesitations and flowering of a love affair between two women—a professor of English who has come to Reno for a divorce and a young cartoonist who works in a casino. Their commitment is explored in the context of attitudes (such as the necessity of marriage and child-bearing) which linger when they have become irrelevant and attitudes (including attachments to place, or people, or work) which must always be taken into account. Mirror and desert images are employed in aid of complex, carefully modulated themes.

This Is Not For You (1970), Rule's second novel, takes the form of an unmailed letter to Esther from Kate. Self-protective, determined at all costs to be conventionally right, Kate refuses to transmit what she perceives as the stain of her lesbianism to the relationship with Esther. This is an intense, earnest book; behind Kate's oppressive, wrong-headed integrity, one senses the author's own liberating anger. The cardinal error in Rule's world is a refusal to risk making mistakes.

Against the Season (1971) marks a turning point in Rule's career. She abandons here the focus upon a single character or a single relationship; point of view becomes more flexible, and the canvas grows. This is a gently iconoclastic novel about community and about unconventional categories of attachment, particularly when these defy one's expectations about what behavior is appropriate to the various seasons of human life.

In 1975 Rule produced a collection of thirteen stories entitled *Theme for Diverse Instruments.*

The author's short fiction—witness, for instance, the title story and "Invention for Shelagh"—tends to be more experimental than her novels, although many of these stories (culled from two decades of work) are traditional in form. In *Theme for Diverse Instruments* generally, more attention is paid to a dialectic between freedom and involuntary relationships—with one's family most often or with one's country. The house is a recurrent image, most often signifying constriction or imposed ideas. The titles of some of the most interesting stories reflect this preoccupation: "My Father's House," "House," "Housekeeper," and "In the Basement of the House."

Lesbian Images (1975), a volume of criticism, is a lucid, scholarly examination of the ways in which lesbian experience has been reflected in the life and work of selected lesbian writers. It begins with a personal introduction, in which Rule gives an account of her own sense of herself as lesbian, the difficulties she has faced, and the critical response to lesbian material in her novels. The next two chapters trace religious and psychoanalytical attitudes to lesbianism. Then twelve individual chapters are devoted to the works of writers such as Radcliffe Hall, Gertrude Stein, Willa Cather, Vita Sackville-West, Colette, and May Sarton. The book concludes with omnibus chapters entitled "Four Decades of Fiction" and "Recent Nonfiction."

Rule's 1977 novel, *The Young in One Another's Arms*, continues in the direction pointed by *Against the Season*, but the community won in this novel is considerably more precarious, as the title suggests, in its allusion to the "dying generations" of William Butler Yeats. As in the earlier novel, people of widely varying ages combine to support and enjoy one another. But political threats (of the Vietnam war, of law, and the engines of progress), as well as abiding natural dangers (the loss of life, of limb) are more prominent here. As in *The Desert of the Heart*, Rule employs a boarding-house as a microcosm of society. Originally located in Vancouver, the group becomes more self-conscious, more aware of its vulnerability and its potential for love, when it reassembles on one of the Gulf islands.

Contract with the World (1980) is an ambitious novel. It concerns again a group of friends and lovers, mostly artists of some kind, and mostly in late youth—at a time when they must make a contract with the world or opt out. Their love relationships and the direction of their creative work are the central issues. The novel is divided into six sec-

279

Page from the manuscript for Rule's novel-in-progress "Memory Board" (by permission of the author)

Dust jacket for Rule's novel about a group of Vancouver artists in the mid 1970s

tions, each assigned to a principal character who becomes the center of interest for that section and then fades back into the supporting cast.

Outlander: Stories and Essays (1981) contains thirteen short stories which are often more interesting as contexts for the discussion of lesbian themes than as fiction and twelve essays concerned with lesbian issues. In this book Rule seems to be addressing other lesbians most particularly.

Inland Passage and Other Stories (1985) is Rule's most recent collection of short stories. Many of the works focus on the simple pleasures of home life. Harry and Anna, parents of two small children, are two of the author's most appealing protagonists; in several of the stories collected here they suffer the vicissitudes of raising children in a material world, doing what they can to introduce genuine human compassion into their lives. Other stories treat a wide variety of les-

bian themes in a compassionate and open-minded way.

Rule's collection of essays, *A Hot-Eyed Moderate* (1985), consists of forty-seven short essays—three pages each on the average—grouped under four headings: "On Writing," "Writing for the Gay Press," "Profiles and Recollections," and "Reflections." Many of these essays appeared first in the magazine the *Body Politic;* others appeared in *Canadian Literature, Branching Out,* and *Room of One's Own,* and still others are published here for the first time. In the section "On Writing," in an essay entitled "Before and After *Sexual Politics,*" Rule argues that literature must be read "seriously and personally," and she warns against the specious objectivity of a formalist approach: "A work of art is not a clever puzzle to be solved by clever readers; it is a passionately articulated vision to be intensely shared." Particularly distinguished among the "Profiles" are her essays about two painters, Judith Lodge and Takao Tanabe. In the essay "You Cannot Judge a Pumpkin's Happiness by the Smile Upon Its Face," in "Reflections," Rule describes the glow-in-the-dark skeleton costumes that her father made for her and her brother on Halloween. The darkness and the light as Rule remembers them, together with the fact that the skeletons were anatomically correct, suggest something of Rule's own clear-sighted approach to life.

Jane Rule's fiction offers a "passionately articulated vision." For all its cool intelligence, her work invites a warm, personal response. Both her essays and her fiction have a particular fascination for women. The voice that speaks in Rule's work is characterized, above all, by honesty and tolerance; and the attractiveness of her work is very much a function of that voice.

Bibliography:

Helen Sonthoff, comp., "A Bibliography," *Canadian Fiction Magazine,* 23 (Autumn 1976): 133-138.

References:

Geoff Hancock, "An Interview with Jane Rule," *Canadian Fiction Magazine,* 23 (Autumn 1976): 57-112;

Helen Sonthoff, "Celebration: Jane Rule's Fiction," *Canadian Fiction Magazine,* 23 (Autumn 1976): 121-132.

George Ryga

(27 July 1932-   )

Jerry Wasserman
University of British Columbia

BOOKS: *Song of My Hands* (Edmonton: National, 1956);

Hungry Hills (Toronto: Longmans, 1963; London: Joseph, 1965; revised, Vancouver: Talonbooks, 1974);

Ballad of a Stone-picker (Toronto: Macmillan, 1966; London: Joseph, 1966; revised, Vancouver: Talonbooks, 1976);

Indian (Agincourt, Ontario: Book Society of Canada, 1967);

The Ecstasy of Rita Joe (Vancouver: Talonbooks, 1970);

The Ecstasy of Rita Joe and Other Plays (Toronto: New Press, 1971)—includes *The Ecstasy of Rita Joe, Indian,* and *Grass and Wild Strawberries*;

Captives of the Faceless Drummer (Vancouver: Talonbooks, 1971);

Sunrise on Sarah (Vancouver: Talonbooks, 1973);

Night Desk (Vancouver: Talonbooks, 1976);

Ploughmen of the Glacier (Vancouver: Talonbooks, 1977);

Seven Hours to Sundown (Vancouver: Talonbooks, 1977);

Beyond the Crimson Morning: Reflections from a Journey through Contemporary China (Toronto & Garden City, New York: Doubleday, 1979);

Two Plays: Paracelsus and Prometheus Bound (Winnipeg: Turnstone, 1982);

Portrait of Angelica / A Letter to My Son (Winnipeg: Turnstone, 1984);

In the Shadow of the Vulture (Vancouver: Talonbooks, 1985).

PLAY PRODUCTIONS: *Nothing But a Man,* Edmonton, Walterdale Playhouse, 8 March 1967;

The Ecstasy of Rita Joe, music by Ann Mortifee, Vancouver, Queen Elizabeth Playhouse, 23 November 1967;

Grass and Wild Strawberries, music by The Collectors, Vancouver, Queen Elizabeth Playhouse, 10 April 1969;

Captives of the Faceless Drummer, Vancouver, Van-

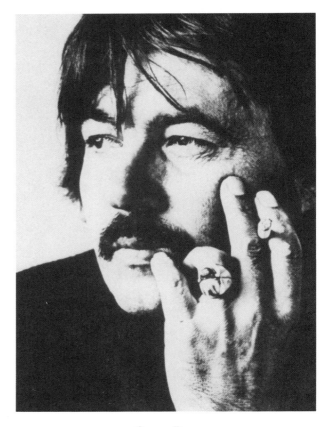

George Ryga

couver Art Gallery, 16 April 1971;

Sunrise on Sarah, Banff, Alberta, Banff School of Fine Arts, 29 July 1972;

A Feast of Thunder (oratorio), lyrics by Ryga, music by Morris Surdin, Toronto, Massey Hall, 9 June 1973;

Portrait of Angelica, Banff, Alberta, Banff School of Fine Arts, July 1973;

Indian, Winnipeg, Manitoba Theatre Centre, 3 May 1974;

Ploughmen of the Glacier, Vernon, British Columbia, Vernon Community Centre, April 1976;

Seven Hours to Sundown, Edmonton, University of Alberta Studio Theatre, 27 May 1976;

The Last of the Gladiators, Summerland, British Columbia, Summerland United Church, June 1976;

Jeremiah's Place, Victoria, British Columbia, 17 October 1978;

A Letter to My Son, North Bay, Ontario, Kam Theatre Lab, 2 October 1981;

One More for the Road, Vancouver, Firehall Theatre, 10 October 1985;

Paracelsus, Vancouver, Queen Elizabeth Playhouse, 27 September 1986.

OTHER: *The Collected Plays of Gwen Pharis Ringwood,* edited by Enid Delgatty Rutland, preface by Ryga (Ottawa: Borealis, 1982).

PERIODICAL PUBLICATIONS: "Theatre in Canada: A Viewpoint on Its Development and Future," *Canadian Theatre Review,* 1 (Winter 1974): 28-32;

"Canadian Drama: Living Art or Academic Curiosity?," *Canadian Drama,* 1 (Fall 1975): 76-78;

"Contemporary Theatre and Its Language," *Canadian Theatre Review,* 14 (Spring 1977): 4-9;

"The Need for a Mythology," *Canadian Theatre Review,* 16 (Fall 1977): 4-6;

"The Artist in Resistance," *Canadian Theatre Review,* 33 (Winter 1982): 86-91;

"The Village of Melons: Impressions of a Canadian Author in Mexico," *Canadian Literature,* 95 (Winter 1982): 102-108.

George Ryga is best known for *The Ecstasy of Rita Joe,* one of the most successful plays written in Canada. It established that an English-Canadian play could address serious social issues in vernacular language and nonrealistic style and still be commercially appealing, helping make possible the explosion of Canadian drama that occurred in the late 1960s and early 1970s. Ryga's other dramatic works and his fiction are similarly distinguished by a strong social consciousness and the attempt to create folk art using contemporary themes.

Ryga, the son of George and Maria Kolodka Ryga, was born and raised on his Ukrainian immigrant parents' Deep Creek homestead in northern Alberta. He left school at twelve, spending the next five years studying by correspondence and doing day labor, often alongside local Indians: "we were struggling exactly the same way to get out of the ghetto as they were from the reserve." In 1949 he won three creative-writing scholarships from the Banff School of Fine Arts, but his awards were withdrawn during his second

summer there because of a poem he wrote protesting the Korean War.

In Edmonton from 1950 to 1954 Ryga worked as a radio producer, again running into trouble for his political activism, and in 1955 he visited Scotland, where he researched Robert Burns's uses of folk language. From there he went to Helsinki for the World Peace Assembly, meeting other politically committed writers, including Chilean poet Pablo Neruda. Although Ryga broke with the Communist party over the Hungarian revolt in 1956, his politics would continue to cause him difficulty: seventeen years later he would be refused permission to enter the United States for the 1973 Washington, D.C., premiere of *The Ecstasy of Rita Joe.*

Back in Edmonton in 1956, he saw publication of his first book, a volume of poems entitled *Song of My Hands.* For the next six years, between night jobs, he wrote mostly fiction, including over forty short stories, many of which were adapted for production by CBC radio. His breakthrough came on 25 November 1962 with the critically acclaimed CBC-TV production of his first play, *Indian,* originally written as a story entitled "The Pine Tree Ghetto" and subsequently adapted for radio and stage. *Indian* concerns the clash of a transient Indian laborer, the white farmer who employs him, and an uncomprehending Indian agent, a "comfortable civil servant" who reappears in a variety of guises in many of Ryga's later works. The Indian, first seen as a stereotype, gradually reveals a profound and desperate humanity. Superficially the most naturalistic of Ryga's plays, *Indian* is also characterized by abrupt plunges into memory, a technique which in more stylized form would become a trademark of Ryga's drama and fiction.

Ryga moved to Summerland, British Columbia, in 1963 with his new wife Norma Campbell Ryga, with whom he eventually had five children. During the next few years he produced his first two novels. *Hungry Hills,* written in 1961 and published in 1963, is the more conventional of the two. Its narrator, Snit Mandolin, tells the harsh story of his return to the drought-ridden family farm in northern Alberta during the dust-bowl 1930s. After years in a welfare home he hopes to rebuild his life; but an abortive bootlegging scheme, a hostile community, and the land itself—"the cowardly greed of these hungry hills"—defeat him. *Ballad of a Stone-picker* (1966) has similar themes but a more interesting technique. Composed of fourteen anecdotal stories Ryga had written for radio, the novel has the effect of a ballad as the narrator interweaves tales about the agricultural community he has never left with confessions of guilt and resentment concerning his dead brother and parents. Both a plaint for and celebration of the brutality of life, the novel was praised for its concentrated power and feeling.

The year 1967 marked a threshold in Ryga's career as he had his first stage plays produced. His initial effort, *Nothing But a Man*, opened in March 1967 at Edmonton's Walterdale Playhouse. Adapted by Ryga from one of his earlier television scripts, it traces the symbolic life's journey of a "Canadian Peer Gynt" in an ambitious but ultimately confusing melange of styles. At about the same time, Ryga was approached by the Vancouver Playhouse Theatre to write a play for Centennial Year. The result was *The Ecstasy of Rita Joe*, his first play written specifically for the live stage. *The Ecstasy of Rita Joe* premiered at the Queen Elizabeth Playhouse on 23 November 1967 and quickly became a landmark in Canadian theater. Using expressionist and Brechtian stage techniques, it tells the harrowing story of a young Indian girl who comes to the city only to be tried and destroyed by the white man's alien culture. The rape and murder that Rita suffers at the end are implicit from the start in the attitudes of the magistrate and the other whites. Nothing that her father does to tempt her back to the old ways of her people can save her. Some critics complained about Ryga's one-dimensional presentation of whites. And, indeed, the real power of the play resides in the well-rounded, never romanticized Indian characters. After its Vancouver run, *The Ecstasy of Rita Joe* was chosen to open the new National Arts Centre in Ottawa; the play was published in 1970, and it has been produced with continued success across Canada, in the United States, and in England. Since 1971 a version of Ryga's play has been in the repertoire of the Royal Winnipeg Ballet. "*Rita Joe*," wrote Neil Carson in a 1970 article in *Canadian Literature*, "establishes Ryga as the most exciting talent writing for the stage in Canada today."

Ryga's next play, *Grass and Wild Strawberries*, was less well received critically but a great box office hit at the Queen Elizabeth Playhouse where it was first performed in April 1969. In its multimedia presentation of the conflict between hippie youth culture and the adult establishment, neither side comes out looking good. Realistic scenes mingle with those of memory and fantasy as the young protagonist gropes his way toward

Cover for the published version of Ryga's 1967 play about the destruction of the Indian girl Rita Joe by the white man's alien culture

selfhood. The play went on to successful runs in Toronto, and more recently it has been produced in Prague. *Grass and Wild Strawberries* is included in Ryga's 1971 volume, *The Ecstasy of Rita Joe and Other Plays*.

On the basis of Ryga's two hits the Vancouver Playhouse commissioned another play, and in the spring of 1970 Ryga submitted an outline for "Litany for Harry Farmer," the story of a superficially successful man hollow at the core. But a month after the October crisis over the separatist movement in Quebec, Ryga sent the Playhouse a revised script entitled *Captives of the Faceless Drummer*, in which the protagonist is held hostage by nationalist revolutionaries. The theater's executive board rejected it. After months of public controversy and accusations of artistic censorship, *Captives of the Faceless Drummer* was finally performed at the Vancouver Art Gallery in April 1971 and subsequently in Toronto and Lennoxville. It is the most static of Ryga's plays, though broken up by flashbacks and the use of a rather ineffectual chorus: a long dialogue between two men who are really doubles, both in their own ways captives.

Ryga kept busy during the 1970s writing for radio, television, and stage, teaching play writing, and traveling. At Banff in the summers of 1972 and 1973 he wrote two plays which the School of Fine Arts produced, *Sunrise on Sarah*, a psychodrama about a middle-class woman which Ryga considers the best work he has done for the theater, and *Portrait of Angelica*, a comedy about a Canadian in Mexico. These were published in 1973 and 1984 respectively. In Mexico himself in 1973 he completed *Paracelsus*, a play he had been working on for thirteen years. A large-scale historical play mostly in verse, it celebrates the Renaissance doctor whose concern for the poor and scorn for corrupt tradition set him in conflict with the medical establishment. *Paracelsus* was published in a volume with the later *Prometheus Bound* in 1982, but went unperformed until September 1986 when it was given a major but disastrous production by Vancouver's Queen Elizabeth Playhouse. Ryga's versatility is illustrated by his other major work of this period, his lyrics for the highly praised oratorio *A Feast of Thunder*, with music by Morris Surdin, performed by the Schevchenko Ensemble at Toronto's Massey Hall in June 1973. Ryga's verses, wrote the critic for the *Toronto Globe and Mail*, managed "with complete success to capture the hope and longing of New Canadians . . . struggling to cope with the potential of a new land."

From his twelve-part radio series entitled *Miners, Gentlemen and Other Hard Cases*, Ryga developed the play *Ploughmen of the Glacier*, a rather fuzzy allegory set on a surrealistic mountainside, in which a newspaperman and a prospector represent the forces that developed British Columbia. First produced in Okanagan beer parlors and community halls in April 1976 and published the following year, it went on to great success in Germany, where it won best play awards in 1979 and 1980. Spring 1976 saw the premiere of another new play, *Seven Hours to Sundown*, produced by Edmonton's Theatre Network. Based on an incident in Ryga's own community and published in 1977, it is an interesting exploration of small-town politics—"an examination," Ryga has said, "of how village fascism begins."

In 1976 Ryga's third novel, *Night Desk*, appeared. Begun in Edmonton in the late 1950s while Ryga was working as a hotel desk clerk, it is the dramatic monologue of Romeo Kuchmir, re-

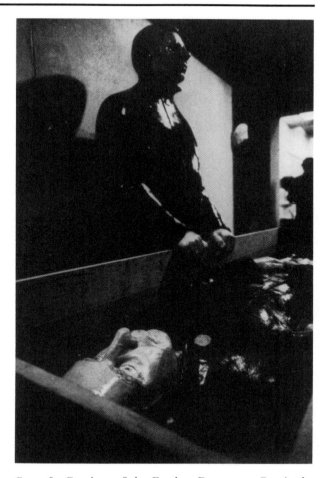

Cover for Captives of the Faceless Drummer, *Ryga's play in which the protagonist is held captive by nationalist revolutionaries*

tired wrestler and fight promoter. He is an extraordinarily vital character who celebrates life's difficulties with humor and gratitude, summing up the theme of much of Ryga's work: "If there's no sorrow, where's the joy comin' from?" The novel was well received. A one-act stage version, entitled *The Last of the Gladiators*, was first performed in Summerland, British Columbia, by the Giant's Head Theatre Company in June 1976.

Ryga traveled to China in 1976 and again in 1978. *Beyond the Crimson Morning: Reflections from a Journey through Contemporary China* (1979) is his impressionistic account of those trips, which includes excursions into memory similar to those in his fictional works. Perhaps also inspired by his Chinese experience was an unsuccessful modern adaptation of *Prometheus Bound*, a highly rhetorical paean to the revolutionary spirit that remains unbroken though the revolution itself is corrupted and betrayed. The play has yet to be produced. The year 1978 also saw production of

Ryga's children's play *Jeremiah's Place*, toured by Kaleidoscope Theatre through Victoria schools in the fall of that year.

Much more in the vein of Ryga's best work is the stage version of a teleplay Ryga had written for *The Newcomers* series in 1978, *A Letter to My Son*, commissioned and first performed by Kam Theatre Lab of North Bay, Ontario, in October 1981. Interior monologues, memory sequences, and musical mood changes mark the attempts of fierce old Ivan Lepa, a Ukrainian immigrant farmer, to address a letter of reconciliation to his educated, Canadianized son. These scenes overlap with Ivan's confrontations with a female social worker, a figure very unlike other government agents in Ryga's drama, who ultimately helps Ivan resolve his guilt and get on with his life. Justly nominated for a Governor General's Award, the play is in many ways Ryga's best since *The Ecstasy of Rita Joe*.

Despite his early successes, George Ryga has remained largely outside the Canadian literary mainstream. With the exception of *The Ecstasy of Rita Joe* his writing is probably more popular in Europe than in Canada. But lately there have been signs of a domestic resurgence for Ryga. *One More for the Road*, a one-character picaresque musical, opened at the Firehall Theatre in October 1985, the first premiere of a Ryga play in Vancouver since the furor of the early 1970s over *Captives of the Faceless Drummer*. This was followed a year later by the Playhouse's *Paracelsus*, the most expensively mounted production of a Ryga play to date. Late 1985 also saw the publication of his ambitious new novel, *In the Shadow of the Vulture*, a tale of exploited Mexican migrant workers in the southwestern United States, and Christopher Innes's *Politics and the Playwright: George Ryga*, the first book-length study of Ryga's work. It remains to be seen whether these developments will result in a much-needed reassessment of the writer *Maclean's* has called "a prophet denied in his own land."

References:

Neil Carson, "George Ryga and the Lost Country," *Canadian Literature*, 45 (Summer 1970): 33-40;

Peter Hay, "George Ryga: Beginnings of a Biography," *Canadian Theatre Review*, 23 (Summer 1979): 36-44;

Christopher Innes, *Politics and the Playwright:*

Cover for Ryga's third novel, based on his experience as a hotel desk clerk

George Ryga (Toronto: Simon & Pierre, 1985);

Brian Parker, "The Ballad-Plays of Ryga," in Ryga's *The Ecstasy of Rita Joe and Other Plays* (Toronto: New Press, 1971), pp. vii-xx;

Laurie Ricou, *Vertical Man / Horizontal World: Man and Landscape in Canadian Prairie Fiction* (Vancouver: University of British Columbia Press, 1973), pp. 121-124;

David Watson and Christopher Innes, "Political Mythologies: An Interview with George Ryga," *Canadian Drama*, 8 (Fall 1982): 160-172;

Bonnie Worthington, "Ryga's Women," *Canadian Drama*, 5 (Fall 1979): 139-143.

Papers:

Ryga's papers are housed at the University of Calgary Library.

Francis Sparshott

(19 May 1926-   )

Wendy Robbins Keitner
University of New Brunswick

BOOKS: *An Enquiry into Goodness and Related Concepts* (Chicago: University of Chicago Press, 1958; Toronto: University of Toronto Press, 1958);

The Structure of Aesthetics (Toronto: University of Toronto Press, 1963; London: Routledge & Kegan Paul, 1963);

A Divided Voice (Toronto: Oxford University Press, 1965);

The Concept of Criticism (Oxford: Clarendon Press, 1967);

A Cardboard Garage (Toronto: Clarke, Irwin, 1969);

A Book, as Cromwell Kent (Scarborough, Ontario: Privately printed, 1970);

Looking for Philosophy (Montreal: McGill-Queen's University Press, 1972);

The Rainy Hills: Verses after a Japanese Fashion (Erin, Ontario: Privately printed by The Porcupine's Quill, 1979);

The Naming of the Beasts (Windsor, Ontario: Black Moss, 1979);

New Fingers for Old Dikes (Toronto: League of Canadian Poets, 1980);

The Theory of the Arts (Princeton: Princeton University Press, 1982);

The Cave of Trophonius and Other Poems (Coldstream, Ontario: Brick, 1983);

The Hanging Gardens of Etobicoke (Toronto: Childe Thursday, 1983);

Storms and Screens (Toronto: Childe Thursday, 1986).

OTHER: John M. Robson, ed., *Essays on Philosophy and the Classics. Collected Works of John Stuart Mill,* introduction by Sparshott (Toronto: University of Toronto Press, 1977).

PERIODICAL PUBLICATIONS: "Plato as Anti-Political Thinker," *Ethics,* 77 (April 1967): 214-219;

"The Unity of Aesthetic Education," *Journal of Aesthetic Education,* 2 (April 1968): 9-21;

"Basic Film Aesthetics," *Journal of Aesthetic Education,* 5 (1971): 11-34;

"Every Horse Has a Mouth: A Personal Poetics," *Philosophy and Literature,* 1 (Spring 1977): 147-169;

"Poets as Readers," *Royal Society of Canada,* fourth series 17 (1979): 149-158;

"Last Word in Criticism," *Royal Society of Canada,* fourth series 20 (1982): 117-128.

Philosopher, critical theorist, and poet, Francis Edward Sparshott has written on a wide range of moral, aesthetic, and intellectual issues. Some of his theoretical writings have appeared in publications alongside those of Northrop Frye, whose influence on him has been considerable. Yet he prefers to describe himself as "primarily a poet, secondarily a writer of miscellaneous prose, and a teacher by necessity."

Born in Chatham, England, to Frank Brownley Sparshott, a teacher, and Gladwys Head Sparshott, Francis Sparshott was educated at King's School, Rochester, and entered Corpus Christi College, Oxford, in 1943. He spent several months early in 1944 writing poetry (work later collected in *A Divided Voice*), but he interrupted his writing and studies to join the British Army Intelligence Corps, serving in Palestine and earning the rank of sergeant before returning to Oxford in 1947. As a teenager he had felt poetry to be his calling; but by his early twenties, he confesses with typical wry humor in the 1977 article "Every Horse Has a Mouth," he made a deliberate choice to be merely a "minor poet" and to take up "the inwardly farcical but outwardly respectable career of the academic philosopher."

Sparshott graduated from Oxford in 1950 with a B.A., first-class honors in *Litterae Humaniores,* and an M.A., and was appointed lecturer in philosophy at the University of Toronto, where he has remained ever since, except for short leaves spent at Northwestern University, the University of Illinois (Urbana), and Sir George Williams University in Montreal. In 1953 he married Kathleen Vaughan whom he met on

an archaeological dig in Peterborough, Ontario. They have one daughter, born in 1954. In 1955 Sparshott became an assistant professor at University of Toronto's Victoria College. Rising through the ranks at the college, he was appointed full professor in 1964 and served as chairman of the Department of Philosophy from 1965 to 1970. In addition to teaching philosophy, he lectured in classics from 1955 to 1970.

His first book, *An Enquiry into Goodness and Related Concepts* (1958), written early in his career as a professor of moral philosophy, was well received, being warmly praised in a *Times Literary Supplement* front-page review for its humanistic approach and its lucid, lively style (a sharp contrast to the scientific language used by contemporary philosophers following Sir Alfred Jules Ayer). *An Enquiry into Goodness and Related Concepts* provides an analysis of the concept and usage of the word *good*, highlighting the imprecisions and ambigui-

ties that are to be encountered in its application in everyday thought and speech, and examining one central, relativist formula: "To say that *x* is good is to say that it is such as to satisfy the wants of the person or persons concerned."

Sparshott's second book, *The Structure of Aesthetics* (1963), is a guide to the structure and problems of the whole field of aesthetics and is empirical in its approach. Defining aesthetics as "that part of philosophy which deals with problems arising mainly out of the existence of beautiful things, and men's response to their beauty," Sparshott does not intend to "solve any of the problems with which aesthetics deals," but rather to clarify "what the problems are, how they are related to each other, what kinds of answers to them have been proposed by others, and how these answers are related." Key issues are beauty, art, and the function of art. The discussion is enriched by frequent allusions and illustrations chosen from a wide range of periods and forms of art, especially the visual arts.

In *A Divided Voice* (1965), Sparshott's first collection of poetry, the struggle between opposites emerges as a principal theme. The speaking voice is often that of a philosophical young man torn between the claims of mind and body, thought and emotion, logic and imagination. Critics have commented on Sparshott's cerebral poetic style, and his subjects, too, suggest the academic and the thinker: the nature of reality, memory, perception, change, and unmerited pain. Most of the verse is traditional and impersonal.

The Concept of Criticism (1967), which again unites Sparshott's literary and philosophical interests, developed out of a graduate seminar in aesthetics he conducted in 1963-1964 and is a first-rate discussion of the crucial matters of description, interpretation, and evaluation of works of art. He starts from a general notion of what criticism is before developing a theory about the scope and rationale of art criticism or literary criticism in particular. His "framing" concept is the notion of "performance," and he proposes that "criticism is essentially discourse about performances but is also itself performance." Given this partnership between creation and criticism, a key problem becomes that of reconciling the artistic integrity of the critic with his critical responsibility to that of his subject.

A Cardboard Garage (1969), Sparshott's second collection of poems, includes "Brittle Bodies," a group of poems with regular metrics and rhyme schemes, and the slightly more experimental "Soft Engines." The poet's main concern is philosophical as he tries to piece together the meaning of life. The poems were written from 1943 to 1969, but most date to early 1966—his second period of concentrated poetic activity—during a hiatus in teaching engagements. In Sparshott's view, expressed in "Every Horse Has a Mouth," the work of this period confirmed that he could, "given a clear mind, sit down with a sheet of paper and be sure that in no more than an hour I would . . . come up with a poem or a substantial part of one." Several poems, however, describe silences, loss of meaning, and the poet-persona's failure to touch other people with his words.

Throughout his career, Sparshott has been a prolific writer of literary and philosophical articles; the best-known of these, entitled "Basic Film Aesthetics," was published in the *Journal of Aes-*

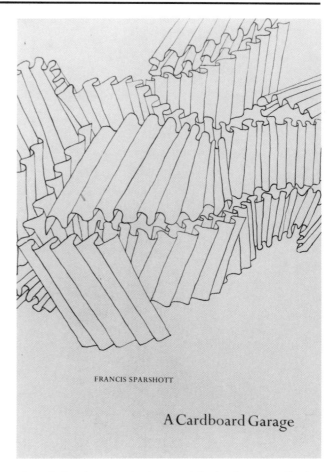

FRANCIS SPARSHOTT

A Cardboard Garage

Dust jacket for Sparshott's second book of verse, collecting poems written from 1943 to 1969

thetic Education in 1971. Typical of his approach to critical problems, Sparshott takes the widest possible grasp of the variables and variations accessible to filmmakers, starting from an examination of the mechanisms employed and moving to discussion of the illusions created in terms of space, time, motion, and other dimensions. *A Book* (1970), privately printed under the pseudonym Cromwell Kent, is a mere *jeu d'esprit* comprising two whimsical, satirical sketches, the longer one being a Canadian thriller.

Looking for Philosophy (1972) combines poems, interludes, glosses, and three core essays as it traces "one literary man's attempt to find himself as a philosopher, only to discover that the attempt itself was all that his philosophy could be." One reviewer described the book as "a kind of film of thought in action." It ends as the philosopher-as-poet vanishes into "the shrieking air" on the midway Ferris wheel of eternity. He

Manuscript for Sparshott's sonnet "The Comedy of Art," collected in The Hanging Gardens of Etobicoke, *1983 (by permission of the author)*

has found that meaning is something attributed to language, not events.

Inspired by his reading of Matsuo Bashō's *Journey to the Deep North*, Sparshott wrote *The Rainy Hills: Verses after a Japanese Fashion* during the summer of 1969. The brief, impressionistic poems composed in the Japanese verse forms of haiku, tanka, and renga form a loose series centered on journeying, myth, and nature. The collection was privately printed in 1979 with the calligraphy by Sparshott himself.

The Naming of the Beasts (1979) was written during Sparshott's fourth burst of poetic activity from June to October 1970. The poems are fashioned in many forms and include a substantial range of subjects. Some poems are drawn from Canadian history, some deal with philosophy (such as the fine "Reply to the Committed Intellectual"), and one quietly moving poem ("Three Seasons") provides a rare personal glimpse of the poet in middle age confronting his aging and losses.

A varied suite of poems published in February 1981 in the *Canadian Forum* shows a new involvement in sociopolitical events, illustrating Sparshott's contention that the poet must be a "restless scanner" whose style is "a style of search, not a habit of acceptance." But his most recent volumes of poetry continue to elucidate his concerns with love and age. *The Hanging Gardens of Etobicoke* (1983) shows in its title allusion to a Toronto suburb his scholarly wit; *The Cave of Trophonius* (1983) is a set of four meditations, primarily on classical themes but also on the Glooskap legends of North American Algonquin cultures. His 1981 reading tour of Scandinavia and his winning of the CBC's third annual literary competition indicate that Sparshott's poetry is becoming more widely known. *Storms and Screens* (1986) further demonstrates his versatility; some poems are written in free verse, some in regular metrics, and the subjects and structures range from longings for transcendence to anagrams, found poems, and spirited word play.

A major new philosophical work, entitled *The Theory of the Arts* (1982), confirms his reputation in aesthetic theory. Announced as the third and final volume in his series of enquiries into aesthetics, *The Theory of the Arts* is a massive, 726-page survey. Whereas *The Structure of Aesthetics* examines the kinds of questions that the study of aesthetics can logically be expected to posit and *The Concept of Criticism* asks what it is that critics do, by asking what it means to criticize, the new book is at once a conclusion to these earlier works and an exploration of a self-referential theory by which to read the earlier volumes again. By examining what "theory" is, Sparshott produces a theory of theory, based in large part on Plato and proceeding primarily by means of a system of classification. Differentiating first of all between what he calls Classical and Expressive lines in art–whether visual, aural, or verbal–he probes under the first category (which itself subdivides) such notions as place, performance, and beauty; under the second (also a plural notion), he considers the character of art as an intuitive process, a sacred symbol, and a political weapon. An extensive appendix examines the nature of such notions as pleasure, judgment, education, and experience as they bear upon people's understanding of what art is and does. Such questions have their impact on Sparshott's sense of poetic design, line, and order; the precise ways in which they shape Sparshott's own poems, however, have yet to be examined critically.

Papers:

Sparshott's manuscripts are housed in the E. J. Pratt Library, Victoria College, University of Toronto.

Peter Such

(29 April 1939-)

Leslie Monkman
Queen's University

BOOKS: *Fallout* (Toronto: Anansi, 1969; revised Toronto: NC Press, 1977);
Soundprints: Contemporary Composers (Toronto: Clarke, Irwin, 1972);
Riverrun (Toronto: Clarke, Irwin, 1973; revised, Toronto: Irwin, 1982);
Vanished Peoples: The Archaic Dorset & Beothuk People of Newfoundland (Toronto: NC Press, 1978);
Dolphin's Wake (Toronto: Macmillan, 1979).

PLAY PRODUCTIONS: *Elephant's Graveyard*, Toronto, University of Toronto Hart House Theatre, December 1963;
Union Station, Toronto, Tarragon Theatre, July 1975;
Island Follies, Toronto, Shadowland Repertory Company, July 1984.

MOTION PICTURE: *Free Dive*, screenplay by Such, Horus Productions, 1980.

TELEVISION: *Home Fires*, CBC, 1981;
"Free and Clear," *The Campbells*, CTV, 1986.

OTHER: "Please Feel Free," in *The City. Attacking Modern Myths*, edited by Allan Powell (Toronto: McClelland & Stewart, 1972).

PERIODICAL PUBLICATIONS:
NONFICTION
"Last Year Another Pyramid Fell Down," *Dialog* (Passover 1971): 19-21, 37;
"The Short Life and Sudden Death of Harold Ladoo," *Saturday Night*, 89 (May 1974): 35-38;
"One Score and Five Years Later," *Canadian Forum*, 56 (December/January 1976-1977): 6-10;
"News From Nowhere," *Canadian Literature*, 78 (August 1978): 103-109;
"Shakespeare Never Went to Verona," *Globe and Mail*, 22 September 1979, p. 6;
"Carrying on Regardless," *Poetry Canada Review*, 5 (Fall 1983): 20.

Peter Such (photograph by Jo Gladding)

FICTION
"Floating Bears," *Impulse*, 2. no. 3-4 (1973): 47-59;
"The Death of Nonasabasut," *Canadian Forum*, 53 (November/December 1973): 28-29;
"Last Year Another Pyramid Fell Down," *Descant*, 10, no. 3-4 (1979): 141-155.

Peter Such is a member of the influential generation of contemporary Canadian writers who introduced new vitality into the creation, publication, and appreciation of Canadian literature in the 1960s and 1970s. None of his contemporaries has been more eclectic than Such, whose work includes poetry, short stories, and novels, a biographical study of six contemporary Canadian composers, an anthropological history of the aboriginal peoples of Newfoundland, a recently completed retrospective on the McMichael Gallery of Kleinburg, Ontario, as well as plays, an opera libretto, and scripts for television and film.

Peter Such was born in London, England, and immigrated to Canada in 1953. After completing secondary school in Toronto and earning B.A. and M.A. degrees in English at the University of Toronto (1960, 1966), he withdrew from formal postgraduate work in 1967 to pursue interdisciplinary studies independently. Interspersed with his graduate studies in the 1960s were a variety of teaching positions at high schools and colleges in Ontario, and from 1970 to 1972, he was writer in residence at Erindale College, University of Toronto. In 1976 he became a founder and coordinator of the Canadian Studies Programme at Atkinson College, York University, where he is currently a professor in the Department of Humanities.

The commitment to Canadian studies reflected in Such's teaching career has also found expression in a variety of initiatives and endeavors in Canadian publishing. While serving as writer in residence at Erindale College, he founded *Impulse*, a magazine of contemporary Canadian writing which he edited from 1971 to 1974. In 1973 Such was the founding vice president of the Canadian Periodical Publishers Association, a group of more than one hundred publishers committed to ensuring that Canada's journals serve effectively as "transmitters of Canada's culture." An extension of this concern with establishing and maintaining forums for the examination and discussion of Canadian culture can be seen in Such's work from 1975 to 1977 as managing editor for the review journal *Books in Canada*.

The concern with the state of culture in Canada is also central to Such's first novel, *Fallout* (1969). Based on his experiences working in the uranium mines of northern Ontario in 1957, when Such was a student, the book explores the impact that the economic collapse of the region's boomtowns had on their native and white inhabitants. Described by an early reviewer as "the archetypal Canadian novel," the book reinforces Northrop Frye's suggestion that a pastoral myth lies at the center of Canadian experience in its concern with the opposition between the landscape and the technology introduced by the white man and with the conflicting visions of the landscape and human freedom arising from red and white cultures. In the preface to the revised edition of 1977 Such notes that the book was mainly written while he was living in the English Lake District for several months in 1968, and the novel is framed by two passages in which the author-persona combines memories drawn from this ex-

Cover for the novel Such based on his experiences working in a northern Ontario uranium mine. Fallout *was the fifth title published in the Spiderline series of first novels.*

perience with observations made in 1968 on a return to the landscape he had last seen as a teenage student. Thus, pastoral images of idyllic English countryside are coupled with antipastoral images of the desecrated landscape of Eliot Lake and its environs. Despite the images of dislocation and destruction, *Fallout* ends with a vision of the resurgent vitality of nature, an expression of persevering faith in human potential for love and freedom, and an image of the artist as one who brings cohesion, if not order, to fragmentary insights and disparate memories.

Such attributes the inspiration for his second book, *Soundprints* (1972), to Canadian composer Walter Buczynski who was the musician in residence at Erindale during Such's tenure there. *Soundprints* attempts "to give the reader some experience of how it feels to live as a contemporary composer in Canada" by examining the careers of Buczynski, John Weinzweig, Harry Somers, John Beckwith, Norma Beecroft, and Murray

Schaefer. An important contribution to a relatively unexplored area of Canadian culture, the book acknowledges the international tradition in which the composers participate and also shows the impact of contemporary experience in Canada on their music.

Both *Riverrun* (1973) and *Vanished Peoples* (1978) reflect Such's continuing interest in archaeology and anthropology, and they extend his concern with documenting Canadian culture by focusing on the peoples of Newfoundland. *Riverrun*, his most widely praised novel, traces the final years of the last family of Newfoundland's Beothuk tribe, extinct since 1829. *Vanished Peoples* is a documentary study of the Beothuks and of the Archaic and Dorset peoples who preceded them. While this later work insists explicitly on the need for "a sense of our past, of how our present and indeed our future grow out of it," *Riverrun* evokes the ancestral past through an elegiac re-creation of the final years of Beothuk culture using the resources of both fiction and documentary history. The initial word of *Finnegans Wake* gives Such his title, and in James Joyce's work "riverrun" links the opening and closing phrases of the book and suggests the cyclical flow of continuing existence. Such's novel, however, chronicles not continuation but extinction; the last Beothuks, whose lives have cyclically followed the river linking their inland lake to the sea, confront the catastrophic breaking of the cycle as "the riverrun ends."

This preoccupation with time and the past recurs in *Dolphin's Wake* (1979). Reviewing his forty-year career as an archaeologist in Greece, the protagonist sees himself as a "rootless one" who has ironically attempted through his work "to define whole civilizations." When he and his wife agree to aid guerrillas opposing the Greek junta that seized power in 1967, they become caught in the "wake" of Nikos, "the dolphin," the symbolic leader of the antifascist forces. The protagonist's vague dissatisfaction and frustration give way to despair as his wife experiences a sense of the elemental renewal of earth itself after years of service and submission and leaves her husband for the guerrilla leader. Based in part on his travels in the Mediterranean in 1967, *Dolphin's Wake* represents a significant departure for Such in its use of a setting outside of Canada and in its exploitation of many of the conventions of adventure fiction. Such acknowledged this conscious departure in a 1979 essay entitled "Shakespeare Never Went to Verona," in which he argues that the era

Dust jacket for Such's novel about an archaeologist and his wife involved with guerrilla forces in 1960s Greece

has ended when he and his contemporaries needed "to express our vision in explicitly Canadian terms." No longer literary colonials, Canadian writers must now also explore a larger world: "Remember Shakespeare and the groundlings. Remember he never went to Verona. . . . As Canadians, we have a unique sensibility and a unique perspective on the world. We have to believe it's important and also *exportable*."

The articulation of various facets of that sensibility serves as the unifying focus for all of Such's work. In a 1978 article entitled "News from Nowhere" he describes Canada as "a country deeply committed to humanist struggles and [to] a concern with documenting the essential human quandaries of culture clash." In recent work that includes the libretto for an opera, "Loom, Sword, River," a script for a film entitled *Free Dive*, released in conjunction with the International Year of the Disabled in 1980, and a series of eight television scripts entitled *Home Fires*, about Torontonians during World War II, Peter Such continues his exploration of these values and of new media and contexts for expressing them.

Interviews:

Bernice Lever, "A Man For All Genres: Peter Such," *Canadian Author and Bookman*, 56 (Winter 1981): 4-5, 10;

Patricia Keeney Smith, "WQ Interview with Peter Such," *Cross-Canada Writers' Quarterly*, 7, no. 2 (1985): 5-6, 26-27.

References:

Arnold E. Davidson, "Crosscurrents in Peter Such's *Riverrun*," *Journal of Canadian Fiction*, no. 31/32 (1981): 194-202;

John Moss, "Genocide: The White Man's Burden," in his *Sex and Violence in the Canadian Novel* (Toronto: McClelland & Stewart, 1977), pp. 256-261.

Papers:

The manuscripts and personal correspondence of Peter Such are at the library of McMaster University, Hamilton, Ontario.

Audrey Thomas
(17 November 1935-)

Constance Rooke
University of Victoria

BOOKS: *Ten Green Bottles* (Indianapolis: Bobbs-Merrill, 1967; Ottawa: Oberon, 1977);

Mrs. Blood (Indianapolis: Bobbs-Merrill, 1970; Vancouver: Talonbooks, 1975);

Munchmeyer and Prospero on the Island (Indianapolis: Bobbs-Merrill, 1971);

Songs My Mother Taught Me (Vancouver: Talonbooks, 1973; Indianapolis: Bobbs-Merrill, 1973);

Blown Figures (Vancouver: Talonbooks, 1974; New York: Knopf, 1975);

Ladies & Escorts (Ottawa: Oberon, 1977);

Latakia (Vancouver & Los Angeles: Talonbooks, 1979);

Real Mothers (Vancouver: Talonbooks, 1981);

Intertidal Life (Toronto: Stoddart, 1984; New York: Beaufort Books, 1984);

Goodbye Harold, Good Luck (Markham, Ontario: Viking/Penguin, 1986).

RADIO: "Once Your Submarine Cable is Gone, What Have You Got?," by Thomas, Linda Sorenson, and Keith Pepper, *CBC Stage*, CBC, 27 October 1973;

"Mrs. Blood," *CBC Stage*, CBC, 16 August 1975;

"Untouchables," *Audience*, CBC, 5 December 1981;

"The Milky Way," *Vanishing Point*, CBC, 26 November 1983;

"The Axe of God," in "Disasters! Act of God or Acts of Man?," *Stereo Theatre*, CBC, 24 February 1985;

"The Woman in Black Velvet," *Vanishing Point*, CBC, 17 May 1985;

"In the Groove," *Vanishing Point*, CBC, 4 November 1985;

"On the Immediate Level of Events Occurring in Meadows," in "Sextet," *Sunday Matinee*, CBC, 26 January 1986.

OTHER: Cathy Ford, ed., *Canadian Short Fiction Anthology*, foreword by Thomas (Vancouver: Intermedia, 1976);

"Trash," in *Vancouver Fiction*, edited by David Watmough (Winlaw, British Columbia: Polestar Press, 1985), pp. 145-150.

PERIODICAL PUBLICATIONS: "Through a Glass Darkly: Canadian Art Criticism," *Canadian Literature*, 46 (Autumn 1970): 62-72;

"African Journal Entries," *Capilano Review*, 7 (1975): 55-62;

"The New Adventures of Elisabeth Hopkins: Dis-

covered, At 80, To Be an Artistic Talent,"
Maclean's (August 1975): 54, 56-57;

" 'My Craft and Sullen Art': The Writers Speak.
Is There a Feminine Voice in Literature?," *Atlantis*, 4, no. 1 (1978): 152-154;

"Clean Monday, or Wintering in Athens,"
Capilano Review, 13 (1978): 68-87;

"An Open Letter to Dorothy Livesay," *Room of
One's Own*, 5, no. 3 (1980): 71-73;

"Graven Images: A Memoir," *Capilano Review*, 20
(1981): 44-51;

"Spring Break," *Chatelaine* (March 1981): 40-41;

"Spaghetti and Meatballs for Christmas?," *Chatelaine* (December 1981): 70-71;

"Untouchables," *Room of One's Own*, 7, no. 3
(1982): 2-17;

"Basmati Rice: An Essay about Words," *Canadian
Literature*, 100 (Spring 1984): 312-317;

"A Fine Romance, My Dear, This Is," *Canadian Literature*, 108 (Spring 1986): 5-12.

Audrey Thomas's fiction is largely and con-
spicuously autobiographical. It tends to be woman-
centered, although sometimes Thomas adopts a
male persona. Her work is often thought of as experimental, mainly because of a fondness for discontinuous narration, word play, fragmented
narrators, and the incorporation of such matter
as etymologies, nursery rhymes, advertisements,
and recipes. The fiction is highly allusive, much
given to play with literary references, most of
them widely accessible. Thomas functions both as
a collector or connoisseur of the fragments of external reality which interest her, and as a custo-
dian of a precarious inner reality.

Audrey Thomas was born to Donald Earle
Callahan, a teacher, and Frances Corbett
Callahan in Binghamton, New York, on 17 November 1935. She received a B.A. from Smith College in 1957; during 1955-1956 she was a
nonmatriculating student at St. Andrew's University in Scotland. In December 1958 Audrey
Grace Callahan married sculptor and art teacher
Ian Thomas. They came to Canada in August of
1959, settled in British Columbia, and had three
daughters: Sarah (1959), Victoria (1961), and
Claire (1967). In 1963 Thomas received her
M.A. in English from the University of British Columbia; later, at U.B.C. she did work toward a
Ph.D. in Anglo-Saxon language and literature.
From 1964 to 1966 she lived in Ghana, where
her husband taught art at the University of Sci-
ence and Technology in Kumasi. Five years later
Thomas returned to Africa alone and traveled ex-

Audrey Thomas (photograph by Victoria Thomas)

tensively in the former French West African colonies. She and her husband separated in 1972. In
recent years she has lived principally in Vancouver and on Galiano Island and has intermittently
taught creative writing at the University of Victoria and at U.B.C. Thomas has also been writer in
residence at Concordia University, at Simon Fraser University, at the David Thompson University
Centre, and at the University of Ottawa. In 1986
she was the Canada-Scotland Literary Fellow, in
residence in Edinburgh.

The title of her first collection of stories,
Ten Green Bottles (1967), implies the author's fear
of collapse or disintegration—of nothingness if
that last green bottle should happen to fail—and
her use of fiction as a container for experience.
The first and last of the ten stories are set in hospitals, in Africa and Upstate New York: "If One
Green Bottle . . ." describes a miscarriage, and in
"Salon des Refuses," which draws upon Thomas's
youthful employment in an asylum, the line between sanity and madness seems to have vanished for all concerned. Fears of incompetence,
of unattractiveness, of death, and of the unknown dominate the book.

Mrs. Blood (1970), which elaborates upon
the miscarriage story, is set primarily in Ghana.

The novel is presented in brief sections labeled either "Mrs. Blood" or "Mrs. Thing." The former is the protagonist's visceral self, so that Mrs. Blood's sections are more poetic and brooding; Mrs. Thing is her objective, but alienated self, and these sections provide most of her ordinary narration. As the protagonist lies in her bed, obsessed by images of blood–those she sees around her as well as other, literary ones–and glimpsing the anomalies of Africa, she recalls her painful affair with Richard and the difficulties of her marriage to Jason.

In 1971 Thomas's two interlocking novellas entitled *Munchmeyer and Prospero on the Island* were published in a single volume. In *Munchmeyer* she adopts a male persona–that of an unappealing, vain, unhappy, and unsuccessful writer. In *Prospero on the Island* she is Miranda, a woman on an island suspiciously like Galiano (and alluding to the island of Shakespeare's *The Tempest*), who is writing a novel about Munchmeyer, of whom she is surprisingly tolerant. The principal interest of this book is in the elaborate, shifting, and subtle parallels which exist between the character configurations of the two novellas and implicitly between the fiction-writer's life and her work.

Songs My Mother Taught Me (1973) is the revision of a novel written early in Thomas's career. Although this is the most straightforward of her books, the narrator, Isobel Cleary, is sometimes addressed as Isobel by the author's voice, and there are occasional temporal dislocations as well as minor typographical oddities. The portrait of a beloved grandfather whose ease and self-acceptance provide a taste of what life ought to be, the hysteria of Isobel's disappointed mother, and the efforts of both her parents to purchase familial happiness are especially poignant. Isobel triumphs over her own fears in the final scenes of the novel, set in the asylum where she works; there she learns something of compassion and something of the madness which has been concealed in her family. Finally, she chooses to be vulnerable.

Blown Figures (1974) is a sequel to *Mrs. Blood*. The protagonist, now called Isobel, makes either a literal or an imaginative return journey to Ghana, to find or "exorcise" the child which she miscarried in *Mrs. Blood*. She is now clearly schizophrenic and addresses many of her remarks to a Miss Miller–an imaginary confidante. Blatantly experimental, *Blown Figures* has numerous nearly blank pages which serve to isolate the fragments (cartoons, one-liners, and so forth)

Dust jacket for Thomas's 1973 novel. In the family photograph used to illustrate the jacket, Thomas is on the left.

which appear there. The novel depends heavily on Africa as a metaphor for the unconscious.

Ladies & Escorts (1977) contains eleven stories set in British Columbia, Africa, and Mexico. Many of the stories are concerned with questions of age difference and sexual politics and reveal an increasing strength in the female characters. In "Aquarius" and "A Monday Dream in Alameda Park" the protagonists are nervous male academics, worn down by the vitality of their wives; in "Kill Day on the Government Wharf" and "Green Stakes for the Garden" the sexual confidence of the female protagonists is fascinating to younger men; and in "Initram" two boisterously confessional women writers meet at the exit point of their marriages.

The gap between male and female seems to have widened in *Latakia* (1979), a novel which takes the form of an "imaginary monologue" addressed to a departed lover. It is the postmortem of an affair between a successful woman writer and an unknown, younger male writer. The narrator conducts her postmortem in order to understand what caused the relationship to end and also to exorcise the pain of loss. The reader

Dust jacket for Thomas's third novel, the sequel to Mrs. Blood

manipulative, and controlling qualities. In "Out in the Midday Sun" and "Timbuktu" the author follows the struggles of two women for whom walking a few steps behind attractive, intelligent husbands is no longer a satisfying mode of existence. These women choose to abandon mothering altogether; the price they pay for wanting more is ultimately the destruction of their marriages. One possible emotional repercussion of this stab an independence is depicted in "Déjeuner sur l'Herbe". Here the middle-aged protagonist, having once known intimacy, suffers from the constant pain of being unloved. Thomas is no pessimist, however, and her strong-willed heroines give themselves the psychic "medicine" they require. Ignoring rules of etiquette and the laws of polite society, which would only perpetuate their isolation, these women find new ways of engaging the world. The final story, "Crossing the Rubicon," combines the issue of balance between private and parenting responsibilities with the theme of independence; the narrator contemplates baking cupcakes for her daughter's Valentine Day party, while trying to write a story describing a girl meeting her ex-lover. In the story within the story, the woman demands that her ex-lover admit that he has missed her, and after he confesses this, she waves goodbye, without looking back.

Like *Latakia*, Thomas's most recent novel, *Intertidal Life* (1984), concerns a successful writer who is suffering the end of a relationship. The story is set on Gulf Island in British Columbia (we think inevitably of Galiano) where her fourteen-year marriage came to its close. Thomas uses nursery rhymes, echoes of *Alice in Wonderland*, camp songs, and excerpts from the diaries of early Spanish explorers, splicing these into the story of Alice, which is again (as in *Latakia*) temporally fragmented. The juxtaposition of texts is both elegant and psychologically intriguing. For example, we are told that "abandon" means "to set at liberty": though her husband Peter has left her, Alice has actually been set free. In this way she is linked to the explorers who are quoted throughout the novel. But Alice is a *female* explorer, and Thomas seems to suggest that explorers of that sex do not act in heroic isolation; they are inextricably involved with others and most particularly with their female friends and children. The novel ends with the scene of Alice's youngest daughter, Flora, in a boat with her father. Flora is crying, but Peter cannot understand why and is incapable of comforting her. At last he pro-

shares her immersion in a love which is over, for which the ending is written and cannot be changed. Thomas avoids telling the story in chronological order: she keeps backing up, and she denies readers the usual climax. Precisely because the moment of separation never quite occurs, it seems to happen continually. *Latakia* is also a kind of travel book (set largely in Greece) and a meditation by the narrator on her experience as material for fiction.

Thomas's collection of short stories entitled *Real Mothers* (1981) outlines the difficulties involved in various types of relationships. Out of the ten stories in this collection, four examine the complex task of balancing one's role as a mother with one's role as a single woman. In the title story, "Real Mothers," a middle ground is never located, and the heroine loses her children because she neglects their emotional needs. "Harry and Violet" explores the opposite problem: the heroine's relationship with her lover suffers because he is not enamored of the idea of sharing his time, or his bed, with her child. In addition to her interest in the difficulties of maintaining a balance, Thomas investigates aspects of mothering itself—often revealing its darker, more

poses that she row, and "they carefully changed places." The new world into which Flora and Alice are moving is one in which women will be not only more independent (as the image of the child and her father in the boat suggests) but also (as Thomas implies throughout the novel) *inter*dependent and able to comfort one another on their journey.

Thomas's most recent collection of short stories, *Goodbye Harold, Good Luck* (1986), is perhaps the author's most varied and complex achievement to date. The sheer diversity of the stories in this collection is remarkable. No two share a common style or tone; the settings range from northern British Columbia, to Greece, Paris, Africa, Scotland, and even into the world of pure fantasy. The common thread linking these tales is that of obsession and the pain of separation and alienation. Thomas's prose is clear and convincing; in the story "Elevation" one shares Clayton's unusual passion for hummingbirds. In "Compulsory Figures" Thomas delves into the mind of a man with a foot fetish, and in the poetic story "The Man with Clam Eyes" she submerges the reader in the grief of a heartbroken woman. In "One Size Fits All" the narrator, suffering from a nervous breakdown, reads everything as if it were a message sent to her alone. This theme of obsession blends smoothly with Thomas's familiar concern for separation and isolation. In "Local Customs" the story is told through the point of view of a young boy, acutely sensitive to the disparity between the Greek and American culture, as well as to the distances between himself and his father and his father's new lover. The desire to belong and "fit in" is starkly depicted in the story "Degrees" in which an East Indian woman, living in Africa with her British husband, tries to be more British than the British. This notion of painful exclusion is echoed in "The Dance." In this case a mother and daughter on vacation in Greece visit the disco Romantika, but the mother, because she is older and "on the shelf," must be content to watch her fifteen-year-old daughter dance; yet she remembers a time when she participated in that communal activity. In the majority of the stories in this collection, the dull ache of loneliness pulses just below the surface of the text. Always Thomas portrays a painful yet magical reality.

Thomas's career to date has revealed her consistent interest in female experience and in the zestful possibilities of language. Though much of her work concerns women, her experimentalism in particular has attracted the interest of readers and critics of both sexes. One may suppose with some certainty that Audrey Thomas will continue to chart the matter of her personal life and to do so in a sophisticated, flexible, highly individual style.

Interviews:

Pierre Coupey, Gladys Hindmarch, Wendy Pickell, and Bill Schermbrucker, Interview with Audrey Thomas, *Capilano Review*, 7 (1975): 87-109;

Elizabeth Komisar, "Audrey Thomas: A Review/Interview," *Open Letter*, third series, 3 (1975): 59-64.

George Bowering, "Songs and Wisdom: An Interview with Audrey Thomas," *Open Letter*, fourth series, 3 (Spring 1979): 7-31.

Bibliography:

Robin V. H. Bellamy, "Audrey Thomas: A Select Bibliography," *Room of One's Own*, special issue on Thomas, 10, nos. 3-4 (1986): 154-175.

References:

Anne Archer, "Real Mummies," *Studies in Canadian Literature*, 9 (1984): 214-223;

A. F. Bellette, "Some Observations on the Novels of Audrey Thomas," *Open Letter*, third series, 3 (Late Fall 1975): 65-69;

Brigitte G. Bossanne, "Audrey Thomas and Lewis Carroll: Two Sides of the Looking Glass," *North Dakota Quarterly*, 52, no. 3 (1984): 215-233;

George Bowering, "Snow Red: The Short Stories of Audrey Thomas," *Open Letter*, third series, 5 (1976): 28-39;

Pauline Butling, "Thomas and Her Rag-Bag," *Canadian Literature*, 102 (Autumn 1984): 195-199;

Joan Coldwell, "Memory Organized: The Novels of Audrey Thomas," *Canadian Literature*, 92 (Spring 1982): 46-56;

Robert Diotte, "The Romance of Penelope: Audrey Thomas's Isobel Carpenter Trilogy," *Canadian Literature*, 86 (Autumn 1980): 60-68;

Lois C. Gottleib and Wendy Keitner, "Narrative Technique and the Central Female Character in the Novels of Audrey Thomas," *World Literature Written in English*, 21 (1982): 364-373;

Wayne Grady, "Journies [*sic*] to the Interior: The

African Stories of Audrey Thomas," *Canadian Fiction Magazine,* 44 (1982): 98-100;

Coral Ann Howells, "Margaret Laurence: *The Diviners* and Audrey Thomas: *Latakia," Canadian Woman Studies,* 6, no.1 (1984): 98-100;

Wendy Keitner, "Real Mothers Don't Write Books: A Study of the Penelope-Calypso Motif in the Fiction of Audrey Thomas and Marian Engel," *Present Tense: A Critical Anthology,* edited by John Moss (Toronto: NC Press, 1985), pp. 185-204;

Elizabeth Komisar, "Audrey Thomas: a review/interview," *Open Letter,* third series, 3 (Late Fall, 1975): 59-64;

Robert Kroetsch, "The Exploding Porcupine: Violence of Form in English-Canadian Fiction," in *Violence in the Canadian Novel Since 1960/dans le roman Canadien depuis 1960,* edited by Virginia Harger-Grinliny and Terry Goldie (St. John's: Memorial University of Newfoundland, 1981), pp. 191-199;

Louis K. MacKendrick, "A Peopled Labyrinth of Walls: Audrey Thomas' *Blown Figures,"* in *Present Tense: A Critical Anthology,* edited by Moss (Toronto: NC Press, 1985), pp. 168-184.

W. H. New, "Equatorial Zones and Polar Opposites," in *Articulating West* (Toronto: New Press, 1972), pp. 216-233;

Gaston Renaud, "Translating Audrey Thomas into French," in *Translation Perspectives: Selected Papers 1982-1983,* edited by Marilyn Gaddis Rose (Binghamton, N.Y.: Translation Research and Instruction Program, State University of New York at Binghamton, 1984), pp. 125-130;

Room of One's Own, special issue on Thomas, 10, no. 3-4 (1986);

Eleanor Wachtel, "The Image of Africa in the Fiction of Audrey Thomas," *Room of One's Own,* 2, no. 4 (1977): 21-28.

John Thompson

(17 March 1938-26 April 1976)

Douglas Barbour
University of Alberta

BOOKS: *At the Edge of the Chopping there are no Secrets* (Toronto: Anansi, 1973);
Stilt Jack (Toronto: Anansi, 1978).

OTHER: "Life Outfaced," "Go on Living," and "Beginning to Live," translations by Thompson of poems by Roland Giguère, *Ellipse* 2 (Winter 1970): 11,13,15,17,21.

John Thompson was born 17 March 1938, in Manchester, England. He lost his father during World War II and endured an unhappy relationship with his mother, who eventually remarried and moved to Australia. After attending Manchester Grammar School on a scholarship, Thompson completed his two years of national service in the British Army, working as a code clerk. He then took a B.A. (with honors) in psychology at the University of Sheffield. In the early 1960's he entered the doctoral program in comparative literature at Michigan State University, where he completed his Ph.D. in 1966. His dissertation, "Translations from René Char's 'La Parole en Archipel' and Other Works, with an Introductory Essay" was supervised by A. J. M. Smith.

Thompson joined the English department of Mount Allison University, at Sackville, New Brunswick, in the fall of 1966 and remained there till his death ten years later. He moved into a rented farmhouse at Wood Point, west of Sackville, with his American wife and their daughter; then in 1972 he purchased a farmhouse on the High Marsh Road, in Jolicure, about five miles east of Sackville. The landscapes and wildlife of the Tantramar Marshes are the groundwork of all his poems. In 1973 his first collection of poems, *At the Edge of the Chopping there are no Secrets*, was published; that same year his wife separated from him, taking their daughter with her. Thompson had already begun working on *Stilt Jack*, his second and final book, the poems of which were based on the *ghazal*—a well-known form of Persian and Urdu lyric. In 1975, suffering from stress, caught up in work on *Stilt Jack* and on a proposed research project on the French surrealists, Thompson took a sabbatical leave in Toronto. While he was working there, his house in Jolicure, containing most of his books and manuscripts, burned to the ground. He returned to Mount Allison in the fall of 1975 and completed the final draft of *Stilt Jack* by April 1976. On 25 April Thompson was rushed to the hospital, having mixed prescription pills and alcohol and called for help, but he went into a coma from which he never recovered. He died on 26 April 1976 and was buried, according to the Anglican rite, in Jolicure Cemetery, overlooking the Tantramar Marshes he had come to love.

As a number of younger Maritime poets and many of his students have pointed out, Thompson exerted a powerful influence, both through the example of his art, and through his dedication as a teacher. Where he is personally remembered, friends and colleagues describe him as a man often tormented by demons he could exorcise only in his writing, yet to read his poems autobiographically would be to do his art a great disservice. No doubt a great deal of his personal suffering as well as joy enters into them, but close study reveals the carefully wrought works of an artist who took his craft very seriously indeed. A student of such literary mentors as Char (who rejected surrealism, as Thompson also did in the preface to *Stilt Jack),* William Carlos Williams, Roethke, Lorca, Neruda, Rilke, Stevens, Yeats, and other modernists, including the line of writers deriving from Ezra Pound, Thompson wrote with great understanding of the open line as well as a profound concern to pack his images and phrases with as much allusive weight as possible. Indeed, in 1986 Peter Sanger, a student of his work, produced *Sea Run*, a volume of annotations on *Stilt Jack* (1978) intended to make the poems more accessible.

When *At the Edge of the Chopping there are no Secrets* appeared in 1973, not all critics recognized its power. Although Dennis Lee, in a long re-

Covers for the first paperback edition of Thompson's 1973 poetry collection, which includes verse originally published in such magazines as Fiddlehead, Prism International, Quarry, *and* White Pelican

view of new poets in *Saturday Night* and Robert Gibbs, in his review of Thompson's book, paid tribute to the poems' spare imagery and emotive force and to their frightening engagement with the pressures of silence, many reviewers simply found them obscure yet rustic, a judgment which undoubtedly disappointed Thompson. Although many were originally published in periodicals as separate lyrics, they are ordered in the 1973 collection so as to offer a specific journey through darkness to a kind of light. Beginning with an evocation of mystery in a woman making bread, Thompson offers symbolic readings of bread, wine, and salt before leaving the safety of the household for the dark dangers of the outer world. Animals, vegetables, bones, the earth itself; all are mysterious and frightening, images of the broken life, the broken relationship. Yet, though the poems dig through a wintry environment to reach some kind of nadir in such poems

as "The Brim of the Well," in which "coldbroken, I lie you / lie" and the very earth is held in question, the volume turns away from such despair to return to a vision of harmony in "The Bread Hot from the Oven" and "The Onion," in which "you are by me, unfolded / to a white stillness, remade warmth on warmth." As the text concludes:

So we turn from our darkness,
our brokenness,
share this discovered root,
this one quiet bread
quick with light, thyme, that deep
speech of your hands which always
defeats me, calling me through strange earths
to this place suddenly yours.

Although in *At the Edge of the Chopping there are no Secrets,* nothing is what it seems and language itself is unstable, language is all the poet finally has, even if he would prefer silence; even if "the poet names, almost / without speech," he does name, he must. And it is Thompson's accomplishment in this book to have named so much mystery without dissipating its presence.

In *Stilt Jack* Thompson transforms the personal pain of his life into the pure speech of poetry, partly through a series of exhaustive allusions (many of which are pointed out by Sanger in *Sea Run: Notes on John Thompson's* Stilt Jack) and partly through a complex use of the *ghazal's* power to assimilate a vast texture of voices and tones. Moreover, by turning both "I" and "you" into "floating signifiers" (as he also did in his first book), he is able to subvert simple autobiographical readings and avoid the lyric solipsism which might otherwise have burdened the sequence with too much sentimentality.

The *ghazal*, which Thompson discovered in its American incarnation in the works of Adrienne Rich and Jim Harrison, is a form rich in possibilities for a poet seeking to escape the bonds of the traditional Western lyric, as Thompson points out in the preface to *Stilt Jack*. But Thompson obviously studied the original writing of such masters as Hāfiz and Ghalib, and his deliberate mixing of the sacred and the profane owes more to them than to the American poets. Still, although he alludes to a number of spiritual traditions in the poems, he writes, as Sanger points out, as a Christian.

Sanger's book is invaluable in pointing out how richly "intertextual" Thompson's *Stilt Jack* is, but simply making allusions does not make for true poetry. It is Thompson's grace and wit, his ability to forge couplet after couplet of mysterious power that distinguish this volume: "The small stone in my hand weighs years: / it is dark."

How paratactically open are these lines, are all the lines of these poems. If the reader is invited into a narrative of loss, of fall, the poet rises at the end to a kind of acceptance: "The world is full of the grandeur, / and it is."

Stilt Jack is one of those books which announce an ending of sorts; had Thompson lived he would probably have sought a new direction in his poetry, and according to friends, he had planned to do so. His death was a loss to those who recognized the quality of his talent, but his influence remains. The writers who have paid *Stilt Jack* the highest homage of emulation include Phyllis Webb, whose "anti-*ghazals*" are among her finest work, D. G. Jones, Douglas Lochhead, and others. For them, as well as for the many readers who treasure the poetry, the final line of the book speaks with hope, not despair: "Friends: these words for you."

References:

Margaret Atwood, "Last Testaments: Pat Lowther and John Thompson," in her *Second Words: Selected Critical Prose* (Toronto: Anansi, 1982), pp. 307-312;

Allen Cooper, " 'Way back the woods are wine-dark'–The Poetry of John Thompson," *Arts Atlantic*, 17 (Summer 1983): 38-39;

Robert Gibbs, "Almost Without Speech," *Fiddlehead*, 104 (Winter 1975): 134-137;

Dennis Lee, "The New Poets: Fresh Voices in the Land," *Saturday Night*, 88 (December 1973): 33-35;

Peter Sanger, *Sea Run: Notes on John Thompson's* Stilt Jack (Antigonish, Nova Scotia: Xavier Press, 1986).

Michel Tremblay
(25 June 1942-)

Renate Usmiani
Mount Saint Vincent University

BOOKS: *Contes pour buveurs attardés* (Montreal: Editions du Jour, 1966); translated by Michael Bullock as *Stories for Late Night Drinkers* (Vancouver: Intermedia, 1977);

Les Belles-Soeurs (Montreal: Holt, Rinehart & Winston, 1968); translated by John Van Burek and Bill Glassco (Vancouver: Talonbooks, 1974);

La Cité dans l'oeuf (Montreal: Editions du Jour, 1969);

En pièces détachées et La Duchesse de Langeais (Montreal: Lémeac, 1970); *En pièces détachées*, translated by Allan Van Meer as *Like Death Warmed Over* (Toronto: Playwrights Co-op, 1973); *La Duchesse de Langeais*, translated by Van Burek in *La Duchesse de Langeais and Other Plays* (Vancouver: Talonbooks, 1976);

A toi, pour toujours, ta Marie-Lou (Montreal: Leméac, 1971); translated by Van Burek and Glassco as *Forever Yours, Marie-Lou* (Vancouver: Talonbooks, 1975);

Trois Petits Tours, includes *Berthe, Johnny Mangano and His Astonishing Dogs*, and *Gloria Star* (Montreal: Leméac, 1971); translated in *La Duchesse de Langeais and Other Plays* (1976);

Demain matin Montreál m'attend (Montreal: Leméac, 1972);

C't'à ton tour, Laura Cadieux (Montreal: Editions du Jour, 1973);

Hosanna, suivi de La Duchesse de Langeais (Montreal: Leméac, 1973); *Hosanna* translated by Van Burek and Glassco (Vancouver: Talonbooks, 1974);

Bonjour, là, bonjour (Montreal: Leméac, 1974); translated by Van Burek and Glassco (Vancouver: Talonbooks, 1975);

Les Héros de mon enfance (Montreal: Leméac, 1976);

Sainte Carmen de la Main (Montreal: Leméac, 1976); translated by Van Burek as *Sainte Carmen of the Maïn* (Vancouver: Talonbooks, 1981);

Damnée Manon, sacrée Sandra, suivi de Surprise! Surprise! (Montreal: Leméac, 1977); *Damnée Manon, sacrée Sandra* translated by Van Burek (Vancouver: Talonbooks, 1981); *Surprise! Surprise!* translated in *La Duchesse de Langeais and Other Plays* (1976);

La Grosse Femme d'à côté est enceinte (Montreal: Leméac, 1978); translated by Sheila Fischman as *The Fat Woman Next Door Is Pregnant* (Vancouver: Talonbooks, 1981);

L'Impromptu d'Outremont (Montreal: Leméac, 1980); translated by Van Burek as *The Impromptu of Outremont* (Vancouver: Talonbooks, 1981);

Thérèse et Pierrette à l'école des Saints-Anges (Montreal: Leméac, 1980); translated by Fischman as *Therese and Pierrette and the Little Hanging Angel* (Toronto: McClelland & Stewart, 1984);

Les Anciennes Odeurs (Montreal: Leméac, 1981); translated by John Stowe as *Remember Me* (Vancouver: Talonbooks, 1984);

La Duchesse et le Roturier (Montreal: Leméac, 1982);

Oncle Vania, translated and adapted from Anton Chekhov's play by Tremblay and Kim Yaroshevskaya (Montreal: Leméac, 1983);

Des nouvelles d'Edouard (Montreal: Leméac, 1984);

Albertine, en cinq temps (Montreal: Leméac, 1984); translated by Van Burek and Glassco as *Albertine in Five Times* (Vancouver: Talonbooks, 1987);

Le Gars de Québec, adapted from Gogol's *Le Revizov* (Montreal: Leméac, 1985);

Six heures au plus tard (Montreal: Leméac, 1986);

Le Coeur découvert: Roman d'Amours (Montreal: Leméac, 1986; Paris: Grasset, 1987);

Le Vrai Monde? (Montreal: Leméac, 1987).

PLAY PRODUCTIONS: *Messe noir*, Montreal, Théâtre du Gésu, 1965;

Cinq, Montreal, La Patriote, 1966; revised as *En pièces détachées*, Montreal, Théâtre de Quat' Sous, 23 April 1969;

Les Belles-Soeurs, Montreal, Théâtre du Rideau Vert, 28 August 1968;

En pièces dètachès, Montreal, Théâtre de Quat' Sous, 23 April 1969;

photograph by Robert Laliberté

Lysistrata, adapted from Aristophanes' play by Tremblay and André Brassard, Ottawa, National Arts Centre, September 1969;

La Duchesse de Langeais, Montreal, Théâtre de Quat' Sous, March 1970;

L'Effet des rayons gamma sur les vieux-garçons, translated and adapted from Paul Zindel's *The Effect of Gamma Rays on Man-in-the-Moon Marigolds*, Montreal, Théâtre de Quat' Sous, 1970;

A toi, pour toujours, ta Marie-Lou, Montreal, Théâtre de Quat' Sous, 29 April 1971;

Les Paons, Ottawa, *L'Atelier*, 1971;

Le Pays du Dragon, translated and adapted from four one-act plays by Tennessee Williams, Montreal, Théâtre de Quat' Sous, 1971;

Demain matin, Montréal m'attend, Montreal, Théâtre Maisonneuve de la Place des Arts, 16 March 1972;

Et Mademoiselle Roberge boit un peu, translated and adapted from Zindel's *And Miss Reardon Drinks a Little*, Montreal, Place des Arts, 1972;

Hosanna, Montreal, Théâtre de Quat' Sous, May 1973;

Mistero buffo, translated and adapted from Dario Fo's play, Montreal, Théâtre du Nouveau Monde, 1973;

Bonjour, là, bonjour, Ottawa, National Arts Centre, 22 August 1974;

Surprise! Surprise!, Montreal, Théâtre du Nouveau Monde, Summer 1975;

Les Héros de mon enfance, Eastman, Quebec, Théâtre de la Marjolaine, Summer 1975;

Sainte Carmen de la Main, Montreal, La Compagnie Jean Duceppe at the Montreal Cultural Olympics, 20 July 1976;

Mademoiselle Margarita, translated and adapted from Roberto Athayde's *Apareceu a Margarida*, Ottawa, National Arts Centre, 1976;

Damnée Manon, sacrée Sandra, Montreal, Théâtre de Quat' Sous, 24 February 1977;

L'Impromptu d'Outremont, Montreal, Théâtre du Nouveau Monde, 11 April 1980;

Les Anciennes Odeurs, Montreal, Théâtre de Quat' Sous, 4 November 1981;

Albertine, en cinq temps, Ottawa, National Arts Centre, 12 October 1984;

Le Gars de Québec, adapted from Gogol's *Le Revizov*, Montreal, La Compagnie Jean Duceppe at Théâtre Port Royal de la Place des Arts, Fall 1985;

Le Vrai Monde?, Ottawa, National Arts Centre/Montreal: Théâtre du Rideau-Vert, 2 April 1987.

MOTION PICTURES: *Françoise Durocher, Waitress*, screenplay and dialogue by Tremblay and André Brassard, National Film Board, 1972;

Il était une fois dans l'est, scenario and dialogue by Tremblay and Brassard, Ciné Art, 1974;

Parlez-nous d'amour, scenario and dialogue by Tremblay, Films 16, 1976;

Le Soleil se lève en retard, scenario and dialogue by Tremblay, Films 16, 1977.

OTHER: Aristophanes, *Lysistrata*, adapted by Tremblay and André Brassard (Montreal: Leméac, 1969);

Paul Zindel, *The Effect of Gamma Rays on Man-in-the-Moon Marigolds*, translated and adapted by Tremblay as *L'Effet des rayons gamma sur les vieux-garçons* (Montreal: Leméac, 1970);

Zindel, *And Miss Reardon Drinks a Little*, translated and adapted by Tremblay as *Et Mademoiselle Roberge boit un peu* (Montreal: Leméac, 1971);

Roberto Athayde, *Apareceu a Margarida*, translated and adapted by Tremblay as *Mademoiselle Margarita* (Montreal: Leméac, 1975).

PERIODICAL PUBLICATION: *Les Socles*, French text with translation as *The Pedestals* by Renate Usmiani, *Canadian Theatre Review*, 24 (Fall 1979): 53-56.

Michel Tremblay is the first Canadian playwright to have won international recognition. His plays have been translated into many languages and performed successfully on three continents. Starting from the tradition of social-psychological drama begun by Gratien Gélinas and Marcel Dubé, Tremblay has transcended the work of his predecessors, achieving a successful synthesis between realism and theatricalism in style, the regional and the universal in theme, naturalism and lyricism in dramatic idiom. Within Quebec his work is frequently classified as "theatre of liberation" and given political significance due to his introduction of the Montreal working-class French *joual* as a stage idiom, as well as to his merciless naturalism and the political parables that underlie many of his plays. Viewed from a wider perspective, Tremblay's work impresses particularly because of its memorable characters, its sophisticated methods of dramatic composition, and the richness and complexity of its levels of meaning.

The prolific Tremblay wrote eleven plays from 1965 (*Les Belles-Soeurs*) to 1977 (*Damnée Manon, sacrée Sandra*), as well as two musicals, several film scripts, television plays, adaptations, and some fiction. Since 1977 his main interest has shifted from drama to the novel. It appears likely that his important contribution as a dramatist ended with his shift to another genre. His later work does not have the impact of the earlier plays. Of the five dramas he has created for the stage in the 1980s, *Albertine, en cinq temps* (1984) is the most imaginative, consisting of five monologues all spoken by the same character, Albertine, at various stages of his life.

Tremblay's dramatic world is firmly rooted in his own life experience in Montreal, in the rue Fabre neighborhood where he grew up and in the Main district off Sainte Catherine Street with its colorful night life. The first provides the setting for his analysis of "monstrous family" situations. The Main provides the background for the cheap entertainers, whores, and transvestites who appear in Tremblay's work. In his attacks on the institution of the family, as well as in his fascination with marginal characters, Tremblay is within the mainstream of contemporary drama. His work takes on special significance in the context of Quebec history and culture, however: the family plays may be seen as conscious efforts to counterbalance the traditional myths of the French-Canadian family created and encouraged by the Catholic Church; and his transvestite characters, beyond their symbolic significance for modern alienated man, carry heavy political overtones. For Tremblay the transvestite best exemplifies life in Quebec since the conquest, with its foreign dominance, foreign models, and cultural colonialism.

Tremblay combines a basically naturalistic view of the world with a variety of stylistic devices which reflect his chief models: Greek tragedy, Shakespearian monologue, and theater of the absurd. His originality lies, in part, in his method of composition. He conceives his plays in the manner of musical compositions, as "scores" for voices rather than as conventional dialogue. This method of composition gives his drama a poetic quality and puts the burden of visual interpretation of the text on the director. All Tremblay's scripts have been freely interpreted for stage by his friend André Brassard: "He doesn't talk in about my texts, I don't talk in about his staging." The musical quality of his plays is in no way hampered by his use of *joual* or of the somewhat less extreme *québecois* dialect; in fact, the few early works written in "academic" French are of inferior quality.

Michel Tremblay, the son of Armand and Rhéauna Rathier Tremblay, was born on 25 June 1942, on rue Fabre, part of the colorful Plateau Mont-Royal neighborhood of East Montreal. His father, fifty-three years old at the time of Tremblay's birth, worked in a print shop. Because of the acute housing shortage of the 1940s, the family lived in extremely crowded conditions: twelve people, all related, shared seven rooms and a balcony. Tremblay had to eat in a high chair until he was six and had to sleep in a crib until he was nine. But he did get plenty of attention; as he remarked in a 1979 interview, "I was brought up by five women." His childhood and the difficulties of life in a poor neighborhood during the war and immediate postwar years left an indelible impression. All of his significant works reflect his early experiences.

Two plays, *En pièces détachées* and *Bonjour, lá, bonjour*, are fully autobiographical, as is the cycle of novels he has been working on since 1977. He began writing as soon as he was able to read: as a young child, he would spend his holidays inventing variants to familiar fairy tales, which he loved. When television came to Montreal in the mid 1950s, he became an avid fan: at the age of

fourteen he was writing plays modeled on television serials.

Tremblay won a C.E.C.M. scholarship but he left his new school after only two months, indignant over the snobbish attitudes of his fellow students. However, his education did not suffer: sharing the books of a friend who attended the *cours classique*, Tremblay read his way through the curriculum on his own. The classical influence is readily apparent in his work, both in the construction of many of his plays and in his frequent use of the chorus.

After he left school, Tremblay worked as a linotypist and began to write seriously. His adolescent works, short stories and short plays, are all written in a carefully elaborated version of "correct" school French. The crucial break in dramatic style came in 1965. Tremblay and André Brassard had been trying to pinpoint the reason why French-Canadian films invariably left them feeling dissatisfied. Finally they realized that the cause lay in these films' use of an artificial language far removed from the language actually spoken by the people of Quebec. Tremblay went home, sat down to work, and three weeks later he had finished *Les Belles-Soeurs*. The play was refused by the jury of the Dominion Drama Festival in 1967; but in 1968, following a successful reading at the Centre d'Essai des Auteurs Dramatiques, it was finally accepted for production. When it premiered at the Théâtre du Rideau Vert that year, it aroused a storm of both praise and protest which made Michel Tremblay instantly famous.

Critical controversy centered on two issues: Tremblay's excessively naturalistic description of milieu and his use of *joual* as a dramatic idiom. While radical critics (Michel Bélair, Jean-Claude Germain) hailed *Les Belles-Soeurs* as the most important breakthrough to date toward a "theatre of liberation" for Quebec, conservatives condemned the play as crude and vulgar. In Paris, where it was produced in 1973, the play received excellent reviews; the critic for *Le Monde* praised the universality of its appeal and particularly the appropriateness of the language. *Les Belles-Soeurs* was published in 1968 and translated into English in 1974.

Although a simple slice-of-life on the surface, *Les Belles-Soeurs* is a complex work which functions on many levels at once and achieves a synthesis between realistic and theatrical elements. The basic story line is simple: Germaine Lauzon, an ordinary East Montreal housewife,

Cover for Tremblay's first book, a collection translated in 1977 as Stories for Late Night Drinkers

has won a million gold bond stamps in a contest and invites her friends, relatives, and neighbors to a stamp-pasting party. Envious of Germaine's good fortune and resentful at her boasting, the other women steal the stamps, and the play ends in a violent free-for-all. This framework provides Tremblay with an opportunity to develop the characters in detail and examine the fates of the fifteen women assembled in Germaine's kitchen; this series of gripping minidramas is of considerably more interest than the frame story itself.

The basic language of the play, *joual*, is given theatrical impetus by the use of choral speaking. Surface structure is fully realistic, with the duration of the dramatic action corresponding to performance time; within the play, however, movement and rhythm are determined by the carefully controlled ebb and flow of speeches as they are developed, singly and in groups, to harmonize or in counterpoint. The most significant elements of the play lie fully outside the realistic

framework; they are the stylized monologues and the choral "odes." In the monologues, individual characters, singled out by a spotlight while the rest of the stage is blacked out, address the audience directly, revealing their innermost thoughts and feelings. The monologues expose the inner workings of individual characters, while the two choral recitations, "Maudite vie plate" and "Ode to bingo," give insight into the collective unconscious of the group. Both of the recitations serve to underline the central theme of the play, that of *la maudite vie plate*: the essential absurdity and meaninglessness of life. "Maudite vie plate" achieves this through the reiteration of events in the senseless daily routine, which all of the women share, "Ode to bingo" by pointing out the irony of lives whose highest points are found in bingo games. *Les Belles-Soeurs* is a deeply pessimistic play, not so much because of the physical deprivations endured by the women (the basic necessities are there) but because of their total incapacity for emotional fulfillment. Unloved and unable to love, the women have family lives that are daily rounds of frustration. Superstition and conservatism fostered by adherence to outdated religious values and practices further contribute to making their lives joyless, their relations to others bitter and intolerant. As many critics pointed out at the time, *Les Belles-Soeurs* was probably the most scathing indictment of Quebec society ever to appear in literature.

While the "battle of the *joual*" set off by *Les Belles-Soeurs* raged in Montreal, Tremblay traveled to Mexico on a Canada Council grant. There, he wrote the fantasy novel *La Cité dans l'oeuf* (1969) and his first transvestite play, *La Duchesse de Langeais*, based on a person he had met in a bar. A grotesque tragicomedy, *La Duchesse de Langeais* is a dramatic monologue in two acts. Through the speeches of the single character, La Duchesse, Tremblay is able to create for the audience both a vivid, and enormously pathetic, personality and an entire life experience. Variety in point of view is provided by the character's shifts in attitude, from sincerity to more or less conscious role playing, to full self-deception. These shifts are accompanied by linguistic change, from *joual* to a satirical version of "good" French.

The setting is the terrace of a café "down South." It is siesta time, and the place is fully deserted except for the Duchesse de Langeais, who sits alone in the blazing sun, halfway through a bottle of whisky. Thus, the sense of loneliness and isolation is created from the beginning. La

Duchesse is about sixty years old, her appearance quite ridiculous, but, as the stage instructions specify, the caricature should be "moving." As she (he) begins to speak, the pathos of her situation becomes apparent. La Duchesse, after a long and successful career as a transvestite prostitute, is now suffering the ultimate indignity: rejection by a young partner with whom she has allowed herself to fall genuinely in love. As she analyzes her present situation and reminisces about her past, a strong, pathetic, but also admirable character emerges, full of dreams and illusions but capable of facing reality when necessary.

The immediate appeal of the play is that of psychological drama. The central problem of decline and the pathos of an older person who suffers rejection by one younger and more attractive are universal; because of the special situation of La Duchesse, however, these difficulties gain poignancy since her professional pride is involved. The sense of isolation and alienation is reinforced by La Duchesse's transvestism, which pushed her into a position that is marginal beyond that of the ordinary old person. In Quebec this aspect of alienation and marginality carries specific overtones of cultural colonialism, as does the role playing which La Duchesse has developed to perfection. Tremblay was well aware of the multiple implications of the transvestite character, whom he brought back in several later plays, most successfully in *Demain matin, Montréal m'attend*, his 1972 musical about the false glamour of night life.

Since his return from Mexico, Tremblay has made several European trips; a sizable portion of his writing has been done abroad (Paris, Greece, Spain). He also goes regularly to New York to keep abreast of American theater life. But in spite of his extensive travels and his current address in Montreal's fashionable Outremont district, he has never truly abandoned home base; his artistic and emotional roots have remained in the rue Fabre district of East Montreal. His central preoccupation remains the family, which he sees as both product and source of the personal and collective traumas of his society. In his view, liberation of the individual is possible only by liberating him from the bondage of the family. In many of the plays which follow *Les Belles-Soeurs*, the family tragedy is set against the background of the same nauseous *maudite vie plate* we find in the earlier work: family relations are described as a nightmare of negative emotions in the total absence of love; and the institution of the family itself is viewed by its members as an almost escape-proof trap. A gallery of impotent father figures is counterbalanced by a corresponding set of embittered, frustrated females, while the younger generation makes fruitless attempts to escape from a hell of their parents' making.

En pièces détachées, the first of the family plays, was produced at Montreal's Théâtre de Quat' Sous in 1969. (An early version, entitled *Cinq*, had been staged in 1966.) *En pièces détachées* is a powerful domestic tragedy on the theme of emotional attrition, with "chus pas capable"–"I just can't"– the refrain repeated by all the characters as its leitmotiv. Classical in its concentration of time and place, the play is a slice-of-life rather than drama of action: an afternoon and evening in the life of a doomed family. The setting is half realistic, half symbolic: at center stage there is "la cour," an inner courtyard where housewives lounge at their windows malevolently watching their neighbors; these women serve as a chorus for the play. The other locations represent aspects of the central character Thérèse's life: the cheap delicatessen where she works; the bar where she drinks; and the family living room which she shares with her husband, her daughter, and her mother, Robertine. Each evening as she returns home, drunk and angry, Thérèse provides the neighbors with relief from their *maudite vie plate* with her violent attacks on her family.

Once a beautiful and intelligent girl, Thérèse has gone steadily downhill since her catastrophic marriage to Gérard. Gérard, in turn, copes with the situation by total withdrawal: half lame after an accident, he has given up communicating with his family and comes alive only when his favorite cartoon characters appear on the television screen. Robertine, the old mother, is probably the most pathetic of them all. In a moving monologue which Tremblay describes as "the best thing I've ever written," she exposes the drabness of her life—a life of hard work and privations, without joy or fulfillment ever, all within the confines of the same house.

With the appearance in the second act of Thérèse's brother Marcel, a madman who has escaped from his institution, the tone of the play changes; in a somewhat heavy-handed use of symbolism, the author makes the lunatic stand for everything the "normal" members of the family lack. Marcel imagines himself all-powerful; he is sure of himself; and he demands that Thérèse and her mother dress in white. It becomes apparent that Thérèse, in spite of her emotional arid-ity, does love her brother very much—a first indication of the incest theme which is fully developed in *Bonjour, là, bonjour*. Throughout Tremblay's work, the only love shown as possible between the sexes is that between brother and sister—the ultimate taboo; a scathing comment on the failure of conventional love and marriage; a vigorous plea for marginality.

Tremblay's most bitter attack on the institution of the family is in his next play, *A toi, pour toujours, ta Marie-Lou*, produced and published in 1971 and translated as *Forever Yours, Marie-Lou* in 1975. Here, the emotional desert is fully unrelieved. The author considers this work his best play to date. It is a masterpiece of technical perfection, a "string quartet," in Tremblay's words, in which four voices speak and converse from two different time periods, ten years apart. The characters are Léopold and Marie-Lou, the parents, and Carmen and Manon, their daughters. All four are on stage for the duration of the play, which consists of sets of parallel dialogues: Lèopold and Marie-Lou speak immediately before they commit suicide in a planned car crash; Carmen and Manon converse ten years after their parents' death. The central event, the accident/suicide, functions as the terminal point for the parents' dialogues and the take-off point for the children's, creating a sense of forward and reverse motion at the same time. Four times in the course of the play, the ten-year time lapse is erased as the daughters enter into the parents' conversation: these four crucial episodes serve as explanation/motivation for both movements of the play. The play as a whole creates a sense of fatality akin to that dramatized in *Oedipus Rex*. This sense of tragic inevitability is reinforced by classical concentration: the entire drama runs through without intermission, and there is only one setting, the kitchen of the parents' house. The stylization of performance (the actors neither move nor look at one another) and careful composition of the four-part dialogue structure elevate it above the level of the basic subject matter—the tragic consequences of parents' sexual incompatibility for themselves and their children.

The dialogue between Léopold and Marie-Lou is constructed as a careful crescendo of accusations, beginning with the trivial irritations of conjugal living and leading up to the central problem, Marie-Lou's inability to accept a normal sex life (the sexual history of the marriage can be reduced to four encounters followed by four pregnancies). Having raked up all the bitterness accumulated throughout their unhappy marriage, Léopold and Marie-Lou find no way out but suicide. Ten years later, Carmen and Manon attempt to come to terms with what has happened. Manon, permanently traumatized, has continued to live in her parents' old home, devoting her life to pious exercises and to imitating her mother, whom she considers a saint and a martyr. Carmen, on the other hand, has been able to free herself from her past. She has left the house and established herself as a singer of Western songs in a café on the Main, thus gaining freedom and independence. Because she has found happiness, Carmen is eager to convince Manon to break away too and make a life for herself; but Manon condemns Carmen as a "whore" and refuses to change her joyless life-style.

Beyond its sociological indictment of working-class family life, its misery, taboos, and sexual ignorance, *A toi, pour toujours, ta Marie-Lou* is a political parable. The parent generation suggests Quebec in the past, impotent and helpless; the two daughters represent possible options for the present. Ultimately, however, the play depends for its effects on Tremblay's original and compelling use of dramatic technique.

Following the success of Tremblay's plays in Quebec, English translations began to appear. Although the author specifically forbade the performance of his work in English in Quebec until after the victory of the Parti Québécois in the 1976 elections, there were Toronto productions of *Forever Yours, Marie-Lou* in 1972 and of *Les Belles-Soeurs* in 1973; *En pièces détachées* was staged in Winnipeg in 1973. Since 1976, his plays have been televised and produced across Canada.

Following *A toi, pour toujours, ta Marie-Lou* Tremblay returned to the transvestite theme with *Hosanna* (1973), another play of psychological analysis that suggests the political/cultural "transvestism" of Quebec. As in *La Duchesse de Langeais*, the fact that both characters are male is incidental to the analysis of the love relationship, though the transvestite couple Claude/Hosanna serves as a symbol of collective alienation. A central theme of the play is the search for identity, represented by Hosanna's compulsive role playing.

Although it is a two-act play, *Hosanna* presents just one moment of psychological crisis in the lives of the two characters, Hosanna (Claude) and Cuirette (Raymond). All action takes place within a few hours and in one place, the shabby one-room apartment which the lovers share. The crisis is brought on by events at a transvestite Hal-

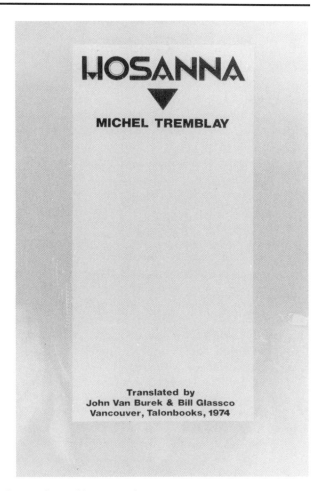

Frontispiece and title page for the English translation of Tremblay's second tranvestite play

loween party, for which Hosanna had made long and painstaking preparations. Her disguise represents the fulfillment of a dream of many years: she appears as Elizabeth Taylor in the role of Cleopatra. However, her secret has been betrayed by Cuirette, and when she makes her grand entrance, she is greeted by a room full of people wearing the same costume as she is. Hurt and humiliated, Hosanna rushes home, pouring out bitter accusations against Cuirette, whose behavior she considers high treason.

The incident serves to bring into the open all the hidden bitterness, hostility, and ambiguity in the relationship between Hosanna and Cuirette. The play develops as an emotional boxing match between the partners; like Léopold and Marie-Lou, they begin by skirting the central issue—Hosanna's inability to accept herself and her compulsive need to create false personalities. Ultimately, Hosanna does accept herself for what

she (he) is, and the lovers return to their real names, Claude and Raymond. Although *Hosanna* is an excessively long play whose subject might have lent itself better to one-act treatment, it was well received in both French- and English-Canada. In New York, where the political implications were less obvious, it enjoyed two short runs.

Bonjour, là, bonjour (produced and published in 1974, translated to English in 1975) returns to the theme of everyday family life. Dedicated to the author's father, this play is even more overtly autobiographical than *En pièces détachées*. The central theme is the difficulty of communication in the father-son relationship, with a subtheme of sociosexual liberation. The plot focuses on the two central issues in the life of Serge, the twenty-five-year-old central character: his strong but never expressed love for his father and his unorthodox love for his youngest sister, Nicole. In the course of one stormy evening, he comes to terms with both. Having first decided to accept his relationship with Nicole, he is then able to break through the long-established communications barrier that separates him from his father.

Tremblay's father-and-son drama is acted out against the usual family background of impotence, frustration, inability to communicate, and desire for liberation. In the case of the father, Gabriel, impotence is suggested symbolically by the fact that he is old, retired, and quite deaf. Charlotte and Albertine, the spinster aunts who keep house for him, have lost all sense of individuality to the point of speaking the same words at the same time or referring to themselves in the third person as "ma tante." Serge's older sisters, Lucienne, Denise, and Monique, resort to conventional escape mechanisms: love affairs, tranquilizers, overeating. Serge, a combination child/lover and sex symbol, becomes the target of all these frustrated females' repressed sex drives; he himself finds fulfillment only in his incestuous love for Nicole, the only kind of male/female love dramatized in Tremblay's work.

The theme of lack of communication is subtly developed through the Chekhovian manner in which Tremblay handles dialogue: the characters follow their individual trains of thought without ever establishing contact. In keeping with the author's usual method of composition, the play is not divided into acts and scenes but into thirty-one short sections labeled according to the number of "voix," voices or characters, who participate: "duo," "trio," and so on, up to "octuor."

Following some slighter works produced in 1975, the playlet *Surprise! Surprise!* and the satirical musical *Les Héros de mon enfance*, a spoof on the traditional fairy tale created especially for summer theater, Tremblay returned to the theme and characters of *A toi, pour toujours, ta Marie-Lou*. With *Sainte Carmen de la Main* and *Damnée Manon, sacrée Sandra*, he closed his cycle of family plays and also arrived at the end of an important period of his career as a creative artist. These two plays clearly present a progression toward a more spiritual view of the universe and of human life. The figure of Carmen stands out in modern dramaturgy as a rare example of a tragic heroine; *Damnée Manon, sacrée Sandra* presents the dual path toward mystical ecstasy—religion and sex—and in so doing questions the validity of the concept itself.

Sainte Carmen de la Main, first produced in 1976, presents the final tragedy of Carmen, daughter of Léopold and Marie-Lou, sister of Manon. The play is set in the Rodéo, a cheap cabaret on the Main, where Carmen performs to an audience of bedraggled, down-and-out characters. As the play opens, Carmen refuses to go on singing the cowboy songs of her usual repertoire, which are alien to her public and only provide a false sense of escape. Instead, she presents them with songs she has written herself, addressed directly to the audience, in their own language—songs with which they can identify, which will give them a sense of dignity and self-worth. The reaction is electrifying. However Maurice, her boss and gangster-king of the Main, orders Carmen to return to the status quo: when she refuses (in a gripping showdown reminiscent of the Antigone-Créon confrontation) Maurice has Carmen killed by his henchman, and life returns to "normal" on the Main.

Despite setting, plot, and language (*joual*), *Sainte Carmen de la Main* is far removed from the realistic play. Tremblay's method of composition is based on the two most elevated genres of Western theater, opera and Greek tragedy. The play is constructed as a series of episodes alternating with choral recitations, the chorus being made up of "the transvestites of the Main, led by Sandra" and "the whores of the Main, led by Rose Beef." The speeches are constructed like operatic scores. Besides these dominant elements of classical tragedy and grand opera, a strong liturgical element also runs through the work in the gospellike recitations by Carmen's dresser. *Sainte Carmen de la Main* is Tremblay's most poetical drama to date; the rhythm, imagery, and verbal music of the choral poetry is in no way diminished by the fact that the language used is *joual*. In this drama the author achieves a synthesis of apparently clashing aesthetic styles and devices. Carmen emerges as a symbol of salvation and liberation on many levels, from national and artistic to human.

There is a clear progression in Tremblay's thinking from the first play in which Carmen appears to the second: while Carmen's escape from the family and successful singing career appeared as sufficient liberation in the 1971 *A toi, pour toujours, ta Marie-Lou*, by 1976 the author is no longer able to accept such a simple solution. The tragic ending of *Sainte Carmen de la Main* reflects his disillusionment with the politics of the Parti Québecois and his increasing pessimism. Heroic death now appears as the only viable option. However, the original finale of the play (the vulgar Gloria Star takes over noble Carmen's place) has since been softened. A 1978 production ended with a proclamation of Carmen's message of hope, that the people of the Main need a spokesman if they are to come to terms with their human worth: "La Main a besoin qu' on y parle de la Main."

Sainte Carmen de la Main was received negatively by critics and general public alike when it was first performed by the Compagnie Jean Duceppe as part of the Montreal Cultural Olympics in the summer of 1976. This stylized production emphasized the classical element, with all-white costumes and sets, and audiences resisted the excessive classicism. The more realistic 1978 production by the Théâtre du Nouveau Monde enjoyed greater success. The play was published in French in 1976 and in English translation in 1981.

Damnée Manon, sacrée Sandra, produced in 1977, is set within the mind of the playwright himself, with the two protagonists representing opposite and complementary aspects of their creator's personality. The stage setting is rue Fabre, where Manon, last surviving child of Léopold and Marie-Lou, and Sandra, a transvestite recently returned to that neighborhood from the Main, live across from each other, each one aspiring to transcendence through her own particular brand of mysticism: religious for Manon, sexual for Sandra. As the play progresses, the two characters engage in separate, but parallel and complementary monologues, until they finally come together to reveal that they are really one, each one having been "invented by Michel." The play not only makes the obvious equation of sex and religious mysticism but it also brings out strongly two great absences in the modern world, particularly significant for Tremblay in the context of Quebec, with its history of repression and clerical domination: the absence of healthy sexuality and the absence of healthy spirituality.

Technically, this one-act play is a masterpiece of construction, its central portion made up of a series of "confessions" by the characters which make clear the interchangeable, complementary nature of their aspirations. The play ends with all opposites and contradictions resolved in the crucible of the author's mind. It was published in French in 1977 and in English translation in 1981.

With the closing of the cycle of family plays, Tremblay turned from drama to the novel, embarking on a narrative cycle which combines realism and fantasy, as his best plays combine realism

Cover for John Stowe's translation of Tremblay's 1981 play,
Les Anciennes Odeurs

and theatricalism. The setting is again rue Fabre; the characters are based on members of the author's family. The first volume, *La Grosse Femme d'à côté est enceinte* (1978; translated as *The Fat Lady Next Door Is Pregnant*, 1981), was a bestseller in Quebec. The novel gives a detailed, picturesque account based on Tremblay's memories of life in the crowded apartment where he was born ("la grosse femme" is his mother). But the novel also contains an element of the supernatural in the presence of three invisible women—the Fates of rue Fabre, who knit endlessly as they sit on a balcony overlooking the street; and animal characters, especially the cat Duplessis, take on human characteristics. Its sequel, *Thérèse et Pierrette à l'école des Saints-Anges* (1980, translated as *Therese and Pierrette and the Little Hanging Angel*, 1984), continues the same theme with a condemnation of the system of religious education. The next two novels, *La Duchesse et le Roturier* (1982) and *Des nouvelles d'Edouard* (1984), remain within the same enclosed universe of life on the Plateau Mont-Royal, while *Le Coeur découvert: Roman d'Amours* (1986) follows several love relationships in Montreal in the 1980s. Tremblay is conscious of the closeness of his fictional universe, and, at present, he has no intention of moving beyond it. His purpose, he says, is and has always been "to create an epic of my people."

Michel Tremblay is recognized as one of the major writers of contemporary Canada. Radical and politically minded critics emphasize his importance in bringing out the specifically Quebecois problems of lack of identity, feelings of impotence, and the need for liberation, whether linguistic or political. Reviewers generally tend to emphasize the naturalistic quality of his work, his lucidity, pessimism, and cynicism. Academic critics emphasize the technical merits of his drama, especially his blending of naturalistic themes with lyricism and theatricalism. He has received many major awards: Toronto's Chalmers Award (1986); Montreal's Prix Victor Morin (1974); the Ontario Lieutenant Governor's Medal (1976, 1977); the Canadian Film Festival Award for best scenario (1975 for *Françoise Durocher, Waitress*); and the Prix France-Québec (1981 for *Thérèse et Pierrette à l'école des Saints-Anges* and 1985 for *La Duchesse et le Roturier*.) Additionally he was named "Chevalier de l'order des arts et des lettres" in France in 1984 and won Montreal's Prix de la Critique in 1986 for *Albertine, en cinq temps*, which was named best play at Le festival du théâtre des Ameriques in 1985.

His work has been successfully received abroad. *Les Belles-Soeurs*, *La Duchesse de Langeais*, and *Hosanna* have been performed in Paris. His plays have been produced in translation in many countries including the United States, Italy, Holland, Belgium, Switzerland, Zaire, Australia, Brazil, Finland, and Japan.

Interviews:

J. C. Germain, "Michel Tremblay, le plus joual des auteurs et vice-versa," *Digeste-Eclair*, 15 (October 1968): 15-19;

Marc F. Gélinas, "Je pense en joual," *Magazine Maclean*, 10, no. 9 (1970): 46;

Rachel Cloutier, Marie Laberge, and Rodrigue Gignac, Interview with Tremblay, *Nord I* (Autumn 1971): 49-81;

Michel Beaulieu, Interview with Tremblay, *Perspectives*, 17 February 1973, pp. 6-9;

Geraldine Anthony, Interview with Tremblay, in her *Stage Voices: Twelve Canadian Playwrights Talk About Their Lives and Work* (Toronto & Garden City: Doubleday, 1978), pp. 275-291;

Renate Usmiani, "Where to Begin the Accusation?," *Canadian Theatre Review*, no. 24 (Fall 1979): 26-37.

References:

Michel Bélair, *Michel Tremblay* (Montreal: Presses de l'Université du Québec, 1972);

Ronald Bérubé, "*Demain matin Montréal m'attend*, de Michel Tremblay," *Livres et Auteurs Québecois* (1976): 116;

Gilbert David, "Notes dures sur un théâtre mou," *Etudes Françaises*, 11 (May 1975);

Jean-Cléo Godin and Laurent Mailhot, *Le Théâtre québecois* (Montreal: HMH, 1970), pp. 191-202;

Naim Kattan, "Le Théâtre à Montréal," *Canadian Literature*, 40 (Spring 1969): 45;

J. P. Ryngaert, "Du réalisme à la théâtralité: la dramaturgie de Michel Tremblay dans *Les Belles-Soeurs* et *A toi, pour toujours, ta Marie-Lou*," *Livres et Auteurs Québecois* (1971): 97;

Adrien Thério, "Un Joual fringant à la scène en 1968," *Livres et Auteurs Canadiens* (1968): 78;

Renate Usmiani, *Michel Tremblay. A Critical Study* (Vancouver: Douglas & McIntyre, 1981);

Usmiani, "Michel Tremblay's Sainte Carmen: Synthesis and Orchestration," *Canadian Drama*, 2, no. 2 (1976): 206-218;

Usmiani, "The Tremblay Opus: Unity in Diversity," *Canadian Theatre Review*, 24 (Fall 1979): 12-25.

Pierre Trottier

(21 March 1925-)

Jacqueline Viswanathan
Simon Fraser University

BOOKS: *Le Combat contre Tristan* (Montreal: Editions de Malte, 1951);
Poèmes de Russie (Montreal: Editions de l'Hexagone, 1957);
Les Belles au bois dormant (Montreal: Editions de l'Hexagone, 1960);
Mon Babel (Montrèal: HMH, 1963);
Sainte-Mémoire (Montreal: HMH, 1972);
Un Pays baroque (Montreal: La Presse, 1979).

Pierre Trottier was born in Montreal, the son of Louis Trottier, a businessman, and Marie-Rose Lalumière Trottier. He studied law at the University of Montreal, from which he graduated in 1945. He married Barbara Theis in 1952. They have three children: Anne-Hélène, Maxime, and Jean-Philippe. In 1949 he went to work for the Department of External Affairs, Ottawa. He was posted at the Canadian Embassy in Moscow (1951-1954), in Djakarta, Indonesia (1956-1957), in London (1957-1961), and as cultural counselor in Paris (1964-1968). After another period in Moscow (1970-1973), he was appointed ambassador to Peru (1973-1979). In 1979 he became the Canadian ambassador to UNESCO in Paris.

Encouraging an attitude of both detachment from and attachment to the home country and affording opportunities for prolonged in-depth contact with different societies and cultures, Trottier's diplomatic career seems to have fostered his gifts as a poet and essayist. Although sometimes overblown in their rhetoric, his works give expression to a vigorous, original, and independent voice among contemporary Quebec writers. His achievement as a poet has been recognized by his receiving the Prix David in 1960.

In his first volume, *Le Combat contre Tristan* (1951), the poet rejects the illusions and warped idealism of his youth, rebelling against the dualism of the body and soul, flesh and spirit which have often been considered a hallmark of French-Canadian ideology.

In many poems he rejects the debasement of sexuality, the guilt and alienation which he associates with the Jansenist Catholicism that has been a strong influence in Quebec culture. At a time when most Quebec poets were absorbed with writing about the inner life to the exclusion of any topical reference, some of Trottier's early poems strike an original and vital note of social concern for the status of French-Canadians as a minority in Canada. Sometimes humorously, as in "Le cortège du vingt-quatre juin," describing the parade on Quebec's national holiday, or lyrically, as in "Pour une jeune protestante de mon pays" and "Femme aux couleurs de mon pays," Trottier explores, before the era of its popularity, the theme of Canadian dual ethnicity with an open-mindedness void of the usual parochial overtones.

Trottier's second book, *Poèmes de Russie* (1957), was published after his return from diplomatic assignment in Moscow. The poet notes in his foreword that the title alludes only to the place where these poems were written. They are concerned with a spiritual experience which transcends both geography and the life of a single individual. As in his first book, familiar French-Canadian demons of misguided spirituality are exorcised. Several poems, "Métiers," for instance, and "Etat de siège," express symbolically the tragedy of what could be called French-Canadian Jansenism: the burden of a divided, introverted psyche, powerless and frightened when confronted with death, love, and life. Courage in the face of death emerges as a key test of moral strength; hence the many "danses macabres" which haunt Trottier's poems. *Poèmes de Russie* presents a characteristic blend of intellectual and moral reflections with warm, sometimes gushing lyricism. In spite of the author's remarks, his mention of Russia in the title is not dictated by geography alone. The remoteness of the poet's homeland and the encounter with Russian culture seem to have triggered a profound meditation on the experience and meaning of time, also a dominant theme in the later poetry: *Les Belles au bois dor-*

mant (1960) and *Sainte-Mémoire* (1972). "Le Retour d'Oedipe," published in *Ecrits du Canada Français* in 1962 and collected in *Sainte-Mémoire*, was inspired by Trottier's return to Canada after many years of absence. It is a powerful and eloquent piece with a wealth of literary and historical allusions–to ancient Greece, Elizabethan England, and Baroque France, to Russia, to Asia– in order to elucidate the Quebec experience.

Sainte-Mémoire contains the first and the latest of Trottier's poems. The latter celebrate the recovery of a long-lost part of the self: a "soeur siamoise," or siamese twin, the female part of an androgynous soul used by Trottier to suggest that man's love for a woman is love of self as well as of the other.

Trottier's essay collections, *Mon Babel* (1963) and *Un Pays baroque* (1979), have been recognized as stimulating and intellectually challenging discussions of Western tradition and especially of French- and English-Canadian identity and culture. Trottier touches upon many topics of contemporary debate: East-West relations, democracy and totalitarianism, ecology, and feminism, bringing to bear on all of his subjects an impressive erudition in the humanities. His new Babel, unlike the chaotic biblical city, will present a harmonious synthesis of all great civilizations, from Tristan's Middle Ages to the apocalyptic modern era. A major source of inspiration for essays in both collections is Trottier's sense of parallelism between the Baroque period, when Europe was torn by civil and religious wars, and the contemporary age, which he sees as fragmented and unstable. Trottier defines the Baroque as a questioning of stable, existing forms, a search for a new form

while a state of instability prevails. He finds neo-Baroque features in all areas of contemporary Western society: the search for a new form within the Canadian Confederation is a prime example as is the problematic shifting of the status of minorities or the relationship between sexes. Not given to sweeping generalizations or far-fetched analogies, Trottier keeps the debate at an elevated level, without, as befits a diplomat, specific commitment, political or otherwise.

For Trottier, the Baroque spirit is a positive force, mainly because of its aspiration to identify with the Other, a process of metamorphosis typical, according to Trottier, not only of Baroque theater in general but also of some of the characters created by contemporary Canadian playwright Michel Tremblay. The complementarity of self and other, eternity and temporality, masculinity and femininity are themes which repeatedly inform Trottier's writings, his poetry as well as his numerous essays. Hence the Baroque functions politically and psychologically as well as literarily as the two epigraphs to *Un Pays baroque* imply. One of these is Jean-Paul Sartre's dictum "L'enfer, c'est les autres." The other is from Germain Bazin's *Bestens du Baroque* (1968): "Etre soi-même et l'autre." In the work of Trottier, it is the power of the Baroque to overcome the antagonism inherent in Sartre's position and to achieve a different kind of harmony.

Reference:

Gilles Marcotte, "Pierre Trottier," in his *Le Temps des poètes* (Montreal: HMH, 1969), pp. 136-140.

W. D. Valgardson

(7 May 1939-   )

David Jackel
University of Alberta

BOOKS: *Bloodflowers* (Ottawa: Oberon, 1973);
God Is Not a Fish Inspector (Ottawa: Oberon, 1975);
In the Gutting Shed (Winnipeg: Turnstone Press, 1976; revised, 1981);
Red Dust (Ottawa: Oberon, 1978);
Gentle Sinners (Ottawa: Oberon, 1980);
The Carpenter of Dreams: Poems (Victoria: Skaldhus Press, 1986).

PERIODICAL PUBLICATIONS: "The Revolutionary," *Grain*, 3 (December 1975): 4-9;
"Afternoons," *Canadian Forum*, 58 (March 1979): 17;
"Personal Gods," *Essays on Canadian Writing*, 16 (Fall-Winter 1979-1980): 179-186.

During the 1970s William Dempsey Valgardson established himself as one of Canada's foremost writers of short fiction. His forceful presentation of lives shaped by isolation and the brutal effects of a northern environment, his careful control of narrative method, and his respect for his audience have won him both a wide readership and high praise from critics and reviewers.

Valgardson was born to Dempsey Alfred Herbert and Rachel Smith Valgardson in Winnipeg, Manitoba, and was raised in Gimli, a fishing village on Lake Winnipeg in the northern part of the province. Gimli was formerly known as Nya Island, or New Iceland, and Valgardson's father was of Icelandic descent. Both the community and his ancestry have strongly influenced Valgardson's writing, providing him not only with settings and themes but also with a vision of human life. "Is it any wonder," he has asked, in "Personal Gods" (*Essays on Canadian Writing*, Fall-Winter 1979-1980), "that having grown up in an Icelandic-Canadian community that suffered, in its migration to the new world, hardships every bit as great as those which were left behind, I write stories which have been described as being governed by a dark vision?" Valgardson's ancestry is, for him, a determining force and a source

W. D. Valgardson

of strength: "In *Njal's Saga*, which was written somewhere around the year 1280, there is a Valgardson. I am tied to an old tradition, I do not complain. It has served me well."

In 1961, the year after his marriage to Mary-Anne Tooth, Valgardson graduated with a B.A. from the University of Manitoba. He subsequently taught English and art at several schools in rural Manitoba during the years 1961 to 1970. During this period he also completed the requirements for a degree in education (B.Ed., University of Manitoba, 1966). In 1968, one year after matriculating at the University of Iowa, he received a scholarship and a Canada Council grant that enabled him to attend Iowa's Writers' Workshop and to complete work for an M.F.A. in 1969. Valgardson's writing career began during these years; although his output was not extensive (he has described himself as "a very slow writer" and said that for a long time "I was writing four stories and destroying three"), his work did attract some attention.

A poem, "Paul Isfeld: Fisherman," received first prize at the Rochester Festival of Fine Arts in 1968, and another poem, "Realization in a Spinning Wheel," obtained honorable mention in the Hallmark poetry competition in 1969. The poem "Raspberries" received second prize from the Manitoba branch of the Canadian Authors' Association in 1970. Valgardson also won the *Winnipeg Free Press* Non-Fiction Contest in 1969 for an article entitled "The Hitchhikers."

From 1970 to 1974 Valgardson taught English at Cottey College, Nevada, Missouri, beginning as an instructor and spending his final three years there as chairman of the department. It was while he taught in Nevada that Valgardson began to establish his reputation as a short-story writer in Canada. "Bloodflowers" (*Tamarack Review*, 1971), which presents with restraint and understatement the growing awareness of a young teacher from the mainland that the inhabitants of a Newfoundland outport have selected him as the appropriate victim for ritual spring sacrifice, won the President's Medal from the University of Western Ontario that year for the best short story in a Canadian publication. (It was also included in the annual *Best American Short Stories* collection for 1971, edited by Martha Foley and David Burnett.)

This story appeared, with nine others, in Valgardson's first collection, *Bloodflowers* (1973). The other stories are set, for the most part, in the northern Manitoba of his upbringing, and most of them exhibit Valgardson's "dark vision." An out-of-work fisherman dies of a heart attack while trying to work as a pinsetter in a bowling alley; a retarded young man is tormented because he buys and wears an air force jacket, and he too dies, under the wheels of a train; two brothers find their father crippled from exposure after surviving a winter storm on Lake Winnipeg, and when he begs his sons to leave him to die, and the eldest son dies in the course of the rescue, the youngest angrily and deliberately refuses the act of mercy demanded by his father. These characters live in isolation, and in an often vio-

Cover for Valgardson's second collection, ten stories set mostly in northern Manitoba

lent natural world; their expressions of emotion are in turn stunted or warped by their environment, and their actions are understandably violent and destructive—even self-destructive.

There are small moments of triumph in some of the stories. In "The Burning" an elderly man has the satisfaction of setting his old home on fire before it can be burned by the local fire department—in the interests of progress. And in "Dominion Day," the only story in the collection that comes close to presenting an optimistic view of life, a young couple are taught by their older relatives the importance of enjoying life and maintaining contact with their community. Such instances of affirmation are outweighed, however, by the pervasive impression of a world in which human beings must struggle, without much hope of success, against the elements of nature and the implacable force of destiny.

Valgardson's second collection of short stories, *God Is Not a Fish Inspector*, appeared in 1975. The previous year he had moved back to Canada, to take up a position in the creative writing department at the University of Victoria in British Columbia; he still teaches there and is now a professor. He chaired the department from 1982 to 1987. Valgardson's second book makes use of the same themes and settings as the first, and the cumulative effect of the stories is, if anything, even grimmer. Violent death, suicide, deformity, and frustration are seen in combination with a stubborn instinct for survival that comes close to being tragic, mocked as it is by the primeval landscape and the operation of destiny.

In the Gutting Shed (1976) collects some of Valgardson's poetry from the late 1960s and early 1970s, taking by surprise reviewers who had thought of him only as a writer of short stories. Part of the volume is made up of poems that parallel, in their settings and themes, Valgardson's characteristic fiction. Other poems are considerably different, offering meditative insights into the author's domestic life and conveying a sense of a personality that had been resolutely excluded from the short stories. This latter group of poems varies in quality, Valgardson seeming to have some difficulty with matters of form when dealing with personal subject matter. The collection was, however, a successful venture; a second edition appeared in the same year as the first—not a common occurence with first books of poetry by Canadian authors. Valgardson's only other volume of verse, *The Carpenter of Dreams*, appeared in 1986.

A third collection of short stories, *Red Dust* (1978), resembles the first two but exhibits at the same time Valgardson's growing maturity and confidence. Some reviewers of the book took Valgardson to task for not striking out in new directions stylistically and for not attempting to deal with different themes. Yet, as Margaret Atwood states in her discussion of this book for *Essays on Canadian Writing* (Fall-Winter 1979-1980), the author has rightly and deliberately chosen to develop his characteristic voice: "If you look at what most writers actually do, it resembles a theme with variations more than it does the popular motion of growth. Writers' universes may become more elaborate, but they do not necessarily become essentially different. Popular culture, based on the marketing of novelties, teaches us that change is desirable in and for itself. Valgardson is its antithesis."

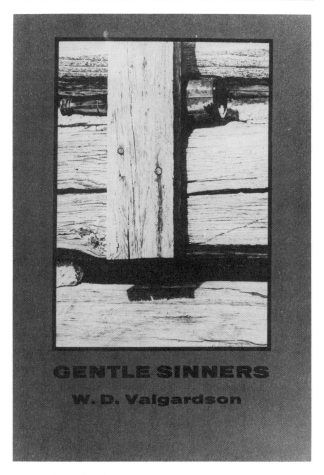

Cover for Valgardson's novel about a boy whose rejection of the fanatical Protestantism of his parents leads him to discover the values of ancestry and community

Valgardson's first novel, *Gentle Sinners* (1980), received the *Books in Canada* award as the best first novel of the year. Although some reviewers commented that Valgardson had not yet mastered the longer form, most agreed that *Gentle Sinners* was moving and impressive, auguring well for the author's future development as a novelist. In its account of a boy fleeing from the fanatical Protestantism of his parents and discovering, largely through the influence of his uncle Sigfus, the values of ancestry and community, the novel stands as something of a departure from Valgardson's "dark vision." There are scenes of pain and brutality, and some of the characters recall in their stunted humanity figures from the short stories, yet the movement of the book is toward affirmation, ending with the promise of human fulfillment—a promise that avoids sentimentality by setting the potential happy ending in a larger ironic context.

Valgardson is a painstaking writer; his stories rise, in his words, from the "strange, seething world of the unconscious," but he uses "art and craft" to communicate his visions. Writing, he says, "may be easy for others; for me, it is so difficult that I rewrite thirty and forty times and must use every device available to me." The form of his short stories he defines as "traditional"; conscious experimentation he rejects as hindering "the bond of understanding" he wishes to create with his audience. He has also deliberately rejected the first-person narrative method in most of his fiction. "I mistrust the first person very much. The first person gives the writer the temptation to fall into writing a summary rather than a story that needs to be dramatized. Also my stories are set in a very small locale, which most readers haven't experienced. That requires a very authoritative tone. I also have a strong Lutheran, and conservative, background that needs to make the statement of belief that the omniscient voice has."

The critical view of Valgardson's work has been best stated by Sam Solecki, who notes that the author sometimes overwrites, relying too extensively on similes, and that he can at times lapse into a monotone style that combines awkwardly with melodramatic effects; at his best Valgardson deals, in an understated yet moving way, with characters whose ordinary lives are treated in Solecki's words, "without any condescension."

Solecki notes, as others have, what seem to be the influences of Hardy and Faulkner on Valgardson's work. The author himself has admitted to possessing a Chekhovian sense of destiny: "My writing has been compared to many Russian writers and I think that's fair. The Interlake area is probably similar to some parts of Russia, with people of a similar background, especially Slavs, facing the cold, the poverty, the isolation, and so on. I speak out of that environment."

References:

Margaret Atwood, "Valgardsonland," *Essays on Canadian Writing*, 16 (Fall-Winter 1979-1980): 187-190;

Anthony Bukoski, "The Canadian Writer & the Iowa Experience," *Canadian Literature*, 101 (Summer 1984): 15-34;

Geoff Hancock, "Interview with W. D. Valgardson," *Books in Canada*, 6 (November 1977): 38-39;

Sam Solecki, "Fiction," in "Letters in Canada," *University of Toronto Quarterly*, 48 (Summer 1979): 324-326.

Gilles Vigneault

(27 October 1928-   )

Alexandre L. Amprimoz
Brock University

BOOKS: *Etraves* (Quebec: Editions de l'Arc, 1959);

Contes sur la pointe des pieds (Quebec: Editions de l'Arc, 1960); republished with *Contes du coin de l'oeil* (1966) in *Les Dicts du voyageur sédentaire* (1970); bilingual edition of *Contes sur la pointe des pieds,* with translations by Paul Allard, published as *Tales sur la pointe des pieds* (Erin, Ontario: Press Porcépic, 1972);

Balises (Quebec: Editions de l'Arc, 1964);

Avec les vieux mots (Quebec: Editions de l'Arc, 1964);

Pour une soirée de chansons (Quebec: Editions de l'Arc, 1965);

Quand les bateaux s'en vont (Quebec: Editions de l'Arc, 1965);

Contes du coin de l'oeil (Quebec: Editions de l'Arc, 1966); republished with *Contes sur la pointe des pieds* (1960) in *Les Dicts du voyageur sédentaire* (1970);

Les Gens de mon pays (Quebec: Editions de l'Arc, 1967);

Tam ti delam: Paroles de chansons (Quebec: Editions de l'Arc, 1967);

Ce que je dis c'est en passant (Quebec: Editions de l'Arc, 1970);

Les Dicts du voyageur sédentaire (Yverdon, Switzerland: Editions des Egraz, 1970);

Exergues (Montreal: Nouvelles Editions de l'Arc, 1971);

Les Neufs Couplets (Montreal: Nouvelles Editions de l'Arc, 1973);

Je vous entends rêver (Montreal: Nouvelles Editions de l'Arc, 1974);

Natashquan, le voyage immobile (Montreal: Nouvelles Editions de l'Arc, 1976);

A l'encre blanche: Poèmes (Paris: Stanké / Montreal: Nouvelles Editions de l'Arc, 1977);

Silences: 1957-poèmes-1977 (Montreal: Nouvelles Editions de l'Arc, 1978);

Les Quatres Saisons de Piquot (Montreal: Nouvelles Editions de l'Arc, 1979);

La Petite Heure: 1959-contes-1979 (Montreal: Nouvelles Editions de l'Arc, 1979);

Quelques pas dans l'univers d'Eva (Montreal: Nouvelles Editions de l'Arc, 1981);

Autant de fois que feuille tremble au vent: Paroles de chansons (Montreal: Nouvelles Editions de l'Arc, 1982);

Comptine pour endormir l'enfant qui ne veut rien savoir (Montreal: Nouvelles Editions de l'Arc, 1983);

Tenir paroles: Chansons, 2 volumes (Montreal: Nouvelles Editions de l'Arc, 1983);

Assonances (Montreal: Nouvelles Editions de l'Arc, 1984).

RECORDINGS: *Gilles Vigneault,* Columbia FS 538, 1962;

Gilles Vigneault chante et récite, Columbia FS 544, 1963;

Gilles Vigneault, Columbia FS 612, 1965;

Gilles Vigneault à la Comédie Canadienne, Columbia FS 632, 1965;

Mon Pays, Columbia FS 634, 1966;

Gilles Vigneault enregistre à Paris, Columbia FL 348, 1966;

Bobino, 3 octobre 1966, CBS 223, 1966;

C'est le temps, CBS GFS 90125, 1966;

La Manikoutai, CBS FS 652, 1967;

Le nord du nord, CBS FS 681, 1968;

La Manikoutai, CBS 63302, 1968;

Les Voyageurs, CBS, 1969;

Du milieu du pont, ESX 70501, 1969;

Le nord du nord, CBS S 63634, 1970;

Le voyageur sédentaire, ESX 70502, 1970;

Le temps qu'il fait sur mon pays, GVN-1000, 1971;

Les Grands Succès de Gilles Vigneault, CBS GFS 90003, 1972;

Poèmes et chants de la résistance, Re-604, 1972;

Qui êtes-vous, Gilles Vigneault? Radio-Canada Int. F-678, 1972;

Gilles Vigneault. Enregistrement public au Théâtre du Nouveau Monde, GVN 1005, 1974;

Le Québec en chanson. Gilles Vigneault et d'autres, CBS 80376, 1974;

J'ai vu le loup le renard le lion, Productions du 13 août, VLC 13, 1975;

Gilles Vigneault (photograph by Kèro)

Gilles Vigneault "J'ai planté un chêne," GVN 1007 / KD, 1977;

Gilles Vigneault à Bobino, GVN 1008 / 09 / KD, 1977;

Comment vous donner des nouvelles, GVN 1010 / KD, 1978;

Avec les mots du dimanche, GVN 1011 / 12, 1979;

Je vous entends chanter, KD 507-508, 1980;

Combien de fois faut-il parler d'amour, GVN-1013, 1982;

Un jour je ferai mon grand cerf-volant, GVN-1014, 1984.

OTHER: François Lafortune, *Où la lumière chante,* text by Vigneault (Quebec: Presses de l'Université Laval, 1966);

John Glassco, ed., *The Poetry of French Canada in Translation,* includes poems by Vigneault (Toronto: Oxford University Press, 1970);

"Sur le premier voyage de Macé Jalobert . . ." and "Les Explorateurs," in *Gilles Vigneault, conteur et poète,* by Donald Smith (Montreal: Québec / Amérique, 1984), pp. 141-143 and 145-146.

Gilles Vigneault is mainly known as a singer; but he also represents the rich vein of French-Canadian folk culture as a poet and writer. Vigneault's 1965 song "Mon Pays" was the most popular contemporary Quebec song—"Mon pays ce n'est pas un pays, c'est l'hiver," runs the refrain—until 1976 when his "Gens du Pays" became the unofficial national anthem of Quebec. It is also for his career as a chansonnier, *conteur,* actor, and poet that he has been so often honored: with a Governor General's Award and the Prix Calixa-Lavallée (both in 1966); the grand prize of the Academie Charles-Cros (1970); honorary degrees from the University of Trent and the Université du Québec à Rimouski (1975 and 1979); the Molson Prize (1982); and membership in the French Legion of Honor. "He is the most gifted poet in Canada since Emile Nelligan, whether in English or French," wrote Louis Dudek in 1967.

Gilles Vigneault, the son of Placide-Joseph-William and Marie-Appoline-Adelaïde Landry Vigneault, was born at Natashquan, a tiny fishing village on the north shore of the Gulf of St. Lawrence, 1300 kilometers from Montreal. Originally from Poitiers, branches of the Vigneault family had settled in Ile d'Orléans in the seventeenth century and in Acadia in the eighteenth, reaching the gulf by 1855. In Natashquan Vigneault's father "Willie" was a fisherman and fisheries inspector, mayor of the town, and a school commissioner. In 1941 Gilles Vigneault began his studies at the Petit Séminaire de Rimouski and expressed his early love for theater when he played a small role in Molière's *Les Fourberies de Scapin* when Les Compagnons du Saint-Laurent toured Rimouski. He went on to enroll in the literature program at Quebec City's Université Laval from which he graduated in 1953. There he read the Symbolist poets and in particular learned to love the medieval songs of France.

Even though he had been writing poems since his early days at the Petit Séminaire de Rimouski, Vigneault served his apprenticeship as an artist and writer during the 1950s. From 1950 to 1958 he wrote poems, stories, and a few plays, as well as some "monologues" which he recited for friends. During this period he earned his living as a bookstore clerk, a publicist, and an algebra instructor—first at the military school at Valcartier and then at the Ecole Technologique de Québec. In 1955 he married Rachel Cloutier, with whom he subsequently had four sons. By the age of thirty Vigneault was writing his monologues for television and teaching literature at the Université Laval. During the same period Vigneault began a parallel career in the theater that culminated in 1956 when he became the director of Quebec's Troupe des Treize. This group won the Calvert Trophy in 1958 at the Festival National d'Art Dramatique.

The year 1959 was an important one for Vigneault. He founded *Emourie*, one of the few poetry magazines of Quebec's literary renaissance. Jacques Labrecque, an important folklorist he had just met, recorded Vigneault's first song, "Jos Montferrand." And *Etraves*, his first collection of poems, was published by Les Editions de l'Arc, a house recently founded by Vigneault.

Etraves is a substantial book of 107 poems divided into six sections. The first twelve poems of "Ressacs" find their unity in the water imagery that culminates in "Natashquan," the prose poem that evokes the founding of Vigneault's village by a Spanish pirate. The quest for origin is the dominant theme of this section of *Etraves*, and it is often expressed through simple and delicate images. "Coquillage cassé" is a good example of the young Vigneault's fine craftsmanship:

> Coquillage cassé
> Sur les sables lointains
> De la haute mer
> Où donc est passée
> La limace
> La limace ourlée et fragile
> Qui t'habitait?
>
> (Broken shell / On the distant sands /
> Of the high sea / Where did the
> Slug go / That rimmed and fragile
> slug / That dwelled in you?)

The twenty-four texts that make up the second section, "Villes," are urban poems in which Vigneault contrasts the present with his memories of a fishing village. Here and there some images seem vaguely reminiscent of the poetry of Lawrence Ferlinghetti, but there is also in this troubadour of contemporary Quebec a touch of classical meditation:

> Nous dépensons dix fois le temps de vivre
> A discourir sur l'ennui de mourir
> Et nous passons le reste dans les livres
> Ah! Seulement ne plus se souvenir!
>
> (We spend ten times the time to live /
> Speaking about the boredom of death /
> And we spend the rest with books /
> Oh! If I could only forget!)

"Nuages" is a suite of sixteen poems, and its subject can best be defined as love for love's sake. In "Madrigal," "Chanson," and "Chanson vieillotte," Vigneault tries to capture old, popular melodies that echo medieval grace. In this section of delicate imagery and poetic lists that allow the Quebec troubadour to say "J'ai fait un bouquet du monde," there is a sense of the traditional code of courtly love songs.

After "Nuages," "Sabliers" is a series of ten poems that are classical either in form or in content. However, the theme of passing time occasionally opens onto nightmarish and surrealistic visions. "Fissures" is made up of nineteen poems that describe interior landscapes. In them the poet writes of "Ton coeur parallélépipède" (Your parallelepipedec heart) and "la conscience de mourir / Dans le geste le plus banal" (the awareness of dying / With the most trivial gesture), while trees and humans share the same suffering, the same anguish. There are also formal experiments with *mise en abyme,* as in "Scène," and prose poems that demonstrate a delicate and surrealistic twist, such as "La Sagesse sera ma perte . . . ."

The twenty poems of "Existences" offer a preview of Vigneault's later poetry in which inventiveness is sometimes cloaked by such sentimental clichés as the comparison of a woman's figure to an hourglass. However *Etraves* remains Vigneault's most substantial poetry book, and the choices made by most anthologists tend to confirm this judgment.

In 1960 Vigneault published a collection of forty-one short tales, *Contes sur la pointe des pieds.* A bilingual edition of this work, with a critical introduction and English translations by Paul Allard, was published by Press Porcépic in 1972. Also in 1960 Vigneault founded the first *boîte-à-chanson* of Quebec City. A *boîte-à-chanson* is more lively than a coffeehouse and less stuffy than a select nightclub or a *café-concert.* It was in such an establishment that the author of *Etraves* became known for some of his first songs: "Jean du Sud," "Jos Hébert," and "La Danse à Saint-Dilon." His first record appeared in 1962, and in the same year Vigneault received the Grand Prix du Congrès du Spectacle.

In 1964 he published two new books: *Balises* (poems) and *Avec les vieux mots* (song lyrics). *Balises,* in French Canada, are fir trees planted in the snow in order to indicate the road during a storm. Throughout the collection the poet develops and expands upon this symbolic title: he wants to plant his "balises" (words) in order not to lose his traditions under the snow of oblivion. Since time has closed the roads for the poet, he must try to remember the past through love. This premise perhaps explains why the first part of *Balises* is devoted to women and the second to his native Natashquan. This collection reveals a poet able to capture the ephemeral moments of intense life; it is a gallery where every pale watercolor hides an epiphany.

Avec les vieux mots is also divided into two sec-

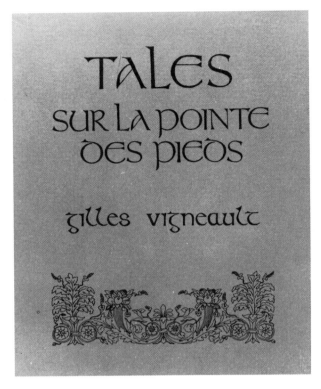

Dust jacket for the bilingual edition of Vigneault's 1980 collection of brief tales

tions, but Vigneault reverses the thematic order established in *Balises:* first come poems about love of the native land, then those dealing with love of a woman, taken as the symbol of universal love. At this time the poetry of Vigneault could have been described by the Spanish proverb: "El pasado fué siempre mejor." The poetry of this period is nothing less than a refined expression of nostalgia.

One of the songs from *Avec les vieux mots* made Vigneault's international reputation in 1965. Sung by Monique Leyrac at the International Song Festival in Sopot, Poland, "Mon Pays" was awarded first prize. The same year two new books were published: *Pour une soirée de chansons,* a thin volume of monologues and songs illustrated by Claude Fleury, and *Quand les bateaux s'en vont,* a new collection of song lyrics that earned Vigneault a Governor General's Award for poetry. It was about this time that Vigneault gave his first concert at the Comédie Canadienne.

In 1966 Vigneault published his second collection of tales, *Contes du coin de l'oeil:* seventeen short fantasies that might best be described as parables. The same year he provided the text for *Où la Lumière chante,* a volume of photographs by

François Lafortune. The year 1966 also marked the first concert Vigneault gave in Paris, at the Bobino theater. The following year Vigneault presented his show *Vive le Québec* in Paris and published two new volumes of song lyrics: *Les Gens de mon pays* and *Tam ti delam.*

From 1968 to 1973 Vigneault toured Quebec, North America, and Europe. During this period Arthur Lamothe made a film on the bard of Natashquan. Vigneault published *Ce que je dis c'est en passant,* a new book of song lyrics, in 1970, the same year that his two collections of short tales were illustrated by Richard Aeschlimann, gathered into one volume under the title *Les Dicts du voyageur sédentaire,* and published in Switzerland. In 1971 Vigneault published *Exergues,* a volume of poems and song lyrics, and two years later, a new collection, *Les Neuf Couplets.*

On 13 August 1974, at the Plains of Abraham in Quebec City, Vigneault sang for the Premier Festival Mondial de la Jeunesse Francophone in front of 150,000 spectators. The same year he published an important collection of song lyrics: *Je vous entends rêver.*

On 23 June 1975, the feast day of Saint-Jean-Baptiste, the patron saint of Quebec, Vigneault participated in the Mont Royal (Montreal) concert and performed for 300,000 spectators. The following year he published *Natashquan, le voyage immobile* illustrated with photographs by Anna Birgit. The "Natashquan universe," as Donald Smith describes it in *Gilles Vigneault, conteur et poète* (1984), is more than just a folk vision of the Quebec countryside; it is an attempt to record, by means of a glimpse of the countryside and the characters of the village past (a past that the author himself knew well), the values that continue to guide Quebec society and to which contemporary Quebecois still, if they *choose,* can have access. Such a sense of country and values helps explain the emotional appeal of Vigneault's songs, poems, and *contes*—an appeal that goes beyond even their technical skill and which gives his contemporary and traditional roles as chansonnier and *conteur* such social force.

These same values continue to inform his more recent writings. From 1977 to 1987 he published nine more volumes. Three of these are collections of previously published works: *Silences* (1978) assembles his poems from the period 1957-1977; *La Petite Heure* (1979) gathers together his *contes* for the two decades from 1959

to 1979; and the two-volume *Tenir paroles* (1983)—its title redolent with appeal to the values of the ordinary citizen, the need to retain the *speech of the people*—collects the texts of his songs from the years 1958 to 1983. *Autant de fois que feuille tremble au vent: Paroles de chansons* (1982) also collects songs, stories, and poems about nostalgia and time; while *A l'encre blanche* (1977), illustrated by Hugh John Barrett, and *Assonances* (1984), which Vigneault illustrated himself, are new collections of poems. In *Assonances,* a series of poems reflects associatively, melodically, on clay, water, tree, and air, bringing them all to focus on "issues": the character of contemporary life, life lived. Perhaps even more clearly, Vigneault's three record / book sets for children—*Les Quatres Saisons de Piquot* (1979), *Quelques pas dans l'univers d'Eva* (1981), and *Comptine pour endormir l'enfant qui ne veut rien savoir* (1983)—express the values he desires for his community. Space, birds, air, and trees are more than merely surroundings; they are opportunities. Take the time to love, his children's books urge, as do all his works. And loving requires remembering. Quebec's provincial motto is "Je me souviens"—I remember. Perhaps Vigneault is one of Quebec's most important cultural figures because all his creative activities are directed toward putting this motto into practice.

References:

François-Régis Barbry, *Passer l'hiver: François-Régis Barbry interroge Gilles Vigneault* (Paris: Editions du Centurion, 1978);

Roger Fournier, *Gilles Vigneault mon ami* (Montreal: La Presse, 1972);

Marc Gagné, *Gilles Vigneault: Bibliographie descriptive et critique, discographie, filmographie, iconographie et chronologie* (Quebec: Presses de l'Université Laval, 1977);

Gagné, *Propos de Gilles Vigneault* (Montreal: Nouvelles Editions de l'Arc, 1974);

Lucien Rioux, *Gilles Vigneault* (Paris: Seghers, 1969);

Aline Robitaille, *Gilles Vigneault* (Montreal: Editions de l'Hexagone, 1968);

Fernand Seguin, *Fernand Seguin recontre Gilles Vigneault* (Montreal: Editions de l'Homme / Editions Ici Radio-Canada, 1969);

Donald Smith, *Gilles Vigneault, conteur et poète* (Montreal: Québec / Amérique, 1984).

Yolande Villemaire
(28 August 1949-   )

Kathleen L. Kellett
University of Toronto

BOOKS: *Meurtres à blanc* (Montreal: Guérin, 1974);

Machine-t-elle, Les Herbes Rouges, 22 (July 1974);

Que du stage blood (Montreal: Editions Cul Q, 1977);

Terre de mue (Montreal: Editions Cul Q, 1978);

La Vie en prose (Montreal: Les Herbes Rouges, 1980);

Ange Amazone (Montreal: Les Herbes Rouges, 1982);

Adrénaline. Poésie et prose 1973-1982 (Saint-Lambert, Quebec: Noroît, 1982);

Du côté hiéroglyphe de ce qu'on appelle le réel, suivi de Devant le temple de Louxor le 31 juillet 1980, Les Herbes Rouges, 102-103 (April-May 1982);

Rrose Sélavy; Spirale d'écrivantes, by Villemaire, Claudine Bertrand, Lorraine Cadotte, Denyse Delcourt, France Gélinas, Isabelle Larrivée, Claire Le Roux, Céline Ménard, Lisette Ménard, Marie-Madeleine Raoult, Colette Tougas, with the collaboration of Gabrielle Roth and André Gervais, *Arcade,* 6 (October 1983);

Belles de nuit (Montreal: Les Herbes Rouges, 1983);

Les Coïncidences terrestres (Montreal: Editions de la Pleine Lune, 1983);

Rrose Sélavy à Paris le 28 octobre 1941, by Villemaire, Lorraine Cadotte, Marie-Madeleine Raoult, Denyse Delcourt, Lisette Ménard, Isabelle Larrivée, Claudine Bertrand Colette Tougas, Jacquie Minner, Céline Ménard, Claire Le Roux, and Giovanna Masella (Montreal: Editions de la Pleine Lune, 1984);

Jeunes Femmes rouges toujours plus belles, Lèvres Urbaines, 8 (Third trimester 1984);

La Constellation du Cygne (Montreal: Editions de la Pleine Lune, 1985);

Quartz et Mica (Trois-Rivières, Quebec: Ecrits des Forges / Pantin, France: Le Castor Astral, 1985).

RADIO: *Les Egouts de New York,* Radio-Canada FM, 11 May 1979;

Yolande Villemaire (photograph by Michel Lemieux)

Belles de nuit, Radio-Canada FM, 27 May 1983.

OTHER: "les paramythes des j. The Pyramyths of iiis," translated by Ray Chamberlain, in *Les Stratégies du réel / The Story so far 6,* edited by Brossard (Montreal: Nouvelle Barre du Jour / Toronto: Coach House Press, 1979), pp. 35-55;

"La Version d'amour," introductory essay by Villemaire in *French Kiss. Etreinte/exploration,* by Nicole Brossard, second edition (Montreal: Quinze, 1980), pp. 7-10;

"Ça devient clair en 1984," in *Dix Nouvelles humoristiques par dix auteurs québécois,* edited by André Carpentier (Montreal: Quinze, 1984), pp. 119-220.

PERIODICAL PUBLICATION: "My Heart Beats like a Bolo," translated by Barbara Godard, *Room of One's Own*, 4, no. 1/2 (1978): 111-128.

Yolande Villemaire has contributed to Quebec literature in several ways—as a theater critic, a literature teacher, and, especially, as a poet and novelist. The daughter of Normand Villemaire, a carpenter, and Evangeline Larose Villemaire, a schoolteacher, she was born in 1949 in Saint-Augustin, Comté des Deux-Montagnes, just outside Montreal. She finished her studies at the Collège Sainte-Marie in 1969 and in 1970 received a B.A. (with a specialty in the dramatic arts) from the Université du Québec à Montréal (U.Q.A.M.). In 1974 she completed her M.A. at U.Q.A.M., having produced a thesis on the Quebec playwright Michel Tremblay. She pursued her studies at the doctoral level from 1978 to 1980 at the Université de Montréal and plans to undertake a thesis there with an essay on creative writing under the direction of Professor Lise Gauvin. Since 1971 she has taught in Montreal at the collegiate level, first at the Cégep de Saint-Jérôme, then from 1974 to 1983 at the Cégep de Rosemont. She currently teaches at the Cégep André-Laurendeau.

Most of Villemaire's works are characterized by a preoccupation with popular culture and formal experimentation. Her first novel, *Meurtres à blanc* (1974), contains all the elements of a conventional thriller, but the plot is complicated to the point of parody, and the line between reality and fiction is confused as the characters of a mystery novel begin to invade the life of the main character, a secret agent writing a mystery novel in her spare time. Villemaire's poetic works, such as *Machine-t-elle* (published as a special issue of *Les Herbes Rouges* in 1974), *Que du stage blood* (1977), *Terre de mue* (1978), and *Adrénaline. Poésie et prose 1973-1982* (1982), are less concerned with narrative technique than with linguistic experimentation, though her poetry generally contains narrative elements. For example, *Que du stage blood* can be seen as a series of prose poems in deconstructed language which form a narrative to be decoded by the reader. As *Meurtres à blanc* draws upon the popular thriller novel, so Villemaire's poetry makes reference to characters from children's literature and popular culture such as Alice in Wonderland, "Vicki secrétaire,"

Snoopy, the Bionic Woman, and, especially, Wonder Woman. The prevalence of female heroines is indictive of the feminist perspective, which is a dominant feature of Villemaire's work, expressed very clearly, for example, in "Matrice Vierge" from *Adrénaline*.

Villemaire's best-known novel, *La Vie en prose* (1980), which brought her the Prix des Jeunes Ecrivains du *Journal de Montréal* in 1980, examines the relationship between life and prose, multiplying the images of life by the proliferation of characters, settings, and events. Feminism plays an important role in this book dominated by women. Feminine solidarity is evident, for example, in the collective work at a women's publishing house and in the women's self-defense class depicted in the text. In fact, the title suggests an association of feminism, writing, and life by its evocation of the song title "La Vie en rose," pink being for Villemaire a color that represents women's power and also carries a personal association with the female subculture by its link with her mother's maiden name, Larose. Lise Potvin's article, "L'Ourobouros est un serpent qui se mord la queue x 2," provides a useful key for the decoding of the complex system of signs in *La Vie en prose*, which she refers to as a "roman sémiologique."

Some elements from *La Vie en prose* appear in the three radio plays collected together in *Belles de nuit* (1983). In particular, *Un Jour de printemps l'hiver* includes familiar characters from the novel, while the scene of the Wen-do class recalls the self-defense class in *La Vie en prose*. The play *Belles de nuit*, which brought Villemaire the prize for the Radio-Canada radio-play competition in 1980, offers an amusing glimpse into a night in the life of telephone operators at Bell Canada, where Villemaire worked in the summers from 1967 to 1969 while she was a student. *Belles de nuit* was broadcast on Radio-Canada FM in May 1983.

Published in 1982 in an issue of the magazine *Les Herbes Rouges*, *Du côté hiéroglyphe de ce qu'on appelle le réel* is a collection of prose pieces, many of which had been published previously. Familiar characters from *La Vie en prose* reappear and heroes from modern mythology, including Wonder Woman, mix with others from ancient mythology, such as the Egyptian god Ptah, the namer. The title piece inquires into the relationship between the sacred and the profane. In the same issue, *Devant le temple de Louxor le 31 juillet 1980* attempts to respond to the question "What

Cover for the poetry collection Villemaire has described as cabalistically constructed: each page has seven lines and each line is governed by seven "laws"

is Egypt?" This preoccupation with Egypt is also evident in works such as the poetry collections *Terre de mue* and *Les Coïncidences terrestres* (1983).

The theme of reincarnation, a minor element in *La Vie en prose*, dominates the novel *Ange Amazone* (1982), in which the narrator, a student of meditation and mysticism, remembers her past lives. In fact, the twin themes of past lives and memory gain increasing importance in Villemaire's work from *Ange Amazone* on. The importance of mysticism in *Les Coïncidences terrestres* is evident even at the structural level. In an interview with Louise Blouin and Bernard Pozier, Villemaire claimed that this collection is constructed cabalistically, with seven lines per page and each line governed by seven laws. At the same time, the picture "Greta Garbo as the Sphinx" (1965) by Clarence Sinclair Bull on the cover of *Les Coïncidences terrestres* underlies the syncretic character of this text which speaks as readily of Egyptian gods as of the fictional space creature E.T. But most of all, Villemaire speaks here of writing and language, of love and desire.

Villemaire does not conform to the stereotype of the introverted writer working in isolation but is an active member of the artistic community. For example, in 1982 she established a telepathic network known as L'Ombre Jaune whose members are primarily writers. Villemaire also leads a women's writing group called Rrose Sélavy, which she organized in 1982 to encourage women friends who wished to write. The name of the group refers to a pseudonym created by the French surrealist Marcel Duchamp and recurs frequently in Villemaire's work; its encoded meaning, "Eros c'est la vie," corresponds to the constant theme of desire in her writing. According to Villemaire, each of the members is a "jeune femme rouge toujours plus belle," a recurrent expression in her work which, in the plural, provides the title for her collection of poems about an unexpected reunion of former lovers. *Jeunes Femmes rouges toujours plus belles* was published in 1984 as a special issue of *Lèvres Urbaines*. Out of the collaborative work of this group of writers have come *Rrose Sélavy; Spirale d'écrivantes*, pub-

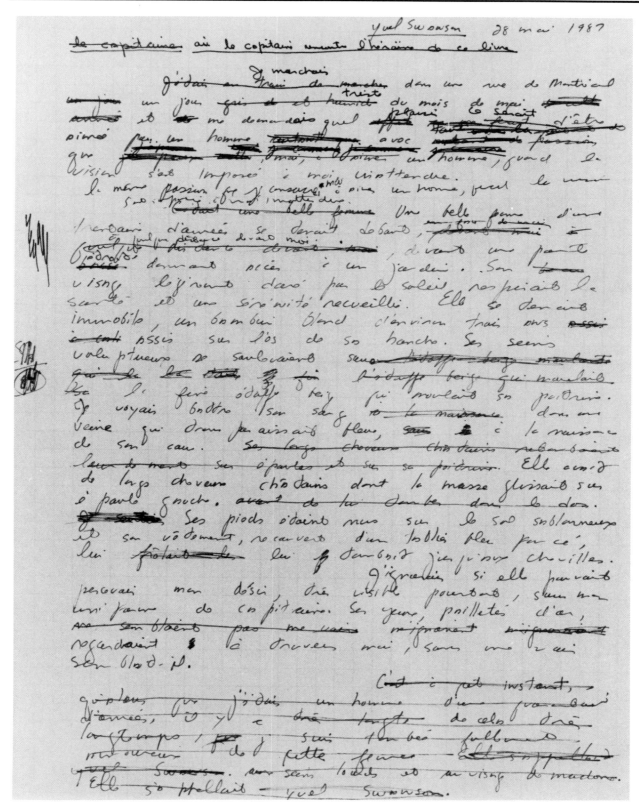

First page from the manuscript of Villemaire's novel-in-progress "Yvel Swanson" (by permission of the author)

lished as the October 1983 issue of the journal *Arcade* and *Rrose Sélavy à Paris le 28 octobre 1941* (1984). To the latter Villemaire contributed the text of the character Celia Rosenberg, who is mentioned in *Ange Amazone* and is the central character of Villemaire's *La Constellation du Cygne* (1985).

Set in Europe during World War II, *La Constellation du Cygne* tells the story of Celia Rosenberg, a young French prostitute. Totally blind to the danger she faces as a Jew in Nazi-occupied Europe, she falls in love with a member of the German S.S., to whom she had apparently pledged fidelity in a previous lifetime. The classical, linear structure of this novel is in sharp contrast to the experimentation with language, narrative technique, and genre characteristic of the author's earlier works. *La Constellation du Cygne* was awarded the Grand Prix Littéraire du *Journal de Montréal* in 1985, for the category of the novel.

Villemaire was chosen by the Ministry of Cultural Affairs in Quebec to spend six months in 1985 at the Studio du Québec in New York, a stay which culminated in the performance on 28 August 1985 of *Rrose Sélavy, New York 1921*. During the same period, Villemaire wrote the poems of *Quartz et Mica* (1985), in which the urban landscape of New York figures prominently.

Since the publication of *La Vie en prose*, Villemaire's importance as a Quebec writer has steadily increased. In 1986 the literary journal *Voix et Images* published as issue devoted mainly to critical studies of her work. Though her reputation is now established, there is no doubt that Villemaire continues to evolve as a writer. As the classical style of *La Constellation du Cygne* contrasts with the twists and turns of *Meurtres à blanc* and the relative simplicity of *Quartz et Mica* contrasts with the fragmented language of *Machine-t-elle*, it would seem that Villemaire has moved to a style which is increasingly accessible to the general public, while maintaining a certain thematic continuity by her concern with feminism, mysticism, and ancient and modern mythology.

Interviews:

Lise Maisonneuve, "Entrevue avec Yolande Villemaire," *Prétexte*, 2, no. 2 (1981): 9-17;

Louise Blouin and Bernard Pozier, "Entretien avec Yolande Villemaire," *Atelier de Production Littéraire des Forges*, 19-20 (1985): 6-16;

Lucie Robert, "Entrevue avec Yolande Villemaire," *Voix et Images*, 11 (Spring 1986): 390-405.

Bibliography:

Lucie Robert, "Bibliographie de Yolande Villemaire," *Voix et Images*, 11 (Spring 1986): 455-463.

References:

Claude Beausoleil, "Yolande Villemaire; Pour une cartographie du futur," in his *Les Livres parlent* (Trois-Rivières, Quebec: Ecrits des Forges, 1984), pp. 219-225;

Anne Elaine Cliche, "La Lutte avec l'ange. Le corps à corps avec le Nom dans la prose de Yolande Villemaire," *Voix et Images*, 11 (Spring 1986): 440-453;

Lise Potvin, "L'Ourobouros est un serpent qui se mord la queue x 2," *Voix et Images*, 11 (Spring 1986): 406-427;

Claude Sabourin, "Le Côte Centripète de ce qu'on appelle l'écriture: proses et poésies villemairiennes, d'un texte l'autre," *Voix et Images*, 11 (Spring 1986): 428-439.

Fred Wah

(23 January 1939-   )

Laurie Ricou
University of British Columbia

SELECTED BOOKS: *Lardeau: Selected First Poems by Fred Wah* (Toronto: Island Press, 1965);
Mountain (Buffalo: Audit East/West, 1967);
Tree (Vancouver: Vancouver Community Press, 1972);
Among (Toronto: Coach House Press, 1972);
Earth (Canton, N.Y.: Institute of Further Studies, 1974);
Pictograms from the Interior of B.C. (Vancouver: Talonbooks, 1975);
Selected Poems: Loki is Buried at Smoky Creek, edited with an introduction by George Bowering (Vancouver and Los Angeles: Talonbooks, 1980);
Breathin' My Name with a Sigh (Vancouver: Talonbooks, 1981);
Owners Manual (Lantzville, British Columbia: Island, 1981);
Grasp the Sparrow's Tail: A Poetic Diary (Kyoto, Japan: Privately printed, 1982);
Waiting for Saskatchewan (Winnipeg: Turnstone, 1985);
Rooftops (Nobleboro, Maine: Blackberry Books, 1987);
Music at the Heart of Thinking (Red Deer, Alberta: Red Deer College Press, 1987).

OTHER: Daphne Marlatt, *Selected Writing: Net Work*, introduction by Wah (Vancouver & Los Angeles: Talonbooks, 1980);
"Which at First Seems to be a Going Back for Origins: Notes on a Reading of Some American Women Writers," in *A Mazing Space: Writing Canadian Women Writing*, edited by Smaro Kamboureli and Shirley Neuman (Edmonton: Longspoon, 1987);
"Contemporary Saskatchewan Poetry," in *Essays on Saskatchewan Writing*, edited by E. F. Dyck (Regina: Saskatchewan Writers Guild, 1987), pp. 197-219.

PERIODICAL PUBLICATIONS: "Mrs. Richard's Grey Cat," *Open Letter*, third series, 9 (Fall 1978): 53-63;

Fred Wah (photograph by Tim Lee)

"Music at the Heart of Thinking," *Open Letter*, fifth series, 7 (Spring 1984): 33-39;
"Making Strange Poetics," *Open Letter*, sixth series, 2/3 (Summer/Fall 1985): 213-221;
"Subjective as Objective: The Lyric Poetry of Sharon Thesen," *Essay on Canadian Writing*, 32 (Summer 1986): 114-121.

Among the poets who have adopted and reimagined the William Carlos Williams-Robert Duncan line in Canada, none has so thoroughly sustained and extended the American school's commitment to the local as Fred Wah. The nature of that commitment is summarized in the preposition which provides the title for one of Wah's early books, *Among* (1972). "Among" is a word with no referent, which does not so much signal connection as a surrounding; it signifies association with, and the word itself is associated with mixing and with joint and reciprocal actions. Wah's home ground is British Columbia's Interior, where he is surrounded, "in a mind of mountains," as he puts it. Wah's reader is always aware of his local geographies, but aware of them as they are perceived in the mind of the observer, *as he thinks* them, in language, and as the language shapes his thinking. The reader is among perceptions. In "The Level" the poet is reading a map and mapping with survey instruments, and through the vocabulary of these activities he is writing his way into, and out of, the mountain's mind.

Among, as a book, is visually/conceptually involving. The poems are printed in forest green over a light green photographic tracery of trees which changes from page to page (themselves, of course, a product of the forest). Wah's sense of the local, as in the poem "Forest," is less a matter of place names than of general nouns and verbs, less a matter of specific details than of surrounding:

> And we just stood there
> in the Forest
> look
> at everything around us
> looking
> surrounding

The observer (writer *and* reader) is one living thing amid a complex of vital reciprocal and equal actions: the unexpected verb form in the third line overlaps declarative with imperative, plural and singular, poet's voice with that of community, noun and verb. To look at the forest is to be looked at; to name is to be shaped by the words spoken and written. As Wah summarizes the complexity of the local in the afterword to his *Selected Poems: Loki is Buried at Smoky Creek* (1980): "Writing has a lot to do with 'place,' the spiritual and spatial localities of the writer, ... All of it, out there, is measured from in here. In the particularity of *a* place the writer finds revealed the correspondences of a whole world."

Frederick James Wah's "in here," in the sense of his genetic (and therefore, cultural and linguistic) background, is increasingly evident in his books published in the 1980s. *Waiting for Saskatchewan* (1985) is his richest writing of his diverse spiritual and spatial localities, an essential extension of the "facts" which, Wah says, "seem partially unreal." They are that Wah was born 23 January 1939 in Swift Current, Saskatchewan, to the former Corrine Marie Erickson (born in Goteborg, Sweden) and Frederick Clarence Wah (who was born in Medicine Hat, Alberta, but lived in China from age five to twenty-three). In 1943 the family moved to British Columbia, where Wah was raised in the small resource-industry cities of Trail and Nelson. From 1958 to 1963 Wah studied at the University of British Columbia receiving a bachelor of arts degree in music and English and became a founding editor of the poetry newsletter *Tish*, now generally recognized as the primary vehicle for the introduction of the poetics of the Black Mountain poets Robert Duncan, Charles Olson, and Robert Creeley into Canadian literature. One of his colleagues at the University of British Columbia was Pauline Butling, whom he later married. (They have two children, Jennifer Ann and Erika Robin.) Wah studied for a year at the University of New Mexico, Albuquerque (where he edited *Sum* magazine), before going to the State University of New York at Buffalo, from which he received an M.A. in English (linguistics and literature) in 1967. During his master's studies he continued to be involved with small local magazines (as coeditor of *Niagara Frontier Review*, 1965-1966, and the *Magazine of Further Studies*, 1966-1967) and produced *Lardeau* (1965). This first book culminates in a sequence of poems (some anecdotal, some loosening into unclosed parentheses and series of ampersands) which anticipate the process of all his books: a crowd of perceptions locates Lardeau, a region in the Kootenays, "as I see it"–that is, mediated through the poet's complex personal contact with his world and yet evoking the singular moment of his perceiving.

In 1967 Wah moved back to the Interior of British Columbia and began teaching at Selkirk College in Castlegar. He has taught linguistics and language, both creative and applied writing, interdisciplinary humanities courses and, in the 1980s, various applications of computer technology to writing and publication–interests which also are evident in his editing and critical writing, especially as founding and contributing editor of *Open Letter*, the most important magazine of the postmodern movement in English-speaking Canada. As teacher and poet in a relatively rural setting, Wah continued to develop convictions about the necessary connection between the processes of the poem in composition and the processes of the natural world, perceiving an infinite series of dependent and supporting interrelationships among living things, each, in itself, continually in process. These connections manifest themselves in the poems and titles of several carefully conceived but syntactically daunting chapbooks, such as *Mountain* (1967), *Tree* (1972), and *Earth* (1974).

In 1975 Wah began to come to wider attention with an unusual book, *Pictograms from the Interior of B.C.*, a series of restrained verbal responses to the restrained Indian rock paintings in John Corner's *Pictographs in the Interior of British Columbia* (1968). By facing a reproduction of a pictograph with one of his own pictograms, Wah makes evident his interest in the ideogram, in its making of meaning by juxtaposing images/signs which invite the reader to compose or recompose a story, its formulas and its spontaneity, its roots in locale and in biology (the pictographs were often literally written in blood). As semiotics developed as an area of study in Canada, readers found ways to read Wah's relationships to language. A new series of selected writings from Talonbooks included a volume by Wah, *Selected Poems: Loki is Buried at Smoky Creek* (1980), with a sensible and appreciative introduction by his long-time friend-in-poetry George Bowering.

In 1978 Wah became coordinator and instructor in the writing program at David Thompson University Centre in Nelson. This move, and the growing responsiveness of a more prepared readership, spurred Wah to more active and diverse writing. *Owners Manual* (1981), a sequence of "how-to" poems, demonstrates most clearly his method of continually shifting the mood and tense and person of his verbs. *Breathin' My Name with a Sigh* (1981; published in earlier manuscript editions, 1978, 1979) and *Grasp the Sparrow's Tail: A Poetic Diary* (1982) became constituents of *Waiting For Saskatchewan* (1985), which won a Governor General's Award for poetry. In this book the poet's feeling for the local and interior is found in an interplay among structures: the narratives of remembering his father, the alphabets of his personal heritage of languages, the psychobiography of his own history in place, and the sound patterns of his own surname. Within his inheritance—"your name is my name"—Wah finds and exploits a much wider variety of forms than in his earlier books. The second section, "Grasp the Sparrow's Tail," is an *utaniki*, a poetic diary

Cover for the 1980 collection edited by the poet George Bowering

of mixed poetry and prose; the third series, "Elite," is a prose poem in ten sections; the final section, "This Dendrite Map," a series of *haibun*, "short prose written from a haiku sensibility." Here we find the most "theory" in Wah's work, the strongest metacritical element, a discussion of the way he/we/language sounds the words, the biology and breath involved. The opening section, about half of the earlier *Breathin' My Name With a Sigh*, is an anticipation of all these forms as they variously figure a series of love poems to his family, especially to his father. *Waiting for Saskatchewan* is an improvisation on phonemes, as sounds become both subjects and signs, and on typographical devices—the book in which Wah's enthusiasms as jazz musician are most evident.

In 1984 the David Thompson University Centre was closed, in a move Wah protested in his Governor General's Award acceptance speech as the action of a "vindictive" government. Wah returned to teaching at Selkirk College and about

MUSIC AT THE HEART OF THINKING #14

Try all the objects/people except speed the/my
mind or morning which will merely lock into the
heart for editing train after train so don't think
knowing will tell you rock along the beach
meaning is everything finally like muffins are
(sweet especially) with berries except sighing does
just what you want how sharpen those oriental
exercises or match the pebble eating its world
even the river in this case lake gets it as thought
skipped over the surface numbers and then sunk
but there's the arm sinking too simply out of
habit that's perfect clarity things around us plus
persons and places Vancouver maybe a little
Italian lunacy shades of Prague watch Steve
carefully essaying how symbol clouds the sky yet
signs the size of sandwiches or grannodiorite
rocks we dive from pool into the same canyons
migration of the soul i.e. Ocean and maps of
trailing training currents currants

Revised printout for one of the prose poems included in Wah's 1987 volume Music at the Heart of Thinking
(by permission of the author)

the same time became a contributing editor of *Swift Current*, Canada's first and only computerbank literary magazine. The possibilities here for extension of Wah's interest in language in action are immense, since the technology shows the language still more evidently to be in process, changed from moment to moment by creator and reader with words that can literally move on the screen.

In his concern for the whole book, in his attention to the intricate linguistic ecology of the local, Wah is the most overtly holistic of those who have adapted, however distantly and independently, the Black Mountain proprioceptive tradition in Canada. His lines are shorter, less fluent and flowing than Daphne Marlatt's; he shows less interest in fiction than George Bowering; he uses less obvious wordplay than B. P. Nichol and less humor than Frank Davey. To compare him, thus, to those who have been his closest poetic allies is a reminder that in the midst of his language one of his most noticeable signatures is the "ah" in "Wah," the apostrophe, which is both address to absent person or thing (personified) and an ecstatic means of making the absent present and part of self. Among this group of contemporaries and friends, Wah's language is the most direct, that is, it calls up fewer literary associations (despite some allusions to other writers and especially to characters in the oral tradition). In these senses, he gets closest to the speaking language of his interior. But those signatures, too, are changing and in process, waiting for the next word.

Interviews:

B. P. Nichol, "Transcreation: A Conversation with Fred Wah: TRG Report One: Translation (Part 3)," *Open Letter*, third series, 9 (Fall 1978): 34-52;

Meaghan Baxter, Jeff Derksen, and Angela Hryniuk, "An Interview with Fred Wah," *Writing*, 9 (Spring 1984): 45-49;

Pamela Banting, "An Interview with Fred Wah," *Brick*, 27 (Spring 1986): 13-17.

References:

Pamela Banting, "Fred Wah's Grammatological Practice," M. A. thesis, University of Manitoba, 1986;

Frank Davey, "Fred Wah," in his *From There to Here: A Guide to English-Canadian Literature Since 1960* (Erin, Ontario: Press Porcepic, 1974), pp. 258-261;

Smaro Kamboureli, "Fred Wah: A Poetry of Dialogue," *Line*, 4 (Fall 1984): 44-62;

Warren Tallman, "Wonder Merchants: Modernist Poetry in Vancouver During the 1960s," *Open Letter*, third series, 6 (Winter 1976-1977): 175-207.

George F. Walker
(23 August 1947-)

Chris Johnson
University of Manitoba

BOOKS: *Three Plays by George F. Walker* (Toronto: Coach House Press, 1978)—includes *Bagdad Saloon, Beyond Mozambique,* and *Ramona and the White Slaves;*
Zastrozzi, The Master of Discipline: A Melodrama (Toronto: Playwrights Co-op, 1979);
Criminals in Love (Toronto: Playwrights Canada, 1984);
The Power Plays (Toronto: Coach House Press, 1984)—includes *Gossip, Filthy Rich,* and *The Art of War.*

PLAY PRODUCTIONS: *Prince of Naples,* Toronto, Factory Theatre Lab, 8 July 1971;
Ambush at Tether's End, Toronto, Factory Theatre Lab, 8 December 1971;
Sacktown Rag, Toronto, Factory Theatre Lab, 5 April 1972;
Bagdad Saloon, Toronto, Factory Theatre Lab, 28 March 1973;
Demerit, Toronto, Factory Theatre Lab, 9 April 1974;
Beyond Mozambique, Toronto, Factory Theatre Lab, 11 May 1974;
Ramona and the White Slaves, Toronto, Factory Theatre Lab, 13 January 1976;
Gossip, Toronto, Toronto Free Theatre, 20 January 1977;
Zastrozzi, The Master of Discipline: A Melodrama, Toronto, Toronto Free Theatre, 2 November 1977;
Filthy Rich, Toronto, Toronto Free Theatre, 20 January 1979;
Rumours of Our Death, Toronto, Factory Theatre Lab, 19 January 1980;
Theatre of the Film Noir, Toronto, Factory Theatre Lab at the Adelaide Court Theatre, 11 May 1981;
Science and Madness, Toronto, Tarragon Theatre, 30 September 1982;
The Art of War, Toronto, Factory Theatre Lab at Toronto Workshop Productions, 23 February 1983;
Criminals in Love, Toronto, Factory Theatre, 7 November 1984;

George F. Walker

Better Living, Toronto, CentreStage, 15 May 1986.

TELEVISION: *Sam, Grace, Doug, and the Dog,* CBC, 1976;
Strike, CBC, 1976;
Capital Punishment, CBC, 1977;
Overlap, CBC, 1977.

RADIO: *The Prince of Naples,* adapted from Walker's stage play, CBC, 1973;

The Private Man, CBC, 1973;
Ambush at Tether's End, adapted from Walker's stage play, CBC, 1974;
Quiet Days in Limbo, CBC, 1977;
Desert's Revenge, CBC, 1984.

OTHER: *Prince of Naples*, in *Now in Paperback: Canadian Playwrights of the 1970's*, edited by Connie Brissenden (Toronto: Fineglow Plays, 1973), pp. 61-102;
Ambush at Tether's End, in *The Factory Lab Anthology*, edited by Brissenden (Vancouver: Talonbooks, 1974), pp. 89-183.

PERIODICAL PUBLICATIONS: *Rumours of Our Death: A Parable in 25 Scenes*, Canadian Theatre Review, 25 (Winter 1980): pp. 42-72;
Theatre of the Film Noir, Canadian Theatre Review, 34 (Spring 1982): pp. 120-164;
The True Nature of Home Repair (excerpt from *Better Living*), Descant, 50 (Fall 1985): pp. 20-27.

George F. Walker has dominated Canadian English-language stage comedy of the late 1970s and the 1980s in a manner unprecedented since Robertson Davies achieved his comic preeminence in the 1940s and 1950s. Like Davies, Walker takes his comedy seriously, using it to present a coherent vision of the world, and, like Davies, Walker is an acute social satirist. There the resemblance ends. While Walker's vision is coherent, the world he sees is not; his is a dark comedy peopled with larger-than-life, obsessive characters addicted to self-analysis and hilariously misguided pseudophilosophical observation. Lineal plot and logical, psychological character development are seldom found in Walker's work, as the characters leap hysterically from thought to thought and action to action in a state of perpetual *non sequitur* and crisis. His dramatic style draws heavily on pop-art forms (cartoons, gothic melodrama, detective novels, B-movies), giving the plays their lurid coloring and frenzied energy. Walker has been compared to Tom Stoppard, for his acrobatic dialogue, and to Sam Shepard, for his use of pop-art icons.

Walker, the son of Malcolm Walker, a laborer, and Florence Braybrook Walker, was born in Toronto and raised in the city's East End, a working-class neighborhood. Walker is shaped by and loyal to this background, urban in his sensibility (in contrast to the rural naturalism prevalent in Canadian dramatic literature) and antagonistic to all political systems (in contrast to the left-wing

sympathies of most Canadian political and working-class drama, like that of George Ryga, Michael Cook, David Fennario, and Rick Salutin). He left high school before graduation, married at the age of eighteen, and worked at a variety of jobs while writing poems and stories. None of this early work has been published. He was driving a cab when he saw a handbill inviting submission of scripts to the Factory Theatre Lab. The result was Walker's Nietzschean teacher / student dialogue, *Prince of Naples* (first produced in 1971), and the beginning of his long association with that theater. He was playwright-in-residence from 1971 to 1974, and his first seven plays, as well as four later ones, were premiered by that company. Walker feels that then artistic director Ken Gass's policy of committing the Factory Lab to production, no questions asked, was the primary force behind his early development as a playwright. Since the mid 1970s, Walker's plays have been produced by the Toronto Free Theatre, Tarragon, and CentreStage in Toronto, and by theaters across Canada and in the United States, Great Britain, Australia, New Zealand, and Germany.

While Walker's formal education was limited, he is extremely well-read; a common criticism of his early plays (*Prince of Naples; Ambush at Tether's End*, produced in 1971; *Sacktown Rag*, 1972; *Bagdad Saloon*, 1973; and *Demerit*, 1974) is that they are too derivative of Beckett and Ionesco. (*Sacktown Rag* was published in a mimeographed acting edition by Playwrights Co-op in Toronto in 1972; *Demerit* has never been published.) Nonetheless, the energy of these plays won a following, and the Factory Lab took its production of *Bagdad Saloon* on its British tour in 1973, a tour Walker accompanied. Walker's voice emerged clearly for the first time in *Beyond Mozambique* (produced in 1974), focused by his use of the B-movie lens. A mad Nazi scientist; his deformed assistant; his wife, who thinks she is Olga in Chekhov's *The Three Sisters*; a defrocked priest; an ex-RCMP corporal; and a porn-movie star are trapped together at a jungle outpost, playing out their fantasies oblivious to one another and to the jungle which surrounds them. The play has all the trappings of a jungle movie, but beneath them it is an examination and parody of the imperialist assumptions underlying jungle movies; as Walker says: "Not obviously a political play but [one] which makes people think about politics." Adverse and confused critical response to his early work and the fear that there might not be a substantial audience for his brand of comedy depressed Walker to the point that he left Toronto for a year of travel in the United States and Canada; at this time he considered writing novels and wrote a draft of a naturalistic play with which he was not satisfied. Still, when he returned to the Toronto stage, he was unrepentently Walkeresque. *Ramona and the White Slaves* (1976) combines B-movie and opium dream for its portrait of a mother devouring her children in an impossibly decadent turn-of-the-century Hong Kong brothel. The first production of this play, by Factory Lab in January 1976, marked Walker's directorial debut; he has also directed the premieres of *Rumours of Our Death* (1980); *Theatre of the Film Noir* (1981); and *The Art of War* (1983); a production of *Zastrozzi, The Master of Discipline* at the Nimrod Theatre in Sydney, Australia, in 1984; the tenth-anniversary production of the same play at the Factory Theatre in 1987; and other productions of his plays in various theaters in Canada. Walker blames his own confused direction for much of the confusion experienced by audiences and critics of *Ramona and the White Slaves*.

Gossip (produced in 1977), was, in Walker's words, a deliberate attempt to be "more generous" with his audience, and audiences did respond enthusiastically to this detective spoof in which reporter Tyrone Power discovers that high society and the art world are pervaded by baroquely complex corruption. After its initial staging by Toronto Free Theatre, *Gossip* was produced in a number of American cities as Walker at last began to achieve recognition outside Toronto. *Zastrozzi*, also first produced in 1977, was equally popular, although Walker denies that he wrote it with greater accessibility as an objective. Based on a description of Shelley's novel of the same title, *Zastrozzi* is gothic melodrama: the eponym, "the master criminal of all Europe," stalks Verezzi the *artiste* ostensibly to avenge his mother's murder, but more important because Zastrozzi is the "master of discipline" with a mission to make all "answerable" to their own dark sides. Like many of Walker's plays, *Zastrozzi* is a confrontation between good and evil, what original director, Bill Lane, calls "a modern morality," compelling the audience to consider the issues through clever manipulation and division of empathy.

Tyrone Power returns in *Filthy Rich* (produced in 1979), another comic exposé of political corruption; this time the *film noir* antecedents evi-

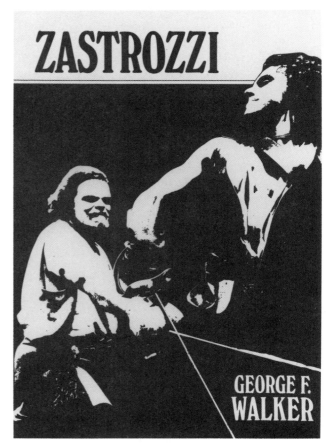

Cover for the published version of Walker's play, a "modern morality" partially based on Shelley's novel

dent in the earlier play *Gossip* are more expertly exploited. *Filthy Rich* is the second work in Walker's series of Power Plays. The third, entitled *The Art of War*, was commissioned to inaugurate the Conference of Art and Reality at Simon Fraser University in Burnaby, British Columbia, 1982. In *The Art of War* the corruption is found in the world of international politics and illicit arms dealing. The forces of evil are clear in the Power Plays, but the forces of good personified by Power's liberalism (with a lower-case l) are progressively shapeless and ineffectual. Walker says there may be a fourth play in the series, but if there is, Jamie, Power's youthful and pragmatic sidekick, will have to take over as the focal point; the antihero himself is inexorably disappearing into his own neuroses.

Rumours of Our Death, a political "parable in 25 scenes," was a great success when Walker directed its 1980 premiere by Factory Theatre Lab as a punk-rock musical with music by John Roby. *Theatre of the Film Noir*, a mood piece set in Paris immediately after World War II, blurs sexual as

Cover for the published version of Walker's play series featuring "political journalist" Tyrone Power

well as ethical boundaries. It was produced by Factory Lab as part of the Toronto International Theatre Festival in 1981 and won a Dora Award the following year. Also in 1981 Walker was playwright-in-residence at Joseph Papp's Public Theatre in New York: Andrei Serban directed *Zastrozzi* for that company, a production Walker disliked because it apparently failed to achieve the vital balance between the comic and the serious. *Science and Madness*, produced in 1982, is another gothic melodrama, a reworking of the Frankenstein story. (The play is available in published form only in a Playwrights Co-op mimeographed acting edition.) Walker saw in *Science and Madness* evidence that he was repeating himself, and *Criminals in Love*, which premiered in November 1984, is a marked change of direction, with the writer returning for the first time since

Sacktown Rag to the East End for subject matter as well as for perspective.

In the 1984 play Gail and Junior are self-described "young lovers doomed." Junior is led into a life of crime by his father and by a bourgeois revolutionary aunt, despite the attempted intervention of Junior's friend, a philosophical bum who argues eloquently against the forces of cosmic or possibly socioeconomic "destiny": the nature / nurture and fate / free-will debates are couched in the terms of high farce. *Criminals in Love* won the Chalmers Award for 1985 (*Zastrozzi* had been nominated in 1977 and *Theatre of the Film Noir* in 1981), and the Governor General's Award for published English-language drama in the same year.

Better Living (produced by Toronto's CentreStage in 1986) is Walker's first play to premiere on a large Canadian "mainstage," and Walker admits that he is uncomfortable with a mainstage audience and its expectations. A "prequel" to *Criminals in Love, Better Living* follows Gail, her mother, and two sisters through their attempts to cope with the return of a man who may or may not be the missing father and husband. Critical and audience response was not enthusiastic, and Walker himself has reservations about the play, although he points out that it is his most ambitious work to date, exploring as it does feminine desire for and submission to power, and, on a personal level, drawing on a childhood in which women played the most important and influential roles. A much different, earlier version of the play was given a partial production at Cornell University in 1982.

Walker is currently working on an adaptation of Turgenev's *Fathers and Sons* called "Nothing Sacred" ("both a title and a warning") and included by CentreStage in its planned 1987-1988 season. Outraged by what he feels real estate developers and the process of "gentrification" are doing to his beloved Toronto, Walker is also writing a play on that subject: "a conflict between big crooks and little crooks; I'm on the side of the little crooks." "Beautiful City" will open the Factory Theatre's 1987-1988 season. Surprisingly, Walker has also left Toronto, moving in the spring of 1987 to Sackville, New Brunswick, with his second wife, actress Susan Purdy, and his younger daughter, Courtney. He says he would like to work on a novel.

References:

L. W. Connolly "Modern Canadian Drama: Some

Critical Perspective," *Canadian Drama / L'Art Dramatique Canadien* 11, no. 1 (1985): 141-149, 221-225;

Chris Johnson "George F. Walker: B-Movies Beyond the Absurd," *Canadian Literature,* 85 (Summer 1980): 87-103;

Denis W. Johnston "George F. Walker: Liberal Idealism and the 'Power Plays'," *Canadian Drama / L'Art Dramatique Canadien* 10, no. 2 (1984): 195-206;

Paul Milliken "Walker's Living Theatre Ignites the Imagination," *Performing Arts in Canada,* 18 (Fall 1981): 43-46;

Gregory J. Sinclair "Live from Off-Stage: Playwrights Walker, Walmsley and Thompson Shout From the Street," *Canadian Forum,* 65 (August / September 1986): 6-11;

Robert Wallace "George F. Walker," in *The Work: Conversations with English-Canadian Playwrights,* by Wallace and Cynthia Zimmerman (Toronto: Coach House Press, 1982), pp. 212-225;

Tim Wynne-Jones, "Acts of Darkness," *Books in Canada* 14 (April 1985): 11-14.

Sheila Watson
(24 October 1909-   )

Dick Harrison
University of Alberta

BOOKS: *The Double Hook* (Toronto: McClelland & Stewart, 1959);

Sheila Watson: A Collection, Open Letter, third series, 1 (Winter 1974-1975);

Four Stories (Toronto: Coach House Press, 1979); republished in *Five Stories* (Toronto: Coach House Press, 1984);

And the Four Animals (Toronto: Coach House Press Manuscript Editions, 1980); republished in *Five Stories* (Toronto: Coach House Press, 1984).

OTHER: *The Collected Poems of Miriam Mandel,* edited by Watson (Edmonton: Longspoon / NeWest, 1984).

Sheila Watson is important to Canadian letters as a novelist, a teacher, and a scholar. A person of strong, independent mind, originality and vitality of imagination, she has made an impression on Canadian intellectual life out of all proportion to her relatively small volume of published work. She is most widely known for her novel, *The Double Hook,* which has made its own place among the handful of Canadian books most often studied and considered essential by younger writers.

Sheila Watson was born Sheila Martin Doherty on 24 October 1909, in New Westminster, British Columbia, where her father was superintendent of the Provincial Mental Hospital. Watson lived there with her parents, Charles Edward and Elweena Martin Doherty, until 1932, when Dr. Doherty died. She took her schooling with the Sisters of St. Anne and the Convent of the Sacred Heart in Vancouver. The place this early experience has taken in her imagination can be seen especially in her short stories. She completed an honors degree in English at the University of British Columbia in 1931, a teaching certificate in 1932, and an M.A. with a thesis on Addison and Steele in 1933. During her studies at UBC Watson developed a breadth of literary interests characteristic of her entire career, encompassing Swift and contemporary authors including Eliot, Pound, Virginia Woolf, Dorothy Richardson, Lawrence, Hemingway, Faulkner, and Dos Passos.

From 1934 until the end of World War II, she taught at various schools in southern British Columbia: St. Louis College in New Westminster and at schools in Dog Creek, Langley Prairie, Duncan, and Mission City. For her readers the most significant of these posts is the one at Dog

Creek, a tiny community in the Cariboo between Ashcroft and Williams Lake which later provided the setting for *The Double Hook*. When she went to Dog Creek for two years in the mid 1930s to teach an ungraded school of nine pupils, she harbored no intention of writing about the place. As Watson said years later, "It was the only place in 1934 that said, 'Come, and teach our children.' "

Christmas 1941 marked her marriage to the poet and playwright Wilfred Watson. After the war the Watsons moved to Toronto where Sheila Watson taught at Moulton College and took up part-time graduate study at the University of Toronto. She taught next as a sessional lecturer at UBC for two years and for one year at a high school in Powell River. From 1951 to 1953 she lived in Calgary where she completed *The Double Hook* (1959).

Watson has acknowledged a complex, paradoxical relationship between *The Double Hook* and her Dog Creek experience. The double hook was "set," as it were, before the writing even began. In her only public statement about the novel, made in 1973 and transcribed in the Sheila Watson issue of *Open Letter* (Winter 1974-1975), she says that long after leaving the Cariboo, "I realized that if I had something I wanted to say, it was going to be said in these images." Yet the novel was also conceived "in answer to a challenge that you could not write about particular places in Canada: that what you'd end up with was a regional novel of some kind." Watson wrote, then, defiantly within the paradox that human universals must, by definition, inhabit the local and particular experience, even in Canada. Her setting was derived from the arid intermountain cattle country in the drought years. Her descriptive metaphors generate a vivid sense of concrete particularity, but the spareness of description and lack of geographical references free the setting from any limitation of place. Her characters interact with a wasteland which is physical, emotional, and spiritual. In critical commentary, comparisons with Eliot, Joyce, and Faulkner are not surprising.

Similarly, the action of the novel is an essence of rural life, as spare and suggestive as a parable. A tiny community is lost among barren hills dominated by the spirit of Coyote, the Indian trickster god of mischief and disharmony. Its members are divided in fear and suspicion under the moral tyranny of an aging matriarch, and though old Mrs. Potter is killed by her son James at the outset, the people remain paralyzed by her ghost,

Cover for Watson's best-known work, written, she remarked in 1973, "in answer to a challenge that you could not write about particular places in Canada: that what you'd end up with was a regional novel of some kind"

moving among and within them. James flees from the responsibility of leadership he has brought upon himself, and the people are left in their individual isolation. In the town below the hills, James learns that the freedom of his escape is an illusion. Meanwhile, his neighbors gather around their reluctant spiritual leader, Felix Prosper, united by the suffering of Lenchen, the pregnant girl James has abandoned, and Kip, a lad he has blinded with a whip in the rage of his escape. As James returns to take up his responsibilities, and the people draw together in real community, the action which began with a death ends with the birth of James and Lenchen's son.

The theme most apparent from the action, of community as a means and effect of redemption from a wasteland of isolation and fear, is appropriate to the life and landscape of the West.

James's necessary rejection of individualism and escape in favor of community is especially appropriate to a Canadian West. But the implications quickly expand beyond the West and beyond that particular theme. References, allusions, images, and ritual gestures associate the action with biblical patterns of sacrifice and redemption. At first the community is under the harsh dispensation of the law, and the story of Jonah is invoked for its suggestions of isolation from God, moral reluctance, sacrifice, and purifying descent. As the action moves from death to rebirth, from Old Testament to New, the typology shifts from Jonah to Christ: community, in effect, becomes communion.

Underlying the theme of community is the more pervasive and universal theme suggested by the novel's title: the paradoxical nature of human experience, its inevitable doubleness, its inextricable uniting of opposites. The paralyzing dilemma the characters initially face is that the community can be renewed only by being destroyed, that individually they can reach life only by sacrificing themselves. This paradox is constantly echoed in the imagery and the action of the novel: death permits life, reason does not explain, blinding leads to vision, violence to harmony, freedom to responsibility, or in Kip's words, "if you hook twice the glory you hook twice the fear." This union of opposites is reinforced by a prominent strain of elemental imagery, of water which drowns or nourishes, fire which consumes but purifies.

Beneath this expression of paradox, the ultimate theme of the novel may be expression itself, a theme which completes the circle by being at once the most universal and the most basic to the problems of the specific people Watson was writing about. She has said that there was something she wanted to say "about how people are driven, how if they have no art, how if they have no tradition, how if they have no ritual, they are driven in one of two ways, either towards violence or towards insensibility–if they have no mediating rituals which manifest themselves in what I suppose we call art forms." It is in mediating rituals or art forms that one can accommodate the baffling paradoxes of existence, subsume them in some form of harmony. The characters in *The Double Hook* have initially no forms in which to understand what is happening to them. They inhabit the capricious order of Coyote, the deceiver who is also self-deceived. Baffled, the more passive attempt to hide in insensibility; the Potters seek relief in vio-

lence. Felix can become the center around which the community coalesces because of his recognition of ritual and form, a quality emphasized by his half-remembered fragments of Catholic liturgy. Felix brings the others back through rituals of hospitality, love, and community, and with his fiddle he is symbolically the source of art and creator of harmony. In a detailed way the problems of form and expression are explored in the dialogue; on a larger scale the ritual pattern of death and rebirth, sacrifice and redemption, through which the characters pass with only faint comprehension, brings them to the stage of precarious harmony and hope on which the novel closes.

The publication of *The Double Hook* in 1959 marked a stage in the development of Canadian fiction, bringing the techniques and concerns of modernism together with rural Canadian experience. The novel's structure has the defined focus of a drama, its style the compression of an imagist lyric. The resulting complexities have attracted much critical commentary since the publication of the New Canadian Library edition in 1969. The novel has a place in most general studies of Canadian literature and has been the object of more than a dozen articles, chiefly devoted to explications of symbolic patterns. No book-length study of Watson's work has been published. The most comprehensive essay to date is Stephen Scobie's "Sheila Watson," published in *Canadian Writers and Their Works*, fiction series, in 1985.

During the 1950s Watson was also writing most of the few short stories she has committed to print. "Brother Oedipus" was first published in 1954, followed by "The Black Farm" (1956), "Antigone" (1959), "The Rumble Seat" (1974), and "And the Four Animals" (1980). The first four were collected with Watson's scholarly essays in the special issue of *Open Letter* devoted entirely to her work. They later appeared in *Four Stories* (1979); the fifth story was separately published in 1980; and all five appeared as *Five Stories* in 1984. Watson's stories are brief, often enigmatic, and marked by the wit with which she brings together classical reading experience and contemporary realities. The recurrent figure of the brother, Oedipus, for example, trails the shadows of Sophocles and Freud into a Roman Catholic family living on the grounds of a mental hospital. Little critical attention has yet been devoted to the stories, though Scobie, in his "Sheila Watson," analyses "And the Four Animals" at some length as a key to the symbolic structure of *The Double Hook*.

After her time in Calgary, Watson lived in Edmonton and in France. In 1957 she resumed her graduate study at the University of Toronto and completed a doctoral thesis on Wyndham Lewis in 1965 under the direction of Marshall McLuhan. In 1968 she also spent a year working with McLuhan at the Centre for Culture and Technology. Her scholarly essays on Lewis and other topics have been published in a variety of journals and are all collected in the special issue of *Open Letter*.

Watson joined the Department of English at the University of Alberta in 1961. Her reputation soon spread beyond the university, attracting graduate students of modern literature from all parts of Canada, to whom she devoted substantial time and energy. From 1971 to 1976 she was the moving force behind the little magazine *White Pelican*, a quarterly devoted to the literary and visual arts. The eighteen issues of the magazine encouraged some of the best new Canadian talent in addition to publishing such established figures as Frank Davey, Roy Kiyooka, Henry Kreisel, Douglas Lochhead, Michael Ondaatje, P. K. Page, Rudy Wiebe, and Norman Yates. *White Pelican* also published two volumes of poetry: Wilfred Watson's *The Sorrowful Canadians and Other Poems* (1972), and Miriam Mandel's *Lions at Her Face* (1973), which won a Governor General's Award in 1974. After Miriam Mandel's death in 1982, Watson edited *The Collected Poems of Miriam Mandel* (1984). The volume, which contains Mandel's previously published poems as well as working papers, is, as Watson notes in the introduction, less a "collection" in the ordinary sense than a "serial poem," composed intermittently from 1969 to 1982.

Watson retired from the university in 1975. In 1978 Western Producer Prairie Books published *Figures in a Ground*, a festschrift in her honor edited by colleagues Diane Bessai and David Jackel. In 1980 the Watsons moved from Edmonton to Nanaimo, Vancouver Island. Sheila Watson's work will no doubt continue to be distin-

guished by the same avidness for new ideas and the same fierce intellectual honesty.

References:

Diane Bessai and David Jackel, eds., *Figures in a Ground: Canadian Essays in Modern Literature Collected in Honor of Sheila Watson* (Saskatoon: Western Producer Prairie Books, 1978);

George Bowering, ed., *Sheila Watson and The Double Hook: A Book of Essays* (Kemptville, Ontario: Golden Dog Press, 1985);

Bowering, "Sheila Watson, Trickster," in his *The Mask in Place : Essays on Fiction in North America* (Winnipeg: Turnstone, 1982), pp. 97-111;

Dawn Rae Downton, "Message and Messengers in *The Double Hook*," *Studies in Canadian Literature*, 4 (Summer 1979): 137-146;

Barbara Godard, " 'Between One Cliché and Another': Language in *The Double Hook*," *Studies in Canadian Literature*, 3 (Summer 1978): 149-165;

Beverly Mitchell, "Association and Allusion in *The Double Hook*," *Journal of Canadian Fiction*, 2 (Winter 1973): 63-69;

Leslie Monkman, "Coyote as Trickster in *The Double Hook*," *Canadian Literature*, 52 (Spring 1972): 70-76;

Margaret Morriss, "The Elements Transcended," *Canadian Literature*, 42 (Autumn 1969): 56-71;

Shirley Neuman, "Sheila Watson," in *Profiles in Canadian Literature*, volume 4, edited by Jeffrey M. Heath (Toronto & Charlottetown: Dundurn,1982), pp. 45-52;

Steven Putzel, "Under Coyote's Eye: Indian Tales in Sheila Watson's *The Double Hook*," *Canadian Literature*, 102 (Autumn 1984): 7-16;

Stephen Scobie, "Sheila Watson," in *Canadian Writers and Their Works*, volume 7, fiction series, edited by Jack David, Robert Lecker, and Ellen Quigley (Toronto: ECW, 1985), pp. 257-312;

Margaret E. Turner, "Fiction, Break, Silence: Language. Sheila Watson's *The Double Hook*," *Ariel*, 18 (April 1987): 65-78.

Wilfred Watson

(1 May 1911-   )

Diane Bessai
University of Alberta

BOOKS: *Friday's Child* (London: Faber & Faber, 1955);

From Cliché to Archetype, by Watson and Marshall McLuhan (New York: Viking, 1970);

The Sorrowful Canadians and Other Poems (Edmonton: White Pelican, 1972);

I begin with counting (Edmonton: NeWest, 1978);

Mass on Cowback (Edmonton: Longspoon, 1982);

Gramsci x 3 (Edmonton: Longspoon, 1983);

Poems: Collected / Unpublished / New (Edmonton: Longspoon/NeWest, 1986).

PLAY PRODUCTIONS: *Cockcrow and the gulls,* Edmonton, Studio Theatre, 29 March 1962;

Trial of Corporal Adam, Toronto, Coach House Theatre, 1 May 1963;

Wail for two pedestals, Edmonton, Yardbird Suite, 3 November 1964;

Chez-vous comfortable pew, Edmonton, Yardbird Suite, May 1965;

Two teardrops frozen in the rear-view mirror, Edmonton, Walterdale Theatre Associates, 15 May 1967;

Canadian Fact, Edmonton, Walterdale Theatre Associates, May 1967;

O holy ghost, dip your finger in the blood of Canada, and write, I love you, Edmonton, Studio Theatre, 4 December 1967;

Soul is my button, Wolfville, Nova Scotia, Acadia Students' Union, July 1969; revised as *Up against the wall oedipus,* Edmonton, University of Alberta Student's Union, March 1970;

Let's murder clytemnestra according to the principles of marshall mcluhan, Edmonton, Studio Theatre, 18 November 1969;

Gramsci x 3, Edmonton, Studio Theatre, 27 March 1986.

OTHER: "The Canticle of the H. of History," *Poetry 62/Póesie 62,* edited by Eli Mandel and Jean-Guy Pilon (Toronto: Ryerson, 1961), pp. 1-5;

Woman Taken in Adultery, in *Prairie Performance: A Collection of Short Plays,* edited by Diane Bessai (Edmonton: NeWest, 1980).

PERIODICAL PUBLICATIONS: "The Lice," *Prism,* 2 (Fall 1960): 34-57;

Wail for two pedestals, Humanities Bulletin, 16 (Autumn 1965): 64-92;

"Preface: on radical absurdity," *Canadian Literature,* 30 (Autumn 1966): 36-44; republished in *The Dramatist in Canada,* edited by W. H. New (Vancouver: University of British Columbia Press, 1972), pp. 79-81;

"Towards a Canadian Theatre," *White Pelican,* 1 (Winter 1971): 55-59;

The Canadian Fact, White Pelican, 2 (Winter 1972): 53-63;

Over prairie trails to the just society, White Pelican, 3 (Winter 1973): 42-62;

"Marshall McLuhan and Multi-consciousness: The Place Marie Dialogues," *Boundary 2,* 3 (Fall 1974): 197-211.

Wilfred Watson, playwright, poet, teacher, and literary theorist, has steadily conducted a one-man revolution in Canadian letters from the late 1950s to the present. As poet and experimental dramatist, he shows remarkable versatility in his inventive explorations of the media-conditioned sensibility of contemporary man. Watson's first gathering of poems, for which he received a Governor General's Award for 1955, gave but slight indication of the radical writing which was to follow. During the 1960s his controversial satiric verse plays alternately astonished, perplexed, and delighted Edmonton audiences; with more than a dozen such dramas, Watson ushered in an avant-garde in Canadian theater years before the rear guard had fully emerged. Throughout this period and since, he has continued writing poetry, notably lyric and satiric verse, that combines verbal and typographical intricacies in a highly disciplined, often dramatic, style.

Watson was born in Rochester, England, the oldest child of Frederick Walter Watson, a sailor in the Royal Navy, and the former Louisa Clayton. He attended Maldon Grammar School, Maldon, Essex, until his family immigrated to

Dust jacket for Watson's first book, winner of a 1955 Governor General's Award

Duncan, British Columbia, in 1926 when he was fifteen. After a year at Duncan High School, he was employed as a worker in a Vancouver Island tidewater sawmill. He attended the University of British Columbia from 1940 to 1943, earning an honors B.A. in English literature. Subsequently he served in the Canadian navy, continuing his education after the war at the University of Toronto and receiving an M.A. in 1946 and a Ph.D. in 1951. In 1941 he married Sheila Martin Doherty, who as Sheila Watson published *The Double Hook* in 1959. In 1949 Wilfred Watson began his university teaching career at the University of British Columbia as special lecturer in English; from 1951 to 1953 he held an appointment at the University of Alberta campus in Calgary. He transferred to the Edmonton campus in 1954, remaining there as professor of English until his retirement in 1977. From 1971 to 1975 he was

coeditor (with Norman Yates, Douglas Barbour, and others) of the little magazine *White Pelican*. He now lives in Nanaimo, British Columbia.

The poems in Watson's first book, *Friday's Child* (1955), were immediately recognized both at home and abroad as formally accomplished renderings of mythopoeic verse in the best modern tradition. Hindsight, however, reveals that his habit of wrenching the language of biblical and literary tradition into contemporary contexts also marks Watson's first step toward theatrical experiment. For example, in such plays as *Cockcrow and the gulls* (produced in 1962), *Trial of Corporal Adam* (1963), and *Wail for two pedestals* (1964), various versions of Judgment Day are comically thrust into surrealistic contemporary settings; traditionally sacred questions are filtered through the distorting lenses of modern-day secularity.

Two important factors entered into Watson's development in the mid 1950s: his introduction to the theater of the absurd during his tenure of a Canadian government overseas fellowship in Paris, 1955-1956, and his growing interest in the theories of Marshall McLuhan. He was to have a long personal association with McLuhan, culminating in their collaboration during 1968-1969 on *From Cliché to Archetype*. The combined effect of these interests is succinctly indicated in two essays by Watson on the drama: as precisely related to his own plays in "Preface: on radical absurdity" (*Canadian Literature*, Autumn 1966) and in the more general speculations of "Towards a Canadian Theatre" (*White Pelican*, Winter 1971). In the latter Watson suggests that "What theatre of the absurd is about, is the birth of a new kind of mind, through the labour pangs of the old simple-minded book mind." The key to his own conception and practice of "radical absurdity" in the theater lies in his development of McLuhan's view of the "multi-consciousness" of contemporary media man.

Watson's plays demonstrate his curiosity about modern man's perceptual shifts from a traditional centralized consciousness to new, off-center or "eccentric" modes of awareness; for him the combinations of multiple consciousness now possible are innumerable. The play *Let's murder clytemnestra according to the principles of marshall mcluhan*, produced in 1969, reflects this idea most directly, although, ironically the work is also a satire, both on McLuhanism and Watson's own deviations from it, as Watson indicates in "Marshall McLuhan and Multi-consciousness: The Place Marie Dialogues."

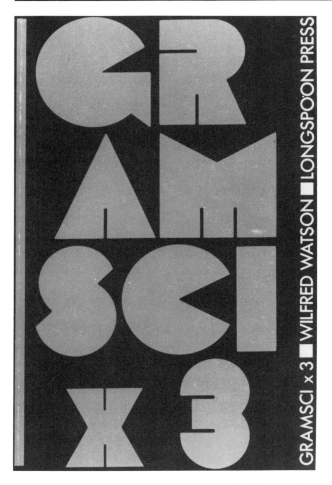

*Cover for Watson's trilogy of plays based on the life of Italian
Marxist Antonio Gramsci*

There is also a strong element of Artaud's theatricality in Watson's drama. The work *O holy glost, dip your finger in the blood of Canada, and write, I love you* (1967) explores and reverses the 1960s flower-power trendiness in a successful early attempt in Canadian drama at total theater. With its assault on the sensibilities and the bigotries of the day, its combination of satiric sketch, chorus, music, and projections, the work focuses on big business, the Vietnam war, and the modern dehumanization of professional life; nail-ins replace sit-ins; peaceniks become violent; and Canadian nationalism (in the country's centennial year) shifts from diffidence to aggression with menacing North American gusto.

At the time of *O holy ghost, dip your finger in the blood of Canada, and write, I love you* Watson indicated in an *Edmonton Journal* interview with Barry Westgate that he wanted to use the theater "as if it was a new medium." Always concerned with

"the maximum use of language," he therefore added in the same interview, "I have tried to see the word as a sort of detonator that explodes itself into something much bigger." Dramaturgical explosions into past-present multiple environments, into fantastic plots involving "caricatures" rather than characters, and into the multimedia bombardment of the audience all became signatures of the typical Watson play. However, a retrospective view of the 1960s drama also reveals a coherent pattern in the work as a whole, of almost epic proportions. Watson was offering a comprehensive satiric comment on the popular trends and attitudes of twentieth-century society, particularly as popularized through Canadian media experience, ranging from print to television. Other examples include the play *Cockcrow and the gulls*, in which the figure of Higgins, the armchair socialist from Nanaimo, offers a comment on the failure of the common man to fulfill his social and spiritual potential; *Another bloody page from plutarch* (1963, unproduced), which asserts the impossibility of democracy; *Wail for two pedestals*, a play that makes present two famously absent characters of modern drama, Godot and Lefty, in order to satirize theater of the absurd; and the unproduced work *Over prairie trails to the just society*, which makes fun of the heroic stances of both Frederick Philip Grove and Pierre Elliott Trudeau. The satiric revue *Chez-vous comfortable pew* (1965) in its day was an apt comment on the trendy liberalism of Canadian journalist Pierre Berton.

The verse of Watson's second collection, *The Sorrowful Canadians and Other Poems* (1972) provides an interesting corollary to the drama, not only in subject matter, but also in Watson's curiously analogous handling of space: the blank page, like the empty stage, invites experiment with new spatial and verbal components. Verbal intensity is modulated by the size or positioning of various typefaces so that the eye is bombarded by a typographical "voice" that speaks with the insistence of the choral utterances in the plays.

In his more recent explorations of the word as detonator, Watson is till transforming the environment of the printed page in novel ways through what he has designed as a number-grid system. Each stanza, or grid, consists of seventeen words typographically juxtaposed to numbers from one to nine. Thus the poem becomes a physical presence on the page, a configuration demanding an almost kinetic involvement from the reader. Since the grids can also be stacked, for

ISBN 0-919285-32-5 LONGSPOON PRESS   ISBN 0-920316-91-3 NEWEST PRESS

Covers for the 1986 collection that includes Watson's fugitive verse from the late 1950s

multiple voices as it were, the possibilities for contrapuntal choral effects also make the poem attractive to actors; there have been several effective performances of the work in an engaging choreography of language with movement. The subjects are wide ranging: simple imagistic responses to the physical world, subtextual "portraits" of personal friends and public personalities, as well as minidramatic satires that characteristically integrate past/present environments. The first number-grid poems were collected in *I begin with counting* (1978), followed by *Mass on Cowback* (1982); the latter is selected from a series of self-illustrated notebooks begun after the poet's removal from Edmonton to Sandpiper Lagoon (on the edge of Nanaimo) in 1980.

While still in Edmonton, Watson began to apply his number-grid structures to dramatic form, completing *The young man from Cagliari* in 1978. This is the first play of Watson's trilogy based on the life and political times of Antonio Gramsci, the Italian Marxist intellectual who died

in 1937 from excruciating abuse during his incarceration in the Fascist prisons of Mussolini. This and the additional plays, *Finding Tatiana* and *The doing-to-death of Antonio Gramsci*, were published in 1983 as *Gramsci x 3;* they were given their premiere performance under the direction of Thomas Peacocke (an actor in Watson's first play) in the spring of 1986. The trilogy, a combination of satire, documentary, and fiction, marks the apex of Watson's experiments as a poet-dramatist. In the tight, economic plain style developed from his number-grid experiments, he variously converts the traditions of Greek tragedy, the medieval morality play, and modern political drama into a series of iconoclastic statements on the intellectual failure of contemporary mass man and its dehumanizing consequences.

Wilfred Watson is still one of the most energetic creative talents writing in Canada today. It is unfortunate, therefore, that his general reputation as a poet still rests primarily on *Friday's Child,* a work cited with particular interest by

Northrop Frye in his annual *University of Toronto Quarterly* resumé of new poetry in 1955. The neglect of the later work is partly because during much of his writing career Watson was perhaps most aptly described as "a prolific poet who publishes little" and partly because he quickly moved outside the commonly recognized mainstream of Canadian poetry. There is one comprehensive study of Watson's early verse, "Vision of Clarity" by John W. Bilsland (*Canadian Literature,* Spring 1960), and another essay, Stephen Scobie's "Love in the Burning City" (*Essays in Canadian Writing,* Summer/Fall 1980), exploring the whole body of Watson's published volumes to 1980. Watson's recent volume, *Poems: Collected / Unpublished / New,* published in 1986, includes a much-needed gathering of Watson's fugitive verse from the late 1950s on and provides a new critical overview by Thomas Peacocke.

During the 1960s Watson's plays were given lively (if sometimes uncomprehending) reviews in the daily press at their times of first performances, but they have not been widely produced since. This may in part be attributed to the underdeveloped state of native theater before 1970, to the limited publishing facilities in Canada for drama at the time, and also to the conservative nature of Canadian theater generally. Only two of Watson's earlier performed plays have been published, *Wail for two pedestals* (*Humanities Bulletin,* Autumn 1965) and the short satire *The Canadian Fact* (*White Pelican,* Winter 1972); two other published works are *Over prairie trails to the just society* (*White Pelican,* Winter 1973) and *Woman Taken in Adultery* (in *Prairie Performance,* edited by Diane Bessai, 1980), both unperformed. The publication of *Gramsci x 3* three years before its first performance is also an indication of the Canadian theater community's continuing reluctance to concern itself with radical dramatic forms.

Interviews:

Barry Westgate, "Another World," *Edmonton Journal,* 27 November 1967;

Helen Melnyk, "Best Sellers Never the Dream of Wilfred Watson," *Edmonton Journal,* 20 January 1979.

References:

Douglas Barbour, "The Sorrowful Canadians," *Open Letter,* second series 5 (Summer 1973): 15-18;

Diane Bessai, "The Prairie Playwright in the Theatre," in *Prairie Performance,* edited by Bessai (Edmonton: NeWest, 1980), pp. 181-182;

John W. Bilsland, "Vision of Clarity: The Poetry of Wilfred Watson," *Canadian Literature,* 4 (Spring 1960): 40-51;

James Dickey, "Opinion," *Poetry,* 89 (November 1956): 110-117;

Northrop Frye, *The Bush Garden* (Toronto: Anansi, 1972): 46-48;

Shirley Neuman, "The Number Grid Kids," *NeWest Review,* 5 (January 1979): 6;

Stephen Scobie, "Love in the Burning City: The Poetry of Wilfred Watson," *Essays in Canadian Writing,* 18-19 (Summer/Fall 1980): 281-303.

Rudy Wiebe

(4 October 1934-)

Lawrence Mathews
Memorial University of Newfoundland

BOOKS: *Peace Shall Destroy Many* (Toronto: McClelland & Stewart, 1962; Grand Rapids: Eerdmans, 1964);

First and Vital Candle (Toronto: McClelland & Stewart, 1966; Grand Rapids: Eerdmans, 1966);

The Blue Mountains of China (Toronto: McClelland & Stewart, 1970; Grand Rapids: Eerdmans, 1970);

The Temptations of Big Bear (Toronto: McClelland & Stewart, 1973);

Where Is The Voice Coming From? (Toronto: McClelland & Stewart, 1974);

The Scorched-Wood People (Toronto: McClelland & Stewart, 1977);

Far As the Eye Can See, by Wiebe and Theatre Passe Muraille (Edmonton: NeWest, 1977);

Alberta / A Celebration, photographs by Harry Savage, edited by Tom Radford (Edmonton: Hurtig, 1979);

The Mad Trapper (Toronto: McClelland & Stewart, 1980);

The Angel of the Tar Sands and Other Stories (Toronto: McClelland & Stewart, 1982);

My Lovely Enemy (Toronto: McClelland & Stewart, 1983).

PLAY PRODUCTION: *Far As the Eye Can See*, by Wiebe and Theatre Passe Muraille, Edmonton, Theatre 3, 12 April 1977.

OTHER: *The Story-makers: A Selection of Modern Short Stories*, edited by Wiebe (Toronto: Macmillan, 1970; second edition, Toronto: Gage, 1987);

Stories from Western Canada, edited by Wiebe (Toronto: Macmillan, 1972);

Stories from Pacific and Arctic Canada, edited by Wiebe and Andreas Schroeder (Toronto: Macmillan, 1974);

Double Vision: An Anthology of Twentieth-century Stories in English, edited by Wiebe (Toronto: Macmillan, 1976);

Getting Here: Stories Selected by Rudy Wiebe (Edmonton: NeWest, 1977);

Rudy Wiebe (photograph by Edwina Frankeford)

"The Death and Life of Albert Johnson: Collected Notes on a Possible Legend," in *Figures in a Ground: Canadian Essays on Modern Literature Collected in Honor of Sheila Watson*, edited by Diane Bessai and David Jackel (Saskatoon: Western Producer Prairie Books, 1978), pp. 219-246;

More Stories from Western Canada, edited by Wiebe and Aritha van Herk (Toronto: Macmillan, 1980);

W. J. Keith, ed., *A Voice in the Land: Essays by and About Rudy Wiebe* (Edmonton: NeWest, 1981);

West of Fiction, edited by Wiebe, van Herk, and Leah Flater (Edmonton: NeWest, 1983);

War in the West: Voices of the 1885 Rebellion, edited by Wiebe and Bob Beal (Toronto: McClelland & Stewart, 1985);

"Canada in the Making," in *Encounters and Explorations; Canadian Writers and European Critics*, edited by Franz Stanzel and Waldemar Zacharasiewicz (Würzburg: Konigshausen & Neumann, 1986), pp. 112-127.

PERIODICAL PUBLICATIONS: "Songs of the
Canadian Eskimo," *Canadian Literature*, 52
(Spring 1972): 57-69;
"On Death and Writing," in *Canadian Literature*,
100 (Spring 1964): 354-360;
"The Blindman River Contradictions," *Camrose Review*, no. 5, pp. 40-44.

Rudy Wiebe's unique contribution to Canadian literature has been to articulate an intense
and comprehensive vision of human experience
rooted in his Mennonite Christianity. For his
seven novels, three volumes of short stories, and
one play, Wiebe has drawn his subject matter
from contemporary society and from Canadian
and Mennonite history. He has given voice to a
myth of the Canadian West that will undoubtedly
find a permanent place in the national imagination, but his deepest interests go beyond questions of nationality or locale. For Wiebe the
major issue is always how an individual or community fares in the endeavor to live according to authentic spiritual values.

Rudy Henry Wiebe was born 4 October
1934 in Fairholme, Saskatchewan, near the Mennonite community of Speedwell-Jackpine, to Abraham and Katarina Knelsen Wiebe, who had
emigrated from Russia four years earlier. His
first language was German; he learned English in
the one-room schoolhouse he attended until he
moved with his family to Coaldale, Alberta, in
1947. There he was a student at Alberta Mennonite High School, where his interest in writing
was encouraged by Peter Bargen, one of his teachers. After graduating, he enrolled at the University of Alberta, intending to become a doctor.

Wilfred Watson, his first-year English professor, convinced Wiebe that he should switch from
premed to arts. Later, as a graduate student, he
took a creative-writing course from F. M. Salter,
who emphasized, as Wiebe recalled in an interview collected in W. J. Keith's *A Voice in the Land*
(1981), that "the way to be genuine writer" was
to "write about the stuff that you know, that
you've lived yourself." In 1956, the year he graduated with a B.A. in English, Wiebe won first
prize in a national writing competition with a
story set on a prairie farm. He then studied at
Mennonite Brethren Bible College in Winnipeg,
receiving a Th.B., and spent a year at the University of Tübingen in West Germany, before returning to do graduate work at the University of
Alberta. (In 1958 he married Tena Isaak; they

later had three children, Adrienne, Michael, and
Christopher.) Under Salter's supervision, he
wrote his first novel, *Peace Shall Destroy Many*
which earned him an M.A. and which was published in 1962 by Toronto's McClelland and Stewart, the firm which has produced nine of Wiebe's
eleven books.

Peace Shall Destroy Many is set in 1944 in the
fictional Mennonite community of Wapiti in northwestern Saskatchewan. The central character,
eighteen-year-old Thom Wiens, is certain of his
basic Christian commitment but uncertain how
best to live it out. Thom's mentor is Joseph
Dueck, a high-school teacher who is troubled by
the facts that the Wapiti church does not attempt
to evangelize the local métis and that Canadian
troops are fighting a war to ensure that Canadian Mennonites may continue to espouse their
risk-free pacifism. His response is to form a Bible
class for métis children and, later, to join the medical corps, thus aiding those wounded in the war.

Dueck's actions violate "the traditions of the
fathers" as they are interpreted by the autocratic
Deacon Peter Block, the settlement's founder,
who believes that Mennonites should withdraw
completely from the secular world around them.
Block is also a hypocrite. His son—or, rather, the
idea of having a son—is secretly more important
to him than his faith. In crucial situations in his
past, he has failed to trust God and has put the interests of his family before those of his community. His dreams disintegrate in the second half
of the novel. His daughter Elizabeth dies in childbirth, having been impregnated by a métis laborer. His son Peter falls in love with a
non-Mennonite schoolteacher and begins a brawl
on Christmas Eve when he finds her with another man. The fight is Peter's first open gesture
of rebellion, and Block is crushed by it. Thom
Wiens finds in this incident confirmation for his
growing sense that Block's authoritarianism is
wrong and that everyone must perceive for himself "the path of God's revelation."

On one level, the novel outlines a debate between liberal and conservative tendencies in Mennonite thinking, but its major didactic thrust cuts
deeper and foreshadows Wiebe's central thematic
concern in his later work. In Deacon Block, the
novel's most vividly realized character, Wiebe portrays a man whose attempt to achieve self-sufficiency causes him to deny the most crucial
part of his humanity. Block's desire that the Wapiti Mennonites be independent as a social unit
mirrors his personal drive to define his own iden-

tity in terms which make him independent of God. Wiebe's lesson is that such "independence" is always illusory, since it ultimately implies some sort of idolatry–of the values of secular society, of the institutional church, of the family, of the self. For the Christian, direct dependence upon Jesus is the only valid stance, as Thom comes to learn. In the four novels that follow, Wiebe's protagonists–agnostic, Mennonite, Indian, and métis Roman Catholic, respectively–all must struggle against the temptations of an idolatry that would prevent them from responding to the religious vision which alone can allow them to achieve true identity.

Early reviewers tended to see *Peace Shall Destroy Many* as a promising first novel, but its publication generated great controversy within the Mennonite community, and Wiebe was forced to resign as editor of the *Mennonite Brethren Herald* in Winnipeg, a position he assumed in 1962. In 1963 he went into self-imposed exile, accepting a teaching position at Goshen College, a Mennonite institution in Indiana.

It was at Goshen, Wiebe has said, that he "learned what it means to be a thoughtful Christian and not just a dogmatic one," but most critics have agreed that there is too much dogmatism in *First and Vital Candle* (1966). The protagonist is Abe Ross, described by another character as "a kind, moral, decent man." Ross's life has been directionless: he has rejected his past, especially his father's narrow Presbyterianism, but avoids significant commitments of any kind. At forty, he finds himself running a fur-trading post at the small settlement of Frozen Lake in northern Ontario.

The local Ojibway Indians are in bondage to a rival trader named Bjarneson, who supplies them with alcohol. The only other whites in the community are three Christians–the missionaries Josh and Lena Bishop, and Sally Howell, a schoolteacher–who try to influence the Indians by leading exemplary lives rather than by preaching. This approach seems to fail, but after a dramatic climax in which Ross shames Bjarneson in a public confrontation, the Indians suddenly become receptive to the Bishops' "Good News."

Abe Ross is a complex and interesting character who must overcome the demon of "pride and self-dependence." His progress toward conversion is more subtly rendered than most critics have realized, but he–and the reader–must attend to so many theological conversations with Sally and Josh that parts of the novel seem closer to tract than work of fiction. When Ross falls in love with Sally, Wiebe exploits the situation with heavy-handed symbolism: her death by drowning on Easter weekend precipitates Ross's conversion experience.

Wiebe also has difficulty with the social dimension of his theme. A Christian might make a convincing general case that if Indians could be freed from the pernicious influences of white society, they might then be prepared to embrace a gospel which is presented to them devoid of institutional and authoritarian trappings. But Wiebe's translation of this argument into narrative is simplistic: an evil white man's humiliation prepares the Indians of Frozen Lake for mass conversion when they hear a good white man's preaching.

Academic criticism has tended to view Wiebe's first two novels as apprentice work. There are complaints about one-dimensional characters, stilted dialogue, awkward structure, and preeminently, overt didacticism. Wiebe himself has shown some sympathy with this assessment. Speaking in the *Alberta Report* (19 September 1980) of his third novel, *The Blue Mountains of China* (1970), he has commented that "I think I really became a novelist with that book."

In 1966 Wiebe had traveled to Paraguay, where he spent several months in communities settled by Mennonite émigrés from Soviet Russia, an experience he has said "was for me really like being able to go back to the Russia that my parents had left forever, and just talk with the people the way they talked then." These contacts generated ideas for individual stories, but Wiebe at first did not think in terms of a novel. In 1967 he returned to the University of Alberta, where he continues to teach literature and creative writing. As he began to work on the stories, he decided that he had the material he needed "to try to write the entire history of a people, scattered over 80 years of their life and scattered over four different continents." The result was *The Blue Mountains of China* (1970), a short novel of epic scope.

Its central focus is on certain members of the Russian Mennonite community and their descendants. Several of the early chapters describe the persecutions of the late 1920s and early 1930s, when the Mennonites of the Soviet Union were dispossessed and many imprisoned or murdered. The more fortunate escaped to Canada or Paraguay, the settings of the other chapters. The novel's action ends in 1967 with a gathering of a number of characters who represent the entire spectrum of Mennonite attitudes to their collective identity. The questions which Wiebe has been probing through the various narratives are now debated openly, and the debate remains open ended—one of the many signals that his art has matured.

The several protagonists in *The Blue Mountains of China* tend to be faced with clear-cut ethical choices. Right action means dying to self; wrong action involves some species of selfishness, ranging from quixotic gestures of self-assertion to failure to act at all. The most Christ-like figure is David Epp, who in 1932 is one of the leaders of a Russian Mennonite community situated on the Amur River. In order to avoid persecution, the villagers make a successful mass escape across the river to China. Epp decides to return alone in the hope that the Soviet authorities will make him their scapegoat and spare the Mennonites in the neighboring village, who knew nothing of the plans to escape. He is never heard from again. Epp's story contrasts ironically with that of Samuel Reimer. Living comfortably in Canada in the mid 1960s, Reimer is, like his biblical namesake, called by God. The call is direct and comical: his mission is to "Go and proclaim peace in Vietnam." He sincerely tries to obey but is opposed by his wife, pastor, and the local Mennonite community. Everyone thinks he is mad. Finally he gives up without having left the country and dies mysteriously soon afterward; his complacently materialistic wife collects on his life insurance policy and buys a new car.

The contrast between Reimer and Epp points to one of Wiebe's ironic conclusions about the nature of Mennonite community. Prosperity in North America seems to present as great a threat to its integrity as did persecution in Russia. The pressure to assimilate is ubiquitous and insidious. But the lesson of *The Blue Mountains of China* is that for Mennonites to attempt to isolate themselves from secular society is both futile and, more important, immoral: the modern world is in desperate need of the authentic Christian witness they can provide.

Wiebe's third novel represents a major advance over his earlier fiction. He displays mastery of a wider range of styles than previously, uses multiple point of view effectively, and, most significant, skillfully integrates the Christian themes with the narrative material. One suspects that its first reviewers were unprepared to give *The Blue Mountains of China* the attention it requires. In

1973 Wiebe complained that "It has not been very well read," but more recent academic criticism has begun to demonstrate the complex artistry of this work, whose reputation will undoubtedly continue to grow.

But Wiebe's general popularity rests most firmly on *The Temptations of Big Bear* (1973) and *The Scorched-Wood People* (1977), in which he interprets the materials of Western Canadian history. The two novels cover roughly the same period: 1876-1888 and 1869-1885, respectively. Their protagonists, Big Bear and Louis Riel, in their roles as leaders of doomed minorities, both attempt heroically to resist white exploitation.

Big Bear is a chief of the Plains Cree, leader of a people that are, in 1876, still free. He refuses to sign a treaty, choose a reserve, or recognize white "ownership" of the land. The white characters—missionaries, traders, settlers and their families, soldiers, policemen, government officials—have a variety of attitudes toward the Indians, but they are united in their inability to comprehend Big Bear's vision of a Northwest in which Indians, métis, and whites can live together, at peace with one another and with the land. The other Indian characters—Big Bear's sons, his warriors, his fellow chiefs—are ultimately equally incapable of appreciating his wisdom.

Big Bear's "temptations" are versions of the ones that face so many of Wiebe's characters. He can attempt to assert his independence by making war on the whites or he can without protest allow his people to become dependent on white charity, as other chiefs have done. But Big Bear's religious sense, presented as directly analogous to that of a Christian, prevents him from either rebelling or capitulating. The disappearance of the buffalo and the coming of the railway have ensured that the Cree way of life will vanish, but Big Bear struggles to preserve the integrity of his people. Eventually his young warriors become frustrated enough to kill a number of whites in the Frog Lake Massacre of 1885. Big Bear is held responsible for their actions, is tried, and unjustly convicted of "treason-felony," serves a prison term, and dies.

Wiebe's interpretation of Big Bear's story in terms of an authentic spirituality crushed (in temporal terms only) by rapacious white materialism is entirely convincing. Scrupulousness with respect to historical detail is combined with a brilliantly imaginative rendering of Big Bear's inner life. Wiebe makes good use of multiple narrators, stream of consciousness, juxtaposition of styles

Dust jacket for Wiebe's 1977 novel based on the two nineteenth-century rebellions led by Louis Riel

and story lines—staples of twentieth-century fiction. Reviewers identified the novel as a major but "difficult" work, although the difficulty should not be daunting to readers of Faulkner or Joyce. *The Temptations of Big Bear* won the 1973 Governor General's Award for fiction.

The Scorched-Wood People—which followed the story collection *Where Is The Voice Coming From?*—is in a sense a sequel to Big Bear's story. The two novels are virtually identical in theme, but the later one is more polemical in tone, as the narrator, Pierre Falcon, evaluates the action he describes. Falcon is an old métis poet who speaks from beyond the grave, a vantage point which allows him access to the minds of both the insurgent Louis Riel and Gabriel Dumont, the military leader of the métis. This device works unobtrusively and allows Riel's story to flow more smoothly than Big Bear's.

The two "Riel Rebellions" are well-known to most Canadians, and again Wiebe carefully follows the contours of historical fact. In 1869 the métis of the Red River district, who have lived there for generations, are informed by surveyors from the East that the land "belongs" to the Crown. The community coalesces around Riel's political leadership, Dumont organizes an effective fighting force, and the eventual result is the creation of the province of Manitoba. But Riel is forced into exile and the government reneges on many of its promises to the métis people. In 1884 a parallel situation develops farther west. Riel returns from Montana to lead the métis of the Saskatchewan in a political battle which culminates in an armed uprising. The métis forces are defeated by government troops at the Battle of Batoche in May 1885. Riel is convicted of treason and executed.

The narrative focuses on Riel's development from a political leader with strong religious convictions to a spiritual leader whose vision expresses itself in political action. Wiebe enters the controversy about Riel's "insanity," devoting a major section of the novel to the period between the rebellions, when Riel was for a time confined in an asylum. For Wiebe, Riel's visions *seem* to be divinely inspired, and, more important, Riel acts as though they were. The Riel of 1884 wants the métis people to found a "New Nation" whose mission would be to bring "God's perfect kingdom" into being. He breaks with the church because he believes it has ignored the claims of social justice. He convinces his supporters—even the hard-headed Dumont—that divine intervention will bring them military victory over the vastly superior government forces. But Wiebe's Riel is no power-hungry fanatic; he never loses sight of reality, and in defeat he retains his dignity.

Near the end of the novel, Pierre Falcon relates the major thematic issue to the question of Riel's sanity. The vision of the Northwest as a Christian "New Nation" is juxtaposed ironically with the plan of the callous John A. Macdonald, arch-representative of the Eastern power elite, who has designs on a vast hinterland ripe for economic exploitation. Where does sanity lie? Throughout the novel it is Riel who has consistently conducted himself in a humane and selfless way, believing he is doing God's will and advancing the cause of his people. It is the cynical federal politicians who are willing to countenance genocide.

For Wiebe, the visions of Riel and Big Bear are not dead. On the last page of *The Scorched-Wood People*, Dumont remarks, of Riel: "A hundred years and whites still won't know what to do with him." A hundred years, Wiebe seems to be saying, and "white" society–racist, godless, endlessly greedy–is still the enemy of all spiritually awakened people of whatever color. In his writing Wiebe becomes the descendant of Big Bear and Riel, fully engaged in the struggle to bring about a West in which various races and cultures might live freely, respecting one another and the environment, governed neither by bullets nor balance sheets but by their own perceptions of "the path of God's revelation."

Wiebe's other works include the story collection *Where is the Voice Coming From?* (1974); a play, *Far As the Eye Can See* (1977); *Alberta / A Celebration* (1979), a collection of short stories based mostly on the reminiscences of Alberta pioneers, illustrated with photographs by Harry Savage; a novella, *The Mad Trapper* (1980); and another collection of short stories, *The Angel of the Tar Sands and Other Stories* (1982). None is likely to add significantly to his reputation. *Far as the Eye Can See,* written in conjunction with members of Theatre Passe Muraille and performed in Edmonton at Theatre 3, is a play about contemporary Alberta politics which wrestles inconclusively but provocatively with questions relating to the morality of expropriation. *The Mad Trapper* grew out of a screenplay for an unproduced film about the RCMP manhunt for the murderer Albert Johnson in the Northwest Territories and Yukon in the winter of 1931-1932. This time, however, Wiebe does not uncover spiritual depths in his historical material. *The Mad Trapper* is a good adventure tale and nothing more.

Wiebe's most recent novel, *My Lovely Enemy* (1983), is puzzling. Set in contemporary Alberta, it may be an ironic study of self-deceit and bad faith, describing a representative modern man's ludicrous attempt to reconcile his desire for a liberated sex life with his vaguely Christian intuitions. From another point of view, it may be a deadserious attempt to describe a decent man's quest to reconcile the claims of body and soul, an exploration of a redefined Christianity for which sexuality is not to be seen, ultimately, as "the lovely enemy" of the spirit. It is a measure of the novel's failure that this uncertainty should exist.

James Dyck, the protagonist, narrates the first four chapters and is center of consciousness for the other two. Dyck is forty-two, a professor of history at the University of Alberta, happily married for fourteen years, father of a ten-year-old daughter. The serenity of his life is shattered

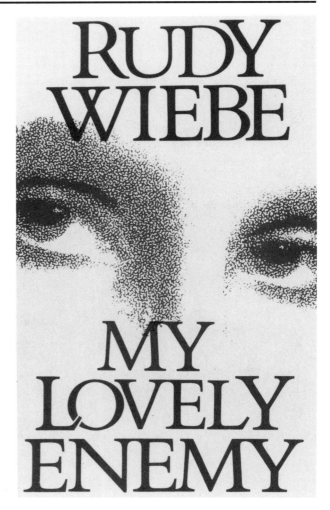

Dust jacket for Wiebe's novel set in contemporary Alberta

when he is seduced by Gillian Overton, a graduate student married to one of his colleagues. The first four chapters, set in what Dyck calls "the merrie Month of Maye," chronicle the origin of the affair. The most striking element in this part of the novel is the appearance (twice) of a mysterious figure who, it is strongly implied, is Jesus–although the reader is left with the option of deciding that Dyck is having psychotic episodes. Dyck's Jesus brings not peace but a seemingly endless series of platitudes: "To live genitally is a beginning, also an end." Dyck is, like so many of Wiebe's characters, struggling with different kinds of temptation–"The certain temptation of Gillian," Dyck observes, "drives me to the possible temptation of the personal Jesus." But by the end of the "May" section, nothing has been resolved.

The two September chapters bear an ambiguous relation to the rest of the narrative and to each other. The first begins as a description of an outing (involving Dyck, his wife, Gillian, and her husband) to a fashionable restaurant in a converted mineshaft. The Mine features all-Alberta cuisine and some strange local customs, as Wiebe uses the techniques of magic realism to disorient his readers. At a certain point in the meal, the diners undergo an experience of the "Long Darkness," which may be Dyck's hallucination, a shared hallucinatory experience, or a transformation of the "real" world. The two couples return to a sexual Eden in an Alberta wilderness where snow and human nudity coexist and sexual partners are exchanged–and enjoyed openly–without jealousy. The last chapter includes no reference to the previous one, leaving open the possibility that the two September chapters provide alternate endings to the sequence of events begun in May. Set in Vulcan, Alberta, it describes the events surrounding the funeral of Dyck's mother, the most remarkable of which is her resurrection when a voice speaks to her as Jesus did to Lazarus. This happens in a cemetery near a field where a farmer is harvesting on the Sabbath; the local mortician, pouring tea out of the farmer's "seemingly bottomless" thermos, opines that in heaven, "you are married to everyone." It is not clear whether he is speaking metaphorically, nor is it clear whether Gillian's presence in this chapter can be explained simply by her status as friend of the family. The traditional Christian language affirming the triumph of life over death may be designed to cast the sensuality of the previous chapter in an ironic light. Or, alternatively, the two kinds of affirmation may be meant to reinforce each other.

But the main source of the novel's obscurity lies in Wiebe's presentation of Dyck himself. He is a figure who demands to be satirized. Too often he is pompous and long-winded in conversation, silly and tedious in his thoughts, selfish and frivolous in his treatment of others. Nor does he change significantly as the novel progresses. Yet there is little evidence in Wiebe's presentation of Dyck that irony is intended. Indeed the fact that readers are forced to pay such close attention to the endless stream of detritus that flows through Dyck's mind suggests that Wiebe expects them to find something valuable there. Neither do we feel sympathy for Dyck; he forfeits that very early when he begins his affair with Gillian in a state of adolescent mindlessness that evokes the image of John Updike's Rabbit Angstrom. But unlike Rabbit, Dyck seems to escape his author's control.

My Lovely Enemy does demonstrate Wiebe's willingness to take risks, to break new ground. And there is, interpolated into the main narrative, a short story about a nineteenth-century Indian named Maskepetoon (the subject of Dyck's historical research) that shows that Wiebe's talent has not deserted him. But *My Lovely Enemy* seems destined to represent a false step in an otherwise impressive development.

Over the course of his career, Rudy Wiebe has developed from a chronicler of an obscure minority group to a forger of the conscience of the Canadian West and one of the few writers in the country to articulate a Christian vision in literature. In 1987 Wiebe was awarded the Lorne Pierce Medal. *The Blue Mountains of China*, *The Temptations of Big Bear*, and *The Scorched-Wood People* will become part of the canon of Canadian literature. Although he is himself uncertain about the specific direction of his future work, Wiebe has said in an interview, "I am still interested in man's spiritual condition, in his relation to his world . . . That sort of interest is not going to change, it's big enough to last me a lifetime. . . ."

Interviews:

Donald Cameron, "Rudy Wiebe: The Moving Stream is Perfectly at Rest," in his *Conversations with Canadian Novelists*, volume 2 (Toronto: Macmillan, 1973), pp. 146-160;

Alan Twigg, "Public Eye," in his *For Openers: Conversations with 24 Canadian Writers* (Madeira Park, British Columbia: Harbour, 1981), pp. 207-218;

Thomas Gerry, "An Interview with Rudy Wiebe," *Rubicon*, 7 (Summer 1986): 126-159.

References:

R. P. Bilan, "Wiebe and Religious Struggle," *Canadian Literature*, 77 (Summer 1978): 50-63;

Sherrill E. Grace, "Structuring Violence: 'The Ethics of Linguistics' in 'The Temptations of Big Bear,'" *Canadian Literature*, 104 (Spring 1985): 7-22;

W. J. Keith, *Epic Fiction: The Art of Rudy Wiebe* (Edmonton: University of Alberta Press, 1981);

Keith, ed., *A Voice in the Land: Essays By and About Rudy Wiebe* (Edmonton: NeWest, 1981);

Francis Mansbridge, "Wiebe's Sense of Community," *Canadian Literature*, 77 (Summer 1978): 42-49;

Patricia Morley, *The Comedians: Hugh Hood and Rudy Wiebe* (Toronto: Clarke, Irwin, 1977);

John Moss, *Sex and Violence in the Canadian Novel: The Ancestral Present* (Toronto: McClelland & Stewart, 1977), pp. 256-269;

Moss, ed., *The Canadian Novel: Here and Now* (Toronto: NC Press, 1978);

Zailig Pollock, "*The Blue Mountains of China:* A Selective Annotated Geneology," *Essays on Canadian Writing,* 26 (Summer 1983): 70-73;

Sam Solecki, "Great Novels and Large Meanings: The Novels of Rudy Wiebe," *Canadian Forum* (March 1981): 5-8, 13;

Pierre Spriet, "Structure and Meaning in Rudy Wiebe's *My Lovely Enemy,*" in *Gaining Ground: European Critics on Canadian Writing,* edited by Rupert Kroetsch and Reingard M. Nischik (Edmonton: NeWest, 1985), pp. 53-63;

Susan Whaley, "Narrative Voices in *The Temptations of Big Bear,*" *Essays on Canadian Writing,* 20 (Winter 1980-1981): 134-148;

"Wiebe's Fables," *Albert Report* (19 September 1980): 40-49.

J. Michael Yates
(10 April 1938-)

Peter Buitenhuis
Simon Fraser University

BOOKS: *Spiral of Mirrors* (Francestown, New Hampshire: Golden Quill, 1967);

Hunt in an Unmapped Interior and Other Poems (Francestown, New Hampshire: Golden Quill, 1967);

Canticle for Electronic Music (Victoria: Morriss, 1967);

Man in the Glass Octopus (Vancouver: Sono Nis, 1968);

The Great Bear Lake Meditations (Ottawa: Oberon, 1970);

The Calling (Toronto: Playwrights Co-op, 1971);

Parallax: Poems (Surrey, British Columbia: Sono Nis, 1971);

The Abstract Beast: New Fiction and Drama (Port Clements, British Columbia: Sono Nis, 1971);

Night Freight (Toronto: Playwrights Co-op, 1972);

Nothing Speaks for the Blue Moraines: New and Selected Poems (Delta, British Columbia: Sono Nis, 1973);

Breath of the Snow Leopard: Poems (Delta, British Columbia: Sono Nis, 1974);

Quarks: Three One-act Plays (Toronto: Playwrights Co-op, 1975);

The Qualicum Physics (San Francisco & Vancouver: Kanchenjunga Press, 1975);

Fazes in Elsewhen: New and Selected Fiction (Vancouver: Intermedia Press, 1977);

J. Michael Yates (photograph by Lois Siegel)

Esox Nobilior Non Esox Lucius (Fredericton: Fiddlehead, 1978);

Fugue Brancusi: A Poem (Victoria: Sono Nis, 1983);

INSEL: The Queen Charlotte Islands Meditations (Moonbeam, Ontario: Penumbra, 1983);

The Completely Collapsible Portable Man: Selected Shorter Lyrics (Oakville, Ontario: Mosaic, 1984).

PLAY PRODUCTIONS: *Subjunction,* Ann Arbor,

University of Michigan, 5 February 1966;
Theatre of War, Winnipeg, Star Players, 14 March 1970;
Night Freight, Toronto, Scarborough Theatre, 7 April 1972;
The Calling, Minneapolis, Guthrie Theatre, 15 May 1973;
Search for the Tse Tse Fly, Montreal, McGill University, 16 June 1974.

TELEVISION: *Smoke Track in the Desert*, CBC, 22 June 1975;
Search for the Tse Tse Fly, CBC, 16 July 1975.

RADIO: *The Broadcaster*, CBC, 6 April 1967;
Theatre of War, CBC, 19 April 1968;
The Calling, CBC, 4 June 1968;
Night Freight, CBC, 11 November 1968;
The Panel, CBC, 22 February 1969;
The Abstract Beast, CBC, 3 May 1969;
The Poet as an Arctic Landscape, CBC, 17 April 1970;
The Border, CBC, 5 February 1971;
Search for the Tse Tse Fly, CBC, 3 May 1974;
The Net, CBC, 13 October 1974;
The Sinking of the Northwest Passage, CBC, 3 July 1975;
The Secret of State, CBC, 13 October 1975;
Pluto's Republic, CBC, 18 May 1977.

OTHER: *Volvox: Poetry from the Unofficial Languages of Canada in English Translation*, edited by Yates with the assistance of Charles Lillard (Port Clements, British Columbia: Sono Nis, 1971).

J. Michael Yates is one of Canada's most prolific and most determinedly experimental writers. He has written in many forms and has been active in publishing, broadcasting, editing, photography, reviewing, and translation. He has traveled widely, performed readings, and had his work published in journals all over the Commonwealth, the United States, and Europe. The son of a U.S. Army Air Force colonel, Joel Hume Yates, and his wife, the former Marjorie Dianne Carmichael, Yates was born in Fulton, Missouri, on 10 April 1938. He took a B.A. (1960) and M.A. (1961) at the University of Kansas City before devoting two years toward a doctorate in comparative literature at the University of Michigan. In 1963-1964 he was an instructor in comparative literature at Ohio University and the following year he served as lecturer at the University of

Alaska. In 1967 he moved to Vancouver where he served until 1971 as writer in residence, professor of creative writing, and member of the Comparative Literature Committee at the University of British Columbia. He founded the Sono Nis Press in 1966 and was an editor of *Prism International* from 1968 to 1971. He also founded *Canadian Fiction Magazine* in 1968. He is now a free-lance writer and a prison guard in Vancouver. Yates has been married three times and has three daughters: Sara, Jaima, and Alexandra.

Yates's work is perhaps more satisfactorily discussed chronologically than generically, since he has often crossed generic boundaries. His fiction has the ring of poetry; his poetry looks like fiction; his drama has the musical quality of verse. He first had work published as an undergraduate and won a number of prizes for this early writing. Much of this material was collected in *Hunt in an Unmapped Interior and Other Poems* (1967), a book of promise despite the overly strong influence of T. S. Eliot and William Butler Yeats. "Basically all my writings," Yates has remarked, "centre around the polarities between absolute wilderness and absolute technology." This preoccupation appears in the early work in which he repeatedly uses the metaphor of wilderness for representing the self: "The shadow of my hand," writes Yates in *Hunt in an Unmapped Interior and Other Poems*, "Reaches forth and imprints/This wilderness of fewer and fewer words."

The concern with technology and wilderness is repeated in his next book, *Canticle for Electronic Music* (1967), which consists of twenty-four canticles, each of which has eight stanzas, three lines long. In this collection Yates's individual style begins to emerge clearly: the verse is increasingly enigmatic and disjointed, the language drawn from a wider variety of scientific and philosophic sources. Yates's obsession with the connection between words and experience, syntax and sense, sound and idea is also fully evident: "How much do the instincts dare absorb?/God was an incomplete sentence and/By and by the wilderness came over me." The poetry is introspective: the poet's concern with the self and the other is expressed repeatedly in metaphors of sea, rocks, and sky. The poems are rhythmical, with a musical beat appropriate to a canticle, but they also demonstrate that abstraction and illogic that are characteristic of electronic music. The language is stripped bare, although it is often plangent and evocative.

Yates's first collection of fiction, *Man in the*

Glass Octopus, appeared in 1968 with an appreciative introduction by his friend and colleague a UBC Robert Harlow. In this book Yates's persona is called Sono Nis, a name which is drawn from Indian legend and also the name which he chose for his press. These stories are all fantasies that take place within the consciousnesses of the characters. In "The Passage of Sono Nis," the first story, the narrator sees a flood of people jammed tightly together running down the street outside his apartment building. He dives over the pile of bodies in the entrance way to join the sea of flesh and runs with them into extinction or oblivion, Yates does not make clear which.

In the second story, "The Broadcaster," the narrator is a disc jockey on a rock program who broadcasts twenty-four hours a day and gradually disappears into the acoustical tile of the studio ceiling. The other stories are about strange obsessive states, and the collection ends with the story "An Inquest into the Disappearance and Possible Death of (The Late) Sono Nis, Photographer." Sono Nis has become an abstraction, a negative, who disappears by going to his darkroom. The tone of the collection is enigmatic, sometimes infuriatingly oblique as Yates explores the recesses of consciousness and the limits of form.

In his next collection of verse, *The Great Bear Lake Meditations* (1970), Yates begins his first prose poem: "The wolves say to the dogs what the madman of me says to the citizen. I need to go fishing until I need to return." Yates uses the long journey to the North and the stay on the remote lake as springboards for philosophical meditations about sexuality, death, wilderness, fear, absurdity, isolation, and consciousness. Too often, however, the abstractions drain these prose poems of movement and meaning.

In 1971 Sono Nis published *Parallax*, a collection of prose poems, and *The Abstract Beast*, a volume in which Yates combines fiction and drama in a surreal landscape that reflects several of his fundamental concerns. *The Abstract Beast* contains eight of Yates's one-act plays, one of which, *The Broadcaster* was adapted from the earlier short story. The best-known work in this collection is *Night Freight* (produced at the Scarborough Theatre in April 1972), a play which Yates describes as "concerned with the subconscious attitudes of men and women who have accrued much time on earth, yet have accumulated little experience." Another successful drama is *Theatre of War* (produced in Winnipeg in March 1970 and separately published in 1972), in which it is argued that war

Dust jacket for Yates's collection of fantasies focusing on the enigmatic character Sono Nis

is the natural state of man. The title play, *The Abstract Beast* (produced by CBC radio in May 1969), consists mostly of a debate between A, the writer intellect, and B, the sensual body. Intellect and body finally reach reconciliation by vanishing into an uncompleted novel. Another play, *The Panel* (produced by CBC radio in February 1969), is a humorous parody of a radio gameshow which ends up in murder and suicide. The most memorable fiction in the collection is "The Pile," in which the narrative voice merges into a huge indistinguishable mass and loses his body, his voice, and his identity. *The Abstract Beast* contains Yates's most accessible stories and plays and is arguably the most successful of his many books.

Three other one-acters are collected in *Quarks* (1975): *The Net*, *Search for the Tse Tse Fly*, and *The Calling*. *The Net* pits a real fisherman against a metaphysical one, and ends with the metaphysician tied and bound in his own absurd net. *Search for the Tse Tse Fly* explores the complex relationships between sleeping sickness, hyp-

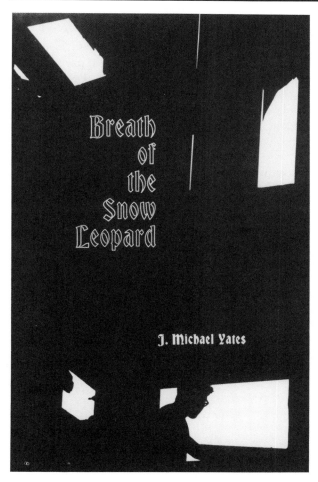

Dust jacket for Yates's 1974 poetry collection, dedicated to "snow leopards and blue-eyed white tigers"

nosis, dreams, and time, and *The Calling* plays on the functions and malfunctions of the telephone–missed messages, broken connections, and faulty receivers–and becomes a metaphor for the mechanization of life itself.

Yates's next collection of poems, *Nothing Speaks for the Blue Moraines* (1973), includes many previously published works and a few new poems. The 1974 collection of new work, *Breath of the Snow Leopard*, was called by reviewer Frederick Candelaria "a bleak book." However, Candelaria, writing in the *West Coast Review*, went on to say that its pessimism "is paradoxically redeemed by the very fact of the book's existence. In its shadows there is light, a 'darkness visible,' of a powerful, poetic intelligence that enlightens the sombre speculations in which the book traps us."

Fazes in Elsewhen, published in 1977, includes previously published work and some strik-

ing new stories. One of these is called "Realia" and is a fantasy in which the world is transformed into a library. The story "Mysteries of the Man Who Walks and the Man Who Watches the Walker" consists of a series of shots, like photos taken at different shutter speeds and with different filters, of a man who walks to a city, gets used to the hurtling traffic, and becomes a practiced dancer between the lines of moving vehicles. In the end the walker is accidentally knocked down and killed by the watcher. This story, like many others by Yates, is an account of the ever-shifting boundaries between the observer and the observed, the real and the illusory.

The question of how one separates the dancer from the dance, art from life, has become paramount for Yates in his later work. It is central to *The Qualicum Physics* (1975) in which the poet puzzles: "How to exact the figure from the stone/Without gravel by the throatful." This long poem is a series of such two-line aphorisms or questions, tenuously connected, which require the utmost attention of the reader to decipher. In Yates's 1978 verse collection, *Esox Nobilior Non Esox Lucius*, the dominant metaphor changes to one of fish and fishing. The collection has a strange, subaqueous aura in which metaphysical problems of perception and portrayal are explored in a variety of poetic forms.

In *Fugue Brancusi* (1983), Yates has moved his closest toward the arts of sculpture, music, and photography. The title echoes two of these arts. The poem is divided into three movements with the traditional fugal developments of statement, variation, and coda; its form resembles the clean, abstract lines of the work of the Roman sculptor Constantin Brancusi. Each section is divided into seven lines. In many cases, each line is one sentence. It seems as if Yates is trying to reach in poetry the purity of line and form achievable in sculpture and music, not surprisingly courting obscurity in the process. The language moves often toward gnomic abstraction, as in "It is sad when a word knows it does not know how not to write." As in earlier poems, the image of the photographer and the photo provides a central metaphor for the creative process. Moving life becomes the still shot; the process of thought is frozen into the phrase. Once again, it falls to the reader to make the connections suggested by the often powerful images of *Fugue Brancusi*.

Yates's most recent books are *INSEL: The Queen Charlotte Islands Meditations* (1983) and *The Completely Collapsible Portable Man: Selected Shorter*

Lyrics (1984). *INSEL* is a series of free-verse observations of the flora and fauna of the remote and largely wilderness islands off the coast of northwest British Columbia. The islands are perpetual centers of controversy between loggers and environmentalists, and, for Yates, they provoke meditations on the situation of the Haida (the native people), on conservation, on love, and on philosophy. *INSEL* demonstrates Yates's ability to deal sensitively with the spirit and meaning of a wilderness landscape and its inhabitants without sentimentalizing. *The Completely Collapsible Portable Man* is a collection of poems assembled from seven previous volumes.

It is clear that J. Michael Yates, as long as he pursues his current recondite paths, will never become a best-selling author. He is on the frontiers of writing, a man who has evoked the admiration of fellow writers and incomprehension from those not so concerned with the craft. As a dramatist and short-story writer, he has shown little interest in characterization and little concern with plot in the traditional sense. However, his imagination, his sense of fun and parody, and his deep awareness of the absurd help redeem the abstraction and obscurity of his writing. Every book that Yates produces is a foray into unknown territory. For some readers such forays can be challenging and profoundly exciting.

References:

John Biguenet, "Yates the Obscure," *West Coast Review*, 11 (October 1976): 36-37;

Ronald B. Hatch, "Beyond Permanence: The Poetry of J. Michael Yates and Robin Blaser," *West Coast Review*, 20 (April 1986): 3-10;

Charles Lillard, "Daylight in the Swamp: A Guide to the West Coast Renaissance," *Malahat Review*, 45 (January 1978): 319-340.

Dale Zieroth

(7 November 1946-   )

Laurie Ricou
University of British Columbia

BOOKS: *Clearing: Poems From a Journey* (Toronto: Anansi, 1973);
Nipika: A Story of Radium Hot Springs (Ottawa: Parks Canada, 1978);
Mid-River (Toronto: Anansi, 1981);
When the Stones Fly Up (Toronto: Anansi, 1985).

OTHER: Al Purdy, ed., *Storm Warning,* includes poems by Zieroth (Toronto: McClelland & Stewart, 1971);
Ann Wall, ed., *Mindscapes,* includes poems by Zieroth (Toronto: Anansi, 1971);
Margaret Atwood, ed., *The New Oxford Book of Canadian Verse in English,* includes poems by Zieroth (Toronto & New York: Oxford University Press, 1982);
Lorne Daniel and Peter Christensen, eds., *Ride Off Any Horizon,* includes poems by Zieroth (Edmonton: NeWest, 1983);
Dennis Lee, ed., *The New Canadian Poets, 1970-1985,* includes poems by Zieroth (Toronto: McClelland & Stewart, 1985).

The publication of Dale Zieroth's work in two important 1970s anthologies established him as one of the significant new voices in Canadian poetry of the decade. That Zieroth's poems were included in *Storm Warning* (1971), edited by Al Purdy, and the House of Anansi's *Mindscapes* (1971), edited by Ann Wall, says something about the essential qualities of his work. On the one hand, he has the casual tone and commonplace rural subject matter of Purdy; on the other, his polished metaphors and political concerns are more reminiscent of Dennis Lee, the Anansi editor who was his early mentor. The storm warning, and a glimpse at his mindscape, prepared an enthusiastic reception for Zieroth's first book. The anticipation of a second book of verse almost turned to impatience before *Mid-River* appeared in 1981 to secure Zieroth's reputation as one of the richest poets in the tradition defined by Purdy.

Zieroth, son of Alfred and Christina Ross-

Zieroth with his daughter Laura

nagel Zieroth, was born in Neepawa, Manitoba, the small town remembered by many readers as Margaret Laurence's Manawaka. He was raised nearby, on his parents' farm, where, he recalls in "Father," a man had "to stand in the sun for/ eight hours a day, to sweat through each/cold hail storm without a word, to freeze/fingers and feet to cut wood in winter." In 1964 he left for Winnipeg, "where the world begins," to study at the University of Manitoba, from which he earned a B.A. in 1967. After a year teaching

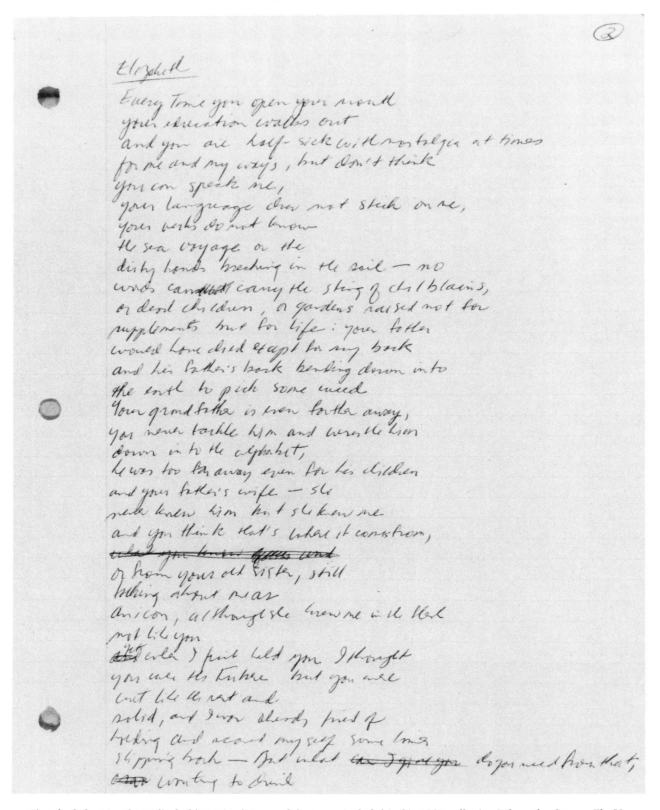

First draft for Zieroth's "Elizabeth/Matriarch," one of the poems included in his 1985 collection When the Stones Fly Up
(by permission of the author)

high school in Kelwood, he moved to Toronto in 1968 and, as he put it in *Storm Warning*, "became involved in the free school movement, part of the counter-culture," but "inside six months I had dropped out, exhausted and dissatisfied." In Toronto he first found himself able to write "objectively" about the prairies. His first book, *Clearing* (1973), traces the journey, from prairie childhood to Toronto, and then back across the country to Invermere, British Columbia, where he moved in 1971. In this work Zieroth's main claim to attention is his directness and simplicity. His poetry lies as much in the astute recounting of an anecdote or personal experience as in the nuances of language. In the first poem, "Prairie Grade School," he describes returning to the abandoned school; he remembers the growing up, the moments of passage: "I was here on the day/things first changed, the day I hid from friends/who learned to play without me, discovering/I controlled nothing and growing afraid/for the first time of ordinary trees . . . ." It is difficult to quote short passages of Zieroth; the delicately, slowly developed perception of himself, of the meaning of the at-first insignificant, is his aspiration. George Woodcock, an early enthusiast, has defined Zieroth's place among contemporary poets as the most representative of a suddenly "identifiable school" of modern prairie poets who "brought effectively into poetry not only the great plains as a visible fact but also the feeling of living among them."

Yet, "Queen Street Trolley," "Downtown," and several poems about his relationship with Margery Patrick, to whom he was married in 1970, showed the limitations of classifying Zieroth solely as a prairie poet. The journey in *Clearing* ends in the Columbia Valley, between the Purcell and Rocky Mountains, although "the mountains have not yet entered/my dreams and become familiar as the cities/and the old places where the land/is flat." Zieroth lived in Invermere until 1978, working from 1974 as a naturalist for the National Parks. *Mid-River* (1981) is the record of that new geography (with its layers of history) becoming familiar. Zieroth still writes mainly what Woodcock calls "geopoems" in a quiet, nostalgic tone. The typical Zieroth poem begins with a description of a landscape and shifts to a personal response. In *Mid-River* the descriptions are vivified by more metaphors, more unusual verbs. But Zieroth's metaphors, often exquisite in themselves, seldom link inevitably to one another, nor is he likely to play variations on a single metaphor through an entire poem. In other words, his poetic language is still comparatively limited in the possibilities it calls up. Many of the poems lament the passing of landscapes and the damage of ecologies, a subject on which Zieroth can be a bit relentless or preachy. Another continuing interest involves the relationships within his family, which includes his daughters Laura (born in 1974) and Marjalena (born in 1984). The growing up of Laura provokes some of the most satisfying poems in the book, fresh in language and startling in perception, and something of a new, more lyrical direction in Zieroth's work.

Other new directions seemed to arise from his move in early 1979 to the West Coast (he now lives in North Vancouver). There he studied at Simon Fraser University (in Burnaby), receiving his M.A. in 1987. Presently he free-lances and teaches creative writing at Douglas College, where he is editor of the literary magazine *Event*. The opening section of his most recent book, *When the Stones Fly Up* (1985), acknowledges the coastal setting, where "the scenery/loses its edge and brings down the rain," but is most notable for containing the most overtly political poems Zieroth has written. Yet, as it did in Toronto, the urban setting stimulates memories of a prairie childhood: the book's second and third sections form a loosely structured serial poem recalling Manitoba-farm, and small-town, and (further back) European ancestry. Although the anecdotal impulse continues to be primary, Zieroth surprises with several interior monologues attempting the voices of distinctive characters—the storekeeper, the Lutheran pastor, and, most memorably, a young female schoolteacher fighting against falling in love with the "tall blond" student. *When the Stones Fly Up* continually shows a slightly more knotted and elliptical syntax and a more obvious attention to language as subject than the earlier books. Zieroth as he enters his forties makes the reading of his poems a degree or two less easy, as if wishing to draw the reader into closer examination of the complexity, and darkness, of his casualness.

Reference:
Peter Buitenhuis, "Attempted Edens: The Poetry of Dale Zeiroth," *Essays on Canadian Writing*, 32 (Summer 1986): 92-105.

Supplementary Reading List

Atlantic Provinces Literature Colloquium. Saint John, N.B.: Atlantic Canada Institute, 1977.

Atwood, Margaret. *Second Words: Selected Critical Prose.* Toronto: Anansi, 1982.

Atwood. *Survival.* Toronto: Anansi, 1972.

Audley, Paul. *Canada's Cultural Industries: Broadcasting, Publishing, Records and Film.* Toronto: James Lorimer, 1983.

Avis, Walter, et al. *A Concise Dictionary of Canadianisms.* Toronto: Gage, 1973.

Beauchamp, Hélène. *Le Théâtre pour enfants au Quebec, 1950-1980.* Montreal: Hurtubise HMH, 1985.

Beaulieu, Victor-Lévy. *Manuel de la petite littérature du Québec.* Montreal: L'Aurore, 1974.

Bélisle, Louis-Alexandre. *Dictionnaire général de la langue française au Canada.* Quebec: Bélisle, 1957.

Bélisle. *Dictionnaire nord-américaine de la langue française.* Montreal: Beauchemin, 1979.

Beraud, Jean. *350 Ans de Théâtre au Canada français.* Montreal: Cercle du livre de France, 1958.

Berger, Carl. *The Writing of Canadian History: Aspects of English-Canadian Historical Writing, 1900-1970.* Toronto, Oxford & New York: Oxford University Press, 1976.

Bergeron, Léandre. *The Québécois Dictionary.* Toronto: James Lorimer, 1982.

Bessai, Diane, and David Jackel, eds. *Figures in a Ground.* Saskatoon: Western Producer Prairie Books, 1978.

Blodgett, E. D. *Configuration: Essays on the Canadian Literatures.* Toronto: ECW, 1982.

Bonheim, Helmut. *The Narrative Modes: Techniques of the Short Story.* Cambridge: D. S. Brewer, 1982.

Bouchard, René, ed. *Culture populaire et littératures au Québec.* Saratoga, Cal.: Anna Libri, 1980.

Bourassa, André G. *Surréalisme et littérature québécoise.* Montreal: Editions L'Etincelle, 1977. Translated by Mark Czarnecki as *Surrealism and Quebec Literature.* Toronto: University of Toronto Press, 1984.

Bowering, George. *Craft Slices.* Ottawa: Oberon, 1985.

Bowering. *The Mask in Place.* Winnipeg: Turnstone, 1982.

Bowering. *A Way with Words.* Ottawa: Oberon, 1982.

Brochu, André. *L'Instance critique, 1961-1973.* Montreal: Leméac, 1974.

Cameron, Barry, and Michael Dixon, eds. *Minus Canadian,* special issue of *Studies in Canadian Literature,* 2 (Summer 1977).

Cameron, Donald. *Conversations with Canadian Novelists*, 2 volumes. Toronto: Macmillan, 1973.

"Canada: Introduction." Annual review. *Journal of Commonwealth Literature*, 1965-

The Canadian Encyclopedia, 3 volumes. Edmonton: Hurtig, 1985.

Capone, Giovanna. *Canada: il villaggio della terra*. Bologna: Pàtron Editore, 1978.

Cappon, Paul, ed. *In Our House: Social Perspectives on Canadian Literature*. Toronto: McClelland & Stewart, 1978.

Chew, Shirley, ed. *Re-visions of Canadian Literature*. Leeds: University of Leeds, 1984.

Codignola, Luca, ed. *Canadiana*. Venice: Marsilio, 1978.

Colombo, John Robert. *Colombo's Canadian Quotations*. Edmonton: Hurtig, 1974.

Colombo, comp. *Colombo's Canadian References*. Toronto, Oxford & New York: Oxford University Press, 1976.

Colombo, et al., comps. *CDN SF & F: A Bibliography of Science Fiction and Fantasy*. Toronto: Hounslow, 1979.

Cude, Wilfred. *A Due Sense of Differences: An Evaluative Approach to Canadian Literature*. Lanham, Md.: University Press of America, 1980.

Davey, Frank. *From There to Here*. Erin, Ont.: Press Porcépic, 1974.

Davey. *Surviving the Paraphrase*. Winnipeg: Turnstone, 1983.

Davey, and Ann Munton, eds. *"Long-liners Conference Issue"* [the long poem in Canada], *Open Letter*, sixth series, no. 2-3 (Summer-Fall 1985).

David, Jack, ed. *Brave New Wave*. Windsor: Black Moss, 1978.

Daymond, Douglas. *Towards a Canadian Literature*, volume 2. Ottawa: Tecumseh, 1985.

Daymond, and Leslie Monkman, eds. *Canadian Novelists and the Novel*. Ottawa: Borealis, 1981.

de Leon, Lisa. *Twentieth-Century Writers of Newfoundland and Labrador*. St John's: Jesperson, 1985.

Dooley, D. J. *Moral Vision in the Canadian Novel*. Toronto: Clarke, Irwin, 1978.

Dorsinville, Max. *Caliban Without Prospero: Essay on Quebec and Black Literature*. Erin, Ont.: Press Procépic, 1974.

Duffy, Dennis. *Gardens, Covenants, Exiles: Loyalism in the Literature of Upper Canada/Ontario*. Toronto: University of Toronto Press, 1982.

Dybikowski, Ann, et al., eds. *In the Feminine*. Edmonton: Longspoon, 1985.

Egoff, Sheila. *The Republic of Childhood: A Critical Guide to Canadian Children's Literature in English*. Toronto, Oxford & New York: Oxford University Press, 1967.

Fairbanks, Carol. *Prairie Women: Images in American and Canadian Fiction.* New Haven & London: Yale University Press, 1986.

Falardeau, Jean-Charles. *Imaginaire social et littérature.* Montreal: Hurtubise HMH, 1974.

Fetherling, Doug. *The Blue Notebook: Reports on Canadian Culture.* Oakville, Ont., New York & London: Mosaic Press, 1985.

Fisette, Jean. *Le texte automatiste.* Montreal: Presses de l'Université du Québec, 1977.

Fogel, Stanley. *A Tale of Two Countries.* Toronto: ECW, 1984.

Frye, Northrop. *Divisions on a Ground.* Toronto: Anansi, 1982.

Gagnon, Serge. *Quebec and Its Historians,* 2 volumes, translated by Jane Brierley. Montreal: Harvest House, 1982, 1985.

Gauvin, Lise, and Laurent Mailhot. *Guide culturel du Québec.* Montreal: Boréal Express, 1982.

Gibson, Graeme. *Eleven Canadian Novelists.* Toronto: Anansi, 1972.

Gobin, Pierre. *Le Fou et ses doubles: figures de la dramaturgie québécoise.* Montreal: Presses de l'Université de Montréal, 1978.

Godin, Jean-Cléo, and Laurent Mailhot. *Le Théâtre québécois. Introduction à dix dramaturges contemporains.* Montreal: Hurtubise HMH, 1970; volume 2. *Nouveaux auteurs, autres spectacles.* Montreal: HMH, 1980.

Gross, Konrad, and Wolfgang Klooss, eds. *English Literature of the Dominions.* Würzburg: Königshausen & Neumann, 1981.

Guillaume, Pierre, Jean-Michel Lacroix, and Pierre Spriet, eds. *Canada et canadiens.* Bordeaux: Presses universitaires de Bordeaux, 1984.

Gwyn, Richard. *The 49th Paradox: Canada in North America.* Toronto: McClelland & Stewart, 1985.

Hall, Roger, and Gordon Dodds. *Canada: A History in Photographs.* Edmonton: Hurtig, 1981.

Hardin, Herschel. *A Nation Unaware: The Canadian Economic Culture.* Vancouver: J. J. Douglas, 1974.

Harger-Grinling, Virginia, and Terry Goldie, eds. *Violence in the Canadian Novel Since 1960.* St. John's: Memorial University, 1980.

Harper, J. Russell. *Painting in Canada: A History.* Toronto: University of Toronto Press, 1970.

Harrison, Dick. *Unnamed Country: The Struggle for a Canadian Prairie Fiction.* Edmonton: University of Alberta, 1977.

Harrison, ed. *Crossing Frontiers.* Edmonton: University of Alberta Press, 1979.

Heath, Jeffrey M., ed. *Profiles in Canadian Literature,* volumes 1-4, ongoing. Toronto & Charlottetown: Dundurn, 1980-1982.

Helwig, David, ed. *The Human Elements*. Ottawa: Oberon, 1981.

Hillis, Doris. *Voices and Visions: Interviews with Saskatchewan Writers*. Moose Jaw: Coteau, 1985.

Isajiw, Wsevolod. *Identities: The Impact of Ethnicity on Canadian Society*. Toronto: PMA, 1977.

Jasmin-Bélisle, Hélène. *Le père Emile Legault et ses compagnons de saint Laurent: Une petite histoire*. Ottawa: Leméac, 1986.

Jensen, Margaret Ann. *Love's Sweet Return: The Harlequin Story*. Toronto: Women's Press, 1984.

Jones, D. G. *Butterfly on Rock*. Toronto: University of Toronto Press, 1970.

Kallmann, Helmut, et al. *The Encyclopedia of Music in Canada*. Toronto: University of Toronto Press, 1981.

Kattan, Naim. *Le réel et le théâtral*. Montreal: Edition HMH, 1970. Translated by Allan Brown as *Reality and Theatre*. Toronto: Anansi, 1972.

Keith, W. J. *Canadian Literature in English*. London & New York: Longman, 1985.

Keith, and B.-Z Shek, eds. *The Arts in Canada: the last fifty years*. Toronto, Buffalo & London: University of Toronto Press, 1980.

Keitner, Wendy, ed. *"Surveying the Territory"* and *"Staking Claims,"* Canadian issues of *The Literary Criterion*, 19.3-4 (1984), and 20.1 (1985).

Klinck, Carl F., ed. *Literary History of Canada*, 3 volumes, second edition. Toronto: University of Toronto Press, 1976.

Kroetsch, Robert. "A Canadian Issue," *Boundary 2* (Fall 1974).

Kroetsch, and Reingard M. Nischik, eds. *Gaining Ground: European Critics on Canadian Literature*. Edmonton: NeWest, 1985.

Kushner, Eva, and Michael Bishop, eds. *La Poésie Québécoise depuis 1975*, special issue of *Dalhousie French Studies*. Halifax: Dalhousie University, 1986.

La Bossière, Camille, ed. *Translation in Canadian Literature*. Ottawa: University of Ottawa, 1983.

Laflamme, Jean, and Remi Tourangeau. *L'Eglise et le théâtre au Québec*. Montreal: Fides, 1979.

Larsen, Christian. *Chansonniers du Québec*. Montreal: Beauchemin, 1964.

Lecker, Robert, and Jack David, eds. *The Annotated Bibliography of Canada's Major Authors*, 6 volumes, ongoing. Toronto: ECW, 1979-

Lecker and David, eds. *Canadian Writers and Their Works*, 6 volumes, ongoing. Toronto: ECW, 1983-

Lee, Dennis. *Savage Fields*. Toronto: Anansi, 1977.

Legris, Renée, and Pierre Pagé. *Répertoire des dramatiques québécoises à la télévision*. Montreal: Fides, 1977.

Lemieux, Louise. *Pleins feux sur la littérature de jeunesse au Canada français.* Montreal: Leméac, 1972.

"Letters in Canada." Annual review. *University of Toronto Quarterly.* 1936-

Lewis, Apula Gilbert, ed. *Traditionalism, Nationalism, and Feminism: Women Writers of Quebec.* Westport, Conn. & London: Greenwood Press, 1985.

Lochhead, Douglas, comp. *Bibliography of Canadian Bibliographies,* second edition, revised and enlarged. Toronto: University of Toronto Press, 1972.

MacDermott, Doireann, ed. *Autobiographical and Biographical Writing in the Commonwealth.* Sabadell, Spain: Editorial AUSA, 1984.

Mailhot, Laurent. *La littérature québécoise.* Paris: Presses universitaires de France, 1974.

Major, Jean-Louis. *Le Jeu en étoile: études et essais.* Ottawa: Editions de l'Université d'Ottawa, 1978.

Mandel, Eli. *Another Time.* Erin, Ont.: Press Porcépic, 1977.

Mandel. *The Family Romance.* Winnipeg: Turnstone, 1986.

Marcotte, Gilles. *Le Roman à l'imparfait: essai sur le roman québécois d'aujourd'hui.* Montreal: La Presse, 1976.

Marcotte. *Le Temps des poètes. Description critiques de la poésie actuelle au Canada français.* Montreal: HMH, 1969.

Marshall, Tom. *Harsh and Lovely Land: The Major Canadian Poets and the Making of Canadian Tradition.* Vancouver: UBC Press, 1979.

Mathews, Robin. *Canadian Literature: Surrender or Revolution.* Toronto: Steel Rail, 1978.

Maugey, Axel. *Poésie et Société au Québec (1937-1970).* Quebec: Presses de l'Université Laval, 1972.

May, Cedric. *Breaking the Silence: The Literature of Quebec.* Birmingham: University of Birmingham, 1981.

McConnell, R. E. *Our Own Voice: Canadian English and how it is studied.* Toronto: Gage, 1979.

McGregor, Gaile. *The Wacousta Syndrome: Explorations in the Canadian Langscape.* Toronto, Buffalo & London: University of Toronto Press, 1985.

Metcalf, John. *Kicking Against the Pricks.* Toronto: ECW, 1982.

Meyer, Bruce, and Brian O'Riordan. *In Their Words.* Toronto: Anansi, 1984.

Moisan, Clément. *Poésie des frontières.* Montreal: Editions Hurtubise, 1979. English version by the author, *A Poetry of Frontiers: Comparative Essays on Québécois and Canadian Poetry.* Victoria: Press Porcépic, 1983.

Monkman, Leslie. *A Native Heritage: Images of the Indian in English-Canadian Literature.* Toronto: University of Toronto, 1981.

Morris, Peter. *The Film Companion.* Toronto: Irwin, 1984.

Moss, John. *A Reader's Guide to the Canadian Novel*. Toronto: McClelland & Stewart, 1981.

Moss. *Sex and Violence in the Canadian Novel*. Toronto: McClelland & Stewart, 1977.

Moss, ed. *Here and Now*. Toronto: NC Press, 1978.

Narasimhaiah, C. D., ed. *Awakened Conscience*. New Delhi: Sterling, 1978.

Nardocchio, Elaine. *Theatre and Politics in Modern Quebec: A History*. Edmonton: University of Alberta Press, 1986.

New, W. H. *Among Worlds: An Introduction to Modern Commonwealth and South African Fiction*. Erin, Ont.: Press Porcépic, 1975.

New. *Articulating West*. Toronto: New Press, 1972.

New. *Dreams of Speech and Violence: The Art of the Short Story in Canada and New Zealand*. Toronto: University of Toronto Press, 1987.

New. *A Political Art*. Vancouver: UBC Press, 1978.

New, ed. *Canadian Writers in 1984*. Vancouver: UBC Press, 1984.

Nicholson, Colin, and Peter Easingwood, eds. *Canadian Story and History 1885-1985*. Edinburgh: Edinburgh University Centre of Canadian Studies, 1986.

Northey, Margot. *The Haunted Wilderness: the gothic and grotesque in Canadian Fiction*. Toronto: University of Toronto Press, 1976.

OKanada. Ottawa: Canada Council, 1982.

Olinder, Britta, ed. *A Sense of Place*. Gothenburg: Gothenburg University, 1984.

Pache, Walter. *Einführung in die Kanadastik*. Darmstadt: Wissenschaftliche Buchgessellschaft, 1981.

Paradis, Suzanne. *Femme fictive, femme réelle: le personnage féminin dans le roman féminin canadien-français, 1884-1966*. Québec: Garneau, 1966.

Petrone, Penny, ed. *First People, First Voices*. Toronto: University of Toronto Press, 1983.

Pivato, Joseph, ed. *Contrasts: Essays on Italian-Canadian Writing*. Montreal: Guernica, 1985.

Poulin, Gabrielle. *Romans du pays, 1968-1979*. Montreal: Bellarmin, 1980.

Powe, B. W. *A Climate Charged: Essays on Canadian Writers*. Oakville, Ont.: Mosaic, 1984.

Reid, Dennis. *A Concise History of Canadian Painting*. Toronto, Oxford & New York: Oxford University Press, 1973.

Reid, Malcolm. *The Shouting Signpainters*. Toronto: McClelland & Stewart, 1972.

Riedel, Walter E. *Das Literarische Kanadabild*. Bonn: Bouvier, 1980.

Riedel. *The Old World and the New: Literary Perspectives of German-speaking Canadians.* Toronto: University of Toronto, 1984.

Riemenschneider, Dieter, ed. *The History and Historiography of Commonwealth Literature.* Tübingen: Gunter Narr, 1983.

Ripley, C. Peter, ed. *The Black Abolitionist Papers,* volume 2 of *Canada, 1830-1865.* Chapel Hill & London: University of North Carolina Press, 1986.

Robeson, Virginia, and Christine Sylvester. *Teaching Canadian Studies: An Evaluation of Print Materials.* Toronto: OISE, 1980.

Robidoux, Réjean, and Cécile Cloutier-Wojciechowska, eds. *Solitude rompue.* Ottawa: Editions de l'université d'Ottawa, 1986.

Robinson, Sinclair, and Donald Smith. *Practical Handbook of Quebec and Acadian French.* Toronto: Anansi, 1984.

Salutin, Rick. *Marginal Notes.* Toronto: Lester & Orpen Dennys, 1984.

Sarkonak, Ralph, ed. "The Language of Difference: Writing in QUEBEC(ois)," special issue of *Yale French Studies,* no. 65 (1983).

Schwenger, Peter. *Phallic Critiques: Masculinity and Twentieth-Century Literature.* London: Routledge & Kegan Paul, 1984.

Shouldice, Larry, ed. and transl. *Contemporary Quebec Criticism.* Toronto: University of Toronto Press, 1979.

Steele, Charles, ed. *Taking Stock: The Calgary Conference on the Canadian Novel.* Toronto: ECW, 1982.

Story, G. M., et al., eds. *Dictionary of Newfoundland English.* Toronto: University of Toronto Press, 1982.

Stouck, David. *Major Canadian Authors.* Lincoln: University of Nebraska Press, 1984.

Stratford, Philip. *All the Polarities: Comparative Studies in Contemporary Canadian Novels in French and English.* Toronto: ECW, 1986.

Stratford. *Bibliography of Canadian Books in Translation: French to English and English to French, Bibliographie de livres canadiens traduits de l'anglais au français et du français à l'anglais.* Ottawa: HRCC, 1977.

Stuart, E. Ross. *The History of Prairie Theatre: The Development of Theatre in Alberta, Manitoba, and Saskatchewan.* Toronto: Simon & Pierre, 1984.

Stuewe, Paul. *Clearing the Ground: English-Canadian Literature after Survival.* Toronto: Proper Tales Press, 1984.

Sutherland, Ronald. *The New Hero: Essays in Comparative Quebec/Canadian Literature.* Toronto: Macmillan, 1977.

Tallmann, Warren. *Godawful Streets of Man,* special issue of *Open Letter,* 3, no. 6 (1976-1977).

Taylor, Charles. *Six Journeys: A Canadian Pattern.* Toronto: Anansi, 1977.

Thomas, Clara. *Our Nature-Our Voices: A Guidebook to English-Canadian Literature*. Toronto: New Press, 1972.

Toye, William, ed. *The Oxford Companion to Canadian Literature*. Toronto, Oxford & New York: Oxford University Press, 1983.

Urbas, Jeannette. *From Thirty Acres to Modern Times; the Story of French-Canadian Literature*. Toronto & New York: McGraw-Hill Ryerson, 1976.

Usmiani, Renate. *Second Stage: The Alternative Theatre Movement in Canada*. Vancouver: UBC Press, 1983.

Wagner, Anton, ed. *The Brock Bibliography of Published Canadian Plays in English 1766-1978*. Toronto: Playwrights Press, 1980.

Wallace, Robert, and Cynthia Zimmerman. *The Work: Conversations with English-Canadian Playwrights*. Toronto: Coach House, 1982.

Wardhaugh, Ronald. *Language and Nationhood: The Canadian Experience*. Vancouver: New Star Books, 1983.

Woodcock, George. *The World of Canadian Writing*. Vancouver: Douglas & McIntyre/Seattle: University of Washington Press, 1980.

Woodcock, ed. *The Canadian Novel in the Twentieth Century*. Toronto: McClelland & Stewart, 1975.

Woodcock, ed. *Poets and Critics*. Toronto, Oxford & New York: Oxford University Press, 1974.

Wyczynski, Paul, et al. *Archives des lettres canadiennes*. Montreal: Fides. No. 2 ("L'école littéraire de Montréal," 1972); no. 3 ("Roman," 1971); no. 4 ("Poésie," 1969); no. 5 ("Théâtre," 1976).

Contributors

Alexandre L. Amprimoz.. *Brock University*
Douglas Barbour .... *University of Alberta*
Neil Besner .... *Mount Royal College*
Diane Bessai .... *University of Alberta*
Allan Bevan... *Dalhousie University*
Peter Buitenhuis... *Simon Fraser University*
Barry Cameron.. *University of New Brunswick*
Cécile Cloutier-Wojciechowska..................................... *University of Toronto*
Fred Cogswell.. *University of New Brunswick*
Hallvard Dahlie.. *University of Calgary*
Gwendolyn Davies.. *Mount Allison University*
Stan Dragland ....*University of Western Ontario*
James Doyle... *Wilfrid Laurier University*
L. H. Forsyth ....*University of Western Ontario*
Richard Giguère.. *Université de Sherbrooke*
V. A. Harger-Grinling ....*Memorial University of Newfoundland*
Dick Harrison.. *University of Alberta*
David Jackel... *University of Alberta*
David L. Jeffrey .... *University of Ottawa*
Chris Johnson ....*University of Manitoba*
J. Kieran Kealy .... *University of British Columbia*
Wendy Robbins Keitner .... *University of New Brunswick*
Kathleen L. Kellett.. *University of Toronto*
M. Travis Lane .... *University of New Brunswick*
Ann Mandel ....*Glendon College*
Alberto Manguel ....*Toronto, Canada*
Tom Marshall.. *Queen's University*
Lawrence Mathews.............................*Memorial University of Newfoundland*
Kenneth W. Meadwell .... *University of Winnipeg*
Patricia Merivale... *University of British Columbia*
Ann Messenger..*Simon Fraser University*
Ginette Michaud............. *Université du Québec à Montréal and Université de Montréal*
Allison Mitcham .... *Université de Moncton*
Leslie Monkman... *Queen's University*
W. H. New... *University of British Columbia*
Andrew Parkin .... *University of British Columbia*
Myrianne Pavlovic...*Quebec, Canada*
S. Penny Petrone ....*Lakehead University*
Brian Pocknell ....*McMaster University*
Valerie Raoul .... *University of British Columbia*
Aviva Ravel ....*Concordia University*
Laurie Ricou.. *University of British Columbia*
David F. Rogers .... *University of British Columbia*
Constance Rooke .... *University of Victoria*
Larry Shouldice .... *Université de Sherbrooke*
Patricia Smart..*Carleton University*
Donald Smith..*Carleton University*
Paul Socken... *University of Waterloo*
Paul Matthew St. Pierre...................................... *University of British Columbia*
David Staines .... *University of Ottawa*

Peter Stevens..*University of Windsor*
Philip Stratford..*Université de Montréal*
Ronald Sutherland ....*Université de Sherbrooke*
Jeannette Urbas ....*York University*
Renate Usmiani...*Mount Saint Vincent University*
Jacqueline Viswanathan...*Simon Fraser University*
Evelyne Voldeng ....*Carleton University*
Wendy E. Waring ....*University of Toronto*
Jerry Wasserman ....*University of British Columbia*
Lorraine Weir ....*University of British Columbia*
Cynthia Diane Zimmerman..*York University*

Cumulative Index

Dictionary of Literary Biography, Volumes 1-61
Dictionary of Literary Biography Yearbook, 1980-1986
Dictionary of Literary Biography Documentary Series, Volumes 1-4

Cumulative Index

DLB before number: *Dictionary of Literary Biography*, Volumes 1-61
Y before number: *Dictionary of Literary Biography Yearbook*, 1980-1986
DS before number: *Dictionary of Literary Biography Documentary Series*, Volumes 1-4

G

I

J

M

N

Q

R

S

U

Y

Z

6977